ON VS
8⁰⁰

Robert

We hope you find some
interesting reading in this book!

Love
Terry & Marie ann
Gerald & Eldine

As
Reported
in
The
Herald

THE CALGARY HERALD.

MINING AND RANCHE ADVOCATE AND GENERAL ADVERTISER.

VOLUME I.   CALGARY, ALBERTA, FRIDAY, AUGUST 31, 1883   NUMBER 1

LOCAL NEWS.

NEW STOCK.—I. G. Baker & Co. have just received 180 wood and coal stoves, which will be sold cheap.

POLICE HOSPITAL.—The hospital contains at present four patients, three civilians and one policeman.

C. P. CONSTRUCTION.—Tracklaying is being vigorously proceeded with by the C. P. R., about 10 miles west of Calgary.

FIRST ARRIVALS.—The first train of freight for Calgary, carried the plant of the CALGARY HERALD, and some goods for Winder & Co.

IN LIMBO.—The guard-room has but one occupant, an Indian named Cut Lip, who is serving his time for stabbing a white man last winter.

TROOP PHOTOGRAPHED.—Immediately after full dress parade, on Tuesday morning, the troop stationed here was photographed by Mr. Bingham.

ANTHRACITE COAL.—We have been shown some fine specimens of what has been pronounced "anthracite coal," lately brought from the mountains.

BIG DRIVE OF LOGS.—The Bow River Mills are now receiving a drive of about 8000 logs, and are sawing night and day to supply the wants of their customers.

PROSPECTORS.—Some of the prospectors have returned from the mountains, bringing fine specimens with them, and glowing accounts of what they have seen.

TREATY MONEY.—The treaty money is to be paid to the Stony Indians, at Morley, to-morrow. The Sarcees receive theirs on the 10th and the Blackfeet on the 25th prox.

PRESBYTERIAN MISSION.—A meeting was recently held in the Hudson Bay store, for the appointment of Managers in connection with the above Mission, when the following gentlemen were appointed : Major Walker, Dr. Henderson, and Mr. Joseph McPherson. The management have adopted the envelope system for their weekly offering.

REGISTRAR DISTRICTS.—We understand that Alberta has been divided into two registration districts. One office will be established at Calgary, the other at Edmonton.

TRAIN SERVICE—A passenger train now leaves Calgary, daily for the east, at 10.80 a.m., and one leaves Medicine Hat for Calgary, every morning at 3 a.m., arriving here about 3 p.m.

EXCURSION.—The Brandon Town Officials purpose visiting Calgary, in a few days. Mr. Egan has placed a sleeper at their disposal. Could not something be done towards giving them a public reception ?

FIRST ENGINE.—On the arrival of the first engine into Calgary, the hill sides were crowded with admiring spectators, many of whom had never seen one before, and others who had not been near a railway for eight or ten years.

ROYAL HOTEL.—Mr. Moulton has just closed his popular hotel for the season, owing to the fact that he could obtain no suitable building site, at present. We believe it is his intention to return to Calgary and erect a large hotel, when the town is surveyed. The outfit was sold by auction on Tuesday last, and owing to the successful manner in which Mr. T. S. Burns wielded the hammer, fancy figures were obtained.

GEOLOGICAL SURVEY.—Mr. J. H. Panton, geologist, of the Manitoba Historical and Scientific Society, spent a day in and about Calgary, and reports a very interesting field of study for men of his profession. He has promised to prepare a paper on his researches in this locality for THE HERALD, which we have no doubt will be hailed with interest by our readers. We hope also to be favored with a paper by the Botanist of the Society.

CALGARY HOUSE.—We have had the pleasure of inspecting the new hotel just completed by Dunne & Wright, and find it a perfect model of taste and neatness. It contains a large comfortable parlour, and a number of bed-rooms, all handsomely carpeted and furnished in the best of style. The dining-room has accommodation for about 40 guests, and the reading room is well supplied with the latest papers. Messrs. Dunne & Wright are well and favorably known to the public, and we have no doubt they will receive the large share of public patronage, which they so justly merit.

THE NAVVIES.—We have to congratulate Mr. G. W. Peterson, of the firm of Peterson & Peterson, Barristers of this place, on his success in securing passes over the C. P. R., for several hundred of Langdon, Shepherd & Co's men. It seems that when engaging, the men were promised passes back on the completion of the contract, but when the work was completed, and pay day came, these were refused and the men were lying here idle, without any shelter day or night for some time, and but for the clever management of the case by the above named gentlemen, might have caused serious embarrassment. Not the least pleasing feature of the affair, was the handsome fee received by Mr. Peterson.

SABBATH SERVICES.—Divine service is held at the Catholic Chapel every Sunday at 10:30 a.m. and 4:30 p.m.

PRESBYTERIAN SERVICE.—The service in connection with the Presbyterian Mission will be held in a tent near the Calgary House on Sunday next at 7 p.m.

CATHOLIC INDUSTRIAL SCHOOL.—Rev. Father La Combe is waiting for the specifications and forms of tenders from Lieut.-Governor Dewdney for the Indian Industrial School at High River. As soon as they arrive parties wishing to tender will be supplied with blank forms.

HUDSON BAY FORT.—The H. B. Fort, at Calgary has lately been raised to the chief post of the district, from which the supplies for 5 posts in the Edmonton district, 6 in the Peace River district, and 1 in the Athabasca district will be forwarded.

THIEVES.—A number of petty thefts have lately been committed in the vicinity, but the smallest thing we have heard of, was the cutting and stealing of the ropes from the foot bridge across the Elbow. This is a matter of some importance, as strangers coming into town are very liable to get a cold bath gratuitously. We hope the ropes will soon be replaced.

METHODISTICAL.—We are pleased to see that the energetic Methodist missionary of this place, Rev. Mr. Turner, is always equal to the occasion. The hospital of the Mounted Police not being longer available, Mr. Turner has secured a tent, and made it comfortable, and will hold service therein next Sunday at 3 p.m. The tent is situated just east of the Hudson Bay store. There is some talk of securing an organ, and forming a choir.

HOUSE RAIDED.—Information was laid a few evenings since, at Police quarters, that a number of men were engaged in gambling in a certain house on the bank of the Elbow accordingly Major Dowling, with a detachment of men, proceeded to the place in question and after entering, found eight or nine persons with cards and checks on the table, he arrested the parties and placed them in the guard-room. The next morning they were up for trial before Supt. McIlree, but as no direct evidence, was forthcoming, they were discharged. Mr. Bleecker of Edmonton defended the prisoners.

A MURDEROUS ASSAULT.—On Sunday afternoon, about 8 o'clock, a telegram was received at the Police Barracks that a fracas had occurred at the end of the track, by which a man named Torrance had committed a murderous assault on another of the gang, knocking him down and kicking him about the head and face. Afterwards drawing a revolver, he "stood off" some men who interfered, and starting down the track, succeeded in gaining a dense bush. A detachment was sent up to keep guard, and see that he did not escape from the thicket, the night being too dark to search for him then. Sergt. Major Lake, with ten men, proceeded at day-break next morning to scour the bush thoroughly, but unfortunately the man had effected his escape and has not since been heard of. The wounded man is progressing favourably.

the recipient, from the citizens of that town, of a gold-headed cane, and a well filled purse, and from the Masonic body, a Past Master's Jewel of gold, accompanied in each case by a very flattering address. The papers give Mr. Swan much credit for the zeal he has always displayed in advancing the best interests of the town, mentioning among other matters that he had a hand in running off the first paper printed by steam in that place—the Confederate. We may say that Mr. Swan arrived here in good health and just in time to render valuable assistance in setting up the first printing press in Calgary. From our personal knowledge of Mr. Swan, we think he is quite an acquisition to Calgary, and have no doubt he will put forth the same efforts to build up this place that he displayed in Mount Forest.

Mr E. H. Talbot, proprietor, and Mr. H. R. Hobart, editor, of the Railway Age, accompanied by their wives, and Miss Nellie Herrick, Secretary, Mr. John A. Fraser, R.C.A., Artist, paid Calgary a visit last week in their magnificent palatial car, the finest ever built in the world. They were informed that they would require to lay in a stock of everything they required in the way of food, as nothing whatever could be grown in this cold climate; but imagine their surprise on receiving from the garden of the Mounted Police a liberal supply of vegetables. They intended remaining only for a day, but the beauty of the spot and the celebrity of the air induced them to prolong their visit from Wednesday till Saturday. Mr. Fraser visited the mountains and made sketches from which he intends to paint a picture to be exhibited at the Chicago Art Exhibition. The rest of the party remained in town, engaged in fishing and visiting the places of interest. Mr. Talbot informed us he purposes returning for the opening of the C.P.R. through British Columbia, when he expects to see Calgary a thriving city.

As Reported in The Herald

Text Compiled
by
Allan Connery

THE CALGARY HERALD

Supervising Editor
Reg Vickers

Design
David Scollard

Production & Marketing
Lorne Kennedy

Editorial Consultant
William F. Gold

Editorial Assistant
Kate Zimmerman

Copy Assistants
Diane Bockman,
Debbie Penno

Special Graphics
Nick Pearce

Acknowledgements

The staff of the Glenbow-Alberta Institute's library and archives were very helpful in the research for this book. A special word of thanks is due Georgeen Klassen of the archives.

This book was made possible by several generations of Herald librarians, who carefully preserved almost every word published in the paper. The present-day library staff gave invaluable assistance in sifting through hundreds of reels of microfilm and thousands of topic files.

A number of books provided historical background, among them *The Timetables of History*, by Bernard Grun; *Canada's First Century*, by Donald Creighton; *Frontier Calgary*, edited by A.W. Rasporich and Henry Klassen; *A History of Alberta*, by James G. MacGregor; *The Roar of the Twenties, Boomtime*, and *Booze*, all by James H. Gray; *The Golden Province*, by Ernest Watkins and *News and the Southams*, by Charles Bruce. C.P. Stacey's articles on the world wars in the *Encyclopedia Canadiana* were also most useful.

While a majority of the photographs appearing in this book are from The Herald's own files, several other sources made pictures available for publication. They are: The Glenbow-Alberta Institute; The Bettmann Archive Inc. in New York; the Provincial Archives of Alberta in Edmonton; Imperial Oil Limited in Calgary; and the Public Archives of Canada in Ottawa. Front pages, cartoons and advertisements were reproduced from microfilm by West Canadian Graphic Industries Ltd.

The type for this book was set in the Goudy face by The Copyfitters, in Calgary. Printing and binding by Hignell Printing Ltd., of Winnipeg.

Contents

Publisher Frank G. Swanson on the terrace at the $70 million Herald newspaper plant.

Foreword

Since 1883, The Herald has kept its readers at the leading edge of history. This is not always a comfortable place for our customers to be, and we don't like to boast about putting them there. However, a newspaper lives to tell its public of the latest remarkable events, tragic or funny, noble or grotesque. In its time, The Herald has compiled a record of a terrible and fascinating century. This book reproduces some of the more striking news and comment that Calgary's first newspaper has published over the years. A short introduction tells the paper's own story, but the rest of the book is devoted to highlights of the news as it unfolded day by day in the pages of The Herald.

Much of this book is the work of men and women who worked for The Herald or its affiliate, Southam News, but there are also dispatches from Canadian Press and other news services. We have leaned toward Canadian stories that were well reported and then, all too often, quickly forgotten. The news stories, the editorials, the cartoons and the advertisements reproduced here are all from The Herald. However, while many of the photographs first appeared in the newspaper's columns, gaps in coverage of historic events have had to be covered with material from archives, especially the Glenbow-Alberta Institute.

In order to compress nearly 100 years of newspapers into one book, we were forced to leave out many things we would have liked to include. Most of the surviving items have been abridged, but the writing style of the particular era has been left intact. We have also made room for trivial stories that may convey some flavor of bygone days. The result isn't meant to be a scholarly history; rather, it is what might be called a collection of souvenirs and snapshots from nearly a century of journalism.

This book marks the dedication of our new plant, an event that means a lot to us at the Herald. For our readers, the paper's gradual transition from a small tent to a block-long building may serve as one small example of the immense changes that a century has wrought.

Since 1883 The Herald's readers have witnessed and read about a remarkable era revealed as events unfolded, day by day. Now, here it is in one book — the news since 1883, as reported in The Herald.

FRANK G. SWANSON
Publisher, The Calgary Herald
April, 1982

Introduction

The Herald story starts in a tent

It is August, 1883. Calgary is a little huddle of tents and wooden buildings at the junction of two rivers. In the spring the streets were little more than mudholes, but now, in late summer, they are only dusty. A sawmill works day and night, cutting lumber for more buildings, because the railroad has come and the future looks bright.

In one of the tents, a thin, quick, nervous man is hand-setting type for the first edition of The Herald. A letter a time, he readies the news for printing. One item notes that there has been a rash of thefts, "but the smallest thing we have heard of was the cutting and stealing of the ropes from the foot bridge across the Elbow. This is a matter of some importance, as strangers coming into town are very liable to get a cold bath gratuitously. We hope the ropes will soon be replaced." Another story tells readers that a geologist from Manitoba has spent a day in the area, and "reports a very interesting field of study for men of his profession."

Calgary has come a long way since that first issue of The Herald, partly because geologists did indeed find the area interesting. The Herald has grown with Calgary, faithfully depositing a daily increment of history and amusement on the doorsteps of the city.

The Calgary Herald, Mining and Ranche Advocate and General Advertiser, as it was grandly called, made its debut on August 31, 1883, proclaiming its duty and pleasure to be, among other things, "The collation of all news items of local interest, the encouragement of all measures religious and moral intended for the welfare of the community, and the exposure of any measures or acts on the part of individuals, corporations or governments, which appear to be framed against the true interest of the place, people or district." The Herald was the third paper in the area that was to become Alberta. The first was the Edmonton Bulletin, founded in 1880 and closed in 1951; the second was The Macleod Gazette, started in 1882 and still publishing.

The Herald's founders were Andrew M. Armour and Thomas B. Braden, boyhood friends who went into the newspaper business on a borrowed shoestring. A Toronto milliner, Miss Frances Ann Chandler, deserves to be remembered for her part in founding The Herald. A friend of Armour's wife, she lent him $500, interest-free, to be repaid if the paper prospered.

The loan was repaid, but Miss Chandler's heirs may have wished since that she had bought a share of the paper instead. However, they would have had to wait some time for a dividend. At the beginning, and for its first 20 years, The Herald was a very shaky enterprise. In an area with only a few hundred prospective readers, working with a hand-operated press and a small supply of type, Armour and Braden turned out a four-page tabloid paper every week from a tent about 14 feet by 20. The Herald's equipment came in on the first CPR freight train to Calgary, and the address on the shipment summed up Armour and Braden's choice of place to go into business: "T. B. Braden, end of track," said the label.

There was no pot of gold at the end of the track: a year's subscription brought in $3, in advance, and an advertisement one column wide by an inch deep was worth about $1.40 for the first publication and $1 a time thereafter. Even at these prices, there must have been some money coming in, because Armour was soon off to the East to buy more equipment. While he was gone, the Northwest Mounted Police detailed Constable Thomas Clarke, who had been a printer, to give Braden a hand with The Herald. Life was simpler then.

Armour and Braden were perhaps typical of the men who came West looking for new opportunities. They grew up on adjacent farms in Southern Ontario. Armour, 35 when he started The Herald, had worked as a printer on Ontario newspapers. Braden, three years younger, had taught school in Peterborough. In 1883 he was turned down for a headmastership, and only weeks later he started The Herald.

By 1884 the founders had replaced their tent with a shack, and hired an editor, Hugh St. Quentin Cayley. A young lawyer from Toronto, Cayley had worked for 18 months on the New York Herald Tribune. In 1885, at the age of 27, he bought The Herald. By then the paper had a building on the main street, Stephen Avenue (later Eighth Avenue).

The Herald had its beginnings in 1883 in this tent. From left are George Rouleau, a Calgary lawyer; Andrew Armour, a founder of The Herald; North West Mounted Police Constable Thomas Clarke, who helped set type; and Thomas Braden, the other founder of The Herald.

Armour went on to establish The Medicine Hat News, and Braden started The Calgary Tribune, a forerunner of the late Albertan. From Medicine Hat, Armour moved to California. He helped to organize the Los Angeles YMCA, and in the 1890s he and his wife Annie travelled as an evangelical team. He preached, she sang and played the organ. Armour died in 1904, leaving two newspapers but no children.

As editor of the Tribune, the Liberal Braden soon found himself feuding with Cayley, who had turned The Herald Conservative. Though he is remembered as a genial, kindly soul, Braden put his case a bit too strongly; he wound up in the police barracks, charged with libelling Cayley. A Tribune retraction restored peace. (Braden went back to The Herald in 1894 and died a bachelor in 1904, the same year as Armour.)

For a few months in 1885, Calgary was a three-paper town. The short-lived Nor'wester, founded in 1884, was then in the last few months of its life. From the beginning it had made The Herald furious. Armour and Braden had tried to take a lofty, dismissive tone. Cayley was more pungent. He called George B. Elliott, publisher of The Nor'wester, a childish egotist, a vampire, and a lilliput from nowhere.

Evidently Cayley could dish out libel better than he could take it.

In the spring of 1885, the Riel Rebellion seemed to threaten Northwest Territories settlers with a bloodbath. Cayley issued extras almost daily, at 10 cents each, and crowds gathered around The Herald office waiting for the latest news by telegraph. The success of the extras may have inspired Cayley's boldest move: he turned The Herald into a daily newspaper. The daily was only a handkerchief-sized sheet, selling for $1 a month, but it was a remarkable step for a weekly with a circulation of about 150. Cayley also replaced The Herald's first press with a new model that could turn out 400 papers an hour, given a strong man turning the crank.

By Christmas, 1885, Cayley was in the North West Mounted Police barracks for contempt of court. The local magistrate, Jeremiah Travis, had tried to enforce the liquor laws of the Northwest Territories. These laws were widely resented as Eastern oppression, the product of Ottawa's pandering to the Ontario teetotal vote. Cayley thought Travis was an arrogant Eastern popinjay, said so repeatedly, and would not repent saying so. Travis sent him to jail. Peter Lougheed's grandfather was the prosecutor in the case.

G.E. Grogan, a Mountie who ran The Herald while Cayley was in custody, later recalled the scene when the editor turned himself in. Cayley rode in a wagon "pulled by stalwarts of the anti-Travis faction in a long procession headed by a brass band. It was a bitterly cold day. As each saloon was reached on the route around town, the band had to adjourn inside to thaw out their instruments at the stove and their insides at the bar. And so on again, Mr. Cayley from the elevation of the wagon box holding forth on the rights of free speech and the liberty of the press with gradually increasing difficulty of utterance until at the last halt at Clark's saloon, he succumbed to his emotions and was finally delivered up in silence by his reluctant admirers."

Cayley spent a couple of weeks in the barracks (as the guest, some believe, of the NWMP commander) and was released when the federal government interceded. According to Grogan's account, Sir John A. Macdonald himself sent a telegram instructing the Mounties to "let the little beggar go."

Cayley's time at The Herald was eventful, but brief. In 1886 he sold to Alexander Lucas, and left journalism to practise law. He was elected to the Northwest Territories Council that year, and served briefly as premier of the territories in 1892. Later he moved to British Columbia, and in 1917, he became a judge himself.

Lucas was another Ontario man who had come West looking for new opportunities. He was active in business and Conservative politics, and combined the two as principal shareholder in The Herald. He found several other investors, including a fellow-Conservative, James Lougheed, later senator and the grandfather of Premier Peter Lougheed. (Lucas, incidentally, was the first local news-media star to become mayor of Calgary; he served in 1892 and 1893. W.F. Orr, who was briefly editor of The Herald under Lucas, was mayor in 1894 and 1895, and again in 1897.)

The Lucas era was a busy time for The Herald. The paper moved several times, first to 811 Centre St. and a year later, in 1887, to 113 8th Ave. S.W. In 1888 it took over the Alberta Live Stock Journal. That year, too, The Herald published its fifth anniversary edition entirely in red ink, a color which may have held a special meaning for its book-keepers. Calgary was booming — it grew from 500 to 3,800 between 1884 and 1891 — but it still wasn't large enough to support two newspapers, The Herald and The Tribune, with any degree of security. Nevertheless, The Herald expanded, putting out four full-sized pages daily.

By 1891 the boom had ended: Calgary grew by only 200 people in the 10 years that followed. Eventually The Herald left 8th Avenue and crawled into a hole in an alley off Centre Street between 8th and 9th Avenues. In 1893 The Herald Publishing Company was in liquidation, and the paper was coming out twice a week at best.

There the story might have ended, but in 1894 a young editor and entrepreneur, John J. Young, came to Calgary. He and his partner, the Conservative politician C.A. Magrath, paid $15,000 for The Herald, and brought it back to life as a daily. Young soon bought out Magrath. In 1895, The Herald moved back to the main street, this time to a building at 134 8th Ave. S.W.

Young was only 27 when he bought The Herald, but he had edited The Regina Leader and The Moosomin Spectator, and owned three small Saskatchewan papers, which he sold to pay for his Calgary venture. He kept The Herald going through some lean years, and in 1903 Bob Edwards wrote in The Calgary Eye-Opener that "Westerners who think editors should be thrown in boiling oil are inclined to make an honorable exception in the case of Mr. J. J. Young who took hold of The Calgary Herald as a moribund fragment and tenderly nursed it into a thing of life." In 1905 Printer and Publisher magazine described him as "a fine example of what can be made in Canada of an Englishman who is caught young."

The Herald continued to suffer from what would now be called cash-flow problems. Mondays, everyone who could be spared was sent out to collect advertising bills. Thomas Braden, by then back at The Herald, once tried to collect $13.50 from a hardware store. He found that the store had applied the $13.50 to The Herald's hardware bill. Norman Luxton (who later founded the Banff museum that bears his name) was a virtuoso collector for The Herald. He cleared up a year-old account with a hotel by drinking with the proprietor from 10 a.m. to closing time. Nothing was said about the bill, but after the last round the hotelman pulled out a roll of cash and paid up. "We parted friends," Luxton recalled.

Sometimes, it seems, The Herald was not so much published as improvised. Whenever the CPR cut off news telegraph service until its bill was paid, Luxton filled the gap. He met the two daily trains through Calgary and got a look at the news bulletins thoughtfully provided for passengers on the CPR. These were the days of tramp printers, some of them first-class craftsmen, who roamed the country, often riding freight trains. When its composing room was short-handed, The Herald sent a talent scout down to the freight yards. Several of the steadier printers belonged to the volunteer fire department, an arrangement that tended to slow down production when the fire bell rang.

After 1897, business had improved so much that The Herald's half-horsepower steam engine couldn't keep the whole print shop running. The answer was to tie down the boiler's safety valve and double the steam pressure. It worked, but it made everyone terribly nervous, especially Braden. One day an apprentice untied the safety valve; the roar of escaping steam convinced Thomas Braden that disaster had finally struck, and he dived through a closed window. When the steam cleared, Young ordered a 12-horsepower engine.

In 1902, The Herald bought the city's first two Linotypes. Until then, every word the paper published was assembled a letter at a time, each letter hand-picked from its own compartment in a type case. When the type had been printed, the letters had to be sorted back into the appropriate compartments. A Linotype allowed a man seated at a keyboard to cast fresh type, a line at a time, from molten metal. After the type was used, it was melted down and used again. It was a revolutionary invention, and a very durable one: The Herald was produced by Linotype for 70 years.

In 1903, The Herald moved yet again, to a new building at 7th Avenue and Centre Street. (At this writing, the building still stands, and bears a faint trace of The Herald's name above its main entrance.) Calgary was booming again: between 1901

9

Three Herald publishers. J.J. Young (left) took over the paper in 1894, when it was nearly bankrupt. He nursed the paper back to health and modernized its plant. In 1907 he sold The Herald to J.H. Woods (centre) and the Southam family. Woods, the longest-serving Herald publisher, retired in 1935. Basil Dean (right) became publisher in 1955, and led The Herald into a new boom era for Calgary.

and 1906, the population tripled to 12,000. The Herald's circulation was 3,600 in 1904, and in 1906 Young installed a new press that could turn out 6,000 12-page papers an hour. By then The Herald was selling morning and evening editions to a news-hungry public.

Young's interests were not confined to the newspaper business, unfortunately. He dabbled in mining also, which made him a natural target, in 1897, for two swindlers posing as prospectors. They fooled Young's assayer, and sold Young a block of worthless yellow metal for $15,000. Max Aitken borrowed this gold brick and displayed it in the window of his Calgary bowling alley. (Aitken later went into the newspaper business himself, took care to buy no gold bricks, and became better known as Lord Beaverbrook.)

In 1906, Young was looking for money to finance his mining and real estate ventures. That summer, an Eastern Canadian journalist and advertising man, James Hossack Woods, 40, visited Calgary on a holiday. He met Young, and within six months had an option on half The Herald and a free hand to find a buyer for the whole paper. In September, 1907, Woods approached the Southam family, who already owned The Hamilton Spectator and The Ottawa Citizen, with an offer to buy a share of The Herald. The Southams were skeptical at first, but early in 1908 they decided to buy. Southams bought 301 shares, Woods 199, and Henry Watson, a banker friend of the Southams, 100 shares. Watson came into the deal with cold feet. His son liked to tell of coming down to breakfast the morning after the decision, and finding Watson Sr. emptying a decanter down the drain. "This stuff cost me thousands of dollars last night," he explained.

He poured too soon. The Herald did absorb a lot of capital in the early Southam years, and in the first of these years it netted only $718.50 on revenues of $70,000. Two years later, however, Woods had doubled The Herald's revenues and

turned a net profit of $7,000. He had moved quickly to trim The Herald's operations. He sold off the job-printing business, the traditional mainstay of small papers, and shut down the morning edition. During his 28 years with The Herald, circulation rose eight-fold, from 3,800 to more than 30,000.

(J.J. Young, meanwhile, fell into bad luck. He bought an apple orchard near Spokane, but a crop failure ruined him, and he moved to Vancouver, where he died in 1923 at the age of 56.)

J.H. Woods, "Bertie" to his friends, "The Chief" to his employees (and later "The Colonel" — he was honorary lieutenant-colonel of the Calgary Highlanders) was very much a public man, very much a philanthropist. He was active with the Belgian Relief Committee in the First World War, and was made a Chevalier of the Order of King Leopold of Belgium. Later he worked with the Red Cross and the Boy Scouts; he won the King's Jubilee Medal for his Red Cross work. In 1935 he was made a Companion of the Order of St. Michael and St. George, and led a Canadian delegation to the League of Nations.

He was remembered as "small but dignified, courteous but firm." For a dignified man, The Herald's staff must sometimes have been a trial. Early in the First World War, for example, they held a party at the Palliser Hotel for a colleague who had joined the army. The guest of honor took exception to the presence of a waiter with a German accent, and from there the party got rough. In the ensuing brawl, Woods was shoved into an open fireplace, evidently not in use at the time. The party dissolved in less than two hours, probably a Herald record. Woods also suffered that nightmare of every publisher, a picture published with a disastrously wrong caption. In this case the caption read "Noted American Burglar Captured," but the picture was that of Sir Henry Thornton, president of the Canadian National Railways. Woods learned of the mistake at the Ranchmen's Club, where he happened to be dining with some gleeful officials of the CPR.

Much worse was the day in 1922 when a Herald reporter, Chief Buffalo Child Long Lance, bombed City Hall. The chief wasn't a real chief, and the bomb wasn't a real bomb, but it was all very exciting nevertheless. The city's top officials and Ralph B. Wilson, a Herald reporter, were in the mayor's office, discussing labor unrest; a brick had been thrown through the mayor's window the day before. The door opened, and a masked figure slowly pushed a black satchel into the office. Even more ominous was a burning fuse protruding from the bag. Thinking quickly, Wilson rushed for an exit. He was bowled over by a city commissioner aiming for the same door. Mayor Samuel H. Adams took refuge behind his desk, joined by the city solicitor. Another commissioner jumped through the second-storey window, and hit the ground running. The city treasurer tried to follow, but got stuck in the window frame. The satchel proved to be empty. The city solicitor, Leonard W. Brockington (later to become first chairman of the CBC and an advisor to Prime Minister Mackenzie King) interceded for Long Lance, but to no avail. That afternoon the chief became the only Herald reporter ever fired on the front page of the paper. He later found work in Hollywood, where he died, perhaps of suicide, perhaps a murder victim, in 1932.

All this was diverting, but not of much help in putting out a paper. Woods had more serious things to worry about. At first, the Southam family wanted to control The Herald's editorial viewpoint, but Woods had a mind of his own, and wanted to speak that mind in the paper. Gradually, the present-day arrangement evolved: each Southam paper makes its own editorial policy, and head office learns of these policies by reading the papers. By 1935, editorial autonomy had reached the point where Southam's Ottawa Citizen was proclaiming Social Credit to be the salvation of mankind, while The Herald was denouncing it as dangerous nonsense. (In later years The Citizen supported the Liberals. The Herald, for the most part, has taken an independent Conservative line, though not automatically. Much to the outrage of the Tories, in 1963 it endorsed Lester Pearson, John Diefenbaker's Liberal rival.)

Woods did have to struggle, early on, with the local Conservatives. They seemed to yearn for the days of Alexander Lucas, when The Herald was essentially a Tory house organ. Woods was a Conservative, but he valued his independence, and for a while he had to contend with the Tories' threats to set up a newspaper of their own. At that time, about 1910, Calgary had two Liberal papers, The Albertan and The News, and another Conservative paper would have further pinched The Herald's market. The Tories' threat evaporated, however, without extracting any serious concessions from Woods.

In October, 1913, came the first hint of vast new wealth for Alberta. A well near Turner Valley produced a small amount of high-grade oil. There was an immediate boom in exploration ventures, many of them foolish or fraudulent. Woods decreed that The Herald would carry no oil company stock advertisements until a useful amount of oil was found. He held firm in the face of charges that he was a tool of big

The Herald building about 1910, at Centre Street and Seventh Avenue. Newsboys are about to hit the streets of downtown Calgary with the latest edition. The paper was growing quickly at this time, and in 1913 it had to move to larger quarters.

business trying to keep the little man from making a fortune in oil. In May, 1914, when the Dingman discovery well at Turner Valley blew in, The Herald relaxed its restrictions.

The oil boom came after a real estate boom. Calgary had grown from 12,000 people in 1906 to 44,000 in 1911, and The Herald's circulation had outgrown its plant. Inspired by this growth, Southams put up two new buildings at 1st Street and 7th Avenue S.W., one across the avenue from the Bay, the other across from Central United Church. In 1913 The Herald moved into the one across from the church. (This structure was later known as the Greyhound Building, and still later was torn down to make way for AGT's Len Werry Building.) Herald circulation reached 20,000 in 1914, nearly double what it was only four years earlier. Unfortunately, the real estate boom had ended in 1913, and the other Southam building was to be a white elephant for some 20 years.

The First World War made extraordinary demands on the newspapers. There was no broadcast radio. Newspaper "extras" were the only source of fast-breaking news. Herald staffers would stumble home after producing a late-night extra, catch a few hours' sleep, then go back to work. Some set up beds in the office and stayed there.

The newspaper extra would eventually be killed off by radio. A few years after the war, The Herald ventured into this new field. On May 2, 1922, radio station CHCQ went on the air, sending its 10-watt signal from the top of the Herald building. In August, "The Station Of The Calgary Herald" boosted its power to 2,000 watts and changed its call letters to CFAC. Over the years, Southam gradually reduced its radio station holdings. In 1959, the company decided not to control radio stations in cities where it published newspapers. Southam reduced its share of CFAC to 40 per cent from 60 in 1961, and this remaining interest was sold in 1971.

Oil and real estate were all very well, but the real prosper-

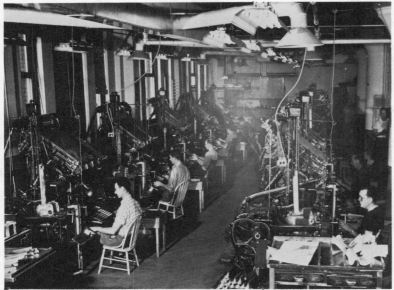

Linotypes (top) set type for The Herald for 70 years. Copy editors (second from top) had to do their job with pencils and glue pots until computer terminals (above) came into the newsroom. The old Herald Building (below) has been a local landmark since 1912.

ity of Alberta still rested on the farmer. In 1923 The Herald played an important part in founding the Alberta Wheat Pool, which gave farmers more leverage to get a good price in the grain market. The United Farmers of Alberta wanted to bring in Aaron Sapiro, an American organizer who had set up marketing co-ops in the United States. Woods enthusiastically lent the paper's support to the idea, and with The Herald's backing, Sapiro came to Alberta. The wheat pool was in business the same year.

By 1930 The Herald's circulation had reached 30,000, and there it hovered all through the Thirties, at one point dropping as low as 27,000. In the depth of the Depression, in 1932, the paper netted less than $50,000 before taxes. In 1929, the net had been $300,000. Only somewhat daunted, The Herald moved again in 1932. This time it took over larger quarters in the other Southam building, on the northeast corner of Seventh Avenue and First Street S.W., just across Seventh Avenue from the Bay. There it stayed for nearly 50 years, until it moved to its new plant in 1981.

The Herald had to scramble for revenue in the Thirties. To hold on to its cash-short farm subscribers, the paper accepted 10 bushels of wheat (delivered to an elevator, not to the paper) for a year's subscription. Circulation salesmen made week-long trips on muddy country roads, trying to keep old subscribers and sign up new ones. The advertising department, The Herald's main revenue source, also faced an uphill fight, with occasional triumphs. Once the paper published a picture and a story boasting of the huge crowd drawn to a furniture store sale by an advertisement "appearing exclusively in The Herald."

These were hard-working, short-staffed days for The Herald's people. Gerry Brawn, who later became news editor, then promotion manager, set a record. One night he did his shift as editor of the 10 p.m. edition (published for the after-theatre crowd) and then was asked to fill in for the ailing night editor. At 5 a.m. he was asked to replace the telegraph editor. Then it was time to work on the 10 p.m. edition again. So it went for 72 hours, with Brawn catching cat-naps at his desk.

In 1935, Social Credit came on the Alberta political scene. The Herald opposed it from the first, firing daily broadsides on the editorial page, but in August, 1935 William Aberhart's Social Credit forces swept into power. The Herald needed a reporter who was on speaking terms with the new premier. Fred Kennedy was chosen: he was the only Herald man who thought before the election that Aberhart had a chance. His speaking terms with Aberhart often became shouting terms. Once, when Kennedy was arguing with the premier over the long-distance phone, Herald editor Robert Somerville was drawn from his office to find what the noise was about. Gerry Brawn shushed him: "Kennedy's talking to the premier in Edmonton." Somerville snapped "Why the hell doesn't he use the telephone?"

Woods retired in 1935, but he kept an active interest in The Herald until his death in 1941. O. L. Leigh-Spencer, a Herald man since 1907, took over as publisher soon after Social Credit was elected. He led The Herald in an epic editorial battle with the provincial government. In 1937, Aberhart turned on his journalistic tormentors with a press-control law. Under this law, the government could order a paper to publish the government's version of the truth, yet at the same time forbid anyone to sue for libels contained in this government-ordered material. The government could require the names and addresses of all news writers and their sources; it could prohibit publishing of articles written by certain persons, or news provided by certain sources. It could even ban an entire publication. In due course the law was thrown out by the Supreme Court, much to the joy of the Herald, which had reached new rhetorical heights in opposing Aberhart.

In 1941, Leigh-Spencer moved on to the Vancouver Province. Peter Galbraith, who had come over from The Albertan as managing editor, succeeded him as publisher. A new generation of writers came up in the Second World War: Ross Munro, who kept going on benzedrine for 30 sleepless hours to report the slaughter at Dieppe; Dick Sanburn, who went with the Canadians as they fought their way through Italy, and was once one truck away from death by land-mine; Frank Swanson, who went into the Canadian Army with a master's degree in journalism from Columbia University, and came out as a major to cover the Belsen trial and later the war crimes tribunal at Nuremburg. A.C. Cummings, the Southam bureau man in London, belonged to an older generation, but he stayed on through the blitz, though in his dispatches he seemed to take every bomb personally.

John Southam, home from the war as lieutenant-colonel of an anti-tank regiment, took charge of The Herald in 1946, and remained publisher until his death in 1954, at the age of 45. For all his establishment credentials, Southam had a resolutely unconventional side. The Banff Springs Hotel had often annoyed him by insisting that he turn his car over to an attendant to be parked: after all, that was the dignified way to do things. Southam borrowed a steamroller from a paving crew, rumbled up to the hotel, descended from the juggernaut, and told the attendant "Park that!" At The Herald, he stood behind his staff against complaints about controversial stories; one of The Herald's notable achievements in his time was a series by David Stansfield on the province's disgraceful treatment of foster children and juvenile delinquents.

Basil Dean succeeded Southam as publisher. An original thinker with an orderly mind — a rare combination — he was fondly remembered by Herald staffers after he moved to The Edmonton Journal in 1962, and died at 52, in 1967. There was Dean the publisher, dealing with a reader's complaint about an undelivered paper by smoothing out his own copy of The Herald and delivering it in person. There was Dean the mathematics specialist, reaching for his slide-rule when Herald columnist Ken Liddell wrote about a tanner who worked with hides 10 feet by 25. Could that be right? Given the diameter of a cow, Dean reasoned, multiplied by . . . Dick Sanburn, editor-in-chief, cut through the mathematical haze: "Liddell, if in your wanderings you should see a cow 25 feet long, by all means photograph it."

During Dean's time as publisher a strange new star, the Herald Weatherizer, appeared briefly above the Calgary skyline. The Weatherizer, a neon-lit spike with a plastic star on top, perched on the Herald Building and signalled weather forecasts to grateful Calgarians. That was the theory, at least. Rings of neon light crawling up the Weatherizer indicated rising temperatures; blue light from the plastic star meant clear

Probably the most famous Herald picture was this one, taken in 1950 by Harry Befus at the scene of a fatal accident in which a pedestrian was knocked out of his rubbers and thrown 35 feet. It won several awards, and was reprinted in Life magazine.

skies, and so on. The forecasts were frequently wrong, because the newsroom staff forgot to set the controls, or set them wrong. In 1959, after three years of predicting snow in July and rain in December, the Weatherizer was scrapped.

Another Herald landmark worked out better. For nearly 50 years, six clocks in The Herald's window on Seventh Avenue told the time in zones ranging from Los Angeles to Paris. The clocks were taken down in the Sixties when the building was renovated, but they were brought back by popular request, mostly from bus drivers who had been setting their watches to Herald time.

All through the Fifties The Herald struggled with a press it had bought second-hand in 1932. The city was getting bigger, and so was the paper. Finally, the press was expanded: in the late Fifties, The Herald bought four more press units — second-hand, again. Three were for production, and the fourth was cannibalized for spare parts. Since three units had been stored for some time in an apple orchard, spare parts were definitely needed. Press foreman Bill Tart and production manager Ty Jackson nursed this collection of scrap metal through some difficult days. Once the cast-iron frame of a press unit cracked and the whole unit dropped several inches out of line with its companions. Production stopped while the press crew threaded paper around the dead unit and through a spare one. After especially bad breakdowns, people recruited from the newsroom and the business offices would help bundle papers to be trucked to the waiting carriers. "We were late sometimes, but we always got the paper out," Jackson recalled when he retired in 1979.

Printing technique has radically changed in the past twenty years. About all that remains of printing as Gutenberg knew it is ink and paper; the process of getting the two together is very different today.

In 1964, The Herald added a press and composing-room annex to its old building downtown. The annex was new, but the equipment inside it had not fundamentally changed since the turn of the century. Linotype operators still transformed words into raised letters running along one edge of an inch-high strip of lead alloy. These lines of type were assembled into full pages — a tricky business, since the page of metal was the mirror-image of the printed page, like a rubber stamp. Then an impression of the whole page was forced into a soft, moist paper mat. This mat, curved and baked dry, served as a mold to shape molten metal into a half-circle printing plate with raised lettering, ready for the high-speed rotary press. (The craft of making these plates, incidentally, is known as stereotyping; this is the original and honorable meaning of the word.)

Continuing growth eventually strained the downtown plant, even with its addition. By 1968, The Herald was selling 100,000 papers a day, and these were large papers. By the early Seventies, the volume of news and advertising pressed hard on the available staff and working space. Fortunately, new technology was coming to printing. Hot metal and thousands of moving parts were being replaced by a new hybrid of electronics and photography.

A good Linotype operator could set more than 200 lines of news an hour, but a Metroset phototypesetting machine can run at up to 1,000 lines *per minute*. Since nobody can type this fast, computers come into the picture. They accumulate the words of dozens of reporters and ad-takers working simultaneously, and feed finished news and advertisements at high speed to the typesetting machines. Instead of a battered manual typewriter, a reporter uses a video

Until the mid-70s, each page of The Herald was built up like this, out of metal slugs bearing raised mirror-image lettering. Today, type is made of photographic paper, not lead alloy.

In 1964, prosperity reached the production department. The Herald opened an addition north of its old building, complete with a brand-new press, the paper's first in at least 50 years. This building was just the beginning of a long period of expansion and technical change for The Herald. Frank Swanson, who was appointed publisher in 1962, probably accounts for more than half of The Herald's capital spending since it was founded — with some reason, since the paper's circulation has nearly doubled in his time. In 1932, The Herald had boasted that its new home across the street from the Bay was "probably the most modern and up-to-date of any newspaper in Western Canada." In 1964, Swanson recalled that claim, and said that the then-new addition to the Herald Building was probably one of the most modern and up-to-date newspaper plants in Canada, if not the continent. It's a claim he could repeat now about The Herald's new $70 million plant.

Frank Swanson has been suspected of carrying a concealed sense of humor. According to one story, possibly apocryphal, a tenant of the old Herald Building met him in the elevator and said "Tell me, Mr. Swanson, how many people work for The Herald?" Swanson paused while the elevator slowed for the second floor, and then, as the door opened and he stepped off, gave his answer: "About half." He is also known for a certain quiet forcefulness. Once, out shooting on his property, he found himself locked out of his garage. Solu-

tion? Shoot the lock off the door. He shot the lock off, all right, but the door still wouldn't budge, so he broke a window. It cost him a cut hand, but he got into his garage.

Despite some picturesque exceptions, the flavor of the newspaper business is becoming more bland. It's been nearly twenty years since three reporters, fed up with Herald pay, took off for Mexico with a piano player from the Wales Hotel, a case of Metrecal, and $40 cash. (They got to Spokane.) People in the business are better-paid now, and they have more formal training. Even in the early Sixties, before a university degree became commonplace among beginning reporters, Merv Anderson, then The Herald's assistant city editor, was running an in-house training program for junior staff in the newsroom.

No doubt this greater seriousness has been good for the paper, and good for the readers, but it has thinned out the ranks of picturesque newspaper characters. Fortunately, there is still John Schmidt, The Herald's agriculture editor, or, as he prefers to style himself, "the manure editor." He's what might be called a practising anarchist. Once, driving a Herald car, he was stopped and rebuked by a policeman in the middle of an illegal left turn. He stepped out, handed over the keys, and uttered the motorist's Declaration of Independence: "Well, then, you drive the durn thing." Then he stomped back to the office. This is the John Schmidt who once desired the atten-

display terminal, which looks like a typewriter keyboard grafted onto a television set. As a reporter types, words appear on the screen, and are stored in the computer. The writer can make changes, additions or deletions cleanly. If he deletes a word, the text on the screen moves up to close the gap. If he inserts a word, everything on the screen is nudged along to make room. Later an editor can call up the reporter's story on another terminal, salvage it (says the editor) or ruin it (says the reporter) and send the finished version to the typesetter. Display advertisements (supermarket ads, for instance) are prepared on more elaborate terminals, whose large screens give printers a preview of the finished job. When a printer (probably an old hand retrained from the days of hot metal) has adjusted the size and position of all the type in an ad, he sends it to the typesetting machine.

In this new age of printing, there is new work for the men who used to take badly-typed, heavily-penciled copy and turn it into metal words. Some now tend the ailments of the new electronic marvels. Others put together pages from the output of the high-speed typesetters. The machines turn out long strips of paper covered with clean black lettering, one column wide. This paper type has to be trimmed and carefully pasted into position on a page-sized sheet of paper. Headlines and picture captions come out on the same machine, and are pasted onto the same sheet. Advertisements, either ready-made from ad agencies or prepared by The Herald, are also pasted in. It is like putting together a giant scrapbook, very carefully, to a close deadline.

The result is one perfect copy of one page, which leaves about 150,000 copies to go. The pasted-up page is photographed, using a mammoth camera that takes film the size of a newspaper. Here the stereotypers take over; but their job, too, has been transformed. From the developed film they transfer the image of a page to new kinds of printing plate. Before The Herald moved to its new quarters and new presses, these plates were a thin sheet of plastic-coated aluminum, with raised lettering etched out of the plastic by a photographic process. Plates for The Herald's new presses are just a flat, flexible sheet of aluminum, whose surface is treated so that print areas pick up ink, while blank areas don't. On the press, the plate picks up ink and transfers it to a rubber "blanket," which then passes it on to the paper. (This offset approach works better than transferring the ink direct from metal to paper.)

The Herald's three new presses are computer-controlled, which helps the pressmen monitor the finicky adjustments that have to be made all through a press run in order to turn out a good-looking paper. Automatic conveyers carry streams of finished papers to the mailroom, where automatic machinery inserts pre-printed news or advertising sections. The papers are automatically counted into bundles and automatically wrapped and addressed to carrier routes.

When the papers get to the carrier, he or she manually puts one copy on each subscriber's doorstep. Nobody has yet worked out a way to automate the carriers. There seems to be no need. And that, to revive an old slogan, is how "The Herald Goes Home."

---

tion of the minister of telephones and utilities. (Schmidt wanted the minister to make people stop calling up to sell him dance lessons.) So, of course, he bought a war-surplus telephone, pulverized it with a large hammer, and began his appointment by pouring pieces of telephone from a shopping bag onto the minister's desk.

Three other Herald reporters, Vern Simaluk, Carl Potter and Peter Michaelson, once had Mount Royal rezoned for high-rise apartments — at least in the pages of The Albertan. They suspected that an Albertan reporter was stealing carbon copies of their work from the press-room at city hall, so they concocted a story announcing that the most exclusive district in the city had been rezoned for high-density housing. The Albertan's man fell for it. The Herald's city hall crew spent the next day explaining to their editors that no, they had not missed a great story, and no, they couldn't imagine how The Albertan could have been so wrong. Readers in Mount Royal may be comforted to learn that this kind of thing doesn't happen much any more.

In the midst of the fun and games, The Herald's staff managed to put out a steadily improving paper, winning a fair number of prizes, including several National Newspaper Awards (Dick Snell for news reporting, Carol Hogg for feature writing, Jack DeLorme, Harry Befus, Gerry Ormond, Kent Stevenson, and John Colville for photography.)

Calgary grew phenomenally in the Sixties and the Seventies. The Herald's circulation reached 100,000 in 1968. By the end of 1980, it was about 140,000, and 173,000 on Fridays. The one-inch advertisement that brought Armour and Braden $1.40 would now cost about $20, but it will reach a thousand times as many readers.

The latest milestone in The Herald's growth is its new building. The new site has eliminated the problem of moving 150,000 large papers through downtown traffic. The plant also makes the most of new technology to produce a more timely and more attractive paper. Armour and Braden would be astonished and, we hope, delighted, to see what they started.

Today's Herald building is about a mile and a century away from the 14-by-20 tent where it all began. No one who remembers that tent, no one who read that first paper with the ink still wet, is now alive. The paper itself is crumbling to dust. Since August 31, 1883, uncounted men and women have brought The Herald, day by day, to the beginning of its 100th year. They left behind them, first on paper, then on microfilm, a memory of their city and their world: a memory that spans two world wars, a great depression, social and scientific revolutions, and the growth of a city still young and hopeful. For a few episodes from this memory, read on.

The Daily Herald

22ND YEAR. WHOLE NUMBER 5,884.   CALGARY, ALBERTA, MONDAY JANUARY 25, 1904   PRICE FIVE CENTS

Special Edition.

Cashel the American Desperado Captured this Afternoon.

SURROUNDED BY POSSE AND DRIVEN OUT BY FIRE.

GRAPHIC STORY OF THE MOST SENSATIONAL CASE IN THE HISTORY OF CANADA.

Birth of a City

1883-1904

Calgary 1883

The Herald began reporting the events of Calgary and the world outside in 1883, just eight years after the North West Mounted Police established a fort at the junction of the Bow and Elbow Rivers.

Calgary and the world outside: that was the order of priorities. The railroad had brought the telegraph, but for thirty years the telegraph brought very little news that would disturb a loyal, English-speaking citizen of the British Empire. The Herald published foreign news, but it devoted most of its attention to local matters and Canadian politics. The Russians and the Japanese might fight a bloody war, the Americans might follow their newspapers into battle against Spain, but if trouble broke out among the un-British races of the Empire,

British ships and British troops would quickly restore the Victorian calm. Queen Victoria had reigned since 1837, and would until 1901; it was the full summer noon of the British Empire. Not even the Boer War, in which men from Calgary fought in South Africa, disturbed the innocence and insularity of this little foothills town.

Meanwhile, there was a city to build. In 1883, Calgary in itself showed no great promise; the promise, as The Herald untiringly pointed out, lay in the surrounding farm and range lands, and in the rich mineral deposits of the Rockies. Calgary itself was the home of some 400 people, who lived and did business in tents and wooden buildings. When the streets were not mud and horse dung, they were dust and horse dung. There were no sidewalks and no streetlights. Water was drawn from wells and delivered in a horse-drawn wagon. After sunset, the only light came from candles and coal-oil lanterns. In winter, Calgary warmed itself with wood and coal; it was a smoky town in those days. Every house and every hotel had a privy out back. Typhoid fever was a constant threat, though it never became an epidemic. There was a bridge across the Elbow, but anyone who had business in the empty land north of the Bow had to take a ferry. The Hudson's Bay and I.G. Baker trading posts might stock a few luxury items, but most of their stock was food and gear for life in a hard country. The population included a complement of drunks, gamblers and prostitutes.

For all this, Calgary never was a Wild West town of the kind so dear to Hollywood. The mounted police arrived first, and they stayed in strength. The forces of respectability, The Herald among them, were strong here. Andrew Armour and Thomas Braden, who started The Herald, were founding members of the First Methodist Church, and early on the paper noted with displeasure that many Calgarians were engaging in sport on Sunday. A year later, it approvingly noted a great improvement in the tone of the local Sabbath. Mrs. Armour, incidentally, is said to have brought the first piano to Calgary. The Calgary House Hotel boasted a reading room, and by 1884, Calgary had a Masonic lodge and a literary society, just like the big cities back east.

In 1883, most of Calgary was East of the Elbow, but it suited the CPR's convenience to put its station west of the river. After protesting in vain, in the winter of 1883-84 Calgarians folded their tents and skidded their wooden buildings across the frozen river to the west side.

In November, 1884, Calgary was incorporated as a town, claiming a population of 1,000, at least double what it had been a year earlier. Readers of The Herald were left in no doubt about the town's great future. Calgary had farm and ranch land; Calgary had coal, iron and precious metals; Calgary had the railroad; Calgary, therefore, would become another Chicago. (At the time, that seemed a good thing for Calgary to become.)

From the beginning, The Herald promoted Calgary and the surrounding lands in terms that nowadays would bring a blush to the cheek of the most hardened local booster. The paper was also quick to respond to pessimism in Eastern or American papers. Did a rancher lose half his stock in bitter cold? Well, that was an abnormal winter; ordinarily the Chinooks ... Did an American homesteader give up in despair and go home? His neighbors stayed, and they didn't think he was much of a farmer anyway. As the number of settlers began to grow in the 1890s, The Herald kept accentuating the positive.

In the 1880s, at least, the facts seemed to justify the local boosters' enthusiasm. Farmers weren't coming in as quickly as they hoped, but Calgary was thriving. By 1891, it had nearly 3,900 people, ten times the figure of seven or eight years earlier. Wooden buildings were giving way to solid two- and three-storey edifices of sandstone. There was electric light, a water system, a sewer system. There were even sidewalks. True, these were wooden sidewalks, and the ones near the river had to be tied down so they wouldn't float away when the Bow flooded, but they were sidewalks. The electric light system was unpredictable, and the water system tended to fall

A wood-burning locomotive brought this work train to Calgary in 1884.

Calgary in 1883 was a clutter of tents, log cabins, and a few frame houses.

short when there was a fire, and the sewers emptied into the river at the foot of First Street East, but nevertheless, these amenities were taken to be the signs of a progressive, go-ahead town, destined for great things.

Doubt must have crept in during the 1890s. Between 1891 and 1901, Calgary's population grew by barely 200. Apparently the population declined in the early Nineties, and the losses were barely made up after times improved about 1897. In that year, Sir Wilfrid Laurier, the Liberal prime minister, appointed Clifford Sifton as his minister of the interior. Sifton put his considerable energies to work on finding settlers for the Northwest Territories. Alberta's population, 30,000 in 1895, reached nearly 75,000 in 1901. Most of the newcomers lived on farms, but the towns, too, were thriving. By the end of 1904, when this chapter ends with Alberta about to become a province, Calgary's population was nearing 10,000, and there was some tentative talk of a real estate boom. (J.J. Young, owner of The Herald, owned a house at the corner of Fifth Avenue and Second Street S.W. Evidently he had a shrewd, if long-range, eye for property values. His house stood in what is now Esso Plaza's courtyard.)

This story of great, though interrupted, progress is not the only story The Herald told in its first 21 years. There were fires and murders and a smallpox epidemic at home, a rebellion close to home, and wars far away. And always there was politics.

The rebellion broke out in 1885, when the Metis, afraid of losing their land to the white man, as they had already lost the buffalo, rallied behind Louis Riel. When he declared a provisional government in March, 1885, a force of North West Mounted Police was sent to quell the revolt. The NWMP suffered several setbacks, and Ottawa rushed 4,000 militiamen to their aid. The fighting never came close to Calgary, though for a time it was feared that the local Indians might join the uprising. The Riel Rebellion was suppressed in May, and Riel was hanged in November, 1885.

In 1892, an outbreak of smallpox was traced to a Chinese laundry. Four people died. There was an outcry against the Chinese in town, an outcry in which The Herald unfortunately joined. In that time and place, the superiority of the white race, especially its British and American branches,

was automatically assumed. The Herald shared this assumption, and said some lamentable things about the Chinese, the Indians, and the Metis. These remarks are part of the record, and they have not been glossed over in the chapter that follows.

International conflict first touched Calgary in 1899, when troops were recruited here for the Boer War, fought between Great Britain and the Dutch-speaking South African republics of Transvaal and the Orange Free State. There was great enthusiasm, especially in Ontario, for Canadian aid to the motherland's cause. The Herald thought that this was all very well, but pointed out that there was plenty of work for able-bodied young men to do at home. It was also concerned that Western breeders should get a fair share of the market for cavalry horses. (Among the 7,000 Canadians who fought in South Africa was a unit privately funded by Lord Strathcona, a founder of the Canadian Pacific Railway. In 1905 the federal government established a Calgary-based squadron of mounted infantry named Lord Strathcona's Horse to commemorate the regiment sent to South Africa.)

Finally, and always, there was politics. The Conservatives were in power in Ottawa from 1878 to 1896; Sir John A. Macdonald was prime minister until his death in 1891. He was succeeded by a series of short-term Conservative prime ministers. (One of them, Sir Mackenzie Bowell, had happened to be in Calgary when The Herald was getting started in 1883, and lent a hand with the type-setting.) The Herald campaigned as vigorously as a good Conservative paper could against the federal government's indifference to the needs of the West. When Sir Wilfrid Laurier formed a Liberal government in 1896, the paper had a freer hand. But even the territorial government at Regina, The Herald often complained, didn't really understand that the Calgary district needed a bridge, an irrigation system, or some other improvement. Most of these battles are long forgotten, but they mattered at the time, and they were fought hard. By 1895, there was a motto running across the top of every front page, just under The Herald's name: Home Rule For Alberta. That battle was being fought a bit too soon. Ten years later Alberta did become a province, but that's getting ahead of the story. First, a look at Calgary and the world, 1883 to 1904, as seen by The Herald.

A Promising Little Town

Calgary was a quiet little town, on the whole, but it did have its moments — some funny, some horrifying. Fires, murders, marvels and oddities stood out from the run of routine news. Still, even the routine news had its own charm, as this selection of items from The Herald's first front page shows. The geologist in the first item was presumably impressed by the coal and metal resources around Calgary. (At the time there were silver mines west of Banff). It would be another 30 years before oil and gas became important.

Mr. J.H. Panton, geologist, of the Manitoba Historical and Scientific Society, spent a day in and about Calgary, and reports a very interesting field of study for men of his profession. He has promised to prepare a paper on his researches in this locality for The Herald, which we have no doubt will be hailed with interest by our readers. We hope also to be favored with a paper by the botanist of the Society.

A number of petty thefts have lately been committed in the vicinity, but the smallest thing we have heard of was the cutting and stealing of the ropes from the foot bridge across the Elbow. This is a matter of some importance, as strangers coming into town are very liable to get a cold bath gratuitously. We hope the ropes will soon be replaced.

We have had the pleasure of inspecting the new hotel just completed by Dunne & Wright, and find it a perfect model of taste and neatness. It contains a large comfortable parlour, and a number of bed-rooms, all handsomely carpeted and furnished in the best of style.

The dining-room has accommodation for about 40 guests, and the reading room is well supplied with the latest papers. Messrs. Dunne & Wright are well and favorably known to the public, and we have no doubt they will receive the large share of public patronage which they so justly merit.

August 31, 1883

The Herald launched itself with this ringing declaration of editorial purpose.

In presenting our first issue to the public, it is only fair and just that, in accordance with usage, we should define the principles which we propose to govern our career. Our position briefly is as follows: Calgary and the district of country, of which she is the acknowledged centre, has long felt the want of a live journal, to faithfully set before the outside public the claims she possesses, from natural advantages, to become one of the greatest centres of the North West.

The duty, then, and pleasure of The Herald, will be, categorically speaking, this:

The collation of all news items of local interest.

The encouragement and support of all legitimate manufacturing and commercial enterprises.

The publication of all agricultural, ranching and mining particulars.

The encouragement of all measures religious and moral, intended for the welfare of the community.

The exposure of all species of vice and immorality that comes to our knowledge.

The exposure of any measures or acts on the part of individuals, corporations or governments, which appear to be framed against the true interest of the place, people or district.

Thoroughly independent in the matter of politics, always ready to give credit to one and all, irrespective of creed, color, race or politics, whose efforts may be worthy of recognition, but under no circumstances neutral.

Having always the courage of its convictions, The Herald will not be found afraid to speak out its mind freely when there are wrongs to be redressed or manifest abuses to be remedied.

The Herald will always lend its influence against the introduction of intoxicating liquors as a beverage in the North West Territories, believing that the liquor traffic engenders vice, immorality and crime.

Whilst open to, and courting correspondence, on questions of public interest, The Herald will never lend itself to become the vehicle for disseminating the views of any one clique or faction, but its columns will be free to all.

Having established The Herald on a purely business basis, with our own capital, and having no ends to serve, other than the prosperity and welfare of the community in which we have chosen our home, and the pardonable desire to place The Herald on a prosperous and respectable basis, we are content, in presenting our compliments to the inhabitants of Calgary and vicinity in particular and the whole North West generally, to leave the result of the enterprise in their hands.

August 31, 1883

Less than a month after its birth, The Herald was already complaining about the post office.

The Calgary mail arrived by stage from Macleod on the 17th of September, bringing to us Toronto papers of August 24th, 25th and 26th, and Winnipeg papers from 27th to 30th of same month. This is certainly a long time to be deprived of our mail matter.

The delay is explained by the stage leaving Medicine Hat on Wednesday, arriving at Macleod on Saturday, and as the stage left Macleod for Calgary on Friday our mail matter would have lain over at Macleod until the next trip, had not one of superintendent McIllree's teams been at Macleod and again conferred a favour on this place by bringing forward two large bags of mail matter.

It will be seen therefore that our mail matter is liable to lie a week at Medicine Hat, three days is then occupied in transferring it to Macleod, it may lie there nine days, and arrive in Calgary three days later. Twenty-two days is employed in conveying the mail from Medicine Hat to Calgary, a distance of 180 miles by rail, with a daily train, and yet our Post Office authorities do not see fit to even give us a weekly mail by train.

September 21, 1883

It has to be admitted that newspapers don't make excuses as well as they used to.

Mr. George L. Frazer, manufacturing confectioner, placed on our sanctum table yesterday some of the first fruits of his labour, consisting of an excellent assortment of cocoanut, sugar loaf, butterscotch taffey, and other varieties of candy. While we gazed on them we smiled all over our face, thinking of the rich feast in store.

We invited all handy to share with us which they did with a gusto, but sad to relate, the richness of the good things proved too much for some of our compositors, and consequently we were somewhat short handed today.

September 28, 1883

Natural gas is much harder to find now that we need it.

At Langevin, 4th siding west of Medicine Hat, a rather singular phenomenon has presented itself. The well-borers have reached a depth of 1,120 feet without finding water, but a gas rushes out of the tube, which, on taking fire emits a flame sufficient to light up the surrounding country. They still purpose going deeper for the water, but have given up working at night, not considering it safe.

December 12, 1883

By 1889, Calgary looked much more substantial that it had just six years earlier, when the first train came through. Builders had started to use the local sandstone, and the centre of town had been moved to its permanent location west of the Elbow River.

In the winter of 1883-84, many Calgarians moved their houses and businesses across the Elbow River to be near the CPR station, which the railway had decided to put west of the river. One anonymous citizen found this a most unsettling experience.

On Saturday, a gentleman went into Dr. Henderson's drug store on business, and after a call of about five minutes turned to go out. On opening the door he was amazed to find himself in a different part of the town. On seeking an explanation, he was informed the doctor was removing, and this had been accomplished so expeditiously and quietly that the ordinary business of the store was not interfered with. We don't quite understand the doctor's object in locating directly in the middle of the present trail and quite out of line with the other buildings in the vicinity.

February 20, 1884

The Herald's founders, good Methodists, were determined to improve the town's morals. So far, the problem they complained of in this editorial has gone unsolved.

It is to be lamented that the vice of prostitution is sullying so deeply the first page of Calgary's history. Already we find the advent of the harlot in town. It may be difficult to stop them from coming here, but it certainly is the duty of the police to stop them from plying their nefarious ways of living in our very midst.

We find the lesser offences of drinking, gambling, etc., crushed by the police with remarkable zeal, yet this greater vice to which we allude, can stalk about our town at noon-day, proclaim to the public its devilish purposes, and yet be winked at by the authorities.

If the den of iniquity which has recently flaunted its sign on Section 15 is not at once swept out of town by the broom of public duty, it will be due to the fact that the authorities are recreant to their trust. If the den to which we refer is allowed to continue its operations, it is merely a question of a few weeks before we have in our midst an exodus from the east of a small army of those characters.

The people of Calgary are asking themselves the question if the police are going to allow this promising town to become the asylum for the harlots and prostitutes of the east.

March 5, 1884

For some time Indians made heavy inroads among "the white man's buffalo." Considering what had happened to the real buffalo, there may have been some rough justice in the situation, but the settlers weren't inclined to see things that way.

We are informed by farmers south of here that the Indians are playing sad havoc among the calves. One gentleman says that out of seventy of last year's calves, he has only seven left, and that a neighbor who last year had one hundred cattle can only count twenty-five. The other day a butcher, noticing that two cows had calved and that two Sarcees were eyeing them, went over to the farmer's boy, telling him what he saw and that he had better go at once and tell his father, who immediately sent him after the calves, and although twenty minutes had not elapsed since the butcher left them, yet when the boy got there one calf was gone and the Indians nowhere to be seen.

These depredations are carried on chiefly by the young bucks, who go in parties of five or six. They will not divulge anything, and think that it is only the one who kills the animal who is amenable to the law, and that by going in parties he cannot be so easily caught. It is a pity that so near to a town of Calgary's size, where there is stationed a force of one hundred police, such depredations should be allowed to continue with impunity.

May 28, 1884

Staying warm in winter was no small problem. The Herald deplored one unofficial solution.

The cold snap and the brilliant business management of our local coal dealers in leaving the town without coal during the severest weather we have enjoyed for two years has proved once more that it only requires opportunity to make fiends of the best of us.

No recognized theory of morality, nor any justifiable worship of midnight Nature in her arctic moods can either satisfactorily explain or adequately account for the extraordinary amount of after-dark prowling around their neighbours' coal-bins which has been the recognized pastime of our citizens during the past week every hour of the night between sun-down and sun-up.

We are aware that the Mountains look well by moonlight. Their castellated pinnacles beneath the pale lunar beams glinting adown their wintry sides, have an irresistible and weird fascination for the poetic soul, but the attitude adopted by the principal poets upon such occasions has not been a crouching stoop, one eye on the eternal hills and the other on your neighbour's kitchen door, with both hands resting lovingly and greedily upon a fifty pound lump of coal which was never paid for by your money.

We cannot insist too strongly upon this. Mountain scenery by night cannot be properly enjoyed in the above attitude, and we cordially invite all interested parties to adopt another.

December 25, 1884

Calgary was once the Sandstone City, before pre-cast concrete became available in so many colors. This item noted the beginning of the sandstone era, and concluded with yet another complaint about freight rates.

The quarries of Messrs. Butlin and May, within two miles of town, are attracting considerable attention in town now that stone buildings are being erected. The bank, Dr. Lafferty's house, the I.G. Baker, Dun and Rankin blocks, the Presbyterian church and the new school house will all be of stone.

The quarries referred to are stated to be freestone equal to the best Ohio freestone, and will presently be another of the many sources of wealth of this district.

Our citizens are rejoicing in a stone and brick craze just now, which may be taken as indicative of disgust at the wooden buildings hitherto in vogue, and an enthusiastic confidence in the future of Calgary. We have, ourself, the utmost confidence in the stone taken from Mr. Butlin's and Mr. May's quarries. It is excellent, and seemingly far ahead of the other stone brought into town.

In the brick line we have little doubt that Calgary will stir herself presently. There is said to be good brick clay on the Elbow, opposite the Mission property, and J.C.M. Davis, for one, is only waiting for a little encouragement to start a kiln, but if the C.P.R. would give good rates from Silverton, we believe the best brick in the territories can be made there. The clay is excellent, lime and water and wood in abundance, and the only thing to complain of is that it cannot be placed on the market at anything like a good figure — say ten or twelve dollars —because of the exorbitant freight. This is a matter for the Board of Trade to take up without doubt.

February 27, 1886

Even though it ignored The Herald's dire warning, the town of Calgary managed somehow not to go broke.

It is evident that the town council receive advice with the cheerful disregard with which a duck receives a thundershower. No doubt the same instinct actuates both, though what the instinct is, one will have to go to the ducks to find out.

It is a misfortune however for the town that the suggestions of the tax-payers should meet with so little encouragement or response. It is pleasant of course to know that the council have so adequate a sense of their own dignity and the respect proper for red tape as to refuse to offer any statement to anybody of the basis upon which they are calculating with so profuse a prodigality as to require $3,000 this year for running the municipal circus.

That it promises to be a circus there is no room for doubt. Men do not incur large expense before they have got at their income or even any idea of what their income will be, without a clearly defined idea of making

Calgary in the sandstone era: in 1929, this building at Eighth Avenue and First Street Southwest was replaced by the Bank of Montreal building.

an edifying show of themselves and their constituents when the books come to be balanced.

Whether it will issue in an auction sale of the corporation, as was the case in Victoria lately, or merely the sale of the councillors' town lots cannot be judged immediately. That it will issue in a burden however which will cramp the growth of the town for some years may be decided on the spot. This town cannot support $3,000 for running expenses alone.

March 5, 1885

The Herald offered a free-enterprise solution to the sidewalk problem. Calgary had recently been incorporated as a town, and an editorial had complained about the number of people on the municipal payroll.

If a man would start a sidewalk along the main street and charge tolls till he had cleared himself he would be a benefactor to this community.

A ditch dug through the snowdrifts between the post office and the Royal would aid materially in drawing off the water. Where are the corporation officers with their shovels? The clerk, the chief constable, the collector, the assessor, the treasurer, and the town solicitor, where are they with their little shovels?

March 12, 1885

Major James Walker (later a Colonel) brought the telephone to Calgary to link his office and his sawmill.

The telephone which Major Walker is erecting between his office and the mills, two miles distant, is all but completed. It is the pioneer telephone of the Calgary district. A telephone from the fort to the station is the next thing in order.

August 12, 1885

The telephone between Major Walker's office and the mill is working, but under disadvantages, since the requisite quantity of wire was not sent up. It is expected though that it will be in complete running order by Monday.

August 19, 1885

A fire in November, 1886 heavily damaged the centre of town. McTavish Street, mentioned below, is now Centre Street; Stephen Avenue is Eighth Avenue South, and Atlantic Avenue is Ninth Avenue South.

At about 5 o'clock Sunday morning flames were observed coming through the roof of a shed between the flour and feed store of S. Parish & Co. and Lamont's tin shop. The fire spread rapidly. In a short time the whole corner block on the southwest of McTavish Street and the Union Hotel across the road were in flames.

The bell was rung in the English Church and the alarm soon spread. The crowd directed their energies to saving the stock in I. G. Baker & Co.'s store and managed to deposit part of it in a place of safety before the flames caught.

Meanwhile the Sherman house at the back of Parish's store, and the buildings on Atlantic Avenue east of the Union Hotel, were rapidly being enveloped in the flames.

A. Carey, one of the proprietors of the Union, lost everything, being even too late to save $500 in bills, which was in his waistcoat pocket. Everything in the Pullman was destroyed.

By this time the whole town was fairly aroused and the police were marched on to the scene. Their discipline and organization made itself felt at once. J. Ellis' store was rapidly cleared of its stock, and the efforts of the crowd were directed to the demolition of Mortimer's bakery and Murdoch's store [to create a fire-break.] An attempt was made to blow the latter up with gunpowder, but failed owing to the force of the charge not being sufficiently concentrated.

Ropes and axes were brought to bear and the buildings were got out of the way just before Ellis' store was fairly in a blaze. Further up the street the Athletic Hotel had been consumed, and set fire in its turn to the Mountain View. The proprietors of the latter house managed to save nearly all of their furniture.

At the Royal Hotel everybody was working with a will; wetted blankets were

Calgary merchants held their first fire sale in 1886, when half the town, such as it was, burned down. Volunteers quickly hauled merchandise into the streets from the threatened buildings. Considering the area it covered, this was probably *Calgary's most dramatic fire; it burned many buildings along Eighth and Ninth Avenues and Centre Street. Fire protection gradually improved, but the fire department was plagued for years by low water pressure.*

---

hung over the roof and out of the windows to protect the walls and every precaution that possibly could be made available, was taken to save the building. Fortunately the portable house formerly occupied by Mr. Riley, which stood between the hotel and I. G. Baker's store, was removed only the day before yesterday. Owing to this, and the fact that the store was built of logs and not of lumber, the preservation of the buildings is in all human probability due.

Dunn and Linehams' butcher shop at the corner of Stephen Ave. and McTavish Street also owed its preservation to sheer hard work. The little building which was formerly Ambrose Shaw's gunsmith's shop was also saved in spite of its close proximity to the Mountain View Hotel, which was totally destroyed.

Mr. C. Sparrow's residence, in the rear of the Athletic Hotel was also saved though much scorched and blackened. Mr. E. Rogers of Rogers & Grant, who was indefatigable in his efforts all day, put out the flames, after they had caught the corner of the building, with a Babcock extinguisher. Inside were the books and papers in Mr. C. Sparrow's charge as treasurer of the town council in 1885.

With the destruction of Mortimer's bakeshop and Murdoch's store, which were hauled bodily away in pieces by the efforts of the police and citizens, the fire began to abate and the Mountain View on the west and Ellis' store on the east marked the limits of its ravages on the Avenue, while it extended down McTavish Street as far as Baker's store on one side and the old Chipman store, now the property of Dunne & Lineham on the other.

November 13, 1886

Calgary hospitality has always had a few small defects.

A gentleman of rather dudish manner says that while he was passing an hotel on Sunday afternoon a pail of water was maliciously dashed from an upstairs window upon him, very much to the discomfort of his new white hat, silk velvet coat, white satin vest and Russia duck lower garments. The party feels so indignant about it, that he will no doubt report it to the New York "Police Gazette."

July 31, 1889

By 1891, Calgary had at least the beginnings of big-city amenities. Still, there was much to be done. The water-works didn't deliver enough pressure to fight fires; power failures were commonplace; and the sewers simply emptied into the river at the foot of Osler Street, now known as First Street S. E. (The next street downstream, by the way, was inappropriately named Drinkwater.) Even so, this editorial took some justified pride in the young city's progress.

With the completion of the Water Works Calgary adds another to her claims to be regarded as the most advanced town on these North-Western plains. We have a telephone service both by day and night. We have two electric light works giving the cheapest light to be had in the Dominion, and this light univer-

sally used in business establishments and churches and largely in private residences. We have a Sewerage system, embracing all the business district and a portion of the residential district.

We have a good Fire Department, the best between Winnipeg and the coast, with both steam and chemical engines, hook and ladder wagon, ample hose reels, and a zealous corps of officers and men.

Finally we have the Water Works system to round off the local improvements and to aid the Fire Department in giving citizens the fullest protection against fire.

When we have done all that is possible to safeguard the health and the property of the citizens generally (especially if compulsory entrance to the sewers be enacted and the old cess-pits that have grown so offensive be closed – both as sanitary measures) the citizens will expect the Town Council to turn its attention to the improvement of the Streets by paving or otherwise, and also to the duty of utilizing the Islands in the Bow as a public park.

The things that are absolutely necessary must first be dealt with – such, for instance, as the public health, the protection against fire, the improvement of the financial situation; after these the citizens will hope to see steps taken to beautify the town and make life in it as pleasant as possible. With a charming townsite, a population keenly appreciative of zeal in the interests of the Town, and already such improvements established as place Calgary ahead of all prairie towns as an agreeable home, we have in sight a prosperous future, which may be greatly helped by enlightened action on lines of practical utility.

June 25, 1891

The following appeared in the Edmonton Bulletin of July 11:
"Reports from Calgary are to the effect that there are thirteen cases of smallpox in that town and two deaths have occurred."

This statement is very far indeed from the truth. There has been no death from smallpox in this town. The only cases that have occurred are the following:

On June 28 a Chinaman living in a shack on Stephen Ave. East, where there was a Chinese laundry, was found to have the disease, from which he was then recovering. He was at once, with the other Chinese inmates, sent out of town to an empty shack at the mouth of Nose Creek, where they have been under strict quarantine, guarded by a detachment of Mounted Police.

The shack and all its contents, including all the washing, were burnt up the same day. Since the Chinamen were sent to Nose Creek one more case has developed among them.

On July 2 a carpenter named Kest, living with a companion in a shack east of the Elbow, took the disease, and both parties were sent out to the quarantine ground.

Last night (July 14) it was found that a man named Pettapiece, who keeps a boarding house two doors west of the Chinese laundry, where the disease originated, was ill of smallpox, traceable, it is believed, to the laundry. He was sent during the night to quarantine; the house has been fumigated, the occupants and clothing and premises disinfected, and a man placed in charge to prevent communication with the place.

July 15, 1892

The following story outlined what was perhaps the saddest case of the smallpox outbreak.

The Calgary Health authorities were notified yesterday that Mrs. Joseph Belmar, a young woman, married only a short time and living in the house of her father David Jerry, about a half mile from Shepard railway station — 12 miles east of Calgary — was down with smallpox. A boy came to Calgary for a doctor yesterday p.m., and Dr. McLean and Professor Shaw of Toronto University went down and pronounced it a case of smallpox.

Arrangements were at once made for Dr. Mackid to go to Shepard and to send an ambulance and another wagon to bring up the people and their effects. Tents were sent over to the quarantine ground during the night to receive the patient and other parties from the house, who arrived there about daylight this morning.

The party consisted of two men, two women and two children. The police are in charge of the house. The poor woman had a miscarriage on the road. One of the men in the house got away and the Mounted Police are out after him.

The case of Mrs. Belmar is said to be traceable to her taking a meal at the Pettapiece house about a fortnight ago, but the disease could scarcely have laid dormant all that time.

August 3, 1892

The laws of self preservation are the "higher law", and all other laws must give way before them. It may be that we cannot say to Chinamen, "You cannot set foot in Calgary," but we can take such measures as will render their stay unprofitable.

The Chinaman who enters our town, if he respects our laws and conducts himself properly, is entitled to the protection of those laws and must receive it. As a law and order respecting community this is imperative. Mob violence is on every account to be frowned upon and put down.

We may, if we choose, levy a special tax on Chinese laundries; we may cause them to be inspected, for sanitary reasons, every month or every week; or even without resorting to law at all we may decide among ourselves that these may become nests of disease and we may abstain from sending washing to them.

In this way, by consulting the interests of the public safety, we may render the stay of Chinamen in Calgary useless and, in a short time, without violence, without any interference with personal liberty, we can be rid of what the majority regard as an obnoxious element.

The late exhibition of mob violence will not drive them forth. The Chinese are quick to know that among well disposed citizens the attack on them has only created sympathy for them, and they expect to profit by that sympathy.

People cannot, of course, shut their eyes to the fact that while there is a strong prejudice against the Chinaman, he seems, to many, to be a necessary evil — to some indeed a necessary good.

He is industrious, apparently never tiring. He is prompt and cheerful in his work and does it well. He obeys instructions quickly. He is civil at all times. In a country where domestic help is scarce, very costly and difficult to manage, it is not strange that many employers rather welcome than resent the advent of the Chinese, through whose labors they get a considerable measure of relief.

Those who object to them point to them as birds of passage, without any stake in the country, having no intention of becoming citizens in the proper meaning of the term.

Whether the Chinaman goes or stays it will be in accordance with enlightened public opinion. If public opinion wills that he shall stay he will receive the fullest protection the laws can give him. If public opinion decides that he shall go the country will not be a loser by his absence.

August 5, 1892

On the information of Alderman Cameron the editor of The Herald was summoned before Magistrate Winter yesterday on a charge of riding a bicycle on the sidewalk.

Alderman Cameron was the only witness. Being sworn, he testified to meeting the accused on his wheel on the sidewalk near the latter's house.

The accused having got permission to cross examine the witness, Mr. Cameron said in reply to questions that he had seen certain criticisms of the city council and of himself in The Herald. Denied that those criticisms had anything to do with his bringing this charge, though he admitted having seen other people riding bicycles on the sidewalk and had not taken action against them. Notwithstanding this he claimed to be a truthful man.

The accused in giving his evidence admitted having been on the sidewalk on the night in question, and intimated that he preferred to pay a fine rather than run the risk of breaking his bicycle and possibly his neck by riding on bad roads when it was too dark to see the stones and boulders which aldermanic indifference allowed to spoil the streets.

The magistrate said as no harm had apparently been done, and as the roads were bad, as he knew from personal experience, he would impose a fine of $1 and costs, which was cheerfully paid.

October 26, 1897

An agreement of the council to listen to any complaints, brought Mrs. Fulham to her feet and without any unnecessary verbiage she strode forward with a manly and virtuous air and presented the council with a letter which set down in precise and correct English a statement of her troubles.

She stated in the letter that while sitting in the kitchen of the New Brunswick hotel, Constables Fraser and Waldon seized hold of her and after forcibly removing her threw her into a wagon and despite her protests removed her to the cells and locked her up.

She was fined in the morning and she stated in her letter that the police charged fees for arresting her, and wound up with an appeal that rang unmistakably of injured innocence, for an investigation.

After the letter had been read Mrs. Fulham went off in a diatribe against the police in general and Constables Fraser and Waldon in particular.

"Sure," she said, "an isn't it mesilf that knows the wickedness of thim both. Dey are bad men." There was a family feud between her relatives and those of Constable Fraser and she was sure that it was in pursuance of it that she was arrested.

Mayor Mackie: "It is a matter for the police and relief committee. Rest assured, Mrs. Fulham, this matter will be looked into."

Mrs. Fulham: "Thank you, Mr. Mackie. Sure an if you don't I'll carry it to the high court at Regina."

Senator Lougheed then addressed the council upon a provision which he wished to see inserted in a bylaw to the effect that a lane situated in a block of which he was the sole owner be conveyed to him, as he wished to make permanent improvements upon it.

The senator had just started well into his speech when Mr. Bernard leaned across and whispered behind his hat to Mrs. Fulham, who was sitting on a bench composedly with an air of work well done. The effect upon her was electrical. She bounded to her feet and rushing toward the council with a package above her head, shouted in strident accents which drowned the voice of the senator:

"Sure, gintlemen this is my hair which thim bastes of policemen pulled out." She accordingly deposited on the table a great bunch of iron grey locks for the inspection of the mayor and council and then withdrew and resumed her seat, while Senator Lougheed continued his argument.

October 25, 1901

In 1902, Twentieth-Century technology had not yet reached the city's electric system, and The Herald was growing impatient.

It is really time that the city council took up seriously the matter of lighting. The service at present is simply execrable, and the lights always seem to go out when they are most wanted. The members of the fire, water and light committee should make it their business to interview the manager of the electric light plant, and arrive at some definite understanding in the matter.

If people knew that there were not going to be any lights, provision could be made to meet the case, but, as it is, they never know when they are to have light and when they are to have darkness. It is to be hoped that the new council will take immediate steps to have the present inferior service improved.

January 9, 1902

Another technological miracle reaches Calgary.

A few evenings ago a Herald man was privileged to witness Dr. Ings operating the X rays which he has in his office. The instrument consists of a large and complicated arrangement of glasses, wheels, pulleys, etc., which seems when stirred up to be perfectly alive with electricity. It is really one of the most marvellous inventions produced by modern science.

The newspaper man placed his hand within the scope of the rays, and was horrified to be able to see clearly through it. All the flesh seemed to have disappeared, and nothing was visible save the bones. Any mineral substance may be seen by this means, and the X rays are simply invaluable in locating foreign bodies in the human anatomy. It makes nothing of substance, so long as it is not composed of mineral matter.

The Herald man took an enormous book, many hundred pages thick, and placed it between his hand and the rays, but it did not make the slightest difference. For all the effect it had of obscuring the vision it might have been composed of transparent glass.

July 4, 1902

This has become a familiar kind of Calgary story. Only the numbers have changed, and the street names. Stephen Avenue is now Eighth Avenue.

A large increase has taken place in the value of Calgary real estate, both business and residential, during the past few weeks. In fact, prices have been steadily rising during the last two years.

Inside lots (25 by 130) in the two principal blocks on Stephen Avenue are held at $6,000 each, and upwards, while corner lots command almost fabulous prices.

A feature of the real estate situation during the past few weeks has been the rapid increase in values in the block east of the post office. Last year, 25 foot lots in this block could have been bought for a thousand dollars each; now, it is impossible to buy lots between the post office and the Queen's hotel, on either side of the street, for less than from $2,000 to $3,000.

The block on Stephen Avenue, west of the Alberta Hotel, is also experiencing something in the nature of a boom, although a solid boom. Several sites have been purchased here by large wholesale firms, who intend to build this season, and it is altogether likely that this part of the city will become a centre for wholesale and warehouse businesses.

April 6, 1903

Cars were still very rare in Alberta in 1904. Billy Cochrane had brought the first one in only the year before. An ingenious American overcame the lack of a Trans-Canada Highway, and drove to Vancouver.

From Boston, on the Atlantic seaboard, to Vancouver, on the Pacific, in an automobile, is the feat which Charles J. Glidden, a wealthy Boston banker, is bent on performing.

Just about dark on Saturday evening a dark green automobile whizzed along the C.P.R. track into the station. The machine was travelling faster than any of the express trains are in the habit of arriving.

In a remarkably short distance the auto came to a stop, a rather stout man about the medium height, attired in a big fawn colored automobile coat, stepped to the platform. A lady wearing a big tweed ulster followed.

The gentleman was Charles J. Glidden, and the lady was his wife. With them in the automobile travelled their chauffeur and Conductor Stone, of the C.P.R., from Moose Jaw.

In conversation with a Herald reporter Mr. Glidden said they had had a splendid trip so far, and were looking forward with much interest to the trip through the mountains. He was proud of his achievement in running from Portal to Moose Jaw faster than any of the trains. On this part of the journey his car was frequently speeding along at 45 miles an hour. He covered the distance between Medicine Hat and Calgary, 180 miles, in seven hours, and in that time had a bang at a few of the ducks which covered the sloughs along the way.

The Napier auto which Mr. Glidden drives weighs a little over four tons and is fully equipped for touring. From Boston to Minneapolis he covered the distance on the regular roads. Reaching the Minnesota capital, the ordinary wheels were taken off and a set of flanged steel wheels substituted. These wheels were made in Britain, and resemble the ordinary wheels of a railway car.

Before the automobile of Mr. Glidden sped up the track yesterday morning, a large crowd at the depot gathered around the machine. The car which Mr. Glidden is making his long tour in differs little from the heavy touring cars so frequently seen nowadays in the eastern cities. Of course, the heavy flanged wheels which hold to the railway track look strange, but outside of that there is nothing to change its looks from other autos.

"That's the second section of No. One," remarked a local man, as he watched the auto go speeding along in pursuit of the regular train.

September 12, 1904

The Editor Went to Jail

It all began innocently enough, with Mounties searching a saloon for unlicensed liquor; within two months the editor of The Herald was in jail and two rival town councils were claiming to be the legitimate government of Calgary. In the centre of this storm stood Jeremiah Travis, the stipendiary magistrate (that is, a full-time, paid magistrate.) Travis was evidently a stern and stubborn man, with no small opinion of himself. He strictly enforced the Northwest Territories liquor law, which imposed stiff and often-ignored restrictions on liquor supplies. John Clarke, a Calgary saloon-keeper, was also a town councillor. When plainclothes Mounties tried to search Clarke's saloon one night without a warrant, Clarke apparently resisted. Travis gave him six months at hard labor, a sentence that outraged half the town. The ensuing factional warfare was waged in Travis's courtroom and the pages of The Herald. Travis had the last word, until Ottawa intervened.

The case of Regina v. Clarke came up for hearing before Judge Travis Friday. The charge was of assaulting the police in the execution of their duty. Messrs. Bleecker & Davis for the defendant. Mr. Lougheed for the Crown.

Const. Allwood detailed the circumstances of the alleged assault, which consisted in Clarke's taking him by the shoulder to put him from behind the counter and holding a bottle over his head to strike him.

Corp. Sunderland of the mounted police corroborated the evidence of Constable Allwood with regard to the alleged assault. In fact his testimony was to a certain extent even stronger than that of the constable.

After the lawyers had addressed the court the Stipendiary summed up. He said that he was more inclined to censure the mounted police for being too lax than too zealous in carrying out the liquor law. He then sentenced the prisoner to six months imprisonment with hard labor.

November 11, 1885

Outraged by this sentence, local citizens petitioned the mayor to call an indignation meeting, which he did.

Two hundred citizens assembled in the Boynton Hall, including representatives of all callings and professions carried on in the district.

Mr. Bleecker made a speech of great eloquence, in which he pointed out that the present law as interpreted by the Stipendiary left the people in the Northwest at the mercy of any tramp who chose to force himself into a house, even at the dead of night, and who, by merely stating that he was a mounted policeman, would have full power to search the whole place from cellar to bedrooms. He also dwelt upon the severity of the sentence even had the alleged of-

Magistrate Jeremiah Travis, in a caricature by R. Randolph Bruce.

fence been committed and also on the slur cast upon the witnesses for the defence.

The meeting unanimously passed a five-point resolution protesting Travis's verdict and the sentence he imposed.

November 11, 1885

Two weeks after the Clarke sentence, the Weekly Herald published this editorial, presumably the work of the owner, Hugh S. Cayley, himself a lawyer. The week after this editorial, The Herald reported that Cayley had been fired from his position as clerk of the court.

We do not impugn in any way the motives of Judge Travis, but merely look at the judgment in the Clarke case as public property.

It is a judgment commenced by the Judge's reading of his commission, then going on to speak of the evils of intemperance and the beauty of the Northwest Mounted Police Act as regards prohibition, then branching off into the great wickedness of horse stealing and incidentally condemning a brother Stipendiary for inflicting light sentences; after that finding great fault with

a jury for not finding a man guilty who was charged with a crime in a case previously tried before him; then excusing the severe sentence imposed by him on Sheehy and McGrath.

Finally the Judge paid some attention to the case before him, intimating that the witnesses for the defence, or a number of them, swore falsely and that Clarke was clearly guilty, and that his being a Councillor was no extenuation of his crime, as he did not know but that he was elected by a whiskey ring.

It was decided, by the Judge, that a policeman in plain clothes or without any badge of authority, at any time, day or night, could enter a private house under orders of a commissioned officer, and could enter a saloon, etc. on information merely or reasonable grounds of suspicion, without any orders.

Let us look for a moment at this judgment from a layman's point of view. Under such a law a man, calling himself a policeman, at midnight may enter a saloon and search it from end to end, and even dig in it, without any uniform to show who he is, or without anything to identify him. It may turn out he is a thief, and may have emptied the till, and in the morning the saloon keeper would find himself minus his money and without any means of redress. If he had demanded a warrant or anything to identify him as a policeman, and none being produced, had very properly kicked the intruder out, he would run the chance of two years in penitentiary for "assaulting a policeman." We may well ask, what is a man to do?

The Judge's sympathies are no doubt with a stringent liquor law, and his private opinions no one will object to. For us however we merely deal with the law as laid down by him, and as laymen content ourselves for the present with objecting to the construction which he has placed upon it.

November 25, 1885

In due course, Judge Travis's not very extensive patience ran out, and Editor Cayley was arrested for contempt of court.

The case of Queen vs. Cayley under a rule to show cause why the defendant should not be committed for contempt of court for certain articles that recently appeared in the Calgary Herald, came up before Stipendiary Magistrate Travis on Tuesday afternoon.

Long before court opened the room was crowded with citizens and residents from all parts of the district, who manifested by the close attention which they paid to the proceedings the interest attached to the case. Numbers were unable to obtain entrance to the court room at all and had to go away disappointed.

[Cayley's lawyer argued that the stipendiary magistrate had no jurisdiction in cases of contempt committed outside of court. Travis was not impressed.]

A lengthy judgment concluded this case on Thursday, the judgment allowing the respondent an opportunity to apologize and pay costs this morning or be sentenced as the court might see fit on Tuesday next.

No apology was made and sentence will be passed on Tuesday.

December 30, 1885

Sentenced to three months for contempt of court, the editor of The Herald went to jail in style.

On Monday, the day appointed for Mr. Cayley's incarceration, his friends in town determined to give him a good send-off before he went down to barracks. A large crowd accordingly got together and put Mr. Cayley in a wagon by the Boynton Theatre, from which position he stated in a few forcible words why he was going to prison, rather than pay a fine, which could be collected in town inside of an hour if he chose to say the word.

The brass band then got into the wagon with Mr. Cayley and the crowd proceeded to the town hall, where halt was called for the instruments to thaw out. The time was occupied by cheers for the Mayor, the old council and Mr. Cayley. The procession then reformed, the band leading, followed by the wagon, in which were Messrs. Cayley and Leeson and Chief Ingram, the rear being brought up by the crowd marching four deep.

In this order they paraded past Judge Travis' house, where three groans were felt to be in order, then up McTavish Street to the Royal, where another halt was called on account of the instruments of the band being frozen up.

Here Mr. Cayley again made a short speech, after which the procession re-formed and marched up McTavish Street and Atlantic Avenue, and so down the town to the town hall again, the Mayor joining the party in the wagon at Martin Bros. store. Cheers for the Mayor and old council and Mr. Cayley were frequently given and Calgary certainly on this occasion recorded her verdict unmistakably on the case of Regina vs. Cayley.

January 6, 1886

During the Cayley affair, Calgary briefly found itself with two town Councils. The losers in the election of December, 1885, complained that the voters' list had been rigged. Judge Travis threw the winners out of office, and declared the losers the legal council. Another election a month later returned the thrown-out council by a large margin. For three months both factions tried to govern. It was probably no coincidence that

Hugh S. Cayley, editor, convict, premier of the Northwest Territories, and B.C. judge.

---

members of the disqualified council had protested against Cayley's imprisonment. In the middle of the squabble, Ottawa ordered Cayley released.

It is now a little over three weeks since Mr. Cayley was sent to gaol by Mr. Travis for contempt of court. The commitment was effected the day after the people of Calgary, by an overwhelming majority, had defeated at the polls the municipal faction which Mr. Travis once designated "the respectable party," and in spite of the fact that that blow was levelled at a loyal Conservative press, which had had a strong fight to maintain for the preservation of the commonest personal and civic liberties.

Yesterday, Mr. Travis was directed by the Minister of Justice, that Mr. Cayley was to be released and his fines remitted. We understand that this sudden destruction of Mr. Lougheed's hundred dollar counsel fee was due to the representations of Chief Justice Ritchie of the Supreme Court, before whom an application for Habeas Corpus by Mr. Cayley's lawyers had previously been heard, the Chief Justice having intimated that it was a case for interference on the part of the Government. It may be a comfort to the Tribune [the Liberal paper in town] to know that it was not political influence but The Justice Of Our Cause which has secured this result.

We do not see that the action of the Chief Justice and the Minister of Justice can have any other meaning than that Travis' views on contempt of court and the power of Stipendiaries are not considered sound at Ottawa. If it has any other meaning we would be very glad to know it. We have had some doubt ourselves on the soundness of the Stipendiary's law on these points and have not hesitated to express it. We rather

imagine there will be a good deal more to express presently.

February 6, 1886

The Herald received a complaint from a distinguished subscriber, and dealt briskly with it.

Sir: I noticed a statement in the Herald a short time since that I had ordered the Herald to be no longer sent to me. This, like the usual statements in the Herald relating to me, was simply a falsehood. But, as I can never rely on receiving it, it might almost as well be stopped.

Apparently, whenever the copies which should be sent to me and other subscribers, can be sold at 5 cents each, we are defrauded out of our copies. Notwithstanding the general worthlessness of the paper, I pay for it and take it, as many others do, for its telegrams.

The Herald's reply was vintage Hugh S. Cayley.

The foregoing letter is not signed, but the handwriting is that of J. Travis, and the expressions are in J. Travis' peculiar and unrivalled style, not to be mistaken for anybody else's. We publish it, because we would not do even such a paltry creature as J. Travis an injustice. Our newsboy was told by a member of J. T.'s household not to deliver the Herald there any more. That J. Travis had given instructions to that effect, we do not doubt in the slightest, for as most of the denials he has made to our statements about him have been deliberate falsehoods, we do not look for any better from him in this particular.

J. Travis calls us in this letter a liar and swindler. He has written a letter to Mr. Smith calling him pretty much the same, and Mr. McCoskrie has also had the pleasure of coming under the lunatic's lash, for demanding payment for work done for him.

We see J. Travis only in the light of a buffoon. It seems to be the light in which he wishes to be regarded. He has the pleasure of knowing that all Calgary now regards him in that light. A carpet-bagger, intriguer and hunter of offices, he is beneath contempt as it is beneath us to do him even an unintentional injustice.

We will henceforth deliver the Herald to J. Travis for nothing. By so doing we are aware that we make him our life-long friend, but we can stand even this, knowing, as we do, that he is presently to give up his position to a man who has the distinguishing feature of being a gentleman.

Editor, The Herald.

March 20, 1886

Travis soon retired from the bench, but he stayed in Calgary, writing law books, enjoying a pension, and perhaps enjoying even more the knowledge that he had bought a large tract of Calgary land before prices began to rise.

Rebellion on the Frontier

The Riel Rebellion broke out in March, 1885. The Metis of the West, who had already lost the buffalo, were afraid that they would now lose their farmland to incoming white settlers. Government land surveys had already dispossessed some Metis squatters. Louis Riel had led a minor Metis uprising in Manitoba in 1870; later he served briefly as a member of Parliament. He was expelled from the Commons in 1874 and banished from Canada for five years in 1875. In 1884, Metis and white settlers invited him back to lead a protest against Ottawa's indifference to the West's problems. His campaign, at first peaceful and constitutional, became more threatening in 1885.

Riel has openly defied the Queen's authority. He claims that the halfbreeds and Indians are under his complete control and that they will fight for their rights. The white settlers are alarmed. They have no arms or ammunition but remain loyal.

A meeting was held at Prince Albert today, at which 500 men were present. They stated their determination to enroll against Riel if the government will find them arms and ammunition. There is great excitement in the settlement.

Prince Albert, March 18, 1885

In the following editorial, The Herald argued that Riel had to be stopped, but conceded that he might have a point.

Riel has at length, according to the reports, thrown off the mask. Defying the Queen may be an amusing freak on the part of a crank, but when it comes to starting, as Riel has evidently done, an insurrection, the freak loses a great many of its amusing features.

Besides it is not at all certain that Riel is a crank. There are plenty of people who hold that he did good to his race in Manitoba, and it is possible that the claims of the halfbreeds may not be so unreasonable. If they are not unreasonable, a moderate insurrection is probably the only way by which they will win them consideration.

Reasonable or otherwise the insurrection has to be put down, for the lives and property of the whites cannot be jeopardized because Riel thinks his compatriots have been badly treated.

The causes of dissatisfaction amongst the halfbreeds and Indians are not numerous although they may be considered important. The halfbreeds have had a bad season and are hungry.

It also seems that the Hon. Lawrence Clarke, formerly member of the Northwest Council, made some indiscreet promises to the halfbreeds concerning the granting of lands to them by the government. No one knows that he was authorized to do anything of the kind, but there is certainly a

Louis Riel, who briefly set the West on fire. Whether he was saint, martyr or madman, his rebellion and his death on the gallows left an indelible mark on the history of western Canada.

reason for agitation in the fact of the promises having been made. This occurred three years ago and the government had not followed the line of action indicated by Mr. Clarke, and the halfbreeds conclude that the government has been false to them.

In regard to the Indians, it cannot be supposed that agrarian troubles agitate them much, nor is it probable that a desire for territorial acquisition is a very powerful motive for casting in their lot with the halfbreeds. It may seem a paltry reason, but if the agitating cause amongst the breeds is the approximation of "hard times," it will not be considered surprising by those who know anything about the Indians, if a lack of government tobacco and tea were not the agitating cause with them.

That the Indians are large consumers of both is not a secret, neither is it a secret that the means they employ to obtain them are by no means creditable to civilization. It is in fact a doubtful question if the Indians would either leave their reserves or engage in agitation if these two necessary luxuries of tea and tobacco were afforded them.

March 26, 1885

On a Sunday morning in March, 1885, The Herald issued its first "extra." Word of the fighting at Duck Lake had just been released in Ottawa. It was the first major engagement of the Riel Rebellion, and the North West Mounted Police lost it.

In the Commons last night, on the speaker taking the chair, Sir John Macdonald said that he had received a telegram that afternoon from Col. Irvine from Carlton, via Winnipeg.

He then read as follows: "The party under my command have just arrived. When near Fort Carlton I found that Crozier with a party of 100 men went to Duck Lake to secure a large quantity of supplies stored there. They were met by some hundred rebels, who had an advantage of position at Beardy's reserve, and endeavored to surround the police and volunteers.

"The rebels fired first, when it became general. Major Crozier, owing to the disadvantage at which he was taken, retired orderly, arriving at the Fort the same time as my party. Ten civilians of Prince Albert and two policemen were killed, and four civilians and seven police wounded.

"The number of rebels killed is not known, but is estimated at between fifty and sixty. The police and civilians acted with the greatest bravery under the heavy fire."

Sir John continued, and said that a telegram in cypher had been received from Major General Middleton, conveying the announcement of these facts, and asking that B. Battery be sent forward immediately. Hon. Edward Blake inquired as to the position of supplies in the Northwest Territories, and as to the defensibility of the centres of settlement. Sir John said that the food supplies were scattered over a country as vast as the whole of Ontario and Quebec together, and that it would be impossible for him to say where they were, but he would have a statement prepared.

Mr. Blake said he did not want information given in the House which might be sent away for the advantage of the rebels, who, he presumed, did not know where these supplies were. Sir John stated that the rebels, as he would not call them, did not know where the supplies were. As for the Indians, Mr. Dewdney [lieutenant-governor of the territories] telegraphs that they were quiet.

General Superintendent Egan telegraphed that a halfbreed had been arrested near Oak Lake for placing an obstruction on the track, presumably to upset the train carrying the military westward. This halfbreed stated that Riel had 1,500 men, well armed and six American cannon. The statement of the halfbreed must be accepted with qualification.

Ottawa, March 29, 1885 (Extra)

Another extra brought bad news from Battleford, and word of new mobilization against the rebels.

Lt. Governor Dewdney has just arrived in Qu'Appelle from Regina. He and Gen. Middleton had a conference together, at which, it is stated, they decided to ask the government immediately for 2,000 more troops.

The reports from Battleford are bad. The Indians are raiding the stores for food and firing on the citizens. A man named Haynes, and another not known, were killed. Indian Agent Rae went out to confer with them, but was fired on. The Hudson Bay store was gutted. The Industrial School has been burnt. The citizens are all housed in the barracks for refuge.

Four doctors leave for Prince Albert by one of Leeson & Scott's teams this morning.

Qu'Appelle, March 31, 1885 (Extra)

The belated news of the massacre at Frog Lake must have heightened fears, if only briefly, that a general Indian uprising was imminent.

Telegraphic communication with Battleford was resumed last Thursday, April 8, and news came of a massacre at Frog Lake on April 12. According to the report, the Indians invited Acting Sub-Indian Agent Thomas T. Quinn and others to a conference in their camp, and shot them as soon as they entered. Eleven persons were killed.

Father McCombe and some ten settlers are entrenched in the Hudson Bay building at Fort Pitt and are surrounded by large numbers of savages. Big Bear's band is amongst them. Great fears are entertained for their fate as well as the fate of the besieged at Battleford who are holding out, but according to the telegram on Thursday were very anxious.

April 13, 1885 (Extra)

Altogether, about 4,000 militiamen came west on the CPR to suppress Riel's rebels. A force from Montreal disembarked at Calgary.

Calgary was all agog Sunday morning last waiting to see the arrival of the 65th, of Montreal, the first body of troops to come to the Amphitheatre City, who were billed to arrive by special train at midday.

True to the time table the train came up to the station, the boys waving their hats and cheering as if they had not been eleven days on the journey and had not had a square sleep or a decent bed since they left their native snows 2,000 miles away. With faces grimed with the dust of travel, with sun-skinned noses and frost-bitten ears, with hair unkempt and headgear awry, they were a pretty spectacle for their mothers and cousins to see and the "girl they left behind them" to smile at.

Nevertheless they trooped out on the platform, and paraded on the square behind the station, with a jaunty step and merry air that spoke volumes for their spirits and constitutions, and promised well for their performance of the hard duties ahead.

The crowd of course put on their most approved air of western indifference and farthest west criticism, while everything that could put on chaps curvetted around on Cummings' and Sandy McDonald's horses in a style that made the Sarcee squaws' eyes water.

Three squaws took up their location by the track and proceeded to mash the military. They had red checked shawls over their heads and beaded moccasins on their little feet and bangles on their wrists. A pencilled ochre line beneath their dark orbs, and tinted cheeks of the same, heightened the charms which nature had bestowed on their Greco-Roman faces.

A full private came to us and asked if they "were all like that," and being answered in the affirmative, lifted up his voice like our ancestor Jacob, and said that "down Montreal way, now" — but then he got blasphemous and we left.

The squaws stayed, however, and maintained a most creditable gravity considering the amount of French and English hurled at them. The boys came at last to think they were statues. They clustered around and patted their ochred cheeks, and pulled their raven locks, and examined their barbaric ornaments, until finally one with a win-or-die resignation, pulled out his watch and his knife and 65 cents Canadian legal tender and requested that in exchange for all his worldly wealth he be permitted to kiss one of the maiden's blushing cheeks.

The effect was elegant. With a vivacity and insouciance strangely at variance with pre-conceived notions of her, the untaught daughter of the foothills broke into our native vernacular with a vigor which seriously disturbed the serenity of the Sabbath.

April 16, 1885

Father Albert Lacombe, a Roman Catholic missionary, and Chief Crowfoot of the Blackfoot tribe were instrumental in keeping the Indians of the foothills and western prairies out of the Riel Rebellion.

Lt. Governor Dewdney and the Rev. Father Lacombe went down to the crossing last week to have a talk with Chief Crowfoot. They were met at Cluny by 150 Indians with Crowfoot at their head, all mounted. The Indians gave their "white brothers" an enthusiastic reception and escorted them to the reserve 2½ miles distant, where all the young warriors, women and children were assembled. The council was held in the Catholic Mission.

Before Mr. Dewdney entered the Mission, Crowfoot addressed his people, advising them always to remain at peace with the white men of this country. Then the Governor entered, and after the usual shaking of hands, explained the purpose of his visit.

He assured them that the government intended to protect them as well as the whites, lest they should suffer an incursion from the northern disturbers. They must shut their ears to all the rumors they might hear in different quarters as to the Crees coming to molest them.

The soldiers, coming into the country, were not coming to hurt them but to punish the bad Indians for killing the whites. They had nothing to fear as long as they remained faithful to their treaty. After a few more remarks explaining the situation, he concluded. William Gladstone interpreted the governor's speech.

Crowfoot then arose, and after another shaking of hands, made some excellent remarks. He said he had only to repeat what he had said to Father Lacombe a few days before when on a mission from the government to him. They had not dreamed of giving trouble to the government or anyone else.

If the government wanted help from them, they were ready to do all they could. He had already sent some of his young men to the Bloods and Peigans to induce them to follow the same line, so that there was no fear in this part of the country of any trouble.

Father Lacombe then addressed a few words to them, saying that he was proud and pleased with what he had seen and heard.

April 16, 1885

The fighting at Batoche, southwest of Prince Albert, was to prove decisive. On May 12, 1885, Riel's main force was defeated there. This April 25 extra describ-ed the combat as the militia fought toward Batoche.

Fighting here has commenced in dead earnest. The rebels were en-countered this morning (April 24) at 9 o'clock by Major Boulton's scouts who were in advance of the main body of the light column, about 15 miles from Batoche, and the east side of the (South Saskat-chewan) river. The rebels occupied a strong position on the banks of a ravine, and com-menced firing, but an answering volley from the scouts induced them to mount horses and retire at once into the ravine where they concealed themselves and kept firing.

The remainder of the troops having come up about noon, the enemy were im-mediately attacked, the troops advancing in skirmishing order. The attack was made on both flanks simultaneously, but the enemy had secured so strong a position that the work of dislodging them was extremely dif-ficult.

Nevertheless the troops advanced steadi-ly, No. 5 company of the 90th, the School of Infantry and "A" Battery on the right, with the other corps on the left flank. The fight was a hot one throughout, the half-breeds keeping up an incessant fire from their con-cealed position in the bush.

The Battery was at first unable to reach them, but after securing better position, they shelled the bluff with good effect. A desperate fight was maintained for over an hour, when the rebels began to scatter. They made another stand in a small post in the woods, but did not hold out long and were soon beyond reach of the volunteers' bullets.

By 2:30 p.m. the attack had been repell-ed and opportunity was given to view the situation. Lord Melgund crossed the River with the 10th Royals and the Winnipeg Bat-tery, during the engagement, and arrived on the scene, but too late to take part.

The troops behaved splendidly, but be-ing new at the work, the number of killed and wounded was very large.

Clarke's Crossing, April 25, 1885 (Extra)

As this extra reported, Riel was captured in mid-May; however, the rebellion continued for another six weeks.

The capture of Riel today caused great excitement in the camp. The three scouts who effected the cap-ture came upon him and two young men in a bluff a short distance north of here. One of his companions was armed, but no resistance was made to the arrest.

While Riel was talking with the three men he saw Boulton's and French's troops approaching, and grew alarmed lest he should be shot out of revenge. He begged the men to take him quietly and quickly before Gen. Middleton. He also expressed his fears of a military trial, and eagerly asked

The capture of Louis Riel by scouts Armstrong and Howie as depicted by a newspaper artist of the time. His captors were careful not to let other soldiers lynch him. Six months later, he was hanged.

the scouts what they thought his chances were of coming before a civil court.

In order to prevent accidents one of the scouts took Riel up behind him on his horse, and he and one of his comrades took an un-frequented path back to the camp, which they reached shortly after three o'clock.

Gen. Middleton was apprehensive of Riel being shot by someone in the camp, as many were known to have sworn openly that they would shoot him down on sight. However the men all remained quiet and nothing occurred while the prisoner was taken before the General. He explained to Gen. Middleton that he had been hiding in the bluffs along the river side on Tuesday.

Batoche, May 15, 1885 (Extra)

Riel and a number of his followers were hanged. His trial and sentence caused a bit-ter political controversy. Most of his fellow French-Canadians favored clemency, while English-speaking Canada generally wanted him executed.

Riel was hanged Nov. 16, the warrant having arrived from Ottawa by special train the night before. Your correspondent obtained admission to Riel's cell that night, accompanied by Sheriff Chapleau. The condemned man was quite calm and stood talking cheerfully to Dr. Jukes.

On our entering the cell Riel looked up and said cheerfully to the Sheriff, "So you have come with the terrible announcement. Well, I am glad to go and be relieved of my suffering."

The Sheriff asked if he had any wishes with regard to the disposal of personal pro-perty. Riel, laying his hand on his breast, said "I have only this. I was willing to give it to my country fifteen years ago and it is all I have to give now."

Your correspondent asked him if he was prepared to die and he replied, "I long ago made my peace with God and am as

prepared now as I can be at any time. You will see that I had a mission to perform."

The morning opened bright and clear. A slight frost had fallen. At eight o'clock the execution party went up the rickety ladder to the scaffold, with Pere Andre and Father McWilliams reciting the prayer for the dying.

At 8:05 Pere Andre administered the last sacrament to Riel. Riel gave the responses firmly. Although pale he was firm. He was dressed in a black coat, brown tweed pants and moccasins. The figure of the hangman now appeared out of the gloom of the loft holding straps to bind Riel. He wore a mask over his face.

At 8:15 Riel rose to his feet and was pi-nioned by the hangman, deputy sheriff Gibson supervising the operation, Riel standing with eyes open praying in French, the priests standing in front.

He then walked firmly to the scaffold repeating "In God do I put my trust." His head was erect, his step firm, never showing the least tremor. As he repeated the prayer-ful exclamation half a smile lit up his face. Descending down a few steps of the scaffold, he stood on the drop with his face turned northward.

Pere Andre and Father McWilliams con-tinued to pray and Riel said in English "I do ask the forgiveness of all men and forgive all my enemies." He then prayed a short time in French.

The executioner now took his place, the white cap was drawn over Riel's head, both priests holding lighted candles continuing to repeat prayers for the dying.

Exactly at 8:23 the drop fell giving a shock to all present. The rope shook violent-ly for a moment, swaying back and forth, then quivered. The length of drop was eight feet. At the first moment of the fall Riel's body remained still. His knees were drawn up violently three or four times, the body swayed to and fro quivering and Riel was dead. From the first moment the drop fell to the time when the body became quiescent was under two minutes.

Regina, November 18, 1885

A Voice From The West

Westerners have never been reluctant to speak up when they feel neglected or mistreated by Ottawa. They have felt this way more often than not. Most of the political battles recorded in The Herald over the years have long been forgotten, but some complaints go on forever, as the following editorial shows.

One of the most distressing features of life in this country is that while all the necessaries of life cost us much more than they do in any other part of the Dominion, the rate of wages is not only not higher, but decidedly lower than elsewhere.

The reason for either fact is on the surface. The goods we purchase of Canadian manufacture are charged with a freight rate practically from Montreal, and such as are of American manufacture are charged with not only a freight rate of considerably over 1,000 miles, but with a duty as well ranging from twenty-five to thirty-three per cent.

On the other hand, fully two-thirds of the men at work in this country have work only during the summer months, when their wages average pretty much the same as their wages in the east. The effect of a customs union scheme of the kind proposed is readily discernible. It would totally bar out American goods and render Montreal our only supply market.

The duty payable on Chicago and St. Paul goods is sufficiently felt in this country already, but the effect of raising this and throwing us back entirely on Montreal and England until such time as we have manufactures of our own would be to bring home to us more than ever how much more this district belongs to the Pacific, or even the American territorial system than to that of the Eastern Canadian Provinces.

January 8, 1885

The Herald frequently took issue with its Liberal rival, the Tribune. In this editorial, the question was whether Alberta and Saskatchewan should become separate provinces, as proposed by Dr. R.G. Brett of Banff, a member of the Northwest Territories legislature.

The Tribune's attempt on Saturday to play into the hands of Regina by opposing the setting apart of Alberta as a separate government with Calgary as its capital, was probably the weakest effort of the kind that has yet been attempted. Its closing paragraph was as follows:

"It might seem favorable to the immediate prosperity of Alberta if she were divided from the rest of the Territories and given the management of her own internal affairs, as proposed in Dr. Brett's scheme. The people of Alberta, however, are not afraid of their future, knowing the richness and fertility of their possession, and will not, we feel sure, take a merely mercenary view of this question, but, while not losing sight of their own interests, will not forget that they are part of Canada, and that their future prosperity is indissolubly connected with that of the whole Dominion."

It is here plainly intimated that in advocating the erection of Alberta into a separate government something is being done that is inimical to the interests of other parts of Canada. Could anything be more ridiculous than such a suggestion? And is it not a remarkable thing that this opposition to what is admitted to be a movement that tends to "the immediate prosperity of Alberta," comes from a Calgary and an Alberta journal?

What we want, what all are working for, is that something which will promote "the immediate prosperity of Alberta." It is for the immediate prosperity of its own locality and territory that every city, district and province of the Dominion are working; and if the people of any locality of the east, who are running the race of wealth and prosperity, were asked to halt and wipe themselves out on the plea that they were injuring some other part of Canada, they would regard the local obstructionist as a fit subject for a lunatic asylum.

We believe in a Government and a Legislature for Alberta with Calgary the Capital as the greatest factor for the immediate prosperity of the new Province.

We know that many local grievances would in that event immediately disappear. If we had a Government and Legislature of our own would we have to wait ten years for a bridge over Sheep Creek?

Would the delays and foolery in connection with the construction of the bridge of High River be tolerated? Would every man who has in his possession a bottle of wine be treated as a criminal? Would we bend our backs to somebody in Regina and beg him for Heaven's sake to permit us to take a glass of liquor?

Would we be dependent upon the good graces of somebody in Ottawa as to whether a court house should go up in Lethbridge, or a bridge should be erected over Old Man's River?

These can all be answered with an emphatic negative; but we shall know no freedom of action as long as the right to deal with Alberta's affairs is withheld from Albertans, the exercise of this right being the one thing still necessary (in the words of the Tribune) to ensure "the immediate prosperity of Alberta."

July 9, 1891

Long before Alberta became a province the name was already being used, and people were pressing for independence from the Northwest Territories government at Regina.

The people of the North West are at last awakening to the fact that the country they live in deserves to be considered no longer in the prosaic light of an appendage to the Department of the Interior. This vast expanse of prairie and foothills has been reclaimed, cultivated and rendered a source of income to the central government through the hard toil of the individual settler who has until recently had no real voice in the councils of those who have directed legislation on North West matters.

The limited power of law-making reposing in the North West Assembly at Regina, has, in its small way, been exercised in a manner calculated to improve the status and opportunities of the settlers in the various districts comprised in the Territories, but the population has increased to such an extent, the country has developed in so many directions and the consequent needs of the people have become so pronounced that the general consensus of those who take more than a passing interest in our public affairs is that a further extension of the powers of local self-government is essential to further progress.

Ignorance, misrepresentation, impudent insult and mossback unprogressiveness, are some of the characteristics of the anti-autonomists in the Territorial Assembly. Some of their speeches are odoriferous of the 7 x 9 politics of an eastern backwoods county council.

Mr. Insinger, who should be careful that he does not earn the title of Mr. Mudslinger, thinks Alberta's claim to self-government rests on the fact that her people "drink more whisky and are more ignorant than the rest of the Territories."

Mr. Haultain, whose claim to speak with authority for Alberta is open to dispute, airily dismisses the case of the provincial government party with the statement that they are "seeing visions and dreaming dreams." The Herald has no doubt this convincing style of argument must appeal forcibly to the prosaic people of Regina and its suburbs, but in the West it will be taken as an admission that the critics of Autonomy are driven to concealing their poverty of argument by a profusion of ridiculous misstatement.

The present position of Alberta is an extremely unfortunate one. Its people are strongly imbued with the spirit of goaheadiveness but they are tied to a corpse. If the Assiniboia and Saskatchewan M.L.A.'s truly reflect the attitude of their constituents the people of Alberta may conscientiously pray to be delivered from any such stick-in-the-mud, fly-on-the-wheel policy as prevails in those parts.

October 30, 1896

Crime and Punishment

For this, the first murder in The Herald's time in Calgary, the paper bordered its news columns in black, and gave all the literally gory details. (It should be said that the story would have been treated much differently today: the gratuitous reference to the accused man's race, the pre-trial publication of evidence, and the publication of the accused's confession are now dire journalistic sins.)

On Friday evening the people of Calgary were thrown into a state of the wildest consternation by the report that a murder had been committed, and the sickening details of which were appalling in the extreme. The excitement was roused still higher, when it became known that James Adams, one of the most respectable and promising young men of the town was the victim.

Mr. Adams was a friend of Mr. McKelvie, a merchant of this place, with whom he slept, and in the evenings assisted in the store. Friday evening Mr. Ed. Francis called there, and while chatting with Mr. Adams a negro known as Jess Williams entered the store for the purpose of paying an account. The victim opened the cash drawer, and Williams endeavoured to obtain a view of its contents. Mr. Francis then left the store.

About 8:30 Malcolm McNeil, T. Spearon, and S. Hogg, who had been on the east side of the Elbow, were returning towards home. McNeil, said he would stop at McKelvie's store and see Adams. On opening the door young McNeil saw Adams lying on the floor, as he thought, asleep; but on nearing him was horrified to see steam rising from the victim's blood.

McNeil called to his companions. On entering the premises they found the young man sweltering in his blood. The police were then notified and the premises searched. A small axe, with its handle and back bloody, was found. Dr. Kennedy and Major Dowling with a posse of police arrived on the scene.

A short distance from the store some person had removed their overshoes and approached the premises in their stocking feet, and the same tracks were observed leading from the building. The people now adjourned to Clark & Beaudoin's hall to devise means to ferret out the murderer before he had time to escape. A determined look marked every countenance, and lynching the culprit was spoken of. Mr. Francis hereupon expressed to the people his fears that Williams committed the tragedy, his reason for thinking so being the remembrance of the wicked gleam from the negro's eyes on seeing the money in the till. [Williams had returned briefly to the store after the body had been found. Some things he said aroused suspicion; a posse was gathered and arrested him at the teepee outside town where he lived.]

Sergt.-Major Lake placed him under arrest and left a sergeant and men in charge of the other inmates of the teepee, till they could be sent for. On reaching the guard room, his clothes and person were carefully examined. A small quantity of blood was found on the breast of his coat, which he said was caused by some beef he was carrying that day. On turning out his pockets a bloody mark about the shape a razor case would make was plainly discernible. None of the missing money, however, was found on his person.

Early on Saturday morning both police and citizens were on the alert to discover further evidence of guilt. The fresh tramped snow where the assassin had resumed his overshoes was the starting point, and a few feet further west Constable Macrae's eyes rested on the razor with which the fiend had performed his hellish mission. (This instrument was slightly imbedded in some snow at the southwest corner of the Herald building.)

On Tuesday morning Mr. Braden of The Herald called on Inspector Steele for permission to interview the prisoner, which was readily granted, and in company with Sergt. Smart proceeded to the prisoner's cell. He met his visitors with an air of the coolest nonchalance that cannot well be imagined, and made the following statement for publication:

"I am forty-three years of age, was born in Texas, but lived in Dakota about two years, previous to coming to this country; about a year and a half ago, I got a position as cook on the C.P.R. and cooked in the Virginia Chop House and Far West Hotel till about two weeks ago, since which time I have done nothing.

"I have confessed the crime to the Commanding Officer voluntarily, and I may as well tell you. On Friday night I went to McKelvie's store to settle a little bill I owed, and saw deceased and another gentleman present; after paying the account I asked deceased for a pencil which was given me. I went forward and scratched out the account which was recorded on the wall; deceased said I should not have done this; I answered the debt was paid, and I wanted it blotted out.

"The other gentleman then went out; deceased and I began wrestling or fooling, and in the fray, Mr. Adams received a slight hurt, and got angry, saying that this must be stopped or there would be a fuss. I said there was no fear of a fuss; seeing a razor on the counter I picked it up and struck at him, not meaning to hurt him, but cut a gash on the left side of his throat.

"Seeing I had injured him more than I intended, I thought I would finish him, which I did with the razor; I then went out but seeing no one, I came back, and as the deceased seemed to be suffering, I picked up the axe and struck him with it to put him out of pain; I then went to the drawer and took out the money; went to the bank of the Elbow River and hid it; I then started for home."

February 13, 1884

In another interview and at his trial Williams gave rather different accounts of the crime, but never denied that he had murdered Adams. On March 29, 1884, he was hanged at the North West Mounted Police fort in Calgary.

The murder of Rosalie, a young Cree woman, was an exceptionally nasty business from beginning to end. The accused, William Fisk, a white man, was found not guilty by the first jury in the case. Justice Rouleau found this an incredible decision, in light of the evidence, and sent the jury back to reconsider. They could not reach a verdict, and Rouleau ordered a new trial. The second jury found Fisk guilty of manslaughter, and he was sentenced to 14 years in Stony Mountain penitentiary.

Probably owing to the fact that Calgary is an exceptionally orderly town and has been singularly free from crime, was largely due the profound sensation which was created Thursday night when the report circulated that the mutilated body of a murdered squaw had been found in a room over the Turf Club restaurant on McTavish Street [Centre Street].

Chief Dillabough of the town Police Force was patrolling Stephen [Eighth] Avenue eight Thursday evening when accosted by a well-known character about town named William Fisk, commonly known as "Jumbo" Fisk, an appellation he has to thank his great size for. Fisk, who appeared considerably excited, told the chief that he had come to deliver himself up.

He explained that he had been spending some time with a dissolute squaw, in a room in the Turf Club and that "she had died on his hands." The chief at once took charge of the man and proceeding with him to the Turf Club, was directed to one of the upstairs rooms. On entering, some blood stains were remarked on the walls while the dead body of a squaw lay spread on a bed.

Upon a closer examination of the room in which the murder was committed the room was found to be more or less spattered with blood. The examination of the body went to show that the wound was made entirely by the fingers, and a couple of pieces of flesh were found by the chief of police under the bed.

Dr. Lafferty says that the post-mortem revealed the fact that this is a regular Jack-The-Ripper case. The organs were terribly mutilated, the hand or instrument used having penetrated as far as the cavity of the peritoneum.

The body of the unfortunate young squaw was interred about dusk Friday evening in the Protestant cemetery. The poor creature in the innocent days of youth had been baptized into the faith of the Roman Catholic Church, and Chief Dillabough applied to the clergy at the Mission to have her buried in the graveyard there. As she had "died in sin," the priests, as usual in such cases, refused her body interment in consecrated ground and her grave was dug in the Protestant cemetery.

While the post mortem examination was still in progress, Mayor Marsh and Chief Dillabough busied themselves making arrangements for the disposition of the body. The coroner telegraphed the officials of the Indian Department at Regina, asking whether the government would assume the cost of the funeral; but as it was necessary to have no delay, the town officials proceeded at once with the arrangements. The Indians, as was natural, showed a disposition to view the murder of their kinswoman as an injury to their race by the white man, and for the purpose of pacifying them it was decided to gratify the national weakness for display by providing a showy coffin for the deceased.

It was about six o'clock when the handsomely polished casket with silver mountings, containing the mutilated remains of the murdered squaw, was carried out of the house in which she had met her cruel death, and placed in a wagon. Seated on the sidewalk in front of the Turf Club were the aged father and mother of poor Rosalie, her sister and two or three other relatives, while standing around were a number of other Indians, and several halfbreeds.

Besides these mourners, a large crowd of sightseers had gathered. The members of the murdered squaw's family had been on the spot most of the day and had squatted there on the sidewalk maintaining that stoicism which is the chief characteristic of their race, in spite of the gaping and quizzing of the crowd of sightseers. Now and again, a sob would come from one of the squaws, or a blanket be raised to moist eyes to wipe away a truant tear. Not a word, however, escaped the lips of one of them, and they sat there hour after hour, their blanketed heads bowed down in expression of a woe which was undoubtedly keenly felt.

Justice moved quickly. An inquest was held immediately after Rosalie's death, and on the Tuesday after the incident Fisk was arraigned. He was committed for trial the same day. At the arraignment, a witness who had also figured in the inquest told a tale of remarkable callousness.

George Kelsey, barkeeper at the Turf Club, gave about the same evidence as at the inquest. Speaking of the moaning he had heard Thursday evening, witness deposed: "I did not know what was causing the noise. I had no dog tied up around the building. I was downstairs when I heard the moaning and there were two or three more there. Someone made the remark, wondering what the noise was or what made it. I think it was Mr. Lee if I am not mistaken. I told them it was a dog. I did not want to tell them that Jumbo was up there with a squaw, that was my reason for saying that the noise was made by a dog."

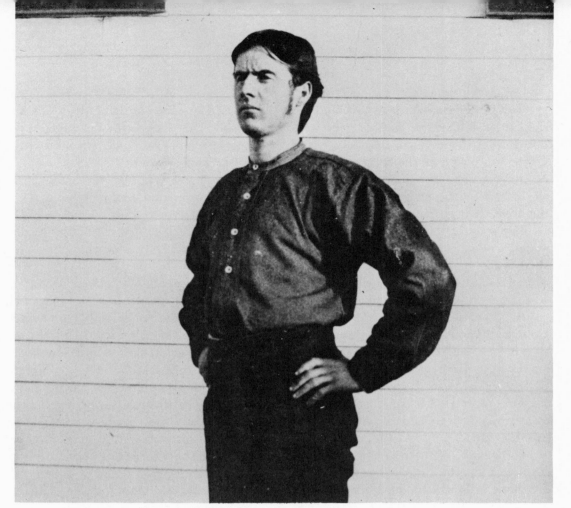

Ernest Cashel, 21 years old, shortly before he died on the gallows. His escape from the Calgary jail won him a few more weeks of life, and started one of the greatest manhunts in Alberta's history.

Referring to the circumstances connected with the unlocking of the room in which the squaw's body was found, he deposed: "It was about half an hour after I locked it that I went up and unlocked the room. Jumbo came out of the room. He made the remark that there was blood on the bed. He asked me then to go into the room as he believed the woman was dead. I went into the room and put my head down to her mouth and I thought she breathed.

"She was lying with her head down at the foot of the bed. I noticed a little blood on the bed clothes. I noticed some blood on the wall at the head of the bed. Jumbo said he would go to supper.

"The moaning was going on for close to an hour. I waited at the head of the stairs till Jumbo came down from washing and he said he would go to supper. We went together. The door of the room was not locked. I went to the Windsor Hotel for supper. I found Jumbo in there eating his supper. He got through eating before I did and left, and was at the Turf Club when I returned from supper.

"I went into the wash room at Donohue's and washed when I went to supper. I saw a little blood on the towel when I went to wash.

"When I got back to the club Jumbo asked me to go upstairs and see if the woman was dead or alive. I told him if he would go with me I would go up. We went into the room; it was not locked. I looked at the woman and told him she was dead. She was still lying in the same position that she was when I was in the room before. We came out of the room and Jumbo asked me what he had best do. I told him he had best go and see Mr. Murdoch and he said he would do so. He went right off."

The evidence of the other witnesses of inquest was taken, and at half past six the presiding justices committed Fisk for trial at the April term of the High Court.

March 6, 1889

Ernest Cashel, a young American drifter who had been sentenced to death for the murder of a local rancher, escaped from a Calgary jail. His escape, and his six weeks of freedom before he was caught and hanged, caused a great stir in Calgary. His brother was convicted of supplying the revolver that got Cashel out of jail.

Ernest Cashel, sentenced to be hanged on Tuesday next for the murder of a rancher, Isaac Rufus Belt, escaped from the guard house of the North West Mounted Police barracks last night.

[Cashel had been taken out of his cell so that it could be searched before the guard change. During the search he sat under an open window. The search found nothing, and Cashel was told to return to his cell.]

When Cashel did not enter his cell promptly, the constables took a step towards him, and were confronted with Cashel covering them with two long-barrelled .38 calibre revolvers. Cashel ordered them to make no move on a threat of blowing their brains out. Calmly he took two or three steps backward, and got Constable Phillips in line with his weapons.

He then ordered the three men into his cell. Getting them there, he demanded their revolvers and cartridge belts, which two of the constables carried. Securing these, he backed out of the cell, keeping his men covered, even while he locked the cell door.

Going along the corridor, Cashel secured the keys with which to unfasten his shackles.

Just before he left the guard room, Cashel went to his own cell, and with a light hearted "Goodbye, boys," he bid farewell to the constables.

"Where did the revolvers come from?" was the question which was on everybody's lips, after hearing of Cashel's escape. Two visitors were to see Cashel yesterday, Rev. G.W. Kerby, who has been visiting him daily since his conviction, and his brother, John Cashel.

The watch were sure that nothing was left with Cashel during these visits, and the supposition is that the two revolvers were handed in through the window when Cashel was placed on the bench at the end of the corridor. To support this theory, tracks were found outside of the window in the snow, but they could not be followed far.

The sole topic of conversation on the streets today is the escape of Cashel. Everybody wants to know the latest developments in the case, but they are forced to go with very little new information.

At the Police Barracks all is bustle. Descriptions and information are being sent to every part of the country, and particular attention is being paid to all trails, and railways which lead to the United States, because most people suppose that the escaped man will endeavor to cross the line into Montana.

The anxiety of the people for information was demonstrated by the many telephone calls which The Herald had to answer today. "Is it true that Cashel has escaped?" dozens have asked over the phone, and when the report has been confirmed, several asked which direction did he go, and other questions of a similar character which the scribes in the newspaper office are unable to answer.

December 11, 1903

The men searching for Cashel were nervous and determined, a combination that nearly led to disaster.

An old lady, who is very deaf, went over to the homestead of her son to put the house in proper shape, and prepare a meal for him. The son, who lives alone, was seen by the police quite·a way from the house, and when they rode along and saw smoke coming from the chimney, they were sure that somebody was in the house, and that the somebody must be Ernest Cashel. Several times the police called on whoever was inside to come out, but nobody appeared. They fired two or three shots, and still there was no sign of life.

Finally, one of the police approached the house, opened the door, and found the deaf woman to be the sole occupant. Her deafness had prevented her hearing even the rifle shots.

December 18, 1903

For weeks The Herald carried daily stories about the unavailing search for Cashel. Then it fell silent, for reasons that later became apparent. When the NWMP was sure it knew of Cashel's approximate whereabouts, it sent out four search parties, consisting altogether of sixteen NWMP men, sixteen civilians, and six soldiers from the Canadian Mounted Rifles. Their hunt was successful.

Ernest Cashel is caught at last! He was brought into the N.W.M.P. barracks this afternoon shortly after two o'clock, and is now safely and securely lodged in jail.

The story of his capture is a most dramatic one. After being at large from the 10th of December to the 24th of January, with all kinds of opportunities to get out of the country, he was finally landed through his own foolhardiness.

During the last two weeks the police have had several traces of him, but as it was found that he was reading the paper regularly, The Herald at Col. Saunders' request published no news of the chase for several days.

Over a week ago Cashel went to the ranche of Mr. Coppock's, south of Sheppard, and held up the family with his revolver, taking what cash there was in the house, and examining Mr. Coppock's cheque book. On Thursday last he held up James Wigmore, at whose place he slept. He followed Mr. Wigmore with his guns every time he went out. Two weeks ago he was in Calgary, and during his visit he wrote a letter to Rev. Mr. Litch. The letter was written on a sheet of paper bearing the imprint of a city hotel. In it he asked Mr. Litch to advise Radcliffe (the hangman) to go home, as he (Cashel) expected to live a while longer. He said he was very comfortable, and had plenty of friends, read the Daily Herald, and knew all that was going on.

During the past few days the police were sure they were on the right track and waited until today when they could secure a number of good riders to assist them in capturing the escaped murderer.

The party headed by Inspector Duffus, consisting of eight men, started out this morning at 8:30, crossed the Langevin bridge, took the Edmonton trail for a few miles, branching off east across Nose creek and began a systematic search of every house.

Suddenly they saw a policeman riding full gallop toward them. He told Inspector Duffus that they had Cashel surrounded in a shack a mile and a half south on the Langdon trail, about seven miles due east of the city.

Cashel had been living for several days in a large hole which he had dug out in a hay-stack. On the approach of the police and civilians, Cashel took refuge in the cellar of the house. After searching the house Constable Biggs went down the cellar with a lamp making the remark that "Here's where the fellow must be."

He heard a voice saying "Who are you calling a -----" and immediately after Biggs heard a shot and a bullet whizzed past his ear.

Naturally Biggs lost no time in scrambling out of the cellar, shouting for the other men as he went out.

Inspector Duffus and Mr. Heald carried hay to the lean-to of the house and set fire to it, but the wind being in the wrong direction they started a fire on the other side.

Meanwhile the posse gradually closed in, although they knew they were taking desperate chances, there being windows on two sides of the house.

On reaching the house Mr. Chamberlin smashed in one of the windows with the butt of his rifle and Inspector Duffus broke in another.

After some talk, during which the inspector advised Cashel not to kill himself, the desperate convict came up out of the cellar with his hands above his head, saying:

"God, boys, I don't want to be hanged, and I don't want to kill any of you, but I guess I'll have to give myself up."

Cashel then came out of the house and shook hands with the whole party, commencing with Constable Biggs. He said:

"I'm sick of the whole business."

He was then placed in the buggy, and brought quietly into town, sitting on Mr. Chamberlin's knees.

January 25, 1904

Cashel was given a week's reprieve the next day, and his brother was given a year in jail for aiding the escape. Cashel said that he could easily have left Alberta in the six weeks that he was free, but he stayed around in the hope of freeing his brother, who was in jail awaiting trial. However, Cashel also carried a list of policemen and jurymen who were involved in his case. On February 2, Cashel, 21 years old, went to the gallows in Calgary.

Ernest Cashel was hanged this morning, and satisfied with his life the demands of justice. He died firm, but with an easy conscience, for shortly before the fatal moment he told the Rev. Mr. Kerby that he was guilty of the murder of Isaac Rufus Belt.

The whole hanging was quietly done and from the time the condemned man left the guard room until the drop fell two minutes were not consumed.

When all was ready Radcliffe (the hangman) warned everyone away from the trap and gave the signal to Mr. Kerby to start the Lord's prayer.

This the reverend gentleman did. He repeated the words: "Our Father, which art in Heaven," and on down in a slow, and distinct voice. When the words "Lead us not into," were spoken, Radcliffe let down the trap and Cashel dropped below, a distance of 10 feet.

After Cashel had been hanging about two minutes, Dr. Rouleau, the N.W.M.P. physician, felt the pulse of the hanging man, and said it was still throbbing, but very faintly.

Radcliffe said "Let him hang about 20 minutes," which was done. At the expiration of this time he was cut down and carried into a tent in the yard.

The limp body was laid on a stretcher and a block of wood placed under the head. Then the coroner, Dr. Mackid, and his jury filed in and viewed the corpse.

After the jury had retired, a Herald representative entered the tent as Radcliffe was examining the body and turning it over.

"Is his neck broken?" asked the newspaper man.

"Feel it," said Radcliffe, as he gripped it in his big hand.

"No thanks," said The Herald man.

"Well, you asked me if his neck was broken and I ask you to feel it for yourself."

The reporter however expressed his willingness to take the hangman's word for it.

February 2, 1904

Alarms and Disasters

Little by little, Calgary grew out of its preoccupation with local affairs. The telegraph, which spanned the continent and later the oceans, brought news of the world beyond the Prairies. Men from Calgary fought in the first war of this troubled century. But the young city's first link with the world beyond the oceans was the Canadian Pacific Railway, completed in 1885.

The last spike in the C.P.R. was driven at Craigellachie near the Eagle Pass on Saturday. Track laying was commenced at six o'clock in the morning on the last half mile of the road. At nine o'clock the last rails had been brought forward and measured for cutting to make the connection.

One rail was cut and placed and the other left until Vice President Van Horne and the party arrived. Major Rogers made several blows with a heavy sledge hammer on the last rail, helping to cut it. One hundred and twenty feet of rails were then taken up and left on lorries to be placed when Mr. Van Horne and the party arrived.

Immediately afterwards the eastern train made its appearance with the magnates on board. The train drew up close to the end of the track and the party came forward. At twenty-two minutes past nine everything was in readiness to complete the connection.

Hon. D.A. Smith took the maul in hand to drive the last spike and after missing it a few times, drove it home amid cheers from all present. After congratulations had been exchanged on the completion of the great work Mr. Van Horne's special passed over the connecting link and departed for Port Moody, where they will take a special steamer for Victoria.

Chips from the last tie were carried away as mementoes by those present. Much speculation was indulged in as to what was the length of the last rail. It proved to be 25 feet 5 inches, and considerable money changed hands on the head of it. Photographers were on hand and took views of the proceedings from various positions.

November 11, 1885

The Herald's correspondent in Ottawa recorded this giddy moment in a long House of Commons debate over tariff policy.

Before the division was taken on the reciprocity resolutions at Ottawa everyone was tired. Some members slept, others went to the smoking room or saloon to pass the weary hours away.

Perly, of Ottawa, talked till there were none but the Hansard reporters awake, even they had to fix carpet tacks in the backs of the seats to prevent them falling back asleep.

From midnight till 4:30 a.m., when the division bell rang, fun and frolic reigned supreme. Guillet, Clark, Wallace and Charles Tupper led off, while Col. Tyrewhitt, commander of the North York Battalion slept while the battle raged.

Tupper let fly a blue book at the recumbent man's head, but missing the mark, struck Wallace between the eyes, who not knowing where the shot came from let a legal document fly at the ear of Guillet. From then on the fun was fast and furious and mirth was unrestrained.

But the great central figure of the evening was D. W. Davis, M. P. for Alberta. Any attempt to fully describe his antics would be futile. He danced the Blackfoot Indian war dance. The dancer held his body in an erect position, but dropped his head on his breast, separated his feet several inches and without a motion of his body jumped along the table on which he was performing, uttering blood curdling yells. Sir John, who came in to witness the dance, enjoyed it immensely.

Ottawa, April 18, 1888

The Herald's telegraph news kept readers in touch with disasters in far-away places: the Russo-Japanese War, the Boxer Rebellion, the Boer War, the Spanish-American War. There was also a short item, a body-count,

Donald Smith, president of the Canadian Pacific Railways, drives the last spike on the line from Montreal to Vancouver. As the Herald noted, "photographers were on hand and took views of the proceedings."

from the French colonial era in Southeast Asia. Some sixty years later, Vietnam would be back in the news.

The New York Herald prints the following cable from Bangkok: "Saigon papers say that there was some severe fighting between the Siamese and French on July 20th on the Mekong River. It is said that three hundred Siamese were killed, while the French losses were slight. The latter have occupied several more islands."

New York, August 7, 1893

When The Herald's revenues couldn't cover its telegraph bills, reporters had to scrounge out-of-town news from the bulletins issued to passengers on the CPR. The resulting column of news perhaps aroused more curiosity than it satisfied.

Forest fires surround Duluth. Germany does not want Samoa. Japs have captured the Corean King. Brockville will not permit Sunday boats to run. Wheat cutting has commenced in Manitoba.

Big forest fires are raging in British Columbia.

Senator Foley of Nebraska was killed yesterday by a widow.

Lindsay had a slight shock of earthquake on Thursday night.

Just $4,750,000 in gold left New York one day last week, for Europe.

The overthrow of the government in San Salvador is looked for daily.

Mr. Hofmyer, the delegate, is saying nice things of Canada in England.

The cholera is spreading at an alarming rate in Turkey. Several fresh cases are reported at Ardiana.

Patrick Purcell's body, stolen from the grave on May 14, 1891, has been found in the St. Lawrence river.

Several small towns in Wisconsin have been destroyed by forest fire. Trains cannot be moved on the Wisconsin Central.

At Bradshaw, West Virginia, Nellie Keene, aged 9 years, hanged herself because she was kept from school to attend two babies.

The Miranda, with Dr. Cook's expedition on board, ran into an iceberg off the Labrador coast, and had to put back to St. John's, Nfld.

A duel with swords has been fought at Paris between M. Paul Deschanel and M. Clemenceau. M. Deschanel was wounded in the neck.

August 3, 1894

The Northwest Territories were at low ebb in the early 1890s. The settlement of the Prairies had barely begun. Some businessmen, discouraged, had left the fledgling cities of the West. In the gloom, The Herald could be heard still beating the drum for prosperity.

The three things above all others that are of the most vital importance to Alberta at the present time, and before which all other questions sink into insignificance are: provincial government; immigration; irrigation.

The Herald regards these three planks in the Alberta platform as of the very highest and almost equal importance. The success of any will assure the success of the other two. With irrigation placed on a practical footing, immigration will be boomed and Provincial independence hastened.

The writer is as yet a comparative stranger to Alberta, but he has watched events here with sufficient care to be convinced that Alberta can never accomplish what she would and could accomplish in regard to both immigration and irrigation until her shackles are thrown off and she is placed in a position to help herself.

At present her hands are tied. She cannot send out immigration agents, she cannot advertise herself in the countries from which she seeks population, she cannot charter railways, she is powerless to develop her vast mining wealth, she cannot pledge her credit to bring in capital for the construction of irrigation and other public works.

True she has a right to a single representative in the Ottawa legislature and also to a handful in the apology for a legislature at Regina. But against overwhelming numbers and opposing interests the little that they can do is but a drop in the bucket compared with what should be done.

With our lands going to waste through lack of settlers and irrigation, our industries crippled for want of capital, business of all kinds languishing and the country losing ground instead of progressing, are our public spirited citizens expecting, like the children of Israel, to be fed in the coming day of continued depression by showers of manna, while they raise no hand or voice to help themselves in this the hour of their adversity? If there is amongst us any man insane enough to believe that business will revive without more population, or that population will come uninvited and without effort of ours, he cannot too soon be disabused of that idea.

God knows times are bad enough. But as sure as tomorrow's sun will rise they will become still worse unless an heroic and united effort is made by the people of Alberta — and that immediately — to secure their rights, the greatest of which is self-government.

February 19, 1895

Alfred Dreyfus, a French army officer, was convicted in 1894 of selling military secrets to the Germans, and sentenced to life imprisonment on Devil's Island. His trial was highly irregular, and the evidence scanty. In 1899, five years of public outcry won him a new trial. He was convicted again, and the controversy raged on until another trial cleared him in 1906. During those 12 years, almost everyone had an opinion on the Dreyfus affair, including The Herald.

Dreyfus has been found guilty. By those who have been following the reports of the court martial proceedings, the announcement will be received with indignation and disgust rather than surprise. There was absolutely no evidence to justify the conviction, and in the opinion of the lord chief justice of England, "not even sufficient evidence to justify an honest magistrate in committing the accused for trial."

But the "honor" of the army was at stake and Dreyfus was made the victim. The taking of what the court was pleased to term evidence was frantic farce. The fate of the accused had been sealed before a single witness had been examined, although as the trial progressed, the innocence of the accused was clearly established. The sentence imposed is no less farcical than the rest of the proceedings. He has already suffered five years of solitary confinement which counts as ten years of ordinary imprisonment and consequently will be released at once.

The fact which is most clearly established by the trial which has just concluded is that France is now at the mercy of an army of hypocrites and scoundrels whose existence is a blot on modern civilization and a disgrace to the country which tolerates them.

September 11, 1899

Some American newspapers played a considerable part in stirring up the Spanish-American War of 1898. Lurid tales of Spanish misrule in its colonies stirred up American public opinion. When the war ended, Cuba had won its independence from Spain, and the United States had won Guam, Puerto Rico and the Philippines, former Spanish colonies. On the day war was declared, The Herald took the American press to task.

The American nation is beginning to realize that it has been dragged into a war which has already cost millions of dollars and which may cost thousands of lives, solely through the mercenary sensationalism of the yellow jingos who run its newspapers.

Yellow journalism has been exploited to the highest degree by the New York World and the New York Journal. These papers have issued edition after edition printed in colors so gaudy and indiscriminate that each page looks like a dish of fried eggs with the yolks smashed.

The so-called illustrations are of soldiers, sailors, exploding bombs and ironclads (battleships) in action, which the reading matter is alcoholic, vitriolic, electric and sensational. One editor broke down under the strain and actually issued an edition declaring war several weeks ago. He was taken from the office of The World to the madhouse — a merciful change of scene, because he will not notice the difference and the public will.

April 25, 1898

In October, 1899, the long dispute between the Boers (the Dutch settlers in South Africa) and the British, who were trying to settle there, climaxed in war. The siege of Mafeking was one of the famous events of the Boer War. The British, led by Colonel Robert Baden-Powell (later the founder of the Boy Scout movement) held out at Mafeking until a Boer siege was broken after 217 days.

A despatch to the Daily Mail from Mafeking, sent by way of Magaipye because the runners who had been sent southward were unable to traverse the Boer lines, gives an interesting account of the fighting during the last week of October. The correspondent says:

After a failure to rush the town the Boer General Cronje had recourse to tactics similar to those employed during the siege of Potchefstroon in the war of 1881, making an advance to the town by a succession of trenches in echelon. Such a move had been an-

British troops from the South African campaign are welcomed back to London in Nov., 1900.

ticipated for some time and for that reason there had been sent out parties to worry the Boers constantly by night attacks.

The little force stole out silently in the darkness. Not a shot was fired. The men with fixed bayonets creeping rather than walking along, gradually approached the chief Boer position near the race course. Then as they closed in there was a shrill screech. It was FitzClarence's signal for the onslaught. There was a fearful struggle, the attacking force catching and bayonetting the Boers under the tarpaulins where they were crouched crying for mercy. At least 50 bayonets got to work and the havoc they wrought was terrible. Again the whistle sounded. It was "cease firing and scatter homewards." The British forces scattered back under a furious fire in the darkness to where the roll was called.

Cronje's attack is described as follows by a correspondent: The end came after five hours' fighting, when the enemy retired, being heavily beaten for all time in so far as Mafeking is concerned. It was the hottest day of the siege, the Boers recognizing that the way into Mafeking, if any, was by the Kopje which was gallantly defended by Colonel Walford's men.

The garrison is jubilant, while the Boers have been hurled back in disorder and will have to content themselves with a long range bombardment unless they are strongly reinforced.

The enemy lost heavily. For hours after the fighting line had rolled back, two wagons went slowly along their position picking up their dead and wounded. The Kopje resembled a shambles after the fight. All the men were killed by bullets or shells.

The lookout tower was shot to pieces while even the saddles of the horses were fearfully battered. The whole place was simply smashed up by the concentrated fire of seven guns and thousands of rifles. The Boers at first held on their advance pluckily but could not live when they came to short range, many of their men being shot down at 300 yards.

London, November 16, 1899

Queen Victoria ruled for 63 years; her death was indeed the end of an era.

The Queen is dead. A despatch to The Herald just as we go to press confirms the sad news. She passed away about 6:55 at Osborne House, Isle of Wight, surrounded by the members of her family, including her grandson the Emperor of Germany.

In anticipation of the sad event, the government had prepared a proclamation declaring the Prince of Wales king, which will be promulgated tomorrow morning.

The news, though not altogether unexpected, has come as a shock to the whole empire. Queen Victoria had come to be regarded as part of England's national life, and her death makes a break and void that it will take many years to fill. Our fathers and their fathers before them were brought up strong in the principles of loyalty to Victoria and now to the people of the Empire it seems as if the centre of the corner stone

were gone, and things were crumbling to pieces.

January 22, 1901

At the time of this editorial, all of Ireland was still under British rule.

Parliament at Ottawa, by a very large majority, passed resolutions last week in favor of granting home rule to Ireland. The resolution was introduced by the Hon. John Costigan, and the reports of the debate indicate that fervent speeches and eloquent pleas were made in favor of relief for Ireland.

Sir Wilfrid, it appears, made one of his usual careful speeches and extended a serious appeal to England now to trust the people of Ireland, give her home rule and allow her to manage her own affairs.

This almost seems a travesty. Here we are in the North West, making appeal after appeal for provincial or self government and Ottawa not only turns a deaf ear but is even unwilling to discuss the question with us. Though time and zeal can be found for Ireland, both hands being extended to help her, nothing of the kind for the good Canadians of the North West. Hon. Clifford Sifton has said in effect that we are unfit to govern ourselves and has passed the word to his colleagues, and this has been accepted at Ottawa by the government.

April 14, 1903

Limestone boulders bigger than a house obliterated half of Frank, a little mining town in southwest Alberta, on an April night in 1903. In the foreground, CPR crews begin repairs on the railway's Crowsnest Pass line. In the background are some of the remaining buildings in Frank.

Early in the morning of April 29, 1903, tens of millions of tons of stone broke away from Turtle Mountain in the Crowsnest Pass, and slid into the valley below. Huge rocks, many of them larger than houses, obliterated part of the little mining town of Frank, about 110 kilometres west of Lethbridge. At least 76 people were killed. Perhaps coal mines in the mountain somewhere triggered the slide; perhaps it was a purely natural disaster brought on by erosion of Turtle Mountain's limestone peak. Today, the highway and the railroad make their way through a desert landscape piled deep in rock that swept down into the valley and part-way up the other side. In the horrible confusion that followed the disaster, early reports were understandably confused.

About 4 a.m. a terrible explosion occurred in the mines at Frank, N.W.T., due to some volcanic disturbance or earthquake. The explosion was followed by a serious outbreak of flames, and whole rows of cottages, belonging to private families, have been destroyed.

The debris of earth, rock and other matter thrown up has entirely dammed up the river. It is said that between fifty and sixty men are imprisoned in the mines, and about 75 people killed.

Doctors and nurses are being rushed through to aid the wounded and suffering from Macleod and Cranbrook. The wires are down east of Frank, and the railway line is reported to be covered for a mile and a half east from ten to fifty feet in depth.

Later: At 2 o'clock this afternoon the wires are working, and P. Burns & Co. received the following despatch from their representative:

"Earthquake almost destroyed town. Hundred killed. We are all safe."

Cranbrook, B.C., April 29, 1903

Gradually the confusion cleared, and the exact shape of the disaster became plain. Six days after the Frank slide, The Herald published this account by a survivor.

The Herald's special correspondent while in Macleod on his return from the Frank catastrophe was fortunate in securing an interview with George Bond, an Ottawa man who was a guest at the Imperial Hotel in Frank on Wednesday. Mr. Bond evidently kept a cool head throughout the trouble and being a keen observer his description is perhaps more valuable than some of those given by residents of Frank, the majority of whom, as may be easily conceived, became panic-stricken at the first report of what they believed to be either an earthquake or a volcanic explosion.

Mr. Bond, whose story has been published in an extra of the Macleod Advance, says:

We felt a violent shaking motion, and there was a loud crashing report, followed by a succession of noises which I can only compare to the continuous bumping noises of freight cars being brought together, with an occasional louder report, accompanied by a loud, roaring noise, which we at the time imagined was caused by the escape of a vast body of steam under great pressure, which was actually caused by large rocks and boulders tumbling down the mountain side.

This all occupied about one minute and a half of time, being over by the time we reached the sidewalk. On reaching the street the first thing I noticed was a dense white cloud overhanging the east part of the town. Then I noticed a blaze starting about 200 yards distant, so a party of us started off in that direction.

On arriving at the scene of the fire we heard a man calling for help. Some of our party went to his assistance, finding that his house had been wrecked, and that the man, his wife, and a baby and three other children had been caught in the wreck. The man had released all but his wife, who was pinioned down to the bed by a large beam which had been thrown across the bed. With the assistance of those of our party, who went to his aid, the woman was released. The children escaped with but slight bruises, but the woman was more seriously injured, though not considered fatal.

In the meantime, we had arrived at the Leitch home. We found what appeared to be the rear end of the house, which contained three rooms, had completely collapsed. We effected an entrance at the west side, where we found two girls, one of whom we extricated with but little difficulty, and who was practically uninjured. The other, pinioned down by one leg, after considerable difficulty was released. She was perfectly conscious and spoke to the rescuers. The injury to the leg is not considered serious.

We then started to locate the remaining members of the family. We came across the wreck of an iron bedstead, and after removing part of a partition which had been thrown diagonally across the bedstead, we removed a considerable amount of plaster, mud, splintered boards and other debris, and discovered the remains of two boys, of ages from 6 to 9, who had evidently been crushed to death as they lay.

We removed this partition, and on the other side, buried deeply among the ruins, and after a great deal of hard labor we discovered the remains of Mr. and Mrs. Leitch. The damage to this house was apparently caused by a wave of mud which had been forced ahead by the falling mass of rock. The house had been pushed or carried over the grass a distance of perhaps a hundred yards. Outside the house, about twelve feet distant, a little infant child of the Leitch family was found, apparently uninjured and crying piteously. It was at once taken care of.

My share of the morning's work consumed about four hours' time, when I returned to the hotel and partook of breakfast, after which I went up towards the railway depot in order to get a better idea of the amount of damage done.

From the top of a hill east of the station, some 500 feet high, I obtained a magnificent panorama view of the whole scene.

Directly in front of me lay, at a distance of about a mile the Turtle mountain, which rears its magnificent proportions fully 4,000 feet in the air. The east end of the mountain, which was the highest point before the disaster, contained at one time, it is estimated, twenty million tons of limestone more than it does today. This immense wedge-shaped mass of rock must have measured at least 1,200 feet from top to bottom and slid and dropped from the top down the almost perpendicular face of the mountain side. This mass of rock at the thickest part of the wedge must have been fully 500 feet thick.

In falling it struck the inclined base of the mountain, the force of the impact smashing huge masses into boulders of all sizes, down to pebbles and dust, throwing it with terrific force and speed clear across the valley, a distance of over two miles, at a depth ranging from 75 to 150 feet, completely demolishing everything in its course.

With the exception of a few houses already mentioned, in which we were engaged in the work of rescue, not a vestige remained of that part of the town east of a line a hundred feet from the main street, and east of it, but a vast field of white lime and limestone boulders, reaching high up on the north side of the valley, completely covering with boulders the C.P.R. tracks and those of the Frank and Grassy Mountain railway, for a distance of a mile and a half.

The Canadian-American Mining Company's works were directly underneath the fall and received the full force of the avalanche and were completely buried, there being nothing in sight after the disaster to show that a mine had ever existed there.

There were 21 men at work in the mine at the time, and four horses. Gangs of men made repeated attempts to liberate the imprisoned miners, but were forced to desist from the work, owing to the continual falling of immense quantities of rock, which came bounding down the mountain side past the point where the rescue parties desired to effect an entrance.

Later on in the day the efforts of the rescue parties were crowned with success. The imprisoned men were themselves working desperately to effect their escape, with the result that they had found a small opening between several large boulders, which

allowed the passage of a man's body. Through this narrow opening 17 men emerged from the mine, mostly in a very weak state.

They relate a terrible experience, with falling boulders that had entered the mine higher up at the manholes, and that were continually rolling down, imperilling the lives of the miners. Four men were killed in the mine. Three horses are still in the buried mine alive, and according to later reports the bodies of the dead miners and their dumb companions had not been removed.

At the time of the accident a C.P.R. locomotive and crew were engaged in shunting cars on the siding leading to the mine. They heard a loud noise and on boarding the engine and cars to make their escape, they observed some lights and heard shouts supposed to come from men who were caught in the avalanche.

The engine pulled out quickly to the main line, and after a time backed up to the station, where they found that a caboose they had left standing with other cars a little east of the station, had been hove off the track, but not damaged. They coupled up, pulled the cars clear of the debris, replaced the caboose on the track, and used it during the day in making trips between Frank and Blairmore carrying refugees.

May 5, 1903

This editorial proposed a cure for Eastern alienation.

This is the season when so many Canadians from the big cities of the east are rushing off to Europe. The capacity of the steamships is insufficient to handle this traffic.

Hundreds of these people make this trip annually and at the same time they have never been west of Toronto. They prefer to be familiar with things across the water.

A Canadian ought to be ashamed to admit that he is well travelled and yet has never visited that portion of his country that is today such a tremendous factor in the industrial and commercial development of the hemisphere.

Eastern provincialism is the curse of Montreal, Ottawa and Toronto. They think, in too many instances, of the West as big but ungainly, progressive but uncultured, self-conscious but not self-contained, honest and manly but somewhat vulgar.

When this stream that annually turns toward Europe seeks the Western domain, when this element investigates and learns what material and refining arts the Canadian West possesses, then will come a tie that will bind the country together for the prosperity of the whole.

June 29, 1904

J.J. Young, who took over The Herald in 1894, believed that he had found the promised land. He wasn't alone in this belief.

Like every newcomer to Alberta we have had to run the gauntlet, during the past few days, of such questions as "Well, what do you think of Calgary?"

No man with eyes to see and ears to hear can walk down Calgary's magnificent main avenue, or stroll through the suburbs of the city and see its splendidly substantial buildings, its extent, its situation, its rivers, its surroundings with the clearcut peaks of the Rocky mountains against the western sky, and feel the indescribable exhilaration of its balmy climate, at no time more keenly pleasant than in these last days of the old year, without having forced upon him, willingly or unwillingly, a boundless and abiding faith in its future.

God never so richly endowed a country without intending it for the habitation of a numerous and prosperous people. He never placed in convenient proximity a soil of such fertility and a flowing body of water of such purity only to lie and run waste. He never laid up so inexhaustible a store of natural fuel without decreeing in His Providence that an enterprising people should take posses-

sion of the land and put its wealth of resources to practical use for the benefit of humanity. It was said of the Pilgrim Fathers when they landed on the shores of New England that they fell first upon their knees and then upon the aborigines. The people who have come here to carve the destinies of Alberta have done better than the fathers of New England. They have cared for the aboriginal Indian and are keeping him at least in comfort if not in happiness. Is it presumptuous to dare to hope that Providence will be even more propitious regarding the rise and progress of a nation on the prairies of the Northwest than it has been towards the evolution of a great people on the now semi-barren soil of New England?

Whatever we may have thought of Calgary before coming here to make it a home, since comprehending its matchless opportunities we have no misgivings as to its magnificent future. To satisfy one as to the tremendous possibilities ahead of the city it is only necessary to look at its ten years' substantial growth and to remember that hardly a fraction of its marvelous resources has yet been developed. Probably no city of its size in Canada can show the solid and rapid advance that Calgary can. Certainly no city in the Dominion, with the same population, can boast such valuable buildings. In no city within our knowledge has private enterprise and private capital

done so much. The citizens of no town of its size can point to such natural advantages, such prospects as a railway centre; to such vast beds of hard and soft coal as are on every side; to such mineral deposits of iron, copper, lead, silver and other ores so near; to such a wealth of rich native grasses, capable of feeding millions of head of cattle; to such pure water, and never-failing springs and streams as surround us; to such a delightful climate; to such invaluable building stone as is quarried here — in short, to such incalculable possibilities as lie before Calgary and Alberta. It is impossible to write on the subject without enthusiasm.

While there may be a temporary stringency of money, while all the sanguine hopes that have been entertained have not been immediately realized, and while Alberta may meet with momentary setbacks through the masterly inactivity of our public guardians, yet, with the aid of irrigation, the vigorous young province is inevitably bound to progress. Alberta cannot be checked, and Calgary cannot go back. Their future is as certain as the good man's hope of heaven. Let people and government each do their duty and there is no fear of the future.

December 19, 1894

The Daily Herald

Best Seller of the Season

IN SCOTT P...

The Daily Herald

HAVE YOU EXAMINED OUR $10.00 SUITS? J. M. HILL & CO.

TWENTY-THIRD YEAR No. 6,334 — CALGARY, ALBERTA, FRIDAY SEPTEMBER 1, 1905 — 10 PAGES

I MUST RED CF MY STOCK OF LUMBER R. C. THOMAS

AN IMMEDIATE ARMISTICE ASSURED IN THE EAST

ALBERTA DECLARED A PROVINCE AND LIEUTENANT GOVERNOR BULYEA SWORN IN 'MID GREAT APPLAUSE

Inaugural Ceremonies Declared to Have Been Celebrated With Three Inches of Snow.

The Daily Herald

WEATHER FORECAST FAIR

YOU Have watched this spot belongs to J. A. COCKBURN The Famous Photographer

33RD YEAR, WHOLE NUMBER 6,232 — CALGARY, ALBERTA, WEDNESDAY, MARCH 1, 1904 — PRICE FIVE CENTS

Resignation of Sifton Filed With the Premier and Will be Accepted.

Walter Scott, M. P., Slated for the Position of Minister of the Interior—Political or Personal Considerations have influenced Sir Wilfrid's Cabinet Officer in Making His Decision—Resignation Filed Three Days Ago—Came as Tremendous Surprise...

IN EXTRA EDITION OF THE HERALD WILL APPEAR ABOUT 4 P.M. WITH LATER DETAILS

The Daily Herald

LETHBRIDGE COAL R. C. THOMAS

Makers of Candy and Ice Cream ROCHON

TWENTY-THIRD YEAR No. 6,??? — CALGARY, ALBERTA, WEDNESDAY, APRIL 18, 1906 — WEATHER: Thursday: Fair, Cold — 8 PAGES

SAN FRANCISCO CITY DESTROYED!

A Terrible earthquake struck San Franciso shortly after 5 this morning sending into ruins the entire business section. Many big buildings are in flames. No water is procurable as the reservoirs are in ruins. The loss of life is terrible. Los Angeles and Sacramento are also visited.

RED DEER'S GREAT BANQUET TO ALBERTA LEGISLATORS

Citizens Display Their Well Known Hospitality—Fine Site Offered Free for the Capital Building.

DETAILS DIFFICULT TO SECURE AS YET

Telegraphic Communication Cut Off—Several Calgary Citizens Visiting in California.

RUSSIA RAISES MONEY

ZULU CHIEFS HAVE JOINED THE REBELS

Natal Question in Becoming Serious and Other Blacks Join Bambata.

Young Corbett Defeated in Hot Fight by Nelson.

Five Thousand People Watch the Pugs Batter Each Other Through Nine Fast Rounds.

CUT PRICE SALE

A Reputation Worth Having

What we say, we do

MACLEAN'S La Grippe Mixture

Price, 50c.

Wendell Maclean, LIMITED

MAPLE SYRUP and BUCKWHEAT FLOUR THEY ARE VERY NICE

Just Received SEVILLE ORANGES. For Marmalade.

CALGARY MILLING COY. LTD. Phone 232

STUART'S MALTO PERUVIAN TONIC

Price 50c. and $1.00

Bott's Drug Store 124 East 8th Ave. CALGARY, ALTA. DRUGGISTS AND OPTICIANS

---

5 p.m. Edition

THE CALGARY DAILY HERALD

5 p.m. Edition

TWENTY-NINTH YEAR, No. 3104 — CALGARY, ALBERTA, FRIDAY, APRIL 19, 1912 — 32 PAGES

THE TITANIC'S DEATH ROLL IS OVER 1,500

ON REACHING RAFT WIRELESS OPERATOR DIES

The Boat Which Rescued Survivors

Stuck to His Post to Last and then Jumped

STRANGE STORY OF FIGHT FOR BELT

WITH LIGHTS ABLAZE AND BAND PLAYING LEVIATHAN MADE BY MAN FOUND A RESTING PLACE IN ATLANTIC

"Bert" Dick Tells His Story of Experiences For People of Calgary

Look as Saw Berg, but Too Late to Avoid Impact with Tremendous Block of Ice—Shock was Really Imperceptible According to Survivors

OFFICERS DID NOT REALIZE POSITION FOR SOME TIME

Some of the Passengers Refused to Get Up When Roused From Beds by Stewards—Liner Broke in Two Amidships Before Foundering

THE ROLL OF DEAD AND LIVING

NEW YORK, April 18...

---

5 p.m. City

THE CALGARY DAILY HERALD

5 p.m. City

THIRTIETH YEAR No. 3113 — CALGARY, ALBERTA, MONDAY, FEBRUARY 10, 1913 — FAIR AND COLDER TONIGHT AND ON TUESDAY — 20 PAGES

CAPTAIN SCOTT AND BRITISH ANTARCTIC EXPEDITION LOST AFTER REACHING POLE

MEXICO CITY IN HANDS OF THE REBELS

Army Rises in Revolt and Takes Possession of Country's Capital

GEN. DIAZ RELEASED FROM CELL IN JAIL

Review of Former President Assumes Leadership—Pres. Madero Hiding

City Will Have to Sell About $4,000,000 of Debentures This Year

LATEST CABLES HOLD OUT HOPE THAT ONLY EXPLORER HIMSELF AND FOUR OF HIS PARTY PERISHED IN ANTARCTIC

Captain Scott and Scenes of His First Expedition

News of Appalling Disaster Which Befell Captain Scott and His Companions Brought by Terra Nova, Ship That Carried Explorer to the Antarctic

TOTAL NUMBER OF DEATHS INVOLVED IN CALAMITY UNKNOWN, PARTY NUMBERED 66

Lieut. Sir Ernest Shackleton, Who Served Under Captain Scott on a Previous Expedition, Declares Party Must Have Been Weakened... Attack of Scurvy

Those Who Perished With Captain Scott

DEPOSED RULER

DISGUSTING CONDITIONS IN LOCAL SCHOOL WHICH THE M. H. O. ORDERED CLOSED

Hundred Children Crowded Into Room Twenty Feet Square Amid Squalor and Filth—Air Is Hot and Foul, and Pupils Sit With Overcoats on—Premises Are Officially Closed

FRANCISCO MADERO

CANNOT BELIEVE TRUTH OF REPORT, SAYS SHACKLETON

British South Pole Explorer, in New York, Discusses Tragedy

MAY PURCHASE JAM PLANT

PARTIAL HISTORY OF EXPEDITION AND SKETCH OF LEADER

CAPT. AMUNDSEN IS HORRIFIED ON RECEIPT OF NEWS

British Explorer Discovered Norwegian Flag Left at Pole by Rival

TORONTO MAN ONE OF THE VICTIMS

BEREAVED WIFE OF DEAD EXPLORER ON

The Book-Lore Catalogue

Provincehood

1905-13

On September 1, 1905, Alberta became a province. The Herald's cry of 10 years before, "Home Rule For Alberta," had finally come true — more or less. Through the years, Ottawa rule in Alberta would continue to provide a rich supply of grievances.

Alberta prospered in its early years as a province. Settlers poured in to create new farms; in percentage terms, Calgary and Edmonton grew faster than they ever had before — or have since. For Albertans the world, with its wars and catastrophes, was still an off-stage noise. At centre stage was Alberta itself.

After years of agitation from the West, Prime Minister Wilfrid Laurier finally saw the merit of creating new provinces in the southern part of the North West Territories. In the election campaign of 1904, he promised that Alberta and Saskatchewan (which were then administrative districts of the Territories) would be made provinces. Laurier was re-elected, and in 1905 the Alberta Act and the Saskatchewan Act became law. The law hadn't been easily written.

The new provinces resented Ottawa's continuing hold on their natural resources, a restriction that had not been imposed on the older partners in Confederation. This grievance festered until 1930, when Alberta and Saskatchewan finally were given possession of their resources. Even more bitter was the dispute over school policy. Laurier wanted minorities to have strong rights to set up publicly-funded schools in their own language. Clifford Sifton, the Manitoba Liberal who was Laurier's minister of the interior, joined the western opposition to the school policy, and finally resigned from the cabinet in protest. Laurier compromised, and the result was the present-day arrangement in which separate school supporters can dedicate their school taxes to their own school system.

Sifton's replacement as minister of the interior was Frank Oliver, a Liberal from Edmonton. These credentials did not delight The Herald, which had often crossed swords with Oliver when he was editor of the Edmonton Bulletin. He soon lived up to The Herald's worst expectations. The Alberta Act specified that the capital would be Edmonton, until the provincial cabinet decided otherwise. So far the cabinet hasn't decided otherwise, but in 1905 Calgary thought it still had a chance to win the capital away from its temporary northern site. Then Ottawa appointed A.C. Rutherford, another Edmonton-area Liberal, as interim premier. Rutherford filled his temporary cabinet with Liberals.

All this was ominous enough for southern Alberta Conservatives, but then Frank Oliver announced Alberta's constituency boundaries, made in Ottawa. The Herald turned purple. Most of the constituencies were narrow strips running east-west across the province, but no less than six were snuggled up to Edmonton.

Alberta's first election was held November 9, 1905. Like most Alberta elections since, it was a landslide. This time, however, it was a landslide for the Liberals, which has since become unusual. The Liberals won 23 of 25 seats. R.B. Bennett, a Calgary Conservative who became prime minister 25 years later, lost a close contest.

The new Legislature first sat in the spring of 1906. When the question of a permanent capital came up, W.H. Cushing, a Calgary Liberal, spoke for his home city. Red Deer and Banff were also proposed. When the vote came, the southern MLAs voted for Calgary, but the carefully-arranged northern constituencies supported Edmonton, and that was that. A year later, Calgary had to bear another disappointment: the University of Alberta was established at Strathcona, just across the river from Edmonton.

Calgarians who needed consolation could look to Alberta's growth. For all his faults, from Calgary's point of view, Frank Oliver continued the work begun by Clifford Sifton's immigration campaign. From the end of 1906 to the end of 1911, Alberta's population doubled to 374,000; about 250,000 of these people lived on farms. By the beginning of the First World War, the population had grown to about 470,000.

Not all of the province was great farm-land. Mormon settlers in the dry south were among the pioneers of irrigation in Alberta. Then the CPR took a hand, with an ambitious plan to irrigate some 6,000 square miles of land between Calgary and Medicine Hat. The railway built thousands of miles of canals fed by a reservoir at Chestermere Lake and a dam at Bassano.

Farmers quickly became a political force in Alberta. The United Farmers of Alberta, organized in 1909, would later become a political movement which would defeat the Liberals and govern the province for 14 years. In the election of 1909, however, they supported the Liberals, who were returned with 37 out of 41 seats. One of the four opposition members was R.B. Bennett.

Even before the UFA, farmers made their wants felt in Edmonton. One thing they wanted very much was railway branch lines that would carry their crops to market. The Legislature heard and obeyed. Early in its first session, in 1906, it granted charters for five railways. Even so, and even with provincial government guarantees to entice cautious investors, the branch lines made a slow start. In 1908, The Herald joined the agitation for more railways. A Herald reporter spent weeks on horseback, criss-crossing Alberta to hear disgruntled farmers' demands for branch lines.

The proposed Alberta and Great Waterways Railway caused the province's first big political scandal. Allegedly some cabinet ministers received payments from the House of Morgan, the New York financial firm that made a profit selling the railway's bonds. The ensuing political hurly-burly temporarily divided the Alberta Liberals. There were feuds and resignations in the cabinet; in the Legislature, R.B. Bennett, a fiery orator of a now-vanished school, delivered a five-hour denunciation of the government. Premier Rutherford resigned (though a judicial investigation later cleared him of any wrong-doing) and A.L. Sifton took over. Even after the scandal, the Alberta railway boom continued, without much regard for economic reality. (However, the Alberta and Great Waterways Railway did reach its goal near Fort McMurray — in 1924.)

The people of Calgary didn't spend much time lamenting the loss of the capital and the university to Edmonton. After all, they had the CPR. Calgary was doing very nicely as the distribution centre of southern Alberta. As early as 1906, city council decided not to put down any more wooden sidewalks; henceforth, only concrete sidewalks and asphalt paving would be good enough for Calgary. (However, in 1909 The Herald was still complaining of a mud-hole at Centre Street and Fourth Avenue South.)

Two ill-fated railways, the Canadian Northern and the Grand Trunk Pacific, laid branch lines to Calgary in 1909. A simmering real estate boom came to a boil. A lot at the corner of Seventh Avenue and Second Street West sold for $2,000 in 1905. In 1912, when the boom was about to run out of steam, the price was $300,000. The land where the York Hotel now stands sold for $12,500 in 1907; in 1910, it cost $100,000.

By 1911, 2,000 people were working in the real estate

Sir Wilfrid Laurier speaks in Edmonton as Alberta becomes a province.

business here. The Herald carried pages of advertising for new neighborhoods: Roxborough, Sunalta, Elbow Park, Bankview, Bowness. American Hill, officially known as Mount Royal, was the choicest part of town. One way to own a house on American Hill was to buy and sell real estate in less choice parts of the city. In October, 1912, the company promoting Tuxedo Park lots at $400 each assured prospective buyers that "within a few years when the bridges across the Bow River are constructed, when the avenues are paved and the sidewalks laid, when hundreds of beautiful homes will be located on the north side, the property . . . will be assessed and marketable at four to five times the price of today." The advertisement also claimed that smart investors were selling over-priced land in south Calgary and buying bargains north of the Bow.

The rise in land prices was supported by astonishing growth. Calgary, a city of 12,000 in 1906, grew to nearly 44,000 in 1911, and to 56,000 in 1916. (Most of the increase between 1911 and 1916 probably took place before the war.) Furthermore, there was construction on many of those increasingly expensive lots. Building permits worth $5.5 million were issued in 1911; in 1912, the figure was $20.4 million; that was the record for a long time to come. In 1929, which started as a very good year, only $11.4 million worth of permits were issued. The total didn't reach $25 million a year until 1950.

Calgary's first two streetcars started until their rounds in 1909. The street car system grew as fast as the city. By 1912 there were 50 cars on 60 miles of track. Some lines ran through empty land to clusters of houses. The Bowness line ran out to a park and a golf course, and not much else. Developer John Hextall's vision of mansions around the park never did come true, and the Bowness line had to pick up revenue by carrying milk from dairy farms along its grassy route. It also carried The Herald.

In November, 1912, the publishers of the Calgary city directory predicted that Calgary would house 100,000 people by 1915. A month later, a Herald editorial noted that the real estate boom was dead, at least for the time being. Calgary had to wait another 35 years for the magic 100,000.

Not many world events dominated The Herald's front pages in those far-off days. The Russo-Japanese war was fought to a bloody conclusion on land and sea in 1905. Russia's defeat contributed to an insurrection at home. The Czar responded with a combination of bloodshed and reform, and kept his throne for another dozen years. An earthquake devastated San Francisco in 1906. The Herald published an "extra" every few hours, bringing the latest news from the shattered city. In 1912 the new ocean liner Titanic struck an iceberg and sank, with a terrible loss of life. Among the survivors were a Calgary couple, Mr. and Mrs. A.A. Dick. Mr. Dick was a real estate investor.

In federal politics, the era was marked by the beginning of another Conservative interlude. The Liberal Laurier had arranged with the United States for free trade in farm products, and lower duties on many other goods. In 1911 he sought Canadians' support for this reciprocity treaty at the polls, and lost. Robert L. Borden became prime minister, and served until 1920. Borden wanted closer ties to the British Empire, and a Canadian contribution to Imperial defence, in return for a voice in the Empire's foreign and defence policies. After a long, rowdy debate, Borden won Commons approval in 1913 for Canada to contribute three ships to the British navy. The Liberal majority in the Senate blocked the contribution, an action which brought bitter recrimination from Conservatives when war broke out in 1914.

By 1913, when this chapter ends, the threat of that conflict hung over the British Empire. The next year, Calgary would send men to the inferno of the Great War. Nothing afterward would be quite the same.

The New Kid Speaks Up

There was more than a whiff of corruption about Alberta politics in the province's early years, though perhaps The Herald's conservative nostrils were unduly sensitive to the odors emanating from Liberal governments in Ottawa and Edmonton. Constituency boundaries for Alberta's provincial election were drawn in Ottawa, chiefly by Frank Oliver, a long-time Liberal and founder of the Edmonton Bulletin. When it published a map of the boundaries, The Herald cried "foul" — and with some reason.

I n the history of Canada no greater political outrage has been perpetrated than that of which the above map tells the story. No printable language can adequately fit the case.

Nobody in the south wants to harm Edmonton or any other part of the north. All we ask is fair play, and we have grave reason to protest against the grossly unfair way in which the Federal government proposes to hive in a lot of small constituencies around Edmonton, and leave important, populous and prosperous communities in the south with outrageously inadequate representation. What right has the Federal government to lay out the constituencies at all? What right has Sir Wilfrid Laurier and his cabinet to interfere in such a purely domestic affair as the selection of a permanent provincial capital? What right have they to load the dice in a game which the respective competitors were prepared to fight out fairly on its merits? Neither Calgary, Red Deer, Medicine Hat, nor Banff, has asked for special favors in this fight.

The fact that the Hon. (?) Frank Oliver and his town, aided and abetted by bishops and railway promoters, have asked for and received special favors in this matter is a confession of cowardice on their part, and of weakness on Sir Wilfrid's. It is more. It is a disgrace to Canada's government and the Liberal party, and it is as strongly denounced throughout the south by Liberals as by Conservatives.

The constituencies grouped around Edmonton and cornering on that town resemble the arms of an octopus. They are deliberately arranged so that Edmonton, with its church and railway co-conspirators, can control five or six members. Look at Stoney Plain. It stretches away down south of Red Deer, but the whole population is in its extreme northeast corner, close to Edmonton.

Equally outrageous is the gerrymander of St. Albert, Sturgeon, Saskatchewan and Strathcona, all of which corner on the town of Edmonton, and broaden out over the whole north.

On the other hand, the constituencies around Calgary have been completely isolated from the city, evidently with a deliberate purpose.

There has certainly been method to the game. While it is possible under the proposed distribution for Edmonton, with its 7,000 people, to elect at least five members,

Calgary, with 12,500, can have but two at the outside.

The bulk of the new population of the last three years has settled in the country between Calgary and Cardston. Yet that vast and populous district remains with but two constituencies — High River and Macleod, while in the same distance on the north line this beautiful gerrymander places six seats, Red Deer, Lacombe, Ponoka, Westaskiwin, Leduc and Strathcona.

A careful computation, based on election returns, the census, homestead entries, and land sales, gives a population of 138,000 to the south, and 99,000 to the north.

Every consideration of right and justice demands that the two constituencies in the wilds of Athabasca should be wiped out, and that Calgary, Banff, Nanton and Claresholm, Cardston and the Crow's Nest districts should be given additional representation.

May 13, 1905

This editorial summed up The Herald's position on the major issues in Alberta's birth as a province. The Liberal government of Sir Wilfrid Laurier had proposed to give minorities the right to establish their own publicly funded schools and to teach in their own language. After a storm of protest, this proposal was modified to create the present-day separate school arrangement. And when Ottawa created Alberta and Saskatchewan, it held on to their natural resources, a grievance that wasn't cleared up until resource control was turned over in 1930. The "schedule" referred to in this editorial is the set of electoral boundaries, drawn up by Frank Oliver, the new minister of the interior, that so heavily favored Edmonton and district.

B ecause The Herald has steadily and unequivocally insisted upon the right of the west to frame its educational policy regardless of the special considerations of any ecclesiastical forces, the weaklings of the coercion crowd insist that the Catholic church is being attacked.

When The Herald expressed the sincere alarm of the west over the well-defined report that Sir Wilfrid had conceded to Messrs. Oliver and Talbot the privilege of arranging the Alberta constituencies, the same little fellows were shocked, and insisted that there was no ground for the suspicion, and that Calgary's chances for capital honors were being lessened by this assumption.

When The Herald declared that the natural resources of the two provinces should be preserved as a provincial asset, a wail went up from the same source, and it was charged that the paper favored radical legis-

lation for the new provinces, which the older provinces had not exacted.

When The Herald alluded to the 10 cents per ton coal bounty which the Dominion government proposed to permanently appropriate in spite of the fact that the other provinces received this revenue, another convulsion was registered from the gang that would handicap the west with any harness the Ottawa conspirators might rig up.

When The Herald opposed a civic banquet to Hon. Frank Oliver upon the ground that the sentiment that promoted the function would be distorted by the partisan element of the east, there was more commotion among the little fellows, who would kiss the hem of Oliver's garments to placate the Ottawa powers. They rejected with scorn the suggestion that Frank Oliver was going down to Ottawa with a cut and dried schedule in his pocket, but when the new minister reached Ottawa the unfair schedule was handed down, and Sir Wilfrid reluctantly admitted that it was Oliver's creature — the product of his treachery to the west.

Now this silly twaddle about "assaulting the Catholic church," "disparaging the Minister of the Interior," "damaging Calgary's chances," and other signals of distress are raised because The Herald insists that a vigorous campaign is necessary if three-fourths of Alberta is not to be disfranchised.

If that considerable portion of Alberta that is dissatisfied with the schedule and disgusted with the unfair methods that dictated the gerrymander, fails to emphasize its disapproval, is there any reason to expect the men who have framed the unjust measure to recede from their position?

It is a part of the Ottawa programme to have the west silenced as long as possible by the hope of fair play. This is essential to the hold-up that was hatched in the interest of a remote section of the north country. It is a part of the game to have every objection belittled and the merits of the controversy clouded at each turn.

To deliberately assert that Alberta is not interested in the principle of a sound educational system of our own choice is to pervert the truth. To say that the majority of the people of Alberta favor handing over the natural resources of the new province to the Dominion government is to question the sanity of the masses. To urge silence and conciliation while the coercion plot continues to tighten around Alberta is to confess the weakness of the west in a moment of extreme peril.

The Herald regards the present situation as dangerous to the prosperity of the west — as a genuine crisis. The paper does not expect the approval of those who believe in coercion, but it does invite the co-operation of all who are opposed to surrendering the great principles of self-government and delegating that authority to the men who are now attempting to impose, for selfish purposes, this unfair system in Alberta.

May 19, 1905

Alberta became a province on Sept. 1, 1905, with all the pomp and circumstance that Edmonton could muster.

Amid the booming of a royal salute of twenty-one guns, G.H.V. Bulyea was at noon sworn in as Lieutenant-Governor and Alberta assumed the provincial status. J.J. McGee, secretary of the privy council, administered the oath in the presence of the most representative gathering the west has ever witnessed.

The Governor-General and his staff in brilliant uniforms, Sir Wilfrid Laurier and a large number of chief officials of the Dominion government were the centre of the group surrounding the new Lieutenant-Governor. A vast throng, estimated at several thousand, surrounded the interesting scene and added to the solemnity of the occasion.

The mounted police and militia guard of honor gave a military aspect to the civic function.

The whole city is in gala attire and flags and banners are flying from every building and flag staff. Nearly every portion of the Dominion is represented and from away into the Arctic circle have come many trappers, missionaries and men of the far north land. The variety of costumes, combining the pioneer and the modern conception added to the picturesque aggregation.

The birth of the province of Alberta was signalled by a military pageant of considerable proportions which was reviewed by the Governor-General. Nothing occurred to interrupt the entertaining programme arranged by the committee.

In the early morning the Governor-General and party were driven around the city and were received everywhere by cheers and demonstrations of pleasure. He repeatedly raised his hat in token of appreciation of the plaudits of the crowds. At eleven o'clock the mounted police parade was reviewed by the Governor-General.

An address was presented to the Governor-General at noon and his response was one of splendid praise for the new province and the enterprising men of the West. This was followed by speeches from Sir Wilfrid Laurier and other distinguished individuals.

This evening the ceremonies will be concluded with a grand ball, the musical ride by the R.N.W.M.P., horse races, ball games, lacrosse and polo games.

Edmonton, September 1, 1905

The Herald added a less enthusiastic conclusion to the foregoing report from its Edmonton correspondent.

In Calgary at noon it was reported that three inches of snow had fallen in the Edmonton district and that as the government train entered the city three inches of snow had to be plowed through. From the same source, considered authentic, it is asserted snow was falling at Edmonton during last night.

And yet the coercion machine insists that Edmonton is the best place in Alberta for the capital.

In Calgary flags were flying and the schools were closed in honor of Alberta's birthday. There was no general holiday however.

September 1, 1905

This editorial officially marked Alberta's birth as a province. Never did optimism burn more brightly. So far, Alberta hasn't quite lived up to The Herald's expectations.

Today Alberta is a member of the sisterhood of provinces in the Dominion of Canada. Big events in other parts of the world will not permit the English-speaking people of other lands today to overlook the introduction of the new provinces in the great Northwest.

From the first they will become tremendous factors in the progress of British North America. Today, wherever a Briton lives, he remembers that the empire is being given new strength in the western world by this development.

Who will undertake to forecast the limitations of the two latest provinces to appear on the Canadian scroll?

When Bernard Snow, that eminent political economist of the United States, in his speech at Calgary Wednesday, registered his solemn judgement that the country embraced in these two new provinces would one day wield the balance of power, political and commercial, in the Dominion, did he draw a picture that is warranted by recent events?

What was but a generation ago the "far west" of the United States, is today the section to which both great political parties of the republic look for their presidential material.

It requires no greater strength of the imagination to contemplate Alberta as the centre of political and commercial influence in the Dominion than it did two generations ago to assign to the central west of the states the lofty position in the affairs of the republic which it now occupies.

September 1, 1905

Alberta politics used to be a much rougher game than it is today. As this story about the first Alberta election shows, the campaign wasn't over even when the polls closed. In the end, R.B. Bennett, the Conservative candidate for Calgary, lost by 25 votes. The Liberals, who had run the interim government that was established when Alberta became a province, won 23 of 25 Legislature seats.

By the worst example of Ottawa interference ever displayed in a provincial election, the coercion plot has been forced upon the electors of Alberta. By the influence of the Dominion machine, probably 15 out of the 25 seats have been carried by the Alberta government.

In Calgary, however, in spite of the most outrageous tactics, the Conservative leader has been elected. There can be no question of the accuracy of this statement. Though W.H. Cushing leads on the face of the returns, by 31, there are several hundred contested votes. These must be counted on Tuesday.

The Conservative management have examined a number of the poll books and in every instance they show that at least seventy-five per cent of the protested votes are those of Conservatives and mostly known friends of R.B. Bennett.

Some of these contests call for the appearance of the voters at the barracks and others at the city hall. The dates range all the way from tomorrow to next Wednesday. In every event the voter should appear for he is liable to criminal prosecution if, charged with having voted illegally, he fails to defend his vote, for in that case he confesses to having attempted to violate the law.

The Conservative headquarters should be visited at once by every friend of Bennett's whose vote was challenged. They will remain open several days. Some fifty well known Calgary men — men whose right to vote must have been understood by the Liberal machine which caused their vote to be challenged appeared at Conservative headquarters last night and received instructions as to the contest.

The local coercion organ (The Tribune) this morning alleges that two hundred of the protested votes are those of Liberals. This, of course, is ridiculous, because the Liberal machine began to challenge votes the moment the polls were opened, by a preconcerted plot, while the Conservatives challenged no votes until late in the day and then only in known or suspected instances of fraud. On the very face of the situation it is clear that the Liberals have contested the bulk of the votes, even if the examination of the poll books did not show this.

The Conservative organization is investigating the report that three ballot boxes, one of them unsealed, were placed in the safe of a well-known man and left in his personal possession several hours last night.

A keen contest will result over the contested votes in Calgary. The Conservative organization is confident of ultimate victory next week in spite of the claims of the coercion management of Mr. Cushing.

A number of voters challenged by Liberals and known to be friends of Bennett's have been told by Liberals that they did not have to appear as summoned to make their vote good. This is merely intended to confuse the Conservatives and help the Liberals.

While it is legal for a challenged voter to make his appearance by authorized agent, the chance of having votes passed in this manner is a hazard no honest elector ought to take.

Conservative headquarters will remain open day and night until this phase of the contest is disposed of. Every challenged voter should appear there, register, and preparations will be made for his defence.

November 10, 1905

The Calgary Boom Begins

After Alberta became a province, Calgary began to live up to the hopes of its pioneers. The first story below expresses some premature — and unusual — pessimism about the real estate boom. In 1906, the boom hadn't even begun, and it would last until 1912. In 1913, the first hints of oil at Turner Valley revived the dreams of speculators disillusioned by real estate. All this time, settlers kept flooding in.

The real estate situation in Calgary continues significantly active. It has, in fact, borne the earmarks of a genuine boom and in the opinion of the more conservative citizens there is danger of its reaching the frenzied stage.

Some people think it has reached that stage and that a slump may occur which would be disastrous to those who failed to get out from under by unloading in time.

There are many others who believe that present prices of real estate are not excessive but that values will be still higher in the spring. They point to Winnipeg and Edmonton, where fabulous prices have reigned for some time. But neither of these cities is an altogether happy example.

It is true Winnipeg has grown marvellously, but late reports are not very reassuring and indicate that building has been overdone. It was recently reported, that there are 1,200 vacant houses in that city. It is said many speculators are having difficulty in unloading and that in some cases prices are on the decline.

As for Edmonton, every unprejudiced visitor gets the same impression, namely that both residential and business lots are held at absurdly extravagant figures, which have been boosted up by the local people buying among themselves, very little outside capital having been invested.

This last feature is to a certain extent true in Calgary, though up to a very few weeks ago the advance in real estate values was fully justified by the steady industrial development of the city and district generally, a development which we believe will continue for some years.

One thing is certain — Calgary does not want a boom. We want all our vacant lands filled up with settlers of means and experience. We want natural gas, cheap coal and cheap electric power, and we want more factories and wholesale houses. We also want more railways and cheaper freight, to bring us nearer to coal and to provide better transportation facilities for outlying settlements. These objects will be assisted by the publicity campaign which has been so successfully inaugurated by the Board of Trade.

The Herald's advice to business men and others having the real interests of the city at heart is that instead of buying lots for speculation they should invest their surplus cash in a movement to attract outside capital and bring in more settlers and local industries.

To build up a great city requires more than swapping lots among the inhabitants thereof.

A round of the real estate offices yesterday revealed some astonishing advances in certain parts of the city, some of them justifiable advances, some otherwise. Twenty-five foot lots on the extreme western edge of the city, a mile to a mile and a half from the post office, which five or six years ago went begging at $25 and even lower, are now selling readily from $200 to $400. On the C.P.R. addition scores of fifty foot lots have changed hands at from $400 to $750 each.

But it is east of the Elbow where the frenzy is at its height. Lots there have advanced from $35 a few months ago to $200, $300, $400 and even $1,000. A site was sold this week for manufacturing purposes for over $5,000.

A very desirable corner in a central business location is reported to have changed hands yesterday for over $30,000, and for certain purposes it is well worth even more. This corner furnishes a striking example of money-making. It was held three years ago for $5,000. It steadily advanced until it was sold last fall for $25,000, and there is a probability of its changing hands again for $35,000 or even more.

One feature of the present flutter is the large amount of money withdrawn from savings accounts for investment in lots. The market at present is certainly active and buoyant. Let us hope nobody will get hurt and to this end it behooves investors, real estate men and property owners to discourage anything in the nature of booming.

February 3, 1906

Settlers arriving in Calgary were greeted by Captain Winn, the immigration agent who ran a half-way house for families waiting to move onto empty land where they would make homes and farms.

Hundreds of new settlers arrived in Calgary yesterday and this morning. Immigration hall was pretty well crowded with those left over from Thursday's and Friday's rush and the newcomers overran Captain winn's hospitable quarters. As a rule only that type from the states which is known as "homesteaders" seek shelter at the hall, but at present the families of a great many investors are taking advantage of these excellent facilities.

While the head of the family goes south or east or north looking for a quarter section of land which "looks good to him" for homesteading purposes, he leaves his wife and children at the hall. They are supplied one week, and after that time, unless unusual circumstances arise, they must make room for others.

The government supplies shelter, light, heat and cooking utensils, and the boarders must supply their bedding and food and a cook. The latter is not a serious question as most of the women are excellent housekeepers and know how to prepare some most tempting food. They are supplied with vast quantities, not one person yet having arrived that needed special attention from Agent Winn.

The quarters are clean, and the women have considerable privacy on the upper floor. In a pinch, little extras are secured for any women and children that do not appear to Captain Winn and his kind-hearted wife to be properly provided.

With the crowds now arriving an assistant at the hall is badly needed. Captain Winn must meet a train at 3:20 a.m., and from that time until the train from the north arrives at 11 p.m. he must be around looking after arriving and departing immigrants, giving them advice, showing them maps, and rendering expert views on the best part of the country in which to seek homesteads or good farms for investment.

The hall presented a very cheerful aspect yesterday afternoon. The mothers were getting their evening meal while the children frolicked on the floor, the older children being out walking. Many of the women are from the same sections and cook their meals as one big family. Roast beef in copious quantities was being served at the long table, and while the facilities in some cases were rather primitive the inmates did not seem to mind such little inconveniences. Appetizing food was plentiful and the women did not seem at all disturbed by their unsettled surroundings.

One sweet-faced woman with a blue-eyed baby was in their midst, apparently disconsolate over the absence of her husband, who was "land-hunting" as she explained. There was an atmosphere of homesickness about this young mother and she hugged her chubby little one close to her bosom as if its presence assuaged her grief in a measure. The other women appeared anxious to cheer her with their conversation and suggestions.

An example of genuine pioneer grit is that of Mrs. Mary Colwin, of Camchester, Oklahoma. She has three children, but no husband, and has come to Alberta to homestead. Her oldest boy is scarcely 16, but he is a manly looking boy and apparently conscious that the family burdens rest on him chiefly.

Mrs. Colwin is of the material of which women of the frontier are made, if her resolution can be determined by her hopeful manner and business-like preparation. Her cheeks are tanned by the heat of the south, and her hands are furrowed by contact with the seamy side of things, but she stands erect and surveys her new surroundings with a complacency that is an example for many of the men of the party.

Mrs. Colwin does not hesitate to tell her dreary story of misfortune in the dry belt of the southwest, when their crops burned up, but her attitude is not one of inviting commiseration. She relates her struggle with life in its hardest form and the death of her husband in matter-of-fact way common to many of the new settlers from that part of the country.

She had gone "into the strip" as she referred to the Cherokee nation, which was thrown open for settlement a few years ago, with her family to make a home. They homesteaded and got a start, but every drouth struck their farm and every cyclone "took a bit out of our wind break," she observed, in detailing the unfavorable conditions which ruined the hopes of the Colwin family in that part of the world.

"When my husband died and I got a chance to sell out I just made up my mind I would come up here, where my three boys could grow up with the country," said Mrs. Colwin, and she laid her withered hand fondly on the head of the youngest, a boy of eight, who was standing near.

March 12, 1906

Alberta's prosperity depended almost entirely on farming; The Herald campaigned vigorously for branch railway lines that would carry homesteaders' crops to market. Jess Dorman of The Herald toured central Alberta, talking to farmers who knew they'd be rich if they had a railway nearby. His travels led to a series of front-page articles.

The Herald's staff correspondent left Calgary today on horseback to accomplish a trip which ought, at this stage of the game, to be done in a palace railway car. The present trip is being undertaken for no other purpose than in the hope of hastening the day when it may be done in a palace car.

The course the rider will pursue runs in a northerly direction, out past Carbon, Ghost Pine, Three Hills and other points on toward Vermilion.

The land department reports that practically all the homesteads in the territory to be traversed are taken, and it is said that the settlers are there, a great many of them actually working their claims, awaiting with the true pioneer patience the coming of the road that will make their land valuable, and encourage them to obtain at least some of the comforts of life their enterprise and fortitude have so fully deserved.

These people came to Alberta as a result of the combined efforts of those of us who were here before them; as a result of the advertising campaign of the government and the land companies large and small; as a result of your efforts and mine. They were told that valuable homesteads could be had for the taking, and were assured, and are being assured, that the railroad will soon pass their doors. They are out there waiting for it, and The Herald man is travelling out to call upon them, to see how they are faring, and to tell its readers.

The Herald's motive is not all philanthropic. Human affairs are so interdependent these days that to help one's neighbor means to help one's self. If the country prospers the city prospers, and if the country stagnates the city does worse. The Herald knows, as well as every man who has pondered the question, that the country's greatest need is railroads. It knows that Alberta will never begin to come into her true value as a commercial asset until her railroad development begins to go forward with very great strides.

The value of our natural endowment is undisputed. It is not denied that we have the material to make us wonderfully rich; neither is it disputed that we need to enter upon a campaign of railway building in order that our agricultural and other resources may begin to realize the good that is in them.

The Herald's purpose is RAILROADS in big letters. Its motive is not political; it is not undertaking to say by whom or by what means, or upon what basis, the roads should be realized; but it is going out to demonstrate the crying need for them. Its interests in the matter are identical with yours, whether you are a merchant, land owner, lawyer, publisher, legislator, or whatever your calling. Its interests are identical with the best interests of Alberta. It wants to see the province grow.

September 3, 1908

Calgary's new prosperity soon flowed through to the dress shops. Seventy-five dollars was a shocking price for an evening gown in 1909 and so was $11.50 for a silk petticoat.

Life in a Very Young City

Calgary's entertainments weren't usually as rough-and-ready as the first item below might suggest. Amateur sport flourished, movies — even a talking movie — supplemented vaudeville, and once Sarah Bernhardt performed at the Grand. A championship boxing match came to a tragic end, but on the brighter side, there was the first Calgary Stampede.

The outcry of the pulpit against the exhibition in the name of sport witnessed last week at Victoria park is worthy of consideration. The particular feature objected to was that in which a huge cowboy grabs a steer by the nose with his teeth and throws the animal to the ground.

This feat has been witnessed several times at the park this summer and has provoked more or less comment. That it aroused a feeling of disgust quite generally is to the credit of the Calgary public. Clean sports are liberally patronized in Calgary. Perhaps no other community of equal size in the country displays more active interest in many sports than the people of this section of the west, but when a man is permitted to make an exhibition of this character in the presence of women and children, the finer sensibilities are outraged.

July 4, 1905

THE STAMPEDE CALL

This irresistible offer came from the Calgary Stampede, which was held for the first time in 1912.

At the time of this editorial, the automobile speed limit in Calgary was 15 miles per hour. High-speed police chases in those days were less spectacular, but perhaps more entertaining.

Ald. Jones, who has recently returned from a visit to British Columbia, complains that the men who drive horses and automobiles on Calgary streets are more reckless than in any city he has visited on his tour.

A case in point came before the magistrate a few weeks ago, when a man who was accused of reckless driving was acquitted as soon as the charge was heard. It seemed altogether likely that the accused was guilty, but no one was prepared to state at what speed the horse was being driven. One witness said it was travelling at eight miles an hour; another said nine miles.

The City of Montreal has devised an expedient that should prove valuable in this city. To put down fast driving and secure evidence that will carry conviction, policemen are now posted at different parts of the city with bicycles. If an automobile comes along at a speed faster than a regulation rate, the driver is asked to stop. If he fails to do as requested, the policeman mounts his bicycle and follows the car. An instrument on the bicycle registers the speed.

December 20, 1906

One of the accused in this case, Longfellow, was convicted, but The Herald seems to have lost interest in the story before he was sentenced.

Last night Herbert Longfellow, who has poetic hair, and Dan Keeley, who hasn't went over to pay a social visit on one Mattie Miller, a lady of evening habits with a tendency toward fancy garters.

They all had a real nice time and became, as usual in such cases, very friendly. But, sad to relate, when captivating Herbert and charming Dan left the presence of winsome Mattie it is alleged that they did not leave behind them certain articles which were indispensible to Mattie.

Her gold garters! Where had they gone? What could she do without gold garters? She would be no different from other ladies if she had not her gold garters.

Those once charming but now horrid young men must have abstracted the hose supporters while Mattie was in a trance. She knew they had admired them, and possibly the temptation had proven too strong. Anyway the garters were gone and they were the ones she suspected.

She hied her to the police station, wearing only the ordinary kind of garters and feeling ashamed of them. She told the heinous tale to the officers, adding that a brooch was also gone.

The two young men with suspected garterish tendencies were apprehended and arraigned before the magistrate this morning. They will appear tomorrow for trial.

November 7, 1907

Thirty miles per gallon is not bad mileage even today. In 1908, it was quite an achievement.

Saturday afternoon, Jan. 18, a most interesting economy test was made of a four cylinder, 12 horsepower, model G Franklin automobile.

The object of the test was to demonstrate that the auto mentioned was able to make the trip from Calgary to Okotoks and return, a distance of approximately 56 miles, on two gallons of gasoline.

Before leaving the Western Automobile

company (who are agents for the Franklin machine) the gasoline tank was examined by Mayor Cameron, ex-Alderman White and a Herald representative. The tank was found to be perfectly empty and then two carefully measured gallons of gasoline were poured in.

The route selected by chauffeur Carl Grasswick was Centre Street to Stephen Avenue, to Second street east, then up cemetery hill to the Macleod trail and on to Okotoks.

No attempt at very fast speed was made, the object of the trip being merely to show that the trip could be made with the two gallons of gasoline.

Okotoks was reached in just 64 minutes and a stop of some 15 minutes made in that thriving town.

The return trip was made over the same route, but did not take quite as long as the outgoing run, the car reaching the garage on Seventh avenue west just 61 minutes after leaving Okotoks.

January 30, 1908

Calgary's first two streetcars began running in July, 1909. Even then Calgarians were looking forward to the day when the streets would no longer be torn up.

Mayor Jameson and the commissioners, as well as the manager of the street railway system are certainly to be congratulated on having the cars running yesterday. The cars had only arrived in the city a few days before and the usual delays incident to starting such an undertaking were expected. That they were so quickly overcome is matter for satisfaction.

Success was not, however, achieved in the last few days. It was during the months of hard but unpretentious work on the city streets that the most important progress was made and in this all the executive of the city shared. The feature of this year's civic administration is contained in the phrase "something doing."

Torn-up streets and blocked sidewalks are not pleasant but they mean work going on, and Calgary is being licked into the shape of a real city with remarkable speed. By fall we will have an up-to-date and presentable metropolis, worthy of its standing as the chief commercial centre in sixteen hundred miles of territory and the most rapidly growing community in Canada.

July 6, 1909

This editorial tried, without much success, to put a stop to the old story of bitter rivalry between Calgary and Edmonton.

It is a favorite habit of strangers from the east, when interviewed in either Calgary or Edmonton, to deplore the rivalry between the two cities, and urge them to come together. These beneficent gentlemen love to spread out their hands in benediction over the two of us and say: "Bless you my children, but don't fight."

As a matter of fact the rivalry to which they refer exists chiefly in their own imaginations. They have heard it spoken of in years gone by, and when they come out here on a trip they look for it, and a person generally finds what he is looking for.

There was a time when Calgary and Edmonton felt somewhat bitter towards one another. The sentiment had little to do with either city, but resulted from circumstances chiefly connected with the competition for the capital site, and the government's deception to Calgary concerning the university.

All that is over now and among the business men of either city will be found almost without exception, a hearty appreciation of the other and the best of good wishes for its progress and prosperity.

Calgary is the larger city, and very much larger in its commerce. The tale is shown by its bank clearings, shipping returns and in many other ways. Edmonton does not deny these facts, but says in effect "Watch us grow, we have a country behind us that will beat you out in time."

Calgary replies: "Go to it and may the best of good luck attend you. We can look after our own end."

That is the situation, and the eastern visitors need not worry themselves about either city. Let them watch us both, and we will give them an illustration of how to grow.

October 28, 1909

Luckily, a Herald reporter was on hand when a civic official handed in his resignation with both fists.

Call me a crook, will you?" said Building Inspector Harrison to Alderman Samis in the commissioner's office, and while the member of the council was making some explanation that did not look as though it would smooth matters over, the building inspector made five passes at the alderman, three of which landed on Mr. Samis' head. The others he avoided by skilfully covering his face with his arms. The alderman did not do any offensive work, but his covering up was above reproach.

After having shown his ability as a "mitt" artist Mr. Harrison showed that his footwork was above reproach. He went out and slammed the door with such force as to imperil the stained glass in the panel.

The mayor hastily summoned the stenographer and dictated a letter to Mr. Harrison stating that he was suspended and the young lady went out to typewrite the letter.

The mayor was still in his private office giving some final instructions regarding the matter when Harrison rushed in again with a letter tendering his resignation. So once again the building inspector showed his proficiency by beating out the civic administration.

[Samis's complaint was about Harrison's handling of a building under construction. Harrison had ordered construction stopped until some already-completed work, which apparently was unsatisfactory, was torn out. Then he had allowed further work to be done after all. Harrison had also tried to get a letter from the owner of the building, saying that Harrison was not to blame for the difficulties. To Samis, all this looked like incompetence or worse. This was the basis of the row in which Samis got punched. It began like this:]

"You practically insinuate that I am a crook," Harrison said.

Mr. Samis was apparently trying to convey another impression when Mr. Harrison stepped over and —

Whiff — bang — bill.

These represent blows that were directed at what real sporting editors call "the block" of the alderman. The first was a right hook, to the jaw, which Samis blocked with his elbow. Samis was sitting down and made no attempt to get up. Harrison tried another with the left, but was blocked, and he came back with a right which landed on top of Samis's head.

Seeing that there was little chance to get in an effectual poke, Harrison stood on the defensive, and Samis glanced out from under his protecting guard, and Harrison sent a straight jab that was slightly effective.

While all this was going on Commissioner Graves and Mayor Mitchell were standing up, and were taking a very lively interest in the one-sided contest. Commissioner Clarke kept his seat and claims he was looking out of the window the whole time.

After blow number five Commissioner Graves went over and laid a somewhat hesitating hand on the shoulder of the infuriated building inspector, whose principal annoyance seemed to be that there was not an open spot on Mr. Samis' anatomy on which to land one.

Then Harrison dashed out of the door.

"Mr. Harrison is suspended from his office," said Mayor Mitchell, and he called the stenographer to put his decision in writing.

After hearing the door slam Alderman Samis abandoned his crouching pose and looked up, smiling. "Never touched me," he said blithely. He smoothed his somewhat ruffled hair, examined his hat carefully and found it was intact.

The letter which was to be slipped over to Mr. Harrison telling him that he was suspended was being written when he dashed into the commissioner's office again with a sheet of paper in his hand.

"There is my resignation," he said, and threw it on the table.

Mayor Mitchell had gone into his office and was not at his seat at the table at the moment.

Before he went out Mr. Harrison again turned to Alderman Samis, who was still in his coat.

"Why don't you come outside," he said. "Sometime I'll get you, and I'll knock your head off," was his parting remark to the alderman.

March 29, 1912

The first Calgary Stampede was held in September, 1912. Guy Weadwick, a young cowboy from Wyoming, promoted the idea, and arranged for $100,000 backing from prominent cattlemen Pat Burns, George Lane, A.E. Cross and A.J. Maclean — the "Big Four." Princess Patricia and the Duke and Duchess of Connaught were the guests of honor. An unnamed Herald reporter saw the first day's events, and came away much impressed.

Majestically superb in all the beauty and wonder of primitive plains life, the greatest historical pageant of western history is now unfolding itself in the most colossal and graphic portrayal of pioneer and range existence that has ever been staged in all the world.

Yesterday the Stampede graduated from a promise into a throbbing reality, pulsating with excitement and featured by riding and roping that exceeded all expectations. Almost 30,000 people were caught in the swaying mass that passed through the portals of Victoria park to witness the opening performance.

Yet grand as was the entertainment afforded by the skill, nerve and dexterity of 150 performers it was not to be likened to the wonder of the spectacle of 2,000 western Indians, who, smeared with paint and decked in the most weird attire of ante-civilized years, passed through the streets of Calgary yesterday morning.

Authentic and seasoned opinions would have it, that never in all the world, since the red man became a dominated instead of a dominant influence, has there been such a gathering of the picturesque aborigines who a few short years ago roamed these western foothills, unmolested by the white.

Verily it was a spectacle that money could not present. Mayhap never again will those who watched yesterday's procession have a similar opportunity afforded them. Ever since the pilgrim fathers invaded New England slowly but surely have the aborigines of North America been driven westward. Silently and with little protest, they have gradually receded from the east until of recent years it has become the prevalent impression that not only were the aborigines a declining race, but one that was nearing extinction.

The pageant of yesterday seemed to question the accuracy of the belief. Over 3,000 manly bucks, buxom squaws and squealing papooses infested our streets and exulted. For them yesterday was the sequel of two months of preparation, two months that had re-awakened in them all the innate love of pomp and primitive splendor that simmered in their souls. Yesterday's parade was the torch that fired the memories of days of yore when the red man was the monarch of all he surveyed on the western plains. And the firing of these memories was the signal for one last grand display of the weird beauties of Indian culture.

Even though the parade of Indians was undoubtedly the outstanding feature of the day, the arena performance at Victoria park was something to enthuse over. Riders who stuck like tanglefoot to the backs of heathenish buckers, employing every artifice indigenous to the genus equus, sent admiring shivers fleeting up the spines of thirty thousand people. Ropers who handled their lariats with amusing dexterity inspired wonder among the spectators. But the coup d'etat of the day was the "bull-dogging" of steers.

Now to the new populace of the west this thrilling pastime was received with admiration by the people present. To see a man drop through space onto the horns of a running wild steer, and to see that man coolly up-end the steer and throw him to the ground is a vision that has all the earmarks of excitement. It was exciting.

The programs of yesterday's events were certainly chuck full of all kinds of thrilling numbers. Not for one moment during the entire afternoon was there a time when the slightest interest was lacking.

Everything was in readiness at 1 o'clock as advertised and the afternoon's proceedings got away to a good start. They were kept up without a hitch until 7 at night, when the shades of evening intervened and the crowd were compelled to disperse and wend their way homeward.

September 3, 1912

Professionals from the United States won most of the events at the first Stampede, but a young Indian won the saddle bronc championship with a spectacular ride.

The last surprise came in the finals for the world's championship in the bucking horse riding. Each contestant had performed miraculously when the last name was called. It was Tom Three Persons, a Blood Indian from Macleod, the only Canadian entry in the finals, who was to ride last.

Then the announcer gave the information that Tom was to attempt to ride "Cyclone," the worst outlaw on the grounds. There were a few moments of apprehension, for "Cyclone" had never been ridden and had thrown 129 riders.

The horse thrown to the ground, Tom jumped across him, placed his feet in the stirrups and with a wild "whoop" the black demon was up and away with the Indian rider.

Bucking, twisting, swapping ends, and resorting to every artifice of the outlaw, "Cyclone" swept across the field. The Indian was jarred from one side of the saddle to the other, but as the crowds cheered themselves hoarse he settled each time into the saddle and waited for the next lurch or twist.

His bucking unable to dislodge the redskin, "Cyclone" stood at rest and reared straight up. Once it looked as though Tom was to follow the fate of his predecessors. He recovered rapidly and from that time forward "Cyclone" bucked till he was tired. The Indian had mastered him.

The thousands created a pandemonium of applause that was not equalled all week. The Princess Patricia and the Duchess, who were in the royal box, leaned far out over the railing, laughing and applauding vigourously at the Indians in the enclosure to the north. It was a thrilling moment, and in it Tom Three Persons had captured the championship of the world for himself and for Canada.

September 9, 1912

These Blood and North Peigan Indians took part in the first Calgary Stampede parade, representing what The Herald called "the beauty and wonder of primitive plains life." With them at right is the well-known missionary, Rev. John McDougall, who acted as their interpreter.

The great French actress Sarah Bernhardt was 68 when she performed in Calgary, but evidently she had not lost her spell-binding powers. She arrived in Calgary in a private railway car, and declined interviews. Her manager assured reporters that she had heard much about Western Canada and intended to buy some real estate here.

That Calgary fully appreciates the honor done it in the visit of Madame Sarah Bernhardt to this city was shown by the warm greeting accorded the greatest emotional actress of modern times at the Sherman Grand theatre yesterday. Despite the fact that Madame Bernhardt's initial appearance was at a matinee, a well-filled house greeted her with spontaneous and whole-hearted applause, which she graciously stepped out of her part to acknowledge with the most charming of smiles.

The selection from her repertoire which Madame Bernhardt selected for her first two performances here was the third act of Victor Hugo's emotional drama "Lucretia Borgia."

To say that Madame Bernhardt filled the role in such a way as to give it all the realism of the actual, is to state a simple fact. Not one of her auditors but felt that the woman before him was passing through the deep and changeful emotions Lucretia experienced in the drama. The fact that perhaps very few in the audience were familiar with the language in which the lines were spoken did not detract from their interest in the piece. The personality of the great actress, her wonderful voice, the magic of her smile, the portrayal, in her lighting changes of expression, of the powerful emotions passing within, united to make a stage presence which kept her audience enthralled.

January 15, 1913

In their early days, movies were short, and ran as an added attraction in a live vaudeville show. Movies with sound didn't really take off until 1927, but an early experiment in the field added a novelty to a vaudeville program at the Grand in 1913.

From the standpoint of "something new" in vaudeville, the talking movies take first place, but even this novelty does not in the least detract from the all-round excellence of the programme.

The talking movies are a perfect synchronization of voice and action, and one can readily imagine the actors are flesh and blood, for there is no brassy gramophonic effect in the voices, which appear to proceed from no other place than the mouths of the men and women themselves. The action and voice are as simultaneous as possible even in flesh and blood. The pictures in themselves as a novelty will draw big houses this week.

April 25, 1913

Arthur Pelkey, left, and Luther McCarty square off in Calgary for the white heavyweight championship of the world. McCarty died less than two minutes later. Pelkey was charged but found blameless.

It was to have been a classic boxing match, the greatest Calgary had ever seen. Luther McCarty was white heavyweight champion. (The title was segregated in those days.) But in the first round of a title fight with Arthur Pelkey, tragedy intervened.

One of the greatest tragedies recorded in modern sport took place at Tommy Burn's Manchester arena Saturday afternoon, when the life of a big, robust youth was flicked out before the gaze of seven thousand startled and amazed persons.

The death of Luther McCarty in the first round of his scheduled 10 round bout with Arthur Pelkey, probably is without precedent in the annals of sport.

The great tragedy was prefaced by an event which has probably never before taken place in any ring, and even now the sinister words of the Rev. William R. Walker, of St. Augustine's Anglican church, as he turned toward the two boxers and told them not to forget in their chase of fame that they had a creator and to prepare to meet him linger in the ears of those who heard him.

With the admonition that the "great referee stood over them in this bout, all powerful above the man selected by them to see fair play," he stepped from the ring and the bout was begun.

Smilingly the two gigantic specimens of manhood faced each other in a trial of skill and strength. They circled, feinted, a few light blows were struck, a couple more in a clinch, and then one tumbled to the canvas mat, never to rise again.

The arena broke into a roar, applause for the new champion, while a dozen doctors rushed to the side of the stricken boy. Even while the crowd shouted, the spark of life had been extinguished in the vanquished form and he lay dead, a victim of a great and unfortunate accident.

The crowd paused in their demonstration to listen to the ugly rumor that McCarty was dead or dying. Thousands of heads were bared and thousands of hearts fluttered and pulsated, with fear and excitement. They filed silently out of the arena and with hushed voices whispered the news to each other.

In another corner of the ring the victor stood, his feet on the ground, but his sense far beyond the reach of men. He was told that his opponent was dying and he was stunned. Arthur Pelkey, conqueror at a terrible price, then would gladly have cast all his fistic ambitions to the winds, if this he could have averted. He was taken into a motor car to the police officials where he placed himself at their command. The authorities held him as a material witness and released him on $10,000 bond.

Sunday night, shortly before twelve o'clock, the arena where the tragedy was enacted, was burned to the ground. The lives of the caretaker and his wife were imperilled and they only escaped with their lives by a narrow margin. The loss is estimated at $6,000, partly covered by insurance. It is thought that an incendiary was responsible.

The death of Luther McCarty ended one of the most meteoric careers on record. Just a short two years ago, Luther, of Piqua, Ohio, had his first match in Calgary. He left the city and started out to gain fame. This he did rapidly. His great determination and aggressiveness won respect for him in the heavyweight division. Only recently he defeated Al Palzer and Jim Flynn, which practically stamped him as the white heavyweight champion of the world.

He was a good drawing card. Always popular wherever he boxed, he soon became to be in great demand. Tommy Burns had Arthur Pelkey in Calgary and the work of Pelkey had greatly impressed the local boxing promoter. Here was a chance to give the Calgary fans a touch of real championship boxing. The men were matched. McCarty returned to the city where he got his start. He returned as the heavyweight champion of the world.

May 26, 1913

An inquest showed that McCarty died of a hemorrhage of the spine, caused by a dislocated neck. The coroner's jury found Arthur Pelkey blameless, but the Royal North West Mounted Police arrested him immediately after the inquest and charged him with manslaughter. On June 24, 1913, a jury found him not guilty, to the cheers of a crowded courtroom.

The World Moves Closer

By latter-day standards, this was a peaceful era, though it did include two great disasters, the San Francisco earthquake and the sinking of the Titanic. The largest war of the time was fought between Russia and Japan. On land and sea, the Japanese drove Russia back from her holdings in China. Unrest in Russia was intensified by these heavy losses. On January 22, 1905, the czar's troops fired on a peaceful protest march in St. Petersburg, killing 1,500 men, women and children. The following dispatch described the beginning of the strikes and riots that ensued. Czar Nicholas II saved his throne, for a time, by making modest reforms. V.I. Ulyanov, better known as Lenin, was one of the leaders of the revolution of 1905. He had more success when he returned to Russia in 1917.

Hundreds have been slain, Emperor Nicholas has fled from the capital, and about 30,000 troops are patrolling the streets. This is the climax of the turbulent scenes which have convulsed St. Petersburg during the last 48 hours.

The empire is in the throes of civil war. The laboring men are unterrified by the fearful execution of their comrades, and display a resolution to carry the fight into the very palace of the monarch whom they reverenced yesterday.

Talk is freely indulged in that a dictator will be appointed by the infuriated populace, and armed resistance to the soldiers of the Czar be made from now on.

The most inflammatory addresses have been issued and the disorders are spreading.

Some of the troops have refused to fire on the mobs.

It is impossible to estimate accurately the number of victims, but figures that were given out run from 500 to 5,000.

The mob has slaughtered many soldiers, using sabres and iron pikes pulled from junk heaps and looted shops. One general and his staff were massacred in the streets.

The mob has erected barricades only to have them destroyed by solid shot, and the defenders slaughtered to a man.

Women and children have been killed in large numbers. They were mixed with the men and the troops shot indiscriminately.

The outburst followed the effort of the laboring men, under the leadership of the priest, Father Gapon, to present a petition to the emperor for redress. He refused to see them, and the thousands of marching men were fired on and charged by the Cossacks. Many streets were choked with dead and dying men, women and children.

At daybreak guards regiments, infantry and cavalry held every bridge across the frozen Neva, the network of canals which interlaces the city, and the gates leading from the industrial section, while in the palace, which was the storm centre, were massed dragoon regiments and Cossacks of the guards.

St. Petersburg, January 23, 1905

The San Francisco earthquake and the fire that followed killed 700 people and destroyed more than four square miles of the city. The fire was eventually brought under control by dynamiting whole blocks to make a firebreak. The Herald published several extras that day, compiled from fragmentary reports sent over hastily repaired telegraph lines.

At 5:10 this morning occurred the most terrific earthquake ever known in the history of the Pacific coast. Buildings toppled and fell in every direction. The police patrol is carrying the dead from the buildings. Fire broke out in the wholesale buildings near the waterfront and other localities, and there is no water to fight it. At 7:30 the communication of a single wire with Ashfork and Los Angeles was restored.

The shock was felt as far south as Santa Barbara, but it was not felt at Los Angeles. All the power lines in the city were wrecked.

The Pacific cable was not damaged, but the loss of power seriously crippled communications. The postal electricians are now at the office endeavoring to restore communication. It is unsafe as yet to remain in the offices.

There has been a slight shock every few minutes since the heavy one.

There was a terrible panic, and everyone rushed to the streets.

Many hundreds are reported killed in South Market street, where the fire is raging.

At eight o'clock fire broke out on the south side of Market Street and is now within one block of the Palace Hotel, one of the most famous hotels in the world.

The water mains have burst, and the fire department is helpless. The utmost confusion exists. All business is suspended. At this moment there is only one wire out of San Francisco, a postal wire. The postal building is badly damaged. The telegraph operating room is a total wreck. Power of every kind is gone, and there are no lights either gas or electric.

The fire is burning on both sides to the east and south of the postal telegraph building.

The damage by the earthquake apparently extends all over the city. The shock occurred at 5:15 this morning, and lasted three minutes. The streets are blockaded with debris.

They are blowing up buildings.

The residential districts are safe so far as heard from.

The shock lasted three minutes, but thousands of buildings were damaged and destroyed.

The loss of life is reported enormous. There is no water and fires are breaking out all over the city.

The city hall costing $7,000,000 is in ruins.

Modern buildings suffered less than brick and frame. The terror and excitement are indescribable. Most of the people were asleep and rushed into the streets undressed. Buildings swayed and crashed, burying their occupants. There is panic in all the downtown hotels.

It is reported that one thousand lives have been lost in the earthquake.

At noon today the damage inflicted at San Francisco was estimated to have reached forty millions. Flames are eating their way along Market street towards the water front, and unless the wind changes nothing can save the wholesale district. The residents are panic stricken, the downtown streets are a mass of debris, while the military are on guard.

The banks and all financial institutions have closed their doors, and refuse to open in spite of the demands made by thousands of panic-stricken people.

The police have been instructed to shoot on sight any one detected in the act of theft.

The only newspaper office able to issue a paper is the Chronicle. All others were put out of commission when the power gave out. They have combined to issue one paper from the Chronicle office.

Thirty-six blocks are burning. The Episcopal church on Eleventh Street is badly damaged. The St. Francis Hotel is partly wrecked. The Empire Theatre Building collapsed. The Gore Block was burned. The Pacific States Telephone Building, the Rialto Building and the National Building were all destroyed.

San Francisco, 2 p.m., April 18, 1906

The Titanic, an "unsinkable" ocean liner, made her maiden voyage from London in April, 1912, bound for New York. On the night of April 14-15, the Titanic struck an iceberg which tore a 300-foot gash along her steel-plated side. Another liner, the Carpathia, heard the Titanic's radio distress call, and rescued 700 people. They were the only survivors. The Titanic sank 2-1/2 hours after striking the iceberg, and 1,500 people drowned. Among the survivors were a Calgary real estate investor, A.A. Dick, and his wife. They told their story to a Herald correspondent in New York, where the Carpathia had taken them.

I was in my berth," said Mr. Dick, "when there came a sudden jar and grinding from the hull about amidships.

"There was no tremendous shock, but it startled the passengers. There was nothing of a panic. The great ship must have continued on her course for a mile or so before it became known to the passengers that there was something wrong.

"The fact is that she had smashed and loosened a number of plates along her sides below the water line by the sideswiping of a dark mass of ice and was doomed from the first.

The sinking of the Titanic, rendered by artist Willy Stoewer. An iceberg tore open the water tight compartments of the supposedly unsinkable ship, which went to the bottom at a cost of 1,500 lives.

"I believe the officers knew she was going down but they did not let the passengers know it.

"Out of the private and staterooms they crowded up to the decks. But there was no panic, but absolute confidence in the boat's ability to stand what appeared for thirty minutes to be but slight damage. Then the great boat began to get out of the horizontal. A settling of the bows was noticed and the order was given that the boats were to be lowered.

"I have nothing but praise for the way the crowds on the deck behaved," said Mr. Dick.

"There was no pushing, no struggling among the first and second cabin passengers. There was still the belief fostered by the officers that taking to the boats was only a precautionary measure. Again and again, women refused to leave their husbands on the ship. Many of them had the idea that the boats would likely come back to the liner and be picked up again. The order was given that the passengers should also put on life belts. As boat after boat got away there was more speed and anxiety shown. One of the loaded boats was smashed, I was told, and some of the people drowned."

Mrs. Dick confirmed her husband's statement that at first there was little or no fear. She three times refused to get into a boat but finally did so. Her husband, she says, was pushed in as the last man to make up the crew.

"Did you see the Titanic go down?" asked The Herald of Mr. Dick.

"Yes, after we had rowed away some distance, we saw lighted deck after lighted deck disappear, till there was nothing but the bleak level of the water with the starry sky lighting the spot where she sank from sight."

"Did you hear anything of the officers being compelled to use revolvers to quell a panic?"

"There was some firing, but I heard of no one being killed. I think it was only to frighten the steerage passengers and keep them in check. The story appears lame in the telling, but behind it is the grim fortitude and bravery of the officers and crew of the Titanic, the discipline and self-control that kept from the passengers the awful fact known to every blue-coated man of them, that there only remained a few boats in which some of the thousand passengers could be given a chance of escape from the ship. They chose to go down with their ship. The band was kept playing up to a few minutes of the time when we saw her disappear."

Mr. and Mrs. Dick told of the cool action of Mr. Andrews, who was the designer of the Titanic. He made frequent trips to the engine room while the ship was sinking, calming the passengers' terror and doing everything possible to pacify the fears of those about him.

Mrs. Dick escaped with only her nightgown and a kimono, but her husband was more fortunate, and was able to save his trousers and a coat.

Mrs. Dick said that the band started to play as soon as the shock of the first great crash somewhat abated, and continued the music until the boat into which she was taken had been lowered away from the Titanic.

"We could plainly see the iceberg after we left the ship," said Mrs. Dick.

"We were six hours afloat, living on bread and water. Another person who was saved told me that three men of the steerage were shot by officers to keep them out of the boats."

New York, April 19, 1912

By 1913, storm clouds were gathering over Europe. This editorial, written in defence of Prime Minister Robert Borden's efforts to contribute Canadian ships to the British navy, pointed to the threat of a great war; a threat that became reality little more than a year later.

The war cloud hangs heavy over Europe, and danger appears imminent. It seems as if another would take the stage from which Napoleon was forced, and that the German kaiser aims to become the overlord of the world.

By the pace he has set in the increase of armaments he has dealt a heavy blow to the commerce of the world, and there seems to be little hope, unless the world's great financial institutions get together and declare that no more private loans shall be negotiated for this purpose. Germany is already groaning under the heavy burden of enormous expenditure for naval and military expansion, and still the work moves on, for there seems to be the determination to usurp Britain's place as mistress of the seas.

Intoxicated with the spirit of military aggrandizement, they now propose to spend $250,000,000 on land armaments and the increase of the army.

On the other hand France has met this spirit of threatening military expansion by the announcement that $600,000,000 will be spent in strengthening the French land forces. There is an old score to settle between France and Germany. France has not forgotten her humiliation. Germany has never been modest about her victories. France seems determined to regain her lost prestige in the consort of powers, and, as well, to break the power of the kaiser in European politics.

Added to this, there is the general unsettlement caused by the Balkan situation, and the menace of the rising power of the Balkan states. It would take but a slight mis-move on the part of either Germany or France to precipitate a war greater than the world has yet suffered; and in the event of such, diplomats say it would be next to impossible for Britain to avoid being drawn into the conflict.

But the Canadian obstructionists continue to hold up any measures that make for relief, and the man in the street tells us not to write and talk so much about war because it is bad for business. But bad business is preferable to war at any time, and the prestige of the Britisher is in danger. To protect our commerce and preserve our prestige we will be compelled to take a strong attitude. This is the endeavor of the government.

March 11, 1913

Over There, a War

1914-19

In 1914, the nations of Europe and the British Empire were plunged into the most terrible war the world had seen up to that time. (It was then known as the Great War, no one being so prescient, or so pessimistic, as to see a Second — and still bloodier — World War only 25 years later.) In the four years that followed, more than 8 million people were killed. Twenty-one million were wounded; some of them spent the rest of their life in hospital with lungs seared by poison gas, or with shrapnel wounds hastily repaired by battlefield surgery. Another 7.5 million were listed as prisoners or missing; many of the missing had no doubt found unmarked graves in the mud-filled shell craters of Belgium and France. The war cost more than $300 billion, for weapons and for the destruction wrought by those weapons.

This chapter spans the war years and the year that followed. That era saw the emergence of today's superpowers, the United States and the Soviet Union. When the war began, the United States tried to hold itself aloof from the troubles of old Europe and her colonies, but in 1917 the force of events drove the U.S. into the war. American troops embarked for Europe to fight on the side of their former motherland, Great Britain. (Perhaps the bands at dockside played a new war song by George M. Cohan, Over There, whose title summed up the still-prevailing attitude toward Europe.) American diplomacy later played an important part in the peace settlement; despite the Americans' refusal to join the League of Nations, despite the renewal of American isolationism in the Thirties, the United States could not wholly retreat from the time when it had taken a decisive hand in the Great War.

In 1917 the czar of Russia was driven from his throne. The comparatively moderate socialists who succeeded him were overthrown in turn by V.I. Lenin and his Bolshevik followers. In March, 1918, Lenin signed a separate peace with Germany. It was a costly settlement, but it left him free to deal with his internal opposition. By 1920, Lenin had consolidated his rule; Russia, half-feudal, half-industrial, had become the first Communist nation. The new regime was economically shaky, and surrounded by nations that were suspicious when they were not actively hostile; even so, in less than 25 years, Russia was able to play a decisive part in winning the Second World War.

An influenza epidemic broke out in the fall of 1918, in the closing month of the First World War. As if to rebuke merely human powers of destruction, in a little more than a year the Spanish flu killed two or three times as many people as the war had. By 1920, when the disease had completed its sweep across the world, it had claimed nearly 22 million lives.

Before any of these large occurrences took place, there was a comparatively small event of great local significance: oil was discovered at Turner Valley, 50 kilometres southwest of Calgary. At 5 p.m. May 14, 1914, the Dingman No. 1 well began to spout natural gas and very high-grade crude oil. The local market in oil stocks, already vigorous on the basis of nothing more than hopeful signs, immediately became feverish. "Calgary is oil crazy!" The Herald reported May 15. Investors, disappointed but obviously not devastated by the collapse of the real estate boom in 1912, responded eagerly. By October, 1914, some 500 oil companies had been formed with a combined capital of $83 million.

Meanwhile, in Europe, much larger events were in motion. On June 28, 1914, a young student, Gavrilo Princip, shot and killed Archduke Francis Ferdinand, heir to the throne of Austria-Hungary. The archduke's wife Sophie also was killed. Austria-Hungary suspected that the assassin had been trained and incited by Serbia (now part of Yugoslavia.) The empire sent an ultimatum to Serbia, demanding to participate in the trial of those involved in the assassination plot. Serbia refused, and Austria-Hungary declared war on the little country on July 28, 1914.

By itself, this episode would have been little more than a footnote in history, but Europe was already at the edge of war. Competition for colonies overseas; conflicting territorial claims in Europe; ethnic minorities clamouring to create nations of their own: all these complications kept Europe in political ferment. A network of military alliances and secret treaties made it virtually certain that a conflict involving one major power would spread quickly. The assassination of Francis Ferdinand was the spark that ignited Europe.

Russia sided with Serbia, and prepared for war. Germany, which was Austria-Hungary's ally, declared war on Russia Aug. 1, 1914. Germany then asked France, Russia's ally to declare neutrality. France stalled, and Germany declared war on her Aug. 3. The following day, German troops marched into Belgium; the invasion immediately brought the British Empire, including Canada, into the war.

Canada went to war in a mood of euphoria. Cheering crowds gathered outside The Herald to wait for bulletins and listen to a brass band playing patriotic tunes. The Herald published a front-page editorial urging kindness toward the Germans and Austrians here, who now found themselves in a country at war with their homeland. (Later in the war, attitudes hardened: after highly-colored stories of German atrocities began to appear, the paper called for the internment of all enemy nationals. Several people who spoke up for Germany were jailed for sedition. In Calgary rioters, including soldiers, wrecked a cafe that had hired an Austrian, and a hotel supposedly owned by a German.)

Germany made rapid gains in the early weeks of the war, driving through Belgium and penetrating within 15 miles of Paris before being thrown back on September in the first Battle of the Marne. Germany having lost the chance for a quick victory, the fighting on the Western Front settled down into four years of grim, slow-moving trench warfare. On the Eastern Front, Russia suffered heavy losses to the Germans, but made gains in Austria-Hungary. In October, 1914, the Ottoman Empire (now Turkey) joined the Central Powers (Germany and Austria-Hungary) and fought the Allies in the Middle East and Russia.

Meanwhile, the first Canadians who went overseas were taking their final training in England. They went to France in 1915, and fought their first large battle in April at Ypres, Belgium. There they held fast against suffocating clouds of poison gas — used by Germany for the first time — and won high praise for their tenacity and courage.

The Herald published reports from special correspondents who followed the Canadian troops on the Western Front; most of the war stories in this chapter are the work of these reporters. (The Herald reported the rest of the war by wire-service dispatches which were generally more perfunctory and less vivid.)

No doubt every technique of battle imposes its own special miseries, but the trench fighting of the First World War can make some claim to being uniquely horrible. As the war ground on, both sides dug increasingly elaborate networks of trenches; these served as bases for desperate hand-to-hand attacks on the enemy trenches a few dozen yards away across "no-man's-land." Men took shelter in the stinking mud of trenches, plagued by rats and lice, sometimes under artillery bombardment, waiting for the order to attack. Many soldiers lost their lives in these attacks, entangled in razor-edged barbed wire, and riddled by machine gun bullets or burned by flamethrowers.

It was a hideously slow and costly war. When the Germans

threatened the French city of Verdun in 1916, for example, General Henri Petain vowed "They shall not pass." In the six months that followed, the Germans gained about six kilometers of ground. The French sustained more than half a million casualties — dead, wounded, captured or missing — and the Germans more than 400,000.

In those bloody years, Canadian troops wrote European names into Canada's history: Ypres, Vimy, Passchendaele, the Somme, Cambrai. These and other battles gave the nation an example of triumph and sacrifice unlike anything it had known before. Admittedly at a hideous cost, the war helped Canada take another step toward national maturity; in 1917, for the first time, Canada and the other dominions won a voice in the British Empire's foreign policy.

Sir Robert Borden, the Conservative prime minister of Canada, wanted the country to make a still greater contribution to the war effort. Until 1917, volunteers had been enough for a war that used men as lavishly as it used bullets. Borden, deciding that conscription was needed to win the war, imposed it in 1917. It was a bitterly divisive measure, especially in Quebec, where there were protest riots. Nevertheless, Borden's Union slate (a Conservative-Liberal coalition) won the federal election of December, 1917, over the opposition of Sir Wilfrid Laurier and the Liberals who stayed loyal to him.

The United States, goaded by German submarine attacks on its ships, had entered the war in the spring of 1917. The following spring, Germany launched a final huge offensive, intended to win the war before American troops could shift the balance of power.

Months of fierce battle followed, and the pace of the fighting changed: in August, 1918, at Amiens, Canadian troops made one of the largest advances of the war, about 13 kilometres in a single day. On August 26, "the black day of the German army," the Germans began to retreat to the fortifications of the Hindenburg Line. The Allies, strengthened by American troops, broke the line. The end was in sight. Riots broke out in Berlin, and Kaiser Wilhelm abdicated. Finally, on November 11, 1918, an armistice was signed, and the guns fell silent.

In imposing a peace settlement, the victorious Allies were torn between idealism and vindictiveness. The American president, Woodrow Wilson, had proposed "Fourteen Points" for a post-war world order. These included arms reduction, a league of nations, and national independence for the subject peoples of the Austro-Hungarian and Ottoman Empires. On the other hand the Allies, with the Treaty of Versailles, imposed a crushing burden of war-damage payments on Germany. Allied vengeance led to German misery and resentment. The settlement of the First World War helped prepare the ground for the Second.

This soldier's arm, broken by shrapnel, was splinted with a bayonet, scabbard and entrenching tool handle.

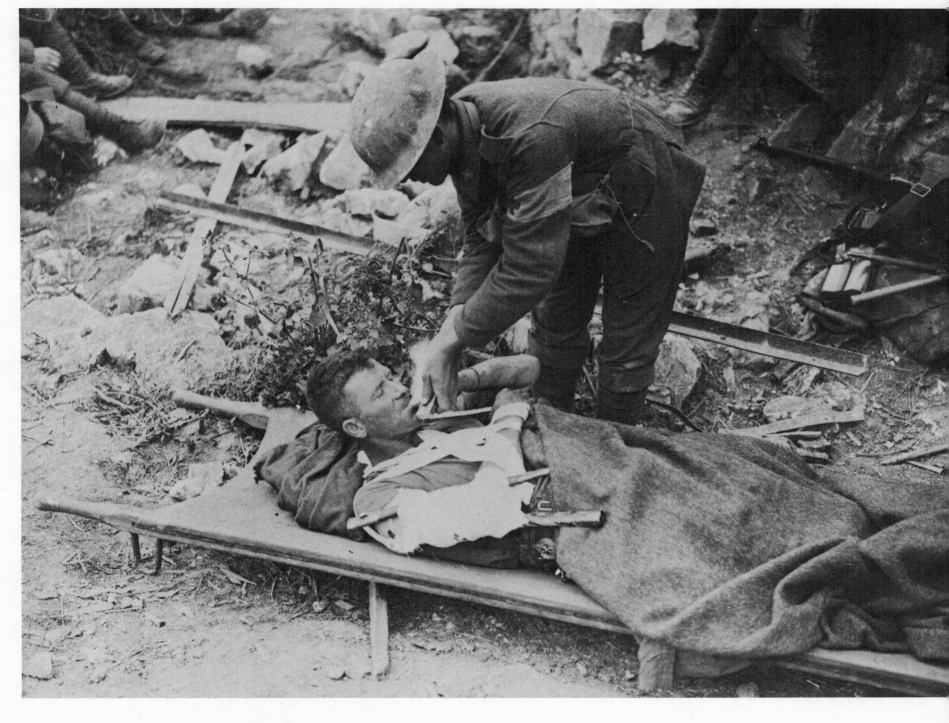

Death, Glory and Mud

By the summer of 1914, Europe was ripe for war. An assassination in an obscure corner of the Austro-Hungarian Empire finally brought about the calamity. Five weeks after the shooting in the streets of Sarajevo, Europe — and Britain's Dominions — were plunged into fighting. Gavrilo Princip, the assassin, died in prison in the spring of 1918.

Archduke Francis Ferdinand, heir to the Austria-Hungarian throne and the Princess of Hohenberg, his morganatic wife, were shot dead in the main street of the Bosnia capital by a student Sunday, while they were making an apparently triumphal progress through the city on their annual visit to the annexed province of Bosnia and Herzegovina.

The archduke was hit full in the face and the princess was shot through the abdomen and throat. The wounds proved fatal in a few minutes after reaching the palace.

Those responsible for the assassination took care that it should prove effective as there were two assailants, the first armed with a bomb and the latter with a revolver. The bomb was thrown at the royal automobile as it was proceeding to the town hall, where a reception was to be held, but the archduke saw the deadly missile coming and warded it off with his arm. It fell outside the car and exploded, slightly wounding two aide de camps in a second car and half a dozen spectators.

It was on the return of the procession that the tragedy was added to the long list of those that have darkened the pages of the recent history of the Hapsburgs. As the royal automobile reached a prominent point of the route to the palace, an 18-year-old student, Gavrilo Prinzip, sprang out of the crowd and poured a fusilade of bullets from an automatic pistol at the archduke and princess. Both fell mortally wounded.

The first attempt against the archduke occurred just outside the girls' high school. The archduke's car had restarted after a brief pause for an inspection of the building when Nedeljo Gabrinivics hurled the bomb. This was so successfully warded off by the archduke that it fell beneath the following car, the occupants of which, Count Von Boos Waldeck and Col. Merizzo, were struck by slivers of iron.

Archduke Francis Ferdinand stopped his car and making inquiries as to their injuries and lending what aid he could, continued his journey to the town hall. There the burgomaster began the customary address, but the archduke sharply interrupted and snapped out: "Herr Burgomaster, we have come here to pay you a visit and bombs have been thrown at us. This is altogether an amazing indignity."

After a pause the archduke said: "Now you may speak."

On leaving the hall the archduke and his wife announced their intention of visiting the wounded members in their suite at the hospital on their way back to the palace.

They were actually bound on their mission of mercy, when at the corner of Buldol Strasse and Franz Josef Stratte, Prinzip opened his deadly fusilade.

It is said after the attempt with the bomb near the girls' high school the duchess tried to persuade the archduke from venturing in the car again. To allay her fears, M. Potiorek, governor of Bosnia, said:

"It's all over now. We have not more than one murderer in the city," whereupon the archduke decided to go on.

Sarajevo, Bosnia, June 29, 1914

The assassination of Archduke Francis Ferdinand brought about the final crisis in relations between Austria-Hungary and Serbia (the southeastern part of present-day Yugoslavia). Serbia, reassured by promises of Russian military support, refused an Austrian ultimatum. Austria declared war on Serbia July 28, 1914. In the frantic week that followed, Europe slid inexorably into war. By July 31, as the following collection of dispatches, shows, all hope of peace had been abandoned.

All hope of averting the war catastrophe has been abandoned. All Europe will soon be involved in the greatest conflict the world has ever seen. Efforts for peace are still going on, but it is expected that they will be fruitless.

A dispatch from Vienna saying "The hope of localizing the war between Austria and Servia is very dim" was received today. The mobilization of the German army has begun. Foreign offices in Vienna and Berlin have been in constant communication for forty-eight hours, keeping each other advised of all developments.

Dispatches stating that the Russian premier replied to Germany's ultimatum with the statement that the mobilization of the czar's troops could not be stopped is regarded as a final blow to peace efforts.

A dispatch has been received from Berlin, stating that the rupture in diplomatic relations between Austria and Russia was complete, accompanied by reports that Austria would declare war against the czar today. The following dispatch from St. Petersburg failed to relieve the tension to any extent — "The following official statement is authorized: 'Russia desires no war. Our partial mobilization is a precautionary measure to preserve the independence of Servia.'"

Premier Asquith called a meeting of the cabinet at Downing street. The first lord of the admiralty, Winston Churchill, carried a large package of documents to the session. These are supposed to relate to the war measures taken by the naval chief during the last ·twenty-four hours. The premier, who also is minister of war, conferred with

several attaches of the war office before the cabinet meeting began.

London, July 31, 1914

President Poincare and his full cabinet held an extended session this afternoon. The war minister made a complete report on the nation's readiness for war. The belief prevails here that if Prince Henry's visit to St. Petersburg fails, war between Germany and Russia is certain.

Paris, July 31, 1914

It is reported that the yacht of the king of Montenegro is being pursued by Austrian war ships.

Athens, July 31, 1914

Military movements on the German side of the frontier were very active today, and the French covering troops sent out outposts. A German patrol at one point actually crossed the border, probably owing to a mistake.

Paris, July 31, 1914

The Cunard liner Lusitania arrived today, bringing the report that the German cruiser Dresden, recently in Mexican waters, was lying off New York harbor, just outside the three-mile limit. This caused the rumor that the Dresden was lying in wait to capture vessels leaving this port if war were declared in Europe.

New York, July 31, 1914

In Calgary, the coming of war was greeted as enthusiastically as the return of peace would be four terrible years later.

Calgary went wild with excitement last night. The news that Great Britain had declared war upon Germany and that the German and the British Empire were finally at grips, acted like magic upon a city already tense with suspense and expectancy.

The flash was bulletined on The Herald's bulletin boards shortly after 7 o'clock, and an "extra" was almost immediately afterwards on the street with the momentous news. Newsboys rushed madly to all quarters of the city, flooding the streets with the pink sheets, and boarding street cars where the papers were eagerly snapped up.

At once the crowds began to pour into the centre of the city on foot and in motor cars, and the newspaper offices were magnets whose power seemed to reach to

Crowds swarmed into downtown Calgary the night war was declared. They gathered outside newspaper offices to wait for special editions and the latest bulletins from Europe.

ious cars and cheering was spasmodic. It would break out at one point and then travel down the whole length of the train. A noticeable feature was that absolutely no signs of intoxication were seen. It was a sober, earnest send off, and one of which the men can feel proud.

The train started to pull out promptly on time and then the cheering reached its greatest volume.

As the coaches pulled out of sight the crowd seemed reluctant to depart. With the excitement all over and the knowledge that the brave men were now on their journey towards the battlefields of Europe came the thought that many may not return. Many ladies were led from the depot weeping and a few men were showing signs of an emotion which revealed the truth that the men are on a grim errand and are risking their lives in the empire's cause.

August 14, 1914

---

the remotest centres of population. As fast as they were received the bulletins were posted, and by 9 o'clock the crowds that gathered in front of the bulletin boards were so great as to completely block traffic.

Not even in the height of the real estate or oil excitement was there such an outburst of pent up feelings. Each fresh bulletin was greeted with enthusiastic cheering and the streets were soon thronged for blocks with people eager for more particulars.

Led by The Herald's brass band the crowds gathered in front of The Herald bulletin boards and joined in the singing of patriotic songs, and the impromptu chorus could be heard many streets away. Fresh outbursts of cheering broke forth as successive bulletins announcing that war had actually commenced were put out, and the most intense excitement prevailed.

The tenor of the crowds was one of grim exultation, not unmixed with a sense of what serious results the war into which the world is being plunged will entail.

"It is going to be a terrible war, but it will clear up a lot of things," was the conclusion of one group who were overheard discussing the situation in front of The Herald bulletin board.

The street cars had difficulty in making their way through the crowds that collected on Eighth Avenue in front of one of the newspaper offices, and many flocked away to The Herald's bulletin board on First Street West, where the constant interruptions of the street cars were absent, and where a band made the night air musical with patriotic tunes. Reports of the excitement and patriotic enthusiasm in Toronto, Montreal and other Canadian cities, where it was announced that such uproarious scenes had never before been enacted, sent a thrill through the crowds. The sense of kinship and common sentiment was stimulating and gave a fresh impetus to the fervor of Calgarians. The knowledge that London and Paris were also seething with excitement and determination to stand by the right and champion the oppressed, and that Canada was one with the Mother Country and the

other Dominions in the hour of action, was like an electric current passing through the crowds, and raised the patriotic elation to fever pitch.

Away over in the southeast, across the roofs of buildings, and above the heads of the cheering crowds, the round summer moon, blood red, formed an ominous symbol in the sky. To the onlooker gazing in that direction, the emblematic touch could not fail to be striking.

The smoke of our forest fires seemed to be the smoke of battlefields, in which Canadians too shall take their place by the side of their brothers across the sea in the defense of liberty and in opposition to tyrannic domination. It was a symbol horrible yet stimulating to those who saw it, as the band played "God Save the King" for the last time, and the crowds dispersed to their homes to prepare for fresh announcements on the morrow.

August 5, 1914

The first of Calgary's soldiers were soon on their way to the war.

Amidst scenes of the wildest enthusiasm the Calgary contingent of the Princess Patricia's Own Light Infantry regiment left the C.P.R. prompt at 1:45 o'clock this afternoon. Nearly three hundred veterans in charge of Major Duncan Stuart, thus have the honor of being the first men of western Canada to leave for the front.

The honor is the striking compliment to both Hamilton Gault, of Montreal, and R.B. Bennett, K.C., M.P. of Calgary, who have financed the regiment, and are making this handsome present to the empire.

Calgary will have an opportunity to witness the departure of her volunteers, as moving pictures were taken of all that occurred. The crowds were bunched around the var-

---

At sea, as on land, warfare became more terrible than it had ever been before. Most accounts of sea battles (such as the Battle of Jutland in 1916, in which Britain lost 14 ships and 6,000 men) tended to deal with ships as if they were pieces on a chessboard. An exception was this harrowing account from 1915 of what it was like aboard a ship being torn apart by exploding shells.

A Times correspondent who has had the opportunity of talking with many of the wounded from the German cruiser Blucher which was sunk in a recent engagement in the North Sea, writes as follows:

The British ships were away some 15 or 16 kilometres distant when they started to fire. Shots came slowly at first. They fell ahead and over, raising vast columns of water. The British guns were ranging. The men on deck watched the water spouts creep nearer with a strange fascination. Soon one pitched close to the ship and a vast watery pillar, a hundred metres high, one of them affirmed, fell on the deck. The range had been found.

Now the shells came thick and fast, with a horrible droning hum. The electric plant was soon destroyed and the ship plunged into a darkness that could be felt. Down below decks there was horror and confusion, mingled with gasping shouts and moans as the shells plunged through the decks. They penetrated the decks. They bored their way even to the stoke-hold. The coal in the bunkers was set on fire. In the engine room a shell licked up the oil and sprayed it around in flames, scarring its victims. Men huddled together in dark compartments, but the shells sought them out, and there death had a rich harvest.

The terrific air pressure resulting from the explosion in a confined space left a deep impression on the minds of the men of the Blucher. The air it would seem, roars through every opening and tears its way through every weak spot. All loose fittings are transformed into moving instruments of destruction. Open doors bang to and jamb — and closed iron doors bend outward like tin plates, and through it all bodies of men are whirled about like dead leaves in a winter blast, to be battered to death against the iron walls.

There were shuddering horrors, intensified by the darkness or semi-gloom. As one poor wretch was passing through a trap door a shell burst near him. He was exactly half way through. The trap door closed with a terrrific snap.

In one of the engine rooms — it was the room where the high-velocity engines for ventilation and forces draught were at work — men were picked up by the terrible luft-druck, like the whirl drift at a street corner, and tossed to a horrible death amidst the machinery. There were other horrors too fearful to recount.

London, February 25, 1915

German stretcher-bearers, wearing gas masks, carry a wounded man away from the front. Canadian forces were ill-prepared for the first poison-gas attack, launched at Ypres.

Canadian troops fought their first major battle of the war at Ypres, beginning April 22, 1915. For the first time, Germany used poison gas in warfare. French colonial troops were driven back by clouds of lung-destroying chlorine gas, leaving the Canadians' left flank exposed. The Canadians held out against the German onslaught until May 4, when they were relieved. By then they had suffered 5,700 killed, wounded, captured or missing. War correspondent Rowland Hill sent this account of the early days of the battle.

Thursday and Friday have been glorious but costly days for the Maple Leaf. In the most terrific battle on the western front, surpassing even the ferocity of Hill 60, and vastly more important to the Canadian troops, I am told that practically the whole division was engaged in a day and night struggle. They have thrown themselves at the enemy after being forced to retire through the giving away of the French line, and have recovered most of the lost ground, have recaptured their own guns, which they were forced to abandon, have taken over one hundred prisoners, and have gathered in two French seventy-fives (artillery pieces) which the Germans were preparing to take back in triumph to their line.

All this happened on the fluctuating front just north of Ypres. Sometimes our men were forced back within sight of the Yser canal; at others their lines were along the Peelcappelle road. It was a case of sheer weight of numbers, several German and Austrian army corps being suddenly brought down from Belgian garrisoned towns, combined with a terrific artillery fire, directed from the forest of Houthulst, and acid asphyxiating shells and bombs, which broke the section of the French line to the Canadians' extreme left on Thursday afternoon. The Canadians, who were in that section declare that the attack was like "hell let loose" and that no infantry could have taken it.

The din of the guns (the French and Canadian artillery were doing terrific damage to the Germans concentrated for the advance) was far worse than Neuve Chapelle, of which the Canadians have had a taste. The Zouaves broke from their trenches, staggered and blinded by gas grenades, and the enemy followed this up to such great advantage that they drove the line back two miles and then southward, until a large body of Austrian troops, who had been resting in Bruges and Ghent, according to prisoners taken, was actually beside the Canadian trenches.

For about an hour, our men were actually fighting back to back. Then the break in the Allied human dam was closed and all the Germans who had broken through were either killed or captured. Some lighter Canadian guns were abandoned when we fell back to join up with the reorganized French line. As soon as the Canadian reinforcements had come up, and the line behind had been backed up by the French, fresh British troops hurried from the reserve. Divisional headquarters sent word that an attempt might be made to recapture the guns if feasible. The Canadians made a heroic charge through the sheets of fire and grenade explosions, had a hand to hand fight with the Germans which lasted half an hour, and later reached the guns, which they triumphantly bought back. Two French guns of the famous "75" pattern, which the Germans were removing, were also retaken, according to my informant.

The Germans were themselves caught by the fumes of the gases which hovered over our left extreme trenches and scores were killed. Many of our men were left on the field between the lines for several hours, but some managed to crawl back to their comrades in safety, despite the tremendous rifle fire. Many others were recovered when we drove the Germans back and recaptured the guns. There were thrilling scenes at the field hospital yesterday. Everywhere the bronze maple leaf cap badges were seen. There were cheers for Canada and Canada's soldiers. The same greeting was given to the mangled men who were being brought down to the base hospital last night.

France, April 24, 1915

Sir Max Aitken, later to be Lord Beaverbrook, was a Canadian correspondent during the First World War. He sent a long account of the Canadians' bravery at Ypres. Here are excerpts.

An officer who took part in the attacks describes how the men about him fell under the fire of the machine guns, which, in his phrase, played upon them "like a watering pot." He added, quite simply, "I wrote my own life off." But the line never wavered, when one man fell another took his place, and with a final shout the survivors of the two battalions flung themselves into the wood. The German garrison was completely demoralized and the impetuous advance of the Canadians did not cease until they reached the far side of the wood and entrenched themselves in the position so dearly gained.

They had, however, the disappointment of finding that the guns had been blown up by the enemy, and later on in the same night

Allied troops move through the ruins of Ypres, Belgium in 1917. In the background is the famous Cloth Hall, devastated by artillery bombardment during the several major battles fought in this area. This landmark was completely reconstructed after the First World War.

a most formidable concentration of artillery fire swept the wood, as a tropical storm sweeps the leaves from a forest, making it impossible for them to hold the position for which they had sacrificed so much.

The fighting continued without intermission all through the night, and to those who observed the indications that the attack was being pushed with ever growing strength, it hardly seemed possible that the Canadians fighting in positions so difficult to defend, and so little the subject of deliberate choice, could maintain their position for any length of time. At 6 a.m. Sunday it was more apparent that the left was becoming more involved and a powerful German attempt to outflank it developed rapidly. The consequences if it had been broken or outflanked need not be insisted upon. They were not merely local.

It was therefore decided, formidable as the attempt undoubtedly was, to try and give relief by a counter attack upon the first line of German trenches, now far, far advanced from those originally occupied by the French. This was carried out by the Ontario first and fourth battalions of the first brigade, under Brig.-Gen. Mercer, acting in combination with a British brigade. It is safe to say that the youngest private in the ranks, as he set out for the advance, knew the task in front of him, and the youngest subaltern knew all that rested upon its success.

It did not seem that any human being could live in the shower of shot and shell which began to play upon the advancing troops. They suffered terrible casualties. For a short time, every man seemed to fall, but the attack was pressed closer and closer. The fourth Canadian battalion at one moment came under a particularly withering fire. For a moment − not more − it wavered. Its almost gallant commanding officer, Lieut.-Col. Birchall, carrying after an old fashion, a light cane, coolly and cheerfully

rallied his men, and at the very moment when his example had infected them, fell dead at the head of the battalion.

With a hoarse cry of anger they sprang forward (for, indeed, they loved him) as if to avenge his death. The astonishing attack which followed, pushed home in the face of direct frontal fire, made in broad daylight, by battalions whose name should live forever in the memories of soldiers, was carried to the first lines of German trenches. After a hand-to-hand struggle, the last German who was seen was bayoneted and the trench was won.

A trench was won, but the battle continued. Later in his account, Aitken had another story of extraordinary heroism.

The last attempt of the Germans was materially reduced in strength on the left, but they managed to slip in between the wood and St. Julien and caused some anxious moments in the long drawn out struggle, and indeed for a moment it looked as though the Canadians were lost.

In the stand made by the third brigade during this supreme crisis, it is almost impossible to single out one battalion without injustice to others, but the efforts of the Royal Islanders of Montreal, 13th battalion, were only equal to those of other battalions which did such heroic service.

Joe Norworth, almost disabled by a bullet wound, was bayoneted and killed while he was rallying his men with easy cheerfulness. That of Capt. McCuaig of the same battalion was not less glorious though his death can claim no witness. This most gallant officer was seriously wounded in a hurriedly constructed trench, at a moment when it would have been possible to remove him to safety, but he refused to be moved. But the situation grew instantly worse and peremptory orders came for an immediate withdrawal. But he knowing, it may be bet-

ter than they, the exertions which still lay in front of them, and unwilling to inflict upon them the disabilities of a maimed man, very resolutely refused, and asked of them one thing only, that there should be given to him as he lay alone in the trench two loaded Colt revolvers to add to his own, which lay in his right hand as he made his last request. And so, with three revolvers ready to hand for use, a very brave officer waited to sell his life, wounded and racked with pain, in an abandoned trench.

London, May 1, 1915

The capture of Vimy Ridge was one of the Canadian army's most brilliant successes of the First World War. This report by Rowland Hill, sent the day after four Canadian divisions attacked along a four-mile front, was somewhat optimistic about the toll, however. By April 14, the operation had cost 11,000 Canadian casualties. Canada's principal war memorial in France stands on Vimy Ridge.

The Canadians today were perched well over the top of the Vimy Ridge, thousands of prisoners have been taken, and, according to the first summing up of our casualties, it has been the cheapest victory the troops from the Dominion have won. The first of the wounded have begun to arrive in England and yesterday at an English port I spoke with some of our men, but most of them had been hit in the early part of Sunday morning. Since then the more serious fighting has developed but as yet our corps have hung on and even gained slightly towards the railway which runs on the far slope of the ridge, part of the line from Arras to Lens.

Canada's division started the attack just as a rainy, stormy dawn was breaking. It followed what one of my informants, who has been through three great bombardments, describes as "the Somme's most terrific day multiplied by five." The Huns' first lines, with which the Canadians were well acquainted after many raids, were gained with slight casualties.

The Bavarian garrisons were dazed into surrender and, in the first hour over a thousand prisoners were hustled back and five machine guns captured. The second and third lines, which had been crumpled almost beyond recognition by the sudden increase in what had been a steady, heavy bombardment, were defended with greater tenacity, but the driving rain which for once came from behind and was in the Canadians' favor, helped considerably. Our heavier guns then started another concentrated bombardment; it must have caught the Huns' complicated system of light railways, for according to one wounded man from Vancouver, his battalion captured a small train of supplies with a little deserted engine in which steam was still up.

London, April 10, 1917

Midway through the battle for Passchendaele Ridge F.A. McKenzie sent this dispatch. The ridge was secured Nov. 10, 1917, but two square miles of land had cost 16,000 casualties.

The second stage of the great battle for Passchendaele Ridge was ended in another glorious, bloody and hard-won victory in which Canada had a great part. We have taken all our objectives and at points gone beyond them. We remain masters of the line, despite furious German counter-attacks from the neighborhood of Vapour Farm to that of Vienna Cottage. Our men are entrenched on the outskirts of Passchendaele village in name only, for it's now nothing but one great ruin.

Our advance since last Friday morning is one mile at the widest point, tapering somewhat on either flank. This may sound little for the tremendous effort necessary to reach only from Centre street to Tenth street west, on Eighth avenue, with a front a little over 3,000 yards, but anyone who witnessed the nature of the German defences or knows how hitherto they have resisted attempt after attempt to pierce them will acknowledge it is an accomplishment rarely equalled in this war. The Germans, recognizing the importance of our attack, concentrated many troops, an enormous amount of artillery and a very strong force of aeroplanes against us.

These aeroplanes are playing an important secondary part in this fight, not merely for reconnaissance, but as active weapons of war. They come over in relays hour after hour, dropping bombs by the hundreds. No responsible soldier who comes out of this scrap will fail to realize how important a strong force of aeroplanes is for any offensive movement.

Our barrage opened shortly before daylight. Less than five minutes afterwards the enemy replied with a tremendous fire. Troops from every part of Canada, from Nova Scotia to the Pacific, engaged immediately. Our barrage lifted while the men were going over the top. The Germans, rushing out of their concrete shelters, opened up machine gun fire. Where the rain of shells swept the line in the rear of each advancing battalion they made it difficult to maintain communication, yet runners usually slightly wounded, went quickly and unhesitatingly to and fro.

No man hesitated. On the right flank the Canadians fought the 346th German regiment with bayonets. Fritz usually shirks steel; on this occasion he fought fiercely, but vainly. The Canadians went through them. At another point the first advance was largely shot down and sent back for supports. The combined force fairly swept the Germans out. By about 8 o'clock practically the whole of our objective had been carried. The troops then dug themselves in. One very strong bunch of concrete positions fronting Gouldbourg was still untaken. These were left till later.

The weather now changed, becoming much colder. Clouds gathered and shortly before noon rain began, cold, miserable and continuous, which soon made the mud worse than ever, adding the crowning touch of physical discomfort for all. The Germans, furious at our success, now prepared two considerable counter-attacks, one from the direction of Passchendaele and the other from behind Gouldbourg.

I want you to picture the scene of the field of battle. The main fight took place upon a long ridge. Black mud in great columns, debris, stones and metal, were flung high in the air along the front line like one great continuous earthquake from bursting shells. The gathering storm blew aeroplanes furiously about, finally compelling many monster triplanes to take cover. You could not hear the approaching shells owing to the continuous roar of bursting charges which drowned every other sound. Our men, with box respirators fastened high on the chest and yellow shell-wound first aid cages hanging from them, sheltered themselves as best they could in shell holes or shallow trenches. They knew they had won a great victory, but there was no loud exulting among them. Wearied and muddy, they waited watchfully.

Not far from this was a Canadian Y.M.C.A. advanced post. I examined these posts going from one to another. They do exceedingly useful work, supplying hot cocoa and biscuits to both wounded and stretcher bearers.

It was good to see the tender way the stretcher bearers lifted the heads of the men, holding the cups to their lips. Many of the men whose heart-beats were slackening and circulation lowering as death approached, and wounded recovering from the first shock of pain, unwounded, like the stretcher bearers and myself, chilled and hungry, found comfort Tuesday from these mugs of cocoa. Y.M.C.A. workers planted their stations at several dangerous points of the line because here their presence was most needed. People may rest content that our wounded had every attention possible. Elaborate preparations were made to promptly rescue them; they were brought down carefully and with the utmost expedition.

Here and there one saw a smiling face, some lay a ghastly yellow and unconscious, others were wearied with shut eyes. Pools below were red with blood from their wounds. Farther down at the big collection point I saw a long procession of walking wounded. During battle time every man must walk who can. Some helped others along. Here were faces badly torn, quickly bandaged — broken men who a few hours before had been whole.

They give themselves for Canada; may Canada never forget.

With the Canadians In the Field, November 3, 1917

Canadian soldiers man machine-gun posts during a lull in the battle of Passchendaele. Much of the war was fought in conditions like this: slow, costly advances were made across acres of stinking mud.

The Halifax explosion of 1917 killed 1,630 people, injured thousands more, and damaged every building in the city. Many people were drowned by a tidal wave thrown up by the exploding munitions ship, the Mont Blanc. Damage was estimated at $35,000,000.

Halifax was wrecked by an explosion of a munition ship at 9 o'clock this morning with heavy loss of life, and a large section of the city is on fire. This is the information which reached the government this morning from the Intercolonial officials at Moncton, N.B. Direct wires from Ottawa to Halifax are down. The report states that all of the city north of the Queen's Hotel is more or less wrecked and that the north end of the city is a mess of wreckage and dead bodies.

Apparently the explosion was a result of an accident. The dispatch states that a munition ship was backing out of Pier 6 when it collided with an incoming steamer. The munition ship caught fire. A desperate effort was made to sink her before the fire reached the explosives, but without success, and the ship blew up about 9 o'clock.

Both telegraph offices at Halifax were blown up and the only available wires are apparently over the railways. No further definite information is expected at Ottawa until the special train from Moncton reaches Halifax. There is no estimate as to any loss of life, but it is feared it may be heavy. There is also anxiety as to the possibility of troopships in the harbor being wrecked.

Ottawa, December 6, 1917

The weather compounded the misery of the homeless and injured of Halifax. Many had to live in tents. Relief trains bringing supplies and doctors were snowbound.

Following the wake of death and destruction yesterday in this city, a heavy snow storm set in early this morning adding to the discomfort of the homeless and impeding the work of the rescuers. Fires are still burning in the devastated area and the fire department is still at work. The fall of snow, however, will assist them in subduing the fires in the ruins. The devastated area extends from North street to Africville, on the shores of Bedford basin, and about two miles from the waterfront west to Gottingen street about three-quarters of a mile. Special trains from Moncton, Truro and Windsor have arrived here, bringing doctors, nurses and medical supplies.

The munition ship was bound from New York for Bedford basin when she collided with a Belgian relief ship bound for sea.

Following the collision, the explosion occurred and in an instant the whole city was shaken from its foundation. Thousands of people have been rendered homeless. The Academy of Music and many other public buildings have been thrown open to house the homeless.

Five hundred tents have been erected on the common and these will be occupied by the troops who have given up the barracks to house the homeless women and children.

Shattered buildings stand empty in Halifax after the disastrous explosion of 1917. A shipload of munitions bound for Europe exploded in the harbor, sending a devastating shock wave across the city.

In the main portions of the city, where the buildings are more or less of stone or concrete, the damage was confined to the blowing in of windows and the injuries sustained by the citizens were in the main due to cuts from flying glass. Proceeding south to the extreme end of the city the same thing was observed.

In the west end and northwest the damage was more extensive and the walls of houses were in places blown to atoms and the plaster and laths strewn on the streets, more like a small section of Flanders than a town or city of Canada.

The main damage, however, was done in the north end of the city known as Richmond, which was opposite the point of the vessel's collision. Here the damage is so extensive as to be totally beyond the field of description. Street after street is in ruins and flames swept over the district.

Here and there by a cracked and shattered pole was the cloth-wrapped body of a tiny tot, scarred and twisted by the force of the horrible explosion which had withered all in its path. By the side of many of the burning ruins were women who watched with horror the flames as they consumed the houses, which in many cases held the bodies of loved ones. With dry eyes they watched as others passed with inquiries as to whether they could render any aid, they shook their heads in a dazed manner and turned their gaze once more to the funeral pyre of all those whom they held dear.

The rescuers who were early on the scene say that the sights in the public schools at the north end of the city were pitiable. They found the bodies of dozens of little children and scores of others with broken limbs and covered with blood. The force of the explosion was felt 75 miles from Halifax, glass being broken in the Learmont hotel at Truro. All the telegraph wires were destroyed and when the explosion occurred the operators jumped from their keys and raced for the open. All the telephones also were put out of order. For a time Halifax was completely isolated from the outside world.

Halifax, December 7, 1917

Fred McCall went on to become the city's first air ace. He was credited with shooting down 37 enemy planes. The Calgary airport was later named McCall Field in his honor.

Lieut. Fred McCall, the only son of J.F. McCall superintendent of the city's electric power plant, has succeeded in bringing down his first Hun airplane after a most exciting struggle. This is related in a letter from the intrepid young lieutenant just received by his parents.

"I was over the enemy lines at about 9,000 feet," he writes, "when suddenly two Hun machines of the fastest and best German type came for me and what a glorious battle we had among the clouds with gunners and infantry on both sides watching their respective representatives going for each other.

"The fight lasted about fifteen minutes and oh, what a warm time it was, but God seemed to protect me from the three hundred bullets the Huns fired, and after putting about one hundred and fifty at him his engine stopped and down he went. He waved good-bye when he went down, and I waved back at him, so I suppose there was no hard feeling. I saw him crash into the wire in front of the trenches. He may not have been killed, but his machine was in an awful mess after striking the ground.

"When the other Hun saw his pal go down he didn't take long to clear off the horizon I can tell you. When I landed, I found six bullet holes in my machine and my wireless had been cut off. A general shook hands with me and complimented me on my fight with superior numbers and the fact that I got down. He saw the fighting from the ground.

"I didn't mind the rumpus at all and rather enjoyed it. It hasn't affected my nerves and has taught me a lot about aerial fighting," concludes this gallant officer.

January 30, 1918

Both sides used poison gas in the First World War, spraying it across the front lines from gas "projectors" when the wind would carry it toward the enemy trenches. At the time of the attack reported here, the United States had just entered the war, and Germany had launched its last, futile offensive.

Saturday the Canadians carried out the biggest combined projector gas and shell bombardment in the history of the western front. From early Friday night until early Saturday morning our heavies and howitzers rained shells upon the hostile battery positions, using lethal gas, lachrymatory (tear) gas and high explosives, while at 2 o'clock Saturday morning more than 1,200 drums of lethal gas were projected against the enemy trenches and support areas in an intensive concentrated bombardment of the area immediately north of Lens.

Bombardment followed bombardment at greater and lesser intervals, in a scientific, carefully-thought-out programme of destruction designed to silence the enemy guns and kill the gun crews, or at least make the operation of their batteries impossible.

In the midst of this destructive operation special units carried out a projector gas bombardment against Lens. In the few seconds occupied in releasing the gas, flares went up all along the enemy front line and the men in our trenches could distinctly hear cries of distress from the enemy caught without masks. When quiet had been restored and the enemy were presumably emerging from their dugouts and other special retreats our artillery sprayed the hostile front, support and assembly areas with shrapnel.

Hun prisoners have already testified to the effectiveness of other like measures. The Ypres account is slowly being settled.

Canadian Headquarters In France,
April 22, 1918

Germany signed an armistice at 5 a.m. French time, Nov. 11, 1918. At 11 a.m. that day, according to the armistice, both sides were to cease hostilities. Word of peace reached Calgary in the small hours of the morning.

The ear-splitting and continued screeching of a whistle on a C.P.R. locomotive, passing through the downtown section shortly after 1 o'clock this morning, was the first notice the citizens of Calgary received of the signing of the armistice imposing virtually unconditional surrender on Germany. Other whistles followed suit, the news spreading like wildfire, and in a few minutes there was a bedlam of bells ringing, whistles blowing, and cheering of belated pedestrians on the downtown streets.

The flash, coming over the C.P.R. wires, was picked up all along the line, and similar impromptu celebrations were staged from the Atlantic shores of Canada to the Pacific coast.

An impromptu procession was started, headed by a drummer and bugler who had been commandeered at the Veterans' Club, and the celebrants paraded through the downtown streets, cheering, yelling and singing. Guests in local hotels, hearing the turmoil, flocked out on the streets, adding to the crowd, and soon automobiles bearing citizens from the residence districts began to arrive downtown.

The influenza mask order was totally forgotten in the excitement, and a good deal of horse play was indulged in by the jubilating throng. Most of this took the form of overturning of Commissioner Samis' garbage tins at the downtown street corners, pulling down flags to use in the parade and similar good-natured exuberances.

Mayor M.C. Costello this morning also issued a municipal proclamation, declaring a half-holiday for today to enable citizens to celebrate the triumph.

November 11, 1918

The Treaty of Versailles sealed the peace between Germany and the allies — and sowed the seeds of another war. The heavy war damages demanded by the victorious powers contributed to economic chaos, political upheaval and resentment in Germany. The desire to avenge Versailles played no small part in Adolf Hitler's disastrous plans for Germany.

The treaty of peace between the 27 allied and associated powers on the one hand, and Germany on the other, was handed to the German plenipotentiaries at Versailles today.

It is the longest treaty ever drawn. It totals about 80,000 words divided into 15 main sections and represents the combined product of over a thousand experts working continually through a series of commissions for the three and a half months since Jan. 18.

Germany, by the terms of the treaty, restores Alsace-Lorraine to France, accepts the internationalization of the Saar basin temporarily and of Dantzig permanently; agrees to territorial changes toward Belgium and Denmark, and in East Prussia, cedes most of Upper Silesia to Poland, and renounces all territorial and political rights outside of Europe, as to her own or her allies' territories, and especially to Morocco, Egypt, Siam, Liberia and Shantung.

Her army is reduced to 100,000 men, including officers; conscription within her territories is abolished; all forts 50 kilometres east of the Rhine razed and all importation, exportation and nearly all production of war materials stopped. Allied occupation of parts of Germany will continue till reparation is made, but will be reduced at the end of each of three-year periods if Germany is fulfilling her obligations. Any violation by the Rhine will be regarded as an act of war.

The German navy is reduced to six battleships, six light cruisers and twelve torpedo boats, without submarines, and a personnel of not over 15,000. All other vessels must be surrendered or destroyed.

Germany accepts full responsibility for all damages caused to Allied and associated governments and nationals, agrees specifically to reimburse all civilian damages, beginning with an initial payment of 20,000,000,000 marks, subsequent payments to be secured by bonds to be issued at the discretion of the reparation commission. Germany is to pay shipping damage on a ton-for-ton basis by cession of a large part of her merchant coasting and river fleets and by new construction, and to devote her economic resources to the rebuilding of the devastated regions.

Paris, May 7, 1919

Flying the Union Jack, and the occasional Stars and Stripes, a victory parade makes its way through Calgary on Nov. 11, 1918. The mayor had proclaimed a half-day holiday to celebrate the end of the war. Several in the parade wore masks to guard against the flu.

A Communist Revolution

The war was going badly for Russia, which was allied with Britain and France. There was defeat on the eastern front, and governmental breakdown and hunger at home. Finally a committee of the Duma, the Russian legislature, called on Czar Nicholas to give up his throne. The czar abdicated, and a comparatively moderate provisional government under Prince George Lvov was set up. This was the first of two Russian revolutions of 1917; the second would establish the Communist regime.

A successful revolution has taken place in Russia. The reactionary party has been overthrown. Reports from Petrograd state that the duma, backed by the army, has succeeded in overthrowing the government completely. The revolution centred in Petrograd and Moscow. Prominent reactionaries, including former Premier Sturmer and M. Protopopoff, minister of the interior, have been imprisoned. The government is now in the hands of a committee of safety.

The garrisons at Petrograd and Moscow went over in a body to the revolutionaries.

The question of the dynasty has been left unsettled thus far. It is reported there is a possibility of the abdication of Emperor Nicholas, who would be succeeded by the crown prince, with Grand Duke Nicholas acting as regent.

The revolution was comparatively bloodless. Some fighting took place on the first day, during which bridges in Petrograd were blown up in order to isolate certain sections of the city. As far as is known here no prominent persons were killed.

London, March 15, 1917

The provisional government of Russia inherited the problems that had led to the overthrow of the czar. After more military defeat and more civil disorder, the provisional government was reorganized under Alexander Kerensky, a moderate. He suppressed the radical Maximalists — now remembered by their Russian name, the Bolsheviks. In October, Bolsheviks leader Nikolai Lenin returned from his temporary exile in Finland. On Nov. 7, 1917 (October 25 by the old Russian calendar) the Bolsheviks seized power.

The Maximalists have obtained control of Petrograd and issued a proclamation saying the new government will propose immediate peace, the semi-official Russian news agency announces.

The Maximalists were assisted by the Petrograd garrison, which made possible a coup d'etat without bloodshed.

A proclamation sent out through the wireless stations of the Russian government today and picked up here, states that the garrison and proletariat of Petrograd have deposed the Kerensky government.

Nikolai Lenin addresses a crowd after the revolution that brought Communism to Russia.

The Maximalist element comprises the most extreme class of the Russian revolutionary Socialists. It first sprang into prominence in the early days of the revolution under the leadership of Nikolai Lenin, the radical agitator, who later was put under the ban of the provisional government because of his ultra-radical preachments and his suspected pro-German leanings.

Meanwhile the Maximalists were under the leadership of his chief lieutenant, Leon Trotsky, whose home was in the United States when the revolution broke out, but who sailed for Russia shortly afterward.

Kerensky's task at the head of the provisional government since his assumption of the premiership on July 20 has been a formidable one. Hailed as the savior of Russia in her hours of need, he labored with ability and patience to keep the diverse elements comprising the revolutionary democracy together.

Nikolai Lenin, who received prolonged cheers, outlined the three problems now before the Russian democracy:

"First, immediate conclusion of the war, for which purpose the new government must propose an armistice to the belligerents; second, the handing over of the land to the peasants; third, settlement of the economic crisis."

London, November 8, 1917

The October revolution was followed by civil war in Russia as the Bolsheviks tried to consolidate their power. The so-called "White" opposition to the Bolsheviks was intensified by the revolutionary government's peace treaty with Germany in March, 1918. The Bolsheviks bought peace by yielding huge tracts of land, including the Ukraine, to Germany. The following story describes some of the horrors of life in Russia at that time. In 1918 and 1919, troops from several Allied countries, including Canada, fought in Russia in support of the Whites. The Bolsheviks' Red army defeated them. By 1920, virtually all opposition to the Bolsheviks was over, and Communist rule had been established in Russia.

The brutal excesses of the Bolsheviks, as cited in the British White Paper, recall the Bryce report with its ghastly account of German brutality in Belgium. A British subject who left Moscow on December 1, says in a memorandum: "The number of people who have been coldly done to death in Moscow is enormous. Many thousands have been shot, but lately those condemned to death were hung instead, and that in the most brutal manner.

"They were taken out in batches in the early hours of the morning to a place on the outskirts of the town, stripped to their shorts, and then hung one by one by being drawn up at the end of a rope until their feet were a few inches from the ground and then left to die. The work was done by Mongolian soldiers. Shooting was too noisy and not sure enough."

The British consul at Vladivostok reported on January 14: "The number of innocent civilians brutally murdered in Ural towns run into hundreds. Officers taken prisoners by Bolsheviks here had their shoulder straps nailed into their shoulders, girls have been raped, some of the civilians have been found with their eyes pierced out, others without noses, whilst twenty-five priests were shot at Perm, Bishop Andronick having been buried alive there."

The following conditions are reported by eye witnesses in Petrograd where the present population is probably not more than 600,000, and wholesale starvation has only been prevented by illicit trafficking in food by "sack men." All newspapers except the Bolshevik ones have been closed, and their plant and property confiscated. All government securities have been annulled and all others confiscated. Payments by the banks for current or deposit accounts have been stopped. It is forbidden to sell furniture or to move it from one house to another without permission. Hundreds of houses have been requisitioned for official or semi-official use, and thousands of unhappy residents have been turned out on the streets at an hour's notice with permission to take with them only the clothes they stood in, together with one change of linen. All hotels, restaurants, provision shops are now closed after having had their stocks and inventories confiscated. The food question in Petrograd has gone from bad to worse. Elaborate food cards are given out each month covering all kinds of products but for months past nothing has been given out on them except bread, which has for the last few weeks consisted of unmilled oats.

London, May 27, 1919

Calgary in Peace and War

In the last few months before the war, Calgary was returning to its boom-town optimism, inspired this time by the Turner Valley oil discovery. In 1915, despite the distractions of the war, Alberta found time to embark on two major social experiments: prohibition and votes for women. One major project, however, was doomed by the war. In 1914, Thomas Mawson, an English city planner, proposed a design that would turn Calgary into a pretty fair imitation of a minor European capital. It was the wrong time to dream great dreams — the real estate boom was over, and soon the war distracted everyone from visions of the City Beautiful.

The preliminary plans of the city of Calgary prepared by Thomas Mawson and Sons for the city planning commission are now in the hands of the secretary together with a report which deals exhaustively with the various phases of city planning, especially as applied to local conditions.

This report is prefaced by the following statement:

"City planning is not the attempt to pull down your city and re-build it at ruinous expense. It is merely deciding what you would like to have done when you get the chance, so that when the chance does come, little by little you may make the city plan conform to your ideals," and this is emphasised by Mr. Mawson frequently throughout his report.

"Never before has there been such a phenomenal development and such rapid peopling of the hitherto waste places of the earth under the conditions provided and imposed by modern civilization, as in the great west of Canada at the present time. Not only is this so, but Calgary stands right at the centre of this development. It is the keynote of the situation, and we feel that, on its success or failure will hang the success or failure of the whole of the territory so rich in every kind of material wealth, which surrounds it on every side, stretching from the snow-capped Rocky mountains on the one hand to Winnipeg on the other, and from Edmonton in the north to the border of the Dominion on the south."

The Herald's account went on to describe Mawson's renderings of his plan.

There are various perspective drawings illustrating the possibilities of the scheme with regard to the C.P.R. depot, Centre street and proposed new market situated on Centre street south of the C.P.R. track.

Many of these drawings are beautifully colored and the perspectives, while they illustrate buildings which are not likely to be erected for a long time, are invaluable as illustrating what can be accomplished in the future, it being pointed out that Paris is still working on Hausmann's plans prepared about 80 years ago and that the city of Boston, U.S.A. has undertaken a scheme which is intended to spread over a period of 80 years.

These highlights of the Mawson plan show what might have been.

A civic centre between Second and Third avenues and Third and Sixth street west, with a broad avenue running north along the line of Fourth street west, across a big bridge resting on Prince's Island.

Centre street adopted as the main north and south artery of the city, this street to be widened on each side.

A spacious circle or "circus" between Second and Third avenues at their intersection with Centre street.

A wide avenue or "mall" connecting this Centre street circle with the civic centre to the west of it.

A new market place south of the C.P.R. tracks at the intersection of Centre street with Twelfth and Fourteenth avenues.

Extensions of the parks system by purchasing of large areas within the city parking and boulevarding both sides of the Bow and Elbow rivers.

Sketch plans for future public buildings, such as the city hall, auditorium, etc., placed around the civic centre and along the avenue or "mall" between the civic centre and the widening of Centre street into a circus or circle at Third and Second avenues.

Provisions for numerous diagonal highways throughout the city, which is regarded by the city commissioners as well as Mr. Mawson himself as one of the most important features of his plans tending to relieve traffic congestion.

April 30, 1914

The Dingman No. 1 well was the first hint of a new era in Alberta. The pace of oil discovery was rather slow for three decades after Dingman's find in Turner Valley, but speculators and wildcat drillers never entirely lost faith that Alberta would make them rich some day. The oil era here almost began with a disaster, as the following story shows. A few days after the discovery, Dingman estimated that the well was producing about 120 barrels a day of light crude — so light, in fact, that it could be used as gasoline. Dingman's chauffeur reported getting 41 miles per gallon "and the machine went up hills like a shot."

At 11:40 a.m. the derrick of Dingman well No. 1 caught fire at the top. The fire was discovered when some sparks fell to the floor of the derrick. A tragedy was narrowly averted by the heroism of one of the drillers, Dinsmore, and Mr. Horndyke, who climbed to the top of the 84 foot derrick with buckets of water amid the fumes of the gasoline gas, and extinguished the flame. The men took their lives in their hands by this act, as the derrick was saturated with the gasoline oil, which had been flowing from the well since five o'clock last night. This oil, which was struck by the drillers at five o'clock last evening at a depth of 2718 feet, is the most remarkable discovered in the history of the world.

The oil is almost pure gasoline, and is of a bluish color, which is due to the sediment displaced by the drill. If allowed to stand and settle, it comes out of the well practically a pure white gasoline.

Last evening when the drill pierced the oil bearing strata at 2718 feet at five o'clock, the oil rose so rapidly in the well that it rose above the 1562 foot level. At this level the gasoline gas is flowing into the well. The gas forced the oil up into a gusher, which shot up fifteen or twenty feet above the floor of the derrick. The drillers immediately stopped drilling and notified the directors that oil had been struck at that time.

Manager A.W. Dingman of the Calgary Petroleum Products company, was at the well, and took immediate steps for confining the oil. All available tanks at the well, consisting of about eighteen, holding forty gallons each, were brought at once to the well, and work of filling them began.

The drillers then baled out with the iron baler about two tanks of forty gallons each of the oil, and capped the well.

They stopped operations, and began again this morning shortly before seven o'clock.

When the capping was removed from the well nothing extraordinary was apparent. The drillers hauled down the baler and were getting ready to let it down into the well when the oil suddenly shot up in a violent spray fifteen or twenty feet above the floor of the derrick.

The walls and all the tools and drillers were soaked with oil, or rather gasoline, and the crowds scattered, fearing an explosion. In a few minutes the pressure died down, and the drillers then resumed their work of baling out the gasoline.

Someone in the crowd noticed a spark of fire fell down from the top of the derrick, 84 feet above the ground. The drillers looked up to the top of the derrick and saw a cloud of smoke shot through with fire furling about the upper works. Confusion reigned for a moment, and it was then that Drillers Dinsmore and Horndyke displayed their bravery. Manager A.W. Dingman had left for Calgary some hours previously, and director O.S. Chapin was in charge. Mr. Chapin called for volunteers to up and extinguish the fire. Without a moment's hesitation Driller Dinsmore secured a bucket of water and started climbing the ladder of the lofty 84-foot derrick. He was followed a second later by Driller Horndyke with another bucket of water. The frightened group around the bottom of the well could see the fumes of the heavy gasoline flowing out of the well and shooting up towards the top of the derrick. The men climbing the ladder were in danger of instant annihilation, as if a spark had dropped down the orifice of the well a terrific explosion would undoubtedly have resulted.

The men were successful, however, and

The oil boom hits Calgary. In just a week after the Turner Valley discovery, more than 100 stockbrokers took out licences. Storefront offices, like these ones on Ninth Avenue, blossomed downtown. Even some travellers on the CPR trains strolled across the street from the station to buy oil stock.

extinguished the fire before any serious damage had been done.

Manager Kelso of the Kelso laboratories, has examined the oil and pronounces it to be the most remarkable ever discovered in the history of the world. It is not a crude oil. It's almost pure gasoline, but the mere fact that this oil has never before been discovered in the history of the world does not go to prove that it is not in larger quantities. On the other hand, some geologists contend that this western Canada field is entirely distinct in its characteristics from any other oil field, geographically speaking in the world. As a result of this it is not a remote possibility that great quantities of this enormously profitable gasoline oil may be found beneath the hills stretching southwest of Calgary.

Parties of automobilists, including the most prominent citizens, have been visiting the well in a great string. The roads from Calgary to Okotoks and then to the Dingman well have been lined with automobiles all last night and this morning, and the hotels and bars in Okotoks are doing a rushing business.

Calgary was soon engulfed in a wave of oil-stock speculation. Not even the war would discourage local investors. The scene on the morning after the Dingman discovery was frantic.

Calgary is oil crazy!

In offices, in street cars, shops and on the streets this morning, nothing can be heard but gossip of oil. Not the idle talk of the last few weeks, but this time the repetition of cold, hard facts regarding the strike of oil in the Dingman well. Everybody,

whether interested directly in oil or not, is talking and thinking of nothing else, and it proves a universal subject which is interesting everybody from the financier to the man sweeping the streets.

The various oil companies of the city, who have, to some extent, been preaching to a doubting public for the last month, this morning were doing a roaring business, and in many places it was necessary to have police in front of the offices to keep the waiting crowds in check. In one office the flow of real money was said to be so fast that it was impossible to keep in any order. A waste paper basket was being used into which bills and cheques were poured as fast as they came.

Oil stock is taking leaps by the minute, and the scarcity of stock in the lucky company is only exceeded by the extreme excitement which prevails. In the broker's office this morning business was very slow. There is no selling. Everyone wants to buy, and the newer companies are the only people who are willing to sell. Private owners of mineral rights on land and also of stocks are holding on for dear life, and have not sufficiently recovered from the first surprise to figure out what they should ask for their rights. Everything relating to values is in confusion.

Wild prices are being asked and wilder bids for stock are being turned down flat. Stock that was bought for $25 one month ago is now little under $1,000. But in spite of the frantic efforts of the people who want to buy, those holding refuse to budge, and it is not expected that the conditions will steady until a few days have passed.

All the directors of the Calgary Petroleum Products company have left for the scene of the gusher. Before leaving several of these gentlemen expressed themselves

to friends as being pleased and confident that their well was at last in the right stuff, and that Friday, in spite of the fact that it is alleged to be a very poor day for things in general, would mark another great step in the development of the resources of the province of Alberta. Samples of the oil have been received in the city, and in one office, where they were on exhibit, the whole place reeked of gasoline. The oil is very clear and slightly amber in color. The smell may well be described as exaggerated gasoline, for it is exactly like gasoline, only much stronger.

May 15, 1914

Oil stocks lured countless thousands of dollars out of bank accounts and mattresses. For a few heady months, the oil boom took over where the real estate boom had left off. A week after the Dingman discovery, more than 100 brokers had paid city licence fees — $50 for inside brokers, and $10 for those who did business on the curb.

The oil fever from which Calgary is suffering at the present time is being reflected at the city hall, where little business is being transacted, owing to the fact that people seem incapable of thinking and talking about anything but oil shares, leases and prospects. The general rush to invest savings in oil shares and stocks is reflected in the receipts of the electric light department, where the revenue has fallen off about half and it has been found necessary to put on a number of extra collectors to bring receipts up to the normal. The receipts in the waterworks department show a similar falling off.

Stories of small fortunes made by lucky or far sighted persons in oil stocks are heard on every hand. A sweeper in the street cleaning department drew his "pile" — $1,000 to wit — out of the bank Saturday and invested it in stocks. The same evening he sold out at exactly double the price at which he had bought, returned his $1,000 to the bank and reinvested the $1,000 he had made. This is only one example of the small fortunes that are being made by men in humble positions.

"I know a chap who borrowed $100 and gave a note which he could not redeem last fall," said an official in the city health department. "He held 350 shares in a newly-formed company, which he had purchased at about a dollar a share. These he gave to his creditors in lieu of payment on the note. Today the 350 shares are worth easily $2,500, and the creditor is congratulating himself on the deal."

Arrangements were completed yesterday for providing Calgary with a big oil exchange and workmen are busy today preparing the first floor of the new steel skyscraper Mackie block at Eighth avenue and Second street west for the exchange. The plans provide for 30 offices and a big rotunda capable of providing for a crowd of more than 1,000 people.

A balcony will run all around the rotunda for the convenience of women buyers and sellers and also as a rendezvous. Blackboards, telegraph wires, messenger service and all the equipment of an up-to-date exchange will be afforded and some exciting scenes are promised when the exchange gets down to business, especially if another of the wells now drilling should bring in oil in the next 30 days as promised.

All hotels in the city are crowded to capacity, reservations are made in advance and all the trains are full bringing in the crowds. The Canadian Pacific is straining every effort to get the new hotel [the Palliser] opened up as soon as possible and it is probable that the big hostelry will receive guests on the first of next month.

May 21, 1914

The Hillcrest coal mine, about two kilometres from the Frank Slide, was the scene of a terrible explosion in 1914. Apparently a spark ignited coal gas. This blast threw up coal dust, which in turn exploded. Nearly 200 men lost their lives.

What bids fair to rank as one of the worst mining disasters in the history of western Canada took place this morning at Hillcrest, Alta., at 9:30, when a terrific explosion wrecked the mine, into the workings of which three hundred men had just gone forth to work out their eight hours' shift.

The scenes around the mine tell a terrible tale of the havoc wrought and the fearful force of the explosion. With the greatest difficulty the gangs of rescuers, armed as they are with the latest scientific devices for saving life in such cases, can make any headway. Men, horses, timber, rails and wagons are jumbled in chaotic mass and the path is so strewn at every step with the debris that only those men who were fortunate enough to have been working near the pit mouth have any chance of being brought out alive. In fact, old-time miners declare their belief that after such a holocaust no man now unrecovered from the innermost workings of the pit can possibly emerge alive.

Immediately on receipt of news of the disaster rescue trains were made up from Calgary, Lethbridge and Fernie, while a special car was rushed to the scene from Blairmore. In a short time there were six gangs at work. Carrying pulmotors and clad in the special dress which protects the rescuer from the noxious fumes, these men went to work with great energy but little speed owing to the chaos which prevailed.

After much effort, however, sufficient debris was cleared away to enable the men who were alive to be reached. These were within easy reach of the shaft and were not subjected to the full force of these explosions which seem to have practically buried their fellow workers farther in. Altogether forty were brought out alive within two hours of the occurrence, and at half-past two this afternoon ten dead bodies were brought up and reverently laid down while a throng of distracted wives and mothers crowded round to see if perchance the victims were of their family.

Hillcrest, Alberta, June 19, 1914

A few days after the blast, a handful of survivors told their terrible stories.

Perhaps the narrowest escape was that of Joe Atchison who was the first man to be recovered from the mine unconscious after the explosion. He was only brought round after he had been worked over for three hours.

"I was working some distance in slant No. 2," said Atchison when asked for his story, "and did not hear the report of the explosion. It was just as if two four inch nails had been driven in my ears. That is how it felt. I was bowled over by the shock but scrambled to my feet. Almost instantly thick black smoke began to come around the slant No. 1.

"I was almost overcome by the shock and the smoke but started to run towards the mouth of No. 2. There were several working with me and they did the same as I did. A short distance ahead we came on Billie Neal, he was lying on the ground overcome. We tried to lift him and carry him along with us but by this time we were too weak with gases. We carried him for a short distance, dragging him over a dead horse that had been killed in his tracks and then we had to drop him.

"I shouted, 'come on boys, we're all in anyway,' then we came to the after-damp, a solid wall that drove us back, nearly suffocated us, and we lay down and rolled back with what strength we had left to a pool of water about 50 or 60 feet back, and here we crawled into the water soaking our shirts and sucking them to keep off the effects of the after-damp.

"Gus Franz, a German was about overcome and we tried to get him down near the water but he had no strength left and at last he became unconscious and we had to let him go, he was finally drowned by falling face down in the water. While we were lying at the water we could see one man not far away who had been almost cut in two. What really saved us was that they reversed the fan outside and we had a little air where we were. We became unconscious and I was carried out later — how long after of course I don't know." The rescuers got Atchison and worked for some time before they got him extricated. He was carried out and the artificial respiration apparatus was used for three hours before he came round. He was very sick of course, but by Saturday afternoon he was helping with the washing of the bodies that were still being brought out.

Hillcrest, Alberta, June 22, 1914

Royalty visited Calgary in July, 1914, and naturally they were taken to see the new wonder at Turner Valley. It must be said that safety standards at the wellhead have improved considerably since 1914.

In the presence of royalty yesterday, Dingman discovery well spouted oil like an inexhaustible gasoline fountain forty feet high until Driller Hovis, at the direction of Managing Director A.W. Dingman ordered the remarkable well turned off.

His Royal Highness, the Duke of Connaught, the Duchess and the Princess Patricia and their retinue were fascinated with the sight of a natural oil fountain and asked a string of questions that kept Mr. Dingman talking at high speed to answer.

As Mr. Hovis, the driller, began to turn the valve over, he told the crowd not to be afraid at the noise, that there was no danger and that they need not run until they saw him run. Mr. Dingman suggested that if the noise of the gas was unendurable, the visitors might place their fingers to their ears.

A few did so, but the most appeared to enjoy the novelty of the sensation. Almost simultaneously with these words, Driller Hovis began to turn the valve at exactly 2:31 p.m.

A slight hissing sound rapidly developed into a hurricane roar and shriek that seemed sufficient almost to burst the ear drums. In ten seconds this roaring began to die away and in a moment longer had resolved itself into a gentle hissing. No one uttered a word. A slight vapor then began to mount above the orifice of the pipe and occasionally Managing Director Dingman passed his hand over it to feel for the uprising oil.

At 2:32 just a minute after the valve was turned, the oil began to come. It was first announced by a light spray of drops fizzing out of the mouth of the two-inch pipe and then a steady stream of oil, or rather gasoline arose with a slight hissing noise, mounting higher and higher, until it reached an estimated height of at least forty feet.

"It's remarkable," ejaculated the Governor-general. "Isn't it pretty?" remarked Princess Patricia. The princess was right. The sight was a beautiful one. Where the brilliant afternoon sun struck through the openings in the west side of the derrick shed and flooded across the cooling fountain of gasoline, the fluid showed a dazzling white in contrast to the dark interior of the derrick shed. The spray fell in iridescent drops, much of it seemingly evaporating before it fell back to the derrick.

Princess Patricia kept urging members of her party with kodaks to get good pictures of the phenomenon, remarking that they ought to turn out well because of the contrast of light and shade between the dazzling white of the gasoline fountain and the darkness of the derrick interior.

The royal party then visited the Dingman No. 2 well, which was still being drilled. It had reached gas, but had not yet penetrated the oil-bearing rock.

July 29, 1914

Two days of heavy rain created havoc in Calgary and the district around. The old Centre Street Bridge was washed away; city commissioner J.H. Garden and city engineer G.W. Craig, who were on the bridge at the time, narrowly escaped drowning.

Calgary's supply of gas entirely cut off this morning as the result of a washout at Okotoks of the Calgary Gas Company's big sixteen-inch line from Bow Island.

A tornado at Redcliff, six miles east of Medicine Hat, resulting in the death of two people, injury of a dozen others and great property damage.

The Bow river in the most extraordinary flood condition since thirteen years ago, and still rising at the rate of four inches per hour.

The Sunnyside and Hillhurst districts of Calgary are threatened with a flood, and the old Centre street bridge closed to traffic because of danger of it going out.

The Elbow river flooded to within a few inches of the top of the arches of the new concrete Mission bridge and still rising.

Cave-ins on various streets all over the city and hundreds of basements flooded.

Washouts on the Canadian Pacific railway west of Calgary and south on the Calgary-Macleod line that will require probably 48 hours to repair.

Such, in brief, is a partial record of damage caused last night and this morning as the result of terrific wind, thunder and rain storms that swept this section of Alberta.

A total rainfall of 1.32 inches was measured in less than 48 hours. The total rainfall for the month of June, so far, measures 2.49 inches. When it is considered that 15 inches of rainfall is counted a heavy rainfall for an entire year in this district, it can be seen what extraordinary rain conditions have prevailed during the last 48 hours.

All rivers in the district are roaring torrents and water from rainfall in the mountains continues to cause them to rise.

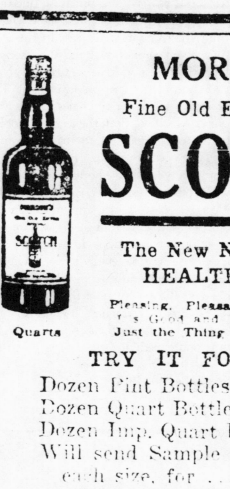

Prohibition did strange things to the liquor trade. Was the product advertised by the Saskatoon Bottling Works real scotch, or was it really a "non-alcoholic health tonic?"

Sheep creek, running through the oil district and the town of Okotoks, has become transformed from a placid streamlet to a flooded river, rising to the top of the bridge, covering the main street of Okotoks with water, and washing out the Canadian Pacific railway tracks between Okotoks and Sandstone, the next station north of Okotoks.

It was here that the greatest inconvenience to Calgary residents resulted through the washing out of the Calgary Gas company's big main line from Bow Island.

The gas line crosses Sheep creek by means of two 12 inch pipes, sunk in the bed of the river and protected by a crib filled with rock.

All gas in the city immediately went off, and residents who arose to cook their early morning breakfast by means of gas found themselves minus hot coffee and warm edibles.

June 26, 1915

Prohibition came to nearly all of Canada during the First World War. In Alberta, the campaign leading up to a vote on the question was short and quiet — and decisive. The "drys" won by a landslide. The Herald opposed prohibition, partly on the grounds that business conditions were already bad, and would be worsened by shutting down bars and breweries. A Calgary landmark, The Alberta Hotel, did close forever, apparently a victim of the "dry" vote. There were peculiar loopholes in the law: physicians could prescribe liquor, and for a time it was legal to order liquor for personal use from outside the province.

By a landslide of dry votes, the magnitude and suddenness of which was only equalled by the great Conservative turnover in the Dominion election of 1911, the Province of Alberta yesterday voted that after July 1, 1916, there shall be no more liquor sold in this province. Every bar, club or other place at the present time licensed to sell spirituous liquors will cease to exist for this purpose after that date next year, when the Alberta Liquor Act will come into full force. Next year Alberta will go back to the state of dryness which existed until 1892.

From almost every corner of the province and even some of the district which were regarded as wet strongholds, the results were the same and it was only in a few that the liquor forces gained any majorities. The decision was pronounced and definite. The majority for the bill will be difficult to accurately estimate until the returns from all the outlying districts are received, but with the last of the returns which were received last night the majority was placed at over 20,000. As far as could be ascertained the province went dry by vote of 2 to 1.

In Calgary and Edmonton probably the greatest surprises were experienced. It was expected by many that the cities would more or less go strong against the bill, but in both Calgary and Edmonton the "drys" were dominant.

Of the cities of the province, Lethbridge was the only one which gave a majority to the forces of the license victuallers. Lethbridge city gave the "wets" a margin of over two hundred votes.

The new liquor age, which comes into force on July 1, 1916 abolishes 320 hotel, club and wholesale liquor licenses in the province. No liquor can then be bought in Alberta except for medicinal, scientific or sacramental purposes. For these purposes liquor will be handled by dispensaries under control of the government. The act, however, does not prevent individuals importing liquor for their own use from outside of the province. The act provides for no compensation for those who lose their licenses.

The fight was the hardest campaign of its kind ever held in the province. For the "wets" C.A. Windle, of Chicago, has been touring the province for some weeks, and has been assisted by other speakers. For the "drys" Rev. F.W. Patterson, of the First Baptist church, Edmonton, took a leading part campaigning all over the province, while others who assisted him were Ben S. Spence, Toronto, Mrs. Nellie McClung, late of Toronto and now of Edmonton and Clinton S. Howard of Rochester.

July 22, 1915

In 1915, the government of Alberta decided to let women vote. The year before, campaigners for women's suffrage had presented the government with a petition bearing 50,000 signatures. As the following editorial shows, The Herald, like the rest of Alberta, took the change calmly.

Premier Sifton's announcement that the full provincial suffrage would be granted to women is a natural evolution of events. It has been apparent for quite a while past that the time for female suffrage in Alberta was at hand.

Exactly what the scope of the measure will be is as yet uncertain. The question is raised as to whether or not women will have the right to be elected to sit in the legislature. Even should such be the case, The Herald does not believe that any harm would be done to the public interest. There are quite a number of bogies in the world, one of which has been the fear lest women if permitted to participate in public affairs would proceed to make a mess of them and disrupt any legislative body with which they were connected. Experience of women serving as school trustees and in other municipal offices has upset that idea. The fundamental question in connection with woman suffrage is not the possible effect it may have upon public matters, but the possible effect it may have on the character of the women themselves and their highest usefulness in the world. That question can only be solved by time and experience.

September 20, 1915

The Alberta Provincial Police enforced the prohibition law. They swept bootleggers and moonshiners into their net, and occasionally, with some simple undercover work, they caught a doctor.

Dr. Albert Rose was found to have been guilty of illegally issuing a prescription for an imperial quart of Scotch whiskey in the city police court this morning, and fined $50 and costs with the option of 30 days imprisonment. The doctor paid, but strongly protested that he had issued the prescription for medicinal purposes, thinking the alleged "Mr. Jones" was in danger of a chill enroute to Banff on a fishing trip.

The court held that a full quart was probably more than sufficient for one first-class chill and that an anticipated chill on a fishing trip was not purely an emergency.

Provincial Detective J.F. Tiderington testified that on the evening of July 6, he and Corporal Norsworthy went to the doctor's office near the Holy Cross Hospital and that (Tiderington) said they were contemplating a fishing trip to Banff and desired all the liquor they could get under prescription to make the trip more enjoyable. He also stated that it was likely to be a chilly morning and the cup that cheers would do much towards the comfort of the expedition.

He testified that the doctor asked him whether he wanted Scotch or Irish whisky, and informed him that he could get a full imperial quart on the prescription at almost any drug store. Tiderington expressed a preference for Scotch and got the same, and the result of the prescription was shown in court, it had been filled with no difficulty.

Dr. Rose went on the stand in his own defence and declared he issued the prescription because he thought Jones was "likely to have a chill" and had no intent that the liquor should be used as a beverage.

July 13, 1918

The year 1919 may have been the high-water mark for Canadian labor radicalism. The One Big Union held its organizing meeting in Calgary, of all places. The OBU, impatient with American-style trade unions that concentrated on the bread-and-butter concerns of their own trade, wanted to organize the whole working class.

The most momentous things that have happened in the annals of the labor movement in Canada occurred this morning at the interprovincial conference at the Paget Hall, when every delegate present voted solidly for breaking away from international affiliation, subject to the approval of the general membership of the delegates' respective unions.

This very definite pronouncement was received with the utmost enthusiasm, wild cheering being continued for a lengthy period.

Not only this, but a new organization was formed, subject to a referendum, with equal gusto, to embrace the whole of the workers. It will be known as "The One Big Union."

Several other important resolutions were adopted, mostly without discussion. These included freedom of speech and the lifting of the ban on certain literature, and the release of political prisoners; the expression of an open conviction that the system of industrial soviet control by the election of representatives from industries was more effective than the present system of government: the demand for a 6-hour work day of five days a week: and sympathy with the Russian Bolshevik and German Spartacan revolutions.

The convention considered a recommendation of the committee in connection with Soviet control. This read:

"Whereas, holding the belief in the ultimate supremacy of the working class in matters economic and political, and that the light of modern developments have proved that the legitimate aspirations of the labor movement are repeatedly obstructed by the existing political forms, and clearly show the capitalistic nature of the parliamentary machinery, this convention expresses its open conviction that the system of industrial Soviet control by selection of representatives from industries is more efficient and of greater political value than the present form of government."

This resolution was adopted with loud cheering and without discussion.

Another recommendation of the committee which was unanimously adopted and without debate read:

"That the interest of all members of the working class being identical, that this body of workers recognizes no alien but the capitalist; also that we are opposed to any wholesale immigration of workers from various parts of the world and who would be brought here at the request of the ruling class."

The resolution demanding a six-hour work day, five days a week, to come into effect on June 1 this year, was adopted by the conference with acclamation.

March 14, 1919

The Year After the War

While statesmen negotiated the peace terms they would dictate to the defeated Central Powers, and laid the basis for the League of Nations, ordinary citizens returned to their peacetime pursuits. The year after the war was not an especially good time, except by comparison with what had gone before. The Winnipeg General Strike dissolved in bloodshed, but worst of all was the worldwide epidemic of Spanish influenza, which killed nearly 22 million people — millions more than the war had. In those days before antibiotics, many died not of the flu itself, but of pneumonia and other complications. In Calgary, public health authorities did what they could — little enough — to stop the spread of the disease.

Masks like these, worn by High River telephone operators, were compulsory in the influenza epidemic of 1918. They may have slowed the spread of the deadly infection.

Theatres, dance halls, public libraries, pool rooms, and all such centres of congregation will be closed throughout the city tonight, as a preventive measure against the spread of Spanish influenza. Notices to this effect are being sent out by the health department this afternoon, and it is expected that all such will be distributed by 5 o'clock.

There were several more influenza cases reported this morning as supposed cases of the Spanish type, but these, like the others, have developed none of the genuine Spanish symptoms of the disease. The amendment to the Public Health Act, announced yesterday, does not require that more than modified quarantine be given the disease.

The officials say that unnecessary alarm is being aroused in the city which is not warranted by conditions although they urge that precautions be not relaxed for a moment.

October 18, 1918

People were required to wear cheesecloth masks on streetcars and in other public places. Merchants advertised disinfectants, and the city made plans to spread disinfectant on main streets. By October 25, two weeks after the outbreak began, 400 cases had been reported in Calgary, but there were certainly more. Two hundred had already recovered and been released from quarantine. By the end of October, 67 deaths had been reported. The city's hospitals, nurses and doctors were hard-pressed, and there was worse to come.

There are about 60 doctors in the city, and it is reported that some 14 of these are confined to their homes through illness, though it is not stated that all have the "flu". Another physician stated this morning that there were 11 doctors down with the disease.

In future, the doctors will not answer calls after midnight except for emergency and maternity cases. They wish the citizens to put their calls in as early as possible, so that they will be able to obtain a reasonable amount of rest.

A large shipment of the influenza vaccine is expected to arrive in the city at any time. Dr. Mahood is constantly receiving requests from various points in the province for supplies of this. He wired to Toronto this morning for a still further supply.

Owing to the large number of cases in homes where there are several children, the Children's Aid Society has been asked to take charge of a large number of juveniles. In most cases the children have not as yet contracted the influenza, and are not expected to do so providing they can be taken and cared for properly. The society appealed to the mayor and commissioners this morning for money to fit out the Stanley Jones School on the north hill, which will be put in charge of a matron.

Volunteer nurses are greatly needed at present and if 50 offered their services this afternoon they could all be utilized at once. Either unmarried women or women without children are needed who could devote either all or part of their time to helping the regular graduate nurses and doctors. Medical Health Officer Dr. C.A. Mahood this morning signed an order commandeering the Good Eats Cafe on Eighth avenue east. It is located immediately opposite the headquarters of the Red Cross and will be used mainly to supply soups, junkets and custards, which will be distributed where needed. So far soup has been the main nourishment distributed, but custards and junket will also form part of the regular supplies from now on.

The court house presented a peculiar appearance this morning, lawyers and witnesses in and about the building all having the regulation "flu" mask, while in the courtrooms the judges were scarcely recognizable behind the cheesecloth with which their features were draped.

The police are endeavoring to compel pedestrians to wear the mask, and are no respecters of persons, a judge of the Supreme court having been tapped on the shoulder by a constable as he entered a barber shop, and ordered to wear the regulation covering.

October 28, 1919

In outlying areas, where there were small hospitals, if any, conditions were far worse. A volunteer nurse in the little coal-mining town of Wayne, near Drumheller, wrote the following letter to a relative.

"I am sitting up in bed writing this. I am so tired I could not be on my feet any longer. This is a terrible place.

"Our hospital only holds eight beds, and, of course, there are only two of us now to look after these cases, and they are pneumonia cases. It is a pitiful sight, and the other nurse is very ill and is lying in a fearful old box addition to the hospital. We cannot do anything with her and her sister had a breakdown, so I was left in charge of the hospital until someone found a German person to come and help me out.

"I was up at 5 o'clock this morning to look after the sick workmen, and Mike Newas is dying tonight. I had to get the little German to help him to the garret and put him on a board stretcher, as there is nowhere to put him. Poor thing, he is a great big Slav, with a mop of black hair, and he has been suffering agonies. I think one of the girls will help the little man to nurse him in the garret tonight.

"Three women died here last night, and there are families upon families all laid down, without any care, but we cannot do any more. I am all right so far. Tonight I looked into an old picture gallery and one or two boys have been looking after the people there, but it is pitiful. That place is packed full of men, some with pneumonia, and some dying, and there is no place to put them. They screamed 'Oh nurse, come and help us.' I was nearly falling over as I had not sat down since 5 that morning.

"Some of those chaps were down on their knees praying, and one poor young man, about 17, was lying on the floor, on a coat, with his shoes and socks off. I don't think he will live. I sent them a great bottle of cough medicine and fever tablets, but cannot do anything, and I expect they will pass away.

"I am going to try to make the poor wretches some soup, and have someone take it down to them. I think some of them are starving to death. There is no place we can get milk, the milk people are all sick, and the women passed away last night. I will not be able to stick to this much longer. There are only two of us among all this, and we have outside patients by the score. We want six nurses and three doctors.

"Don't get the flu."

October 30, 1918

By December 23, the epidemic seemed to be past its peak. Fewer new cases were reported. However, the pneumonia season had arrived, and on Monday before Christmas local undertakers reported 27 flu deaths since noon the previous Saturday. There were nearly 250 flu cases in the hospitals, and more victims were confined to their homes. Then the disease faded out as quickly as it had struck. By January 28, 1919, The Herald noted that "According to the health authorities, Spanish influenza seems to have quit the city entirely. But before we begin to boast about this fact we had better touch wood."

The first trans-Atlantic flight was made by John Alcock, an Englishman, and Arthur W. Brown, a Scot. (Charles Lindbergh, who made his more famous flight in 1927, was the first to make the flight alone.) Alcock and Brown shared a $10,000 prize offered by the London Daily Mail, and both were knighted. Alcock was killed a few months later in a plane crash.

Captain John Alcock and Lieut. Arthur Brown, in their Vickers-Vimy biplane, landed at Clifden, Ireland, Sunday morning, completing the first non-stop airplane flight across the Atlantic. Their trip from St. John's Nfld., was made in 16 hours and 12 minutes.

The landing was made at 9:40 o'clock, British summer time. In taking the ground the machine struck heavily and the fusilage plowed itself into the sand. Neither of the occupants were injured. Much of the flight was through a fog, with an occasional drizzle. This hampered the airmen considerably during their journey.

Describing the experiences of himself and Lieut. Brown, Capt. Alcock, in a message from Galway to the Daily Mail says:

"We had a terrible journey. The wonder is we are here at all. We scarcely saw the sun, or moon, or stars. For hours we saw none of

them. The fog was very dense and at times we had to descend within 400 feet of the sea.

"For four hours our machine was covered with a sheet of ice caused by frozen sleet. At another time the fog was so dense that my speed indicator did not work and for a few minutes it was very alarming.

"We looped the loop, I do believe, and did a very steep spiral. We did some very comic stunts, for I had no sense of horizon.

"We encountered no unforeseen conditions. We did not suffer from cold or exhaustion, except when looking over the side; then the sleet chewed bits out of our faces. We drank coffee and ale and ate sandwiches and chocolate.

"Our flight has shown that the Atlantic flight is practicable, but I think it should be done, not with an airplane or a seaplane, but with flying boats. We had plenty of reserve fuel left, using only two-thirds of our supply."

The Vickers-Vimy machine, which completed the trans-Atlantic flight, has a wing spread of only 67 feet and is equipped with two 350-horse power Rolls-Royce engines, said to be capable of developing a speed of more than 100 miles an hour.

London, June 16, 1919

The Canadiens played an exhibition game against the local hockey all-stars. The Herald's sports writer did what he could for the local boys, who were on the wrong end of a very lop-sided score.

Four thousand Calgarians were given a glimpse of Stanley Cup hockey last night when George Kennedy's highly polished Canadiens, led by the redoubtable Newsey Lalonde, used a local team of All-Stars as a foil for their brilliant and scientific exposition of the sport. The score of 12 to 1 was only an incident to the game. That it became quite one-sided as the struggle surged along into its dying moments was a condition that did not cause much heart-burning among the enthusiastic spectators.

It was not a partisan crowd. Rather it was one which attended the game for the purpose of seeing a finished, smoothly work-

ing professional team, of championship calibre, in action. The fans and fanettes were not disappointed. They witnessed an exhibition of clean-cut hockey skill that will be regarded locally as setting a standard to be emulated.

They saw Lalonde the peerless in action, and he lived squarely up to the reputation that had come ahead of him. His bursts of speed, his superb stick-handling and his cool calculated attacks, frequently fatal in respect to bulging the nets awakened in the spectators a sincere admiration. There were no false motions and no wasted energy.

Indeed the same might be said of the entire Canadien team. While they attacked with the utmost vigor and repulsed onslaughts with equal energy, there was method in their offensive and in their defensive. In point of mechanical skill, they were letter perfect. Their defence dove-tailed into their offence and never could a Calgary skater get a clear right-of-way.

However, it was this science, plus speed and scoring ability, which the Calgary crowd paid to see and the unanimous opinion was that they got more than their money's worth, which is an excellent impression to take away from any match.

What struck the spectators perhaps most forcibly, was the easy flow of players on the Canadiens' team. There was what might be termed a fluidity about their entire play that excited the warmest praise. Nothing stiff or brittle was to be observed. The whole aggregation moved easily and gracefully. It was poetry of motion combined with hundred per cent efficiency in scoring and in preventing the other fellows from scoring.

March 15, 1919

Captain Fred McCall, the Calgary air ace, gave flying exhibits after the war. On one occasion at least, he showed the skill and steady nerve that had made him Canada's fourth-ranking fighter pilot.

Capt. Fred McCall, D.S.O., M.C., D.F.C., and the two young sons of Manager E.L. Richardson, of the Calgary exhibition, as well as scores of other people, escaped death or injury by a hair's breadth Saturday evening, when Capt.

When air ace Fred McCall had to make a forced landing at the Calgary exhibition midway, he chose the only safe place — the top of the merry-go-round. There were no injuries.

McCall's airplane was wrecked on top the merry-go-round just west of the race track.

Capt. McCall was forced to make a sudden landing immediately after leaving the field either by the accidental cutting off of his power or a sudden shift in wind.

Compelled to make a lightning decision between colliding with wires over the motordome, dropping in the midst of a crowd of people in the midway, where scores would have been killed and injured, or alighting on top the merry-go-round, Capt. McCall chose the latter instantly. The same judgment and cool nerve which made him victor over more than thirty-five Hun airplanes in France brought the young airman and his youthful passengers safely through the thrilling experience on the Calgary exhibition grounds without even a scratch.

Herbert Richardson, aged 13, and Ronald Richardson, aged 11, were sitting in the passengers' seat in the airplane when it flopped on top of the merry-go-round.

Among those watching the flight was E.L. Richardson, manager of the fair, whose two young sons were in the airplane. When he saw an accident was about to occur, Mr. Richardson ran with all his might for the scene, fighting his way through the crowd of thousands that quickly surrounded the place.

His eldest son saw him coming, and when he arrived near enough to hear, shouted to him:

"We're all right, Dad."

"Right ahead of me," said Capt. McCall, "was the race track around which the racing motor cars were going then at full speed. To land there was impossible without a terrible accident. On the other hand, farther ahead was another bunch of wires over the motordrome. I saw that in the short space I had to go, it would be impossible to put on the power sufficiently to cause the machine to rise and clear those wires. It was either land or hit them. At the same time, I saw no place to land except in the crowd in the midway or on top of the merry-go-round.

July 7, 1919

The Winnipeg General Strike of 1919 lasted six weeks; it climaxed in a bloody riot between strikers and police on "Black Sunday," June 21, 1919. Five days later the strike was called off. It had begun with the refusal of employers to bargain with metal-workers' and building-trades councils, each representing a group of unions. The employers wanted to negotiate with one union at a time. Sympathy strikes spread to a number of other cities, including Calgary, but the most dramatic events took place in Winnipeg, as the following account, compiled from three Herald stories, shows.

In a desperate street battle arising out of the strike, one man shot dead Saturday afternoon, more than thirty were wounded, two probably fatally, and three hundred prisoners were lodged in the cells at the city police station.

The Riot Act was read and mounted police and military were called out in aid of civil authorities. Militiamen with fixed bayonets were under orders to keep Main street clear of pedestrians right from Portage avenue to the C.P.R. subway.

Scenes of disorder, unparalleled in the history of Winnipeg, precipitated military control, though the city is not actually under martial law. Martial law has not been proclaimed, and the reading of the Riot Act does not automatically bring it into effect.

Twenty-four wounded lie in the General hospital, two are expected to die. Three more are in St. Boniface hospital, and several in the Military hospitals and police stations. Machine guns and cavalry are posted in the streets, and an airplane, loaned by the military, is keeping watch from air until night fall.

The strikers were organized for riotous disturbance and for killing. They were at first directed by a man with a whistle. The whistle was used to signal that the mounted police were charging, and every time it sounded the strikers ducked for the side streets and closed in again after the mounted men had passed.

Strikers armed with pistols, stood upon nearby roofs and fired into the mob, wounding several returned soldiers and special policemen.

The heat of the battle occurred right on Main street in front of city hall. The strikers having previously given notice of their determination to parade great throngs gathered upon the sidewalks on both sides of Main street. At 2:30 the parade began to line up, and the R.N.W.M.P. under Inspector Mead, acting under orders from Ottawa to prevent any parades in Winnipeg cantered north on Main street and passed through the crowd.

They wheeled at Alexander avenue and started south again just as a street car going north was intercepted by the strikers, its crew forced from the car and the car windows smashed. The strikers were trying to overturn the car when the police charged, the mounted men rode again through the crowd, which parted as its signal whistle blew, and immediately closed in behind the redcoats again.

After a few minutes, sticks, bricks and bottles began to fly through the air. The Allies' jitney bar was raided and every bottle taken out for use as a missile.

Missiles were thrown at the redcoats, and at this stage Mayor Gray read the Riot Act from the steps of the city hall and the police were ordered to use their revolvers instead of the baseball bats they had used up to that stage.

Two salvos of revolver shots rang out in rapid succession and the crowds fled in all directions.

The police charged the crowds again and again, and finally succeeded in scattering them to the side streets. Special police were turned out to patrol the riot area from Portage to Higgins avenue on Main street. They were closely followed up by a squad of mounted police and Inspector Mead, in charge, stopped every hundred yards and re-read the riot act and warned everybody to be off the streets within thirty minutes or take the consequences.

Winnipeg, June 23, 1919

With the world once more at peace, this Herald editorial considered the prospect of future wars. Unfortunately, the modest hopes expressed in the editorial came to nothing.

Major-General McRae, an officer who has had exceptionally fine opportunities for observing the situation in Europe and of hearing the diverse and frequently conflicting views of leaders among the nations concerning their peace ideals, comes to us with a warning. We must not imagine democracy has won a great fight against autocracy and because there is in process of formation over in Paris a league of nations, that the millenium is at hand. It is possibly just as well that we should be told this; at times we are prone to become too optimistic following the long four years of struggle.

As a military man the major-general feels certain that while there is not likely to be another great war within the next half century, there will ultimately be more wars. He evidently has not the faith of some others who believe that with the formation of the league of nations will be ushered in a perpetual reign of peace. His doubt has justification. Human nature is much the same as it was before the European war and in its belligerent phase will no doubt reassert itself in time to come as it has in the past.

But though it may not be possible to altogether prevent future conflicts there is surely cause for hope that they may be both localized and minimized. It is inconceivable that among the great nations which have been warring during the past four years there should ever be found one which in years to come would willingly enter upon such another horrible conflict. The league of nations, once in full operation, will be a powerful aid in preventing such a calamity while the will of the people under the new and more dem-ocratic regime now being ushered in in every country, will be utterly opposed to a recurrence of such black disaster.

And after all, it will be the people who will decide the business. With no more secret treaties and with the masses in control of governments, we may rest assured that there will be predominating objection to any more fighting. War brings nothing but trouble and sorrow to the common people and for any other than defence purposes they want none of it. Under control of the league of nations it should be impossible for a conflict to start up as did the last one as a sudden conflagration. If there are disagreements they will be discussed and effort made to adjust them. Unsatisfactory as the outlook for the future may be it is infinitely more hopeful than it has ever been in this connection, for which cause we should be profoundly thankful.

February 1, 1919

THE CALGARY DAILY HERALD 5 O'CLOCK EDITION

CALGARY, ALBERTA, MONDAY, JUNE 28, 1926

FORTY-THIRD YEAR, No. 4712

MACKENZIE KING GOVERNMENT RESIGNED THIS AFTERNOON

Meighen Witholds Notice Of Action When Called on To Form New Gov't

Conservative Lobby Joyous Over Victory

Meighen and Stevens Centre Of Wild Ovation When Government Falls

GLOOM REIGNS IN THE LIBERAL CAMP

Highlights and Shadows of Dramatic Political Moves in Ottawa

In the Limelight at Ottawa Today

Rumored Liberal Leader Has Given Up Party Control

Earthquake in Mediterranean Area Is Felt

Districts Shaken from Italy to the New

NUMEROUS PERSONS REPORTED KILLED

Herald Telephone Service

For Election Information, After 7 p.m. Call M7481

For Business or Routine Calls, After 7 p.m. Call M6861

THE CALGARY DAILY HERALD 5 O'CLOCK EDITION

CALGARY, ALBERTA, TUESDAY, NOVEMBER 8, 1923

FORTIETH YEAR, No. 4905

CHIEF POLLS GIVE 25,131 "WET" MAJORITY

NOT MORE THAN 25,000 VOTES IN RURAL AREAS REMAIN TO BE COUNTED

Crowds Throng Street to Hear First Bulletins On the Liquor Plebiscite Through the Herald

NEWSPAPERS PLEAD FAIR TRIAL OF NEW LIQUOR LAWS

Provincial Returns

Regular Session to Frame New Liquor Law

THE CALGARY DAILY HERALD 5 O'CLOCK EDITION

CALGARY, ALBERTA, SATURDAY, MAY 21, 1927

FORTY-THIRD YEAR, No. 246

LINDBERGH SPANS ATLANTIC OCEAN IN GREATEST AERIAL EPIC

Lands Plane Paris

Lindbergh and His Mother

Odds of 10 to 3 Quoted Against Flier's Success

"Flying Fool" Wins Hearts Of Frenchmen

Last Trace Hostile Sentiment Vanishes as Airman

HOME TOWN IN U.S. PLANS CELEBRATION

LINDBERGH'S PLANE IN FLIGHT

Seeded Area Larger Than Anticipated

Wheat Seeding 85 to 100 Per Cent. Completed in South Alberta

MOISTURE PROMISES EXTRAORDINARY YIELD

BAROMETER STILL RISES; WIND N.E.

Despite Steady Rise of Glass, Wind Stays in Storm Direction

COLD HOLDS BACK SOUTHERN FLOOD

DE PINEDO WILL HOP OFF TONIGHT

Previous Flights Across The North Atlantic Ocean

Bellanca Plane to Start Early on Sunday Morning

Conservatives Not Planning Fusion to Beat Farmer Party

BED AWAITING FLIER IN PARIS

THE CALGARY DAILY HERALD 5 O'CLOCK EDITION

22 PAGES

FORTY-THIRD YEAR, No. 5416

LARGEST AIR LINER SPANS ATLANTIC

Canada Asks Board Of Imperial Jurists To Harmonize Laws

French Orator Final Winner Great Contest

Argentine Lad Second, and Wm. Fox, of Canada, Given Third Place

CLOSEST MARKINGS ANY CONTEST YET

Equality of Status Basis of Agreement

Would Be Used to Reconcile Differences Between Various Gov'ts

Makes Historic Ocean Flight

Graf Zeppelin Big Business

FORTY NEW SCHOOL AREAS IN ALBERTA

More than 5,000 School Rooms Operating Now, Department States

Threshing Machines Humming

WOMAN DROWNS UNDER CAR AS HUSBAND FAILS IN FRANTIC RESCUE

THE CALGARY DAILY HERALD 5 O'CLOCK EDITION

22 CALGARY, ALBERTA, MONDAY, JUNE 3, 1929

FORTY-SIXTH YEAR, No. 5816

22 PAGES

HUNDREDS OF CITY HOMES MENACED BY RIVERS

Baldwin Gov't Votes to Hand In Resignation

Cabinet Confers Monday Decides to Ask King for Official Release

MacDONALD TO AGAIN TRY MINORITY GOV'T

For Second Time in Five Years British Labor Will Try to Carry On

Ghost River Dam Menaced by Floods

Worst Floods Since '02 Ravage Calgary And South Districts

All Residential Areas Near Rivers Are Completely Covered Monday

Bowness and St. George's Parks Wrecked—Animals At Zoo Drowned

Rivers Still Rising On Monday Afternoon

Two Streams Pouring Flood Waters Over Big Sections of the City

Twenty-Fifth Avenue Bridge Is Washed Out

THE SITUATION AT A GLANCE

THE CALGARY DAILY HERALD 5 O'CLOCK EDITION

CALGARY, ALBERTA, FRIDAY, OCTOBER 18, 1929

FORTY-SIXTH YEAR, No. 5725

Five Alberta Women Win in Senate Claim

WIN IMPORTANT CASE

Canada Supreme Court Decision Is Overruled

Privy Council Judgment Goes Thoroughly Into Question Of Women's Rights

Where Premier Is Guest at Capital

British Experts Say World Wheat Stocks Ample for 1930 Need

Canned Big Carry-Over Will Take Care of Requirements

Storage Facilities Of Continent Choked

Early Retirement Of Labor Chieftain Not Thought Likely

Judgment on Rates Appeal Case Reserved

SASKATCHEWAN DIFFERS ON MOUNTAIN TARIFFS

Manitoba, Ontario and the Railways Opposed to Granting Requests

HEAVIEST RAIN IN YEARS STRIKES SOUTHERN ALBERTA

Bow and Elbow Rivers Continue to Rise Far Above Danger Levels

MRS. MURPHY SAYS DECISION HELPS NATIONAL UNITY

Breakwater and Pier To Be Built by Gov't At Gull Lake in Winter

Labor Chief Sworn in as Canada P.C.

The Weather
HERE AND ELSEWHERE

SHOWERY

A Fleeting Golden Age

1920-29

The Roaring Twenties: the age of jazz, the age of flight, the age of the automobile, the age of radio. Gangsters, bootleggers, and bathtub gin. Fast cars, flappers with bobbed hair, and Scott Fitzgerald's sad, rich young men. A frenzy of money-making on the stock exchange, ending overnight in the shattering crash of October, 1929. A decade with flavor.

A reader glancing through some 3,000 editions of The Herald from the Twenties would find a somewhat quieter story. The great events and some of the larger lunacies were duly recorded, but they were islands in the flood of day-to-day business and politics. Calgary slowly recovered from the war and the short depression that followed. Alberta elected a new government, which, true to the Alberta pattern, would rule for a long time and then vanish with hardly a trace. Canada, with a new confidence born in the Great War, cut many of the remaining ties with the British Empire and became, for most practical purposes, an independent nation. The Twenties also saw the rise of Canada's most durable politician, Prime Minister William Lyon Mackenzie King.

On the international scene, statesmen tended a troubled peace and negotiated treaties which, they hoped, would prevent another world war. The fascist dictator, Benito Mussolini, came into power in Italy. An obscure demagogue, Adolf Hitler, made a comic-opera attempt to seize control of Germany.

The Twenties began slowly for Calgary. In 1921, the population was 63,000; in five years that followed it grew by scarcely 2,000. Farm prices had dropped after the war, and Calgary's prosperity depended on farming. The oil business was still tiny and uncertain, and it had trouble finding investors. The upturn was gradual, fueled largely by better crops and better prices. In 1927, Alberta farmers' wheat income reached a peak that wouldn't be equalled until 1945. The oil business, too, began to look more promising. In October, 1924, the spectacularly productive Royalite No. 4 blew in.

The trade in oil stocks became brisk again. Speculators here also shared in the huge, though short-lived, profits to be made on the American exchanges. By 1929, prosperity was clearly in sight once more. That year the CPR added to its Palliser Hotel, the Bay doubled the size of the store, and Eaton's built its downtown store. The value of building permits reached $11 million, more than half of what it had been in the record year of 1912. The 1931 census showed Calgary's population as nearly 84,000; most of that growth (from 65,000 in 1926) probably took place before the crash of 1929.

Alberta as a whole moved through the same cycle of postwar depression, renewed hope, prosperity and collapse. Crops were poor from 1919 through 1922. Dry weather forced many farmers to sell out and look for literally greener fields.

In the middle of this bad time, a new force emerged in Alberta politics. The United Farmers of Alberta had been founded in 1909, but until 1921 the organization had been content to act as a pressure group on Alberta's Liberal government. That year the UFA, which had enrolled one-third of the province's farmers, lost its patience. It ran its own candidates, and won three times as many seats as the Liberals. The cities elected four Labor candidates who were generally sympathetic to the UFA. The Herald, which had warned darkly against the UFA and "government by a single class," had trumpeted the Conservatives as "the new force in Alberta politics," an opinion that was about 50 years ahead of its time.

The UFA victory was especially remarkable considering how deeply its leader distrusted party politics. Henry Wise Wood had become president of the UFA in 1916. An American, he had moved to Alberta the year of provincehood, when he was 45, and became a Canadian citizen in 1911. He held that farmers should act co-operatively to defend themselves against the exploiters who surrounded them; but he did not believe that farmers or any other interest group, should try to form a government. In 1921, Wood's followers swept past that article of his faith. Wood himself never ran for office. Herbert Greenfield was chosen the first UFA premier.

The roar of the Twenties was fueled partly by gasoline. By 1925, Alberta had 65,000 cars, and the number was rising quickly. The Herald devoted two or three pages a week to advice and advertisements intended for would-be motorists. (One local dealer warned against buying little-known makes that would soon vanish from the market. He had a Studebaker franchise.) Most of the roads were terrible, and would remain so for 20 or 30 years. A drive to Banff and back was a long day's adventure, enlivened by mudholes and flat tires.

Cars brought Alberta into fleeting contact with the world of Dillinger and Capone and Bonnie and Clyde. Occasionally robbers roared north across the American border to crack safes in small-town banks. More often, cars loaded with booze roared south across the border into a thirsty United States which had opted for prohibition in 1919. (Albertans, who had voted for prohibition during the war, threw it out in 1923.) One bootlegger, Emilio Picariello, was a man of some standing in the Crowsnest Pass area. He and a woman accomplice were hanged for shooting a Mountie who chased them while they were making a liquor run.

Pilots back from the war, men like Wop May and Fred McCall, pioneered commercial aviation in Alberta. They flew forest fire patrols and delivered urgent supplies to isolated settlements. Some toured country fairs, thrilling crowds with stunt flying, and taking the more affluent and adventurous up for a short flight in an open cockpit. By 1928, larger planes were making regular passenger flights between Regina, Calgary and Edmonton. This airline may not have been as comfortable as the train, but it was somewhat faster, and much more dashing.

In 1920, Prime Minister Robert Borden resigned, exhausted by the war and the peace conferences. He was succeeded by another Conservative, Arthur Meighen. In the 1921 elections the Conservatives lost heavily. The Liberals' new leader, Mackenzie King, formed a minority government. Supported by the Progressives, who were gentle radicals of the UFA stripe, King managed to last out the Twenties as a minority prime minister, even surviving a nasty, complicated parliamentary crisis in 1926.

King was no activist, no innovator. In the 1920s, federal spending actually decreased while the provinces' spending doubled. The old age pension bill of 1927 was an exception, introduced under pressure from the Progressives. King excelled as a survivor. As the poet F.R. Scott wrote,

Truly he will be remembered
Wherever men honor ingenuity,
Ambiguity, inactivity and political longevity.

Much of King's ingenuity in the 1920s was devoted to weaning Canada from the British Empire. At the 1923 Imperial Conference, he won a declaration that the conference was a meeting of separate governments, not an Imperial cabinet. The 1926 conference declared that all nations within the Commonwealth enjoyed individual status. In 1928, London appointed a high commissioner — effectively an ambassador — to Canada, replacing the governor-general as the principal channel between Ottawa and the British government. Such were King's accomplishments in the Twenties.

In 1929, a group of five Alberta women won a ruling that women are persons in the eyes of the law, and are thus

Downtown Calgary in the Twenties: Eighth Avenue and First Street West before the south half of the Bay was built.

qualified to be senators. The Supreme Court of Canada had ruled against them, but they won by appeal to the British Privy Council. (Such an appeal was a remnant of the Imperial past that was later swept away.) Alberta women were by that time experienced campaigners for reform — earlier they had been a driving force behind prohibition.

In the world at large, the Twenties were a time of great accomplishment and wonderful nonsense. Two Canadians, Frederick Banting and Charles Best, discovered the insulin treatment for diabetes. A Scottish bacteriologist, Alexander Fleming, discovered penicillin. Charles Lindbergh flew alone across the Atlantic; a year later, in 1928, Amelia Earhart did the same. A new generation of American novelists flourished: Sinclair Lewis (*Babbitt*), Scott Fitzgerald (*The Great Gatsby*), Ernest Hemingway (*The Sun Also Rises*.) In Europe, Thomas Mann published *The Magic Mountain*, and James Joyce, *Ulysses*. Radio and the phonograph spread popular songs across the continent: *Makin' Whoopee, Tea for Two, Stardust, Tiptoe Through The Tulips, Yes, We Have No Bananas.* Everyone was playing a new game, mah-jongg. Women swooned over Rudolph Valentino, the last of the great silent-movie stars, and wept at his funeral. (Mussolini sent a wreath.) The first experimental television broadcasts were made, and the movies learned to talk, their first words uttered by Al Jolson in *The Jazz Singer*. Mickey Mouse and Alfred Hitchcock made their first films.

Sports buffs still remember the Twenties as a golden age. Jack Dempsey, Gene Tunney, and Luis Firpo were just some of the decade's top boxers. Babe Ruth, also known as "The Bambino" and "The Sultan of Swat," had a spectacular season in 1917, hitting 60 home runs for the New York Yankees. Red Grange and Knute Rockne were famous names in football. Nels Stewart, Frank Nighbor and Howie Morenz played some great hockey. Even golf caught on as a sport to be watched rather than played: Walter Hagen, Bobby Jones and Gene Sarazen were among the top pros. Johnny Longden, a coal-miner's son from Alberta, started his record-breaking career as a jockey. Percy Williams, a 19-year-old Canadian schoolboy, won a spectacular victory in the sprints at the 1928 Olympics.

All through the twenties, statesmen tried to learn the lessons of the Great War, tried to ensure that another would never be fought, tried to adjust the consequences of the harsh peace imposed on Germany — all, of course, without yielding too much of their own nations' interests. In little enough time, all these efforts would be mocked by another world war.

In 1921, Germany was ordered to pay the Allies $33 billion in reparations for damage done by the war. The Germans' protests that the payments would wreck its already battered economy were ignored. In 1923, France occupied the Ruhr, her old enemy's industrial heartland, to enforce payments. That year, inflation ran wild in Germany. Postage stamps sold for billions of marks; workers were paid daily, because money lost much of its value literally overnight. A committee of the principal allies, led by an American, Charles G. Dawes, then arranged aid to stabilize the German economy and set up a more realistic schedule of reparations payments.

Meanwhile, Adolf Hitler's thugs, the Brownshirts, were fighting in the streets with thugs from other parties. Hitler's attempted coup of 1923, the "beer-hall putsch," was an inglorious failure; he persisted, unfortunately, and a decade later he triumphed.

In 1925, Germany was treated for the first time as a friendly power; at the Locarno conference, the German government agreed to join the League of Nations, and signed a treaty with France and Belgium agreeing never to fight again. In 1928, 15 nations signed the Kellogg-Briand pact, renouncing war. Unfortunately, the pact provided no way to deal with the likes of Adolf Hitler. It came into effect in the hopeful year of 1929.

Lively Years in Alberta

CFAC, the first privately-owned radio station between Winnipeg and Vancouver, was established by The Herald (which no longer owns it.) After a few months of experimenting with the low-powered transmitter, the station officially went on the air with a 2,000-watt system. An anonymous Herald writer did his best to convey the wonder of the occasion.

To the sweetly modulated tones of the Salvation Army Silver Band, to the voice of a contralto soloist, to congratulatory messages sounded abroad through the ether from Mayor Adams and Frank Freeze, president of the Board of Trade, the big two kilowatt radio broadcasting machine of The Calgary Herald was officially and formally opened to thousands of listeners-in on Tuesday evening. Hundreds in Calgary heard the music and the spoken messages of congratulations; receiving sets from the Radio Corporation of Calgary, in the care of experts, were stationed in Lethbridge and Medicine Hat, and it is certain that for a radius of several hundred miles listeners-in caught every word and tone from the new broadcasting station of The Herald.

"I feel certain I express your wishes in thanking The Calgary Herald for the part it is playing in the development of this most useful art. I wish also to convey to my hearers who are not Calgarians the greeting and good wishes of the people of Calgary. I now have great pleasure in declaring this plant to be formally opened." Thus, Mayor Adams, at the close of a remarkably thoughtful speech, in which he traced briefly some of the wonderful developments of radio.

It was a wonderful scene for the imagination to conjure with as one sat and watched and listened. Here was a popular band, seated in a room scores of feet from the ground, and playing exquisite music – for whom? Apparently no one in particular. Outside on the roof top, one could glimpse a figure leaning against the parapet of the high building, silhouetted against the summer sky of deepening splendor. Someone was sitting on a window sill, listening intently. A small boy crouched on the steps leading into the room, absorbed in thought. That was all. Music for the summer air, with the lights of the city flashing up into the sky.

But in behind the dark green curtains, stood a machine, glittering with lights, gleaming on copper wires and reflecting back on the polished darkness of the electrical switches. Beside the machine stood the operator, with a pair of ear phones clamped over his head listening intently, his eye never leaving the electrical indicators.

Here was the secret of it all. This is the machine, which by long night vigils and patient strivings of scores of inventors, has been brought to the pitch of perfection whereby thousands might sit in their homes, by the fireside, and listen to the music broadcast into that yet unknown mystery the ether. The machine whereby men travelling in desert places may hook their receiving wires to trees and hear music and voices from the great centres of the earth.

The machine whereby men who go down to the sea in ships and do business in great waters may send out their messages when the ocean waves beat upon them, and they are hurrying down the gulfs to destruction. Messages that are caught up by listening ears and stout vessels leap forward to rescue and succor of shipwrecked men.

And the music on the roof of The Herald building, pouring in liquid notes from the polished instruments of the Salvation Army band; the sweet notes of the contralto singer; the swift bowing of the violinist, and the words that fell from the lips of Mayor Adams and Frank Freeze went in through that wide mouthed horn, traveled the wires to that glittering machine, passed in some wonderful manner through the vacuum tubes, out over the burnished copper wires, and up and out – out – out through the mysterious ether in long swelling waves.

Upwards and downwards and in all directions, penetrating every obstacle, through brick and stone and steel; out over the hills; out over the far lake waters; over mountain tops, over running rivers and roaring mountain torrents and deep, lonely forests; out until those mysterious waves, laden with music or the human voice, found a resting place on some simple piece of wire mysteriously tuned in with the delicate waves of ether-borne sound.

Others heard it not, it passed through them and over and around them, and only those in tune with the infinite could catch the message. And standing on the roof of the building, scores of feet above the earth, one could see those wires stretched from pole to pole, dumb and insignificant symbol of the two poles between which the human voice is destined to reach, traveling by a mystery which is yet elusive of human ken.

Wonder of the Twentieth century! Wonder of the ages! A wonder that even now has become a commonplace toy with the veriest ragamuffin of the streets, a wonder that is now passing into the ranks of those things which serve us every day, and the populace stands and waits; waits for the next child of the brains of science, and idly speculates on its achievements.

August 30, 1922

Radio won fans quickly, despite its technical shortcomings. Except for the simple crystal set, which a bright youngster could build, radios were an expensive luxury. A good receiver was as big a purchase for the average family as a color television set today.

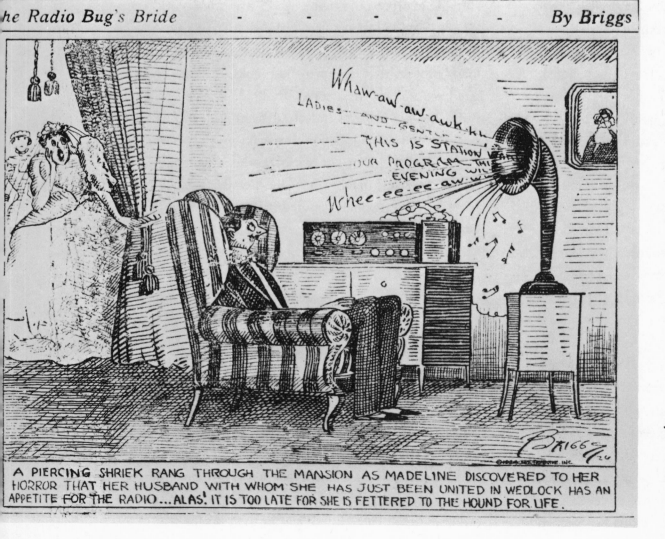

he Radio Bug's Bride - - - - - By Briggs

A PIERCING SHRIEK RANG THROUGH THE MANSION AS MADELINE DISCOVERED TO HER HORROR THAT HER HUSBAND WITH WHOM SHE HAS JUST BEEN UNITED IN WEDLOCK HAS AN APPETITE FOR THE RADIO...ALAS! IT IS TOO LATE FOR SHE IS FETTERED TO THE HOUND FOR LIFE.

In the early days of radio, there were far fewer stations contending on the same frequency, and CFAC's signal did indeed reach across mountains and forests. A Texas man heard the station on a simple crystal set, and more sensitive receivers picked up the Calgary station in Samoa and New Zealand.

In the 1915 alcohol plebiscite, prohibition won an easy victory after a quiet campaign. By 1920, sentiment was beginning to turn; a plebiscite that year decided that Albertans could order liquor by mail from outside the province. By 1923, temperance and pro-liquor forces were squaring off for a decisive battle, and Calgarians flocked to hear the following lively debate.

Prohibitionists and the users of alcoholic liquor as beverages, represented by Rev. Hugh Dobson, of Regina, and Dr. Michael Clark of Olds, respectively, met in strenuous and vigorous debate in the Victoria pavilion on Tuesday night, before an audience of at least 3,800 persons of both sexes, crammed into the building until scores stood in the aisles and alley way, and outside another five hundred roared and clamored for admittance, beating vainly on the doors with their fists, and then sending up rousing ironical cheers when they found their efforts of no avail.

So great was the press at the doors that the principals in the debate, including his worship Mayor George H. Webster, even found difficulty in obtaining admittance, the stolid policemen refusing to believe that the men on whom the meeting depended were not safe and sound within the building.

Considering the nature of the subject under debate, "Is prohibition desirable, attainable and calculated to be beneficial," the meeting was orderly and in general gave a patient hearing to both speakers, though toward the end, interruptions, particularly when Rev. Hugh Dobson was speaking, were many and frequent.

Once he was most unmercifully booed when, in illustrating his idea of liberty, taking physical exercise as his vehicle of explanation, his fists approached perilously close to the nose of Dr. Clark, and the crowd roared its wrath. Sympathetic cheers greeted Rev. Dobson when he asked if the roads of Alberta were to be paved with the hearts of women and the innocent bodies of the little innocent children.

Terrific cheers rose and thundered through the building when Dr. Michael Clark said in tones which echoed through the building, "The race of men has never been born who could say to Britishers, you must live as I want you to."

But the audience seemed to grow restless toward the end. Cries were heard for Dr. Clark to "Go on, go on" when his time was nearing conclusion, and when Rev. Hugh Dobson, under the rules laid down by the committee for the debate was given his last ten minutes of summing up, the immense audience could no longer be restrained, and the speaker's voice was finally drowned in an enthusiastic singing of the national anthem, and the people streamed from the pavilion joking and laughing as they went, apparently well satisfied with the value they had received for their humble and nimble quarters.

And so it came to an end. On the whole it was orderly and well conducted, and both men had a fair hearing. No decision was given, but it was evident that both sides had listened with care and absorbed the arguments presented by both sides with skill and intelligence.

Bootleggers stayed in business even after prohibition ended. The Alberta Provincial Police made this haul in the Crowsnest Pass in 1925. The sacks apparently contained raw material for an illegal still.

The Herald devoted two pages to the debate, including boxes giving the highlights of each speaker's position. Here are some of the points Clark made.

I believe it is undesirable to allow force to invade the region of morals for forced morality has no virtue at all.

Liberty is the method of God Himself in building great nations and great peoples.

Mr. Dobson can drink all the ginger ale he wants to; he can stand up to his neck in water all day long, for all I care. I won't bother him.

The steps of moral reform have been dogged by lawlessness and the lawbreaker has been made rich.

It's no use having law unless there is a strong public opinion behind it.

We sold last year in Alberta $2,500,000 of liquor to people on prescription. What a sick people we are!

If prohibition has done anything, it has driven an evil underground. We see and know this. What's the good of studying statistics in a cloister. We know the facts.

It used to be that farmers used to come to town to get drunk. Now they come in drunk. They own their stills.

The world was very wicked once and the good Lord made a covenant with Noah and promised that the people would never be drowned again. Now comes Dobson and his friends slopping their tanks of water all over the country.

When Noah came from the ark, we are told he got drunk. He found the vine all ready to hand. Who put it there?

Fermentation has been given to us by God, but evil is not in it, it is in the individual!

The man that takes a drink can look after his family as well as any teetotaller I ever met.

Mr. Dobson is a puritan born three hundred years too late.

And on the side of continued prohibition, Dobson made these points.

For more than a hundred years there has been a struggle toward prohibition in Canada.

The man in the street says that crime has greatly increased. I have figures to prove something different.

The sum total of crime from before the war until afterwards meant a decrease of eighty per cent.

With a decrease in crime, how do you account for the very serious assumption that a serious crime wave is sweeping the country?

What I have told you is very measurable evidence as to the attainability of prohibition in this country.

The police are bad, say the liquor interests. We have better police forces now than we ever had before. I have had a lot to do with them. (Loud and continuous laughter.)

I am as thirsty as any of you fellows, quoting from Hon. George Langley, but I am in favor of prohibition. (Terrific noise from the bull pen and a violent kicking on the door.)

I concede the charm of Dr. Michael Clark, but not his logic.

Under prohibition the people have more money to pay for their doctor's bills. (Ironical laughter.) But there is a tragedy behind this.

A revenue raised from appetite takes the burden from the wealthy and puts it on the shoulders of the men of moderate means.

After all, the root problem is deeper than all this. Are you going to risk your chances on the rising generation?

Are we to pave the roads of Alberta with broken hearts of women and the souls of little children?

February 28, 1923

Bathtub gin, Mount Royal style.

For more than an hour on Saturday morning inland revenue officers and city police brought crocks of whisky, buckets of gin and barrels of mash, as well as the complicated machinery of the biggest illicit still ever seized in Alberta, from the basement of a big house in South Mount Royal, where George Packwood Sr. and his son are alleged to have carried on moonshine operations.

The house, standing at 2917 8 Street west, is isolated. Perched on the top of the hill, it overlooks the Mount Royal Golf Club and Elbow Park. It is a few blocks south of Prospect Avenue and the big residential district on the hill.

With a capacity of from 75 to 100 gallons of liquor a day, the plant is declared by revenue officers to be by far the biggest ever grabbed in this province. The officers were almost dumbfounded at the complete layout they discovered when they entered the premises suddenly on Friday night. Packwood and his son were in the midst of operations and a great quantity of liquor was on hand. The plant takes up most of the room in the basement of the big house.

Packwood and his son had little to say when they were surprised in their distilling operations on Friday night. The elder member of the household is reported to have commented laconically that he voted for prohibition but made no other statement.

The product of the Packwood plant is declared to be of very high class, as moonshine goes. Their methods were very thorough and they left nothing undone. They manufactured quantities of gin, buckets of the liquor being removed from the basement where they were evidently awaiting bottling. The still produced large quantities of good alcohol, which was diluted and colored to make the finest lines of old Scotch whisky.

In the main part of the basement 12 great barrels of mash arrived and there was about 75 gallons of finished liquor ready for shipment.

May 12, 1923.

The Packwoods were fined a total of $1,868 for breaches of the Inland Revenue Act.

In the plebiscite of November, 1923, a record turn-out voted to have the provincial government sell liquor. On May 12 of the following year, provincial liquor stores opened. The Herald reported that trade was "quite meagre" at first, but evidently it picked up quickly.

The clerks were kept busy wrapping up samples of the government's bottled goods. By noon the shelves were beginning to look depleted. However, there is a big enough supply of liquor in the city to assure even the most nervous.

There was much merry jesting among the gay throng that besieged the vendor. Some of the applicants came in merely to purchase their permits, which they displayed to their friends with great glee, but the majority stayed to look over the stock and take away some samples.

Along first street west, it was a new spectacle to see a man trampling home with the familiar brown package, sometimes a bulky one that must have contained at least half a dozen bottles. The more opulent loaded their purchases into waiting automobiles.

The permits are very similar to those in use in British Columbia. They bear the signature of the holder in two places and expire at the end of the present year.

Few people took out the "beer only" permits which cost $1.00, as against the $2.00 for a general permit for the purchase of both beer and spirits.

Calgary along with the rest of Alberta woke up "wet" on Monday morning after an alcoholic drought of eight years, all but two months. The province entered the prohibition period in July 1916, after the vote of the year before. On November 5, 1923, the voters turned down prohibition for government control and the act has now been proclaimed.

Following a meeting on Sunday evening, local breweries announced a reduction in the price of beer from the prices announced at their first conference.

Draught beer will remain at $25 a barrel.

Case beer will be sold at the following prices:

Case of two dozen pints $4.20, less 60 cents on bottles, or a net price of $3.60, as against the net price of $4.15 as previously decided upon.

May 12, 1924

In 1923, the Calgary Stampede was combined with the Calgary Exhibition. The combination has been an annual event ever since, but it's been years since anyone rode a horse into a restaurant.

Way back about 1905, Alberta cowboys visiting Calgary gave up the practice of hitching their ponies on Eighth (then Stephen) avenue; the traffic became so congested that it was safer and more convenient to leave them in livery stables. But on Tuesday morning, July 10, 1923, they all came back, parked their chuck wagons in front of modern retail establishments between First street west and First street east, tied their horses outside dignified bank buildings; literally pitched camp on the main drag.

Late egg hunters in the Club cafe got a rude jolt when a black pony, with a kindly white splash down his face, wandered into the establishment, made his way down a row of stools, past the kitchen door and out through the tables, posing for a moment for The Herald staff photographer at the door. More than one nervous breakfaster hitched forward nearer the "two boiled" and offered up a silent prayer that the pony was not one of those he watched at the Stampede on Monday and dreamed about that night after eating an indigestible late supper.

But there was no cause for alarm. The pony was "Tony" and he was ridden by Ed King of Calgary. "Tony" is complete restaurant broke and even smiled at the cashier and reached over for the tooth picks. He was the guest of the management.

July 10, 1923

Chuckwagon breakfasts downtown during Stampede week are a tradition dating back nearly 60 years. The first downtown Stampede cheered up a city that had been suffering a recession ever since the end of the First World War.

When Jack Morton, the man who wears the brightest orange shirt yet exposed to view, galloped the CX chuck wagon down Eighth avenue on Friday morning, he started the final performance of the "Morning Stampede" in a way that Calgary will never forget. Just how many city bylaws and statutes were broken by the howling, whooping, rip-snorting bunch of cowboys that he brought with him will never be known; and it is not likely that anybody will ever inquire. It was just what the thousands of people who thronged the thoroughfare wanted.

Four plunging horses, dragging behind them a complaining chuck wagon, flanked by howling cow punchers who rode across the car tracks as if such modern improvements did not exist, made the turn around Traffic Officer Dan Finlayson, and pulled with a jerk on the south side of the avenue, between Centre street and First street west. Out came the old cookstove, and soon the pungent odor of wood smoke filled the air, to be followed shortly by the inviting aroma of sizzling hot cakes.

"Who wants em — Who's hungry?" queried the cook. They wanted them, and they were hungry. Spectators fought to get to the front in order to bite into the luscious flap-jacks that were being turned out by the outfit's cook.

It was the last "morning stampede" of the week, and the thousands who gathered to watch it were not disappointed. It is fine to sit up in the grandstand, clutching your reserved stub in your hand, and watching these cowboys perform at a distance. But it is a grand and glorious feeling to get right down with 'em. Calgary crowds demonstrated that they wanted to meet cowboys, talk to them, risk being kicked by their horses. They warmed to the personal touch.

The "morning stampedes" are responsible for putting new life into the citizens of Calgary.

Visitors were the first to appreciate the significance of these displays. Then the inhabitants began to wake up to the fact that after four years of slumber things were happening in their little old town. They donned their glad rags, took a hitch in their belts, and joined in the fun.

"I guess," remarked Fire Chief "Cappy" Smart, as he gave his Stetson another hitch to port, "that this is the turn."

July 13, 1923

In the early 1920's, long before the Canadian Wheat Board became a permanent
fixture, farmers had to accept prices set on
the Winnipeg Grain Exchange, an institution they deeply distrusted. Prices had dropped sharply since the temporary wheat
board, set up in 1917, was shut down in
1920. Farmers were ready to set up their
own marketing agency. Under pressure from
its members, the United Farmers of Alberta
promised to set up a provincial wheat pool.
The Herald, suspecting the UFA of foot-
dragging, and perhaps wanting to needle
the UFA government, took a hand. It en-
listed the aid of The Edmonton Journal,
and brought in a brilliant American co-op
organizer, Aaron Sapiro, to rally farmers to
the wheat pool. Even allowing for a
sponsor's pride, the following story suggests
that Sapiro was a real spell-binder.*

Alberta can be organized for a
wheat pool within thirty days. It
can be done. I am not telling you
of guess work. I have seen these movements
of co-operative marketing and it will go. I
never saw a province so ripe for it as this
one. Do this, men, and you are making the
greatest contribution to the world's freedom,
and in the right handling of its greatest commodity that has ever been."

Such was the ringing peroration of
Aaron Sapiro in closing an absorbingly brilliant speech on the burning subject of the
day, that of co-operatives marketing, before
a large audience in the Victoria pavilion on
Thursday night; an audience which literally
hung on every word the man spoke to them.
The two hours in which he spoke passed so
rapidly that few realized that this little,
black-haired, bright-eyed man had held
them in the thrall of his racy eloquence for
that length of time.

Without needless words or phrases or
platitudes, like the man of concentration
that he undoubtedly is, Mr. Sapiro went
straight to the heart of his subject.

His story of the wonderful organization
of the growers of Burley tobacco was like listening to a story of the magic of the genie
from the Arabian nights; he told of the
misery of those who were forced to take
what was offered them, and how, when
gaunt famine stared them in the face, they
made their tobacco pool, and in a few short
months sold their product at a price which
made them a fair return for their labor.

He made the startling comparison of the
average earnings of the California farmer
under co-operative marketing of $2,200 a
year, as against the pitiful income of $390 by
the tobacco grower of Kentucky. A storm of
cheers greeted him when he said he regarded
wheat not as wheat, or tobacco as tobacco,
but ordinary human life.

"It is human life," he declared, "it is the
whole standard of living. It means boots and
shoes and good food, and education and a
share in the better things of life. It is human.
I tell you co-operative marketing is a system
which works with specialties and it works
with national products. It has never failed
with any commodity if applied with the
right principles. You must have your aim,
the right technique, and the right man. You
have the right men, and the rest can be
done."

He told of the intricacies of the wheat
markets of the world, and how those who
handled these markets, thought not of
locality, but of commodity.

He emphasized the fact that today
Canada is the key to the wheat markets of
the world, and if Canada organizes right it is
on the way to reasonable prosperity for all
the nation.

"Remember," he said in encouragement,
"you do not need to contract all the wheat
in the world to get the right prices. But it
will eliminate most of the gambling, and all
there is left will be so small it will not hurt
you."

"Do this," he said, "and it will be the
greatest contribution ever made to life, and
Alberta can do it, for you have the government behind you, you have the farmers' organizations and you have the press and you
have the merchants."

Aaron Sapiro made a wonderful impression on his audience. The man is an evangelist, consumed with zeal for the cause he is
engaged in. He fires the imagination with
the thought of the possibility of what might
be. He seems to be not only the prophet of a
new age, but a prophet who fulfils his own
words.

August 3, 1923

*The UFA got busy two weeks later, and
signed up nearly half the 1923 wheat crop
for a voluntary pool that would hold out for
better prices. The Alberta Wheat Pool had
been born.*

What price safety?

When is a canary worth $20?"
Answer — "When the bird is used at the city hall to test a gas
appliance." At least, that is the reluctant
decision arrived at by Mayor George Webster who found himself recently called upon
to investigate a bill for $20 paid by the city
for one canary.

The bill bore the O.K. of former city engineer George W. Craig, who has long been
gone from the wild and woolly west.

Investigation finally brought to light the
fact that the bird had been used to test out a
certain make of gas appliance. Canaries are
particularly susceptible to gas fumes in atmosphere and the former city engineer, evidently advised by former City Chemist Fred
Field, who conducted the test, had shouted
for the canary.

A stenographer in one of the city hall
offices had been sent post haste to buy a
small bird. Apparently not being apprized of
the use to which the canary was to be put,
the young lady picked a good one. In fact, it
was such a lovely singer that the dealer
figured it at $20. Or, perhaps he knew it was
the city that was doing the buying.

The climax of the story is that Mr.
Canary was put to bed in the same room
with the gas appliance and failed to answer
when called the next morning. In fact, he
was upside down in his cage. The tragedy
was concealed and a secret burial held from

which reporters were excluded. Then the
chemist reported that the gas stove was the
bunk.

October 12, 1923

---

*On one of his visits to Canada, the then
Prince of Wales, later King Edward VIII,
bought a ranch near Calgary. Over the years
the prince, a popular but perhaps rather
lonely man, visited the ranch whenever he
could. (In January, 1936, he became king,
but he abdicated in December of the same
year to marry Wallis Warfield Simpson. He
was then given the title Duke of Windsor.)*

The gates of the E.P. Ranch, out in
the Alberta foothills, where Edward, Prince of Wales, will soon
shed the trappings of royalty, are swinging
ajar, awaiting the arrival of the ranch's
young boss.

"Carlyle," said the prince one day last
year — Professor W.I. Carlyle is manager of
the E.P. — "This has been the happiest day
of my life."

Carlyle, a practical farmer with 25 years'
experience in big farm experimental stations
all over Canada and the United States, was
inclined to be sceptical.

"I mean it," the prince insisted, "this is
the first time in my life that I've felt like a
real man. I've met all the neighbours and I
like them. What's more, I think they like me,
not because I'm a prince, but because I'm
one of the gang."

That's why the prince is coming back to
Alberta this year.

The E.P. Ranch is his only "own" home
— the one place in the world that is entirely
his own, to do with as he wills.

He calls it home!

"The prince isn't altogether the gay,
carefree laughing young man that people
think," says Mrs. Carlyle. "He's a man of the
world, with a wonderful grasp of world problems and politics. He knows a good deal
more about the affairs of state than he does
about dancing."

This ranch of the prince's is something
new to him and gives him a freedom that he
never dreamed of before, but it's far from being a toy.

Another reason why the Prince of Wales
likes the west: Out here, as he says, he's one
of the gang. His Alberta neighbours read the
newspaper stories about the great receptions
he is given in the United States and Eastern
Canada, and realize how glad he's going to
be to get out where the people think of him
as a he-man, rather than a prince.

Last year, a young man who had just
found his freedom and tasted, perhaps for
the first time, the joys of life as an ordinary
human being, the prince moved about as he
liked, rode his own horses on his own
ranch, with some lively bucking thrown in;
fished and explored his 4,000 acre property;
ran up to Calgary to play golf when he felt
like it; took a jaunt to Banff in the Rocky
Mountains, and danced and swam there to
the delight of the debutantes and others;
rushed back to the ranch; cut oats with a

mower, helped feed the silo; dug post holes.

Up at 5:30 in the morning, and through a day's activities that would knock most athletic men cold: democratic to a degree that would stagger many self-styled democrats on this side of the water — that's the prince that the people of Alberta know.

There is always a welcome for the prince's friends and neighbours.

George Lane, who owns the big Bar-U Ranch, near the E.P., was late in getting around last year. In fact, he didn't pay a visit until just before the prince was leaving for England.

"You're a h——— of a neighbour," said the prince, when Lane finally arrived. "Where've you been all this time?"

There is nothing pretentious about the ranch itself, although it's a good building as ranch houses go. There is no gilded furniture scattered about the comfortable living room, or the low-ceilinged, raftered dining room, but everything there stands for solid comfort.

September 13, 1924.

The great stock boom of the Twenties was just getting under way when The Herald published this story on the front page. Speculators had another five years of gorgeous prosperity before the great crash of 1929.

Mushroom" fortunes reminiscent of war times, were reported with the stock market's unprecedented activity. George F. Baker, who owns large blocks of shares of American Can, was reputed to have made several millions on Can's spectacular rise of 13 points in the last seven days. Harry F. Sinclair has profited in Mammoth Oil, which has shared in other oil stocks' rise.

Charles M. Schwab is among many others reported to have cleaned up a fortune in the last week.

In two minutes a simple gesture of the hand had made Alexander Low, a curb broker, $5,000 during the excited trading Wednesday. Low watched the 38 point decline of United Bakeries, bought 500 shares at 115 and signalled "sell" two minutes later at 125.

Wall Street entered another hectic day today with brokerage houses still swamped with an avalanche of orders on the eighth day of the great post-election business boom. Traders were astounded at the strength of the market which showed a net gain of approximately 4 1/2 on an average since the election, despite heavy profit taking all along the line.

There were some breaks in prices yesterday, but the market on the whole showed a gain with some special issues soaring to great heights. From a speculative standpoint the street was baffled as to what the market will do next and today's developments were awaited with some anxiety although many conservative traders believed the rush of buying from all over the nation would be more than enough to absorb the widespread profit taking.

New York, November 13, 1924

The flood of 1929 was dramatic, but brief. The day after this story appeared, the rivers were returning to normal, and the city was preparing to count the damage.

With Bowness Park and St. George's Island completely submerged beneath the roaring, swirling, muddy waters of the Bow river, and bridges and scores of houses menaced by the flood waters of the Elbow river, Calgary, on Monday, faced the worst flood crisis since the big flood of 1902.

Thousands of dollars' worth of damage had been done up until Monday noon, and while anxious city officials and householders in the districts affected scanned the measure sticks, officials of the water power branch of the Dominion government reported that the rivers were still rising.

The flood condition is widespread throughout the southern part of the province. High River is three feet under water, the main highway is washed out in places, small bridges spanning the rivers have been washed away, and late reports indicated that no relief was yet in sight.

Calgary will sustain a substantial loss as a result of the floods. Bowness Park, which had been brought to a high standard of perfection in late years as a summer resort, was swamped beneath a muddy, swirling flood of water early Monday morning. Both dams on the west end of the park broke under the pressure, and within fifteen minutes the whole park was submerged. The bathhouse crumpled up like a pack of cards, and was swept away. In the big dance pavilion, the expensive hardwood floor crumpled under the pressure and tables and chairs danced around in the swirling waters.

At St. George's Island a scene of desolation presented itself. The whole island is now part and parcel of the river. The zoo animals, which were turned loose when the waters menaced the park late Sunday, are believed to have perished. The two bears were not released, but it is believed they will be able to cling to the tops of their cages until the water recedes. The whole park is one wild racing river.

Flood conditions in the Elbow Park, Roxboro Place and Rideau Place, are serious. Fortieth avenue, Elbow Park, was under three feet of water Monday afternoon, and firemen were rescuing householders from their homes by using flatbottomed boats. A dozen furniture vans were pressed into service, but it was found that only horse-drawn vehicles could make any progress through the flooded streets. The water was up to the horses' shoulders, and when one team struck a hole, the horses had to swim their way to higher ground.

Residents of Rideau Park and Roxboro Place, whose homes fronted the river bank, saw the flood waters slowly creep towards them Monday morning, and a number locked up their homes and went to spend the day with friends. Every house facing the river from the Mission bridge to the Twenty-fifth avenue bridge, and right north almost to the second street east bridge, sustained damage as a result of the flood.

In the Hillhurst district, the Bow river overflowed its banks Sunday afternoon just west of the Louise bridge, and on Monday the water was lapping along the roadway on Tenth street.

June 3, 1929

Winston Churchill spoke in Calgary in 1929. He was then 54 years old and a veteran politician, but the greatest achievements of his career were still ahead of him.

If the nations within the British Empire continued along their individual paths of development on a basis of equality and co-operated wholeheartedly, but voluntarily to protect the interests and ideals of the whole, there was nothing to fear for the future of the Empire, declared Rt. Hon. Winston Churchill, former chancellor of the British exchequer, soldier, author and statesman, when he spoke before a gathering of 750 persons at a luncheon held in his honor at the Palliser hotel Monday noon.

Mr. Churchill recalled his former visit to Canada, almost thirty years ago, when he visited the "fringe of the Canadian west." Upon his present visit, he was astonished at the enormous expansion which had taken place during those 30 years. During his first visit there were solemn politicians who assured the people of Canada that the country was of too vast area and too slimly populated to amount to a great deal unless absorbed with another nation.

"I do not hear any croaking like that now," Mr. Churchill said amidst applause.

The political and social status of Britain stood ahead of every country in Europe. The status of living of the mass of the people provided greater refinements of life, and greater protection of individuals against strikes, death of the breadwinner and other catastrophes than any other country in the world, the speaker said.

"Also in the political sphere, I am not afraid. I am sure that the working classes will eventually cast aside that barbarous delusion, Socialism, which has been imported into Britain from such unhappy countries as Russia and Germany, which did not know our political freedom. British security will not be fatally reduced because of it. We can trust the people and need never doubt the English democracy.

"The British Empire's first interest is for peace. We want peace. We have had all we want of fame and glory and we want to have peace to develop the tremendous resources of the Empire. We need peace and I cannot see why we should not get it.

"We can expect troubles such as in China and Russia and among the barbarous nations of the world, but speaking of the polite peoples (laughter), those nations upon which civilization depends, can be expected to maintain a prolonged period of peace.

"But let us be on guard that those who in their enthusiasm for peace do not afford a cover for them to preach for peace but not have it as their ideal. We have got to be a little more careful in standing up for our rights, and though we desire peace it should not induce us to lose what is our due."

August 26, 1929

Some of Our Champions

Calgary's Hillhurst team won the 1922 Dominion soccer championship defeating Toronto Ulster United 2-1 in a two-game total-point series. In the process, they proved that soccer is not a game for the faint-hearted.

The one goal lead obtained by the Hillhursts in Thursday night's game enabled them to win the Connaught Cup, as Saturday afternoon's game resulted in a scoreless draw, although there is no doubt that all the breaks were in the favor of the new holder. Hunt sustained a broken leg in the first half, and two minutes after the second half commenced, King, who has been the most brilliant of the local forwards, sustained an injury, and for the remainder of the game Ulster was compelled to play nine men against eleven. Despite this handicap the locals had as much, if not more of the play, than did the visitors, who can credit their successful journey east to their sound defense.

Both clubs fielded the same teams as played on Thursday night, the line-up being:

Ulster United – Stansfield, Hunt and Johnson, Dierdan, McAdam and Martin, Sims, MacAvoy, R. Lavery, P. Lavery and King.

Calgary Hillhursts – Wilson, Foster and Stephens, Austin, Mitchell and Scott, Deluce, Gough, S. Wakelyn, Cartwright and Wright.

The crowd had increased to around the 10,000 mark when the Hillhurst team, led by Captain Wakelyn, came on the field.

The Calgary team were soon on the attack, but their first attempt was spoiled when Wright pulled up for offside. A rush by Ulster looked dangerous, but McAvoy put his cross too far over and the ball went out. The Hillhursts' goalie had to move swiftly. King was pulled up for charging the goalie. The whole of the Calgary forward line went down in a line, but Hunt took the ball off the toe of Wakelyn and the danger was over.

Hunt was hurt when he stopped Gough going down the field, and had to be carried off the field.

Billy Sims took up the position at right back and Ulster continued with ten men.

Wakelyn set the ball in motion for Calgary at the start of the second half. The Irishmen commenced to attack and King was hurt right in the Calgary goal mouth when he was attempting to shoot. The doctor had to be called and it was found that his right leg was fractured above the knee. It is one of the hard rules of the game that no substitutes are allowed. The game was held up fifteen minutes while the doctor put the fractured leg into splints and had the injured player carried off the field.

The game began to get rough and fouls were being frequently called against both teams. The Calgary goalie pulled off a marvelous save from a beautiful shot by Phil Lavery.

Lavery put in a splendid exhibition

tricking three of the Calgary players with the ball on his toe, but was unable to shoot in the right direction. Another attack and Lavery was pulled up for an offside. Stansfield handled the ball outside his area which gave Calgary a free kick. McAdam got his head to the ball and cleared. Just before the close Lavery made a couple of brilliant runs in an effort to score but his shots were wide. Final score, Ulster 0, Calgary 0.

This gave Calgary the round by 2 goals to 1 after one of the hardest exhibitions of football ever seen in Canada. The misfortunes of having two players break their legs in one game is a hard one, and has been seldom duplicated in soccer titular games before.

Toronto, August 14, 1922

Canadian Olympic star Percy Williams.

A young Canadian runner starred in one of the most dramatic moments of the 1928 Olympics.

Percy Williams, Vancouver school boy sensation, who was crowned King of Sprinters in the 100-metre final at the Olympiad here, came on in a

sensational finish Wednesday to win the 200-metre final, performing the remarkable feat of winning both of the Olympic sprints, a feat performed only once before, in 1912 by R.C. Craig, of the United States.

Williams won the furlong final in the greatest fight of the games, beating Rangeley, of Great Britain, in a great finish. They came up the stretch neck and neck, but Williams won driving at the tape.

Johnny Fitzpatrick just placed fifth. Rangeley, of England, was second in the race with Jackson V. Scholz, of the United States, and Helmut Koernig, of Germany, in a dead heat for third place. Fitzpatrick was fifth with Schuller, of Germany, sixth.

The run into the stretch found Williams, Koernig, Scholz and Rangeley running four abreast. At fifty yards from the tape it looked as though Rangeley or Koernig might have had it, but from there on Williams came through, although Rangeley's challenge was a hard one. Fitzpatrick fought hard, but was out-classed in the world-beating finish.

Canadians broke past the policemen in the stands and draped Williams in the Union Jack. P.J. Mulqueen fought his way through and kissed the victor.

It was the first time in history that the world's double sprint championship came to Canada. Williams' victory today in the 200 metres shows the Canadian to be the greatest of all. He won in the face of almost unbelievable odds, against specialists who did not compete with him in the hundred metres; in the face of the great heat in the two hundred Tuesday, which had sapped the strength of the great German, Koernig, so utterly that he failed entirely before Williams' withering finish. Williams did today what he did before, winning without the slightest fuss or bother.

He went to the marks calmly, and when the delay caused the other sprinters to chafe impatiently, Williams stood still, calmly awaiting the starter's pleasure. When they started he burst ahead, running magnificently from start to finish, easily, swiftly and close to the ground in perfect style. Outside and ahead of him was his team-mate, Johnny Fitzpatrick, fighting for the lead. They started in lanes and as they rounded the first turn there didn't appear to be a change in the places, and Williams seemed behind at the stretch. There Fitzpatrick challenged for the last time, going down fighting.

One German was out in front and another was coming, and Rangeley was second and Williams third. Somehow then, Williams came up to his full stature and forcing every ounce up he hurled himself ahead in one last burst. He made it, beating them all. He came into the stretch without the terrific finish, but this came later when he drew upon the last great reserve which had already brought him one great championship.

Amsterdam, August 2, 1928.

King, Byng, and the UFA

Herbert Greenfield, the first UFA premier of Alberta, was not a notably effective leader. The Herald, no friend of the UFA government, had been shaking its head over his shortcomings for years. In 1925, Greenfield's followers decided that he had to go, and replaced him with John E. Brownlee, an action which inspired the following editorial.

The Farmer's Party's shifting of the Premiership from Mr. Greenfield to Mr. Brownlee is one of the most curious events in Canadian political history.

Much dissatisfaction with the rule of the Farmer Party in Alberta has been expressed, and this feeling has been growing stronger with the passing of time, but the public has felt that Greenfield was as good as his party. Fear of what may happen at the next provincial election has induced the Farmer members to lead Greenfield to the slaughter. Weak members have sacrificed the leader of their own weak party.

What a spectacle it is! This group of farmer politicians, who have always claimed to be more pure than those of other parties, who claimed that possession of higher ideals than ever before guided political parties, throwing their leader to the wolves in the hope that they may save their own skins!

No government ever went into office in this country carrying better wishes for its success than the Greenfield government. The people of Alberta looked forward to an era of better administration than it had ever had. But before one year had passed they knew that they were to be disappointed. The high protestations evaporated. The fine ideas were kicked aside. Both decision and courage were lacking. And there is now this climax, this scene of a power-seeking party thrusting all the blame for its misdeeds upon one man, making him the sacrificial goat.

What improvement in government may we expect now that the Farmer members have completed their decapitating act? Certainly none with the ministers who served Greenfield. And none with any others who may be induced to join Brownlee, so long as the present standard of ability marks the Farmer membership in the legislature.

Greenfield was not a good political captain, but he had a poor set of officers land a mutinous crew.

November 24, 1925.

Alberta Premier Herbert Greenfield.

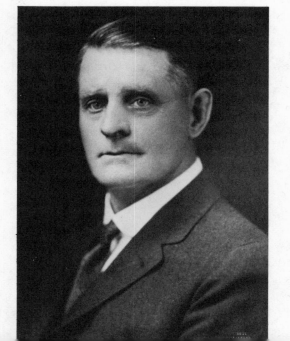

Prime Minister Arthur Meighen.

Defeated in 1921 by the Liberals under their new leader, William Lyon Mackenzie King, the Conservatives made a strong comeback in 1925. They won more seats than the Liberals, but fell short of a majority. Mackenzie King, with the aid of Progressive MPs. clung to power. Then a scandal broke out in the customs department. Officials were accused of theft, smuggling and bootlegging. A former customs minister was accused of illegally receiving liquor samples. Faced with a vote of censure in the House of Commons, Mackenzie King went to Lord Byng, and asked him to dissolve Parliament and thus bring about an election. In an extraordinary move, Byng refused his prime minister's advice. He ruled that Parliament would continue to sit. King resigned, and the governor-general asked Arthur Meighen, the Conservative leader, to form a government. Charles Bishop of The Herald's Ottawa bureau filed the following report.

Refused a dissolution of parliament by His Excellency the Governor-General Premier Mackenzie King this afternoon tendered his resignation to Baron Byng and it was accepted.

The house adjourned very soon after the prime minister made his announcement, and efforts by Mr. Meighen to secure a conference with Mr. King were rejected on the grounds that he is only a private member and that there is no longer a prime minister. After a very brief parley the house adjourned amid a wave of Conservative cheering.

Canada is in the throes of an interregnum. For the first time in her history, and for the first time in 114 years in any British country, there is no government.

Rt. Hon. Arthur Meighen returned to the house of commons at 4 o'clock this afternoon after a conference with His Excellency the Governor-General lasting more than an hour. He was sworn in. No official statement was available at that time, but it was stated that Mr. Meighen had been asked to assume the responsibility of forming a government and had accepted, but that he had stipulated that he would not be sworn in until the house is closed.

Thus he can enter the house as a private member, the most logical one for the task, to represent the crown in closing up the session. This includes passage of supply and essential legislation. He can carry on with the full power of a prime minister in the circumstances, but can stay in the house and thus save his own vote. If he were sworn in he could not re-enter the house until after re-election.

The point is that he will need his own vote. It is believed that Mr. King and his strategists plan a vote of want of confidence at the resumption of the house tomorrow to impress upon the country their claim that Mr. Meighen should not have dissolution because he has not the confidence of the house. In many quarters preparations are being made for fireworks from the moment the house resumes tomorrow, and there is even talk of His Excellency being asked to adjourn it for several days until the situation created by the interregnum has been clarified.

The constitutional issue promises to loom large in the discussion in parliament tomorrow if there is to be any discussion at all. Liberals claim that in refusing the advice of Mr. King to dissolve parliament, Lord Byng has violated the precedents for a hundred years, and they further claim that having further refused dissolution to the former premier, His Excellency, constitutionally, cannot grant it to Mr. Meighen. They maintain that a Governor-General is bound to accept the advice of the prime minister, and that while refusal to do so automatically entails resignation of that particular advisor, the crown cannot follow the identical advice from his successor.

They hold that the office of Governor-General is an institution bound by precedents and not one where the vice-regal representative can exercise his own discretion. Conservatives say that Lord Byng, having given Mr. King a chance to carry on for six months is entitled to give Mr. Meighen a similar opportunity.

Ottawa, June 28, 1926

Meighen faced an awkward situation. At the time, (though no longer) newly-appointed members of the cabinet had to resign from the Commons and run in a by-election. Meighen could not appoint a cabinet without disastrously weakening his already shaky position. He sought to get around the requirement by appointing "acting" ministers. The Liberals bitterly attacked this manoeuvre, and the Meighen government was defeated on the question by one vote. The outcome hinged on the practice of "pairing," an unofficial arrangement which assures that the balance of power in

William Lyon Mackenzie King campaigning in 1926, after the "King-Byng crisis." (At that time, apparently, not all of his supporters knew how to spell his name.) King's Liberals won and held on until their defeat in 1930. They came back in 1935, and stayed in power for another 22 years.

the Commons will not be upset by the unavoidable absence of some MPs. An MP who has to be away arranges a "pair" with one of his opponents, who refrains from voting in his colleague's absence. The Meighen government was brought down by a breach of this practice. Charles Bishop sent this report.

Parliament was dissolved this afternoon but the date of the elections was not fixed.

The proclamation for dissolution was signed by His Excellency the Governor General, shortly after 1 o'clock. It means abrupt termination of parliament. Dissolution was granted on the advice of Rt. Hon. Arthur Meighen, who will form his government and appeal to the country. Neither house nor senate will meet this afternoon. Everything is over. All the legislation unfinished in the senate and awaiting royal assent goes by the board. Supply for the public service will be secured by governor general's warrants.

Dissolution today was the inevitable sequence of what has gone on in the house this week. When Mr. King was forced to resign and subsequently when the new government was defeated in the house, dissolution became the only possible means of exit from the constitutional cul de sac in which parliament found itself. It was only a question of who would get it. Meighen or King.

The procedure now to be followed is for Mr. Meighen to form a cabinet and to assign different ministers to the various portfolios. When that is done, the date of the elections will be formally filed and the campaign will be on. Not only the delays that are called for by the Election Act, but also the fact that the active period of harvesting has to be considered will operate as deterrent factors. The election cannot be before September.

It has been a thrilling week of almost dramatic intensity. On Monday, Mr. King resigned and Mr. Meighen took hold. Liberal members packed up hurriedly and moved that very night. Mr. Meighen took over the quarters of Mr. King in the eastern block and others of the embryonic cabinet went to their departments.

Everything looked hopeful up to late last night. The Meighen ministry got one majority of 12, and another of 10, with Progressive aid and there was talk of it meeting another session, although this was not at all relished by the party as a whole. They viewed with suspicion the Progressive element whose aid enabled them to get into office. In the first two votes of the week, it seemed as though the new ministry was relatively firm in the saddle, but this morning it was dislodged.

If Rev. T.W. Bird, Progressive, had kept his pair with Kennedy, of Peace River – he claims he forgot about it till it was too late – the vote would have been a tie. How Speaker Lemieux would have cut the knot is not clear. He is not called on to do so because the recorded division stands.

Although the house went home only at 3 o'clock, and in Liberal quarters the celebration was kept up till daylight, members were around again early today – eager, anxious and inquisitive.

Ottawa, July 2, 1926

In the ensuing election campaign, both parties struggled to gain the high ground. The Conservatives pointed to proven corruption in the customs department under the Liberals, and called on the people to throw the rascals out. The Liberals seized the constitutional issue: the governor-general had no right, they cried, to refuse Mackenzie King's advice to dissolve Parliament, and then to grant dissolution to Meighen a week later. Is Canada an independent nation, they asked, or is it a Crown colony? In the course of the election campaign, Mackenzie King gave a two-hour speech in Calgary. The Herald printed most or all of it, filling two pages with small type. Then it replied, at more merciful length, in the following editorial.

Mr. King struggled valiantly to put the best color possible upon the disclosures of the customs inquiry. His major claim was that his government had co-operated with the Commercial Protective Association to unearth the nefarious operations of the smuggling ring, but he made no reference whatever to the fact that, with knowledge of much that was transpiring in that crooked circle, his government so far failed to take remedial measures, so far failed to punish the guilty parties, that, at last, in despair of getting any action from the Liberal government, the Commercial Protective Association delivered all their evidence of the startling fruits of their investigations to Hon. H.H. Stevens and only then secured action by Parliament.

Everything that subsequently developed could have been done long before if Hon. Mr. King and his government had set in motion the wheels which Mr. Stevens set in motion. The Liberal government would take no responsibility. According to Mr. King's own story last night, it did not itself set the detectives on the trail of the malefactors; it left first to the outsiders of the Commercial Protective Association and next to Hon. H.H. Stevens the responsibility of digging up the information, making the investigation, and laying the charges.

What the former Prime Minister said respecting the constitution sounded more important than it was.

Lord Byng's position, as defined last night by Mr. King himself, from the first has appealed to the common sense of the average citizen. Mr. King takes objection to it and has built upon it a ponderous superstructure of fancied assaults upon the liberties of the Canadian people, of a return to the status of a crown colony, and what not.

Governor-general Lord Byng.

Notwithstanding this the lesson undoubtedly has been learned, the lesson that other members of a cabinet must be vigilant in watching the transactions of all departments respecting the administration of which they have to bear responsibility. The hope respecting stable government may materialize. The Herald declared during the campaign that it would be better to have an independent Liberal government free from the necessity of dealing, bargaining and compromising with a dictating minority, if a Conservative majority were not to be elected.

Liberals have much reason for being pleased with the election. It was clear triumph for their party, and The Herald ungrudgingly congratulates them upon a victory won in open fight. It is to be hoped now that the country may have political tranquility, with all of our people working as Canadians, not as Conservatives or Liberals, for the advancement of Canada in the coming years.

September 15, 1926

sion such as this is to allow the elation which, in the event, is natural, to draw one from a proper reserve. In Calgary we are so close to Mr. Bennett, he has for so long been a dominating personality in this community, that we might have thought the choice of him to be inevitable. Here in Calgary where he is known best we believe that the choice has been wisely made. To know that the estimation of him which is locally held is also that of the country at large is decidedly pleasing. He has impressed his character, his intellectual power, his capacity for leadership, upon the Dominion as a whole.

The Herald, with great sincerity, records its gratification in the election of Hon. R.B. Bennett, a citizen of Calgary, to the high and honorable position of leader of the Conservative Party and records also its confident belief that he will lead the party with distinction and success, presently, as leader of the opposition, and, at a not distant date, as Prime Minister of Canada.

October 13, 1927.

Canadians know as well as they know anything that Lord Byng would not be a party to any action which might, by one iota, impair this country's right of self-government. They know equally well that if any further right of self-government is desired by the people of Canada, all that they have to do is to ask for it through the government of the day and the British government will grant it. We are not in a shadow of danger of losing a single liberty now possessed, a fact better known to Mr. King than to most other citizens.

August 17, 1926

When the voters had their turn to speak, they gave the Liberals 116 seats and the Conservatives 90. Mackenzie King did not have a majority in the 245-seat House, but he had ample support from Progressives and members of the United Farmers of Alberta. Editorially, The Herald consoled itself with the thought that at least Canada once more had a stable government.

The Liberal victory at the polls yesterday was decisive in all respects. The party held its own in Quebec repulsing every effort of the Conservatives to make gains in that province. It added to its strength in the Maritimes. Conservative losses to Liberals in Ontario fixed the outcome of the election.

It is as apparent as it is suprising that the electors declined to be affected by the customs situation. The election was brought about by the customs exposures. These were of a most serious nature. Wrong-doing in government departments in the past has always been condemned by the Canadian people. The inexplicable has happened in this instance.

Apart from details of its election campaign, this paper appealed for clean government and for strong stable government. The Canadian people have refused to administer the expected rebuke for all that has transpired in one of the government departments during the King administration.

R.B. Bennett, a 30-year veteran of Conservative politics, was named leader of the federal party in 1927. The Herald, a longtime Bennett supporter, hailed the choice in an editorial.

The election of Hon. R.B. Bennett is an impressive personal story when viewed from the aspect of his lonely eminence as the only Conservative member of parliament from Lake Superior to the Rocky Mountains. Examined from another angle he was less isolated than the other candidates for the leadership.

Mr. Bennett was born in New Brunswick and spent his early life in the Maritimes; he has lived during his mature years in Alberta; his business interests have compelled him to keep in touch with both Ontario and Quebec. He is by far the dominant figure as compared with his competitors in the race for the great prize of the greatest political contention in the history of the Dominion.

The temptation present upon an occa-

Conservative leader R.B. Bennett.

Five Alberta women led a determined struggle to eliminate a strange piece of discrimination from the Canadian constitution. The British North America Act says that "persons" may be summoned to join the Senate. The Supreme Court of Canada ruled that for the purposes of the BNA Act, women were not persons, and could not be senators. The Alberta five appealed to the British Privy Council (a route of appeal which is no longer open) and won.

Women are eligible to be summoned and become members of the Senate of Canada. Their lordships of the judicial committee of the Privy Council rendered this opinion today on the appeal by five representative women of Alberta against an adverse decision of the Canadian Supreme Court.

Contrary to the supreme court, the privy council today came to the conclusion "that the word persons includes members of both the male and female sex."

The appeal hinged upon the meaning to be placed on the word "persons," as contained in the clause of the British North America Act.

The Lord Chancellor of Great Britain, Lord Sankey, delivered the judgment, taking the unusual course of reading it in full before the court. For some years it has been the practice merely to announce the general result.

The appellants were Hon. Irene Parlby, of Alix, Alberta, one of the first women in the Empire to become a cabinet minister; Mrs. Louise McKinney, of Claresholm, Alberta, first woman elected to the Alberta legislature; Mrs. Nellie McClung, Calgary, writer and lecturer, who represented Edmonton in the legislature; Mrs. O.C. Edwards, of Macleod, Alberta, veteran expert, who has been convenor on laws for the National Council of Women, and Magistrate Emily Murphy, of Edmonton, one of the first two women in Canada to be appointed magistrates.

The five who proved women are persons: from left, Nellie McClung, Henrietta Muir Edwards, Irene Parlby, Louise McKinney and Emily Murphy.

The privy council ruling said in part:

"A heavy burden lies on the appellant who seeks to set aside an unanimous judgment of the supreme court, and this board will only set aside such a decision after convincing argument and anxious consideration but having regard to: British North America Act –

"First – The object of the act – to provide a constitution for Canada, a responsible and living state.

"Second – That the word "persons" is ambiguous and may include members of either sex.

"Third – That there are sections in the act which show that in some cases the word must include female person.

"Fourth – That in some sections the words "male persons" are expressly used when it is desired to confine the matter in issue to males.

"And having regard finally to the provisions of the Interpretation Act (of 1889), their lordships have come to the conclusion that the word "persons" includes members of the male and female sex, and that therefore the question propounded by the governor general must be answered in the affirmative; and that women are eligible to be summoned and become members of the Senate of Canada."

London, October 18, 1929

An editorial.

The judgment will remove an anomaly in the public life of the dominion which was both striking and absurd. A woman sits as a member of the House of Commons, members of the sex have served as provincial cabinet ministers. At the present time there is a woman in the cabinet of Alberta. The Dominion government sent Miss MacPhail, MP, as a member of the parliamentary delegation to the League of Nations last summer. Women magistrates are not a phenomenon in Canadian jurisprudence.

With these evidences of the capacity of the fair sex for public service on record, there has not been, and could not be, any question raised as to the fitness of women to serve as members of the Senate. The opposition to their being called to the upper chamber has been lukewarm at best. It rested entirely on the interpretation of a clause in the British North America Act, drawn at a time when women had not yet attempted to enter the lists of public life. Among men of all professions except that of the law there has been no tendency to exclude women from the right to be known as a "person."

Their lordships of the Privy Council have shown impatience with legal hairsplitting. They have taken a common sense view of the problem submitted to them.

October 18, 1929

This tender thought was brought to Herald readers by the life insurance industry of Canada. Presumably it was grateful for the existence of women and children, and expected that its customers would feel the same.

IF IT WERE NOT FOR WOMEN AND CHILDREN THERE WOULD BE NO LIFE INSURANCE —

LIFE INSURANCE SERVICE

Conflict and Adventure

Burdened by war reparations imposed by the victorious Allies, Germany slid into economic chaos in the early Twenties. Inflation reached grotesque proportions. Workers had to be paid daily, and had to spend their pay the same day before it lost much of its value. Germany fell behind in reparations payments, and the allies accused it of foot-dragging. In 1923 France and Belgium sent troops into the Ruhr industrial area to force more payments out of their old enemy. The Herald published a series of articles by Whiting Williams, an American sociologist, who went to work in the Ruhr coal mines.

Here for more than a year we miners worked regularly an extra shift and a half every week, just in order to help meet France's reparations demands. That meant an extra million tons every month. And then, just because they found it a few hundred tons too short, they march in upon us to make us slaves."

I had hardly got my pick into my hand, in the guise of a visiting mining student, before my companions began to do precisely what I had hoped for: tell me their troubles.

"Yes, I should be working now instead of talking," said one old man who had been digging in these veins for more than thirty years, "but, unhappily, I find that I must rest more often now-a-days. The reason is that I can no longer afford meat every day, as of course I used to, back in the good old days before the awful war. Now—ha! Well, if I can have a little of the precious stuff of a Sunday, I thank the dear God.

"Back in those days you could get a suit of clothes for less than five shifts of work," broke in a younger chap. "But now — now you must save up all your wages of a month, hundreds of millions! And then by that time the price has doubled. How can one go upon the street?"

"Yesterday," testified another, "I saw a woman crying in a store. She had come in with the 15 millions they had asked her for the shirt her man must have if he was to go out of the house. But she found that the same shirt had gone up from the day before to 20 millions. The poor old woman, she just sat down and cried."

I confess that more than once in such discussions I have found it hard to keep back the tears.

"Beer? I have not known the taste of it for months," the father of several children burst out one day. "And I like beer, too. Just last night, I had a few hundred thousand marks we had not contrived to spend. But when I said, 'Let's go in and have a glass,' my wife looked at me. 'We should better get a little candy for the children, what?' she said. We didn't go in."

"Not only beer, but also a cigarette occasionally, I like,"came from another, "but for months both of them have been beyond me."

Gelsenkirchen, Ruhr, Germany, October 26, 1923

In 1925, as this editorial noted, splendors which had been hidden for more than 3,000 years were brought back into the light of day.

Perhaps the supreme moment in modern archeological research came on November 11, 1925. On that day Howard Carter, in the presence of government and scientific representatives, began the examination of the mummy of Tutankhamen in the Valley of Kings at Luxor. From the musty tomb where the boy king's remains had lain for 3,273 years, the splendours of ancient Egypt were brought to light, dwarfing in richness and magnificence all that had gone before.

The matter-of-fact official report telling of the finding of the Egyptian crown jewels failed to conceal the dazzling character of the beautiful and precious objects discovered. There are passages which read like extracts from a tale of wonder.

"Among the objects brought to light were...gold amulet and collarettes ... superb gold dagger with crystal handle, bracelets of intricate workmanship...a large number of finger rings of intricate workmanship, some having scarabs bearing the king's name...a second dagger more beautiful than the first...several large inlaid pectorals, bead-work ornaments, circlets, etc....

And again, "both forearms were loaded with magnificent jewels...jewelry discovered upon the king, who lies in a coffin of gold, is far beyond expectations...on the feet are golden sandals and on the fingers golden stalls...

No living man has ever before gazed on such a find as this. The splendour of the jewels and precious objects must have bewildered those who first gazed upon them. Their intrinsic value is no doubt fabulous, but far greater is their artistic worth. The art of the best lapidaries and goldsmiths of Egypt went into the ornamentation and embellishment of the jewels which were buried with the youthful king. But only the merest details have been given to the world. Comparative secrecy is being preserved, it is obvious, when one remembers the wealth of description concerning the opening of the outer chamber three years ago. When the full story is told, it will form a narrative unrivalled in all archeology.

November 24, 1925.

When the British government cancelled wage subsidies to the coal industry, mine owners demanded that miners work for lower wages. When the miners refused, they were locked out. The Trades Union Congress called a general strike, and nearly three-quarters of Britain's union members stopped work. To many (including Sir Philip Gibbs, the former war correspondent

who wrote the following dispatch) the general strike of 1926 looked like the beginning of anarchy in Britain. In fact, the strike lasted nine days, though the miners themselves stayed out for about six months.

The first day of the general strike throughout Great Britain began that paralysis of industrial activity upon which the life of the nation depends. A struggle had begun between the forces of organized labor, led by revolutionary minds, which are acting behind the scenes, and the great majority of the British people who stand loyal to constitutional government and peaceful methods of political argument.

Those of us who have wireless sets, especially those of us who live in country districts, as I do, have been sitting up late at night to get any word over the wireless waves which might give hope and peace, and while the destiny of our nation is on the scales of fate there comes through our receivers jazz tunes and negro songs, or dance music to a gay rhythm. It's like the mockery of Nero playing a fiddle while Rome burns.

So far the tragic significance of this struggle — for no matter what happens it will be heavily weighted with tragedy — has not affected the good humor of ordinary citizens.

The first morning of the strike when there were no trains and no trams and only a few pirate omnibuses, hundreds of thousands of men and women had to walk to offices and shops in London. Many walked five or six miles — young girls in high-heeled shoes and silk stockings striding out, like young Dianas, and laughing and joking as they went.

Others had bought or borrowed bicycles for which there is a great demand. All roads into London were thronged with motor traffic and every old crock or pre-war date was brought out from country garages, while luxurious cars gave lifts to working men and girls.

I have been watching the faces of the crowds in London today, east and west. On the whole they are good-natured and not much worried nor yet inflamed by political passion. But here and there I have noticed other kinds of faces, those that are furtive and sullen and rather criminal in type. Out in the dark little dens of London slums some of our night birds have stepped into the light of day, scenting trouble, excited by the chance of anarchy.

It is with such types at the present time in all great cities that the British government is taking no chances.

Following the years of unemployment, bad trade, troublesome housing conditions in crowded cities and unfilled promises too freely made in time of war there is a lot of bitterness in many hearts. Political agitators and wild-mouthed men may stir up passion. Criminal instincts may surge up in time of trouble. Hunger and failing of strike pay and inevitable defeat may drive young hot-heads into desperate acts before we are through. Unless there is a quick finish there are bound to be some outbreaks of violence leading to stern and merciless suppression for the sake of law and order.

Meanwhile the most tragic figures are Ramsey MacDonald and his colleagues in the Labor party in the house of commons. They are men of peace. They hate and detest revolutionary methods. They wished to play for England as well as for their own side. But they have been out-manoeuvered by younger and wilder men, who have captured the machinery of the Labor unions and are eager to set it in motion, with all the brakes off.

This general strike will be broken so far as it threatens the life of the nation. The British constitution will prevail beyond any shadow of doubt. The cost will be great and the disaster will be felt by all classes and all who seek the progress of democracy in Europe.

London, May 5, 1926

The final edition of The Herald on May 21, 1927, carried a paragraph of dramatic news.

Lindbergh landed here this evening after his flight from New York. He made a safe landing.

Le Bourget Field, Paris, May 21, 1926

Under this "Flash" appeared an earlier story, relating the 25-year old aviator's take-off from New York. Lindbergh was the first man to fly solo across the Atlantic, a distance of more than 5,000 kilometres.

Alone young eagle, whose daring has thrilled the world, from all indications, winged his way this morning over the 1,900 mile stretch of the Atlantic ocean.

Behind him was New York and the dangerous northwestern Atlantic area; before him was Paris, fame and fortune.

Captain Charles Lindbergh quit the

Charles A. Lindbergh and friends with his famous plane, the Spirit of St. Louis.

Newfoundland coast at 7:15 eastern summer time, last night, entering the most hazardous stretch of his 3,000 mile trip from New York to Paris.

Alone and without a radio or any signalling device, but with all the newest aids to air navigation, the 25-year-old flier, roared on and each hour served to decrease his hazard. As his fuel decreased, his speed would increase. The flier lost 800 of his original 5,150 pounds with the passage of each thousand miles.

Night flying does not worry the young airman. He has flown the night mail summer and winter, and even stepped out of a disabled plane in a parachute in the darkness.

Lindbergh is described by his friends as the perfect picture of clean-cut youth. He does not smoke or drink, and is in perfect trim.

His life of flying, stunting, barn-storming and rigid discipline have made him nearly immune from ordinary physical fatigue.

"A peculiar guy," said Robert Westover of Billings Mont., of the flier. "I don't think he will be lonesome on the trip to Paris. He is just as happy alone. He doesn't care for the company of other young fellows and has no use for girls. Everything he owned was in the pockets of his large overalls."

B.F. Mahoney, the 26-year-old president of Ryan air lines, builders of his plane "The Spirit of St. Louis," today told of the young airman's food supply.

"He is carrying two ham sandwiches, two roast beef sandwiches, and one hard boiled egg sandwich. I had to press the last one on him. He said "four would be

enough," said Mahoney.

"He carried two canteens of water, about four quarts in all, but no coffee or liquor."

New York, May 21, 1927

An editorial.

Young Lindbergh, the "flying fool" made issue with fate in his lone non-stop air flight from New York to Paris, France and won. In two and a half hours shorter time than he had estimated he covered the distance which keeps the traveler by fastest steamship and train moving for several days. Thirty-three and one half hours was Lindbergh's time from take-off to landing.

The most noteworthy result of Lindbergh's feat is likely to be found in the psychologic effect it is bound to have upon his fellows the world over. He attempted what had heretofore been regarded as impossible; in his success he has attained what was supposed to have been unattainable. In him the world now has a new hero to worship, a new master to learn from.

Because in this age, when everything seems to have been accomplished and there is danger that the ancient virtue of hazard and adventuring is being bred out of humanity, it is well that there should appear from time to time a Lindbergh whose personal daring may fan into flame the spirit of adventure in the hearts of his fellow men. For by this spirit and by it alone is human progress possible.

May 23, 1927

As the Twenties neared their end, and the horrors of the Great War faded deeper into memory, an era of peace and progress seemed to be at hand. In the New Year's Eve editorial, The Herald greeted the fateful year 1929.

The close of 1928 is a fitting time for retrospect as well as forward looking. It has been a year of good crops and general expansion in Western Canada. The middle west is opening up rapidly to industry and a more varied development.

One of the epochal events of the year as far as this part of the Dominion is concerned was the inauguration of aerial mail transportation. The few weeks' trial at the end of the year may be confidently regarded as the precursor of a regular mail

service in the prairie provinces.

Only a few years ago the carriage of mail from Winnipeg to Calgary in a few hours would have been regarded as a dream. Today it has become a practical necessity. It is a logical development of the remarkable progress achieved by the west in the past four decades. Old pioneering conditions have been revolutionized. The early appalling isolation of settlers is a thing of the past. The rural telephone, the radio and the automobile have changed life on the prairie. There is immediate and constant touch with the outside world, while labor-saving appliances both in the homestead and on the farm have banished much of the old-time toil.

There are some who think that life is becoming too easy and they fear a decline

in morale. But who would want to go back to the vanished burdens and privations of the past? Electric light is better than the old whale oil lamps. Automobiles are more comfortable and faster than riding on horseback. The modern pullman is a great improvement on the pioneer's stagecoach. It is better to live in security and safety instead of in fear of the Indians and wolves.

There will always be croakers. If life is easier now than it was in the past it should be the cause for rejoicing. Virtue, clean thinking and thrift are not the products of one's environment, but of character. The world is not going to smash because it is moving onward and not backward.

December 31, 1928.

The Depression Years

1929-39

The Dirty Thirties began in the last ten days of October, 1929. The Wall Street crash of that time marked the beginning of a decade that began in economic disaster and ended in world war. On the front pages of The Herald, the stock-market crash shared equal billing with news that was even more alarming for a farm-based community like Calgary: wheat prices were dropping sharply.

So began an economic collapse that would soon be compounded by drought, locusts and hail. It shattered hopes and lives. Families were broken up, farms were abandoned, the work and savings of years were wiped out. At first, it was said that prosperity was just around the corner. The reassurances went on even as the news got worse. Eventually it became clear that nobody knew when or how the depression would end.

William Lyon Mackenzie King, the Liberal prime minister, predicted an early recovery, without government action. King argued that Ottawa was constitutionally unable to help victims of the depression. He was not persuasive, and in 1930, a Calgary Conservative, R.B. Bennett, became prime minister. It was not an opportune time to form a government. Bennett lasted the worst five years of the Dirty Thirties, and gave his name to that Prairie symbol of the depression, the "Bennett Buggy." (This was a horse-drawn automobile, not many farmers could afford gasoline.) In 1935, Mackenzie King was returned to power with a huge majority.

By this time, President Franklin D. Roosevelt's "New Deal" was taking shape in the United States. Ironically, Bennett's own version of the New Deal was a major part of the election platform that sent him to defeat. The Herald took some note of Roosevelt and his recovery programs, but it had its hands full with domestic issues. In any case, Britain was still very much the mother country. Interest in U.S. affairs grew during and after the Second World War, when the U.S. became the dominant world power.

Statistically, the depression reached its depths in 1933, when Canada's gross national product fell to $3.5 billion, from 1929's $6.1 billion. (By 1939, the GNP was back up to $5.6 billion.) Behind these numbers lay the grim reality of people out of work. Men rode freight trains across the country, seeking jobs, or just seeking towns that would let them stay for a short time and do manual labor in return for food. At the depth of the Depression, one-fifth of Calgary's 75,000 people were on welfare.

Food and housing was cheap, but pay was low, so most people made do without expensive pleasures. An outing to Bowness Park on the streetcar, and getting home in time to listen to Amos 'n Andy on the radio, might be the highlight of a week — for anyone who could afford the streetcar fare.

It was a good decade for movies, if nothing else.

Transit revenues fell off in the Thirties; some people had no place to go, and others needed to save a nickel by walking.

In 1934, two pounds of hamburger sold for 25 cents, and a six-room house in Sunnyside rented for $25 a month. A solid brick bungalow on the North Hill sold for $2,200. (It had sold for $4,950 before it was repossessed.)

Many survivors of the era can remember happy times and simple pleasures, which is more than might be expected from a reading of the Thirties' newspapers. For those who could afford a movie now and then, there were movies worth seeing: The Blue Angel (1930) with Marlene Dietrich; Frankenstein (1931) with Boris Karloff; Grand Hotel (1932) with Greta Garbo; Red-Haired Alibi (1932), Shirley Temple's first movie; It Happened One Night (1934); Snow White and The Seven Dwarfs (1937) by Walt Disney; and in 1939, Gone With The Wind, The Wizard of Oz, John Ford's classic version of Stagecoach, and Goodbye, Mr. Chips. The movies were the best thing about 1939.

For anyone who felt like singing, there were songs, and some of them became classics. Brother, Can You Spare A Dime? was painfully close to the facts of 1932, but that same year they were singing Night And Day and April In Paris. Next year came Smoke Gets In Your Eyes and Stormy Weather. In 1934, Blue Moon and Stars Fell on Alabama. In 1937, The Lady Is A Tramp and Harbor Lights. In 1938, September Song and the ineffably lovely Flat Foot Floogie With A Floy Floy.

But when the singing stopped, politics and economics were still there. Wheat prices had hit bottom in 1932, but their recovery was another bitter irony, because from 1933 through 1937, the southern prairies suffered a terrible drought. Hot, dry, unceasing winds carried away topsoil, turning the sky black at noon. Many farmers had nothing to sell for the improved prices.

Tired of trying to outwait the drought and depression, people began to look for economic nostrums to cure it. Technocracy attracted some small attention, and Communism won a few converts. Calgary even elected a Communist alderman for several years. But the real Alberta story was Social Credit.

William Aberhart, the man who brought Social Credit to Alberta, was well-known even before he went into politics. He was principal of Crescent Heights High School and a prominent evangelist. He conducted the Back to the Bible Hour on CFCN radio and preached from the pulpit of his own Prophetic Bible Institute.

In 1932, Aberhart read a book about the Social Credit system of a British amateur economist, Major C.H. Douglas. It was a revelation. Soon something new was added to Aberhart's evangelical message. The fifty big shots who run Canada, the bankers' toadies, the lackeys of the financial interests — they were to blame for the crisis. They were depriving the ordinary man of buying power, the lifeblood of the economy.

Aberhart's version of Social Credit is remembered mostly for printing "funny money" and for the promise of a $25 monthly dividend for every citizen. In fact, Social Credit prosperity certificates never became a major factor in the Alberta economy, and the monthly dividend was never paid. Yet, far from being a failure, the Social Credit party provided a government that people were happy to re-elect for 35 years.

Working with a promising young assistant named Ernest Manning, Aberhart established the Alberta Social Credit League. Powered by Manning's brilliant grass-roots organizing, the Social Crediters launched themselves into Alberta politics. In August, 1935, a record voter turn-out elected 56 Social Credit MLAs, every one of them new to the Legislature. Also elected were five Liberals and two Conservatives. The previous government, the United Farmers of Alberta, was wiped out.

Whether Social Credit could ever have worked is still a theoretical question. Aberhart proved beyond doubt that it wouldn't be allowed to work in one province. Again and again Social Credit measures passed by the Alberta Legislature were disallowed by Ottawa, or ruled unconstitutional by the Supreme Court.

Aberhart was determined to subdue his opponents, notably the newspapers and the banks. He proposed laws that would have deprived newsmen and bankers of rights enjoyed by ordinary citizens. The Herald raised its voice from jeering to outrage — and it was as outraged for bank employees as for itself.

In the midst of the uproar over Social Credit, hopeful signs began to appear. Alberta's 1938 wheat crop was the best in years. Merchants reported seeing $100 bills again. The welfare rolls began to shrink. But relief of a grim, different kind was already on the way. War would soon put everyone to work.

By the mid-Thirties, dictators were on the march in Europe and Asia. Adolf Hitler took over as chancellor of Germany in 1933, and brought in compulsory military training in 1935. In 1936, he sent troops back into the Rhineland, which had been a demilitarized zone since the First World War. These moves defied the Versailles Treaty, which had been intended to bring peace to Europe by crippling Germany's power to make war.

In 1935, Fascist Italy attacked Ethiopia, and managed to conquer it the following year. This was an unimpressive accomplishment in itself, perhaps, but it was a disturbing sign of things to come.

Spain was torn by nearly three years of civil war, begun in July, 1936 by a Fascist revolt led by General Francisco Franco. German and Italian forces fought on the victorious Fascist side, while France and Russia sent aid to Spanish forces loyal to the elected government. Loyalist sympathizers, most of them with no military training, came from abroad to support the government.

Hitler annexed Austria in 1938. Later the same year he demanded that the Sudetenland area of Czechoslovakia be turned over to Germany. Even then, the democracies hoped for peace. At a conference in Munich, France and Britain agreed to let Hitler absorb the Sudetenland, and no more. Prime Minister Chamberlain returned to London proclaiming "Peace for our time." Six months later, in March, 1939, Hitler's army marched into what was left of Czechoslovakia.

Poland was Hitler's next target. France and Britain warned him that they would aid Poland if Germany attacked. In August, 1939, Hitler signed a non-aggression treaty with Russia, supposedly Germany's deadliest enemy. With his eastern flank thus protected, Hitler attacked Poland September 1, 1939. On September 3, Britain and France declared war. Canada came into the Second World War a week later. The Thirties were over.

The German army, dismantled after the First World War, was rebuilt and on the march once more in the late Thirties.

Crash and Consequences

The sudden collapse of stock prices on Wall Street was the opening disaster in a decade of economic depression. The effects of the crash were quickly felt all over the western world. New York's stock-market disaster was echoed in the Canadian exchanges. Southam reporter Paul Reading sent this report on a bad day in Montreal.

The Montreal stock market has just emerged from the most exciting day in its memory and a colony of harassed brokers are still counting the cost of it as I write.

In volume of trading it has probably been a record day and it has been beyond all question the most acute panic in a generation, but these are not the points that are fixing the attention of the board room as the day closes.

It is the pity of it and the needlessness of it that seemed to be uppermost in the minds of the market fraternity. One usually expects a matter-of-fact point of view in a broker, but I have talked to a number of them Thursday afternoon, who had seen so many people in financial straits that sympathy was the strongest emotion an adventurous session had left them.

"Look at that board," exclaimed one member. "Nickel opens at 47 and closes at 45½, a drop of only 1½ points, but meanwhile it has been down to 40, and that means that the little fellow is wiped out. It is the same story all through the list. There was a good recovery but it only benefited the people who were strong enough to get in at the bottom. I have never seen a day bring so much hard luck in all my experience as a broker."

The slump came like an electric storm. For the first hour the tape had been dragging along sluggishly. Then New York commenced its bear raid and people in the board rooms began to forget about their appointments.

The Montreal stocks held at first, then sagged, then broke like a dam at high water. By lunch hour there was standing room only in the brokers' offices and some of the faces there were grey. Here and there a woman was weeping.

When a thunderstorm cut the New York wires about half-past one it looked as though the panic would become a stampede.

The air is still so full of gossip that it is difficult to estimate the truth of what one hears, but one picks up stories of grave losses to important interests, of individual stockholders who have dropped $40 and $50 thousand since morning, and others who are wiped out, of business houses whose reserves invested in stocks have vanished.

How did it happen? I have heard only one plausible explanation, that the public, just as they bought like sheep a year ago, suddenly and with equal unreason took fright and commenced selling like sheep.

Half a dozen of the best market authorities were forecasting a good market on the strength of sound conditions, but some of the sheep took fright, the stop loss orders came into play and last night most of the sheep were shorn or trampled to death.

The brokers' clerks are still at work sending out margin calls. What that will mean to Friday's market most of the traders hesitate to guess. There is a general feeling that the market, while it has steadied itself, will remain very nervous for a day or two.

Regarding the margin calls, however, they point out one significant thing. Many of the weaker accounts will not be asked for extra margin in the morning – they are already disposed of, for the crash was so sudden and so extended that a good many speculators were wiped out before they had time to cover.

A large proportion of those who remain will probably, in a stiffer market, find themselves able to put up extra margin rather than throw their stocks overboard.

Montreal, October 25, 1929

This editorial pronounced the stock-market boom of the Twenties dead. How right it was.

The confidence expressed in New York last weekend, that Thursday's stock market crash had established a firm bottom, was not well-founded.

Ruinous as that decline was, it was comparatively innocuous to the debacle which swept over the stock exchanges on Tuesday. Low levels established last week were many points higher than the lows now prevailing, and the record turnover of shares established on Wall Street last week was far exceeded.

The situation was made worse by the spread of frenzied selling to the leading European exchanges. The severe drop in prices produced forced selling, and values have become depreciated to a degree not justified by dividend returns and business prospects. When a market gets out of hand there are excesses on the down side as there

THE BOY WHO DIDN'T MAKE GOOD

"WITH THE EXCEPTION OF THE BARREL I DON'T SEEM TO BE MUCH BETTER OFF THAN WHEN I STARTED"

This was the 1929 version of the standard New Year cartoon, which The Herald reprinted from The New York World. It spared readers a glimpse of the infant 1930 — a very nasty child.

have been in the past few years in the extravagant valuations placed on stocks.

It seems inevitable that the long speculative boom is over. History has repeated itself. The lambs have been shorn. The bitter experience will keep them out of the markets for a long time. The situation is not one where much comfort can be advanced to those who have lost heavily.

Even local oil stocks have descended to levels far below the intrinsic value of the shares. But that is something that always happens in a general market decline. Everything goes down all at once. The one bright ray in yesterday's record slump was the strength of wheat. Prices closed not far below the quotations on Monday afternoon.

October 30, 1929

Hard times set in quickly.

With orders out for city relief work for married men to be cut to a minimum, and the provincial government unemployment relief scheme gradually being tightened, men flocking into Calgary from farms, towns, and the Turner Valley oilfield in search of work will be disappointed, according to city officials.

Wednesday morning there were between 70 and 75 single men working for the city under the government relief scheme which pays $1 a day, where before there had been as high as 932 employed. The employment service has been culling over its lists for men to go into the brush country, and to go on outlying farms, where work is now available.

Many men, when their names have been called, have refused the brush cutting or farm work, and have been struck off the government relief list. Since Tuesday the list dropped from between 400 and 500 to about 75 men.

With the provincial government taking care of single jobless, the city has endeavored to give work to all married men in Calgary this winter. The men have been employed on shifts, some being laid off for a time and then replacing their mates later.

Orders were issued Wednesday morning from the commissioner's office to cut, and the work of weeding out the less needy has commenced. Newcomers to the city who have taken up residence within the last few months will be among the first to go, unless their cases are very sad or deserving.

Older residents will be given preference generally, but the number of dependents and other aspects of each case will be considered before men are struck off the relief lists.

Single men have more chance of picking up work in Calgary now, with the spring coming on, than the married men have. Contractors and builders get most of their labor off the streets without applying to the employment bureau, and they find single men more suitable in many cases. Hope of employment for married men lies in the farms, officials of the government employment service stated on Wednesday.

March 12, 1930

Herald reporter Fred Kennedy visited some of the luckier jobless in their work camps west of town.

In the heart of the Bow River forest reserve, where the majestic Rocky Mountains form an impregnable barrier to the west and the sullen roar of the famous Elbow Falls comes faintly to the ear, Calgary's army of single unemployed men is under canvas.

Recruited from all nations of the world, the men have dubbed themselves "Premier Brownlee's Foreign Legion," and although their only "weapons" are the lowly pick and shovel, and their "uniforms" are mackinaw coats, overalls and shoe packs, the little army is hacking and blasting a road through the western boundaries of the forest reserve in return for 75 cents a day and board.

Industrial depression, like war, makes queer bedfellows. A diminutive Cockney, who won the Military Medal while serving with a London regiment, swings a pick side by side with a German from whose picket dangles the Iron Cross. He is using it as a watch fob.

The cook in Camp No. 12 was a chef in a well known Calgary club for years. Monday noon, the main dish was "Braised Beef a la Jardiniere." The men were suspicious. They tasted it, liked it, and asked for more. They called it "Mulligan stew." Everybody was satisfied.

In one work gang, a former bank clerk works side by side with a former canned heat artist. [Canned heat, an alcohol-based fuel, was sometimes used by far-gone alcoholics.] The banker had quit to enter a brokerage house. The brokers went to jail. He lost his job, well nigh starved to death and then hit for the brush camps. He traded off his tuxedo for two pairs of overalls and two pairs of shoe packs. He's well and happy and healthy. The canned heat artist almost died the first week. He's one of the best men on the gang now. Three square meals a day and good Alberta sunshine worked wonders with him.

The camps are conducted along military lines. The men are awakened at 7 o'clock in the morning. They wash, have breakfast and are ready for the road by 8 o'clock. They quit work at noon, have dinner and are back on the job at 1 o'clock. They work until 5 o'clock. The evening meal is served at 5:15, and from then until 9:30 o'clock, when lights out is sounded, they play cards, read, or enjoy a little community singing.

Even the most chronic grouch (there are always one or two in every camp) agrees that the food is good, well prepared, and plentiful.

If the men have any complaint at all, it is the rate of wages being paid for the work they are doing. In camps No. 1 and 12, the unemployed are doing real road work. Blasting operations are carried out several times a day and the gangs have to wheel the heavy shale in wheelbarrows to where the road is being graded. They believe that they should get at least 40 cents an hour for their labors.

A commissary department supplies the men with clothing at near wholesale prices. They are fairly well clothed, very well fed, and well treated by the camp bosses, and even those who are always ready to "damn

the government" frankly admit that they are much better off than the hundreds of men who are walking the streets of Calgary, with only one 25-cent meal to look forward to every day.

Bragg Creek, January 20, 1931

This story noted that there is no excuse for panhandling. Except, perhaps, the desire to eat something besides oatmeal.

Every day is porridge day in Calgary to far as the unemployed are concerned.

Two thousand bowls of the breakfast cereal that has made the name of Scotland famous are dished out to hungry unemployed daily at the porridge kitchen, opposite the city hall, and no questions are asked.

The kitchen was started by a well known Calgary citizen, who does not wish his identity made known.

Four men and one woman are kept busy all day long, cooking porridge and serving it.

Between 250 and 300 pounds of rolled oats and about 70 gallons of milk are needed every day.

With the city providing either work or direct relief for married men, relief tickets for single men, and the porridge kitchen being operated for the benefit of all, city officials state that there is no need for "pan-handling" on the part of the unemployed, and every effort is being made to put a stop to this practice.

February 11, 1931

From the introduction to The Herald's 1931 Progress Edition. Unfortunately, worse times were just around the corner.

Like a game fighter, who, although punch drunk and reeling, rallies to the call of the timekeeper's gong, the city of Calgary is making a come-back in a big way.

The stock market crash, the drop in the value of oil stocks and a serious unemployment condition set this hustling western metropolis back on its heels for a time, but with the fighting spirit that characterizes all Calgarians now very much in evidence, the lost ground has been regained, and backed by the grain growing section and the livestock centres of Southern Alberta, Calgary is forging ahead to new heights of endeavor.

Undisputable evidence that the industrial and commercial crisis has been passed, and that Calgary and districts surrounding it are again marching ahead, can be seen on all sides. More than 400 new homes were built in Calgary last year. Nearly 100 additional new homes have been started since January 1. Tax collections show an increase over last year. Business tax collections in 1930 exceeded estimated revenue by nearly $52,000. Calgarians paid the city more than $3,000,000 in property taxes during the year, and sundry revenues brought the city nearly $1,000,000 more.

Local industries were compelled to cut down their staffs when the slump was on, but with the prospect of new orders in sight, the plants and factories will undoubtedly be going full blast again within a short time.

April 16, 1931

Calgary had a small but vigorous branch of the Red Menace during the Thirties. It was a slow May Day that didn't yield prosecutions for illegal parading. The following episode, from June, 1931, was livelier than most, but hardly unique. The names of those charged have been omitted; some were later found not guilty.

Six men, two of them police, were injured and 31 were arrested in conflict between police and unemployed late Monday afternoon and evening.

All injured were reported progressing favorably Tuesday morning.

A man was charged with assault occasioning actual bodily harm to Constable J. M. Carter.

Five alleged Communist leaders were arrested on charges of being members of an unlawful assembly and 21 men were arrested on charges of disorderly conduct.

Two others charged with having been drunk and disorderly were arrested at 9:45 o'clock.

Three Russians and a Lithuanian were taken into custody at 10:20 o'clock and charged with being aliens unlawfully in possession of firearms.

The trouble started at 5:20 o'clock after one of the alleged Communists had addressed a large crowd on the vacant lot near the city hall. Someone set up a shout and the men began to mill about.

In a moment there was a shout for help. The tumult grew. Another shout called for a doctor. Police reserves rushed the vacant lot and men, dodging through traffic in a frantic effort to escape, ran through the streets. Batons were swung freely and at once the police began to return with their first prisoners.

Constable Carter, a gaping wound in his head, lay in the arms of two comrades on the lot. The battle was over as quickly as it had begun. Those who saw him declared that, in their opinion, Carter would have little chance for recovery but word soon came through from the hospital that he had regained consciousness and the tense feeling around police headquarters relaxed.

Following interference with work crews in the morning, warrants had been sworn out for the arrests of several alleged Communist leaders.

At 8:10 police received word that a meeting was to be held in the basement of the David Block and that the men sought were to be present.

Immediately, under Lt.-Col. D. Ritchie, chief constable, a large patrol left the headquarters. The movement took place just as an auto carrying policemen back from dinner arrived, and this was followed by more than a thousand spectators in automobiles and on foot, eager to share the excitement.

The crowds followed the police around Third Street East. Someone on Eighth Avenue began to throw stones, blocks of cement and bricks. Sgt. C.W. Cox, struck in the stomach by a piece of cement, fell groaning to the pavement. He was picked up by two spectators in a car and taken to the hospital.

Meantime the police had entered the front of the block, a strong guard having taken possession of exits on the lane.

Men burst through the rear doors of the building only to stumble into waiting policemen and detectives. One or two, making breaks for freedom, dashed down the lane but were soon overtaken and brought back. One, as though an innocent bystander, stepped from the door, smiled at a policeman nonchalantly and began to brush his threadbare coat. A chunk of iron fell from his clothing to the pavement. The jig was up and the constable nabbed him.

Eighteen were arrested in this raid and no sooner had they been lodged in the cells than the lusty strains of "The Red Flag" came from the basement of the police building.

The next trouble was reported from Eighth Avenue where it was reported that mobs, throwing stones, had smashed some windows. A small patrol dispersed the crowds and reported only one window broken.

Meanwhile the search for the alleged leaders and others continued. One, unaware the police held a warrant for him, walked into the police station and inquired for some of those arrested. He was immediately placed in the cells.

June 30, 1931

Optimism, 1931 style, as seen in a Herald editorial: things may be bad but they are worse elsewhere, and some day they will be better.

The toll taken by drouth and low prices on the value of Canadian field crops is shown by the total valuation for 1931 as estimated by the federal bureau of statistics. The figure given is $431,251,000, which is small in comparison with other years, notably 1919 when the high record of $1,537,169,000 was reached.

There is some consolation in the fact that Alberta, with a field crop production of $92,588,000, stands second in the list of Canadian provinces, Ontario leading with $138,547,000. Taking the smaller Alberta farm population into consideration, Alberta is even ahead of Ontario. While farm conditions are far from being good here, it seems our province is the brightest spot on the agricultural map of the Dominion insofar as

field crops are concerned.

Agriculture is in the doldrums now, but will not always remain there. The providing of food for the earth's inhabitants is too important an occupation to be depressed and impoverished for very long. This is the only word of cheer that can be held out to Alberta agriculturists at the present time. Alberta has an important place to fill in the future development of agriculture and the time will come when the misery and hardships of the present period will be but an unhappy memory.

December 21, 1931

A front-page editorial. Its Scrooge-like tone is perhaps justified by the fact that Calgary was headed for a close brush with bankruptcy only a few years later.

Not without cause has Calgary earned the soubriquet of Santa Claus city of Western Canada for itinerant single out-of-works. Since July 1, 1931, there has been paid out by Calgary's city council not less than $104,000 of the taxpayers' hard-earned cash to maintain in comparative comfort an army of thousands of idle single men, only a small percentage of whom have the slightest claim to citizenship status. At the present moment 1,100 of these men are being fed and housed by the city.

A so-called "tentative agreement" with the Dominion government on May 1 was to the effect that instead of one-third of direct relief costs, the Dominion would pay half.

Thus far the Dominion government has given no sign that it will honor the agreement or that it ever entered into such a bargain. In fact it has not even paid its one-third of direct relief costs since May 1. Meanwhile, the taxpayers of Calgary are paying high interest on borrowed money with which to meet the costs of settling the government's share of direct relief.

The Herald does not believe the city of Calgary was at any time under obligation, moral or otherwise, to house and feed the horde of unemployed single floaters which every year gravitates from one end to the other of Western Canada, stopping longest where pickings are easiest.

July 16, 1932

The Depression soon bit into the middle class. The author of this article was identified only as "Observer"; apparently he or she was a relief investigator.

Contrary to general belief, those who make up the bulk of the applicants for direct relief in our cities are not what the English term the "rag, tag and bobtail of society"; nor are they drawn exclusively from the ranks of unskilled labor. On the contrary, in our city with a population of more than 80,000, representatives from

Anyone who lost a job in the Thirties faced a very uncertain future. There was no unemployment insurance, and not many jobs. For those who lived in dread of being fired, one Herald advertiser offered this simple solution.

Pay your doctor, and keep your credit rating. In the days before medicare, doctors sometimes had trouble collecting fees. This ad in the Herald was sponsored by doctors, dentists and the Calgary Retail Credit Grantors.

---

practically all the trades and professions as well as former merchants are to be found in the relief ranks.

There is at least one minister of the gospel. Then there are lawyers, architects, chemists, electricians, machinists, painters, journalists, butchers, steel-workers, paper-hangers, bookkeepers, accountants, salesmen of every description, clerks and professors of music, farmers, engineers, railwaymen, barbers, furriers, upholsterers, porters, carpenters and laborers.

We have on single relief between 2,500 and 3,000 men and girls, and on married relief in the neighborhood of 2,700 families.

While it may be true that at the commencement of the present hard times the applicants for relief were very largely from the laboring class among whom foreigners predominate, as the Depression lasted, many others, who had at first a small accumulation of earnings, have been forced to come in.

Many and varied are the experiences of the investigator as he goes his rounds. Here is a middle-aged man who worked for 22 years for one of the best-known firms in Canada. He had saved up a tidy sum; and looking at his family, said to himself "If I can make money for the firm, why not make some for myself?" So with his savings and his line of credit he went into partnership with another ambitious man.

They did fairly well until hard times came, and then could not make a living together. He sold out what interest he had left in the business for $30 to his partner, paid a month's rent in advance, and has $2.50 left. This soon went and the morning of the day on which I called the children would have had to go to school without breakfast had the landlady not supplied them with food.

A minister in our town was doing well. He fitted up the basement of his church with beds for the unemployed last year. Then he resigned his pastorate to take up special work but had to abandon this. Coming back to the city, he found his former pastorate filled. No opening occurred. The children must be fed. So he also bowed to the inevitable and sought relief.

A professor of music who has taught two generations of pupils in our city finds that with the introduction of the phonograph and the radio, fewer pianos are bought and fewer pupils think it necessary to learn to play. Then, when a period of stress came, pupils fell off as did his income. He was faced with starvation and finally accepted relief.

On my rounds I found many instances of crowding. In one four-roomed house (foreigners) I found a family of four, and five roomers. In another place of five rooms there were a man and his wife with three children and eight roomers.

There was a young girl who applied for single girls' relief, saying her father had turned her out. I was sent to investigate, and found her parents living in their own home nicely furnished and receiving relief from the city. The father stubbornly refused to have anything to do with the erring one. Then I told him if he had no pity on his own child the city could have no pity on him. He was cut off relief and the daughter put on.

There is a changing attitude toward receiving relief. I was sent to see a family in distress. The father was in the hospital and they were in dire need. I recommended relief and the mother was given the maximum for a family of that size — I think it was $14 per week. But as she had to move and lacked a few dollars she came to me to ask if I could get her more.

I explained she was getting the maximum and suggested that as they were church members, she ask the church officials to aid them out of the poor fund to that extent. She replied "Oh, no, I cannot bear to beg or ask for charity."

February 22, 1932

Hungry men rode freight trains back and forth across the country, looking for work or looking for handouts. The federal government's solution: make them stop.

All single transient unemployed who are not bona fide residents of the city, and who are in destitute circumstances, are being advised by the city of Calgary to get back to their original homes before the freight train ban on transients goes into effect on Sept. 30.

Although a meeting of the special unemployment committee of the council will not be held until Thursday afternoon, it was stated at the city hall Wednesday that no relief to transient single unemployed men would be granted by the city this winter, and that only men who have been resident in Calgary since January, 1930, would be classed as bona fide residents.

As an added measure, the maximum sentences under the Railway Act for trespassing on trains will be imposed by all magistrate's courts throughout the whole Dominion of Canada.

In making the announcement before the conference of premiers and mayors on Tuesday, Prime Minister R.B. Bennett stated that when the ban goes into effect on Sept. 30, police forces of the country would be organized to see that the instructions of the government were carried out to the letter.

September 7, 1932

Like many employers, the city of Calgary cut back staff and wages when hard times came. Even so, the city was at the edge of bankruptcy later in the Depression.

Fifty-five civic employees will be discharged, a number of others, including Fire Chief James Smart and Inspector J.H. Cooper of the city police force, will be pensioned off, and services in many civic departments will be reduced to a minimum, if the economy report prepared by the city commissioners at the order of city council is adopted by the board of aldermen at their regular meeting Monday morning.

In addition, the commissioners are recommending that all civic employees more than 70 years of age be discharged with the usual notice and one month's extra salary; that all motormen in the street railway service, 65 years of age or more, be relieved of

their duties, and that work be rotated wherever possible.

The land department will be amalgamated with the city assessor's department and the services of D.R. Crichton, superintendent of the department for many years, will be dispensed with.

Members of the police and fire departments who are in executive positions and have reached the pensionable age will be retained until Dec. 31, while the rank and file over this age will be pensioned off immediately.

Fifteen civic departments came under the pruning-knife, and only a few escaped the attention of the commissioners. The public works department and the city parks department were hardest hit. Twenty-two men in the public works have received notice, and about a dozen men in the parks department.

In their report to the council, the commissioners stated that after consultation with Fire Chief James Smart and Chief of Police David Ritchie, it had been deemed inadvisable to reduce the manpower of either of these departments, with the exception of the men going on pension.

No economies were effected in the city medical health and school board health departments after it had been proven that there was no over-lapping of work.

September 10, 1932

After some terrible years, long after the false hopes of 1930 had faded, things did begin to get better.

Calgary has fewer people on relief at the present time than it has had at any time since February of 1932. At the beginning of last month, there were 2,034 families receiving relief here.

This was the lowest figure since February

of 1932, when there were 2,089 families on relief.

Harvest employment alone is not responsible for the reduction. A general improvement in conditions, indirectly attributable to the harvest, is seen as the major cause.

Ever since spring rains indicated a good crop year, employment throughout the province has picked up steadily. In anticipation of expanded fall business, merchants have undertaken repairs to premises, have laid in larger stocks and taken on added help to handle the increased turnover.

Farm machine houses have been able to place larger orders. Railways have had to take on more engineers, firemen, repair workers and section men.

As the summer advanced, the expansion in employment increased. In the last few weeks harvest optimism and labor demands have found their most pronounced reflection in employment figures since 1932.

September 2, 1938

Better times, and the cash registers rang out the glad tidings.

Calgarians are buying more clothes, paying off old debts, buying more furniture, attending movies more, and flashing more $100 bills than have been seen for a long time.

A generally cheerful scene in the business world was depicted today in a survey made of business conditions among retail merchants.

Though one or two firms cautioned against regarding the increased prosperity as signs of "a boom", still it was the consensus that the past season had seen the harvesting of an excellent crop, and that as a result people had more money to spend and were doing so to increase their comfort and enjoyment.

The result is that stocks in retail stores are reported to be "moving quickly", and luxury commodities that have suffered some neglect during the past few years are coming back into the trade picture once more.

The spirit of confidence and optimism was reflected by managers of general merchandise stores dealing in groceries, clothing and hardware. One stated: "All lines are moving well, and we have seen more $100 bills during the past few weeks than we have for a long time."

"Spending money and feeling good" was the way in which many shops described the buying public. Customers generally seemed to have more money to spend, and exhibited a more confident and cheerful attitude, it was said.

Furniture stores, especially, reported marked improvements, both in cash sales and collections. One firm stated it had taken in accounts that it had almost given up hope of ever collecting.

October 13, 1938

Unemployed men staged a protest march in downtown Calgary. The seething discontent of the Thirties never broke out into full-scale violence in Calgary, though there were minor incidents.

Another farm blowing away. Drought, wind and poor farming practice all did terrible damage to Western farmland. Soil blew away, and drifted so deeply in places that it buried fenceposts. Sometimes the dust storms blotted out the sun, and there was darkness at mid-day.

If city-dwellers suffered in the Thirties, farmers suffered doubly. Even those who had never been near a stockbroker were hurt as deeply as speculators in the crash of 1929. Grain prices dropped sharply at the same time Wall Street was falling apart. Grain prices recovered in the mid-Thirties, but the improvement was a bitter irony for Western farmers who saw their land racked by drought and wind. They had very little to sell at the new, higher prices. In the days before the Canadian Wheat Board, farmers watched the Winnipeg Grain Exchange with keen interest. From there, in the early Thirties, came bad news about grain prices.

An avalanche of wheat poured into the grain pit here today and prices plunged to levels not reached since July, 1913, seventeen years ago. Closing figures were 4 1/8 to 4 5/8 cents under Tuesday's final levels.

Signs of the decline were evident in the opening few minutes and before the end of the first half hour of trading two cents had been chipped off values. General liquidation from the professionals and the public sent a steady stream of wheat into the pit, and prices crumbled under the weight of it.

During the session there were feeble attempts at rallies, but they speedily died. At the slightest sign of a rally, offerings flooded the pit and prices were again beaten back.

As values faded, stop-loss orders were touched off and this loosened further selling. Trading was on a large scale and buying orders were an exception. At the closing bell prices were only about an eighth of a cent above the low points of the day.

An export business of about 700,000 bushels overnight and this morning had no effect in dispelling the bearish sentiment that overhung the market. The foreign demand for wheat seems to have petered out as importers and millers are satisfied for the time being with the heavy purchases made during the last four weeks.

The statistical situation was encouraging to the bear forces. Broomhall, the Liverpool expert, estimates the world's wheat production this season at about 190,000,000 bushels larger than last year.

Winnipeg, July 30, 1930

After helping to start the Alberta Wheat Pool, The Herald took a fatherly interest in its future. This editorial was evidently intended to shore up morale at a bad time.

This is the testing time for the wheat pool. It has many enemies at home and abroad. Prices are phenomenally low, and the entrance of cheap Russian wheat on the European market has added to the gravity of the outlook.

The initial payment for 1930 wheat was set some time ago at 60 cents a bushel for No. 1 Northern at Fort William, 40 cents lower than the first payment of 1929. Yet, in spite of all these factors, it is a matter of record that pool deliveries this season are the highest on record. There have been reports of bootlegging but the practice apparently is no more prevalent than it was during the recent prosperous years.

The loyalty of the members is highly significant and highly satisfactory. It indicates that they recognize their loyalty is just as much on trial as the pool system itself. They intend to stand by their bargain in a dismal year. It has been established during the past twelve months that the pool cannot control prices on the world market or secure more for grain than the rates created by competitive selling.

But the pool members know that if the pool disintegrates and a great co-operative movement ends in disaster, they will be thrown back into the old condition of utter dependence on the will of the private grain companies. Their experience of old is not one that they wish repeated.

September 25, 1930

This was not the only story of its kind in the Thirties, when a lost job or a lost crop could drive a man to despair. The family's name has been omitted here.

A Camrose district man, about 38, shot and killed his wife and two daughters, aged 8 and 6; left a son, 4, when four men came upon him; ran into the Dried Meat Lake and drowned himself at 5:30 p.m. Friday, according to police allegations.

Dismissal from the managership of a lumber company here Friday morning is believed to have caused the man to worry, which resulted in the tragedy.

The shooting took place at a lonely spot a quarter of a mile from Dried Meat Lake and 14 miles southeast of Camrose. The man had taken his family out for a car ride, and the bodies of the girls were found in the back seat of the car with bullets from a .45 calibre automatic pistol through their chests, and the wife on the roadway 60 feet from the machine.

The little boy, held in the arms of his father when four men in another car came upon the scene after the mother and the girls had been killed, was put carefully back into the front of the machine. Then the father started to run across the fields.

The men took the boy into Camrose, notified police, and left the boy at the residence of a neighbor.

The family had been resident in Camrose for slightly less than a year, the father being appointed to the managership of the lumber yard at that time.

The dead man had served with an artillery division, according to those who knew him, and had been awarded the Military Cross.

Camrose, May 23, 1931

Herald reporter D.A. McCannel toured southern Alberta for a first-hand view of 1931 farm prospects. Here is one of his dispatches.

Crops along the Empress line are needing rain badly. Pastures are very short, and unless rain comes within the next week or ten days, all grain yields will be very light.

Contrasted with the dry land area, the irrigation section along this line east of here and west to Cluny is very promising, and the wheat and alfalfa are making seed growth.

Several good fields of grain are to be seen in the "Little Sweden" district, south of Buffalo, where a number of farm homes have been well improved with good buildings and windbreaks, sharply contrasting with the deserted buildings on nearby farms, mute evidence of the effect of the prolonged drought on the efforts of earlier and less fortunate settlers.

Well-built and painted houses and barns with windows and doors gaping open, stand grouped around dry wells, while miles of wire and posts lie along roadsides and range stock wanders unhindered through weed-grown fields and gardens which testify to the outcome of the unequal battle with nature waged for a time by optimistic settlers in this area.

Further north a more cheerful picture is presented. Atlee, Buffalo and Bindloss districts have had good showers recently and with additional rains in the next week or ten days will still yield a light average crop. Jen-

ner district has not been so fortunate in the matter of rainfall.

One farmer here who has 700 acres of crop expressed the fear that he would have to let his men go instead of keeping them on for fall work unless prospects greatly improved soon.

A variation of the "strip farming" method is being used with apparently good results in a number of fields in the Jenner district as a moisture conservation measure.

Seed is sown from six runs in the seed drill and the next six are stopped up, leaving bare strips three feet wide alternating with three-foot strips of grain throughout the field. The bare strips are kept black with a small cultivator until the grain is well grown, and the effect of the additional moisture from these fallow strips is quite apparent on the growth and color of the grain.

Entry into the irrigation section around Princess, Patricia, Duchess, Rosemary and Countess is a welcome change on a trip along this line. Water has been flowing in the ditches since April and it seems a strange irony that the irrigated belt has had showers denied much of the outlying parched land.

Farmers in the Duchess, Millicent and Gem districts are finding hogs one of their most profitable farming lines. Breeding stock, after the spring litter of pigs is weaned,

are turned into alfalfa fields in many cases. It does not appear to hurt the crops and it is a rich dish indeed for the porkers.

This district will send more hogs to market this year than ever in its history and porkers' cheques will pay a good many local bills.

Bassano, June 16, 1931

Dry humor from the dust bowl.

There is still humor in the drought districts — a humor refreshed by this week's rainfalls. One farmer from the dry belt area east of this city tells the story of the frogs on his farm, which though 17 years of age had never learned to swim.

Another man in the same district is said to have fainted last Monday when he opened his door and saw rain for the first time in many years. All known methods are said to have failed to revive him until he was brought back to consciousness with a glass of dust.

Drumheller, July 17, 1937

BUT WHERE ARE MY CROPS?

GRAIN PRICES U...

Higher prices are of no use to a farmer who has nothing to sell. Many Western farmers found themselves in this ironic dilemma in the Thirties. (September 2, 1933)

In the drought years, once-fertile land baked and cracked under the relentless sun. The sky was empty blue for weeks at a time. Farmers looked anxiously for *clouds, but the few brief rains could not save their crops. After the drought, it took years to restore the eroded soil.*

A really unlucky farmer was one who hadn't enough thistles to feed his stock.

All we have is thistle!" The reiteration of this plaint occurs with painful regularity as one speaks to farmers in the drouth area centring on Youngstown. Russian Thistle has been known to keep animals alive over winter.

Feed is not to be had for the buying in this area, and as Martin Paetz, councillor of Collholme Municipality pointed out, "It has not been the practice of any government to give feed relief for stock before snow-fall."

Typical of the situation is the case of J. Zelinka, a hard-working and adept farmer who has never found it necessary to ask for government relief feed. He has 100 head of cattle and 20 horses.

"Are you going to have feed for your cattle this winter?" he was asked.

"Well, if my cattle have iron stomachs, they will be able to live on this rubbish I am cutting for them," he said as he pointed to a mixture of fox-tail, dried reeds, weeds and grass he was cutting on what was formerly Antelope Lake but is now a dried piece of alkaline soil with a few soap holes.

"Are you going to be able to keep all of your stock?"

"No, I will try to keep 50 head, the others I will have to sell, but I do not want to sacrifice them at a low price or I will be unable to buy what I require to feed the rest," he replied.

Asked if any of his crop grew, Mr. Zelinka answered jokingly, "Our rye didn't look bad until the first rain in July, then it just died of shock. Seriously, though, the sawflies, hoppers and gophers ruined it. We will have to buy oats for our horses and feed for our chickens. We can get along without these just now working the horses easily, and we still have a little chicken feed.

North in the Hemaruka district a similar condition is found to exist. J. Sims told us: "I will have to depend on thistles if I stay here; even these are so short it will be difficult to cut them unless we have more rain."

Martin Paetz, farming 22 miles south of Youngstown, said: "It is almost impossible to exaggerate the need for feed in the district from here south to the Red Deer River. Even the sheep men are going to have to get assistance from the government, and those people with hogs and chickens require immediate help if they are to feed them."

"How many head of stock have you?"

"I have 50 head now, but will have to sell most of them; I'll try to keep the cows." Mrs. Paetz then spoke up:

"Yes, but you can't get any price for thin cattle and how can you get them fat on this range?"

"We haven't had oats for our horses for some time, so we only work them half-days," Mr. Paetz added. The thistles are not growing in abundance in this section.

In the Rainbow district, J. Lynn observed: "I think I can winter mine without any assistance. I am one of the fortunate few, I guess. I have 160 acres of wheat from which I think I'll get three to four bushels to the acre, then I have a field of oats that will make green feed. This with the thistles, I think, will see me through."

Youngstown, August 2, 1937

At last, a sign of hope. The farmer whose crop burst his granary must have had a classic case of mixed feelings.

Elevators in Southern Alberta are filling to capacity. Some are already plugged, and at a few points the high grade grain is being dumped on the ground awaiting cars to move it.

The heaviest crop in years, coupled with a shortage of cars in the south-eastern part of the Lethbridge division, has resulted in most of the elevator space being filled.

Farmers are pleased with the big crop, but are worried over the possibility of rain arriving and causing loss of grade to the wheat piled in the open, according to Norman F. Priestley, vice-president of the United Farmers of Alberta.

Mr. Priestley returned today from an inspection trip in the south during which he visited Vauxhall, Taber, Sterling, Magrath, Cardston, Hillspring, Pincher Creek and other points.

At Sterling, he said, the elevators were filled to overflowing, and huge piles of grain were rising on adjoining ground. In the same district, there were reports that some farmers were emptying their combine hoppers right in the field, the grain being in piles 50 to 75 yards in length.

One farmer dumped so much wheat into his granary that the walls gave way.

The "plugging," however, is considered only temporary, as there is ample storage space at terminals as soon as rail cars can be secured to move the wheat.

September 3, 1938

Hard times brought countless personal disasters, some of them dramatic enough to reach the newspapers. The Herald Sunshine Society conducted an annual Christmas drive to help the poor. Every front page in December carried a grim story of suffering and an appeal for help.

The thermometer touched 15 below in Calgary this morning. In a little house in the Capitol Hill district a man sat crouching over a pitiful little fire that burned weakly in the kitchen stove. Alongside the stove, so close that the dying flames lit up their wan faces, a woman and four children huddled together in a makeshift bed for warmth.

Two of the children gnawed away at pieces of hard bread. One cried softly as the hard crusts bruised its tender mouth. The mother reached forward, dipped the hard bread into a pitcher of water and handed it back to the baby. It munched away at it contentedly.

Dogs have turned up their noses at better fare.

In scores of Calgary houses the same poverty-stricken conditions prevail. Unemployment, illness and poverty, walking hand in hand, are creating havoc in Calgary.

Official investigators of the Herald Sunshine Department have discovered conditions that are almost unbelievable. The city can boast of its $10,000,000 worth of building permits for the year, its new high record for bank clearings, and the hundreds and thousands of dollars that swap hands daily on the stock exchange, but walking in the shadows are hundreds of unfortunates whose main battle at the present time is to keep from starving or freezing to death.

December 11, 1929

Given dry grass and a high wind, a prairie fire could be a terrifying force.

A prairie fire, starting at noon and sweeping across country in the Rowley Morrin district on Friday, took three lives, laid bare twenty-five miles of country and razed five farmsteads.

The dead are Mrs. Oscar Devaleriola, who died on Saturday morning in Drumheller hospital, and her two daughters, Margaret, 17, and Ellen, 10.

A vast amount of farm machinery and at least one horse were destroyed as the fire swept first north, then east, and in the late afternoon headed south as it was fanned by a strong wind which died down as suddenly as it started.

A wall of fire and smoke jumped across a trail about five miles northwest of Morrin when the car in which the three victims were riding and which was driven by the father, Oscar Devaleriola, stalled in a swampy dip. The girls with their mother, alighted from the car while the driver frantically sought to release the vehicle.

Sparks set their clothing afire and sent the girls into a panic. Heedless of the calls of their mother, who dashed after them in a heroic effort to save them, they ran directly into the thickest of the smoke, the elder being fatally overcome only a few yards away from the car while the ten-year old girl was lost to sight over a small hill. She was later found dead 100 yards away.

The mother fell unconscious as she reached her elder daughter and by the time she was rescued most of her clothing had burned. When admitted to the Drumheller hospital she was unrecognizable and suffering acutely from burns and shock.

Devaleriola, who remained in the car and was unable to see the tragedy which was being enacted a few yards ahead due to the density of the smoke, was uninjured, while the car was not damaged.

Had the three victims remained in the car the fire would have passed on within a few minutes as the wind veered suddenly.

The Devaleriola family has lived in the Morrin district for the past twenty-three years, having come to Western Canada from the Dakotas. There are several surviving children.

Drumheller, April 15, 1933

The Herald Sunshine Society gave a little help to this family, driven to the roads by bad times.

They came to Calgary in an antiquated car — estimated value about $10 — mother, father and four children, little more than babies. Their destination was a town somewhere in Manitoba.

But the storm overtook them and they reached Calgary almost frozen to death. Two of the children were so ill that they had to be taken to hospital.

The babies have recovered now, and local organizations have been looking after the family. They are still a long way from home, and unless arrangements can be made for their return, Christmas will see them stranded and desolate.

Sunshine has played its part in helping these parents, along with scores of others. Donations to the Santa Claus fund will make it possible to send them on their way rejoicing.

December 14, 1933

A domestic crisis, made worse by hard times.

Two little girls, aged eight and 15 years, were deserted by their mother in the city police building yesterday afternoon.

Interviewed by Children's Aid Officer Fred Gardiner this morning, the mother said she had left the children because she had no money to feed them.

The children were cared for during the night by Mrs. P. Lennington, of the provincial relief department, and Miss J. Chapman, Travellers' Aid officer of the YWCA.

On June 12, said Clarke Eady, supervisor of provincial relief, the mother applied to the provincial relief office at Calgary to get relief for herself and two daughters. Her husband was employed as a farm laborer at Aldersyde, and she had been living with the children at Blackie.

Investigation disclosed that the husband was willing to support his family to the best of his ability. He said that his wife had sold her household effects and moved to Calgary without his consent. Provincial relief officers offered the woman transportation to return to Blackie or to High River, where she would be near her husband. The mother refused.

Yesterday Mrs. Lennington again offered her transportation to High River, and emergency relief for a few days until she could arrange to move, but again she refused.

Later in the day, city police telephoned Mrs. Lennington, informing her that the two girls had been left in the clerk of court's office in the police building.

"The father told me he was sorry this had happened and that he would try to make arrangements to have the girls boarded near Aldersyde," said Mrs. Lennington. "I talked to the employer, too, who said the man was a good worker who made between $25 and $30 per month."

July 30, 1937

An eye for sale. The youth's name has been omitted.

An offer to sell his injured right eye "for a reasonable sum" was made today by a 19-year-old Calgary youth.

"I am prepared to lie down on an operating table and permit a surgeon to extract my eye and transfer it to a blind man who might regain his sight thereby. If that should prove impossible, I am willing to sell my living eye to any scientific organization for the advancement of medical science," he said.

The young man is at present unemployed, but, he says, he obtains work off and on at a Calgary plant.

"I can't earn money fast enough to pay off medical bills as fast as I would wish," he asserted. "The doctors did me a great deal of good and they should be paid. I want to sell my eye to pay them. The medical services had nothing to do with my eye."

"How much money would you expect for your eye?" he was asked.

"A reasonable sum — just about what I would receive if I received compensation for losing my eye in an accident for which somebody else was to blame," the young man replied. "I should say about $1,500 or anything reasonable."

"I hope there will be some response. Apart altogether from the money, I would like to help out some man or woman suffering from loss of sight and to make a contribution to medical science."

July 18, 1938

The Edmonton Commercial Grads were a spectacularly good senior women's basketball team. Founded in 1914, the team held the world championship for 17 years, winning 502 of the 522 games it played. The founder and coach, J. Percy Page, later was a member of the Alberta Legislature, and then lieutenant-governor. This report describes the Grads in fine form, a few years before they were disbanded in 1940.

Edmonton Grads gained their 13th Canadian senior women's basketball championship here Saturday night when they defeated the Windsor Alumnae, Eastern Canada's best, by 57 to 30. It was a three-out-of-five series, Grads taking the first two games 84 to 20 and 47 to 30.

A passing game with a decided edge around the basket territory gave the Grads their victory after the Alumnae held the play for the first five minutes of the game and then dropped under a drive by the titleholders.

Gladys Fry, sharp-shooting centre for the Grads, was the high scorer of the game, notching 17 points, while her team-mate Margaret MacBurney followed with 16.

Grads dominated the play for the whole game, except for the first few minutes. When the Alumnae rolled in four points to start the game the Grads suddenly came to life and scored 10 points while the easterners could get no more during the first period. At the start of the second period Windsor added one more point on a foul and the Grads then rolled in another five field baskets before the Windsor team found the hoop again.

The Grads had all of the game in the third quarter and their passing was at its best then. Although Windsor played a sturdy defence and knocked down passes frequently the Grads were able to direct the play so that one of their players could get into shooting position. Time after time from a knot of players Margaret MacBurney managed to break away to the side and remain uncovered until she got the ball. Her scoring ability is at its best at a corner of the floor.

Edmonton, April 30, 1934

Jesse Owens, a black American, won three Olympic gold medals, for the running broad jump and the 100-meter and 200-meter dashes. The Nazi hosts of the Olympics found some trouble in reconciling these wins with their racial theories. Elmer Dulmage of the Canadian Press filed this report from Berlin on the first of Owens' victories.

Jesse Owens, the "black bullet" of the United States, won the Olympic 100 metre championship today. It was the negro's first triumph in his try for three Olympic gold medals. Owens also is entered in the 200 metre event and the broad jump.

Owens broke fast and led after the first ten metres, beating his fellow countryman, Ralph Metcalfe, by one yard and a half.

Metcalfe previously had won the semi-final heat that marked the passing of Canada's Howie McPhee from the picture. McPhee finished fourth in a trial run in 10.5 seconds.

Owens feather-footed over the brick red strip before another capacity throng of more than 100,000 in 10.3 seconds, to capture the gold medal in world- and Olympic-record-equalling time.

While Jeannette Dolson was succeeding in staying in the running for the women's 100 metre sprint, another Toronto girl, Hilda Cameron, ran third and out in her heat. Emha Albus of Germany won the latter trial in 12.4 with the Austrian girl, Vancura, 1-10th second back.

"Hustling Howie" McPhee, of Vancouver, Canada's main bidder for sprint honors, was eliminated when he finished fourth in the second heat.

Ralph Metcalfe won the heat in 10.5 seconds to join the other U.S. negro, Jesse Owens, in the final. Owens won the first heat in 10.4 seconds, 2-10th second off his phenomenal time in the quarter finals yesterday. That performance shaved 1-10th second from the world standard, but it was not allowed because there was a wind at the runner's back.

Clocked in 11.4 seconds, Helen Stephens of the United States lowered the world record in winning her heat in the opening trials of the 100-metre sprint for women. Miss Stephens' time eclipsed the listed world standard of 11.8 seconds set by Stella Walsh of Poland in 1933 and the Olympic record of 11.9 also set by Miss Walsh at Los Angeles in 1932.

Jeannette Dolson of Toronto was second, nearly 10 metres back of the Missouri flier, with three others trailing still further to the rear.

The elimination of McPhee from the metric century was a disappointment in the Canadian camp. Despite the brilliance of Owens and several other contenders, there was a fond hope that the big, muscular Howie might duplicate the double win Percy Williams, also of Vancouver scored for the Dominion in the 100 and 200 metre dashes in the 1928 games.

Berlin, August 3, 1936

Champion bronc rider Pete Knight at work. He died in a California rodeo, thrown and trampled by a bronc named Duster, which had thrown him before.

Pete Knight of Crossfield, four-time world champion bronc rider, died at 33 in a rodeo at Hayward, California. The Herald published this eyewitness account by J. Harry Rowell, a rancher and rodeo operator.

Pete Knight died a champion's death Sunday. He was riding "Duster," the best bucking horse in the show and one of the best in the world, and he was winning.

The 5,000 spectators were cheering him and there wasn't one of the boys, not even those who had ridden against him, who wasn't pulling for him to win. It was the last event of the day and Pete had ridden another horse earlier in the day and he had given the crowd plenty of thrills.

The horse was bucking like an eel, but Pete was riding him high, wide and handsome and trying to get "Duster" to pitch even harder. The judges had written him down already as the winner.

Then it happened.

Nobody knows why it happened, I guess. "Duster" was just a little too good that one second. It didn't look as though Pete was in any trouble when suddenly he was out of the saddle. He went over the horse's head and the dust spurted a little as he fell on his back and lay there for a hundredth of a second. He didn't have a chance to move.

When we got to Pete's side he was still. "Duster's" hoofs had landed square in his stomach. A doctor in the crowd called an ambulance but when we got to the hospital Pete was dead.

We're going to bury him Wednesday with a cowboy's funeral. They'll sing the cowboy songs he loved to sing and they'll sing them well because they'll be for one of the finest guys in the world.

Pete knew what he was riding. "Duster" threw him at Elko, Nev., last year, but he had made money on the horse. Pete rode "Duster" because it was what he contracted to do.

In a couple of days we'll be starting on the California rodeo season, then on through the regular old route, but it won't seem the same, though, without Pete.

Hayward, Calif., May 25, 1937

Despite the gloom and doom on the front pages, most people made do, got along somehow, and managed to enjoy themselves now and then. Some got up to the improbable tricks that brighten the inside pages of newspapers even in the worst of times. Some, however, found that apparent good luck could be deep misfortune. Lukin Johnston of The Herald's London bureau wrote this story of an Alberta rancher who inherited an earldom. Fred Perceval's son, the next Earl of Egmont, later returned to Alberta and lived south of Calgary.

As a little group of people, headed by one broken-hearted lad, his son, followed the body of Frederick Perceval, tenth Earl of Egmont, to the grave at Acocks Green, near Birmingham, where he was born, "finis" was written to one of the strangest romances of the British peerage, and one of the most pathetic.

Ostracized by aristocratic "county" families of Hampshire society ever since his return to England, three years ago, Lord Egmont and his son lived the lives of hermits at Avon Castle. No neighbors from nearby great estates called on them. None made an effort to make easier the path which "Fred Perceval" had chosen for himself in his desire to fulfil what he considered the obligations of his inheritance. He came back from his Alberta ranch, he said, because of this and because of the duty he felt he owed his son, who must now assume his father's burden.

Only among the simple villagers of Ringwood, near his castle, did the late earl make any friends. There sometimes he would talk wistfully to cronies in the local inn or store of his life on the Alberta farm. They like him, although embarrassing him by the English villagers' ineradicable respect for a "title." He was always "Sir" even to them and never "Fred" of the Alberta days.

"A finer, straighter man you could never meet," said one of his Ringwood friends yesterday. "If there were more like him this would be a better place."

Loathing the publicity to which the newspapers subjected him unceasingly for weeks after his arrival, he could seldom be persuaded to take part in any public event.

Many stories are told of his life at Ringwood. Once in a local inn he said, "People over here ain't natural. When I succeeded to the title I found I was expected to wash and shave four times daily, ride a poor downhearted-looking horse in the New Forest with a lot of funny looking guys I didn't like and who didn't like me, dress like a dummy attending idiotic meetings about nothing, and act generally as though I was daft. Three pints please, landlord."

Once he was asked why he lived in the kitchen and employed no servants or housekeeper. "Just because a housekeeper or butler would boss me about," he said, "and I'm not going to be bossed. I'm going to get up when I like, eat when I'm hungry, and do things that amuse me."

But Hampshire society could not surmount its dislike of this plain man's rough and ready manners. Probably none will ever know how deeply he was hurt by the treatment accorded him.

London, May 19, 1932

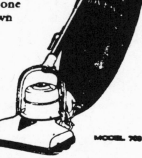
A tender ad for a vacuum cleaner. This woman tells us that she was fast losing her youth to household drudgery. Then, instead of some useless trinket, her husband bought her a Hoover.

Even household hints had a special Thirties flavor. A sack of flour, Elnora Bailey wrote, was more than just a container for food — it was clothing, too.

Governments may come and go, but the flour sack is undisturbed by political changes and its future is unquestionably bright.

One of the most common uses of flour sacks is effectively demonstrated on the clothes lines of both city and country homes each wash day, when dish towels in the process of bleaching advertise their origin, and incidentally, the flour they once contained.

Very often in the country homes the brightly colored drapes that make the windows look so cheery and the rooms so cozy are dyed flour sacks. The material takes the dye readily, and if thoroughly bleached before application, evenly.

Children completely outfitted in flour sacks are a common sight in the Peace River country. In view of the fact that many little girls in rural Alberta wear dresses whose material has been procured in this manner, some milling companies are bagging their flour in red-and-white and blue-and-white checked gingham.

The stamp which proclaims the brand of flour is being applied more lightly, so that it may be completely removed in an ordinary washing, and will not make necessary more rigorous methods of bleaching which might also remove the gingham design.

On one homestead in Southern Alberta, a very voluminous and intimate article, undoubtedly belonging to the matron of the home, graced the clothesline each week and declared to the world at large it was "For Family Use," an advertisement frequently used on the larger weights of flour.

October 30, 1932

Unisex hair stylists? In Calgary? In 1936?

Whether it is the baleful influence of the movie sheik, or the desire to increase their natural claims to pulchritude, the young men of Calgary are taking to "permanent" waves.

And not just the "lounge lizard" type, either. Those nice, fresh-looking youngsters just out of college; the high school boy searching for his first job; the lad who is always a "wow" at the dances. Dozens more. All have succumbed, it appears, to the current fad for wavy hair.

If nature gave it to them, so much the better. If she didn't, there is always the beauty parlor and its staff of skilled operators to transform straight locks into the loveliest curls before you can say "skat."

A Herald reporter refused to credit the story that Calgary's male youth and beauty had "gone feminine." She had been brought up in the school of thought that men — real he-men — detested curly hair and spent their time plastering it down with unguents designed to keep it flat — if they were so unlucky as to possess it.

"Don't you believe that men hate it," she was told by the male proprietor of one of the largest of the city's beauty salons. "They are just as vain as women, and they love it. If they haven't got waves they come to us to get them — just like the women. Why, I give an average of 10 permanents a month to young men of the city, and I have 40 to 50 regular customers. Not only that but lots of them come in regularly for finger-waves. Sure" — in response to the reporter's gasp of horror — "they come in during the regular hours — they're not bashful. No sir!"

September 26, 1936

A man-in-the-street interview.

Almost all Calgary pedestrians are jay-walkers, and almost all think something should be done to discourage them, but just what, they don't know.

Between 11:00 o'clock and 11:15 this morning, 161 persons on foot approached traffic lights which were against them, at the intersection of Seventh Avenue and First Street west. Of these, 157 completely ignored the red light warning them to stop; five of them going so far as to kitty-corner across the intersection.

"It is not the pedestrian who is grievously at fault, but the motorist," said a pedestrian interviewed by The Herald. "In the old days, they used to blow their horns giving the pedestrian ample warning of the approach of an automobile; now they are upon you before you can even think about it.

"Of course," he continued, "I am heartily behind any action which would help to put a stop to jay-walking."

"Thank you," said the reporter.

"You're welcome," the man replied, crossing the intersection against a red light.

January 20, 1938

THE EVENTS LEADING UP TO THE TRAGEDY

Radio had put music in the air, and song-writers seemed to compete to write the most mindless but unforgettable tune. The strongest man might crack under the strain. Boo boo pa doop.

Beware the killer canary.

Importation of Indian hemp seed, from which deadly marijuana plants may be grown, has just been prohibited by the the customs authorities, and Calgary feed stores may no longer sell the seed to farmers for windbreaks or any other purpose, Inspector J.O. Scott of the Calgary subdivision of the RCMP said today.

While the growing of marijuana plants has been prohibited in Alberta for years, the customs authorities have just taken action to prohibit the importation of the seed into Alberta and other Canadian provinces, the inspector stated.

A Calgary feed store informed The Herald today that it had sold about five pounds of the seed each season in the past to farmers who considered the plant an excellent wind-break. Recently the remaining seed on hand in the store was removed by the RCMP.

"We also used it for feeding young canaries," a member of the staff of the feed store said. "It is an excellent food for them. We imported it from England and had no trouble getting it through the customs until about a week ago."

The plant, which thrives in Alberta, has generally been grown innocently by persons without knowledge of the deadly narcotic drug contained in the leaves.

Of recent years, however, the RCMP has been active in uprooting all marijuana plants found growing in Alberta.

Only this week, RCMP officers located the marijuana plant growing in gardens in the town of Macleod under the name of "Iceland Palm." All plants found were destroyed. A year ago a number of plants were located within the Calgary city limits and they were destroyed by the Mounties.

The narcotic drug marijuana, known as hasheesh in Asia, is generally smoked by addicts in this country in cigarettes called "reefers." The habit is very easily acquired. The drug causes a marked stimulation of the brain, resulting, in many cases, in temporary insanity. When "high" on marijuana, addicts have committed murder and other serious crimes.

August 19, 1939

R.B. Bennett, a Calgary business man and lawyer, became Prime Minister of Canada in 1930. His Conservatives won 137 seats, and the defeated Liberals 88. The voters also elected 10 United Farmers, nine of them from Alberta, and 10 miscellaneous independents. It was a setback for the Liberals' durable leader, William Lyon Mackenzie King, but five more years of hardship were to make the public as impatient with Bennett as they had been with King. Charles Bishop of The Herald's Southam bureau in Ottawa filed the following dispatch the morning after Bennett's victory.

The capital city awoke this morning to a realization of the fact that, after nine years of office, the Liberal government of Hon. W.L. MacKenzie King has been defeated, to be replaced in due course by a Conservative ministry under Hon. R.B. Bennett.

Early today the final figures were still somewhat obscure, but the one clear thing was that the government is submerged. Just how badly the next 24 hours will tell precisely.

Different factors and influences entered into the defeat of the government. Business depression, unemployment, the cry of hard times, the call for a change — all these played their part, but more conspicuous than the rest was the havoc wrought in rural Quebec and Ontario, and elsewhere, by the argument that the dairy industry is prejudiced and depressed by importations of New Zealand butter. Seemingly, if the greatest vital factor in the defeat of the government is sought, it lies in this bitter question. Only in recent months did they give heed to an agitation long exploited in parliament.

The government appears to have slipped and fallen on this avalanche of New Zealand butter more than anything else. In the cities unemployment cut a figure, but except for Montreal, Regina, part of Winnipeg and East Edmonton, these places were Conservative anyway.

There is no record in Canada of any governments forced to encounter an election in a period of depression, being able to get away with it; and while the King ministry playing part of the time in good luck stressed the budget and inter-Imperial trade, the alternative issues raised by the opposition cut a wider swath of influence.

Something, it is agreed, happened down there when Conservatives were able to win 23 seats, a few perhaps because of inter-party divisions, but mostly on straight lines; and, moreover, it is considered to be better for the country to spread the Liberal support in place of having such high concentration in this particular province.

Also very noticeable is the Conservative sweep in New Brunswick, the reversal of form in Prince Edward Island and the blocking of anticipated Liberal gains in Nova Scotia. In the Ontario result is seen the influence of the Ferguson government though some losses are checked up against gains and the Conservative net betterment is six seats. This is offset by Liberal gains in British Columbia. On the prairies the Conservatives did what they expected to do.

Ottawa, July 29, 1930

An editorial marking the election of R.B. Bennett's Conservatives.

The record of the King Government and its promises stands condemned. The people have declared for a more vigorous expression of Canadianism and for a more virile management of the country's fiscal affairs. They have declared against a policy of vacillation and indecision, and the verdict has been expressed from coast to coast. Even the province of Quebec has swung away decisively from its old allegiance. The chief dairying counties there have expressed condemnation of the King tariff policy, and the province as a whole has administered a severe rebuke to the effort to revive old racial and religious prejudices. The attempt of the government to talk Imperialism in Ontario and anti-Imperialism in Quebec has met with the punishment it deserved.

The result is a declaration that the people will no longer trust to a government that does not know its own mind on tariff policies. They had decided that the last-moment switch to protection was a weak and insincere move. They have declared for a policy of confidence and courage with regard to fiscal policies. They want a Canada First programme.

July 29, 1930

Calgary was the unlikely birthplace of the CCF, which later became the New Democratic Party.

The Commonwealth Federation (Farmer-Labor-Socialist) organization came into existence at the Sunday morning meeting of the Western conference of Labor political parties, held in the Labor Temple. The report of the committee on Farmer-Labor matters, which was adopted by the conference, brought in the name, the object of the organization being given as follows:

"The federation of organizations whose purpose is the establishment in Canada of a co-operative commonwealth, in which the basic principle of regulating production, distribution and exchange will be the supplying of human needs instead of the making of profits."

The object of the federation was said to be the promotion of co-operation between and correlation of the member organizations with the general viewpoint and program involved in the socialization of the economic life which has already been outlined and accepted by the Labor-Farmer and Socialist groups affiliating.

The question of the desirability or otherwise of a Dominion-wide Labor party and the suitability of the name "Socialist" or "Labor" for that party, occupied the attention of delegates Saturday afternoon.

While all were agreed that the various groups in Canada gathered under the workers' flag had the same aims and objects and belonged to the Socialist movement, there was considerable difference of opinion as to the methods to be adopted to attain a Socialist government.

Following a plea for a Dominion-wide party under the name of "Socialist" by the British Columbia delegates, with other delegates refuting the necessity of one big organization under the name "Socialist," the following resolution, moved by M.J. Coldwell, was accepted by the gathering:

"That believing that the present economic crisis is due to the inherent unsoundness of the capitalist control of production and distribution that involves the payment of rent, interest and profit, that we organize nationally to change this system. We declare further that we recognize that social ownership and co-operative production for use is the only sound economic system."

Under the heading "Pinkish Soviet Plan Launched," The Herald indicated editorially that it was not about to take out a membership.

Canada is to have a Commonwealth Federation, modelled not too remotely on the Russian theory of government. So much was decided at a so-called national Farmer-Labor-Socialist conference in this city over the weekend.

The new organization with the imposing name may be more pink than red at the outset but it is apparent that Russia has provided the inspiration for the new body. Canada is to follow suit in establishing a new and better social and economic order wherein production, distribution and exchange will be subordinated to human needs and not conducted for profit. In fact, the objective is to set up a socialistic state, a modern Utopia, in which selfish individual ambition and private gain will be eliminated altogether.

The successful farmer has always been classed as a capitalist. His whole business ambitions and personal activities have been devoted to the making of individual profit. He has been an individualist par excellence. Now he is to subordinate his personal ambitions and abandon his individualist tendencies to become submerged in a co-operative state. If the Commonwealth Federation ever comes into control in this country, Mr. Woodsworth and a few other obvious leaders of the movement will do his thinking for him. They will also control his activities and distribute his profits, if any.

It is within recent memory that the Laborites and Socialists of Great Britain decided everything was wrong with the body politic over there. The electorate finally agreed to give them a chance to run the country, and everyone will recall what a sorry mess they made of things in a very few years. They brought the old country to the verge of ruin. The sponsors of this new Canadian plan evidently ignore this British example but surely they do not expect the Canadian people to have such a short memory. Is there any reason to expect they can achieve in this country what far better trained Socialists in Britain failed to accomplish?

August 1, 1932

Prime Minister R.B. Bennett was a vigorous campaigner. Southam reporter W.L. McTavish found him at the peak of his form in Vancouver. Bennett won the fight, but he lost the election.

Prime Minister Bennett last night showed Vancouver a new technique in handling a turbulent political audience.

He outshouted his interrupters, insulted them, bore them down until the people of Vancouver, 12,000 of them, were able to hear and appreciate his speech.

He called the interrupters hoodlums.

He suggested they were inmates of the zoo.

He said they chattered like magpies.

He said the kind of relief they required was bread and water.

He called them emissaries of a foreign power, trying to prevent decent citizens from hearing their national problems discussed.

He called them cowards, hiding in the anonymity of masses.

He suggested that those who came to hear would be fully justified in throwing those who came to interrupt "out of that door by the scruff of the neck." And he said all this and more, in a louder and more emphatic voice than any of his victims could muster.

It worked. Before long Mr. Bennett could be heard for half a minute at a time without interruption, then for a minute at a time. Inside twenty minutes he was swinging easily along in his speech, getting a hearing,

and a good hearing, for an address well received by the huge audience.

The crowd that had silenced Premier M.F. Hepburn of Ontario by the same tactics had met its match. Rather significantly, the only interruption after a little while was the noise of feet as several hundred people walked out on him. It was the final gesture.

Vancouver, September 24, 1935

An editorial, following the return of Mackenzie King's Liberals with 171 seats to the Conservatives' 39. The Herald mourned the Conservatives' loss, and regretted that 17 Social Credit members had been elected, but found some consolation in the thought that Mackenzie King deserved the troubles that he had inherited.

The swing of the political pendulum that swept the Mackenzie King government out of office in 1930 was in full reverse yesterday. It was the Bennett administration that was given an even more emphatic repudiation than the Liberals received five years ago.

In view of the fact that periods of depression are almost invariably fatal to the prospects of governments seeking a renewal of mandates, it was perhaps inevitable — and was so regarded in many quarters — that the Conservatives would go down to severe defeat.

However, nothing quite so pronounced in the way of an electoral uprising in favor of the Mackenzie King forces was anticipated. There was a feeling of confidence among many Conservatives inspired by the amazing personal campaign carried out by the prime minister.

His display of courage, vigor and confidence in his cause won the admiration of the great majority of his fellow Canadians. Where he went he won the ovations that were due a gallant fighter, an outstanding personality and a great Canadian.

It was in every respect the most confusing election in the country's history. The addition of three new federal parties seeking the suffrage of the people complicated the situation immeasurably. It is no doubt true that one of the main reasons for the completeness of the Liberal sweep was the determination of the electorate to ensure that federal affairs during the next five years should not fall under the blighting effect of government by group.

Mr. King will probably realize ere long the gravity of the many problems that confronted the Bennett government during the past few years. He will find that governing the affairs of the country at this time is a far cry from administration during the carefree years prior to 1930 when revenues were buoyant, international trade channels still free, and unemployment relief non-existent as a national obligation.

October 15, 1935

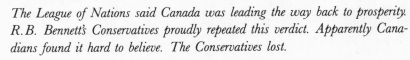

The League of Nations said Canada was leading the way back to prosperity. R.B. Bennett's Conservatives proudly repeated this verdict. Apparently Canadians found it hard to believe. The Conservatives lost.

It's King or chaos, the Liberals trumpeted in the campaign of 1935. When the durable Mackenzie King was returned to power, T.C. Douglas of the CCF commented that Canada got both King and chaos.

A Scandal in Edmonton

John E. Brownlee became premier of Alberta in 1925; nine years later he resigned after one of the most sensational trials in Alberta's history. A year after his own political demise, his party, the United Farmers of Alberta, was swept away by William Aberhart's Social Credit forces. It is hard to say whether the UFA would have survived even if there had been no Brownlee scandal. It had the misfortune to be in power when times grew bad. The scandal, however, was the last straw if one was needed.

Claiming unstated damages and costs and charging seduction of an 18-year-old girl, a writ was issued through Supreme Court channels here Friday morning in which Hon. John E. Brownlee, premier of Alberta, is named as the defendant.

The suit is entered by Allan D. Mac-Millan, father of the girl, and Vivian Mac-Millan, the girl herself, who is now employed as a stenographer at the government buildings.

Rumors of the sensational suit have been heard for some time past, but first intimation that legal action was contemplated in the matter came this morning shortly after 11 o'clock, when Neil D. MacLean, K.C., filed the statement of claim at the courthouse.

September 22, 1933

Brownlee responded instantly with a denial.

"While one regrets to have to face a case of this kind, still it will enable me to come to grips with rumors that have been spread abroad through the province for some weeks. There is not a word of truth in the allegations against me. I will defend the action to the limit, and hope to show before I am through the real cause behind it."

September 22, 1933

The premier followed up with a counter-claim alleging that he was the victim of a conspiracy.

In a statement of defence filed Monday, Premier Brownlee completely denied all charges contained in the seduction action brought against him by A.D. MacMillan and his daughter, Vivian MacMillan.

The statement of defence alleged that "the statement of claim is false, frivolous, vexatious, scandalous and abuse of the process of court, and the defendant will contend at or before the trial of this action that it ought to be struck out and expunged from the records of the courts."

The defendant also counterclaims against Vivian MacMillan and another person, or persons, asking $10,000 damages alleging the statement of claim is part of a conspiracy to injure his reputation.

The claim said in part that "The defendants by counterclaim conspired with each other and with diverse persons to the plaintiff by counterclaim, at present unknown, to secure for the defendant by counterclaim John Caldwell a reward or profit to be paid by one or more of his fellow conspirators in consideration of the defendants by counterclaim, taking such steps as would be designed to bring into disrepute the character of the plaintiff by counterclaim.

"In furtherance of the said conspiracies the defendants by counterclaim invented and made the allegations contained in the statement of claim. . . well knowing each of the said allegations to be untrue."

November 14, 1933

The trial opened in the last week of June, 1934. The Herald covered the proceedings nearly word-for-word, publishing pages of transcript. What follows is a selection from the front-page stories describing the trial.

Obviously nervous and speaking with a quick, excited voice, Vivian MacMillan, daughter of Allan MacMillan, Edson, commenced her evidence this morning in connection with the suit for unstated damages against Premier Brownlee, brought by herself and her father, alleging seduction.

Attired in a plain-checked dress, Miss MacMillan had not a vestige of color on her face and seemed to be at a high emotional pitch. She is a slim, blue-eyed, pretty girl, now 22 years of age.

She declared her parents were Baptists and prior to leaving Edson for Edmonton at the suggestion of Premier Brownlee she taught Sunday school in that town.

Premier Brownlee (who was visiting Edson), she said, told her mother that she had a very beautiful daughter, and wanted to know what she was going to do with her in the future.

According to Miss MacMillan, Premier Brownlee deprecated the proposal that she undertake a musical career. The premier, she said, declared there was little money in music and it would take a long time to earn a living. He also thought nursing was too hard a life for a young girl.

The premier then suggested, according to Miss MacMillan, that she come to Edmonton and take a business college course, following which he would obtain a position for her. He said he would act as her guardian, invite her to his home and see she did not get into trouble and would not be alone in a strange city, Miss MacMillan said.

Later the same day she and Premier Brownlee attended a dance, and he danced with her. At this dance, she said, the premier told her she was beautiful and he hoped she would come to Edmonton and carry out the plans he had suggested.

June 25, 1934

Neil MacLean, K.C., chief counsel for the MacMillans, outlined a sad and squalid tale for the all-male jury. The unhappy suitor was John Caldwell, named as a conspirator in Premier Brownlee's counterclaim.

"There will be evidence put before you, gentlemen, that immediately after Vivian MacMillan came to Edmonton the premier got in touch with her; did invite her to his house; did make her welcome. Mrs. Brownlee welcomed her also, made her feel at home, and encouraged her to come. There will be evidence, shortly after she came to Edmonton, the premier began taking her for rides in the country alone at nights.

"He told her he loved her from the first time he met her, that he was a little lonely and unhappy, and that it was her duty to submit to his desires, and she did. For over 2½ years the premier had connection with Vivian MacMillan in different places: in automobiles, in his own house, and in his office in the Parliament Buildings.

"In the fall of 1932, Vivian MacMillan met a young man, of whom she became extremely fond, and he of her. In January, 1933, he proposed marriage to her. She told him she could not marry him, breaking down and giving him the reason why. She told him the whole story of the relations. She tried to break off with the premier, but he refused to allow it. Finally, the matter so palled on her she broke down and told her mother and father the whole story."

June 25, 1934

Then came the most dramatic cross-examination in the trial.

A grilling cross-examination of Miss Vivian MacMillan by A.L. Smith, K.C., counsel for Premier Brownlee, had to be halted twice this morning as the plaintiff broke down and wept.

The 22-year-old girl who charges Mr. Brownlee with having seduced her when she was 19 years old and having continued an intimate relationship during 2½ years declared she never loved the premier and she believed the premier never loved her after the first six months.

Mr. Smith endeavored to show inconsistencies in Miss MacMillan's story, and succeeded in obtaining an admission that she did not occupy the maid's room in Premier Brownlee's house in October, 1931, when Mrs. Brownlee was away, and come into his bedroom during the night. She said she must have slept in Mrs. Brownlee's room. She insisted, however, that there had been improper intimacies.

Mr. Smith told the witness she should remember the details of this occasion as it was the first time she had occupied a bed with Mr. Brownlee, according to her own story.

The witness replied that even at this date her relationship with Premier Brownlee had become so intimate as to practically constitute a habit.

Miss MacMillan reiterated her statement that Mr. Brownlee had told her (during a drive in the country) that he was a lonely man and his wife was a wife in name only and that if the situation were any different Mrs. Brownlee would die. She said he appealed to her to save Mrs. Brownlee's life, to repay her hospitality, and to help him by granting his wishes for intimate companionship.

When the premier suggested that she get in the back seat of the car, she did so but not willingly, Miss MacMillan said. She thought it her duty to do so and the premier was exercising an influence over her which made it practically impossible for her to oppose him. However, she said, she resisted.

After further acquaintanceship with the premier, she discovered he had a very nasty temper, Miss MacMillan said.

"I never knew anyone else with a temper like his," she said.

"So he dominated you mentally and physically," Mr. Smith stated.

"Yes," the witness replied.

June 26, 1934

Occasionally the Brownlee case sounded like an old-fashioned detective story.

Neil MacLean, K.C., her solicitor, and John Caldwell, her admirer, were in the car which followed the car which she and Premier Brownlee occupied on July 5, 1933, Miss MacMillan stated at the close of her cross-examination by A.L. Smith, K.C.

Miss MacMillan said she was unaware that they were to be followed that night. She had seen her solicitor for the first time on May 24, 1933.

On this occasion, she said, Premier Brownlee suspected they were being followed and he endeavoured without success to shake off the car at the rear.

June 27, 1934

Brownlee denied everything. Still, it was politically embarrassing for a premier to be in a position where he had to deny anything of this kind.

A sweeping denial of the charges by Vivian MacMillan that he enticed her to Edmonton under promise of becoming her guardian, seduced her and continued intimate relations for 2½ years, was made by Premier J.E. Brownlee on the witness stand this morning.

Producing diaries covering the years 1930, 1931, 1932 and 1933, Premier Brownlee read entries which showed, he declared, he was often out of the city or otherwise engaged on occasions when Miss MacMillan declared he was driving her around in his car.

Miss MacMillan, he said, was a great friend of Mrs. Brownlee's, and during 1932 and 1933 she became as close a member of the family as it would be possible for anyone

John E. Brownlee, premier of Alberta from 1925 to 1934. Though he finally lost his case in the Supreme Court of Canada, there are still lingering doubts about what happened.

to be other than a natural daughter. She was regarded as a niece would be, he said.

Going over the entire story told by Miss MacMillan, Mr. Smith questioned the premier respecting the occasions upon which the premier was alleged to have had improper intimacies with the plaintiff, and concerning which Miss MacMillan had given specific dates.

The premier denied that any intimacies had taken place with Vivian in his car or any other car, or his home, or in his office in the parliament buildings.

Edmonton, June 28, 1934

Brownlee's counsel submitted no evidence in the premier's counter-claim alleging conspiracy. He said that he did not want to complicate the issue of whether or not there was a seduction. The counter-claim was dismissed, and on June 30, the case went to the jury. After the Dominion Day weekend, The Herald had dramatic news for its readers.

After four hours and 45 minutes deliberation the jury in the MacMillan-Brownlee seduction suit upheld the action and awarded Miss Vivian MacMillan and Al MacMillan a total of $15,000 damages, $10,000 to the 22-year-old Edson girl, and $5,000 to her father.

Edmonton, July 3, 1934

The consequences of that verdict followed swiftly.

In the richly panelled council chamber of the legislative buildings where, behind drawn curtains, three premiers have been released from office and three others selected as party chieftains during the last 17 years, another dramatic political scene is being enacted today with the resignation of John

E. Brownlee in the hands of practically the same followers who presented him with the premiership after the deposition of Herbert Greenfield nine years ago.

This chamber of memories where, since its opening in 1910, has been cradled practically all of the legislation and government programs now guiding and girding the province, saw the late A.L. Sifton turn over the reins of office to Charles Stewart in 1917; witnessed the departure of Mr. Stewart in 1921 and the incoming of Herbert Greenfield and the U.F.A. regime in the same year, and one evening in 1925 was the setting of an unusual scene when Mr. Greenfield's colleagues in the House asked for his resignation as government leader.

U.F.A. members, solemn-faced and openly apprehensive over the fate of the party under any leadership other than that of John Brownlee in the present crisis, entered the council chamber today divided in their allegiance. It was obvious that the resignation of Mr. Brownlee would be accepted only after a struggle in the minds and feelings of the majority of his followers.

Edmonton, July 3, 1934

The final surprise came from the judge.

Instead of obtaining $15,000 in damages awarded them by a jury here Saturday night against Premier John E. Brownlee on seduction charges, Vivian MacMillan and her father, A.D. MacMillan, of Edson, will not only lose the monetary verdict but will be required to pay the costs of the action, believed to run into several thousand dollars.

This in effect is the judgment of Acting Chief Justice W.C. Ives of the trial division of the Alberta Supreme Court, who presided at the sensational seduction trial in Edmonton last week.

The judge ruled "It is quite clear that the daughter left her home in Edson with the consent and approval of her parents and was accompanied to Edmonton by her mother. It is equally undoubted that no illness resulted from the seduction and no evidence that the ability of the daughter to render services was in any way interfered with."

"In my opinion the law is well settled that damage is the gist of the action and I am also of the opinion that the damage necessary to found a right of action in the woman must be of the same character as gave the master his right of action, that is loss of service, or at least an interference with the woman's ability to serve. I see nothing in our statute to convey a contrary intention of the legislature.

"In my view of the law the action must be dismissed with costs, including costs of discovery, and only one bill should be taxed."

July 4, 1934

The MacMillans lost again in the Alberta appeal court, but finally won damages in the Supreme Court of Canada. By then, Brownlee had left politics, and his successor, R.G. Reid, had been defeated by William Aberhart. Was Brownlee the victim of a conspiracy? The question lives on, though the protagonists are dead.

The Rise of Social Credit

William Aberhart, radio evangelist and principal of Crescent Heights High School, thought he had found the answer to the Depression in the Social Credit theory of an English engineer, Major C.H. Douglas. Aberhart already had a large personal following when the Alberta Social Credit movement was launched into politics at a meeting in the Prophetic Bible Institute in Calgary. In a matter of months, he would become premier of Alberta, and founder of its longest-lived governing party.

Attended by a visible audience estimated at 2,000 people, the first general convention of the Alberta Social Credit League, southern division, reached a rousing finale Friday evening.

While the gathering taxed the capacity of the Bible Institute, two meetings in other sections of the city accommodated the overflow crowd. The program was broadcast, thanks to the sponsorship of the Ogden CPR shop group.

Bringing to a close the first general convention of Social Credit forces in Alberta, radio, song and oratory all combined to send out what movement followers classed as the scientific solution to present economic ills.

William Aberhart, B.A., founder of the theory and leader of the present movement, climaxed the variety program with a general address.

Congratulating the convention on the success of its work and pointing to efforts now concentrating in the north, the leader predicted that approximately 80 per cent of the voters in Alberta are now behind Social Credit.

He turned a verbal broadside at the Calgary Herald, referring to the editorial of Thursday evening announcing its stand on Social Credit, briefly touched on the public debt and the huge interest burden it is causing, charged the U.F.A. government with failing to look after the suffering people of the province and terminated with a plea to Social Credit groups not to reorganize or permit trouble to creep into the ranks.

Among the first items to be placed on the Aberhart grill was the editorial mentioned, and in his opening remarks the speaker said "The Herald does not believe in the Aberhart Social Credit scheme nor does it respect the way it has been promoted up to the present time." The editorial was read.

Mr. Aberhart continued: "That is surely a polite way of saying it. We are very religious down at The Herald. We don't believe in mixing our religion with politics.

"The day is past when religion should be put on the shelf during the week and taken down on Sundays."

Mr. Aberhart thought it ill-fitting of the publication to find fault with the method he utilized to propound the principles of his religion.

Round two of the barrage centred on a news item headed "Ex-Premier Brownlee starts anti-Social Credit campaign."

"Confusion and chaos," said Mr. Aberhart, "are hinted by Mr. Brownlee as the result of inauguration of Social Credit in Alberta — a blue-ruin cry — but why don't he say what he will do?"

"Men and women," he continued, "you have a chance at the next election, and if you have never cast a ballot you'll cast it at this time, or you'll never need to cast another." He warned followers to be aware of political gas bombs and dust. "Are you going to be afraid?"

"No! No!" (from the audience).

In conclusion Mr. Aberhart mentioned the approved platform which, in a few days will be forwarded to Social Credit groups all over the province and particularly to the northern followers.

He asked if the delegates would have any objection to placing the first two verses of the Social Credit theme song, "O God Our Help In Ages Past" at the top of the platform.

Instant approval came from the gathering.

April 6, 1935

The Herald published pages of letters on Social Credit, pro and con. Here are two samples.

It is indeed a relief to know just which side of the fence the Herald is taking on the question of the Aberhart plan for Alberta. An editorial of April 4 clears that up.

We must admit that up to the present time religion and politics have had very little in common, but if the thoughtful observer who wrote this editorial has ever studied Mr. Aberhart's plan he would know that Social Credit is merely Christianity in practice.

Just as God chose Moses to lead the children of Israel out of bondage, we firmly believe God has also ordained Mr. Aberhart a second Moses, who will lead the people of Alberta into a better and higher standard of life and into their rightful heritage.

Mrs. A.M.C., Calgary, April 29, 1935

I trust that you will find room to add my paean of praise to the swelling chorus.

What a glorious thing it is to think that we are privileged to live in a small community that has such a monopoly of brains of this world that it is about to point the way to peace, plenty and prosperity to all the other millions of half-witted humanity who have the misfortune to inhabit less enlightened parts of the globe.

We are doubly fortunate in that we have in our midst a "superman" who is prepared to lead us along these rosy paths, riding in his chariot, clad in fine raiment, preceded by his henchmen, bearing aloft a banner inscribed with the words "I can't be wrong," and strewing the path with brightly-colored pieces of paper for the common people to feed, clothe and shelter themselves with.

Can we doubt that this "superman," with all his vast scholastic experience and gift of prophecy, will be able to guide us along the trail, however it twists and turns, and finally seat us on the top of that mountain called "High Finance," from whence we can see the dawn of another day and the precipitous path back to the point from which we started?

B.U. Loney, Pine Lake, April 29, 1935

William Aberhart speaks at a Social Credit rally. In the background at right is the young Ernest Manning, later to become premier of Alberta. Picnics and rallies were only part of the Social Credit campaign; Aberhart was the first to use radio effectively in Alberta politics.

Just before the election that would sweep Social Credit into power, The Herald took this parting shot. Major C.H. Douglas, the founder of Social Credit theory, had serious doubts about the Aberhart program, as outlined in the Alberta party's official manual. But neither editorials nor theoreticians could stop an electoral landslide.

The main issue to be determined by the electors of Alberta on Thursday is the fate of the fantastic program advanced by a Calgary school principal lacking economic training and political experience.

The Aberhart proposals have been condemned by leading economists in Alberta and other provinces. They are condemned by the inconsistencies apparent in the latest Social Credit manual. They are condemned by Major Douglas, author of Social Credit. Speaking at a dinner in London on his return from Alberta a short time ago, Major Douglas said:

"For anyone to suppose that any useful purpose can be served at this time by putting forward Social Credit, much less any detailed proposals for its application, without a clear idea as to the powers which must be invoked for its success, is absolutely childish."

Yet in view of this declaration, the Aberhart political party continues to dangle a monthly cash promise before the eyes of the unthinking. No one knows, least of all Mr. Aberhart, how this province of about 700,000 people can finance a basic dividend of $25 per month to every adult, or $75 as the leader, in a last desperate bid for power, now suggests.

His explanation of how this unprecedented free hand-out can be financed, as made in his now notorious manual, should fail to convince the most credulous. It is a collection of contradictions.

But Mr. Aberhart insists on giving himself plenty of elbow-room. In the manual he says "I would judge that 15 to 18 months would be required" to introduce Social Credit into Alberta. How does he propose to support the men and women who vote for him in the meantime? He has no plan. He proposes to leave it to some unknown "experts."

August 20, 1935

Aberhart won the 1935 Alberta election. The final count was 56 Social Credit MLAs, five Liberals, and two Conservatives. The United Farmers of Alberta, the previous governing party, was wiped out. The Herald's editorial next day tried to be philosophical, but it reserved the right to say later "We told you so."

It would be foolish to declare that the magnificent support marshalled behind Social Credit candidates was wholly inspired by the lure of cash monthly dividends for all adults. The vote cast for the new political party was too overwhelming to permit of that explanation.

It was an uprising of a people demanding a new deal of some kind. It was a mass revolt

SOCIAL CREDIT
MEETING

-- at --

Macleod Arena

-- on --

TUES., JULY 2ND 1935

Speaker:
W. ABERHART

The New Signalman

--Cartoon by Stewart Cameron, Calgary.

TOP: By the summer of 1935, the words Social Credit and the name William Aberhart were enough to fill an arena. BOTTOM: Calgary cartoonist Stew Cameron flourished in the Aberhart era. This drawing appeared on the day of the election that brought Aberhart to power. (August 21, 1935)

against depression. The rural voters joined with urban electors in a sweeping denunciation of conditions as they are in Alberta today. Farmers who are most likely to feel the weight of application of policies which will inevitably mean heavier taxation on both producers and consumers rallied to this new cause. In the fervor generated for a new party with something entirely new in the way of election programs, the men and women in the rural ridings swept aside fellow farmers carrying the U.F.A. banner like ninepins.

Mr. Aberhart and his colleagues will now be called on to make good their many promises. He enters on the task of meeting these promises with no definite plan announced. He proposes to bring in experts. He will have to form a government from untried and inexperienced material, and he will have to placate the many thousands of supporters voting for the cash dividend system until such time as he has a workable plan of some kind.

It became evident as the campaign progressed that the Social Credit party had built up an organization much superior to that of any of its opponents. As the result of almost two years of intensive propaganda, with a hymn as a battle cry and a pulpit as a forum, the new economic gospel fell on receptive ears. It appealed to the discouraged and the discontented, and because of its origin it was believed in by a people wanting to believe.

Nothing could stand up against that sort of mobilized enthusiasm. The Herald believes the people of Alberta have made a most unfortunate decision, and may soon see the folly of it. They have trusted fantastic promises that can only be carried out at the cost of enormous dislocation of business and trade. Impatient with advice sincerely offered, they have dragged the province into government by experiment, administration without experience.

However, this is a democracy and the will of the majority is supreme.

August 23, 1935

Social Credit will always be remembered for "funny money," though the experiment lasted only a year, and made very little difference to the Alberta economy. The idea was that the government would pay out "prosperity certificates" instead of real money. Some were paid as wages to men doing road work. Once a week (Thursday being the appointed day) anybody holding a $5 certificate had to stick on a special stamp, bought from the government for five cents. After two years, a certificate with $5.20 worth of stamps could be sold back to the government for $5. The Herald was perhaps not alone in finding the idea ridiculous. In an editorial, it proposed a simpler approach.

Until the government has told us precisely what "prosperity bonds" are to be, and how they are to work, it is difficult to discuss the proposed new currency without the risk of unfairness to its authors. The extraordinary fact is that, though we are assured that this experiment

Genuine Social Credit funny money, officially known as a prosperity certificate. Apparently this one's owner lost faith after six weeks of sticking one-cent stamps on the back of his "dollar."

---

will be launched within two or three weeks, the government has not yet given us any very definite or complete idea of it.

As described in government statements thus far it will be scrip — that is, unbacked promissory notes, meant to circulate as money but without either the government authority to make them legal tender or any government promise to redeem them freely in legal tender.

If an Alberta laborer is paid two weeks from now with a "prosperity bond" he cannot compel anyone to accept it for anything. He will find that he goes out to do the week's shopping with a promissory note maturing two years hence.

The man to whom you offer a real $100 Alberta government bond has at last an official assurance that if he keeps it to maturity it will be worth $100. If you offered him a $5 "prosperity bond" he would know that if he kept it two years it would be worth exactly nothing at all. At least, not exactly nothing. It would in fact be worth $5 cash if he meanwhile bought $5.20 worth of stamps from the government and gummed them on the back of the "bond" — otherwise nothing.

That is to say, the "prosperity bond" starts out in life worth nothing minus 20 cents. It breaks even with zero when 20 cents worth of stamps are stuck on its back, and from then on it is worth exactly the value of any further stamps the public affix to it. You can do the same thing for yourself with a large piece of brown paper and be 20 cents ahead of the game.

We await with interest any full-dress explanation of "prosperity bonds" that may improve our present estimate of them. Meanwhile, they look to us like a somewhat intricate way of inducing people to work for the government and pay their own wages.

June 13, 1936

Premier Aberhart said that he and his cabinet ministers would take 20 to 25 per cent of their pay in scrip. The Herald was not impressed.

We can remember a time when, as children, we were occasionally given a dose of very nasty medicine. We did not fall in with the idea very readily but there was one stratagem that helped to persuade us. Father used to "take a dose himself." He never made a face and he always licked the spoon to show us how good it was.

We have learned from our doctors since that we were right about not liking the stuff, for it did us more harm than good, even if Father did believe in it. We have learned something about Father, too. By his own confession he never really took any of that medicine at all. He was just pretending with an empty spoon all the time.

Mr. Aberhart is asking a lot when he invites other people to accept scrip freely, or even buy it with hard cash, while he still pays himself three-quarters or more of his salary in real money. As long as he sticks to this twenty-five per cent acceptance of scrip it will be hard for him to convince any grown-up person that even he himself has one hundred per cent faith in it.

July 13, 1936

As it happened, the premier and his cabinet took all their pay in real money. The Herald recalled its earlier editorial, and went on:

Father at least indulged in an artistic bit of bluff with the medicine spoon. The cabinet members, it appears, are no longer even bluffing about their willingness to be paid in scrip. At any rate, pay-day has come and gone in Edmonton and neither 20 nor 25 per cent of his compensation has been accepted by one member of the government or its party in the House. They all took cash, in full and on the nail.

Of course they were all by law entitled to cash for their services, just as anyone else in the province is entitled to legal tender for any payment that is due. But in exercising their right to cash, the government and its supporters have sacrificed every shadow of right to ask that others forego that right.

September 10, 1936

"Funny money" never did play a large role in Alberta commerce, as a Herald reporter discovered when he tried to find some.

Managers of several "neighborhood" grocery and confectionery stores who have been accepting prosperity certificates told the Herald today the volume had dropped off considerably in the past three days, but even prior to that sufficient was not handled to warrant applying for redemption of the certificates.

In East Calgary six stores reported a total of less than $60 on hand Monday morning. One merchant had one certificate among his cash. He had, he said, received that Friday. Another displayed 10 certificates and one store estimated a total of around 40 certificates on hand.

Two taxi firms said their drivers had been accepting an occasional certificate but no volume had been turned into the office. The drivers themselves generally disposed of the certificates at eating places, etc., and consequently practically none was handled with the ordinary returns.

Several of the places accepting the certificates were willing to take the Alberta tender provided the full amount was taken in goods and no change requested.

Merchants on Eighth Avenue west of Centre street are either not taking scrip or they are accepting it in such small quantity that the question of redemption is not of serious concern, the survey disclosed.

"It doesn't look to me as if scrip is of much importance in boosting business when weeks pass without even a scrip dollar being offered," one merchant said.

The manager of a magazine and tobacco store said he was taking in a little scrip, and getting rid of it constituted no problem at all. "We only take in about $10 or $12 a week in scrip," he said. "Then we pay a few dollars in scrip in the pay envelopes of our clerks. That's how we get rid of it. We did not have enough on hand to bother sending it to Edmonton to be redeemed."

A hardware store reported very little scrip in circulation.

"We had none at all on Saturday and the amount is decreasing," the manager said. "We have great difficulty in passing it. In fact it isn't even in demand for souvenirs. When we run across a government supporter we give it to him and he can't very well refuse it, but even some of them do," he concluded.

September 14, 1936

A letter to the editor. In this case, it must be admitted that The Herald failed to oblige a subscriber.

As I have taken the Herald for over ten years I feel that I should be allowed to speak my piece.

The Herald has consistently and daily belittled and sneered at Premier Aberhart in a most unsportsmanlike manner. After all he is the head of our provincial government and entitled to a certain amount of respect.

The people of Alberta expressed themselves a year ago and they are getting tired of all this propaganda against Social Credit. Most of us take a paper for the news and can form our own opinions without coaching.

Give us the news and lay off Mr. Aberhart. We are getting mighty tired of it.

Open Mind, Calgary, October 29, 1936

Another letter, and another disappointed reader. Stew Cameron's cartoons, if anything, got tougher.

Unlike your correspondent who recently approved of the cartoons appearing in The Herald, I detest this method of entertaining the public.

The New Act—Will She Do It?

"The minister declared the government would proceed very carefully with the issue of certificates. The worst enemies of the plan were not those who opposed it but those who wanted the government to go too fast with it, he stated."

Lucien Maynard was ringmaster, William Aberhart the star attraction in this Stew Cameron cartoon. The government seemed to have cold feet about its prosperity certificates, or scrip. (July 4, 1936)

Knock Mr. Aberhart all you like through the recognized channels, but for the sake of good sportsmanship cut out the political cartoons.

As you well know, this is a one-sided affair wherein the victim is powerless to retaliate.

Tim Longbotham, Baintree, October 29, 1936

"Funny money" was in circulation less than a year, but it became a part of Alberta lore, along with the $25-a-month dividend that was never paid. Fred Kennedy reported the demise of scrip.

The provincial government has abandoned its prosperity certificate plan. Announcement to this effect was made by Hon. Solon Low, provincial treasurer, at noon today. Only about $12,000 worth of scrip is outstanding at present.

The government will redeem this scrip as it comes in, but no certificates will be reissued by the government. The decision to abandon the plan was reached when it became apparent that circulation of the scrip had almost stopped.

"It had nothing to do with Social Credit anyway," one MLA remarked when the decision of the provincial treasurer became known.

The scheme was launched in August, 1936, by the government as a means of financing road work in rural constituencies.

About $500,000 worth of certificates were printed in Calgary. Of this amount only $262,000 worth was actually issued.

Less than 60 days after the first scrip certificate was issued, doubts were expressed as to the success of the plan.

In an effort to keep the plan in operation, individual members of the cabinet announced that they were prepared to accept a portion of their salaries in scrip.

They failed to go through with their part of the bargain.

In a last desperate effort to keep the plan alive, civil servants were "invited" to "purchase" small quantities of scrip every payday.

Edmonton, April 7, 1937

It must be said for Aberhart that he was no separatist, even in the face of strong provocation.

Alberta will fight along constitutional lines in its battle to enforce recent bank legislation, Premier Aberhart asserted at a "social credit" picnic at Lakeview beach on South Cooking Lake, near here.

Told by the Canadian Press at the meeting that the Dominion government had disallowed three acts passed at a recent session of the provincial legislature, the premier announced the Dominion government's action to the crowd a few minutes later.

"You see what we are up against," he added.

"Give us a gun," a man shouted. Other members of the crowd of about 350 persons were silent.

"No, no — none of that," Premier Aberhart replied quickly.

"This is not bloodshed," he continued. "It is constitutional. We'll stand by the constitution and fight it through. May I suggest to you that you never allow anybody to tell you we are going to secede from our great Dominion. We have no desire to leave the home of our forefathers.

"We may disagree with their prejudices but we'll stand together and fight together, and try to solve our difficulties. We want to be allowed to fight out our differences in our own real home."

Mr. Aberhart said the government was determined "with all the force in us" to obtain for the people what they had demanded "if you keep asking for them." He listed as the demands from the people increased purchasing power, a lower cost of living and relief taxation.

The people need not bother how these aims might be accomplished, he stated, but could leave that to the experts chosen to do it.

"Don't let details bother you, ask for results," he said.

"For goodness sake, don't get that inferiority complex," the premier continued. "You cannot get anything if you don't think you can get it. How? That is something you don't need to bother about. You go ahead with your farm work."

Edmonton, August 18, 1937

Premier Aberhart's war with the press came to a head in 1937, when "An act to ensure the publication of accurate news and information" was proposed. The Herald responded with this front-page editorial. The act was quickly passed, but the lieutenant-governor, in a very unusual step, refused to give it royal assent. Eventually it was ruled unconstitutional by the Supreme Court of Canada.

For centuries it has been the unquestioned right of every British subject to speak, write or print statements or opinions on any subject without let or hindrance from his government or his neighbor. The natural and necessary check on that right — and the only one — is that he must answer to the courts for any proved abuse of it. He may not utter slander, sedition or blasphemy without facing the judgment of a jury of his fellow citizens and the punishment of a British court.

That is freedom of speech under Anglo-Saxon law, and it is the only freedom of speech that any newspaper enjoys. Freedom of the press in British countries is no special thing, but merely the freedom of the publisher to say what any one of his fellow citizens may say in words, in writing, or in print. And under the terms of the Aberhart government's new press law that freedom would cease to exist.

For this law provides that without a hearing in court the government may, on the recommendation of one of its employees, prohibit a newspaper from publishing or a writer from getting his articles printed or a private citizen from obtaining publication of any information he may possess, no matter

Inventor Aberhart says "I never thought so many questions could be asked concerning so simple a matter." Social Credit was complex, and Aberhart was not a patient explainer. (June 27, 1936)

how vitally important that information may be to the public or to himself.

This may not be press censorship in the familiar sense of the term; but it is aimed at something worse – press control. It is a weapon cunningly designed for the extinction of responsible journalism in this province. It goes still further than that.

This law proposes not only to crush any newspaper which publishes what it knows to be the truth about the conduct of government and expenditure of public funds in Alberta, but also to compel all newspapers to publish at their own expense and regardless of whether it is true or false, a flood of government propaganda. The government plans to confiscate newspaper space without paying for it, and make whatever use of it will best serve its own ends. It could just as honestly seize a flat in an apartment house and convert it into a liquor store without paying rent.

And further still, this law provides that no one has any protection from libel or slander that may be contained in the government propaganda thus published. It proposes that the government should be able to compel a newspaper to publish anything, however libellous or damaging, about private individuals or concerns without these latter being able to protect themselves in the courts, or obtain redress. This is a freedom of speech such as no British newspaper has ever enjoyed in the whole history of the press.

These things come as the climax of a long campaign in which Mr. Aberhart and his colleagues have sought to brand as rogues and liars any publications which openly criticized them. They have never once in the course of that campaign had the courage to take their grievances into court and seek the legal protection which would have been theirs for the asking if they had really been wronged. Having failed to rebut frank statements regarding them and their policies, they are now bringing in a measure that they hope can be used to prevent the public from reading any statements about the government which are not concocted by its own propaganda bureau.

Characteristically, they would rather try to muzzle their critics than answer them.

October 1, 1937

This editorial gently chided the then-youthful Ernest Manning, later to become premier of Alberta, and later a senator.

Youthful Mr. Manning, who among his other sudden distinctions conducts religio-political services on Sundays, declared in his latest religious oration that the Aberhart government has been given a mandate to carry out its present program – of licensing regimentation and defiance of Federal authority. The youthful provincial secretary must think the public has a short memory. The sole mandate conferred on Messrs. Aberhart, Manning and Company was to pay every adult citizen of Alberta a monthly dividend of twenty-five dollars. In recent months Mr. Manning and his leader have been trying to induce the public to forget all about this promise on which they were elected to power.

Mr. Manning worked himself into a fine state of frenzy in Edmonton on Sunday evening because a storm of criticism of the government's course has developed. He deplored the "tactics" being employed by the individuals who dare to criticize the government's course. Such tactics he charged were rousing feelings of deepest disgust on the part of fair-minded citizens.

The youthful Mr. Manning has discovered, so he assures his hearers from a pulpit, that "there is a growing disgust on the part of the thinking section of the public of this province toward those who are lending themselves to the lowdown, cheap, mud-slinging type of criticism that is being blazed abroad in Alberta today." The answer is that the intolerance and unfriendliness so apparent in this province today are the direct result of the "social credit" campaign of arrogance and deception of two years ago.

The wind was sown then, the whirlwind is in sight today, and nothing Aberhart and Manning can say from a pulpit at this late date will avert it.

October 26, 1937

An editorial. This rather laborious look at the record came at the end of an era. Prosperity was coming, and so was a world war. Economic cure-alls and political in-fighting would lose their obsessive interest. Alberta Social Credit would keep its name, let its doctrine go, and go on to give Alberta another 32 years of sound, small-c conservative government.

Premier Aberhart's persistent reiteration of the charge that his every move to implement election promises has been blocked by "someone with more power than I," is not substantiated by the records. Take his basic dividend promise as an illustration. That promise, by the way, was included in the Social Credit party platform at a convention on April 6, 1935.

In Edmonton Mr. Aberhart told an audience that the dividend might be $75 a month. That was in August, 1935. On August 27, 1935, Mr. Aberhart expressed the hope that the dividend would be possible in from 15 to 18 months. On September 9 of that year Hon. Mr. Manning announced registration for the dividend would start "soon." And the record continues:

Sept. 12, 1935 – In Toronto the premier is thus reported: "The $25 dividend will be paid. We will not repudiate our debts and there will be no defaulting."

Sept. 27, 1935 – Premier announces that first dividend will be paid to persons on relief.

Oct. 7, 1935 – Dividends will be provided for the unemployed during the winter, for which no work will be required.

Oct. 14, 1935 – Premier says eighteen months will be needed for payment of dividends.

Jan. 6, 1936 – Premier asks from four to six months additional time for dividend payments if government so desires.

March 25, 1936 – Registration for dividends postponed indefinitely. Don't hope to start paying until 1937.

April 13, 1936 – Premier says if he can't pay the dividend he will tell the people and let them fire him.

June 17, 1936 – Dividend payment promised by March, 1937.

August 4, 1936 – Premier denies statement that dividend will be paid by Oct. 3, 1937.

Sept. 10, 1936 – Premier tells Fairview audience dividends will be paid in three months.

Sept. 15, 1936 – Premier tells Banff audience first dividend may be for an amount between $5 and $10.

Sept. 23, 1936 – Premier in a Vancouver interview says dividends will be paid within two months.

Jan. 3, 1937 – Premier asks for an extension of six months in which to put Social Credit into effect.

Jan. 18, 1937 – Premier asks for at least two years before being criticized for not delivering the dividends.

Feb. 15, 1937 – Premier says only the Calgary Herald and the Liberals appear to be interested in dividends.

March 1, 1937 – In a Calgary broadcast premier admits failure to pay basic dividends within eighteen month period and asks his followers to tell him what to do about it.

Today Premier Aberhart is blaming his failure on "someone with more power than I." Why doesn't he identify that ignoble "someone?" Leaving it to his audience to do their own guessing probably better suits his purpose. After all he has said about them he can be reasonably sure the guess will be the courts and the federal government. But that wouldn't be a correct guess.

During the whole period of Premier Aberhart's reiterated basic dividend promisings right up to the date upon which he publicly admitted failure, there had been no intervention from either courts or federal authorities that could have in any way affected his basic dividend payment plans.

It was in October, 1936, that legality of his debt reduction legislation was questioned. It was in January, 1937 that the IOOF challenged the legality of his mortgage interest reduction act, and it was not until February, 1937, that the Alberta supreme court declared *ultra vires* his act for the reduction and settlement of debts.

So far as The Herald is aware these occurrences had no connection with Premier Aberhart's basic dividend plan. It would be more honest were he to admit what he well knows to be the truth: that his grandiose schemes, including the something for nothing basic dividend, while they looked on paper and in his brain to be easy of accomplishment, all went cock-eyed when there was serious thought of how they might work in actual practice.

August 12, 1939

Europe Slips Toward War

By the early Thirties, the shadow of another European war could be seen. Hungry, resentful, disillusioned by democracy (as represented by the Weimar Republic), Germany was ripe for dictatorship of the left or the right. When Hitler came to power, the shape of things to come was clear to at least some Germans, who spoke more or less openly to visiting reporters about the prospects of another war. Spain was torn by civil war, and Mussolini's troops had won some easy victories against North African tribesmen. Near the beginning of this dangerous decade, Lukin Johnston of The Herald's London bureau sent the following report on a Germany ripe for Nazism.

Forty thousand flats to let. Beggars at every street corner. "To let" signs plastered in store windows all along the famous Unter den Linden. Palatial new office buildings half empty. Great new factories equipped with the latest machinery silent and ghostly. Tens of thousands of automobiles laid up in enormous garages because the owners cannot pay taxes on them.

Seven hundred thousand unemployed. Almost daily bloodshed in minor clashes between Communists, Fascists and police. Luxurious hotels and restaurants practically deserted. The whole population of four and a half million in a sort of stupor, haunted by nightmares of currency inflation and filled with despair.

Three-quarters of them are so sick of politics that they care not whether Bolshevists or Hitlerites seize control.

That is the superficial picture of Berlin today, while beyond the frontiers Germany's former enemies argue and wrangle as to whether, when and how she shall pay the uttermost cost of a war that ceased 13 years ago.

Meanwhile, Germany alone has ceased to care whether the Lausanne Conference meets or not or whether the United States scales downward First World War debts or not. Even Chancellor Bruening for the time being, at least, has ceased jockeying for position with his political rivals. "We cannot pay. Do your worst," he says in effect to foreign nations, and his own people know well the alternatives to his rule.

But the outside world asks suspiciously "Is this a true picture of Germany? — Are conditions really as desperate as all that — or is it play-acting? What about Germany's huge favorable trade balance?"

France alone is sure it is mostly play-acting. Other foreigners, observing closely without prejudice, are convinced of Germany's peril, but they don't deny there's some play-acting too.

Chancellor Bruening is walking a political tight-rope, leaning this way and that, and likely to fall at any moment. In the Reichstag of something over 500 members he leads the centre "Roman Catholic" party of only 64.

On one side of him are Communists and other elements on the "left," totalling roughly 250. On the other side are "Hitler's Fascists," numbering 114, with others who lean toward his policy totalling in all 248. Inside the Reichstag, Hitlerites and Communists combine in attacking the government, one desiring dictatorship, the other undiluted Bolshevism.

Outside the chamber they shoot each other daily in the streets of Berlin. Nothing but Bruening's courageous moderation keeps these two violent antagonists from turning Germany upside down.

Hitler, unloved and untrusted as a prospective national leader by the mass of the people and with no known followers competent to take office, steadily recruits followers from Germany's youth for whom the past has been one long tale of privation and misery and for whom the future is bleak and hopeless. Hitler, master showman, bides his time to seize control, steadily preying on the sentiment of people whose nerves are almost at the breaking point from years of suspense and uncertainty.

Berlin, January 22, 1932

A dispatch via the Southam news service from the Times of London describes the beginning of a dictatorship.

Adolf Hitler's dictatorship over Germany is now complete. Captain Goering has been appointed premier of Prussia and Franz von Papen, of the Nationalist party, Hitler's allied party, has been set aside.

Thus Prussia is now entirely in the hands of Hitlerites. Socialists and Communists have lost all influence and the brown shirts are in supreme command.

The latest outbreak of Nazi fury has been directed against the national Federation of Youth Hostels, an outgrowth of the great youth movement which swept over Germany after the war.

Headquarters of these hostels has been forcibly occupied by the executive of the rival Nazi youth movement and allegedly "incriminating documents" found. In future, therefore, emissaries of Hitler will be placed in a position to control the youth movement altogether.

Raids on private homes continue in Berlin while the regular police take no action. Meetings of Bible students have been prohibited at Bamberg and 21 students arrested. Similar arrests have taken place in Weiden, Augsburg and Gunsburg.

Alfons Pressburger, Jewish cattle dealer, shot himself dead in his home near Munich as he was about to be arrested on suspicion of having spread "atrocity propaganda" against the Nazis.

Resignations of the present heads of universities are inevitable under administrative changes being inaugurated. A new Prussian students' code, being made public on Wednesday, abolishes parliamentarism and substitutes Nazi "leadership." The Nazi principle of making appointments from above replaces popular election of student leaders.

April 12, 1933

A soup kitchen in Berlin, about 1930. Economic misery and resentment of Germany's humiliation after the First World War provided a rich ground for the growth of totalitarian politics.

By 1933, German morale seemed better, at least superficially, but at what cost? Southam newsman T.E. Nichols sent this dispatch from Nazi Germany.

Light from the burning torches showed up the faces of the marching men, set and determined, now and then breaking into the "Battle Song" of the Nazis. They had been marching a long time (though it was in one of the smaller cities of southwestern Germany) and they were still coming, in hundreds.

Detachment on detachment of the brown-shirt Storm Troopers followed the bands; then a group of the regular German army's cavalry, steel-helmeted and erect. Then a band of the "Shupo," military-trained police.

There were more bands and more men, young and old, many without uniform, but singing the battle song. The procession moved on until nearly an hour had passed and torches were still being carried through the heavily treed avenues to the meeting place of the storm detachments and followers of Adolf Hitler.

They were honoring his birthday. Red, black and white flags, bearing the Swastika, fluttered from countless windows

People crowded the sidewalks and cafe windows, looking on stolidly and without sign of emotion. No one smiled at the parade.

A man who was standing at the edge of the walk frequently raised his arm — "Heil!" The marching men took up his shout, "Heil, Heil, Heil." Near him a smartly dressed woman also raised her arm in salute. Children too lifted their hands to the "Heil," nation-wide salute to the Chancellor

The youngest of the Nazis have joined the march. Many times we see them on the road, led by sturdy youths to the notes of pipes and the beating of drums. The younger ones — some of them tots of nine or ten trudging strenuously to keep time — taking up the rear of the parade. All of them know the salute and "Heil" the Swastika.

Everywhere there are Nazi flags and the shop windows are filled with Hitler paintings, etchings and photographs.

On the news stands it is the same. Current publications carry on their front pages pictures of Hitler standing with arms folded before a group of his picked followers; Hitler thanking a little child for flowers; Hitler in the country with his police dog. There are pictures of German troops leading prisoners, or Richthofen, the great flying ace, or a German soldier "type."

In Munich, Nazi officers come in and out of the Brown House. Above the door of this famous house is the slogan, "Germany Awake!" And although many onlookers will not cheer and say, "It is not good," and others "Those who are with Hitler you see, but those who are not with him you do not see," Germany today is marching in millions behind the banners of Ex-Corporal Hitler.

May 27, 1933

Police Magistrate H. G. Scott of Calgary wrote of a visit to Nazi Germany and what he learned there.

The great Nazi rally at Nuremberg at the end of August went off amid roars of enthusiastic cheering. Hitler and his chief assistants were acclaimed as if they were semi-divine heroes of mythology. No murmurs of criticism, however mild, were allowed to be heard in the chorus of praise.

In the earlier part of August a great rally of the Nazi Youth movement was held at Munich. Something like 40,000 young people, boys and girls, young men and women in the brown Nazi uniforms gathered for the rally.

The newspapers acclaimed the gathering as a triumphant success. "Germany's Youth on the March," said the great headline in the papers — but they failed to say, because they dared not say, that there were over 2,500 casualties caused by over-fatigue and exhaustion in the long marches under heavy packs.

Is this possibly characteristic of the situation in Nazi Germany? Are there casualties unpublished in the triumphant army, which is not thought well to publish?

A taxi drives up a street in a south-German city and stops. A man gets out and pays the driver. The taxi drives away. The man walks slowly along the street a little way, makes certain that the taxi is out of sight, and then goes to a door and rings. The door is opened and he steps quickly inside.

After some time when the street is quiet, he comes out again and walks briskly away. He does not call a taxi until he is well away from the house where he has been.

In this furtive manner the correspondent of a great foreign paper gets some of his information as to what is going on from day to day in Germany. Being well known in Germany as the correspondent of the paper, it is often necessary for him to be very careful that it is not known to the Nazis and their agents from where he is getting his news. Otherwise dire punishment will be wreaked on those who have dared to reveal to non-German eyes what is being done in Germany.

Some of the things so revealed suggest the Middle Ages rather than the Twentieth

Berlin, 1933. Somewhat amateurishly — they had not yet had much practice — a crowd of civilians offered the Nazi salute as Hitler passed by in a motorcade.

At the time, many people, not all of them German, saw the Nazis as the salvation of Germany's dignity and fortunes.

Century. In one German city a large number of Jews were recently arrested on the charge of intending to hold a meeting to protest against the illegal persecution to which they were being subjected. They were marched to the outskirts of the city, and there ordered to dig up an area of ground. The digging was done under the eyes of Nazi guards who encouraged their victims with taunts and threats.

Some of the guards even took the Jews' spades away from them and forced them to dig up the ground with their bare hands, telling them that they would know what German soil was like before they were done. Some were actually forced to lie down on the ground and tear up the grass with their teeth. Comment on such things seems needless.

In a quiet flat in a German city lives a lady who until recently was a member of the parliament of her state, and the head of a number of organizations connected with women's work of one kind or another. She has given the best years of her life to the work. Her reputation is high. She could not even be accused of being a Jewess. The Nazi flood poured over her state, and she was deprived of her seat in parliament, summarily dismissed from all her positions, and permitted only to go to her flat and live there very quietly.

There are thousands of other women who have been treated in much the same way, she says. The Nazis do not approve of women taking part in politics or government work.

There is indeed great enthusiasm in Germany for Hitler, just as there was great enthusiasm in France for Napoleon III at the outset of his government. He was to lead France to avenge Waterloo. Hitler is to lead Germany to revenge for Versailles.

As the years went on in France a certain ominous ground-tone began to be heard underneath the cheers that acclaimed the rule of Napoleon III. When he led France to Sedan that ground-tone burst out into the shouts of the Commune. Is there not a similar ground-tone in Germany beneath the Nazi cheering? What will it become if Hitler fails to lead Germany to victory?

October 7, 1933

M. H. Halton of the Toronto Star visited Hitler's Germany. In this article, reprinted in The Herald, he told of finding a German colleague who had some disturbingly prophetic things to say.

It was my first night in Germany, where I have come in this most important and fateful autumn since the war to describe for readers of this paper the good and the bad in the Third Reich after seven months of Hitler — and I sat in a cafe on the Unter den Linden talking to a German journalist.

My German said "Apart from the harsh measures which we have been forced to take against Jews and socialists, what is it that is making the Anglo-Saxon world ridicule and hate the Hitler movement?"

I said "I believe, and I think most of the Anglo-Saxon world believes, that the Hitler movement, in spite of the flaming idealism which motivates it, and in spite of our sorrow at what Germany has suffered since the war, is a movement of tragic reaction, a going back to 1793.

"The point is, you see, that no matter what crimes the other nations have committed against Germany, the world is presumably moving toward a belief that war is evil."

"There is no doubt about that," the German journalist said. "But I suppose there will never be peace. I suppose war is in the blood of us Europeans. I fought in the last war, and I fully expect that my son, now ten years old, will some day be marching across the Rhine to France."

I felt hot and cold with the stupidity and the futility of it all. "In the next war," I said, "it won't be nearly such a romantic matter as marching across the Rhine toward France. It will be a matter of poison gas, of human beings being destroyed overnight, of the probable destruction of what little civilization we have."

Again the German shrugged. "Is the fact that the next war will be terrible any reason why Germany should not struggle to regain her greatness and her equality?" Then my friend said "You people in the world outside don't know anything of what is happening in Germany. I admit our press is controlled, but tell me anything the outside world

knows that we don't know."

"Listen, then," I said, "do you know that at the Nuremberg rally a short time ago, a blonde German girl had all her hair shaven off, and was paraded through the streets, restaurants and theatres all day, with a placard fastened round her neck, on which were the words 'I wanted to marry a Jew'?"

My German friend jumped up. "That's a lie," he said. "You should be ashamed of yourself for saying things like that."

"You didn't know that," I said. "Well, the rest of the world knows it. The daughter of the American ambassador here saw it with her own eyes. The rest of the world knows it," I said. "You might also be interested to know that the girl is now in a lunatic asylum."

My friend shuddered. "I cannot believe it," he said. And then, passionately, "But what then? What right have you British to talk? What about the British atrocities in India? What about the Black and Tans in Ireland after the war? What about the American prison system? And there is at least some excuse for Germany; she is in the throes of a revolution."

Around a bonfire a few yards off, self-hypnotized Nazis were shouting "Down with France."

My friend shook his head and said "Undoubtedly we are all mad, and all will reap the whirlwind."

October 20, 1933

Adolf Hitler, complete with Iron Cross and swastika armband, salutes yet another cheering crowd at a Nazi ceremony. Banners, ceremonies and precisely drilled marchers by the thousands were the staple of Nazi propaganda. In the end they produced a terrible enthusiasm.

Lukin Johnston was the first Canadian journalist to interview Adolf Hitler in Berlin after he came to power. It was Johnston's last assignment. Two days later he fell from a ship en route from Holland to England.

Germany stands ready to consider favorably any invitation from the other great powers to recommence negotiations for disarmament or limitation of armaments.

She does not care whether negotiations take place within or without the framework of the League of Nations.

Her only condition is that she will enter only on terms of absolute equality.

She awaits a call to Geneva or elsewhere.

She believes the time has come when there is a general feeling some new instrument should take the place of the Versailles Treaty.

Such were the unequivocal statements made to your correspondent by Chancellor Hitler in an exclusive interview here. This is the first statement of Germany's future policy since Sunday's monster referendum made Hitler absolute master of Germany. Incidentally, it is the first interview he had ever granted a Canadian newspaperman.

There was a complete absence of formality about our meeting. He received me in his private office in the chancellory in a room panelled in mahogany, without pictures and without ornamentation. As I entered he rose from his desk and came forward, clicking his heels together as the introduction was made, and we shook hands.

Answering my questions Hitler stated that last Sunday's great vote did not alter by one iota Germany's claims regarding disarmament.

"Our position is just as it was before," he declared. "We demand absolute equality in negotiations which we undertake with other powers – no more or less. Given these conditions we are prepared to resume negotiations at any time.

"The Versailles Treaty," he said, "is only a document which gives legal basis to the present state of affairs. In itself it provides for revision and there is a growing general opinion that as a treaty it has been a danger to both victors and vanquished alike, and that it ought to be replaced by something better."

At this point when I had interjected that Canada was vitally interested in European affairs, I asked the chancellor if he had ever met the Canadians during the war.

He at once forgot he was the chancellor of Germany and became a war veteran, talking reminiscences. He smiled and gesticulated as he reeled off dates and places when he had been opposite Canadians. In effect he said: You bet I met the Canadians in the war. At Armentieres in 1915, at Bapaume and on the Somme in 1916, and later.

To my suggestion that he should know Canadians as virile people he laughed and thoroughly agreed.

These reminiscences brought a flood of words to his lips. "As a Canadian you ought easily to understand," he said, "the attitude of Germany after the revolution. Soldiers who actually faced each other across No Man's Land must surely have a clearer view of each other than politicians who never fought.

"From what I know of Canadians and British as soldiers I cannot imagine that if they had been defeated in the war they would have submitted tamely to the treatment handed out to Germany."

I told the chancellor Canadian opinion was much exercised by statements that school children and storm troops were given military training which went far beyond what could reasonably be considered as defensive training, and also that grave danger to world peace was seen in the new doctrine of race supremacy being taught in Germany. It was considered retrograde and even savage by other nations, I informed him.

With much vehemence of gesture he declared the training he was trying to give young Germany was neither militaristic nor aggressive, but merely educative. It took the form of strict discipline.

"When in opposition," he said, "I had to work with a great mass of men and fight Communism in its most violent form. Do you think I could have done that with a crowd of street preachers?"

Striking the table with his fist, he continued "Now with the success of the revolution I want to keep up that spirit of discipline, but I insist again, it is not militaristic. You cannot have a huge following without some forms of organization, and that organization naturally takes on military appearance."

My next question, in view of the known desire of Germany to have colonies, was which overseas possession he might wish to have returned. He said certainly Germany would be happy to regain the possibility of colonial activity, because it would help world trade. Germany would gladly co-operate in exploiting undeveloped territories. All industrialized nations were more or less congested and must seek new outlets.

Finally I asked the chancellor if he could indicate when he thought the concentration camps, which had aroused so much criticism abroad, would be abandoned. Here again, he become voluble. "In no other country has a government no power to fight against six million organized Communists. Other countries can deport undesirable citizens, but Germany has had no such opportunity, such as France for instance.

"We should be most happy to get rid of our troublesome people, and would gladly pay their fares to Canada if Canada would take them. But Canadians would be rather astonished at the kind of people they would have to welcome. Canada has always had strict immigration laws, and Germany has admitted too many people who have abused the privileges of citizenship."

According to the chancellor there are now only 17,000 persons in concentration camps.

Berlin, November 16, 1933

NAZIS UBER ALLES

This early view of Hitler's swastika and its real meaning came from the Dutch newspaper De Groene Amsterdammer. The Herald reprinted it in July, 1932. Some statesmen continued to hope for at least six more years that Hitler wasn't really an octopus reaching out over Europe.

The abdication King Edward VIII was a bitter pill for many of his subjects, in Canada as well as in Britain. For a time, news of the gathering European disaster was driven from the front pages by this crisis. A.C. Cummings of The Herald's London bureau sent the following dispatch at the height of the constitutional dispute. The issue was whether the King, head of the Church of England, could marry a divorced woman and keep his throne. A week after this dispatch, he abdicated in order to marry. Later, as the Duke and Duchess of Windsor, he and his wife sometimes visited their EP Ranch south of Calgary. His brother succeeded him as King George VI. Queen Elizabeth II is George VI's daughter.

The gravest constitutional crisis that has faced the crown and cabinet for more than a century enthralls all Britain today on the disclosure that King Edward persists in his desire to marry Mrs. Ernest Simpson, former wife of a Canadian ship broker, whom she married in this country after a divorce from her first husband, an American naval officer.

The crisis is so acute that Premier Baldwin and his cabinet threaten to resign rather than allow the King to have his way.

The story of the Royal romance which has filled the world with gossip for months past and which today causes a stock exchange slump, consternation in the Anglican church, and spread of the wildest unfounded rumors of the King's abdication in United States and on the continent, began more than a year ago.

The King met Mrs. Simpson in London and fell in love with her. Scorning usual subterfuges and concealments in such cases, he went about with her openly, took her on a voyage to the Mediterranean last summer, had her name included in the court circular as an honored guest at Balmoral Castle, and constantly visited her in her flat in London. Naturally this gave rise to gossip everywhere and finally both church and cabinet felt impelled to intervene.

Mrs. Simpson in the meantime obtained a divorce that was dismissed in the British press with the barest mention.

Then when the coronation preparations were afoot, certain prelates demurred at administering the Holy Communion part of the coronation ceremony to the King, who as head of the church they insisted should set an example to all his subjects.

Despite all their pleadings, joined with those of Queen Mary, the King refused to give up Mrs. Simpson. He agreed, however, to make his relationship with her one of utmost discretion. He undertook to do his duty as sovereign with the utmost conscientiousness, to be crowned next May without fail, and to follow the advice of the cabinet as a strictly constitutional monarch.

A compromise on this basis had been tentatively arranged when the whole issue was reopened last week by certain bishops and one or two high church cabinet ministers who insisted that a grave scandal would be caused unless the King gave up Mrs. Simpson altogether.

Today the British public and press waits and wonders whether the King will adhere to his decision to marry even in the face of cabinet's threats to resign or whether he will abdicate and give the throne to the Duke of York.

Profound regret is expressed by responsible persons, and newspapers in Britain today that at a time when the world is in such a state of political upheaval, such a grave constitutional issue should disturb the tranquility of British political life.

London, December 3, 1936

A.C. Cummings reported from London on the abdication crisis, one more trial for Britain in an already trying time.

King Edward VIII abdicated today and was succeeded on the throne by his brother, the Duke of York. Abdication was announced in the House of Commons by Capt. Edward Algernon Fitzroy, Speaker of the House.

The dramatic move ended a week of tension such as Britain has not known since the days of the Great War.

Edward, said a report received, intends to leave the country, probably tomorrow night. There was no indication where he would meet Mrs. Simpson or when they will marry.

Around the globe, through sundown and dawn, to those who hear allegiance to Britain's King, flashed this message from their sovereign: "After long and anxious consideration, I have determined to renounce the throne to which I succeeded on the death of my father, and now I am communicating this, my final and irrevocable decision."

Rather than give up the twice divorced American woman who waited today within the rain-splashed walls of a villa on the Cote d'Azur, balked by state and church in his desire for morganatic marriage, Edward VIII this morning signed the decree of abdication.

Prime Minister Baldwin outlined the whole crisis for Commons in a voice low and broken with emotion. He described his discussions with the King and Mrs. Simpson, and told the members how Edward from the outset had declared his determination to marry her.

Cheers rang through the chamber as Baldwin decared: "I reminded him of what I have often told him in years past, and that is this: The Crown over the centuries has been deprived of many of its perogatives, but today — while that is true — it stands for far more than it ever has done in its history."

London, December 10, 1936

An editorial.

There is not a British subject anywhere but will view with keen sorrow the developments of the last few days in London. Whatever other considerations there may be surrounding today's event, the Empire knows that it has lost a great king.

All one can say is that in part it has been a struggle between the new tradition and the old. Just as King Edward had shocked his ministers with his outspokenness regarding the slum conditions he encountered in various parts of the British Isles, he shocked them, and in their opinion might shock the British public, with the idea of marrying a divorcee.

Perhaps in matters of this sort compromise is impossible; certainly that seems to have been Mr. Baldwin's view of the case, and the King himself, who has presented us with such a vivid personality, can hardly have been expected to capitulate in a matter where his heart was sincerely involved.

But for Britishers down the arches of the years the question will forever echo: Was it necessary?

December 10, 1936

A.C. Cummings covered this coronation of King George VI and Elizabeth, the Queen Mother.

Britain crowned her King today! While London's millions thundered cheers from stands and roof tops and windows, half hidden beneath rich, flaunting decorations on masts and house-fronts, and while joybells clanged from spire and tower, bands played loyal airs and the voices of broadcasters carried vivid descriptions of a great historic occasion to the farthest ends of the earth, King George the Sixth and Queen Elizabeth drove in state from Buckingham Palace to the old grey abbey of Westminster and were crowned rightful ruler and consort of the greatest commonwealth of free peoples history has ever known.

It was a spectacle unparalleled anywhere else in the world. Not only was it a vast outpouring of the Empire nations' loyalty to their monarch and to the democratic constitution by virtue of which he wears a crown, but it was a solemn religious festival as well — a festival whose ritual goes a thousand years back, in symbolism and in observance, into the "rough island story" of the British peoples. Above all, it was the renewal of a solemn covenant implicit in the British constitution itself — that the King rules and serves and works for his peoples and they in turn give him loyalty, honor, service and affection.

London, May 12, 1937

In July, 1936 a Fascist revolt started the Spanish civil war, which continued for nearly three years. Italians and Germans fought on the Fascist side. The Spanish Loyalists had the support of leftist foreign volunteers, including Canadians. Ernest Hemingway covered the war for the North American Newspaper Alliance. One of his dispatches, published in The Herald, began like this:

The window of the hotel is open and, as you lie in bed, you hear the firing in the front line 17 blocks away. There is rifle fire all night long. The rifles go tacrong, carong, chaang, tacrong, and then a machine gun opens up. It has a bigger calibre and is much louder: rong, cararong, rong, rong. Then there is the incoming boom of a trench mortar shell and a burst of machine gun fire.

You lie and listen to it, and it is a great thing to be in a bed with your feet stretched out gradually warming the cold foot of the bed and not out there in University City or Carabanchel. A man is singing hard-voiced in the street below and three drunks are arguing when you fall asleep.

In the morning, before your call comes from the desk, the roaring burst of a high explosive shell wakes you up and you go to the window and look out to see a man, his head down, his coat collar up, springing desperately across the paved square. There is the acrid smell of high explosive you hoped you'd never smell again, and, in a bathrobe and bedroom slippers, you hurry down the marble stairs and almost into a middle-aged woman, wounded in the abdomen, who is being helped into the hotel entrance by two men in blue workmen's smocks. She has her two hands crossed below her big, old-style Spanish bosom and from between her fingers the blood is spurting in a thin stream.

On the corner, 20 yards away, is a heap of rubble, smashed cement and thrown up dirt, a single dead man, his torn clothes dusty, and a great hole in the sidewalk from which the gas from a broken main is rising, looking like a heat mirage in the cold morning air.

"How many dead?" you ask a policeman.

"Only one," he says. "It went through the sidewalk and burst below. If it had burst on the solid stone of the road there might have been fifty."

Madrid, April 24, 1937

An editorial.

It is never ill-timed or out of place for advocates of peace to strive for the abolition of war, but it must be recognized that today they face a most discouraging situation. All the great nations of the world are increasing their armaments either for offence or defence, convinced that war on a major scale is unavoidable.

There are two very dangerous factors: the Franco-German deadlock and the aggressive foreign policy of Japan. Thus peace is threatened in Europe and in the Orient, and nations which are most desirous of peace, like Great Britain and the United States, are forced to prepare to meet dreaded eventualities.

The decline in prestige of the League of Nations is deplored and no more so than in Great Britain, which has made heroic efforts to bring about disarmament, but without success. The old country could not reconcile the opposing views of France and German on the question of equality, and as a result all Europe is again springing to arms to meet some unknown contingency.

Canada stands aloof from all this preparation for conflict, and perhaps it is natural enough that a peace movement should assume large dimensions in this country. Unfortunately the Dominion with its bare ten millions of people is not in a position to exert any influence on war-fevered nations. They respect superior force and that alone. A most unfortunate fact is that Canada's fervor for peace and total disarmament would not be the least protection if a war-mad nation decided to use Canadian territory as a base for offensive operations against another nation. We are crying peace when there is no peace.

May 8, 1934

In the last year of peace, Calgarians were anything but eager for war.

If the drums of war were to beat in Calgary today, they would most likely fall on deaf ears.

Mr. and Mrs. Calgary and Young Mr. Calgary are not interested in the prospect of taking part in another European war.

If Canada was invaded, the youth of the country would be found in the front lines fighting in the defence of their homeland, but the prospect of joining an overseas expeditionary force does not strike a responsive chord in the breast of the average Calgarian.

A Herald reporter came to this conclusion today after listening to Calgarians gossip about the war crisis in restaurants, soldier and civilian clubs and on the street corners.

The average former soldier is not interested in another spell of front line duty in France or Germany. The majority of them are anxious to spare their sons the pain and misery which they had undergone during the years of 1914-1918.

A few ex-soldiers stated that they would offer themselves for overseas service if war was declared, but they would prefer a job behind the lines rather than front line duty.

In one local soldiers' club, nearly a dozen former soldiers were discussing the war crisis in subdued tones when the reporter entered.

To the question of "are you prepared to go to war again?" there was a loud and instantaneous "no."

One veteran, however, expressed the view that a response to a call to the colors would be astounding, even in Canada.

"You see," he said, "it is a matter of history that every time Britain has sent out the call, there has always been a good response. The people would grumble and grouse before a war was declared, but they always rallied around the colors at the finish."

Another former soldier said that if war was declared, he would be in favor of calling up for front line duty, immediately, all the officials who had anything to do with the awarding of pensions to soldiers disabled in the last war.

In March 1938, the Austrian government resigned after an ultimatum from Hitler. German troops marched in, and Austria was absorbed into the Reich. Herald cartoonist Stew Cameron was somewhat premature in predicting what Russia, Britain and France would do about Hitler. (March 18, 1938)

As an afterthought, he thought that maybe the professional soldiers should be disposed of first, and then the pensions board officials.

A son of a former soldier told the reporter that although he would certainly fight if Canada was invaded, he would not, under any circumstances, volunteer for overseas service.

"Things are a bit different from the days of 1914," he said. "The youth of the country are taking a much greater interest nowadays in war and the causes of war than they ever did before. The last war ruined my father both physically and morally. I was six years old when he came home from the war. I thought he was a hero.

"The war did something to him. He didn't want to work. He thought the country owed him a living, and then he drank to forget his troubles. There was years of misery at home. Before the war, he was a happy, hard-working man. But the war changed all that.

"I'm not so much interested in that at the moment, but what I am interested in is why the youth of Canada should be sacrificed to the gods of war just because some dictator in Europe starts throwing his chest around. I'm not interested in any European war, and you can print that in letters a foot high."

One ex-officer admitted that he had sent in his name in the event of another war.

"Why not?" he said. "I've nothing to lose. No job, wife dead, no family. I'm 50 years old, but they will need experienced officers if they start to recruit a new army.

"I'll say right now, however, that I'm not interested in front-line duty for the simple reason I don't think that I'm up to it at my age."

This former officer expressed the opinion that only professional soldiers were looking forward to another war with any degree of enthusiasm.

"There is nothing very mysterious about that. They adopted the army as their career, and there is very little advancement in the regular army in times of peace. One can't blame them for hoping that this business in Europe will finally involve Great Britain and her Dominions."

September 26, 1938

The Munich agreement of September, 1938, bought temporary peace by forcing Czechoslovakia to yield the Sudetenland to Germany. "Peace for our time," said Britain's Prime Minister Neville Chamberlain, who joined Hitler in pressing the Czechs to yield. "Munich" soon became a shameful word for the democracies.

Chamberlain and Hitler reached agreement of world-wide importance today. They have decided jointly that Britain and Germany shall never go to war again and pledge themselves to settle and further Anglo-German disputes by diplomatic means.

The Chamberlain-Hitler statement, agreed upon jointly, says they recognize

British Prime Minister Neville Chamberlain returns home from the Munich conference proclaiming "peace for our time." All he had from Hitler, as events proved, was a piece of paper. Less than a year after Munich, Britain was at war with Germany. Chamberlain resigned in May, 1940; he died the same year.

Anglo-German relations as of vital importance in Europe and believe that agreement signed in Munich is to be regarded as symbolic of their joint desire never to go to war again.

This understanding puts the coping-stone on the prime minister's peace efforts and is regarded in London as going far toward eliminating future crises. The whole European outlook is now altered for the better. Stock markets skyrocketed when the news became known and Chamberlain's welcome in London exceeded anything known in history.

A.C. Cummings was willing to join in the cheering for Chamberlain, but he quietly expressed his doubts. Six months later, Germany invaded what was left of Czechoslovakia.

It is peace! Premier Chamberlain flew back to London today amid the heartfelt acclaim of the entire world, his reputation as a statesman prouder and more glittering than any mighty conqueror of continents. The voice of criticism everywhere is silent. Instead a chorus of praise goes up in Germany, Italy, France, Britain and elsewhere. He has kept nations from war and that is all that matters. The rejoicing is as great today as the gloom and foreboding were deep on Wednesday.

Behind the tremendous wave of public relief, however, those best acquainted with the vast complex of European events are by no means easy about the future.

Czechoslovakia, "utterly amazed," has been given yet another ultimatum by friends and enemies. More sacrifices of billions of dollars worth of territory are to be forced upon her. It is true the four-power agreement is not as disastrous to her as Hitler's

ultimatum at the Godesberg meeting with Chamberlain, but it undoubtedly constitutes a tragic bargain for the Czechoslovak people and they have yet to meet the demands of the Polish-Hungarian minorities. Alone among the European nations today, they have no applause for Chamberlain.

One encouraging fact that stands out glaringly in the present rush of events is that, despite the most malignant Nazi propaganda, the German people want no war. Their heartfelt cheers for Chamberlain in Munich proved this. Also in the factories in Hamburg and elsewhere, the word has gone around "away with Hitler — then peace is assured."

Peace has been preserved. My explosive-proof cellar and poison gas mask have overnight become suddenly meaningless. But one cannot forget that behind all this shouting and delight this settlement has been dictated by what the League of Nations was founded to banish from Europe — armed force.

London, September 30, 1938

The day after Munich, a Herald editorial hailed Chamberlain as the man of the hour. "Appeasement" had not yet become a dirty word.

Whatever may happen in the future — near or remote — to disturb the new-found peace of Europe, the whole world breathed a sigh of relief yesterday that an accord had been reached by the four western powers on the Sudeten issue.

And the man to whom the world turned to pay tribute was Neville Chamberlain. It is he who has been accorded rightly the major praise for the Munich agreement by which war on a major scale was averted. His third homecoming to London from conferences in Germany evoked an extraordinary show of feeling and esteem.

The other day a well-known commentator said of him "He is not a popular figure, and, almost seventy as he is, he cannot be expected to kindle the imagination of the electorate."

Sometimes the smartest of critics are confounded. Today, in his hour of triumph, Chamberlain has kindled not only the imagination to the British electorate but of a vaster group throughout the world. By courage and persistency and refusal to admit defeat in his efforts to bring appeasement to Europe, he has won through. Today he is the man of the hour on a much larger stage than Great Britain itself.

October 1, 1938

The euphoria that followed Munich was short-lived, and Britain began to re-arm, barely in time. A.C. Cummings wrote of the new mood in London.

The stark declaration by Nazi Propaganda Minister Goebbels that the German people would have had to fight to crush Czechoslovakia's resistance to Chancellor Hitler's wishes and the broad hint that the next demand from Germany will be for the return of colonies make the British people today almost unanimously welcome the announcement of a new arms drive symbolized by throwing open the whole of the aircraft industry to the manufacture of military machines for the government.

Within a year Britain's weakness in aerial fighting craft should be remedied.

France is copying the United Kingdom's example and proposes to spend $450,000,000 on extending air fleets so that in 18 months she may have 4,000 frontline fighters and bombers.

News of this tremendous speedup arouses bitter comment among the dictatorships. The Nazi-controlled newspapers attack Britain for her failure to live up to the spirit of the no-more-war pact signed between Chamberlain and Hitler.

However, such a drastic policy as this waits on Chamberlain's word. At his official home, Chequers, this weekend he is studying not merely the reconstruction of the cabinet, but whether further appeasement projects are possible in the midst of an arms race calculated to arouse German-Italian suspicion.

Chamberlain's foreign policy is now under bitter attack at the by-election in Oxford City, where, watched by the whole nation, a master of Balliol College, A.D. Lindsay, with the backing of dissident Conservatives and the full support of Liberals and Laborites, asks the electors to say the government's trust in dictators' promises is the height of folly.

London, October 22, 1938

Canadian civilian volunteers fought on the pro-government, anti-Fascist side in the Spanish civil war, but by 1939 the Fascists were winning. The volunteers were ordered out when the government agreed to eliminate foreign intervention in the war.

Keen, bespectacled Major E. Cecil-Smith led a grim battalion through the murky English night toward Liverpool where they embark today for Canada, and expressed the views of the whole bedraggled band when he said, "We are leaving Spain as soldiers following orders, not because we want to."

Dressed mostly in thin, ill-fitting overcoats which hardly hid their tattered uniforms, and what remained of their civilian kit, some were limping, some were led. Some were carried on stretchers as the 272 men disembarked at Newhaven and then were speeded to Liverpool under the close surveillance of the authorities.

"Yes, we are naturally glad we are going home and seeing our families once again, but there was still work in Spain we would have liked to clean up," Major Cecil-Smith said.

"What do we intend to do? Well, we intend to settle down to Canadian citizenship, some on farms, some in offices, some in trades; a few in professions, but we intend to do our part for Spain by telling our story and correcting misinformation which might harm the cause of Spain in particular and of democracy in general."

When they first landed at Newhaven they dismissed inquiries as to how they felt with brief "okays" as they sought anxiously information concerning the plight of Barcelona. When told the city had fallen they incredulously said in unison:

"Impossible! Terrible!"

They admitted this was a severe blow to their cause but insisted there was still a chance of victory. They argued "France must now see the danger of Fascism's threatening spread and in the interests of her own safety and of world democracy send aid in time to keep Spain free."

"If not," added Major Cecil-Smith, "it won't be very long before my boys will be back in uniform — and with earnest willingness, too — only this time it will be Canadian uniform. And the conflagration will be world-wide."

Newhaven, England, January 27, 1939

After his triumph in conquering Ethiopian tribesmen, Italian strong-man Benito Mussolini invaded Albania. The Herald was not impressed. This was perhaps the last time Fascism would seem even faintly comical.

The Italian conquest of Albania must indubitably be reckoned with the greatest military adventures of modern times. Poets, singing of it, will rack their brains to find a rhyme for Caporetto; historians, writing of it, will find only one comparable tour de force, the defeat by Mussolini of the Ethiopian blackamoors.

Great were the disadvantages encountered by the Romans in Africa. Their airplanes and machine guns were limited; the sticks and stones of Ethiopians came from a practically inexhaustible supply. The Ethiopians, being dark-hued, were able to conceal themselves better than their caucasian opponents. The very scarcity of the Ethiopians had a grave effect on the morale of the sons of the wolf — they worried and lost weight trying to figure out whether they were in the right country. To top all this, the Ethiopians refused to admit themselves defeated, even after their national extinction had been officially acknowledged from London and Paris.

Similar difficulties were evident when Italy finally moved to protect herself from the threats of the Albanian mountain hordes. Admittedly, Italy had 50,000 armed men to Albania's 7,000. But the Albanians had threatened to fight with women when their men had all fallen. Italians have always been noted no less for their chivalry than for their daring, and they felt themselves obliged to avert such a state of affairs. They did not exert their best efforts, and snatched victory only under gruelling difficulty.

Nor was this all. Rain fell at many points on the Italian line of advance. Yet they did not falter. We can believe that many of them, with a shrug of disdain for increasingly tremendous odds, refused to don their raincoats, and risked the chance of getting a nasty headcold. Dulce et decorum est pro patria more.

D'Annunzio, alas, is dead. How well the masterful conqueror of Fiume would have immortalized this victory! To the sober historian is left the task of commemoration, and he, after careful study of Italian military history, may pen the comment that it was, after all, worthy of the heroes who achieved it.

April 11, 1939

The year after Hitler annexed Austria, one of his victims, a woman lawyer, told her story.

Before the Nazis came to Austria, we were such a happy, contented family. My father was a well-known ear, nose and throat specialist. My brother, who is also a doctor, held a good hospital appointment.

I was beginning to make headway at the bar, and my briefs brought me in about $1,500 a year. My husband held a good position as the manager of a mineral water factory. Oh, we were so happy!

Then the Nazis entered our country, and in a night everything for which we had worked so hard was brought crashing down.

My brother was the first to suffer. With Austria part of the German Reich, anti-Jewish regulations came into force, and his job at the hospital was taken from him. His private practice, too, vanished, for no patients would dare call on a Jewish doctor.

He and his wife were insulted in the streets and spat upon. They spent most of the days in their flat, afraid to go out.

Twice, young men of the Nazi Party came thundering at the door late at night, demanding entrance. In their searches they nearly wrecked the place. But they found nothing. What was there to find? My brother was not interested in politics. He was interested only in curing the sick.

His wife became seriously ill with fear and worry. Friends of ours were being sent to Dachau, the terrible concentration camp, and he wondered what his fate was to be. Soon he knew. He was given seven days in which to get out of the country or be sent to the camp.

By begging and praying he managed to get from the British consulate a visa to travel to England. They granted it because our great-aunt, with whom we are now living in London, guaranteed that he would not be a charge on the public funds. But no amount of pleading would obtain a visa for his wife.

Well, it was England or the prison camp for him, and his wife insisted he should leave. He did so when his time of grace had three hours to expire.

By this time my father had lost his practice and his savings were taken. Now he is penniless. He, a distinguished doctor, must beg.

Of course, as a Jewess, I was barred from practising in the Vienna courts. But my husband still had his job. Then he, too, was dismissed.

At last we were dragged before a Nazi official and told to leave Austria at once. He was not interested in where we went; whether we starved or managed to live. His only concern was that we crossed the frontier.

Again, because of our great-aunt, the only relative we have outside Austria, my husband and I were able to join my brother in England.

But my great-aunt's income is only $10 a week, out of which she pays rent for part of the old house in which we live.

On what is left, and the $4.50 a week I earned by scrubbing floors, the four of us manage to survive somehow.

My chief worry now is whether my husband will be permitted to remain in England and find work. He is learning English at night school in the hope that Jewish friends will find him something to do as a salesman or agent.

My brother's permit is good for six months. After that, heaven alone knows what will happen or whether he will ever be reunited with his wife. He lives in hope of finding refuge in some country where he will be allowed to practise as a doctor.

As for my father and mother, their plight seems beyond all help. We know they are penniless, almost starving. But what can we do? Except think of them as living dead and mourn.

London, April 29, 1939

The posturing of Europe's dictators, with their uniforms and their special salutes, seemed amusing until it became all too obvious that war was imminent. Herald cartoonist Stew Cameron depicted Hitler and Mussolini in characteristic poses, and suggested something a little more modest for William Aberhart, premier of a province that then desperately needed financial help.

Salutations

The reality of Nazi Germany was less heroic than the banners and torchlight parades suggested. Here a group of Berlin policemen, in a force sufficient for the purpose, arrest a German Jew. This man was probably among the millions who died in the Nazi extermination camps.

On Sept. 1, 1939, Germany invaded Poland, triggering the Second World War. On August 28, Fred Kennedy wrote this story in the last week of peace.

Calgary today began to play its part in the Canada-wide plan of defence in the event of war breaking out in Europe.

As in other parts of Canada, guards were mounted this morning on all principal military and public buildings, while members of the permanent and non-permanent militia units were prepared to move at a moment's notice, the former to proceed overseas if necessary, the latter for home defence work — 10,000 members of the non-permanent militia have been summoned for duty across Canada.

Eight Wapiti bombing planes from the 113th bombing squadron, Royal Canadian Air Force, took the air Saturday afternoon and headed east. In semi-official circles, it was reported that the planes are destined for coastal defence work at Dartmouth, Nova Scotia.

Shortly after the bombers disappeared in a southeasterly direction, after taking off from the Currie Barracks airfield, a Hawker Hurricane fighter also took off and sped east at a high rate of speed.

This afternoon, it is expected that the other two Hawker Hurricane ships, which have been stationed at Currie Barracks airport for several months, will also fly to the east coast.

Some of the ground crew personnel of the air squadrons left for the east last night and the remainder are expected to entrain tonight for Dartmouth. It will represent the first transportation of permanent force troops for possible active service since the days of the Great War.

The Currie Barracks, which houses several detachments of permanent force troops, has been closed to the public for the

King George VI and Queen Elizabeth, the Queen mother, visited Calgary a few months before the beginning of the Second World War. Their two-hour stop in Calgary included a short chat with Indians and Mounties. Saluting soldiers lined the route of their parade through downtown Calgary. Disabled veterans of the Great War of 1914-18 cheered them from the windows of the Colonel Belcher Hospital, which was then a much smaller building on 8th Avenue S.W.

first time since it was opened several years ago. All entrances leading to the barracks proper are closed with the exception of the one adjoining the guard house. At this entrance, a trooper of the Lord Strathcona's Horse (R.C.) stands guard. Civilians must state their business before they are allowed to enter, and the sergeant of the guard makes a note of the licence numbers of all automobiles driven by civilians, before they are allowed to pass through the gates.

Within the barracks, especially in the vicinity of the airport, a scene of intense activity presents itself. Details of the various air force squadrons are busily engaged in "packing up" before leaving for coastal defence duty. Transport trucks race from the barracks to the railway station with squadron equipment of every description. This evening, it is expected that the huge hangar, which for nearly two years housed air force squadrons, will be practically deserted. It is understood that a skeleton guard will stand watch over the building until the crisis is decided and until the building is again occupied by new units.

August 28, 1939

It was, all in all, a bad time, and about to get worse. Yet, as this editorial showed, there was still time and reason to enjoy life.

The other morning, when the Mountaineer snorted into the depot, a young lady got out and looked around the platform. She asked the porter a question. He nodded in affirmation. So she ran back to the doorway of the coach and called to her companions "Come on out! This is the place they told us about!"

This is the place all right. But what they told her about it, or who "they" are, was lost in the bustle of the station.

Maybe they told her it was the loftiest city in Canada (3,439 feet at the depot). Maybe they told her about the high, winey air (don't run for a street car; there'll be another one along soon). Maybe they described to her (and she could have noticed it herself that morning) the electric blue of the sky, the sharp light that cuts the outlines of buildings to a razor-edge. Maybe they told her about the rivers plunging down into the plains, or the hamburgers and five-gallon hats and the guns and saddles in the store windows.

They might have been talking to her about the North Hill, where children and potatoes sprout with prodigal abandon; where they grow rhubarb to shade the house, and a cabbage fits nicely into a wheelbarrow.

Or Riverside, whose streets are daily in blossom with unspeakably beautiful young woman, all wearing slacks.

Or Elbow Park, where evening closes in quietly and painlessly, and the soft gurgle of the river over the rocks awakens nostalgic memories, and voices speak softly under the moth-fluttering lights.

Or the high open fields of Killarney, where the mountains seem within arm's reach, a barricade of blue cardboard.

Who is she? Who are "they"? What did they tell her? Please, miss, whoever you are, when you get back to St. Paul, or Fargo, or Chicago, tell them it is true, it was just like they said. Tell them we haven't sunk so much as an inch, the sun still shines, everything is still here down to the last brown-eyed susan, the last gopher, the last pair of "chapps" in the second-hand store window.

August 12, 1939

THE CALGARY HERALD

CALGARY, ALBERTA, MONDAY, SEPTEMBER 11, 1939

CANADA JOINS ALLIES, DECLARES WAR ON HITLER
FRENCH SCORE ADVANCE

Momentous Move At Ottawa Leads Canadian People

King George Gives Assent to Declaration Uniting Empire in European Conflict.

SEE NO HONORABLE RETREAT

HITLER FINDS EARLY PEACE PLANS UPSET

Conquest of Poland Can Be Deferred Many Months

3-YEAR WAR

Poles Es...
In Fie...
To C...

Step Up Munitions Dep't

THE CALGARY HERALD

2nd EXTRA

...R ON POLAND,
...6,000,000 MEN,

THE CALGARY HERALD

CALGARY, ALBERTA, THURSDAY, MAY 30, 1940

BRITONS REACH HOME PORTS THROUGH SHELLED DUNKERQUE

Allied Ships Keep Channel Ports Open To Embark Troops

Furious German Drives Fail to Cut Allied Force in Two

Today In Europe

SECOND DIVISION OFFICERS NAMED FOR OVERSEAS

THE CALGARY HERALD

CALGARY, ALBERTA, THURSDAY, AUGUST 20, 1942

Wide Control Of Manpower

To Place All but Very Young, Very Old and Disabled Behind War Effort

Calgary Tanks at Dieppe Carry Brunt of Attack

Western Regiments Fight Canadian Fliers Way Into Streets of City Win New Laurels In Dieppe Battle

Many Westerners Scored Hits On Nazi Planes

Reds Attack On North Front, Hold in South

Claim Nazi Advance Across Don Wiped Out

THE CALGARY HERALD

CALGARY, ALBERTA, TUESDAY, JUNE 6, 1944

"Let the hearts of all, in Canada today, be filled with silent prayer for the success of our own and Allied forces, and for the early liberation of the people of Europe." —Prime Minister Mackenzie King

Allies Widen Beachhead, Advance Deeper Into France

Canadian Units Gain

Invasion Moving On Schedule, Churchill Says

Declares Many 'Surprises' Await Enemy

Thousands Here Bow In Prayer

Citizens Jam Street for Invasion Ceremony

Great Air Fleet Finds Little Nazi Opposition

11,000 Planes Provide Cover For Invaders

Many Secret Weapons Are Used in Invasion

THE CALGARY HERALD

INVEST IN THE BEST

CALGARY, ALBERTA, MONDAY, MAY 7, 1945

END COMES TO WAR IN EUROPE

Tomorrow Designated As VE-Day

LONDON, May 7 (CP)—The Ministry of Information announced that tomorrow will be treated as VE-Day.

Surrender Is Unconditional To 'Big Three'

By The Canadian Press.

THE CALGARY HERALD

CALGARY, ALBERTA, TUESDAY, OCTOBER 1, 1946

12 Of Hitler Gang To Be Hanged, 7 Get Prison Terms, 3 Acquitted

6 Stab Wounds Pierced Wall Of Child's Chest

Any One of 8 Knife Injuries Would Have Caused Death

Goering, Ribbentrop Get Death

NUERNBERG, Oct. 1 (AP)—The International War Crimes Tribunal today decreed death on the gallows for 12 leaders of the Adolf Hitler gang, sentenced seven to prison and — with Russia dissenting — acquitted three defendants.

THE LONG NUERNBERG WAR CRIMES TRIAL came to an end today with the sentencing of the German war leaders.

Murderer Sought

The Weather

Farmers Accept

Calgary Official!

A World Again at War

1939-46

On September 10, 1939, Canada entered the Second World War. There was no boasting or cheering, as there had been when the First World War began; this war was just a grim job that had to be done.

Canada declared war this time as an independent nation, by act of her own Parliament. It was another step toward national maturity. In 1914, as part of the British Empire, she had automatically — and enthusiastically — joined in the First World War by Britain's decision.

There was much to be done before Canada could play any useful role in the new conflict. Armed forces had to be built and armed from a tiny, peace-time nucleus. The Royal Canadian Navy, for instance, began with war with only 10 operational vessels.

More than a million Canadians served in the army, navy and air force in the Second World War; of these, nearly 50,000 were women. Under the Commonwealth air training plan, 97 flying schools across Canada turned out more than 130,000 aircrew for the Commonwealth air forces.

It was a total war, and no one at home was allowed to forget it. Advertisements, official pronouncements, editorials all admonished civilians: don't hoard; don't waste; do without if you can; turn in your aluminum pots to make bombers; and buy Victory Bonds to help pay for the war. Sugar was rationed. Meat was rationed. Gasoline was rationed. There were no new cars, and no new tires to put on old ones. And there wasn't much complaining. The war came first.

At the movies, you could escape the war with Charlie Chaplin's satire of Hitler, The Great Dictator (1940), or watch Orson Welles in Citizen Kane (1941). Bing Crosby sang White Christmas for the first time in Holiday Inn (1942), Humphrey Bogart looked into Ingrid Bergman's eyes and murmured "Here's looking at you, kid," in Casablanca (1943), and Ray Milland showed us what a hangover was really like in Lost Weekend (1945).

On records, some of the war-time hits were The Last Time I Saw Paris, Blueberry Hill, Chattanooga Choo-choo, The White Cliffs of Dover, Praise The Lord And Pass The Ammunition, and Mairzy Doats.

When radio fans weren't listening to Lorne Greene, "The Voice of Doom," reading the war news on the CBC, they could listen to Edgar Bergen and Charlie McCarthy, Lum and Abner, Glen Miller and his Orchestra, or Pepper Young's Family.

For those who liked stronger entertainment, politics continued. In Alberta, William Aberhart was re-elected premier in 1940 with a reduced majority, but larger events cut down the amount of attention and passion that could be devoted to Social Credit. In 1943 Aberhart died, and was succeeded by Ernest Manning, who was to be premier for some 25 years.

The great political issue of the war was conscription. Before the war Prime Minister Mackenzie King had pledged that no man would be drafted for overseas service. He wanted no conscription crisis like the one that divided the country during the First World War. The need for manpower grew more pressing, and in 1942 King won a plebiscite releasing him from his pledge. Quebec was still opposed, however, and King avoided sending conscripts to Europe until late in 1944. This delay cost King the resignation of his defence minister, Colonel J. L. Ralston, but he avoided another full-scale conscription crisis.

After Japan entered the war, Canada forcibly relocated thousands of Japanese-Canadians who were living on the West Coast. Some went to work camps in the B.C. interior; some were moved to southern Alberta to pick sugar beets; some were moved as far away as Quebec and Ontario. Their fishing boats, cars, farms and other assets were sold. Even if they were third-generation Canadians, they were moved at least 100 miles from the coast. So great was the fear of a Japanese fifth column, and so great were the powers of the federal government in wartime.

The Canadian army fought primarily in Europe, except for about 2,000 who were sent to Hong Kong shortly before it fell to the Japanese. The Royal Canadian Air Force served in almost every field, from southeast Asia to Europe and the Mediterranean. The navy's biggest role was in the North Atlantic, where it convoyed shipments of food and weapons to Britain through the German submarine wolfpacks, but Canadian ships also saw action in the Mediterranean and in the D-Day invasion of France. (Southam news correspondents were concentrated in Europe and Britain, where the Canadian troops were, a concentration that is reflected in the selection of war stories that follows. The Herald used wireservice reports from the other theatres of war.)

The Second World War was immensely complicated, with great events taking place almost simultaneously in widely-separated fields of conflict. It began on Sept. 1, 1939, when Germany invaded Poland. Keeping their pledge to Poland, Britain and France declared war on Germany Sept. 3. Britain sent 150,000 men across the Channel to reinforce the French.

Then came an eerie pause; the Allies watched and waited, and nothing happened. Finally, in April, 1940, Germany ended the so-called "Phoney War" by invading Norway and Denmark. On May 10, German troops swept into Belgium, the Netherlands and Luxembourg. Winston Churchill became prime minister of Britain the same day, replacing the disillusioned and disgraced Neville Chamberlain, who had hoped that appeasing Hitler would mean "peace for our time."

The Nazis drove British and French forces back to the French port of Dunkirk, where an improvised fleet, including fishing boats and yachts, rescued 340,000 of them from May 29 to June 3. The Germans occupied Paris June 14, 1940, and France surrendered June 22.

In July began the Battle of Britain, fought in the air over the south of England. The Germans wanted to destroy the Royal Air Force to clear the way for their invasion of Britain. Guided by a secret new invention, radar, young men flying the last generation of propeller-driven fighter aircraft shot down German fighters and bombers. They held off the Germans until rough weather came to protect Britain from a cross-channel invasion in 1940. By the time smooth weather returned in 1941, Hitler had his hands full with the invasion of Russia. The Royal Air Force had saved Britain. As Winston Churchill said, "Never in the field of human conflict was so much owed by so many to so few."

In spite of this victory, England still had much to suffer. In September, 1940 the London "blitz" began. Night after night, German aircraft rained down fire-bombs and high explosive. Sometimes square miles of the city were in flames. At sea, German submarines took an increasing toll of supply ships.

The see-saw battle for control of North Africa began in 1941. British forces drove Italian invaders out of Egypt, but one of Hitler's most brilliant generals, Erwin Rommel, turned the tide. In two weeks the tanks of Rommel's Afrika Korps won back what the Italians had lost. At sea, the new German battleship Bismarck sank the HMS Hood, largest ship in the British navy, but three days later the British sank the Bismarck.

In June, 1941, Hitler broke his nonaggression pact with Russia. The invading German troops made huge gains at first, but the terrible Russian winter slowed them. A second winter would complete their ruin.

The United States came into the war on December 7, 1941, when Japan attacked Pearl Harbor, Hawaii. The Japanese made frighteningly quick gains in the Pacific. Hong Kong fell on Christmas Day, 1941. In 1942, Japan conquered Burma and the Philippines. The Americans ordered General Douglas MacArthur to flee the Philippines and lead the Allied forces in the southwest Pacific. He escaped by torpedo boat and plane to Australia, where he made his famous vow: "I shall return."

In May, 1942, the United States won the four-day battle of the Coral Sea. The battle was fought entirely by carrier-based airplanes; the contending vessels never sighted each other. In June, Japan lost four carriers and many aircraft in the battle of Midway, which ended the threat to Hawaii.

On August 19, 1942, 5,000 Canadians raided Dieppe, France, testing the German defences; they suffered 3,400 casualties.

On the North African front, the Germans and Italians captured Tobruk in Libya, but by July they had been halted at Alamein, Egypt. In October General Bernard Montgomery's British forces took the offensive and rolled Rommel back across Libya to Tripoli. In Russia, the Germans reached Stalingrad, and an epic siege began. In occupied Eastern Europe, the Nazis began their "final solution": systematic extermination of the Jews.

A second Russian winter took its toll of the German forces. The survivors at Stalingrad surrendered February 2, 1943, and Soviet troops began to roll the Germans back.

In the Pacific, the war turned in the Allies' favor. In 1943 the United States drove Japan from Guadalcanal, the Aleutians, and other Pacific Islands.

The battle for North Africa was resolved in 1943: German and Italian forces surrendered in Tunisia. This victory cleared the way for the Allies' invasion of Sicily in July, followed by the invasion of Italy on September 3, 1943. Italy surrendered September 8, but German troops continued the war on Italian soil. More than 92,000 Canadians served in Italy, and nearly 5,800 were killed.

The Russians broke the long German siege of Leningrad on January 27, 1944. That year the last German invaders were driven from Russia, and forced back into Yugoslavia and Hungary, with Russian forces in pursuit.

June 6, 1944 was D-Day: a huge fleet carried the Allied invasion force to the beaches of Normandy, France. The fight to liberate Western Europe had begun. Canadian troops played a major role in liberating Belgium and the Netherlands; from D-Day to the German surrender, nearly 11,000 Canadians lost their lives.

In 1944, after the Normandy landing, the first German V-2 rockets fell on London. They made no difference to the outcome of the war, but they should be remembered as the forerunners of the intercontinental ballistic missile.

In 1945, MacArthur fulfilled his promise: American forces landed in the Philippines. In Europe, the Allies continued their drive eastward into Germany, while the Russians pushed westward. By April 22, 1945, the Russians had reached the suburbs of Berlin. Hitler killed himself in his Berlin bunker on April 30. Germany surrendered May 7, and Europe was at peace.

London, 1940

The war continued in the Pacific. On August 6, the United States dropped the first atomic bomb on Hiroshima, and another on Nagasaki August 9. Japan surrendered August 14, 1945.

The first session of the United Nations General Assembly was convened in 1946, amid high hopes for a better world. The Nuremberg trial returned its verdict on the principal Nazi war criminals. Twelve were to hang, seven were imprisoned for terms ranging up to life, and three were acquitted. Hermann Goering cheated the hangman by taking cyanide the night of the executions.

The War's Darkest Days

War came again to Europe on Sept. 1, 1939, when Germany invaded Poland. France and Great Britain declared war on Germany Sept. 3, but they could offer Poland little more than moral support. The country was quickly overrun by Nazi forces. After the fall of Poland came a respite. British and French troops in France waited through the winter for Hitler's next move. Nothing happened; people began to call it "the phoney war." Then, in April, 1940, Germany invaded Denmark and Norway. In May, the German war machine swept through Belgium, Luxembourg, and on into France. The British and some French forces were driven back to the Channel coast, where an improvised fleet evacuated them to England. France surrendered to Germany on June 22. Britain stood alone, her Commonwealth allies an ocean away. On Sept. 1, 1939, The Herald published an "extra" with news of the invasion of Poland.

German hostilities against Poland began shortly after midnight, Calgary time. First dispatches reported German bombing planes had flown over Warsaw and discharged a number of bombs.

The Polish foreign office said today that German planes had bombed Krakow and Katowice, in Southwestern Poland.

The report caught Paris by surprise on a sunny morning when newspapers were proclaiming that "French and British firmness can still save peace."

Immediately after the bombing Poland charged Germany with aggression. The Polish embassy in Paris announced Germany had violated the Polish border at four different points. Military action all along the Polish front had already developed.

About midnight, Calgary time, Albert Forster, leader of the Danzig Nazis, formally announced to Hitler the reunion of Danzig with the Reich. Hitler replied, accepting return of the city and the swastika flag was immediately hoisted over Danzig.

Prime Minister Chamberlain called his cabinet into session and parliament will be called immediately.

Hitler called the Reichstag to meet at 10 o'clock, or 2 a.m. today, M.S.T.

President Roosevelt received word of hostilities at 2:50 o'clock, E.S.T., by telephone from Ambassador Biddle at Warsaw and Ambassador Bullitt at Berlin. The president directed that all naval vessels and army commands be notified by radio at once.

First actual news of fighting came when an army ambulance arrived at Gleiwitz, Germany, at 9:10 o'clock (1:10 o'clock, MST), bearing wounded German soldiers.

London, September 1, 1939

Fuehrer Hitler, in his order of the day to the army, today ordered the German military to meet force with force.

The order of the day to the army read:

"The Polish state has rejected my efforts to establish neighborly relations, and instead has appealed to weapons.

"Germans in Poland are victims of a bloody terror, driven from house to home.

"A series of border violations unbearable for a great power, show that the Poles no longer are willing to respect the German border.

"To put an end to these insane incitations, nothing remains but for me to meet force with force from now on.

"The German army will conduct a fight for honor and the right to the life of the resurrected German people with firm determination. I expect that every soldier, mindful of the great traditions of the eternal German military, will do his duty to the last.

"Remember always that you are representatives of the National Socialist Great Germany. Long live our people and our Reich!"

The German radio announced a blockade of the Polish harbor of Gdynia.

Hitler gave his orders to his army at 5:30 a.m. (9:30 p.m. M.S.T. Thursday) to use "force against force." The command was issued as the order of the day to the army massed on Polish frontiers from the Baltic to the high Thera mountains, and in East Prussia.

The radio announced immediately an indefinite closing of all schools in Germany.

Rapid-fire orders followed commanding masters of German vessels to get out of the Baltic Sea and not to enter the Danzig or Polish harbors.

The radio warned all foreigners that Polish territory is a danger zone and their presence was at their own peril because of the likelihood of military action.

Berlin, September 1, 1939

Britain and France were poorly prepared for war, but at last they lived up to their commitment to stop Hitler. After the Nazi invasion of Poland they declared war on September 3, 1939. It was already too late for Poland; invaded by Germany on the west and Russia (then Hitler's ally) on the east, the country was crushed by early October. On the eve of the war, A.C. Cummings of The Herald's London bureau sent this report on an especially grim preparation for the coming conflict.

The mightiest organized mass migration of human beings in the world's history is transforming the face of Britain today.

By tonight one million women, children and invalids will have been moved from London to country homes and nearly another million from the big provincial cities of England and Scotland.

By tomorrow, those who will conduct the war against Hitler's mad aggression will be relieved to know that three millions of the non-combatant population are safe from the Nazi dictator's bombs and poison gas.

For boys and girls it was an exciting and enjoyable episode, but here and there on railway platforms mothers were quietly weeping at the thought of parting with their little ones.

Irrepressible Cockney humor, however, would break out, and occasionally on the back of a private automobile would be scrawled such words as 'Half a mo', Hitler, until we get the children away.'

The spirit of everyone was magnificent.

Each child had his label, gas mask, food and postcard to send home on arrival, telling his mother where he had got to, for the evacuation was on a plan which did not disclose the destination of any group until it had arrived there.

London, in the darkness of the blackout, with every house shrouded so that no light can be seen from the sky, where the great balloon barrage guards the city from the enemy, is almost childless tonight.

While waiting for formal declaration of war, there is not a voice raised to say Britain should not fight. Admirers of dictatorships — and they were neither few nor without influence a year ago when Czecho-Slovakia was delivered over to Hitler's mercy — have dissolved their Anglo-German organizations, discovering that Hitler is not the great man they once thought him.

There is no cheering in Britain today as there was in 1914. No one wants war. But they know of no other way to get peace than that of frontier days of North America turning out a whole village to suppress a criminal who threatens everyone's life.

London, September 2, 1939

As the Nazi forces swept into France, Taylor Henry of the Associated Press sent this dispatch.

Fleeing crowds of refugees from Belgium and northeastern France are streaming toward the interior, while the French army meets the triphammer blows of the invading German shock forces.

I have just returned to Paris from a week's stay along the sector of the front where the fighting is now heaviest.

The fighting has been terrific, like nothing else before in history. A French officer of the last war told me: "There can be no comparison between this battle and the worst ones of the last war. Two hours of this is worse than two days of the battle for Verdun."

As J.J. Philip of the New York Times and I were setting out for Paris on bicycles, the only available means of transportation, a German plane dive-bombed behind us.

It loosed five bombs on railroad tracks. We were within 40 yards. We threw ourselves flat against a wall amidst a shower of bricks and glass and then raced to shelter to avoid the plane's spraying machine gun bullets as it returned.

Again the planes attacked. They were bigger bombs this time. The force of the explosion knocked me off the bicycle, ripping the back wheel to pieces. A French major who slept in the hotel room next to mine the night before was among those killed.

Screams of the wounded after the bombing were ghastly. One woman with arteries severed in both legs was holding a small baby in her arms. An old man hobbled around trying to stop the flow of blood spurting from the stump of his arm. A child huddled in the corner of the station kept wailing "mama."

I prevailed on a terror-stricken boy on a bicycle to repair my wheel. Philip and I started out again for Paris.

From every hill unbroken columns of refugees could be seen winding down to the main highway. Nazi planes were flying everywhere single and in squadrons up to 30. Time and time again we ducked from our bicycles and flopped in the ditches alongside the roads to hide.

Town criers went through villages ringing great bells and warning everyone to be on the move within an hour. Methodically the peasants closed their homes, loaded their belongings on pushcarts, in old trucks and in great two-wheeled farm chariots drawn by from four to eight farm horses.

What was left they strapped to their backs and with scarcely a look behind started on the same trek that all but the very young had made in 1914.

Paris, May 20, 1940

A.C. Cummings of The Herald's London bureau put the best face on the Dunkirk evacuation. It was a brave affair, and it saved many soldiers to fight another day, but the evacuation was a great setback for the Allies.

All Britain thrills today to the marvelous story of the evacuation of the Anglo-French troops from war-shattered Belgium and Northern France.

For days, in secret, men who were never defeated by Hitler's steel monsters or by his murderous rain of bombs from his numerically superior air force, have been taken in thousands from Continental ports and ferried across the Channel to temporary safety.

French and Belgians have come with them through the storm of high explosives and incendiary bombs, through death in water, air and on land. They have survived and they want to go back as soon as they can to avenge the horrors they have seen Goering's winged murderers inflict on innocent women and children.

The retreat of the Allied armies on Dunkerque was an unparalleled feat of courage, skill and endurance. The French died

By mid-September, 1940, the weather on the English Channel was too rough for a Nazi invasion force to attack Britain from occupied France. Herald cartoonist Stew Cameron summed up Hitler's problem. In 1941, the Nazis shifted their attention to Russia.

that British soldiers might reach the innumerable small craft waiting in the shallow waters along the coast. British died that French might also escape.

Screened by flights of aircraft that flung scores of enemy airplanes out of the sky, the Allied forces, sleepless and exhausted by continual fighting, fell back on Dunkerque, giving ground only inch-by-inch to half a million Germans hurled against them. Round Dunkerque the Allied commanders have let in the waters of the Channel and slowly today, the protective flooded area balks the German tanks from reaching the retreating troops.

Along those low Flanders hills the Canadians of the last war know so well, the thunderous battle rages. Not even war cemeteries nor war memorials have been spared by German fury.

When the evacuation is complete, the war will enter on a new phase. The Nazis have gained the Channel ports. They have won air bases of incalculable value against the United Kingdom. They have forced the bulk of the Dutch and Belgian armies, numbering nearly a million men, to surrender, but, this only means they have won the battle but not the war.

British troops in unconquered France will speedily be reinforced. Britain herself is becoming an island fortress, guarded from treachery within as well as from the menace of parachutists and transport airplanes. And both France and herself are speeding up airplane and tank production — their essential need — at a rate the enemy will discover before the summer is over.

May 31, 1940

After the British retreat from France, Prime Minister Winston Churchill rallied his people with one of the most famous speeches of his career.

The French Admiralty announced tonight that the last Allied naval and army units had abandoned Dunkerque, leaving the city entirely to the Germans after destroying all supplies.

The British admiralty congratulated "all concerned in the successful evacuation of the B.E.F. and Allied Armies" from Dunkerque.

Paris, June 4, 1940

Never surrender and never give up the struggle against German tyranny, Prime Minister Churchill warned the world today from the ancient lofty House of Commons.

"We shall go on to the end," the prime minister declared. "We shall fight in France, we shall fight on the seas and oceans, we shall fight with growing confidence and growing strength in the air.

'We shall defend our island, whatever the cost may be.

"We shall fight on the beaches, we shall fight on the landing grounds, we shall fight in the fields and streets and in the hills.

"We shall never surrender and even if, which I do not for a moment believe, this island, or even part of it, is subjugated and starving, then our Empire across the seas, armed and guarded by the British fleet, will carry on the struggle until in God's good time, the new world, in all its strength and might, sets forth to the rescue and liberation of the old."

In probably the finest speech of his career — several old members said it was the finest delivered in the House in years — Mr. Churchill announced that 30,000 men of the British Expeditionary Force were killed, wounded or missing.

But in the "miracle of delivery," 335,000 men of the British and French armies had been evacuated from Flanders.

But he warned that "wars are not won by evacuations." It was a tremendous effort and a great victory to snatch so many men from the jaws of death, but Britain and France had suffered "a colossal military disaster" on the field of battle. That must not be forgotten; it must not be minimized.

Britain has lost enormous quantities of material, guns and transport vehicles. The effort to make up this loss "will delay expansion of our military strength" and he implored the people of the United Kingdom never to cease their efforts and their exertion.

London, June 4, 1940

With the fall of France, Britain was left with no allies in Europe. A.C. Cummings sent this dispatch.

France has gone down to defeat. The last great bastion of democratic liberty in Continental Europe has fallen. Marshal Petain, who became France's premier overnight, replacing Premier Reynaud, who was all for continuing the struggle, has broadcast to an appalled world the terrible news that France can fight no more.

So black is the outlook that already in Britain people are saying the bulk of the non-combatant inhabitants should be evacuated to Canada and these islands converted into a fortress protected by the British and French fleets and all available aircraft.

It is a grim and terrible picture, but if there is no alternative the British people will not shrink before it.

They will never surrender. That is certain beyond all question. The British people will see their homeland in flame and ruin before they will think of giving in to Hitler.

Nevertheless, what will happen now that France has capitulated no one knows. The British Expeditionary Force must once again be withdrawn.

London, June 17, 1940

Life under the Nazis' bombs inspired this dispatch from A.C. Cummings of The Herald's London bureau.

The blitzkrieg which propaganda-drugged Germans believe to have laid London in ruins was launched again during last night at twenty-four towns throughout the United Kingdom.

A new type of murder bomb was dropped indiscriminately. A passenger train and firemen were machine-gunned from the air. But the actual damage done in comparison with the risks incurred and the effort extended was so small that Hitler will have to carry on his war for another fifty years if he hopes to defeat Britain.

The hostile air fleet arrived over London at almost the same minute as the previous evening. The procedure is now becoming stereotyped and no longer has the charm of novelty.

First there comes the long drawn-out blood-curdling banshee wail of the air raid sirens. Millions of persons, whether in blacked-out streets, in factories or at home preparing to go to bed, seize gas masks and hurry to underground steel and concrete shelters. The noise of traffic dies away. Then overhead is heard the easily recognizable vicious drone of unseen enemy aircraft.

If clouds are thick he is hard to discover and if it is suspected he is trying to find anti-aircraft batteries so that his friends may come back and bomb them he is allowed to wander about until British fighter planes come and go up to challenge him.

Finding enemy aircraft in a cloud-covered night sky is harder than finding the proverbial needle in a hay-stack. If, however, a glimpse is caught of the foe, searchlights fasten on him. You see something like a tiny silver leaf far in space — and then guns go off with a roar that shakes the ground and makes the air shudder around your head.

If bombs come down they whistle alarmingly and you imagine they are directed straight at the very spot you are standing. If from some roof top you are lucky enough to see a Spitfire or Hurricane hurtle itself across the heavens at the enemy machine you may be able to follow the dog-fight beneath the stars five miles overhead.

Already Kent, which is known as the Garden of England, is littered with the ruins of Nazi murder machines. Yet the enemy airmen, because they are misled by Goebbels' propaganda lies into thinking the Royal Air Force can be worn down by endless attacks and that then a large scale sea and air invasion will give them quick victory, come again and again despite the staggering losses.

Since June 18, when they began large scale raiding, they have lost 1,170 planes not counting those damaged that may not have reached home. During the same period the British losses have been only 262 machines — or a couple of days output of British war factories.

In London and other cities residents expect sleepless nights during the continuance of these "jitter raids" which they take so calmly that theatres are arranging "siren parties" after their ordinary evening performances. A young Ottawa-born boy, Aircraftsman Kapinsky, who eight months ago was a shoe salesman, has become momentarily famous as a singer in this connection at the London Hippodrome.

London, August 28, 1940

W.T. Yarbrough of the Associated Press reported on the work of rescue crews in London.

It is feared that casualties may be heavier than in recent nights," said the calm, prosaic official communique. Not so calm, I saw rescue workers bring the still forms of a baby and five women from the basement of a flaming bomb-shattered home in Northeastern London on an ambulance ride to gather up the dead and injured from this moonlight raid.

Then I watched a woman ambulance-driver pump faint signs of life into two of the women victims, while bombs still thundered around us and anti-aircraft guns boomed in answer.

Several hours earlier, as we waited at an ambulance station for the night's first call, a bomb demolished an open air school building just 100 yards away.

A telephoned call of a street address sent an ambulance to a three-storey building, already in flames. One ambulance which reached the scene first was just leaving.

"Two badly hurt," a policeman said. "One of those oil bombs."

Two men with a pick and spade dug frantically at the foundation, hacking through solid concrete.

"There's five down there," one of the workers said.

Then somewhere below a man's voice said over and over:

"All dead. All dead."

The man came up the basement steps holding the body of a baby about six months old. The child's plump legs dangled limply.

Other men in blue uniforms were coming up from the basement. One of them said, "Six altogether — not five. There's five adults and one child."

The woman driver told us, "That's one bomb. We've had worse. We've had absolute hell."

In the grey dawn we had tea and waited for an all-clear signal. As it sounded, swelling to a din, the woman driving said simply:

"There's always hope with the dawn."

London, September 18, 1940

The German air raid on historic Coventry was especially damaging, not only materially but psychologically.

Coventry was a scene of devastation today after Nazi bombers from dusk to dawn had dumped their destructive bombs in ceaseless relays of about 40 planes each.

A full moon shone, but its brilliance was dimmed by a pall of smoke and the glare of fire from burning buildings.

Today there were at least 1,000 dead and injured; victims were buried under vast piles of wreckage, fires licked through the town and the 14th century cathedral, with its 303-foot spire, was but one of many buildings in ruins.

Scarcely a street escaped the pounding of

Duelling aircraft left condensation trails in the skies over London. Flying the last generation of propeller-driven fighter planes, and guided by the first primitive radar, Britain's defenders inflicted heavy losses on the German Luftwaffe during the summer of 1940.

the raiders. It was the worst continuous attack experience by any city — including London — since the seige of Britain began.

(The Nazis, declaring it was a retaliatory attack for Britain's bombing of Munich while Hitler was there, claimed that more than 500 raiders dropped a ton of explosive apiece in addition to 30,000 fire bombs.)

All night long, the narrow streets where Lady Godiva rode on her horse nearly 1,000 years ago trembled and crumbled with the thunder of diving planes, the scream of bombs and their explosions and the roar of anti-aircraft fire.

Searchlights stabbed through the shroud of smoke. Rifles and machine guns crackled as the city's defenders tried to shoot scores of flares out of the sky.

At least two hospitals were hit. There were casualties in one; in another, all glass was blown from the operating theatre.

Two policemen, Fred Rolling and William Timms, were among the hero dead. They worked for hours amid falling bombs, rescuing women and children trapped by debris, survivors said.

At dawn factory workers from night shifts burrowed into the smoking wreckage of their homes, shouting the names of their wives and children and calling "we're coming. . .we're coming."

One young man recovered a body and then tunneled into the wreckage his hands torn and bleeding, to pull out another - his wife.

Coventry, November 15, 1940

The Battle of Britain, fought in the air over the south of England in the summer of 1940, was a turning-point in the war. The Germans had to destroy Britain's air force before risking an invasion across the English Channel. This the German air force failed to do. Winter came, and the channel became impassable for German invasion barges. By the spring of 1941, Hitler had turned his attention to Russia. The Herald published the diary of an unnamed pilot who fought in the Battle of Britain. Dorniers and Heinkels were German bombers; Messerschmitt 109s and 110s were German fighters; Hurricanes and Spitfires were British fighters.

First day, Sept. 2, 1940, at our new station, at 15,000 feet we sighted a large lump of blitz. Solid block of 20 Dornier 215's with a large fighter escort. Attacked en masse, then dived away as fighter came down. Joined Butch again after a frantic tail-watching breakaway, and started after the bombers again.

Suddenly we see a Dornier coming towards us — running for home. We jump on it — Butch sits on its tail, pumping lead at it. I do quarter attacks. He doesn't like this, lumps fall off and smoke pours out. I am awake now, and feeling hungry.

He is a wreck — rudders in ribbons and pieces falling off all the time. One guy comes out at 100 feet. Parachute streams as he hits the ground — bounces. Butch and I are very cocky, go home and shoot a horrid line.

("Shooting a line" is R.A.F. slang for boasting of one's exploits.)

Two more quick sorties, seeing nothing, and then more blitzkrieg on the fourth do. We run into a whole pile of Messerschmitt 110's and Dorniers. Too far to attack the bombers, so we mix it with the 110's. They circle, and come down vertically behind us.

I lose Butch and everyone else as I turn round and round, watching my tail. Then a 110 rears up in front of me, plain view, and does a steep turn. Range is almost point blank as I turn inside and plug him. He disappears under my nose, and, when I see him again, he is diving vertically, starboard engine and wing blazing.

I feel very cocky again, look for the fight, and find it is out of sight. I go home and find that I've only fired 300 rounds.

Fifth Day: Up in the morning over the Thames Estuary to meet another raid. We nip in before the Hun fighters can get at us and do a quick flank attack. Fighters follow at once. I follow behind the bombers, watching two Messerschmitt 109's coming up behind me.

Before they get into range I turn a sharp left and whip under them. Unfortunately C__, who is following me, gets plugged by one of these guys and has to crashland. I get into a circle with two 109's and shoot the second. He starts to dive, so I chase him. Third burst sets him on fire, whole of starboard wing and fuselage. We are down to 50 feet, so I leave him to burn and climb to 10,000 feet at full bore.

Fighting is still going on and two more 109's come for me. They work in pairs, and it seems fairly easy to get number two. Again I pick him out and we tear down to 0 feet. We race along the Pilgrim's Way (Chaucer's old road to Canterbury) and I fire the rest of my ammunition into him.

Both radiators stream glycol. I formate on him when I finish my rounds and he has his oxygen mask off, looking out at me. I leave him to go home and see him crash-land a few miles on.

Going home I see a parachute and circle it – a British one. Later it turns out that it was the C.O., who got shot down by the 109's. In the evening a party, then on to a dance with the boys of another squadron. Slept at ____ and stayed in bed till nine.

Sixth Day: I have the rest of the day off – and a very good thing, too. Squadron gets into big London raids and loses quite a few. F____ died in hospital, W____ missing, several more shot down and bailed out.

S____ and I drove down to Maidstone hospital to pick up the C.O. Coming back we get to the Blackwell Tunnel (connecting North and South London under the Thames) when the trouble starts raining down all around us – no time to get to a shelter. We stand under an arch and watch the bombers approaching in waves, hear the bombs whistle down, and then the explosions.

Fourteenth Day: The best day we've had. We go off at lunchtime with another squadron to meet 16 Dorniers and lots of 109's. We go into the bombers but Butch breaks early as he gets hit. I break with him, lose him, then go for the bombers again. Meet them coming home and no Messerschmitts in sight.

So I attack one on the edge of the formation. Get him straight away and leave the rest of his boys. Follow him, plugging all the time. A quarter attack comes off beautifully, see bullets going in, in a line from the nose back to the tail, at intervals of a foot all the way down.

See that rear-gunner is lying back in his seat, probably dead. Dornier is smoking like a chimney, oil comes back on to my aircraft and pieces fly past me.

Then three blasted Spitfires horn in and drive me away from my own private and personal Dornier. One guy bails out from the Jerry. He has his arms folded and seems quite resigned. His ship crashed in flames and Spitfires shoot a line all round it, probably dropping visiting cards.

Afternoon brings even better pickings. Again we attack Dornier formation and break it wide open. They scatter all over the sky and go for the clouds. I get one straight away with a long burst. He catches fire and goes straight in.

Chase another in and out of the clouds. Port engine catches fire and Butch and I claim him as a probable; damned sure he was finished. Then I see two Messerschmitt 109's behind me and whip around in a left-hand climbing turn.

Horrid moment as I see his cannon winking at me, but he misses. Turn and start circling with the two of them. Gradually tighten the turn until I get a shot at number two from above. See my bullets hit his left

British pilots (above) warned by radar of an incoming German attack, scramble to their waiting fighter planes. These were the men of whom Winston Churchill said "Never . . . was so much owed by so many to so few." Hurricane fighters (below) and the more famous Spitfires held off the threat of a German invasion through the summer of 1940, but they could not stop the waves of bombers that devastated British cities.

wing and he is so shaken he dives into a cloud.

Chase these two again and lose them. Then see two fighters coming straight for me. I think they are Spitfires so I don't fire. Dodge under them and find they are the same two yellow-nosed Messerschmitts. Annoying because they make off and I can't catch them.

Most successful day for the squadron, a bag of ten destroyed, 13 probable and others damaged. Our losses nil. My bag – two destroyed, one probable and one damaged. Beginning to shoot a bit of a line. Celebration in the evening.

Fifteenth Day: Scrambled out of bed in absolute confusion. Cloudy up to 20,000 and mighty cold. We see dozens of vortices but no enemy aircraft.

(Here the diary entries end. A few hours later its author had been killed when his Hurricane crashed in battle.)

January 28, 1941

___

Life and death beneath the bombers.

Attacking only a few hours after King George and Queen Elizabeth had visited the city, the German air force rained high explosive and fire bombs on Plymouth during the night.

A number of children were killed when a bomb hit a hospital, and two children were born during the attack. One of them was delivered by doctors working in a bomb crater where the mother had been thrown.

Plymouth, March 21, 1941

Canada at Britain's Side

Canada entered the Second World War as an independent nation, not as part of an empire. Canadian soldiers fought at Hong King, at Dieppe, in Italy, Normandy, Belgium and the Netherlands. Canadian sailors fought German submarines in the North Atlantic, Canadian airmen flew in virtually every theatre of the war from the Battle of Britain onward, and Canada trained thousands of new fliers from the Commonwealth countries. This contribution became a source of great national pride, but the decision to go to war was made very soberly. H.H.C. "Torchy" Anderson of The Herald's Ottawa bureau reported the momentous decision.

B y official proclamation Canada moved into the world war on Sunday at 10:10 Calgary time (1:10 Ottawa time.)

But it was during a casual, dramatic moment when the Commons' clock pointed to 7:23 p.m., M.S.T., Saturday, that the country actually made its decision to enter its second Great War beside Great Britain and France.

In this half minute of destiny men may some day find the most important moment in the history of this young country. It passed without demonstration.

Canada shouldered arms in silence.

But in that casual moment, Parliament decided that way was forward. It burned its bridges; it marched toward the goal from which there is no honorable retreat.

No recorded vote lies on the record. Officially it was the unanimous decision of a body of men whose duty has weighed heavily on them since Thursday of last week, when they took their seats in special session.

If the fateful Saturday in this great stone pile lacked excitement, it held its solemn moments.

Early in the afternoon, there was that moment when Rt. Hon. Arthur Meighen, veteran of Canada's last war cabinet, held his fellow senators in silent attention as he called on all his great power of language to declare the conviction that Canada's path lay with Britain.

There was no hesitation, no qualification, in the burning words of Mr. Meighen. They were simple, direct, deep. He leaned slightly forward, his face to the Speaker. There were no superfluities in his language. Each word was weighed, aimed to his goal.

A little later, in the green Commons chamber at the other end of the building, there rose another great figure of Canadian Parliament, Hon. Ernest Lapointe, minister of justice.

"I hate war with all my heart and conscience — but in my soul and conscience I cannot take any other course." In those words the Quebec veteran made clear to a solemn House his stern decision.

Ottawa, September 11, 1939

Canadian pilots enjoy a joke during a break in the Battle of Britain. In 53 days, the Canadian fighter squadron destroyed 30 German aircraft. Most members of the squadron were from Montreal.

Captain Cunnington was just one of Calgary's war heroes.

T he first Alberta officer in the Canadian Army to be decorated for gallantry in the present war, Captain Douglas W. Cunnington, R.C.E., of Calgary, has been awarded the George Medal for conspicuous bravery under fire, according to an official announcement made in London today. His companion in the exploit, Lieut. J. M. S. Patterson of Kingston, Ontario was awarded the George Cross.

Captain Cunnington is the son of Major D. G. L. Cunnington, M.C., V.D., G.S.O. of the local military district.

It was learned that Captain Cunnington was in command of a small section of Pioneers when word was received that a time bomb had fallen in the centre of a busy thoroughfare in London and was endangering the lives of hundreds of persons.

Taking only his second-in-command, Lieut. Patterson, Captain Cunnington drove to the crater. He backed the truck and then Lieut. Patterson descended into the crater and tied a rope around the bomb.

Both officers then heaved it onto the truck and with Captain Cunnington at the wheel they set off to find a spot where the bomb could be detonated safely.

German airmen were still dropping bombs all over the place as the young Canadians drove off with their lethal cargo. They drove the truck into an open field, calmly lowered the bomb into another crater and then drove off. A few minutes later it blew up with a tremendous explosion.

December 16, 1940

Flight Lieutenant Hartland Molson was one of several Royal Canadian Air Force men who wrote first-person stories for The Herald. Molson became a senator in 1955.

O n one occasion we split up a formation of Heinkel 111 bombers. On turning around I saw a lone one heading for the coast. I started after it and just before I got in range I saw another Hurricane come in and give him a burst in his right engine, which started to smoke.

As I closed in I thought the smoke stopped and I opened fire on the left engine. The Heinkel started a turn to the right, losing height.

It didn't look very badly damaged so I proceeded to carry out two or three more attacks from different angles until my ammunition was exhausted.

This Heinkel finally hit in the middle of a field and spread a great sheet of flame through the hedge and half way across the next field.

I actually saw this aircraft destroyed and yet I think the Hurricane ahead of me had started him on the downward path so I do not know who was credited.

I am giving you these instances to illustrate the great difficulties of scoring the war, but I think it also serves to indicate that for every machine confirmed there are probably at least two written down as damaged.

Of these damaged machines there must be a large number which never reach home.

One bright day, with only a little cloud at around 5,000 to 6,000 feet, we were sent up to intercept some fighters just south of London. They were Messerschmitt 109's.

It is a great habit of some German ME 109's to hang around in the sun while others are fighting it out below, ready to pounce on any lone machine whose attention is distracted by his fight.

There were a couple of our own trying to get at these vultures and it seemed the most useful place to go, so I went up to join in.

I got short bursts at two Huns and missed and then found a pair working together. I chased them around for a few minutes getting in short bursts whenever the sights were on.

One was damaged and went down so I started on the second. It seemed as though it slowed up and straightened out.

At this point I forgot all I had learned. I slowed up and straightened up too, without looking around.

Not looking around is by far the most elementary way of getting mowed down in a dog fight existence.

There was a gentleman behind just hoping I'd do something stupid and he knocked my machine out of control with his little cannon in about two seconds.

A moment later I was off on the greatest flight of my life, strictly on my own, bailing out at 23,000 feet.

My instrument panel was shattered, one fuel tank punctured, controls useless, and liquid carrying pipes broken.

Perhaps I was lucky to have injury restricted to leg wounds.

With controls useless, I had no other alternatives than to bail out — and quickly.

The nose was headed down vertically, and there was nothing I could do to prevent rapid increase in speed.

It doesn't take courage to bail out. Your one fear is that you may not be able to, and you have a feeling of great thankfulness when you find that you are clear of the machine and your parachute is working.

After slowing up I was able to watch the ground getting nearer and nearer. After a drop of about 12,000 feet, I could not resist the temptation of pulling the rip cord.

There was some cloud at that height so I had no longer any fear of becoming a sort of trap-shooting target for the enemy.

The parachute opened with a slight jerk, but no discomfort. From there on the descent seemed interminable, as though the earth would never arrive.

Fortunately the tree I struck was a sapling, and let me right through with a slight bump to the ground.

I had only been in the woods a few minutes when some soldiers came to my assistance, taking me to their medical officer who dressed my wounds.

May 10, 1941

An army is made up of former civilians.

Maj. Gen. Victor Odlum, noted for his democratic relations with the troops, met two Canadian privates during a walk. One saluted smartly; the other, a cigarette drooping from his mouth, did not.

The commander of the Canadian Second Division congratulated the first. Turn-ing to the second, he put a kindly look in his eye and remarked: "Now how about that cigarette?" The man started, looked embarrassed, and felt in his pockets.

"Sorry, general," he explained. "I'm afraid this is my last."

London, June 14, 1941

The Allies built up their armaments with astonishing speed. Less than three years after the war burst upon a pitifully unprepared Britain, they were able to mount thousand-bomber raids over Germany. Douglas Amaron of the Canadian Press reported on one of these huge operations.

More than 1,000 Canadian airmen took part in Saturday night's aerial smash at the heart of the industrial Ruhr and the Rhineland, it was authoritatively estimated today.

Considerably more than 1,000 bombers, twice the size and with four times the bomb-carrying capacity of any force previously sent against Germany, left Cologne, the main target area, a mass of flames.

Four squadrons of the Royal Canadian Air Force, including one flying four-engined bombers for the first time, and hundreds of other Canadians in the R.A.F., flew in this aerial armada which crossed its target at the rate of one bomber every six seconds.

It was estimated that about one in six of the more than 6,000 airmen taking part in the gigantic raid was a Canadian. The others were Britons, Australians, and airmen from other parts of the Empire and the Allied air forces — Poles, Czechs and Free French.

Returning pilots said planes were over Cologne in such numbers that German gun crews and searchlight defenders were unable to concentrate on any single machine or follow it through as it made its bombing run over the target.

Every Canadian was in high spirits when he got back, for there was no question of the effectiveness of the job done. All agreed there had never been a blaze comparable with the one they had left behind them.

PO L.G. Higginson of Montreal, captain of the first aircraft to return in his squadron, gave the ground crews and station personnel first news of damage done.

He estimated the smoke column over Cologne at 8,000 feet, and Wing Commander Johnny Fauquier, who landed a little later, added another 2,000 feet to that figure. Still later reconnaissance this morning showed smoke had risen to 15,000 feet.

"It was a bigger blaze than Luebeck," said Higginson, referring to the smashing attack last March on the German Baltic port. Others in the squadron who had been in both operations agreed.

Many navigators were able to reach the target without the aid of instruments, as soon as they came within 100 miles of Cologne.

"The glow in the sky told us where it was," said PO W.H. Baldwin of Ottawa, navigator of one huge four-engined bomber. "We couldn't miss it."

It was the second night in succession of heavy activity by Canada's airmen.

Friday night five Canadian squadrons flew with the R.A.F. in smashing factories near Paris and a convoy off the Frisian Islands, the Netherlands.

Wing-Cmdr R.H. Niven of Calgary took his R.A.F. "Dawn patrol" squadron into the shipping engagement in which eight German ships were hit by bombs, four of them apparently being set afire.

It was PO. J.G. Middlemass, of Wainwright, navigator of a four-engined Halifax, who told of destroying a JU-88 which attempted to stop the Canadians. Another crew shook off three enemy fighters.

Middlemass said the German attacked with machine guns and cannon, damaging the Halifax tail turret, port wing flap, and gasoline system. Both mid-turret and tail gunners replied, and saw the enemy machine suddenly dive and explode on the ground.

The Halifax captain was able to land safely despite the fact all three landing wheels were punctured.

June 1, 1942

This dispatch from A. C. Cummings in London was perhaps a symptom of growing impatience among Canadians with their traditional role as Britain's dutiful daughter.

The people of Great Britain are just beginning to realize what they owe Canada in this war. Hitherto little has been heard here of the Dominion's war effort, which has been for the average Briton altogether overshadowed by the gigantic plans and projects given out by the United States' highly efficient publicity services.

Within the past week, however, there has been a sudden realization of what Canada's partnership in the Empire has meant based on the disclosure that the Canadian Navy is doing splendid work in the Battle of the Atlantic and the Canadian airmen are fighting in every battle zone from the Alaskan Islands to Ceylon.

The first lord of the admiralty, A. V. Alexander, has just paid a high tribute to the Royal Canadian Navy and especially to the corvette fleet so rapidly built and so efficiently manned.

The recent decision to make the Canadian units distinctive from the Royal Air Force proper is welcomed here, since it will throw into prominence the extent of Canada's real contribution to the battles of the skies.

There are Canadian airmen defending Britain, Malta, Egypt, Palestine, Syria, Iraq, Ceylon, India, Australia and Alaska at present.

The idea also that Canada can send tanks to Russia and launch a good-sized ship every four days has surprised United Kingdom editors accustomed to look to the United States for such achievements.

London, August 15, 1942

Death and Glory at Dieppe

Ross Munro of the Canadian Press went ashore with the troops who attacked Dieppe, a resort town on the Channel coast of Nazi-held France. Except for a few British commando units, the raiders were all Canadians. The operation, described as a "reconnaissance in force," took a ghastly toll. Altogether 4,963 Canadian soldiers embarked; 3,367 were killed, wounded or captured. It is said, however, that lessons learned at Dieppe were valuable two years later when the Allies mounted a full-scale invasion of Nazi-held Europe.

For eight raging hours, under intense Nazi fire from dawn into a sweltering afternoon, I watched Canadian troops fight the blazing bloody battle of Dieppe.

I saw them go through this biggest of the war's raiding operations in wild scenes that crowded helter-skelter one upon another in crazy sequence.

There was a furious attack by German E-boats while the Canadians moved in on Dieppe beaches landing by dawn's half light.

When the Canadian battalions stormed through the flashing inferno of Nazi defences, belching guns of huge tanks rolling into the fight, I spent the grimmest 20 minutes of my life with one unit when a rain of German machine-gun fire wounded half the men in our boat and only a miracle saved us from annihilation.

A few hours later there was the spine-chilling experience of dive-bombing attack by seven Stukas, the dreaded Nazi aircraft that spotted out the small assault landing craft waiting off-shore to re-embark the fighting men.

Our boat was thrown about like a toy by their seven screeching bombs that plunged into the water around us and exploded in gigantic cascades.

There was the lashing fire of machine-gunning from other Nazi aircraft, and the thunder of anti-aircraft fire that sent them hustling off.

Over our heads, in the blue, cloud-flecked French sky were fought the greatest air engagements since the Battle of Britain, dogfights carried on to the dizzy accompaniment of planes exploding in the air, diving down flaming, some plummetting into the sea from thousands of feet.

Hour after hour guns of the supporting warships growled salvoes at targets ashore, where our tanks were in violent action.

Unearthly noises rumbled up and down the French coast, shrouded for miles in smokescreens covering the fleet.

There was heroism at sea and in the skies in those hours, but the hell-spot was ashore, where the Canadians fought at close quarters with the Nazis. They fought to the end, where they had to, and showed courage and daring.

They attacked the Dieppe arsenal of the coastal defence. They left Dieppe silent and afire, its ruins and its dead under a shroud of smoke.

Here Munro described crossing the English Channel on a calm, clear night, and transferring to an open assault boat, which came under fire nearly an hour before the scheduled attack on Dieppe. His boat got through to the beach.

We were to land in a matter of minutes. Through smoke layers I looked up at the white cliffs, growing higher before us. Anticraft guns up there clattered unceasingly. Machine-guns drilled down bullets that clanged against the armorplate of our boat.

By the time our boat touched the beach the din was a crescendo. I peered out at the slope lying just in front of us, and it was startling to discover it was dotted with fallen forms of men in battle dress. The Royals ahead of us had been cut down as they stormed the slope. It came home to me only then that everyone of those men had gone down under the bullets of the enemy at the top of the incline.

Vicious bursts of yellow tracers from the machine-guns made a veritable curtain about our boats. The Royals beside me fired back with everything they had. One Canadian blazed away with an anti-tank rifle.

The Germans held a couple of houses near the top of the slope and occupied some strong pillboxes. From their high level they were able to pour fire into some boats, ours among them.

Several bursts from machine-guns struck men in the middle of our craft. The boat's ramp was lowered to permit the men with me to get ashore, but German fire caught those who tried to make it.

The remainder crouched inside, protected by armor and pouring return fire at the Nazis. The Canadians' shooting was dead-on and half a dozen men in steel helmets and field grey uniform toppled from windows to the ground.

Other Germans made the mistake of trying to change their positions only to be caught when sighted by Royal sharp shooters armed with Brens.

Caught by this unexpectedly intense Nazi fire the Canadians fought a heroic battle from those craft that were still nosed up on the beach.

I lay behind a flimsy bit of armor plating and heavy calibre bullets cut through it a couple of feet above my head.

An officer sitting next to me was firing a Sten gun. He got off a magazine and a half, killed at least one Nazi, and then was hit in the head. He fell forward, bleeding profusely.

A sailor next to him was wounded in the neck and another got a bullet through the shoulder. Those around the injured tied them up with field dressing. The fire was murderous now and the Canadian's firepower was being reduced by casualties.

There were eight or 10 in our boat who had been hit, and a landing here seemed impossible. The naval officer with us decided to get the boat off the beach. On manoeuvres there were times when it was a difficult task to do it quickly, but by a miracle it slid off and we eased away from the

Landing craft draw away from a motor torpedo boat in the English Channel as Canadian troops start the run to the beaches at Dieppe, France. Nearly three-quarters of them would be wounded, captured, or killed in a day of terrible fighting.

Dead men and shattered weapons on the stony beach at Dieppe. Of the 6,100 men who took part in the ill-fated raid nearly 5,000 were Canadians, among them members of the Calgary Tank Regiment. About 900 Canadians were killed, and almost 2,000 taken prisoner.

hellish fire with nerve-wracking slowness.

The Nazis pegged away at us for a half a mile out. That attempted landing was one of the fiercest and grimmest events in the whole raid and the only spot where the landing was temporarily repulsed.

I will forever remember the scene in that craft: wounded lying about being attended by medical orderlies oblivious to the fire; the heroism of the Royals as they fought back and strove as desperately as any men could to get on the beach and relieve their comrades still fighting ashore; the contempt of these men for danger and their fortitude when they were hit. I never heard one man even cry out.

During the whole raid there were no stauncher fighters than the Toronto soldiers.

Off Dieppe the raid flotilla remassed after putting the troops ashore. Our wounded weren't sent to a hospital ship.

I transferred at sea to another assault landing craft and then another and another.

They were floating about doing jobs at the different beaches.

At one stage 15 soldiers and I tried to get onto one of the beaches near Dieppe but the German cliff-side machine-gun posts which later were wiped out plastered us without hitting anyone and turned back out of range.

Finally we got ashore for a few minutes right in front of the Dieppe Esplanade. The smoke screen was so thick, though, that one could not see much of the town and we took off again. The area in front of the town looked like a first Great War battle ground, with broken buildings gutted or burning in all sections.

By 10 a.m. the Canadians, many of their actions led by tanks, seemed to have the town fairly well under control and to have stabilized the situation on the beaches.

Then 50 minutes later the Nazis sprang their one heavy attack by air. For 45 minutes Stukas, Dorniers, Heinkels and fighters swept up from the south and attacked the fleet, whose terrific bombardment I had been watching from an assault craft just off the main Dieppe beach.

German pilots flying anywhere from 200 to 2,000 feet showered bombs over the British ships, at the same time sweeping them with machine-gun fire. The sky was splotched with hundreds of black and white puffs from exploding shells and the thundering of the ships' guns was deafening.

Sometimes the Nazis picked peculiar targets. At one time even their Stukas were dive-bombing our little craft, which this time carried only one naval officer, four ratings and this lone correspondent.

Their bombs came crashing down on either side of our bouncing craft, making the sea look as if it had been churned by a tornado. Once we almost capsized but we ended up with only a bashed stern and a shattered bow.

We had just picked ourselves up from the deck when a fighter zoomed in and gave us a hail of gunfire. But they added only more scars to our unsteady but still seaworthy craft.

The plane was one which had succeeded in avoiding squadrons of British planes which hovered overhead throughout the operation picking off German machines attempting to get in close. Seven Nazi machines crashed into the sea within the limited view we had of the complete scene.

At noon, final re-embarkation of the troops was under way and the force was taken off the main beach.

While another smoke screen blanketed the raided town, the fleet turned for

England. No German aircraft marred the departure, and the navy gave some coastal installations another bump with heavy guns for good measure.

I lay in the sun and slept, and woke to see the white cliffs of England in the mist ahead.

British planes — fighters and bombers — were swarming south to France again in a steady stream, with more packages for the Germans.

August 20, 1942

Two days after the Dieppe raid, Ross Munro filed this report of heroism and disaster.

Throughout Canadian Army camps in Britain today stories of heroism and courage of Canadians in the hellfire that was Dieppe on Wednesday were recounted by hardened men who now have been battle-tested.

There were countless deeds done on the shores of France and in the streets of Dieppe that never will be told. Too many did not return for a complete picture of Canadians' individual heroic performances ever to be assembled.

But at the bases of the Calgary Regiment (Tank), the Essex Scottish, South Saskatchewan Regiment, Royal Hamilton Light Infantry, Fusiliers Mont Royal, Toronto Scottish, Winnipeg Camerons, Royal Regiment and the Black Watch there were plenty of accounts from fighting men to stamp the action as something rivalling the last war's Vimy in point of valor.

And as eyewitness to the manner these

men faced withering fire from strong Nazi fortifications without a trace of fear — rather, in fact, with sheer enthusiasm at getting into action — I can testify there is no praise too high for the courage of the Canadians.

A wounded regimental sergeant-major, Roger Strumm of Saskatoon, unable to walk, was carried waist-high into the sea and re-embarked by comrades who refused to leave him behind when the withdrawal was ordered.

He landed on the beach with units of his regiment in the early morning of Wednesday's assault.

Shortly afterwards he received a shrapnel wound in the leg, and as he could not walk he was carried by his battling comrades to a captured pillbox.

There the soldiers lay while fortunes of war swayed across the pebble-dappled beaches and through Dieppe's narrow streets. He stayed until mid-afternoon, when, their job done, his men came back for him.

Willing hands lifted him, and then ducking, scrambling and taking advantage of anything offering even the most meagre cover, they carried him to the shoreline, out into the sea, and placed him aboard the landing craft despite heavy enemy fire.

Doctors told of a Canadian private arriving at a dressing station in a pair of army shorts with a blanket wrapped around him. It was all he had after being picked out of the sea, but as they were fixing him he stuck out his hand and said, "I've still got this, anyway."

He clutched a sea-soaked but still intact snapshot of his wife.

The work of the British Commando troops was highly praised by returning Canadians.

The British outfit, commanded by Lord Lovatt, wiped out 150 Germans when it destroyed a German gun position at Varengeville, west of Dieppe.

A special detachment of the Royal Canadian Engineers was trained for the raid and developed demolition equipment with explosives for use in the particular task assigned to them in helping to destroy Dieppe installations.

The R.C.E. landed on the main beach with the Essex and Hamilton men. They blew up wire obstacles which blocked the infantry, checked the promenade for mine fields and then helped the tanks get through road blocks at street entrances.

There were many cases of valor.

There were the men of the Royals with whom I rode who were turned back from the beach by withering fire from the cliffs.

I left them and transferred twice to other assault boats and heard later that they had regrouped, gone ashore and knocked off the opposition which prevented them from landing at the first attempt. They had been badly cut up in that attempt, too, being under fierce fire for 20 minutes.

There were the Fusiliers whose task was to blast German boats in a pool in town. It was a mile from the beach and was called the "Basin du Canad." The survivors who blew up everything they could renamed it the "Basin du Canada."

Twelve of them started for the job, but only four arrived. After they had done their task they bumped into eight other French-Canadians but were promptly surrounded and captured.

They had seen the Germans take a dozen of their comrades prisoner and shoot them in the back.

They were luckier.

Their captors merely stripped them of their clothing, down to their underpants and took their boots from them, then left them in charge of one young German soldier who stood behind them with a rifle.

One big French-Canadian got an idea. In broken English he asked the Nazi if he could speak English.

The German said he could a little and the Canadian asked.

"How about a glass of water."

The Nazi was not as tough as the rest. The question got him for a second. He lowered his rifle and promptly found himself at the bottom of a heap of a dozen half-naked men.

One of them found a length of pipe and knocked the Nazi's brains out.

Then they ran for it through streets piled with dead Germans and swarming with lively ones.

They made the cliff-top and hid among boulders there until the re-embark order came and brought them a smoke screen through which they slid to the beach.

As they ran across the shingle from their offshore station the big man who had the idea that saved them all stumbled on a wounded officer. He slung him over his shoulder and took him aboard.

The Canadians carried with them handbills and posters, advising the French population of Dieppe not to try to help them because this was not an invasion — only a visit.

"Frenchmen!" the text read, "this is a surprise stroke, not an invasion. We strongly urge you to take no part and to do nothing that might invite reprisals by the enemy.

"We appeal to your cool-headedness and good sense. When the hour strikes we will notify you. And then will we act side by side for our common victory and your liberty."

Returning Canadians said the warning worked, except in a few isolated instances.

"Somewhere in England," August 21, 1942

The Calgary Tank Regiment fought at Dieppe. Douglas Amaron of the Canadian Press told their story.

We're going back..." That was the message that came from headquarters of the Calgary Tank Regiment, whose men fought in the bloody battle of Dieppe. A lot of them didn't return and new men have come to fill their places.

The new commander from Calgary, who won his promotion and command of the unit at Dieppe on the fall of the original commander, grimly summed up the survivors' feelings, "It's a personal war with this unit now. We were the first Alberta regiment — and the first armored regiment to see action. Give us time to refit and we're going back."

(From St. Thomas, Ont., it was reported Saturday that the parents of Lt.-Col. John Andrews, 33, had been advised by his wife who lives at Barrie, Ont., that he has been reported missing. Col. Andrews was in command of the Calgary tank battalion at Dieppe. Apparently Major John Begg of Calgary, second in command of the unit, automatically became officer commanding the unit after Col. Andrews was reported missing.)

Andrews' successor (Begg) told the story of the battalion's fight — of its charge ashore in support of the Essex Scottish and the Royal Hamilton Light Infantry in an attack on Dieppe itself; of the withering artillery and machine-gun fire with which the Nazis prevented part of the forces from landing and of the bravery of those who got ashore.

Dawn was just breaking over the area when the attack opened, the battalion's first two waves going in 15 minutes apart and headquarters 30 minutes later, led by the adjutant who was brought up short of the sea-wall.

There was no room to manoeuvre the tanks in the narrow landing craft which had to withdraw from the beach without the adjutant or his crew.

Meantime, other tanks found the ramp near the casino, went ashore and made their way up to the esplanade where they were to fight for the rest of the day.

When the commanding officer learned of this, he decided to take the battalion headquarters ashore, but by this time four hours had passed and the Germans were prepared.

"We got 33 hits on our landing craft in five minutes," the colonel, then serving as second in command, said. "They hit us with everything they had."

Despite this opposition, which one veteran of Gallipoli said was fiercer than anything encountered there, the commanding officer tried to move in, still going forward even after a direct hit on his tank.

The shell blew off his waterproofing material and the tank sank in six feet of water. The heavy vehicle could go no further and the commanding officer radioed, "I'm getting out of my tank — Toodle-oo."

That was the last message heard from him.

It was a grim story as the men in the machines moved up and down the esplanade blowing up pillboxes and covering the withdrawal of the infantrymen. One clear fact emerged: not one of the men stopped fighting while he had any ammunition left.

One tank reported its "tracks are broken, the tank's on fire and the traverse is out of action but I'm still firing and fighting like hell and killing lots of bloody Germans." That crew was still firing when the last infantryman had been withdrawn from the beach.

One conversation between the tank crew particularly emphasized grit and fighting spirit.

An order went out, "Evacuate your tank; blow it up and get back to the beach."

Came the reply, "Why the hell should I blow up my tank? I've still got ammunition."

"Somewhere in England," August 24, 1942

Warfare in the Atlantic

Ships carrying food, weapons and troops to Britain had to make their way through seas infested with German submarines. As the war went on, the Royal Canadian Navy took on most of the task of convoying merchant ships safely across the North Atlantic. Allen H. Bill of The Herald spent some time aboard a Canadian destroyer, and sent this report.

Although destroyers get all the 'dirty work' in war, none of the officers or ratings I spoke to want to serve in anything else.

Many of them have served in large ships of the Royal Navy. 'No. 1,' for instance, Lieut. P.E. Haddon, R.C.N., whose home is in Victoria, has been in the navy eleven years, five, in R.N. ships.

He's still in his twenties, I'd say. He knows battleships and cruisers and many parts of the world. But destroyers are his choice; provided he can get ashore once in a while for a game of golf.

It's a young man's job too. The average age of the eight officers in this ship is probably under thirty; that of the ratings about the same.

After days at sea with them, watching them at work, sleeping, eating, talking with them in wardroom and messdeck, I'll tip a salute to the men who serve in the small ships.

And when I head westward again across the Atlantic in a passenger ship with a destroyer escort I'll make it a double.

The Canadian destroyers on both sides of the Atlantic have done grand work. The ship I was in has served as escort to more than 1,200 ships crossing the Atlantic, and every one of them has reached its port safely.

She has one U-boat to her credit. Her captain, Commander Mainguy, received his mention in dispatches. Across 50 miles flashed an S.O.S. from a merchantman: 'Being shelled by submarine.'

The destroyer put on full speed and tore for the spot. They had covered 25 miles when again the S.O.S. came: 'Still being shelled.' Commander Mainguy then really started "boiling the kettle."

Soon they sighted the merchantman and the U-boat. When he was within range the destroyer opened fire. Shells splashed around the sub and he crash-dived.

The merchantman, undamaged, went on his way and for 12 hours the destroyer tore back and forth dropping depth charges. Night closed in and still the destroyer kept up the hunt.

It must have been a grim night for the sub with those steel barrels packed with death searching him out as he manoeuvred to escape. And towards morning they found him and there he still lies.

And there's more to a destroyer's work in war time than killing subs, of course. Many hundreds of survivors from torpedoed merchantmen have been saved by these ocean scouts. Our ship has done her share of it.

On one occasion two men went far beyond the ordinary risks to save the life of a 14-year-old English cabin boy.

All but the boy had been lifted from the wildly pitching boat. His feet had become wedged under a thwart. Try as he would, he could not free himself.

So over the plunging side of the destroyer went Leading Seaman W.H. Aveling of Burnaby, B.C., and Leading Stoker Stanley Foreman of Esquimalt.

It was like trying to mount a bucking bronco, to get a footing in that boat when a slip probably meant being drowned or battered to death against the ship's side.

But they made it, with the aid of a rope held on the deck end by Petty Officer John Dunick of Winnipeg. Making the rope fast under the boy's arms, they freed his feet and he was hauled aboard. Aveling and Foreman scrambled up after him.

It was only the "guts" of that young cabin boy, who never whimpered throughout the whole ordeal although he was all in from pain and exposure, that Aveling and Foreman would talk about. Their own part in it was "routine."

London, March 12, 1941

Canadian Munitions Minister C.D. Howe narrowly escaped death at sea in 1940. The Herald's Allen H. Bill, then in London, interviewed survivors of the sinking Western Star, the ship carrying Howe. Another survivor was E.P. Taylor, Howe's assistant.

Hold everything!" With the torpedoed Western Prince sinking under him, and a German submarine still lurking nearby in the inky blackness, Col. W.C. Woodward, Vancouver, executive assistant to Hon. C.D. Howe, minister of munitions and supply, shouted these words into the teeth of a howling gale and disappeared down a companion way. He had forgotten something.

Fighting against the mighty heaves of the ship, he stumbled through the blackness to his cabin and then back to the deck, clutching in his hands a gold cigarette case and pencil, gifts from his wife.

"Hell's bells," he told me Thursday. "I wasn't going to leave those."

Col. Woodward, however, is saddened by the loss of Hon. Gordon Scott, Montreal, financial advisor to Mr. Howe, who lost his life.

"Tell Canada Scott died like a hero. He, Taylor and I were getting into the boat when Mr. Scott yelled, 'Where is Mr. Howe?' and disappeared into the blackness to seek the minister. The next second our boat was being lowered into the raging sea, shaking us like peas in a pod and crashing the boat against the ship's side.

"After assuring himself that Mr. Howe was safely in a lifeboat and away, Scott slid down a rope to a another lifeboat, but before he could get in it, he was crushed between the boat and the ship and the rope was torn from his grip. That was the last seen of him. His death is a great loss to Canada.

"While some of us did what we could to make the two women and four babies in our boat as comfortable as possible, others fished in the fast-filling boat for the plug and others bailed for dear life. In a few minutes there was a terrific explosion and the ship went down.

"We had plenty of food and drinking water, but no one thought of eating and all were confident we would be picked up. When the rescue ship was sighted no one was excited. Someone said, 'There's a ship' as our boat soared to the top of a great wave. Then we lost it as the boat shot down into the trough and gallons of water poured over us.

"We fired two flares and then drifted to where we last saw the rescue ship. Finally, somehow, we got alongside and got a line thrown from the rescue ship. The babies and women were hauled about in a coal-basket while the men scrambled up the rope ladders."

Col. Woodward had the highest possible praise for Capt. Reed of the Western Prince, but thinks that the tradition of the captain staying with his ship is foolishly wasteful of brave lives.

Capt. Charlton, a passenger, tried to persuade Capt. Reed to leave the ship, but Reed told him to get in a boat and "stand by in case we need you." But he did not call for aid and as the lifeboats drifted away in the gale, he sounded three blasts on the whistle as a farewell gesture to his passengers and in defiance to the Nazis.

London, December 20, 1940

The Royal Canadian Navy played a large part in convoying cargo ships to Britain through the gauntlet of German submarines. It was dangerous work.

In a blazing close-range gun battle the Canadian destroyer Assiniboine sank a German submarine, killed its commander and captured the crew, Naval Minister Macdonald announced last night.

The battle — described by Rear-Admiral L.W. Murray, flag officer Newfoundland force, as "one of the most spirited actions of the war" — took place at an unannounced location. It was learned from a naval source, however, that the encounter was somewhere in the Western Atlantic.

Mr. Macdonald said it was "only one of the successful actions waged by the Royal Canadian Navy against U-boats." Details of other actions will not be given until it is certain they will not help the enemy.

The submarine in the action was finally sunk by ramming after the two ships hurled shot and shell at one another with the Assiniboine tossing depth charges so close together that the Canadian gunners could see the faces of the Germans.

One man, Ordinary Seaman Kenneth Watson of Revelstoke, B.C., the youngest member of the crew, was killed and 14 others were wounded.

Ordinary Seaman Stanley Gallant, of Prince Edward Island, was operating one of the starboard point five guns. He reached for some fresh ammunition and was hit on the right forearm by an enemy machine gun bullet. He looked at the blood streaming from his arm turned to his mate and said casually, "Hey, Bill, they got my drinking arm."

Later, when the Nazi prisoners were brought on board, one of them walked over to Gallant and said in broken English: "I the fellow who shoot you. I see you at the gun." Gallant had an answer for that too, but it is better left unprinted.

Gallant went on operating the gun. Machine gun fire was all around him, while the shells from the U-boat's Oerlikon also were making their presence known. To quote Ordinary Seaman Albert Lindsay of Hamilton, Ontario: "Gallant got in some pretty good licks at the Nazis."

When "Assiniboine" reached port, Gallant and Leading Seaman William Leggett, of Rocky Mountain House, walked down the gangplank to the waiting ambulance, as their mates cheered and offered words of encouragement. Leggett had also been "winged" in the arm.

The Assiniboine caught up with the U-boat after chasing it in and out of fog and losing sight of it twice. The fog cheated the Canadians when they sighted the enemy at 1,000 yards. They saw him again at half-mile range and tried to ram him but lost him in a fog bank.

Lieut. Cmdr. J.H. Stubbs of Halifax, a native of Kaslo, B.C., commander of the Assiniboine told the rest of the story.

Naval headquarters reported him as saying: "Then we saw him again, right on the surface and almost a stone's throw away.

"From the bridge I could see the German commander plainly in the conning tower, but a short time later he was killed by a shell from one of our 4.7's which struck the conning tower.

"With all our guns blazing, our point five gunners kept spraying the submarine's decks."

The U-boat tried to dive and the Assiniboine started a "criss-cross" action, crossing its stern several times but too close for it to fire its torpedoes. A shell fired by AB. Michael Scullion of Verdun, Que., entered the U-boat's bows and the Assiniboine got in position to ram.

"We slapped right into him then," said Stubbs, "and then for good measure let go charges from our port and starboard throwers which exploded under him."

Seamen manning the throwers said one depth charge bounced onto the deck of the submarine and rolled off to explode underneath it.

Canada's part in the war of the North Atlantic won this recognition from Hollywood. A corvette was a small, hard-riding warship, armed to destroy submarines and built with a shallow draft so that torpedoes might pass under it.

"By this time the Germans had had enough," said the commander. "They had lined themselves along the deck with their hands held high. They were all wearing their escape apparatus. As the Nazis plunged into the sea the submarine went up by the stern, shook for a second and took the last plunge."

Ottawa, September 19, 1942

RCAF patrol planes joined in the battle against German submarines in the Atlantic. F.C. Colborne, the pilot in this story, later became a minister in the Alberta cabinet of Premier Ernest Manning.

Two Calgary airmen, with the aid of a Medicine Hat navigator, are sure they sank a German U-boat in the North Atlantic off the East coast of Canada recently.

The two local fliers in a seven-crewed R.C.A.F. Canso patrol plane were Flight Lieutenant F. C. Colborne of 1507 25th Ave. W. and Sergeant Bob Duncan,

506 Boulevard N.W. Flying Officer W. P. Irving of Medicine Hat was the navigator.

A "flier's flier" is Fred Colborne, for he has been crazy about flying since he was a youngster, and was taking flying lessons before the war. In fact, he did his first solo while taking his private pilot's licence out at the old Municipal airport on the day Hitler marched into Poland.

He got his pilot's licence that October and immediately volunteered for active service and was a member of the first class under the British Empire Air Training Plan.

Here is Colborne's own account of a patrol flight that brought results.

"All was serene and the trip out was uneventful until we received a message from base advising us that a pack of submarines had been sighted. We altered course. Everyone was doubly alert. After another half hour it happened.

"We were at (blank) altitude when I saw the U-boat six miles ahead and slightly to port. As promised by the weatherman it was a cloudless day in this area. No cloud cover! No chance to sneak up on him! I slapped open the throttles and started to dive to gain speed.

"The co-pilot Sgt. Duncan gave the alarm signal to the rest of the crew and prepared to take pictures of the approach to attack. I was sure we could never get him in time. But he was caught napping. Duncan took two pictures as we approached.

"It seemed to take hours to get near him. Why didn't he dive? He must see us now. I began to fear that he was going to shoot it out with us. Could we hold our own against his superior fire power? How close should I go before taking evasive action? The decision was made for me. That tell-tale puff of smoke from the U-boat stern signalled the start of his crash dive. But all too late!

"We were going — miles per hour too fast! — feet too high; I cut throttles, shoved her nose down, and made the attack. Throttles on again as we were in close — then the moment for release of the depth charges! Every pilot knows instinctively as he pushes the release button if the attack was good. I was happy!

"The front gun, conning tower, and all of the stern of the U-boat were visible as we passed over. Then a quick turn to port to give the camera operator his chance to get the pictures which are so important in determining results of the attack.

"As we turned I could see, through the settling water of our explosion, what happened to be the conning tower wallowing through the swirling water. It sank and then came air bubbles, a large boiling mass of them! These lasted for about 10 minutes, then oil spread over the area with bits of debris. We remained in the vicinity for nearly an hour before setting course for base.

"It was a long drag back to base, taking seven hours to complete. But we were all happy. We had dinner on the way in and the rest of the flight was quiet, punctuated at intervals by whoops of joy and bits of song."

April 10, 1943

141

War on the Home Front

As Canada's part in the war increased, civilians were called on to make more and more sacrifices. Meat was rationed, liquor was rationed, gasoline was rationed, tires were unobtainable, and a new car was a post-war dream. Hundreds of everyday items like hairpins were scarce or unavailable. Everyone was urged to buy Victory Bonds to help finance the war. Women learned that they could do men's work, even heavy construction. Conscription was a sore point, largely because of Quebec's opposition. However, a conscript army for home service was created, while only volunteers were sent overseas. (Late in the war some conscripts were sent, too.) Even a home army didn't appeal to some men who were willing to take extreme measures to avoid being called up.

I n the biggest boom in the marriage market ever to hit Calgary in one day, 45 licences were issued by David Ormond, registrar at the department of vital statistics in the court house, to eager prospective brides and grooms on Saturday.

The long lines of anxious couples, that began forming at the marriage licence department even before the doors were opened Saturday morning, stayed determinedly in the building after the doors closed at twelve noon, and the last two did not leave until their licence had been issued to them by an exhausted registrar at 7:30 at night.

As there are only a few chairs and benches in the office most of the waiting couples stood for the greater part of the afternoon, and as they would not be allowed back in after the doors closed, they had to forego lunch and supper. Some had thoughtfully brought along oranges for their refreshment.

In keeping with the rush for marriage licences, jewellery stores and ministers also did a rushing business Saturday and Sunday. Jewellery stores report one of the biggest days in the sale of wedding rings that they had ever experienced. One store reported the sale of 17 rings in two hours.

"They didn't seem to care about the looks or the price. They took anything they could get that looked like a wedding ring," clerks said.

Sunday, ministers worked overtime to take care of all the requests for their services. One minister said he solemnized 15 marriages during the day. Couples were waiting on his doorstep most of the afternoon, he said.

Calgary was not the only place that experienced a rush of applicants for marriage certificates, obviously inspired by the Dominion government's ruling that all men called up for military training for home defence will be considered as single if married after July 15.

From all points across Canada there was a stampede of couples to marriage licence bureaux.

July 15, 1940

A simulated poison-gas attack on 8th Avenue S.W. during the war. There was no immediate danger of a real attack, but giving Calgarians a taste of war helped to increase the sale of Victory Bonds.

A mock gas attack on downtown Calgary was a high-pressure way to sell Victory Bonds, but it worked.

I f you have tears, prepare to shed them now," quoted Captain F. R. Millican, in charge of the gas wing at Currie Barracks.

And that was the first warning that the crowds at the corner of Eighth avenue and Second street west had of their second gas attack of the day. Somebody was pouring something from a bottle into a tin can, and suddenly clouds of acrid tear gas billowed up into the faces of the spectators.

They had tears, it seemed, and prepared or not they shed them. Spectators up wind from the "gas bomb" laughed heartily as those less fortunate spluttered and wiped their eyes.

It was all part of the military display that took place in downtown Calgary today as the issue of Canada's second war loan was launched in the city.

Captain Millican explained that an enemy force was retreating through the city, endeavoring to slow down their pursuers. An army truck backed into the intersection, and four cans of strong-smelling liquid, a harmless training gas, were thrown out on the street.

Immediately Captain Millican sounded the "gas alarm" on a siren borrowed from the fire department, and the decontamination squad came hurrying up in an army truck. Meanwhile, the people were told of the deadly effects of mustard gas on marching troops.

Five "men from Mars," clad in tin hats, gas masks and head-to-foot covering of gas-proof rubber clothing, climbed out of the truck, unrolled a fire hose, and proceeded to flush down the street, sending the spectators scurrying back out of range of the splashing water.

September 9, 1940

Herald writer Fred Kennedy introduced some light relief to the war effort.

A fter successfully passing through every guard post between the Sarcee Indian Agency and the boundary of the Indian reserve two miles north of Priddis, and photographing and "destroying" every bridge and culvert in that area, two "fifth columnists" were apprehended on the return journey by a patrol of the 19th Alberta Dragoons late yesterday afternoon.

Disguised as an Indian rancher and his squaw, and driving a team and wagon, the "fifth columnists" were caught after an exciting three-mile chase over prairie trails.

Their captor was Sergeant James Winthringham of Edmonton, who commandeered another wagon driven by an Indian boy. The chase ended about a mile and a half north of corps headquarters when the soldier drew alongside and shook his bayoneted rifle at the driver.

The prisoners were then escorted to headquarters in the field where identity cards revealed that the Indian rancher was the writer while his "squaw" was J.L. Rosettis, the Herald staff photographer.

The idea of trying to break through the closely guarded military lines was born at Sarcee camp headquarters on Monday while Captain A.S. Jacobs, G.S.O. III, of the local military district was giving an outline of an army exercise to the press.

Captain Jacobs was justly proud of the plan. It involved the guarding of every important bridge and road intersection in a large area southwest of Calgary.

It looked like a fool-proof plan, and there was just a hint of a challenge in Captain Jacob's voice as he said:

"If you do happen to get through one post without being challenged, just let us know at headquarters and we'll give the troops further instructions."

Right there and then the writer decided that he was going to get through those lines.

Right at the outset we averted disaster by an eyelash. Rosettis has a weakness for big strong cigars. He believes that they settle his nerves or something.

So there he was in the wagon smoking a big fat cigar when right ahead of us a strong patrol of soldiers stepped out of the long grass beside the trail. To hesitate was to invite capture so we sailed by them, looking neither right nor left while behind us came the awe-stricken voice of one soldier exclaiming, "Brother, I've seen them Indian women smoking pipes but that's the first one I've ever seen smoking a cigar."

The Herald's "Indians" rolled on through the Sarcee Reserve, pausing only to take pictures and plant fake bombs. Then, unfortunately, the fifth columnists over-reached. They decided to return by the same route. Sgt. Winthringham grew suspicious, and gave chase.

"Maybe we'd better stop," said Joe.

"Indians don't savvy army rifles — we'll just keep on going," I said.

We made the bottom of the hill in safety and out of the corner of his eye, Rosettis saw the soldier coming on the dead run. Off to the left was another Indian team and wagon, driven by a young Indian boy. We saw the Indian turn his team and the soldier climb aboard.

"We're going to make a run for it."

I snaked out the lines and gave them the whip, and those Indian ponies dived into their collars and ran.

With an anguished yell, Joe grabbed his precious camera equipment to his breast and subsided in a heap in the bottom of the wagon.

The team was headed for home and they were really fogging. For nearly three miles the chase continued and once it looked as if we were going to make it, but the signallers and the wireless men had been busy. A quarter of a mile ahead we could see a platoon of soldiers spread across the trail, with rifles pointed in our direction.

I pulled up and "surrendered" to Sergeant Winthringham just before reaching headquarters.

Our identities established, we were welcomed by Colonel W.A. Cubitt, officer commanding the regiment. The sergeant was commended for his good work and we continued our journey back to the office

A lot of hard-sell advertising talent went into the annual Victory Bond campaigns. In 1942, for instance, readers of The Herald were treated to the prospect of Calgary in flames. The bonds campaigns worked: Calgary's target for 1943 was $10,643,000, a huge amount considering the size of the city and the level of wages at the time.

where we reported the successful conclusion of our mission through "enemy" lines.

July 23, 1941

For some, housing in Calgary was literally impossible to get. Families had to live in shacks and chicken coops on the edge of town.

All through the recent cold and rainy weather, a soldier's wife and nine children have been living in a tent pitched in the bush near the Bow River, in hopelessly inadequate living quarters, because they can't find a house in the city at a reasonable rental.

The woman's husband, a veteran of the last war, is a member of the Veterans' Guard, and is now stationed at Ucluelet, B.C.

The family gave up a homestead near Melfort, Sask., which they were unable to farm successfully because it consisted mostly of swampland, and came to Calgary in May of this year, travelling in an old automobile and towing their possessions in a small trailer. They pitched their tent in the bush land near the C.P.R. tracks in East Calgary below St. George's Island.

There are only two beds in the tent, and the bedding has been soaked several times by rain leaking through holes in the canvas. There are no floor-boards in the place, and the only way of warming the tent is by means of an oil-drum stove.

Sanitary arrangements are of the most primitive. The family hauls water for washing from a house several blocks away. The children appeared well-fed and husky.

The operators of a nearby filling-station took some of the children into their home on several occasions during the evenings, when they came over "just to get warm".

September 20, 1941

The Quebec City conference, 1943. Here President Franklin D. Roosevelt, seated at centre, and Prime Minister Winston Churchill, seated right, met to consider strategy for the liberation of Europe. Canada, the host but otherwise a junior partner, was represented at the conference by Prime Minister William Lyon Mackenzie King, seated at left.

British Prime Minister Winston Churchill spoke in Ottawa in December, 1941.

Prime Minister Churchill in his speech in the House of Commons chamber said today the objective of the Allied democratic powers is the total and final extirpation of "Hitler tyranny, Japanese frenzy and the Mussolini flop."

Hundreds upon hundreds of persons in his distinguished audience cheered and laughed at the reference to Italy's war effort.

The prime minister said there would be no compromise or quitting by the Allies until the earth had been "purged of Hitler villainy."

Earlier in his speech Mr. Churchill said that the "evil day" when Britain might have been destroyed is past.

From now on, he declared, the British people would confront the evil-doers with weapons as sharp as any they could bring into use.

Mr. Churchill said the Empire did not seek the land and wealth of any country, but the Empire peoples were a hardy lot.

They could not have journeyed across the years had they been made of "sugar candy."

"Hitler and his Nazi gang — let them reap the whirlwind," Mr. Churchill said.

Mr. Churchill said Canada had done much in men, in ships and in food to support the cause of war. The Canadian army in Britain had "chafed" under its inaction. But the Canadian army stood in a key position.

No reservations had been placed on the use of the Canadian army.

It was "unlikely this war will end without the Canadian army coming to close quarters with the Germans as their fathers did at Vimy Ridge and Ypres," Prime Minister Churchill declared.

The Herald published a full text of the Churchill speech. Here is one famous excerpt.

The French government's generals misled them. When I warned them that Britain would fight on alone, whatever they did, their generals told their prime minister and his divided cabinet, "in three weeks England will have her neck wrung like a chicken."

Some chicken! Some neck!

Ottawa, December 30, 1941

The federal government had forced Japanese — Canadians or not — to leave the Pacific coast. Feeling against Japan was running high, and they weren't wanted anywhere else.

Representation will be made to Ottawa protesting against the settlement of Japanese in Calgary and district, as a result of city council endorsing Monday the recommendation of the city commissioners. Applications from two Japs who want to enter business here were refused.

Ald. E.H. Starr declared "even if the Japs are British subjects, they have been ordered away from the coast and we don't want them here. The army won't take them for soldiers even if they are born here and are British subjects."

He criticized "a local paper" for saying Japs who have come to Calgary are British subjects, "when two of them are working within a half-mile of the Glenmore reservoir and within two miles of the dam. I don't care what they are, we don't want them."

On behalf of the farmer who had employed two young Japs on his farm near the dam, Ald. Freeze explained the man could obtain no other help. The men were milking cows, he said.

April 14, 1942

Fred Kennedy reported on Calgary's answers to Rosie the Riveter.

Operating powered hoists, skipping up and down scaffolding with remarkable agility, and toting wheel barrows loaded with tile and cement like veterans, 15 Calgary women and girls are now being employed on construction of the new military hospital.

The girls are pleased with the opportunity to work for two reasons. The first is that they are being employed on a real war project and the second, they are receiving the going rate of wages for the work they do.

They wouldn't stop work even to have their pictures taken.

"We're not glamor girls, we're here to do a job and we're doing it to the best of our ability," one of them said.

Mrs. Violet McKinnon of 1008 14th Ave. W. was operating a steam hoist with uncanny ability, considering that she had never seen one in her life before yesterday.

Mother of two children, Mrs. McKinnon attends to her household duties, and gets her youngsters ready for school before reporting for work. Her job is to control the operating of a cement carrier high up in the building, and the foot clutch, the foot brake and two hand levers keep her busy.

"I like the job and I'm staying until it is finished — unless they fire me in the meantime," Mrs. McKinnon said.

The men on the job are proud of the new recruits.

"They work like beavers," one of them said when asked if the women were doing good work.

September 17, 1942

An edict from the Co-ordinator of Sundry Items.

In a ruthless simplification move, the Prices Board today lopped handles from cups. An order issued by L.E. Messinger, co-ordinator of sundry items, specified that all potteries must make utility pottery ware — undecorated, simplified in style and with handleless cups in the semi-porcelain varieties.

"The mortality of cups," Mr. Messinger remarked, "is said to be four or five times that of any other piece of dinnerware, and if people take greater care in handling them we might return, before long, to production of cups with handles."

Ottawa, December 21, 1942

A very nice try, but not good enough.

Four German prisoners of war, reported missing after completion of a mass transfer of prisoners from one Alberta camp to another five weeks ago, are back in custody.

They had never left the first camp, and the story of their disappearance and subsequent recovery is one of cunning and resourcefulness on their side outmatched by smartness and determination on the part of a detail of the Veterans Guard of Canada.

The prisoners, all non-commissioned officers of the German army, had burrowed their way underground, but when recaptured they were found to be in first class physical condition.

All were freshly shaved and appeared well nourished. Adequate stores of provisions, blankets and mattresses were found in the dugout which had been constructed alongside one of the sump pits in the big camp.

When the mass transfer of prisoners was completed five weeks ago, it was found that four prisoners had not responded to the roll call. The Veterans Guard of Canada, in charge of security work in this camp, were confident that the men had not escaped.

On Monday, after five weeks of searching the camp foot by foot, the efforts of the Veterans' Guard were rewarded.

On one section of the camp, they came upon a sump pit, the sides of which were boarded. They ripped off the boarding, and there they discovered their first clue.

It was a false wall, about three feet in height. This wall separated the sump pit from a little tunnel which was two feet in diameter. This tunnel was about four feet long, and then opened into a dugout, which was about eight feet six inches by seven feet six inches, and three feet two inches in height.

In this dugout the four prisoners were discovered. At the word of command, the quartet emerged from the tunnel one by one. They blinked as they hit the bright sunshine and then submitted meekly as the guards closed around them and marched them to the guard house.

December 29, 1942

Liquor was rationed, of course, and bootleggers did their best to help the thirsty, for a price.

Here's the latest story on Calgary bootlegging activities vouched for as true by a well-known city lawyer. Thursday night, an elderly man, about to enter the liquor store on Ninth Ave. W. was hailed by a taxi driver.

"I'll pay for your permit and give you $3 for yourself in addition if you get me some supplies," the taxi cab operator propositioned.

The taxi cab man produced the money for the liquor permit, a 40-ounce bottle of hard liquor, some wine and some beer – in fact, all an individual is permitted to buy.

In a short time the man emerged from the liquor store weighted down with bulky parcels, and walked away.

The taxi driver jumped out of his cab and pursued the man. "Give me my liquor" he shouted. "Why it's mine. I bought it on my permit, look see," said the man.

A violent argument developed and soon there was a small crowd of interested spectators.

Then a policeman arrived on the scene. The taxi cab driver hastened back to his cab, sadder and wiser. The elderly man continued on his way.

February 27, 1943

An editorial.

Premier William Aberhart of Alberta is dead, and so ends the career of one of the strangest political figures ever to appear in the public life of Canada.

Whenever in the future the history of this country is recorded, his name will be found written largely in the pages. His contribution to our politics was unique and colorful. In the dark days of the last depression he came from the obscurity of a high-school classroom and a self-founded Prophetic Bible Institute, preaching a new doctrine and promising a new Utopia. That his theories were unsound, impractical and unworkable did not matter so much to the thousands of Albertans who rallied to the sound of his voice, as the fact that he represented protest against a system they believed was not providing them with their share of this world's goods.

Although his attempts at economic changes were all failures, and although his followers never realized the nirvana he had pictured, his death will bring sorrow to many who remained firm in their belief in his sincerity.

No one can deny that Premier Aberhart was the driving force behind the Social Credit Party. With his death the future of that movement is very much in the mists of the days to come. Sometime we may view in retrospect the whole record of the last decade and perhaps accurately estimate the value of Social Credit to the Canadian scene. Now it is too recent, too much current history, to fit into a definite plan.

In the brief life of this province, Alberta people, singly and in groups, have led or fostered many small rebellions and many phenomena. This foothills province has never cradled standard or stuffy thinkers and has never been afraid to break new ground.

Maybe when the pieces of the puzzle come together we will find that all we were really looking for was something akin to Mr. Roosevelt's four freedoms.

The Calgary Herald was one of Premier Aberhart's political enemies, but not such an enemy that today we cannot offer sincere sympathy to his family and his friends.

May 25, 1943

Death in the air over Calgary.

Two Air Force training planes collided in the air over Calgary this morning and crashed in the city about a mile apart, one near the race track in Victoria Park and the other on the front lawn of Mr. and Mrs. Hermon Stevens' home at 839 19th Ave. W.

Three fliers were killed and one slightly injured when he parachuted to the pavement on 19th Ave. beside the wrecked plane. In addition two civilians, a milk-wagon driver and a five-year-old child were injured, presumably by flying debris from the 19th Ave. crash. The driver's horse was burned and bolted, but soon stopped.

Pieces of the smashed planes fell in various parts of the city. One piece of fuselage fell near the Public Building on 8th Ave. East. Another at the rear of the Traders Building.

The actual collision occurred directly over a point at 15th Ave. and 4th St. E. The planes were apparently both flying a good height in a westerly direction when they came together.

As they met, one wing was seen to drop off one plane, and almost immediately residents of the district thought they saw two men take to their parachutes. It is considered certain, however, that only one flier escaped by parachute.

One of the planes continued to the west, while the other veered sharply to the south and then went into a spin directly over Victoria Park.

Scores of horsemen, who were getting ready for the afternoon horse show, scattered as the plane dived at terrific speed.

It hit the ground in the Victoria Park infield, about 35 yards southwest of the manager's residence.

The moment that the plane hit the ground, it exploded, and within a few seconds the wreck was a blazing inferno.

The heat was so intense from the burning plane, that rescuers, who ran to the scene could not approach within 100 feet of the burning wreckage.

There was no sign of life in the mass of twisted and burned debris.

Mrs. Herman Stevens, 839 19th Ave. W., said that the other plane "crashed right in my front garden."

"We heard the crash and rushed to the front of the house. Flames were coming in the front windows and doors, and the burning plane was lying on our boulevard and in the street right in front of the house."

The whole front and porch of 839 19th Ave. was blackened and scorched.

One of the civilians injured, John Tawse, a Union Dairy milkman, had just delivered milk to the Stevens' home and was returning to his wagon on the street when he was hit by part of the falling plane. He was rushed to the Col. Belcher hospital.

The milk wagon horse hit by the falling plane went charging westward down 19th Ave. Several witnesses reported that the horse was on fire.

It was finally stopped by Mrs. John Pugh of 1817 19th Ave. W., with the help of two boys.

August 28, 1943

The Turning of the Tide

In 1942, the war began to turn in the Allies' favor. British forces had fought a see-saw battle with the Germans across North Africa. John A. Montgomery of the North American Newspaper Alliance sent the following report when the British began to win on the El Alamein Front. British and American forces drove the Nazis out of North Africa in 1943, clearing the way for the invasion of Sicily and Italy. Meanwhile, in Russia, the German Sixth Army surrendered at Stalingrad in January, 1943. From England, waves of bombers attacked Germany.

I t is armor against armor and tank gun against tank gun in what might prove to be the most vital tank battle ever fought in the desert. This is the moment that the British Eighth Army has been waiting for ever since it came back to the El Alamein line.

When I came forward here you could sense the nearness of battle. There was an atmosphere of suppressed excitement everywhere. I saw British tanks rolling across the desert with dust flowing away behind them in the tawny boiling wakes. The muzzles of slim guns protruding from their turrets were swathed against the dust. Their crew rode with handkerchiefs bound around their mouths to keep out the grit.

I found a position on a knoll near the Indians. Soon before dusk, tin-hatted Indians were standing about or sitting on the ground cross-legged in groups. Every man held his rifle cuddled against him. They knew they had not long to wait.

The sudden crashing thud of guns smashed the evening quiet like a stone falling in a deep pool. British shells went whistling overhead to enemy positions.

The sun was disappearing now and the horizon was rimmed with gold and pale mauve. Dust spots thrown up where our shells landed rose dark against it. A shell scored a direct hit on some target, which burst into vivid flame.

Enemy were replying now, adding their voices to the clamor. The unbroken thump and rumble were like a surrealist symphony thrashed out by the hands of a monstrous, insane pianist.

A rosy glow burst over the enemy lines like a gigantic, suddenly opening flower. A brigadier commanding the artillery standing beside me said: "That's healthy. It looks as if the enemy has fired one of his ammunition dumps as he went back."

It was seconds afterward when the blast of the exploding dump reached us. It was like a gust of heavy wind. Then, after another pause, a terrific rumble shook the ground underfoot. The enemy must have lost scores of tons of high explosives when he fired that dump.

The enemy's guns were still loud enough, but you could tell they were receding. Now the rattle of machine guns was joining in the noise as the Indians, New Zealanders and South Africans got to close quarters with

British infantrymen capture the crew of a disabled German tank during the battle of El Alamein. Victory in the North African desert was the first step in driving the Nazis back into Germany.

the Axis men. Flares and tracer bullets were scribing red and white patterns across the sky above the fighting troops. Our artillery had ceased fire and the sounds of battle seemed more remote. It was up to the infantry now.

El Alamein Front, July 24, 1942

The Allies knew what was in store for them if they were defeated. Nazi atrocities in conquered nations were well-known early in the war. A. C. Cummings described some of the grim reports smuggled out of occupied Poland. The concentration camp at Oswiecim is better known by its German spelling, Auschwitz.

P hotographs too horrible to publish or even to describe in print, have been obtained secretly by the Polish government in London as proof of the incredible atrocities the Germans have committed in martyred Poland.

Recently, the Nazi "terror" has been intensified. The Huns, fearing defeat in Russia and a rising of the Slav populations of central and southeastern Europe, are resorting more and more to outbreaks of sadistic cruelty which without evidence, would be unbelievable. But the Polish government here has the evidence now. And the Deputy Premier himself, Mr. Stanislaw Mikolajczyk, has shown it to me.

The story it tells is appalling. Not only have the Germans starved and beaten Poles and Jews, but they have hanged them, poisoned them with gas, executed them on the edge of their own graves, inoculated them with deadly diseases and experimented on them with newly-discovered drugs.

In the infamous Nazi concentration camp at Oswiecim, tortures are practised worse than in the inquisitions of the Middle Ages. Prisoners here are worked literally to collapse and death; or they are tortured until they fling themselves against the barbed-wire fences of the camp and are shot by the guards for "trying to escape." Sometimes the Nazi gaolers swing a prisoner against a post until his back is broken.

Last year poison-gas was used. Many people were driven into an underground shelter. In the morning they were all dead — and the Germans had the information they wanted about the effects of the gas.

"In the recent months and especially since Himmler's visit," the Deputy Premier told me, "the Gestapo has intensified its terroristic methods."

The beating and torture of prisoners is so intense that more and more cases of deaths during "cross examination" are occurring. The Gestapo applies not only terrible beatings but also the most ingenious sadistic tortures — the tearing out of nails, hanging by the feet, beating in the stomach, piercing the most tender parts of the body, and kicking with heavy boots so that pieces of clothing are driven into the flesh.

Most of the people return from the torture chamber to prison in a state of terrible physical exhaustion. The torture of persons under examination always aims at the extraction of information concerning secret organizations, so that the next Gestapo terror may the more easily discover fresh victims.

The existence of 23 concentration camps

where Poles are confined, are known to the Polish government in London. These are their names: Belzec, Buchenwald, Ciechanow, Dachau, Dobrzyn, Dyle, Dzialdowe, Dziesienta, Flossenburg, Gross-Rosen, Grudziadz, Hamburg, Hohenbrueck, Mathausen, Nasielsk, Oranienburg, Oswiecim, Plensk, Ravensbrueck, Sierpe, Studhoff, Trawniki, Tramblinka.

The compulsion to dig one's own grave, the mowing-down with machine-guns and hand-grenades, and even the poisoning with gas are common methods of annihilating the Jewish population. In Lwow the Jewish Council also had to provide a list of victims themselves.

The Deputy Premier estimates that the number of Poles executed, murdered and tortured to death during nearly three years of German occupation amounts today to 200,000. The number of massacred Jews exceeds 200,000. From the beginning of war up to date about 400,000 Polish citizens (Poles and Jews) have been killed; 500,000 Poles deported to forced labor in Germany; 200,000 are prisoners-of-war in Germany; 150,000 were killed in the September, 1939 campaign; and 170 Poles compulsorily recruited for the German army from the incorporated territory.

London, July 24, 1942

The battle for Stalingrad was one of the most terrible of the entire war. It was the turning point on the Eastern front: From then on, the Russians drove the Nazi invaders back. It was not an easy campaign for the Western press to cover, but T.C. Cummings of The Herald's London bureau did what he could with official dispatches.

The epic battle of Stalingrad nears its end. A few thousand wretched frost-bitten, disease-ridden, shell-battered and starving Nazis remain of Von Hoth's proud army of over 300,000 men imperiously ordered by Hitler a few weeks ago to take Stalin's own city of the Volga at any cost.

Probably never in history has such sacrifice been demanded of so many. Terrible stories of their sufferings on frozen steppes are now reaching London.

While the Nazis were battering their way into the city they were so certain of victory that their letters home described how they "chased Russians like wild beasts," drove them to earth and "smoked them out again."

A few weeks of actual battles in the streets of Stalingrad itself however, soon undeceived them. Then came the shattering surprise of new Red armies pouring over the Volga to relieve the city and Axis retirement to the west where they were quickly surrounded by Russian tank units, heavy artillery and enormous numbers of men.

Almost 30 divisions were caught. At first they expected early relief from General Von Manstein's army further down the railway towards Rostov. But days passed, blizzards and frosts intensified and food ran short.

Soon men were eating horses and even rats and anything they could trap on wintry

Soviet Premier Joseph Stalin's image had to be adjusted after he became an ally of the democracies. His non-aggression pact with Hitler, signed in 1939, had confirmed him as a deep-dyed villain. When Hitler invaded Russia in 1941, Stalin became, willy-nilly, a gallant friend. Herald cartoonist Stew Cameron made the necessary alterations, but perhaps he suspected that they would be temporary.

steppes. For a time food was flown to them by giant transport aircraft which landed at the airdrome of Tsasinsk. Then, as the Red air forces shot down more and more enemy machines and finally captured the airdrome, famine overtook the badly-clad and half-frozen soldiers.

Russians quickly brought up artillery and soon by night and day terrific fire poured down on the Nazis' snow-covered dugouts. Men began to freeze their hands and feet by deliberate exposure in the hope of evacuation to hospital by the few planes that still carried wounded. Pilots malingered because it was death to fly in daylight. Officers threatened to shoot those who sought surrender. Orders were issued that anyone giving himself up to the enemy would bring heavy punishment on relatives at home. Nevertheless desertions took place daily and bodies of Germans frozen to death at night when escaping to Russian lines were found in the snow every morning.

Thousands fell ill with disease, many with typhus. Von Hoth and his staff had fled by airplane and General Paulus, who was left in command, flew to Hitler's headquarters to explain his men were in such desperate plight they could fight no longer.

Hitler insisted they continue, as it was necessary to hold the Stalingrad area so that the rest of the German armies in the Caucasus could retreat to a new line. So Paulus told his exhausted troops they must sacrifice themselves to the last man as an example to the German army and people.

A generous offer of surrender from the Russians was rejected and the battle resumed. The Red Army, using deadly mortars, rained death on the freezing, starving Nazis, drove them from the hills and slaughtered them in dugouts with bayonets. Overhead Russian aircraft bombed ragged victims of Hitler's military blunders without cessation.

While the men died of hunger as the Soviet iron ring closed tighter and tighter about the doomed army, not even an airplane carried a loaf of bread or packet of medicine to it.

So Christmas passed in terror, starvation and death. In January frosts worsened and local blizzards swept icy wastes. Hunters who had gleefully treated Russians as wild beasts had come to know what it was to be hunted to death themselves.

Now there remain only hidden groups of wounded, dying or exhausted men, enormous quantities of unused war material and many square miles of snow-covered battle debris.

Hitler's Volga army is no more. It died at his orders — uselessly.

So today in Germany Nazis are compelling boys of 16 to become soldiers. Hitler's wastage of human lives has to be made good.

London, February 1, 1943

Fighting as part of the British Eighth Army, the Canadian 1st Division and the 1st Army Tank Brigade invaded Sicily on July 10, 1943. After hard-fought battles on that island, they took part in the invasion of the Italian mainland in September. Richard L. Sanburn, a Herald war correspondent and later editor-in-chief of The Herald, covered the Italian campaign.

When the full story can be told of the 8th Army's invasion of Italy and the part the Canadians played, it will be a tale of sheer audacity that will make a stirring chapter in the Dominion's military history.

I have just returned by air after a five-day jeep trip in Italy over a tortuous route hundreds of miles long, travelled by these Canadian units after their almost unopposed landings.

That route stretched painfully up mountains thousands of feet high, through barren and deathly quiet valleys where the oppressive heat and desolate vistas suggested prehistoric worlds, and again into lofty mountains where the daytime sun sent temperatures over 100 degrees yet the nights brought bitter cold that penetrated several blankets.

All that can be said now is that the Canadians accomplished immeasurably more than was expected of them, travelled by brilliant forced marches distances seemingly impossible, and by their arrival high in interior Italy they threatened to flank German forces in the hard pressed Salerno area. That manoeuvre played a big part in sucking back the pressure on the Fifth Army and helped tip the scales in favor in a situation by no means good.

The roads of the Canadian route writhed like agonized pythons and seemed to go on forever to accomplish a forward advance of only a few miles.

The cunning German system of mine laying, incidentally, brought me and the party with which I travelled closer to death than I ever want to be again. With Fred Griffin of the Toronto Star; Ross Munro of

Armed with a typewriter, Southam war correspondent Richard L. Sanburn followed Canadian troops as they fought northward through Italy, and later as they drove German troops back through Belgium and Holland. Sanburn was to become Southam's London correspondent, and then editor-in-chief of The Herald.

the Canadian Press; Maj. Ian Wilson of Toronto, and our driver, Private Hank Rice, of Collingwood, Ont., we had driven a few miles from the Canadian camp en route to the coast and Algiers.

On a sharp bend a truck coming towards us slowed to let us pass over a mine crater. We did with jarring bumps, and passed on. Less than a minute later a tremendous explosion echoed through the mountains and we looked back to see the truck that waited for us hanging over a cliff by its rear wheels, while a great cloud of smoke rolled to the sky.

The Germans had planted deep mines that explode only after many vehicles have worn down the road and our own car had given all but the final jar needed for detonation. But for the politeness of that unfortunate other driver who waited for us we would have been the second truck over that spot. By such thin threads did life hang for many Canadians who first pushed bravely at top speed over that road.

The country of the toe of Italy is more poverty stricken and barren than anything I had seen in Sicily. The people were almost primitive in habits and dress and undoubtedly they were hungry.

Never a town we passed through that crowds didn't chase the jeeps crying "biscotti per bambini." However, even more often came the cry for "cigaretti." One becomes hardened after a bit for we learned that male members of the family insisted the women beg for cigarettes for them instead of food.

On the long, arduous trip to the Canadian camp our convoy mixed with hundreds after hundreds of Canadian vehicles hauling supplies, and progress slowed down to a crawl and often stopped altogether. These intervals sometimes gave one the opportunity to see the effects of Allied bombing.

Every town where railway yards existed to any extent had been visited with devas-

tating results. The towns were mostly undamaged, but the railway yards invariably were an utter mess with blasted and burned locomotives and freight cars tangled horribly in the steel grip of rails torn up and twisted like tentacles of a Frankenstein octopus.

Our air strength in this theatre is terrifying. During the critical period of the Salerno front our aircraft flew 4,000 sorties in two days. Captured Germans said they could stand it no longer. R.C.A.F. squadrons, of course, were playing a strong part, and never forget the thousands of Canadians in the R.A.F. units in this theatre. At a rough estimate there are 6,000 Canadian airmen in this area alone.

There should be no cause for impatience at the sometimes apparently slow progress in Italy. It is a gruelling struggle in a rugged forbidding country where the enemy has carefully planned defensive strongholds that must be cracked one by one with shells, bombs and blood of British, Americans and our own Canadians.

One fact should stand above all — we are definitely winning.

Algiers, September 27, 1943

Richard L. Sanburn reported on the battle for Ortona, Italy. This dispatch was published a day after it was written.

The battered city of Ortona fell to the Canadians today after eight days of what has been described as the grimmest battle the Canadians ever fought since the last war and perhaps the toughest yet fought by the 8th Army in this war.

When dawn broke today over the masses of rubble and destroyed buildings, with many dead bodies lying in the streets of what once was a city, the Canadians ready to continue the house to house struggles found the Germans had suddenly withdrawn during the night. A Western regiment poured out of the north exit of Ortona in pursuit.

Ortona was captured by Western Canadian regiments supported by Canadian tanks and artillery. Yesterday the big guns poured high explosive into the mouth of a railway tunnel in the cliff below the city, through which the Germans had been bringing reinforcements by night.

Doorway by doorway and brick by brick, the Canadians tore Ortona from the Germans' grip. As they fell back block by block the Germans blasted buildings to ruin, leaving only stout brick walls here and there for their own defensive purposes. As the Canadians advanced block by block they had to blast down these remaining walls to reach the Germans. That is the way Ortona died as a city.

Never had the Germans in this theatre fought so fanatically. They would sandbag one ground floor room in a building, crawl inside and blow the building in on top of them, making a giant rubble pillbox from which they directed streams of machine-gun bullets. They have been known to hide in a narrow doorway waiting for one of our tanks to pass down a street, then rush out and attempt to fix a magnetized "beehive" mine to the tank's armor.

Trapped in the upper floors of a building they would throw Molotov cocktails and hand grenades down into the streets until the overwhelming fury of our attack usually made their fanaticism end in death. Not many German prisoners came from Ortona.

On Sunday the Germans launched a strong infantry counter-attack against a company of the famed Ontario Regiment. In a spread out line of crouching, running figures the enemy came in on the Canadian positions. One by one the Germans plunged dead or wounded into the deep glue-like mud as our small arms opened fire with deadly accuracy.

The crouching line thinned quickly until only one figure continued to charge to our positions. A company officer raised his revolver and fired. So close had the enemy come that this last attacker fell dead right on the doorstep of our company headquarters.

In one area the same battalion cleared out troublesome pockets of enemy resistance, and in many cases it was a matter of mopping up by attacking one isolated farm house after another. More than once it has come to this — one of our tanks noses right up to the corner of the farm house in which the Germans are known to be sheltering, the tank nudges its mighty bulk against a corner of the house till it crumbles; the crew pours machine-gun fire into the interior until the Germans are dead or captured.

And so the battle unfolded hour by hour with startling bright threads of individual experiences standing out in the vast sombre tapestry of war.

Major George Rennison, Toronto, was chatting with brother officers in one of two big trucks parked rear to rear, when a five-inch German shell made a direct hit on the roof of one truck, luckily not the one in which Rennison was standing.

The front wheels were blown off the truck and the cab wrecked as the shell passed through. Shaken but uninjured, Rennison retired prudently to a slit trench to continue the conversation. Later he returned to his own tent to find an ugly splinter of shrapnel imbedded in the tent pole a few inches above his bed.

It is battle weary Canadians who have not eaten hot food for a week who have taken Ortona. But in any army in the world it would be impossible to find soldiers whose spirit and morale is higher.

With the Canadians in Italy,
December 29, 1943

The destruction of the Mohne and Eder dams was one of the most remarkable bombing feats of the war. Wing Commander Guy Gibson, leader of the "Dambusters," told his story in the December, 1943 Atlantic Monthly. It was of special interest to Calgarians because two of Gibson's crew were from the district: Flying Officer Harlo "Terry" Taerum of Calgary (later killed in action) and Squadron Leader Daniel Walker of Blairmore. The Herald reprinted the Atlantic article. W/C Gibson (who died in a later raid) described the preparation for the mission, and the flight through anti-aircraft fire to the target. Then came the bombing.

I spoke to my squadron: "O.K. chaps. Come in to attack when I tell you. I'll attack first." Then I began my approach. As we came in over the tall fir trees, Spam, my Australian bomb aimer, said, "You're going to hit these trees."

"That's all right Spam. I'm just getting my height."

I was looking at the special sight on my windshield. Spam had his eyes glued to the bombsight in front, his hand on the button. The bomb doors were open. Terry, the navigator, was checking the height. The flight engineer was keeping the speed constant.

The gunner saw us coming. It was not exactly an inferno. I have been through far worse flak than that, but we were very low. There was something sinister and slightly unnerving about the whole operation.

My aircraft was so small and the dam was so large; it was so thick and solid, and now it was angry. My aircraft was very small.

We skimmed along the surface of the lake, and as we went my gunner was firing into the defenses, and the defenses saw us coming and fired back. Their shells whistled past us but for some reason we were not being hit. Spam said, "Left...steady...steady ...bombs gone!"

Then it was all over.

Trevor, the rear gunner, said, "I'll get those devils," and he began to spray the dam with bullets until at last we were out of range.

As we circled round I saw that we had not broken the dam, and so far as I could see there was not much damage, but the explosion of my mines had caused a great disturbance upon the surface of the lake and the water had become broken and furious, as though it were being lashed by a gale. I had to wait for this to calm down and it took quite a long time.

"Hello, M Mother, Hello, M Mother. You may attack now. Good luck."

Hoppy began his attack. Hoppy the Englishman, casual, keen now only on one thing, which was war. I saw him approach. I saw him drop his mines. I saw him shot down.

Many minutes later I told No. 3 to attack. He was all right; he got through. It was then that I saw that the dam wall had moved. It had moved back on its axis and I knew then that if we could only go on pushing, in the end it must collapse. Then one after the other, No. 4, No. 5 and No. 6 went in to attack. Each one of them dropped his missiles exactly in the right place. I was flying up and down watching them. My rear gunner was all the time shooting at the defenses and trying to take some of the flak away from those who were attacking.

Now we had been over the dam for more than an hour, and all the while I was in contact with my aerodrome at home.

Suddenly, as the last aircraft attacked and as I watched the mines drop in exactly the right place, a great column of whiteness rose up a thousand feet into the air and the dam wall collapsed. I saw it go, but I could not believe that it had happened. I heard someone shout, "I think she's gone!" And other voices picked up the call and quickly I said, "Stand by until I make a recco."

Now there was no doubt about it. There was a breach 100 yards across and the water was gushing out and rolling down into the Ruhr Valley towards the industrial centres of Germany's Third Reich.

I passed the message home to my station, and I am told that when the news came through, there was great excitement in the Operations Room. I am told that the scientist who designed the special bombs leaped up and danced around the room and shouted the news.

Then I looked again at the dam and at the water. It was a sight such as no man will ever see again. Down in the valley we saw cars speeding along the roads in front of this great wave of water which was chasing them and going faster than they could ever hope to go. I saw their headlights burning and I saw the water overtake them one by one, and the color of the headlights underneath the water changed from light blue to green, from green to dark purple, until quietly and rather quickly there was no longer anything except water.

The floods raced on, carrying with them as they went viaducts, railways, bridges, and everything that stood in their path.

Then I felt a little remote and unreal sitting up there in the warm cockpit of my Lancaster, watching this mighty power which we had unleashed; and then I felt glad because I knew that this was the heart of Germany and the heart of her industries, the place which itself had unleashed so much misery upon the whole world.

February 26, 1944

From Normandy to Berlin

After years of suffering and preparation, the Allies were ready to re-enter Europe. D-Day, June 6, 1944, was the beginning of the campaign to liberate a continent. The first waves of a force of nearly 3,000,000 men landed along a 50-mile stretch of the Normandy Coast. As they established beachheads, more and more men and supplies flooded in. It was the beginning of a campaign that would last almost a year. Nazi troops were slowly driven out of territory they had conquered in a matter of weeks. Ross Munro of the Canadian Press (later to become publisher of the Edmonton Journal and the Montreal Gazette) sent this dispatch.

Allied soldiers faced obstacles like these when they landed on the beaches of Normandy. Many of the barriers, designed to stop tanks and landing craft, were armed with explosives. The plan had been to clear the obstacles away at low tide, but many of the D-Day invaders had to go ashore on a beach still alive with barriers and mines.

Canadian assault forces bounced through the stormy sea in landing craft Tuesday and in broad daylight stormed the French beaches and battled their way inland.

There was some stiff opposition on certain sections of this particular beach but 1½ hours after landing, reports of success came in rapidly to this headquarters ship.

(Actual landing place of the Canadians in Normandy was not revealed but Desmond Tighe of Reuters news agency reported watching "cheerful and smiling tin-hatted British and Canadian troops attacking at Bernieres Sur Mer."

(If that was the Canadian landing place perhaps the objective was Caen, 12½ miles to the southeast.)

One Canadian regiment after another flashed back messages that it was advancing through the coastal defence strip, part of the Germans' so-called West Wall. Hard fighting was likely to be encountered inland, however, but the Canadian forces expected that.

A number of enemy strong points on the beach zone resisted, and they were being fired on by naval craft.

Earlier, naval bombardment and air force bombing blasted the French coast until it shuddered. From the deck of this ship I watched the whole incredible scene from start to the finish and never have I witnessed anything so tremendous in any seagoing attack.

As we were crossing the Channel, R.A.F. heavy bombers struck at the beach defences and specific targets up and down the coastline. When daylight came, U.S. medium bombers took over the attack, and hundreds of planes dropped high explosives all along the beaches.

After that, U.S. heavy bombers went in with a roar that drowned out the sound of the naval gunfire and struck other targets.

Cruisers started off the naval bombardment, which was by far the heaviest coastal shelling of the war. For 40 minutes hundreds of guns were shelling without a let-up.

Under cover of this colossal barrage, Canadian infantry and engineers in the first assault waves plunged through the white-capped Channel water in small landing craft, and the first regiment touched down easily.

Other units followed in rapid succession, some going under heavy machine-gun fire and shelling. They fought their way forward and gained their first objectives on schedule time.

Allied tanks also landed with the assault force and went into action with the infantry.

In two hours and 45 minutes' fighting on the beaches Canadian invasion forces won their beachhead and shoved on inland.

At 10:45 o'clock Tuesday morning the Canadian commander sent this message to Lt.-Gen. H.D.G. Crerar, army commander: "Beachhead taken. Well on way to immediate objective."

The strip of coast won by the Canadians in this initial assault was quite narrow but it gave them beaches and provided a base for further penetration.

There was some stiff street fighting in the little coastal towns and the Canadians also met considerable enemy fire on the beaches and as they worked their way into the German defences they had to overcome numerous steel and wooden obstacles which had been placed out on a tidal part of the beach.

However, the assault went in just as the tide began to rise and many of these obstacles were cleared away by engineers before water covered them, enabling follow-up craft to beach and unload.

The Canadians suffered some casualties from machine guns, mortars and artillery fire.

By 10 a.m. the Canadians were about 1,000 yards inland and going strong, meeting only small pockets of Germans.

On other parts of the front near us the operation is moving along. Canadian and British airborne troops did a good job when they dropped and came in by gliders at 3:30 a.m. They captured and held several important bridges.

Cruisers provided the Canadians with very effective support. One cruiser knocked out a troublesome battery about a mile and a half from the coast with six direct hits.

The first sign I saw of enemy activity was at 4 a.m. when strings of flares were dropped over the convoy miles to the west of us. The red lights hung in the sky but were not shot at by naval gunners, who had been ordered to hold fire.

We were right in the Channel, cleared by minesweepers, for the final run to the beaches.

Everyone was at his post by 5:30 when it was quite light and there was the invasion fleet, stretched out from horizon to horizon.

The French coast still was mist-draped but through the mist appeared the light of bomb explosions as the night raiders finished their task and flew over us to England.

Our grey-and-blue camouflaged ships plunged south in their mine-swept lanes, every ship and the main bombardment ships moving to correct positions to lash the enemy beachline in the 40 minutes before H-Hour which was 7:25 a.m. on our beach. The landing to the west of our sector was scheduled for an hour before that time.

By 6 a.m. I could see the French coast about eight miles ahead. Through my binoculars I spotted a church steeple at a seaside town and could see the strip of white seawall and the town's buildings. The white beach, sweeping along for miles, was our landing place.

"With Canadian forces landing in France," June 7, 1944

These Canadian troops waded ashore at a seaside town in Normandy on the morning of D-Day — June 6, 1944. Some heavier equipment had landed earlier, but this wave of soldiers went in to liberate Europe equipped with nothing more formidable than rifles and bicycles, presumably to speed communications along the country roads of Northern France. In the days that followed, massive numbers of well-supplied men landed via floating, pre-fabricated docks.

Ross Munro sent this report from the Normandy beach where Canadian troops landed.

Canadian assault infantry, engineers and tank crews avenged Dieppe in their magnificent D-day attack on a four-mile strip of Normandy coast here.

I spent three hours Thursday walking through German Atlantic Wall defences seeing what the Canadians had to overcome. They cracked this line in a bloody, two-hour battle and won — through stern courage, technical skill and careful, long preparations.

Formidable concrete placements were dotted along the stretch of coast covering the beach and approaches with heavy guns and between them were scores of pillboxes well sighted and constructed. There were elaborate trench systems, all camouflaged, and observation posts from which the German fire could be controlled.

The defence strip was about a half-mile wide. Behind this correlated defence system were batteries of 88 mm. guns.

On the sandy flat beach itself there were hundreds of obstacles to troop landing craft. Many were uncovered at low tide. First was a row of 12-foot gate-like steel obstacles. These were former Belgian anti-tank fences employed by the Germans in this new role.

Closer to shore were what were called hedgerows — four-foot angle irons stuck into the sand, each with an old French mine or fused French shell tied to it.

There also were many wooden stakes driven deep into the sand with French shells attached as explosives.

Canadian infantry, sappers and tanks sailed in on a rising tide and while many of the beach obstacles were high and dry they had to pass between many others.

It was a terrible ordeal, especially in the heavy sea that was running, and some craft were blown up before they touched the beach. However, the great mass of craft and tanks did get through.

This all was done in broad daylight because of tide conditions and the necessity of having good observation for the tremendous naval barrage that preceded the assault.

Into the face of this fire went the infantry. To see it all and examine the defences minutely makes one wonder how the Canadians ever did it, especially on the western flank where the stiffest resistance was overcome.

I walked through one defence point on the east side of the harbor and the German dead still were lying where they fell by their cannons and machine-guns. The base of the concrete emplacements was 12 feet thick in some places, the walls four or five. The Germans fought to the end.

Burial parties moved through the dunes with a padre and patrols of commando riflemen worked through the catacombs of tunnels linking the defence posts to seek out any Germans holding out there.

Twenty feet from an entrance to a tunnel where there were two Commandoes with fixed bayonets I saw seven Germans suddenly spring from the tunnel mouth, hands high in the air, a terrified look in their eyes as they looked at the cold steel. The attack had passed inland but they had stayed there in the bowels of the Normandy West Wall.

The engineers played a big part in the success. They devised many methods of clearing beach obstacles and breaking up concrete emplacements and an old French seawall which ran across some beaches.

The Allied high command took Dieppe as the basis from which to work and built on the experience of that raid two years ago to find the answer to Germany's Atlantic Wall defence.

With Canadian forces in France, June 10, 1944

Weeks after the D-Day invasion, Herald war correspondent Ralph Allen was finally able to piece together the story of the Canadian paratroops on that fateful day.

In an action that began six hours before the main landing forces touched down by sea and subsided only when the invasion was deep into its second week, Canadian paratroops fought a non-stop guerrilla war on the eastern hinge of the British-Canadian beachead to write the little epic into the larger epic of the sixth airborne division.

The first Canadian paratroops battalion that ever dropped into battle found itself with a regimental history that many units 20 times as old would be proud to own.

In their first engagement with the enemy, the maroon-bereted youngsters —

Canadian troops and French civilians amid the wreckage of Caen. The Canadians fought a bloody battle for possession of this French town following the D-Day invasion.

the youngest soldiers on the average in any Canadian unit serving abroad — fought through the early hours of D-Day, not as a battalion, but in little groups of two, three, four, and up to eight.

In the early hours many were lost and officially leaderless. But they landed together with other lost and leaderless men to battle towards objectives which if untaken, might have threatened the fate of whole armies that came in later on their flank.

As the flat, marshy plain east of the River Orne erupted with dozens of sudden skirmishes, peasants left their beds in the night to guide our airborne soldiers to their first rendezvous.

The battalion fulfilled all its initial assignments, reunited on a fire-swept ridge in its weakened numbers and remained there in the face of shelling and direct counter attacks that continued for 11 days.

The Canadian battalion's role within the sixth airborne divisional role was to blow up two bridges along the network of canals, streams and irrigation ditches meshing out from Dives River, and then establish a battalion guard over the crossroads hamlet of Le Mesnil from the high ground of the Bois de Barnat.

The colonel, a former Regina accountant, who at 32 is the battalion's second oldest member, said, "The hardest part of the job wasn't the fighting, but getting

ourselves organized after we hit the DZ."

DZ means dropping zone. Weird and fateful things can happen just before and just after the jump hatches open over that weird and fateful spot. When the hatches of the Air Fleet bearing the first Canadians into France began to yawn above Normandy at 1:15 on the moonless morning of June 6, chance took over where navigation left off. Hundreds of soldiers inevitably missed their individual pin points, some by miles. A little flak was coming up from the ground. Startled German garrisons fired on every moving object.

In hundreds of ditches and copses kids from Canada squirmed free of their first layers of jumping gear, paused for a minute to try to think which of the hundreds of ditches or copses they had memorized from maps this particular one might be, and moved off to do their jobs.

By 7 o'clock in the morning, the bridge at Varaville had been blown up according to plan. The garrison left there to defend it held out all morning in a strong blockhouse, but yielded 40 prisoners after its officers had been killed. The bridge at Robehomme was demolished earlier. Both these hazardous tasks, originally company assignments, were performed by fragments of companies who recruited their Allies wherever they could find them as they felt their way ahead

through a blackness abruptly broken by sudden ambushes and assaults.

With the Canadians in France, June 26, 1944

Herald war correspondent Richard L. Sanburn followed the Canadians' hard-fought course through northern France and Belgium.

The bitterest Canadian fighting since D-day is going on now for possession of that unfriendly chunk of Holland that juts westward into Belgium along the North Sea. The whole area makes up less than 200 square miles. It is only about 15 miles long and 12 miles deep at its broadest. For Canadians fighting across the Leopold Canal northward toward Aardenbur it is a wet, murderous hell.

Veteran Canadian troops who have experienced the toughest fighting of any Allied soldiers in Europe since last June, frankly say this is worse than Caen, and Caen will be historic for its bloody fighting. Here, for once, Germans have so far had at least as much artillery as we have had. We have suffered casualties in this bridge-head over the Leopold canal, and the only reason we haven't suffered a lot more is because Canadian soldiers have learned so much in the past four and one-half months. Nobody in this war theatre knows more about Hun fighting than these very same Canadians.

Today there is one Canadian unit carrying on the fight like other units have done before in the same horrible spot — waist-deep or neck-deep in icy salt water. They are forced to take each shrub, each tree, each bit of stone fence or dike, as a separate objective.

The Germans here are more offensive-minded than ever before. Prisoners admit they have been told that any thought of surrendering either on their part or on the part of their families in Germany, will bring immediate death to all concerned. So there is no surrendering. Germans fight until they are killed or have no more ammunition.

Today I asked a Canadian officer how, if the going was so tough, our troops had done as well as they had. He answered "Same old story, any Canadian soldier is as good as any two German soldiers. But we respect the Germans around here — they are good. Our boys win every inch of this damn wet ground by sheer guts and that's all."

When the Germans roll back they leave snipers and machine-gun nests dug into rear slopes or dikes commanding the only approaches there are for us along roads that are not flooded or along dike tops.

They infiltrate into our lines at night, every night. Our men getting up in the morning and going a few yards to wash often are sniped or machine-gunned by Germans who have occupied our washing area during the night. Last week it was said that our first task every morning was to spend two hours shooting Germans out of our own lines.

A couple of days ago a Vancouver brigadier was jeeping along a road we had controlled for days when his jeep was suddenly riddled by enemy machine-gun fire. The officer got fighting mad, grabbed a tommy gun as he leaped for the jeep, killed two Germans and captured two more before he continued to drive to his destination.

In another area on Sunday, one of our patrols got up earlier than the Germans and discovered quite a fair number of the enemy asleep in slit trenches not far away.

They called up a couple of light mobile flame-throwers and "fried them where they lay."

"With the Canadians in Belgium,"
October 1, 1944

A month before Germany surrendered, Richard L. Sanburn sent this report from the occupied zone of that shattered country.

Conquered Germans are streaming past the gates of Allied refugee camps back to the remains of their homes in the Rhineland, now that war has sped past and plunged its steel fingers into the Reich.

It's only a fragment of Germany, but what is happening here gives the first broad outlines of what the picture may well be for all Germany in the immediate post-war future. In 90 per cent of the cases life must be started again from absolute zero. Germans accustomed to a solid standard of living are having to revert to almost primitive life on the scarred land.

Just though it is, for we have no pity in our hearts, it is not a pretty picture to see.

The Rhineland that died in flaming agony two weeks ago, has become a backwater of war. A panorama of tumbled chaos in which you may drive for miles in ghostly stillness and never see a live thing.

Within the past three days German civilians have been freed from refugee camps and are going "home." From one camp alone, at Bedburg, they will be released at a rate of 1,800 daily until the camp is empty. They depart in lorries, almost in holiday spirit, laughing and waving farewell as they go.

What are they going back to? How will they live?

The city of Cleve, which normally housed 22,000 people, now is badly smashed, but it might, in a pinch, provide some kind of shelter for 5,000. Actually 1,000 of Cleve's population are accounted for. Thousands are dead. Thousands are just gone.

Cleve, incidentally, will be a plague spot of horror when the hot weather comes. Literally thousands of bodies lie amid the ruins.

In the Cleve jail alone the bodies of nearly 300 prisoners are mangled in the ruins. In piles of grey stone and grotesquely twisted iron bars you can see, in collapsed cells, the ghastly remains of these hapless men.

The industrial population, their factories and homes now levelled in grey dust, will have to become farm workers in order to eat. Frankly, in the majority of cases, there is

The war was driven deep into German territory before the remnants of the Nazi regime surrendered. German civilians, like these ones, packed up whatever belongings they could salvage and tried to get away from the oncoming tide of battle. Many later returned to find their homes and farms shattered by the war.

no place but the farming countryside left in which to live.

Hundreds of people are moving back into pieces of homes that are perilously smashed and may well collapse in a high wind. I saw one family in a two-storey house wth the entire rear half blown away, floors hanging down into space, three sides gone and the roof partly caved in. It will be a miracle if many Germans are not killed by these rickety death traps falling in on top of them.

Yet, the strange and powerful urge that makes people want to go home is just as irresistible in Germans as it is in normal human beings. In Cleve yesterday when 500 civilians in one camp were told the doors were open and they could go home, they stood up and cheered wildly. An officer said "You'd think the war was over and they had won it."

Home — to a disused gunpit with a roof of broken bricks piled on rough boards.

Home — to a cottage with shell holes in two walls big enough to drive a jeep through. Home — to a farm house with 20 strangers billeted in your attic and stable.

And for the city worker, the white collar men and women, "home" to a barn on a strange farm, with pigs and cattle sharing the shelter, to till the soil with awkward unaccustomed hands so that families may eat next winter.

These are the spoils of war for Germany today. This is Germany today.

Occupied Germany, April 7, 1945

The Allies lost a great leader toward the end of the war. Bob Bowman of the Herald's Washington bureau paid the following tribute to the late Franklin D. Roosevelt, who had taken on the burden of the American presidency even though he had been crippled by polio. Vice-president Harry Truman was sworn in as president, and immediately faced agonizing decisions, including the use of the atomic bomb on Japan. The San Francisco conference referred to below was to establish the United Nations.

A great heart stopped beating for the world yesterday. Now it will be hoped that the United Nations will set up the greatest of all monuments to Franklin Roosevelt's memory, an organization, resolution, and the will to make future wars impossible. The San Francisco conference is to be held as the President planned it.

There is no doubt that Mr. Roosevelt's heart did beat for humanity. Perhaps it was a lesson he learned more than 20 years ago through suffering. By rights, Mr. Roosevelt was a wealthy man and needed not to be concerned with the problems of all men.

The illness which would have crushed those who have vilified him, or sent them into pitying retirement, led Franklin Roosevelt to climb a pinnacle from which he could survey the needs of all men. Often as he worked to make things better for even those who sought to crucify him, he turned the other cheek, and carried on.

In spite of his physical handicap and

constant pain, Mr. Roosevelt accepted a challenge when he stepped into office in the darkest days of the depression. He was not afraid. It was the others who were afraid, and it was Roosevelt who said to them, "The greatest thing we have to fear is fear." Yet when he pulled them from the depths of poverty and despair, many turned on him and used their crutches to beat the head of the man who helped them.

The people of the United Nations can mourn the passing of Franklin Roosevelt more sincerely than the people of his own country. Certainly every Canadian in Washington knew they had a friend in the White House, and a man who knew and understood Canada.

When L.B. Pearson, Canada's present ambassador, presented his credentials to the President the written speeches were discarded with a wink, while Mr. Roosevelt kidded "Mike" about his appearance on "Information Please," and his interest in baseball.

President Roosevelt was a real fighter. He gladly carried the troubles of the world on his broad shoulders, and summoned strength into the rest of his body to support them. He pulled the United States through the disaster of the depression and threw more than his share of weight into pulling the world through the war.

His ambition as of yesterday was to finish the good fight, make a just and lasting peace and then take economic steps to make the world a better place for all humanity.

Those are not just glossy sentences, but facts well known to those who have been privileged to talk to Mr. Roosevelt twice a week in his press conferences.

Washington, April 13, 1945

L.S.B. Shapiro of the North American Newspaper Alliance reported a dramatic — and all too rare — re-union.

It was like something out of the movies. It couldn't really happen, but it did happen," said L/Cpl. Erie Cahn of the Canadian Army, field security section, as he squeezed the hand of a pretty girl in blue denim overalls who smiled tearfully beside him.

The scene was the notorious Westerbork transit camp for Jews — the last collecting point in Holland from which Nazi cattle-car trains have carried 105,000 Jews to death camps in Poland.

The girl was Mrs. Hameloa Eisinger, Cahn's sister, whom he had long given up for dead.

In 1938, Cahn left his native Hamburg. He was one of the last Jews in the city to obtain a visa for England, and he departed heavy-hearted because his sister declined to go with him.

When the war broke out in 1939, Cahn joined the pioneer corps of the British Army. He did not know that his sister had fled Germany that year and crossed the frontier into Holland only to be trapped there when Hitler struck in May, 1940. Cahn served with the pioneers until 1944, when the Canadian Army, preparing for the invasion

of Germany, sought German-speaking troops for its field security section.

"The other day," he told me, "I was instructed to investigate the Westerbork camp for Jews, which had just been liberated by our troops. Believe me, I had a premonition as I drove toward the gates.

"Suddenly I heard a shout in a familiar voice and there, struggling through the crowd, was my own sister. I couldn't believe it. I can still hardly believe it."

Westerbork, Holland,
May 3, 1945

A.C. Cummings of The Herald's London bureau compiled this account of the death of a dictator.

The corpse of Mussolini, once dreaded dictator of 42,000,000 Italians, hangs today head downwards from an improvised gibbet in the square in Milan known as Piazza Loreto. Pinned to it is a placard with the words, "Justice has been done." Beside the body hang those of his film star mistress, Clara Petacci, and many of the Fascist leaders who used to greet him with flattering cries, "Duce, Duce", when he presided at the Fascist grand council in his palmy days in Rome.

Mussolini, – the murderer of the Italian patriot Matteotti and of the thousands of his fellow countrymen; jailer of concentration camps in Lipari Islands; would-be conqueror of Africa who killed and gassed thousands of Ethiopians; who seized Albania; who made war without cause upon Greece and France; who boasted of his air fleets which "darkened the skies"; of his army of four million bayonets; of his "mare nostrum", meaning Mediterranean Sea – died a dog's death.

In German uniform he was driving furiously to escape into Switzerland, which, in his Socialist youth, gave him shelter as a political refugee. According to reports reaching London, including those from the Times correspondent who was in Milan, he was seen and recognized by customs guards who reported his whereabouts to headquarters of the Italian resistance movement at Lake Como. They set out in pursuit, headed off the fleeing dictator, placed barricades across the road and brought his car to a halt at a little town named Giuliano Di Mezzegere. Mussolini, looking exhausted and ill, made no attempt to resist.

His guards brought him to San Domino Prison in Como and there he spent the night. Leaders of the resistance movement were summoned and the question arose whether the demand from the Bonomi government in Rome that the prisoner be handed over to it for formal trial should be agreed to. The majority objected and decided for instant trial and the death sentence. They would take no chances, they said, on Mussolini escaping again.

According to some reports the whole party was taken at noon Saturday back to the village where Mussolini was captured and there shot through the back by a firing squad. The dictator's last words are said to

have been "No, no," as rifles were levelled at him. His mistress was shot separately.

The corpses were then flung on trucks and taken to Milan. There, in the square where the dictator had 15 Italian patriots executed some time previously, the bodies were dumped in a contemptuous heap. Mussolini's head, when The Times correspondent saw him, was resting on the breast of his mistress. His face was frozen as if by terror.

The news quickly spread throughout Milan, from which the Germans had already fled. The crowd gathered silently. Then one of those Italian outbursts of hatred, which Anglo-Saxon peoples cannot fathom, led up to an incredible scene.

An elderly woman in the crowd stepped up to Mussolini's body with a revolver and fired five bullets into it. "That's one each for my five dead sons," she screamed.

Immediately the mob swept aside the partisan guard and kicked the corpses in wild fury.

The corpse of Clara Petacci was especially battered as it lay with its masses of long tumbled hair clad in white lace blouse and dark skirt.

"He died too easily," shouted the infuriated crowd. "He should have been handed over to us."

Later the disfigured bodies were taken up and hung head downward like so many slaughtered animals from an improvised gibbet. The Milanese, who were never good Fascists, filed past, spitting and showering curses on the men who had brought Italy to the greatest shame, degradation and destitution she had ever known in her 27 centuries of history.

London, April 30, 1945

Finally, Hitler, too, died.

Adolf Hitler, who vowed to rule the world, committed suicide in the ruins of Berlin with Propaganda Minister Goebbels and the chief of the German general staff, Gen. Hans Krebs, a Soviet communique said today.

Whether Hitler was a suicide or whether he was the victim of a brain hemorrhage, a possibility reported by Allied supreme headquarters in Paris, there was little doubt among Allied leaders that the fuehrer indeed was dead and that he had met death in a manner which would thwart any diehard Nazi attempt to build a Wagnerian legend about him.

The Soviet communique did not say where the reported suicides took place. Hitler had been reported in the depths of the Tiergarten fortifications in the heart of Berlin.

Goebbels, who followed his fuehrer doggedly from Munich on through the ruin of Germany, fulfilled one of his own propaganda pledges if he took his own life. In his last speech he had said he would remain in Berlin to the end and would commit suicide rather than live in a Germany occupied by "Bolshevik terror."

London, May 3, 1945

Pearl Harbor to Hiroshima

Japan brought the United States into the Second World War with an attack on the naval base at Pearl Harbor, Hawaii, December 7, 1941. The United States at once declared war, not only on Japan but on Germany. Britain had a new and powerful ally, but Japan nevertheless made frighteningly quick gains. Hong Kong fell to Japanese troops on Christmas Day, 1941. Through 1942 Japan expanded its hold on the islands of the South Pacific. The Americans had to win control of this vast area, by naval battle and jungle warfare, before an invasion of the Japanese homeland could be mounted. In the end, it was a fearful new weapon, the atomic bomb, that forced Japan to surrender and made an invasion unnecessary. Canadian soldiers played a brief, tragic part in the Pacific war. Two Canadian battalions were sent to Hong Kong three weeks before it fell. Those who were not killed were captured. Many of the survivors suffered life-long damage from their ordeal in Japanese prison camps. Stories of Japanese atrocities hardened attitudes at home toward Japanese-Canadians.

Pearl Harbor, December 7, 1941. Rescue workers try to save a few men from the burning American warship USS West Virginia. About 360 airplanes, launched from Japanese aircraft carriers, attacked the naval base in Hawaii. Their bombs and torpedoes sank 18 ships and destroyed about 170 American aircraft.

T he defence of Hong Kong has broken under relentless assault by land, sea and air and the Crown colony which for a century has been a British bastion off the Southeast China coast has fallen to the Japanese.

"So ends a great fight against overwhelming odds," the Colonial office declared Christmas Day, announcing the surrender.

No further resistance, it said, was possible.

Without estimating the figures, the foreign office said "military and civilian casualties were heavy..."

The announcement said lack of water was one of the great handicaps of the British Tommies, the Canadians and the Indian Sikhs, who fought step by step back across the mainland sections of the colony and then held out desperately and with little hope in the fortified mountain fastnesses of the island.

(Canadian defenders included the Royal Canadian Rifles of Quebec and the Winnipeg Grenadiers. Casualties were not estimated in Canadian announcements.)

As the Japanese wrested away one after another of the Hong Kong settlements and smashed water mains by shelling and bombardment, water supplies of the hard-pressed garrison dwindled until, the announcement said, "Two days ago there remained but one day's supply."

Canadian and Indian troops at Hong Kong, estimated at 6,000, were reported to have been ordered to stack arms by noon today in conformity with yesterday's surrender to the Japanese, said a Tokyo broadcast.

The mainland frontiers of the crown colony of Hong Kong on the southeast coast of China were attacked by the Japanese Dec. 7 when the armed forces of the Japanese empire struck simultaneously at the United States and British empire.

For only the first few days of the fight were hopes harbored that the colony's defences could hold out indefinitely without support.

The sinking of the battleship Prince of Wales and the battle cruiser Repulse off Malaya, which cost Britain her heaviest naval units known to be in Far East waters, prevented any naval stroke to save the colony.

British, Canadian and Indian defence troops, their number estimated by the Japanese at more than 20,000, were pushed back slowly to strongholds on heights rising 1,700 feet.

Japanese broadcasts praised the stubbornness of the garrison's defence, and the defenders, who twice rejected ultimatums to surrender, claimed a heavy toll of the attacking forces.

Crippled communications made their contact with the outside world slow and interrupted. Last word from them came in communiques dated Tuesday and Wednesday.

With the Canadian troops who fought at Hong Kong was one young man, Pte. Harvey J. Perry of Victoria, B.C., who wasn't supposed to be there. He stowed away on the troopship which took the Canadians to Hong Kong.

What has become of him — whether he was among casualties, whether he had been returned home, whether he stayed with the Canadians as they fought, or whether he was taken prisoner, wasn't known here.

December 26, 1941

The Battle of the Coral Sea was the Allies' first major victory in the Pacific. It came just five months after the Japanese attack on Pearl Harbor brought the United States into the war. Stanley Johnston of the Chicago Tribune sent this report. In later dispatches he described the sinking of the Lexington, which was struck by two bombs and two torpedoes.

F rom the deck of an aircraft carrier which was bombed, machine-gunned and torpedoed, I witnessed the Battle of the Coral Sea.

For five full, never-to-be-forgotten days I lived with the American heroes — airmen and sea-men alike — who there won a magnificent victory.

The naval developments of these five days were scattered over 400,000 square miles of tropic seas. The surface fleets which fought the battle never saw each other and during most of the fighting were from 80 to 180 miles apart. This is the story I have to tell — the first of its kind in all history.

First of all this was an engagement of aircraft carriers: two American against three Japanese. It was disclosed how completely the carrier has displaced the battleship in importance in modern war.

It was a battle of dive bombers, torpedo bombers, and fighter pilots. It also was a battle of anti-aircraft gunners.

When it was finished one of the Japanese carriers had been sunk and another was out of action. As for our own forces, the gallant old U.S.S. Lexington, one of the famous old "twin" carriers that laid the foundation for all the navy's aircraft operations, and the destroyer Sims and the tanker Neosho were our only losses.

I stood on the signal bridge of this gallant old ship and watched her crew fight the Japanese, defend her, and make desperate efforts to save her. I saw them beaten by internal fires started by explosions which rocked the ship hours after her Jap assailants had been beaten off.

The total balance sheet for profit and loss of the Coral Sea battle, however, was much more than two carriers to one. Although our forces lost only the Lexington and two other ships, the Japanese, in addition to their carriers, lost at least 15 ships, including three heavy cruisers, one light cruiser, two destroyers, and several transport and small vessels.

Throughout our two-week voyage we had our air scouts ranging the seas for 200 miles or more on all sides of us. When we joined forces these scouts were augmented and on the afternoon of May 3 an aviation ensign spied 15 enemy craft, warships and transports, in Tulagi harbor.

We were up before dawn, airplane motors turning on the flight deck of the carrier. Scout planes were off in the pre-dawn dark. Soon they were reporting the enemy still in position, entirely unsuspicious of our presence. Immediately dive bombers and torpedo planes took the air and in less than 30 minutes were roaring down on the Jap ships.

Surprise was complete. Our boys unloaded, came home, loaded bombs again, and flew off. A few fighters accompanied the second wave and liquidated the minor Jap opposition (five seaplane fighters).

The bombers came back for a third trip and when they had dropped their last missile 14 of the 15 Jap ships were sunk or beached and burning. This occupation threat had been removed.

Photographs and pilots' reports indicated enemy loss of life here must have been terrific, particularly on the crowded troop ships that were blasted from above and below.

On the afternoon of May 6 our scout planes had exciting news. They had located north of the isle of Misima, a Jap carrier and cruiser force. We didn't know it then, but this was the enemy spearhead bound for Jomard Passage.

Back on our carrier, anxiously awaiting the outcome, I crowded into the wardroom with officers off duty. There was a jumble of orders and meaningless calls on the radio between the planes until suddenly Lt.-Cmdr. Bob Dixon, skipper of the scout bomber squadron, identified himself to the carrier.

"Scratch one flat-top, scratch one flat-top," he said, and abruptly signed off.

The ship's loudspeaker system carried the message to the entire crew and the craft rang with cheers. The men knew that Dixon was reporting the destruction the Jap carrier. Our own losses (it seemed even more than a miracle then than it does in writing it now) were only two scout dive bombers.

Our fliers shot down 23 enemy planes in widely scattered engagements. Later in the day we learned that a heavy cruiser was sunk at the same time.

Chicago, June 13, 1942

The Japanese drove American General Douglas MacArthur from Corregidor, a fortified island in the Philippines, in 1942. He vowed then "I shall return." He did, after nearly three years of naval battles and jungle warfare on the islands of the South Pacific.

Gen. Douglas MacArthur announced today that he and every able-bodied survivor of Corregidor have come back at the head of a huge invasion army to drive the Japanese from the Philippines.

Ground forces, landing under air and sea barrages along the east coast of Leyte – 415 miles southeast of Manila and 600 miles north of MacArthur's previous advance base of Morotai – seized three strong beach-heads.

Front line dispatches said the Leyte landings were preceded three days ago by landings on small islands guarding the entrance to Leyte Gulf and mine-sweeping operations of the gulf to make it safe for the passage of convoys.

The Japanese, expecting landings to the south of Mindanao, were so completely surprised that beachheads in the Tacloban area "were secured with small casualties," stated a special communique.

Reinforcements and supplies poured ashore as the Americans started their drive on an estimated 225,000 Japanese troops in the Philippines headed by Field Marshal Juichi Terauchi.

Fulfilling his promise, made two years and seven months ago when he took leave of the islands that "I shall return," MacArthur went back aboard a warship. It was part of a giant convoy, sailing from New Guinea, which stretched as far as the eye could see.

The United States navy, in unchallenged strength, ruled the invasion scene and the seas about it.

Allied air forces virtually monopolized the skies.

Philippines, October 20, 1944

The age of nuclear warfare was announced in this dispatch from the Associated Press. Three days later, on August 9th, a second atomic bomb was dropped, this time on Nagasaki. The Japanese opened peace negotiations on Aug. 10, and accepted the Allied surrender terms Aug. 14.

The United States Army Air Force has released on the Japanese an atomic bomb containing more power than 20,000 tons of TNT.

It produces more than 2,000 times the blast of the largest bomb ever used before.

The announcement of the development was made in a statement by President Truman released by the White House today.

The bomb was dropped 16 hours ago on Hiro Shima, an important Japanese army base.

The president said the bomb has "added a new and revolutionary increase in destruction" on the Japanese.

Mr. Truman added: "It is an atomic bomb. It is a harnessing of the basic power of the universe. The force from which the sun draws its power has been loosed against those who brought war to the Far East."

The base that was hit is a major quartermaster depot and has large ordinance, machine tool and aircraft plants.

The president disclosed that the Germans "worked feverishly" in search of a way to use atomic energy in their war effort but failed. Meanwhile, American and British scientists studied the problem and developed two principal plants and some lesser factories for the production of atomic power.

The president disclosed that more than 65,000 persons now are working in great secrecy in these plants, adding:

"We have spent $2,000,000,000 on the greatest scientific gamble in history – and won.

"We are now prepared to obliterate more rapidly and completely every productive enterprise the Japanese have above ground in any city. We shall completely destroy Japan's power to make war."

The president noted that the Big Three ultimatum issued July 25 at Potsdam was intended "to spare the Japanese people from utter destruction" and the Japanese leaders rejected it.

The atom bomb now is the answer to that rejection and the president said "they may expect a rain of ruin from the air, the like of which has never been seen on this earth."

Mr. Truman forecast that sea and land forces will follow up this air attack in such numbers and power as the Japanese never have witnessed.

The president said that the discovery may open the way for an entirely new concept of force and power. The actual harnessing of atomic energy may in the future supplement the power that now comes from coal, oil and the great dams, he said.

Washington, August 6, 1945

Canada had a significant role in developing the atomic bomb.

Canadian scientists have played an important part in the development of atomic bombs, Munitions Minister Howe announced today.

Mr. Howe said that Canada, in co-operation with the United States and United Kingdom, has undertaken to establish a pilot plant for further investigations near Petawawa military camp, northwest of Ottawa. He said also that government action in taking over the Eldorado Mining and Smelting Co. was part of the atomic program.

The National Research Council had assembled the largest and most distinguished group of research workers known in Canada. One national research laboratory in Montreal had a staff of 350, including 140 scientists, among whom were many internationally known.

More than half the staff were Canadians and the others included a number from the United Kingdom and some French scientists. Others were working at Ottawa, McMaster University at Hamilton, McGill and Toronto universities.

Ottawa, August 6, 1945

The Herald greeted the atomic age with these two editorial comments.

Man stands today at the pinnacle of his scientific achievements. He has learned how to harness the immeasurable power of the atom.

It is a matter for regret — but not, we think, for surprise — that he has made this remarkable discovery while in search of new and better methods to kill other men.

Man the builder is only matched by man the annihilator. Man the savior of human life is only matched by man the destroyer of human life.

It is by God's mercy, says Winston Churchill, that the atomic bomb has been placed in the hands of Britons and Americans, rather than Germans. Or Japanese.

God's mercy it may be. But it is only a temporary mercy. The atomic bomb will not stay indefinitely in the hands of men who detest war. These inventions have a way of spreading about the world. They become, in time, the property of all mankind.

Let the atomic bomb be used, as it is being used, against the Japanese. Let those who were first to take the bomb perish by the bomb. But let us not deceive ourselves into imagining that the atomic bomb is selective, that it kills only aggressors, and leaves peaceful folk alone.

The atomic bomb is capable of killing anyone anywhere, in a bad cause as in a good. It has neither mind nor heart. All it knows is to kill. Hence it may well become, unless men put an end to their quarrels, a noose to hang the entire human race.

What hath man wrought?

Each day, he becomes more skilled, more dexterous, able to travel more rapidly, to compute more accurately, to deal more mercifully — and to destroy more ruthlessly.

In matters like physics and chemistry and engineering, he moves with breathtaking speed from one triumph to another. But in matters like wisdom and tolerance and compassion, he moves with agonizing slowness. If, indeed, he moves at all.

About the art of destroying other men, he knows — and wants to know — so much. About the art of living with them, he knows — and wants to know — so little. Now he stands in the world with his atomic bomb as a child might stand in a schoolroom with a loaded revolver. He has performed his greatest wonder, and its name is death.

"I saw once," wrote Clarence Day, "a photograph of a ship being torpedoed. There it was, the huge, finely made structure, awash in the sea, with tiny black spots hanging onto its side — crew and passengers. The great ship even while sinking, was so mighty, and those specks so helpless. Yet it was those tiny beings that had created that ship. They had planned it and built it and guided its bulk through the waves. They had also invented a torpedo that could rend it asunder."

August 7, 1945

In the atomic era, human beings will behave much as they have always behaved: that is to say, nicely some of the time and badly most of the time. Preachers and such will endeavor to improve them, but will find it mighty tough going.

In the atomic era, people will read the works of Henry David Thoreau and will note one particular sentence: "The mass of men lead lives of quiet desperation." They will be astonished at the shrewdness of this observation, and will wonder how a preatomic man (1817-1862) could see so far, so very far, into the future.

August 8, 1945

Vern Haugland of the Associated Press visited the ruins of Hiroshima less than a month after it was bombed.

Street cars rattle along the streets where not a single building stands. A few deadpan civilians pedal slowly through the rubble.

Block after block contains only a thin covering of rusting tin, a few stones and some broken bricks. The twisted frames of less than a dozen buildings stand forlornly alone in the midst of ruin that was once touted as Japan's most modernized city.

That was the Hiroshima I saw today with the first Allied post-war visitors to the world's first target of the atomic bomb.

For its size, no city in the world was so completely wiped out by bombs as was this war-swollen metropolis of 400,000 whose heart was smashed completely by a single application of atomic power.

The Japanese newspapermen who had visited the city shortly after the levelling told me that the residents of Hiroshima "hate you and think you the most fiendish people on earth."

Hiroshima, Japan, September 4, 1945

Hiroshima. A single atomic bomb, a small one by present-day standards, devastated this city. About 70,000 people were counted as dead or missing; another 70,000 were injured. Others died later of invisible injuries caused by radiation. Three days later, an atomic bomb was dropped on Nagasaki.

Peace and a New World

The war made a new world, though not an altogether better one. There were new alignments of friend and foe, and new, more terrible weapons ranged on both sides. One great fear about the postwar world proved unfounded: there was no relapse into the depression of the Thirties. Work that had been left undone since 1929 was finally done, and goods that people had done without for 16 years were in demand. Returning soldiers started new families, and new houses were built as quickly as a shortage of materials allowed. After a pause to re-tool the war factories for peacetime production, the consumer society was launched. The hates bred by six years of war were gradually forgotten. Old enemies were accepted, uneasily at first, as useful allies. Japanese-Canadians, who had suffered most on the home front, were gradually accepted. Even before the war with Japan ended, Herald columnist Richard J. Needham offered a few unpopular words on behalf of the Japanese in Canada.

We didn't know it was a crime in Canada for a man to visit his wife, but now we learn it is. The Montreal Gazette (April 25) reports: "Judge Omer Legrand doubled the fine on a 28-year-old Japanese-Canadian in Criminal Court yesterday as he pleaded guilty to having entered the province of Quebec from neighboring Ontario without a permit from the R.C.M.P. The accused, Joshiji Jakahashi, of Brantford, Ontario, was fined $50 and costs last fall for a similar offence. This time, the fine was $100. It was explained that the accused came to this city to visit his wife, who resides here."

This report leads to some interesting conclusions. Here is a man who paid $50 to visit his wife last fall, and paid $100 to visit her this spring. In addition, he must have purchased two round-trip tickets from Brantford to Montreal, making an approximate total of $200. On top of all this, he had the disagreeable experience of appearing, not once, but twice, in the criminal courts.

We gather from this that the Jakahashis have a pretty good marriage, the kind which should be encouraged, rather than discouraged, by our righteous governments.

We may imagine that if Mr. Jakahashi was trying to get a divorce, the Almighty State would give him a fair hearing. But because he likes his wife, and tries to see her occasionally, the Almighty State arrests him, and makes him into a criminal. This seems very strange, particularly when you consider that the men who govern Canada are noted for the Christian zeal, and that they frequently hold forth on the blessings of family life, and the sanctity of the home. They do not say anything in their speeches about the necessity of getting a permit from the R.C.M.P.

But perhaps there is an understanding among our rulers and functionaries that Christianity — at least, the Canadian version thereof — does not apply to minority groups. The Heavenly Father of Canadians, it would appear, has strong convictions on the subject of race and color. He draws a dividing line between Canadians who are yellowed by the sun, and Canadians who are yellowed by their natural inheritance.

In this connection, we see that the Japanese-Canadian will be banned from several provinces after the war. Premier Ernest Manning of Alberta has made a statement to this effect; so has Premier George Drew of Ontario and so has Maurice Duplessis of Quebec.

All these men are good Christians: much better Christians than we will ever be. Mr. Manning is a Baptist, Mr. Drew is an Anglican, and Mr. Duplessis is a Roman Catholic. But that does not prevent them from turning their faces against this little group of people, whose only tangible offence is their pigmentation.

The issue is further complicated by the fact that about 10,000 Japanese-Canadians are themselves members of Christian churches, and presumably worship the same Heavenly Father as Mr.Manning, Mr. Drew and Mr. Duplessis. This is enough to confuse anybody, be he Christian or heretic.

The business of banning Japanese-Canadians from this or that province is most interesting. The provincial governments have no right in law to do it, of course, but then, who worries about law and justice where minorities are concerned? These things should not incommode us, any more than they incommoded the Germans. What we need now is an order forbidding people of Jewish origin to live in Nova Scotia, an order forbidding people of English origin to live in Quebec, an order forbidding people of French origin to live in Manitoba, an order forbidding people of Swedish origin to live in British Columbia, and so on all along the line.

Then we can all be happy and pure, and any racially-inferior man who wants to send his racially-inferior wife a bunch of daffodils will have to get a permit from the R.C.M.P. under penalty of ten million years in jail.

May 4, 1945

Peace at last and Calgary goes wild.

Calgarians were caught in a rising crescendo of wild peace celebrations Tuesday, beginning when the first newsboy hit the street, shortly after 5 p.m. with news of Japanese surrender, and climaxing during the late evening when thousands of young people milled through the downtown area, halting automobile traffic, sending street cars back to the barns, building huge bonfires, and littering the pavements with a snow of paper and a barrage of broken glass and bottles.

Most of the revellers were teenagers who knew little of the real reason for their peace day celebrations. They had known almost nothing of the sorrow or suffering of six years of war.

"Listen boy," one of the comparatively few servicemen and overseas veterans in the crowd told a snakedancing youth. "You don't even know what it's all about. You don't even know why you're yelling and screaming. You don't even know what war was like."

Tuesday night's celebration was unparalleled in Calgary's recent history. It surpassed in noise, exuberance and property damage the VE-Day celebrations but was conducted on the same style.

At the height of downtown celebrations, 8th Ave. from Centre St. to 2nd St. W. and 1st St. W. from 9th Ave. to 7th Ave. was a screaming sea of teenagers, plus a number of servicemen, and a few adults who watched the antics from the jammed sidewalks or from vantage points on the roofs and fire escapes of nearby buildings.

Bonfires blazed on the main streets throughout the evening. The first, at 1st St. W. and 8th Ave., resulted in a fire alarm being turned in.

The city's celebration began shortly after 5 p.m. when workers surged from office buildings and learned the news of the Japanese surrender.

Within minutes crowds had congregated in front of The Herald building to read the peace bulletin. Others rushed to the 1st St. W. windows to see The Herald presses roll off an extra edition carrying the news.

A pressman seized the first copy off the presses, held it up to the window so the crowd could see the surrender headline. "It's true," the onlookers said.

August 15, 1945

Home from the wars, and back to the hardware stores and the banks.

Cheering crowds that packed downtown Calgary, masses of waving flags and the rousing airs of military bands combined with the brilliant warmth of a perfect Indian summer day to give a great welcome to the first Calgary unit to return as a unit from overseas, the 1st Canadian Infantry Brigade Company, Royal Canadian Army Service Corps.

Since the first troops began to return from the Second Great War the city has welcomed many groups, large and small, but today's reception to a gallant unit which was the first to go overseas from Calgary in 1939 achieved a new peak of warmth and rejoicing.

Thousands of citizens packed the concourse in front of the C.P.R. station and along Centre St. and 8th Ave. on the route of the march to the Mewata Armories there was a cheering mass of humanity.

PEACE—IT'S WONDERFUL

The war ended, but what followed wasn't exactly peace. There were strikes in major industries, and violent disputes in Palestine and Indochina — trouble spots that nowadays are called the Middle East and Vietnam.

Quickly the bronzed and battle-hardened soldiers who had served through the toughest fighting of Sicily, Italy and Western Europe de-trained and lined up on the station platform to receive a brief welcome from Mayor Andrew Davidson.

Six years of soldiering has left its mark on these eight "old sweats" but they have no regrets. Each was a private in 1939. Seven now bear stripes and one the crown and wreath of a sergeant-major.

S/Sgt. Dave Shepherd, B.E.M., voiced the opinion of all of them when he said: "We have no regrets. We've had a lot of fun. If I had to do it all over again, I would."

S/Sgt. Shepherd won his British Empire Medal in Italy in 1944, but it was on July 13, 1945, that "the biggest thrill of my life" occurred. It was on that day that he received his medal from the hands of the King at Buckingham Palace.

They had their tough times. Some of the toughest ones seem funny to them now. They recalled the time when German planes dropped incendiaries on their ammunition dump. Why the dump didn't go up and with it the ammunition company they still don't know. But they got the fires out and they saved the dump, and a considerable area of the English countryside.

That was their first real experience of working under fire. Near Ortona, in the Italian campaign, they were shelled every night. It was there they fought as infantrymen. To hold the line two officers and 36 other ranks fought up front for eight days. Fortunately casualties were not unduly heavy and the men were able to return to their major job of getting ammunition up to the troops.

The luck of the unit still held. Two days after they had handed over the ammunition dump to a British Indian unit the dump blew up.

Though they now face demobilization their chief concern is not jobs. "We want to look around a bit and size the situation up," they said. Most of them plan to return to their former occupations eventually.

S/Sgt. Shepherd, for instance, will go back to the hardware store his parents operate at Rumsey. He has agreed with himself, however, that when customers buy ammunition they'll carry it themselves.

Sgt. C.A. Mumford's chief interest last night was his wife and two children in Calgary. He expected to find a big change in his sons, Bill, now 13, and Ted, nine. He is going back to banking, his occupation before the war.

October 6, 1945

The Gouzenko case might be called one of the first skirmishes of the cold war. Igor Gouzenko, a code clerk, defected from the Soviet embassy in Ottawa. His revelations led to a series of arrests for spying. Among those convicted were atomic scientists Klaus Fuchs and Allan Nunn May, and a Canadian member of Parliament, Fred Rose.

A shaken, curious and still incredulous Ottawa today found itself in the vortex of the first major spy probe in the nation's history.

The unsuspecting capital was stunned last night by Prime Minister Mackenzie King's announcement that a royal inquiry was under way and arrests already had been made of present and past government employees suspected of supplying secret information to a foreign power.

No indication of the numbers arrested or the governmental departments involved was given in the prime minister's statement, but an Associated Press Ottawa dispatch said twenty-two men had been taken into custody, some known to have been employed by the National Research Council.

Direct suspicion of having participated in the sale of war secrets centres on about a dozen men, including some civil servants of prominence, notably in the now defunct department of munitions and supply, The Herald's Ottawa correspondent said today.

The affair began with Igor Gouzenko's visit to an Ottawa newspaper office. Embarrassingly, they didn't spell his name right the first time.

Canada's "spy hunt" was touched off early one morning last September when an R.C.M.P. squad descended on the home of a member of the staff of the Russian embassy here to find four Russians ransacking his apartment, Reginald Hardy of The Herald's Ottawa Bureau reported today.

Ivor Gosenko, the embassy employee, who is now in protective custody, at the time of the raid was hiding in an apartment across the hall. A few days before he had visited a newspaper office here and has asserted that he had received threats against his life. He was advised to get in touch with the justice department and tell his story there.

Some time after midnight two Ottawa constables who had been watching the apartment found four Russians ransacking it. Two of them, according to the Ottawa police, were members of the Russian embassy staff. The other two were not accredited representatives.

The city constables took the names of the four men, together with the name of the chauffeur of a Russian embassy car parked outside the apartment building.

While the men were being questioned R.C.M.P. men arrived, and, on justice department instructions, the five men were allowed to go.

At this juncture Gosenko, his wife and child "disappeared" into the protective custody of the R.C.M.P.

February 18, 1946

Treaties and Judgments

At last, a terrible war was over. It was succeeded by an uneasy peace, made more uneasy by the spectre of one last nuclear war. The victorious nations resolved to punish the guilty, and to make new arrangements that would prevent mankind from bringing the final catastrophe on itself. The punishments and the arrangements were, however, subject to the customary jockeying for advantage among the major powers. In a series of war-crimes trials, Nazis ranging from Hitler's henchmen to minor prison-camp functionaries were confronted with their crimes and punished. A new organization, the United Nations, was created in the hope that it would be more effective than its failed predecessor, the League of Nations. In the last days of the war, shortly before the destruction of Hiroshima announced the nuclear age, The Herald published the following editorial on the Potsdam conference.

The Potsdam conference has come and gone, leaving behind an aroma of good intentions and excellent brandy.

Various decisions have been made: some large, some small. The small ones have been announced. The large ones we imagine will be announced later. Or found out later.

Reading the 6,000 word report issued by the Big Three, we get the impression that the board of directors of a vast company have met for several days and have emerged with the announcement: "We are going to fix the leaky tap in the gentleman's washroom on the third floor of the Saskatoon warehouse."

An announcement of this nature is, of course, perfectly true. But it leaves much unsaid.

Looking back on the war in Europe, we recollect that a great many people took part in it. Some fought, some worked, some paid. Naturally they are wondering what kind of a victory they have gained.

Their questions have not been answered by the Big Three announcement. They are still wondering.

And doubtless they will continue to wonder.

In the meantime, it may be said that the Big Three have concluded their deliberations at Potsdam. The service was efficient, the steaks were tender, the strawberries fresh and juicy. The diplomats were comfortably housed and there were picked sentries to keep away people who, not being officials, had no official business with the official delegates.

During the proceedings, it is understood an unknown man, wearing some kind of military uniform, was noticed loitering in the vicinity of the conference. Taken into custody, he made an incoherent statement about freedom from want and fear, freedom to speak his mind and freedom to worship God as he pleased. After questioning, he was held for examination by psychiatrists.

The brandy, however, was excellent.

August 3, 1945

Belsen was only one of the notorious Nazi extermination camps. Frank G. Swanson of The Herald's London Bureau covered the trial of the camp commandant and his accomplices. The trial was held at Lueneberg, Germany.

Josef Kramer, Belsen 5 commandant and his aides, saw their handiwork again Thursday. They never blinked an eye or moved in the dark as the grimmest film ever made was shown in the war crimes trial courtroom. In the spectator's gallery German townspeople saw the horrors of the Nazi atrocity camps in complete silence. They saw pictures the rest of the civilized world could never see.

They saw corpses stacked like cordwood inside barbed wire stockade in thousands, saw the degradation and filth of a "rest camp" run by "supermen" of Europe's "superior race." In the grey half light of the big courtroom, the faces of countless dead stared back at the men and women charged with killing them. The wasted bodies, thin to the point of disbelief and emaciated beyond description were silent testimony of the hell that was Belsen.

And Kramer smiled when the lights came on, relaxing in his seat.

Throughout the trial, he has made copious notes of the translated proceedings, frequently passing messages to his counsel, seated directly in front of the dock. Throughout Thursday's sittings he and the others appeared more relaxed and at home than any day since the start.

An eyewitness account by a British internee, a Channel Islands school master, of his stay in the concentration camp told of incredible privations and boundless suffering. He was Harold Le Druillenec, who used a cane to assist him into court and who was committed to Belsen ten days before the arrival of the British.

During his first four days, he said, he received only one pint of soup, receiving neither food nor water during the following five days. He, with the others in his hut, rested on the floor where sleep was virtually impossible.

"The floor was wet and foul and we had only two damp blankets for covering.

"Many slept on boards on the rafters to escape the foul floor below. A night in a hut is something that only men like Dante could describe," he said.

He told of looking into one of the camp huts, and seeing "thousands of bodies" laid in rows stacked in every room. He was able to get a mug from which to eat his soup by going to the pile of dead persons' possessions, taking one which he had to use without washing because there was no water.

After four days, he said, he and others were put to work carrying corpses of dead from the prison compound into mass burial pits. He spent five days on this work and received neither food nor water during the entire time.

"During the dragging of these dead to the pits," the witness said, "I noticed strange wounds back of the thigh in many of them — they looked like gunshot wounds at close quarters, but a friend of mine said many prisoners were cutting chunks off these bodies to eat.

"On the next visit to the mortuary, I actually saw prisoners whip out a knife and cut flesh off the leg of a corpse and put it in their mouth."

"One guard watching this procession wanted to see us go past him at the double. When a prisoner dragging a corpse did not run past at the double the guard shot him and then other prisoners were ordered to carry him to the pits."

He described an S.S. guard administering whippings to a group of women in the female compound because the women had attempted to light fires to cook some turnips they had found.

"The language of blows was the only language we knew. After being in a concentration camp for a while one ceased to wonder about the reasons for things that happened to us. Instead we just accepted things as they were," he told the court.

Dr. Ada Bimko, a Polish Jew, testified today that 4,500 of a shipment of 5,000 Jews were moved into the Oswiecim (Auschwitz) chambers and crematorium on the day of their arrival at that Nazi concentration camp.

Her voice breaking, she said her parents, her brother, her husband and her six-year-old son were among the victims. She was among 250 women and 250 men of the group who were spared at that time.

Kramer and 11 others were stationed at Oswiecim before being transferred to Belsen.

Sophia Litwinska, 28-year-old Jew from Lublin, told of her almost incredible escape from a Nazi gas chamber coming "back from the dead" after being ordered into the infamous shower room at Oswiecim.

Lueneberg, September 21, 1945

Perhaps it was in the trials of the lesser Nazis such as the Belsen staff that the true beastliness of the Hitler regime was made plain. The policy-makers were tried at Nuremberg, but the policy itself had been carried out in places like Belsen.

The German town folk here are at a loss to understand why the British authorities are going through long and complicated legal proceedings to establish the fact that Josef Kramer and his Belsen S.S. Troopers are war criminals.

"If they did these things you say they did why weren't they shot right away" is the opinion of the average German in the street. Nevertheless, he is impressed with the slow moving but painstaking trial procedure.

The Auschwitz extermination camp, part of the Nazis' "final solution to the Jewish question." Here, a grandmother and children walk slowly from the camp toward the gas chamber. Prisoners at the Nazi death camps were stripped and gassed, and their bodies were burned in crematoria.

Daily, about 200 civilians are allowed into the gallery of the war crimes court where they sit high above the accused and peer down silently into the dock. Almost all day long, crowds of others stand about the barricades near the court entrance, waiting for a glimpse of the accused and court officials as they enter and leave the building.

All evidence is translated into German for the benefit of the accused, but the German spectators lean forward in their seats to hear the words for themselves. That they are amazed at the lengthy and comprehensive trial procedure is putting it mildly.

They are amazed too, by the fact that the defence counsel outnumbers the prosecution counsel by about four to one. Each four accused have one defence lawyer, a British army officer with legal qualifications.

They apparently don't understand the accused's right of cross examination of witnesses produced by the prosecution and appear surprised when statements by these witnesses are questioned by defence counsel.

Most Germans who come to the trial go away commenting on the fact they believe the Belsen camp staff are receiving a fair trial, and that the British have apparently gone out of their way to see they get a fair trial. They apparently have not the slightest comprehension that the method of trial being carried on here is standard throughout democratic nations of the world.

Dr. Ada Bimko, Polish Jewish doctor, testified today that Kramer himself took part in catching prisoners who tried to escape death in the Auschwitz gas chambers.

Kramer would hit and kick prisoners be-cause they were not quick enough getting into trucks which were to take them to the gas chambers, the woman physician told the court.

Dr. Bimko, who survived internment at Auschwitz, said prisoners were loaded onto trucks in the presence of Kramer and one of his fellow accused, blonde S.S. woman Irma Grese.

Maj. Ell Cranfield, cross examining Dr. Bimko for the defence, asked, "Do you swear that during the 15 months you were in Auschwitz, apart from gypsies, no person other than a Jew was sent to these gas chambers?"

"Yes," she answered.

It was then suggested to the witness that only persons who were listed as ill and with a limited time to live were selected for the gas chamber.

Dr. Bimko said she had seen quite healthy persons who were on the camp's discharge list for the next day being sent to the gas chambers.

"One cold night a young woman from my native town cut a piece of blanket and put it on her shoulders. As a punishment she was sent to the gas chambers."

Kramer and the 44 others accused revisited the twisted and charred desolation of the camp that has become notorious throughout the world.

With them went some of the former prisoners of the camp, and members of the British military court conducting the trial.

As the party toured the camp, an S.S. woman, Ida Forster, faltered and turned faint near the crematorium.

Driving 80 miles from Lueneberg after Friday's adjournment, the court went round the camp in procession, headed by an armored car, and accompanied by the present commandant, Maj. Leonard Berney, who has transformed part of the former camp into a holiday rest centre for displaced persons.

Kramer and Dr. Fritz Klein, handcuffed together, looked at each other in silence when the procession halted near the graveyard of the victims where a notice in German says: "This is the site of the infamous Belsen concentration camp, liberated by the British, April 15, 1945. Ten thousand unburied dead were found here. Another 13,000 have since died — all victims of the German new order in Europe, an example of Nazi culture."

Lueneberg, September 22, 1945

The surviving leaders of the Nazi hierarchy were tried at Nuremberg, for crimes against humanity. Frank Swanson, Southam correspondent, reported the opening of the trial.

The case against 20 Nazi war lords charged with engulfing the world in a blood bath was opened today by Justice Robert H. Jackson, chief prosecutor for the United States, after the accused, in cold, clear voices, had told the International Military Tribunal they were not guilty. None pleaded guilty.

Justice Jackson, in his 20,000 word statement, said that the Germans planned as far back as 1940 to attack North America. He said Nazi records in the tribunal's possession also disclosed that the Japanese had planned to assassinate Premier Stalin in 1940 through the use of Russian traitors. Justice Jackson promised the "20 broken men" would be convicted by the Nazis' own meticulously kept records.

When Justice Jackson, dressed in a black morning coat, stepped to the centre of the courtroom and began reading his long statement, the Nazi defendants leaned forward and listened closely in marked contrast to their indifference to the proceedings yesterday.

When Justice Jackson solemnly stated that the Nazi leaders would be convicted by their own documents, Hans Frank, Hitler's ruler over conquered Poland, laughed aloud. There were no smiles from the others, however.

Justice Jackson said the 20-odd defendants have so identified themselves with the philosophies they conceived and the forces they directed that "any tenderness to them is a victory and encouragement to all the evils which are attached to their names."

The Nazis ignored the internationally agreed rules of war, Justice Jackson said. For example, he made the charge:

"On June 1, 1944, it was ordered that captured English and American airmen should no longer be granted the status of prisoners of war. They were to be treated as criminals and the army was ordered to refrain from protecting them against lynching by the populace."

In concluding his statement, Justice Jackson told the tribunal: "The real complaining party at your bar is civilization...

"Civilization asks whether law is so laggard as to be utterly helpless to deal with crimes of this magnitude by criminals of this order of importance.

"It does not expect that your juridical action will put the forces of international law, its precepts, its prohibitions and most of all its sanctions, on the side of peace, so that men and women of good will in all countries may have leave to live by no man's leave, underneath the law."

The prisoners exhibited increased friendliness among themselves and engaged in animated conversation before the trial reconvened for the afternoon session.

Only a third of Justice Jackson's opening statement had been read at the morning session. As he continued, Hess alone among the defendants did not put on his earphones to hear the German translation.

The muscles in Julius Streicher's neck twitched and he stared at Justice Jackson as the prosecutor accused him of a part in the Nazi plan to exterminate the Jews of Europe.

Ribbentrop listened to the recital of crimes against the Jews with his eyes closed. Goering occasionally pencilled notes. Franz von Papen removed his earphones and gazed pensively at the ceiling.

Franz shook his head negatively when Justice Jackson spoke of executions in "gas wagons." Then the prosecutor held before the court an open book containing an S.S. general's report on the destruction of the Warsaw ghetto.

Justice Jackson, his voice alternately sarcastic and scornful, expressed the hope that the tribunal would visit the nearby Dachau concentration camp, where 40 other Nazis at present are on trial before a U.S. military court for war crimes.

Justice Jackson read a Hitlerian order that American and British fliers parachuting into Nazi territory were to be treated as criminals instead of prisoners of war. Goering and Keitel, still in uniform but shorn of their decorations, scribbled busily.

Justice Jackson told the court he had the German plan for invading Britain which started with the words:

"Although the British military position is so hopeless, they show not the slightest sign of giving in."

These plans, he said, as well as others for invading Russia in violation of a non-aggression pact, bore the initials of Keitel and Jodly.

At the prosecutor's order, a large chart was placed before the court showing where the Nazis had violated treaties. The prisoners studied it with evident interest.

Nuremberg, November 21, 1945

Kurt Meyer, an SS general, was the only war criminal sentenced by a Canadian court. He was sentenced to death, but this sentence was reduced to life imprisonment. He was released in 1954, and died in 1961, in West Germany. Frank Swanson covered the Meyer trial for the Southam newspapers.

Testimony that Maj. Gen. Kurt Meyer declared "these murderers only eat our rations" and thereupon ordered seven English prisoners immediately taken out and shot was given today at the war crimes trial of the S.S. divisional commander who is charged with responsibility for the murder of 48 Canadian prisoners of war.

The evidence for the prosecution was presented in the form of a statement made by Jan Jesionek, a Polish soldier who once served at Meyer's own headquarters.

The statement was read by the prosecution after a stream of Canadian soldiers appeared on the witness stand before the Canadian military tribunal to describe mass shootings of Canadian prisoners of war by the Germans during the early stages of the invasion of Normandy.

Meyer is charged with having issued orders to his S.S. troops stating that prisoners of war were not to be taken. Today's witnesses told how Canadian soldiers, captured during the bloody battle of Caen, were shot down by German troops as they were being marched under guard to concentration points.

Witness after witness outlined the grim story of helpless prisoners being mowed down on the roads and in the fields around Normandy villages of Authie and Buron.

As the trial went into its fourth day with the prosecution still presenting its case, Cpl. Walter McLeod, of Glace Bay, N.S., told how nine members of their regiment, the North Nova Scotia Highlanders, were cut

SS General Kurt Meyer was held responsible for the shooting of unarmed Canadian prisoners of war, and was condemned to death. When the sentence was reduced to life imprisonment, Canadian veterans protested bitterly.

---

down by German fire at close quarters near Authie, France.

McLeod and Conrad escaped the slaughter which took place after they had been taken prisoner along with Pte. Gus Doolan of Sydney, N.S., and nine others.

They told the Canadian military court trying Meyer that their group, guarded by German soldiers, was moving along a road east of Authie with their hands over their heads when German troops going into battle came out of a wheat field.

One of the Germans out in front pulled his pistol from its holster and shot at the group of prisoners when only 20 feet away. A wounded German also shot at the prisoners with his rifle and Conrad said a German guard seemed to be shooting at them too.

Of the group of 12, only McLeod, Conrad and Doolan moved on to the Abbey of Ardenne where prisoners were being concentrated.

"The other nine were shot down and they never moved," Conrad said.

Aurich, Germany, December 13, 1945

Frank Swanson sent this report from the war crimes trials. Twelve were sentenced to hang, including Martin Bormann, who was tried in absentia. Seven were given jail terms ranging from 10 years to life. Three were acquitted.

As the hour of their judgement approaches, most of the 21 Nazis in Nuremberg jail are showing increasing signs of mental strain and nervousness. This is unanimously the opinion of jail officers who have been on duty here since the trial started last November.

To offset this tendency the rigid jail discipline of the past ten months has been relaxed considerably. Now instead of being allowed one hour's exercise daily they are given four. They are allowed as well to consult defence counsel at any time rather than just once a day, and may see prison chaplains at any time as well. Chapel services are conducted for them nightly now rather than each Sunday as formerly.

Nearly all the prisoners are taking advantage of the chaplain's visits to spend long periods in spiritual discussions. Hess and one or two others are the sole exceptions to this practice.

According to prison officials, Goering continues to lose weight through worry. He is halved in bulk and quartered in arrogance and his clothes flop about him like a bell tent in a gale.

Streicher has altered so much he is virtually unrecognizable. Schirach, although looking none too well, continues to stand up better than most of his fellow inmates, reading assiduously and not paying much attention to the growing strain in the cell block.

Ribbentrop's eyes are even more sunken and are surrounded by darker rings than when the trial concluded. His guards say he looks more like movie actor Boris Karloff every day.

All are looking old, strained and haggard and are showing evidences of prolonged mental and physical suffering. The majority have been touched by the dull grey prison pallor so common to convicts.

Nuremberg, Germany, September 19, 1946

Ten hangings and a suicide marked the end of a black chapter of history.

Herman Goering — flamboyant to the end — cheated the hangman with a capsule of cyanide Tuesday night but ten other ringleaders of the punctured Nazi reich died at the end of a rope in the dark hours before dawn today in payment for their crimes against the world.

Goering, No 2 man of a Nazi regime intended by Adolf Hitler to last 1,000 years, twitched out his life in a prison cell only a few hours before his condemned henchmen plunged through the banging traps of two gallows in a grimy building thirty-five yards away.

The ten who died on the gallows — as directed by the International Military Tribunal which convicted them two weeks ago of war crimes, crimes against the peace and crimes against humanity — went to their deaths without collapsing and making "God save Germany" final declarations.

Joachim von Ribbentrop, Hitler's foreign minister, who replaced Goering as the first man to climb the thirteen steps to doom, dropped through the trap at 1:14 a.m. (5:14 p.m. Tuesday M.S.T.) One hour and 43 minutes later, when Arthur Seyss-Inquart, Nazi gauleiter of the Netherlands was pronounced dead, it was all over.

In the gymnasium, where only last Saturday guards had played a basketball game, stood three scaffolds, only two of which were used. Each scaffold had the customary thirteen steps to the top and each rope the customary thirteen coils.

The executions were carried out with machine-like precision. While one man hung from one gallows — his body concealed inside the structure of the scaffold — another man was brought in.

Every one of the ten men approached death bravely once he entered the room and saw the grim appurtenances of the hangmen. Some quailed and approached hysteria before they entered.

Each of the Nazis was given a chance to say a last word before they were executed.

Only Alfred Rosenberg, Nazi party philosopher, could find no word except a murmured "nein" to leave to history.

Ribbentrop said firmly: "God protect Germany. My last wish is that German unity should remain and that an understanding between east and west will come about and peace for the world."

Keitel and Jodl died as Prussian officers to the last, Keitel shouting "I follow my sons. All for Germany." Jodl cried "I salute my Germany."

Hans Frank, former governor general of Poland, muttered a barely audible thanks for the good treatment he had received as a prisoner and asked God to take him under his "good protection."

Wilhelm Frick, the Nazi "protector" for Bohemia and Moravia, was dressed in a gaudy sports jacket, the same one he wore during the ten months of the war crimes trial in the nearby courthouse. As he got his first glimpse of the gallows he cried out: "God bless Germany always."

Ernest Kaltenbrunner, chief of the Nazi security police, was so pale when he mounted the gallows that the scars on his cheeks shone out a blood red color. He declared:

"I loved my people and my country. I have done my duty toward my country at a difficult time and I have not participated in the crimes I am charged with."

All of the men were tied hand and foot as they made their last drop and each one was escorted to the gallows by a soldier at each elbow.

Where the bodies of the executed Germans were taken will remain a secret, Capt. Samuel Binder of the security police detail, declared emphatically.

Nuremberg, Germany, October 16, 1946

Many hopes that there would be no Third World War were riding on the United Nations, organized by the Allies when the end of the Second World War was in sight. H.H.C. "Torchy" Anderson, who six years before had reported Canada's decision to join the war, now wrote from San Francisco on the eve of the UN's formation.

The forty-niners came for the gold in the hills — hope was their grubstake; the nineteen-forty-fivers are here today, their well-tailored backs bent with the woes of a war-torn world — their hope, world peace.

About the time you are reading this dispatch, when the sun begins its dip towards the vastness of the Pacific, representatives of some 46 United Nations will gather in the gold and crimson San Francisco civic opera house to begin to prepare to lay the first foundation in what they all hope will be permanent world peace.

The thing to remember about the meeting is this: it is not a peace conference.

It is not a final gesture of a group of delegated magicians who can wave the wand of perfection over their deliberations.

It is the first step of a number of gentlemen in frock coats to bring about an agreement by which the world may look for a time when the papers will not be filled with casualty lists and San Francisco harbor won't be filled with the stern, crowded traffic of war.

Flags are still at half-mast here in memory of a great man, the man who called this conference, the man who designated this place facing the Pacific. Perhaps the late president knew the value of facing delegates with the problem of Asia. Here, under their very windows, they see the unbelievable movement towards the Pacific. Here the war against the Japs takes no second place. From here men have a more equal focus on Japan and Germany.

Behind the blare of the bands, the triumphal spirit of the ceremony this afternoon lies the stark, deadly fact of murdered civilians, of soldiers killed and maimed, of millions of ordinary people uprooted and homeless.

When the last nationalistic disagreement sinks to the bottom of the cocktail glass, the question of the departing marine in Oakland rises insistent: "Will my kid have to do this?"

San Francisco, April 25, 1945

Peace Walks a Tightrope

1947-60

The Fifties: cold war and rock 'n roll, Khrushchev and Eisenhower, John Diefenbaker and "Uncle Louis" St. Laurent, Ernest Manning and Ernest Manning again, Elvis Presley and James Dean, Suez and Hungary, the beginning of the Space Age and the beginning of the Television Age.

A world war had ended, and another seemed to be shaping up. There was a Berlin crisis in 1948, and another in 1958. It was a time of air-raid sirens, civil defence evacuation exercises, and fall-out shelters. Since no one can worry all the time, it was also the time of tail-fins on cars, Ed Sullivan on television, crewcuts or greased-down hair on boys, and crinoline skirts on girls.

For Alberta, the Fifties were the beginning of the Oil and Gas Age. The first oil well at Leduc, 25 kilometres south of Edmonton, started a boom that has now run for more than 30 years, transforming Alberta into something beyond the most grandiose dreams of its pioneers.

Leduc No. 1 blew in early in 1947. Calgary's oil business, based mainly on the dwindling reserves of the 33-year-old Turner Valley field, began to flourish again. The Leduc field was bigger than Turner Valley, and a new surge of exploration soon discovered fields even bigger than Leduc.

In 1947, Calgary was a quiet little city of about 100,000 people. Street-cars and horse-drawn milk wagons still contended with cars for space on the narrow streets. The main roads were paved, but some side-streets were still dirt, graded and oiled every year. The Palliser Hotel and the Robin Hood flour mill (where the Gulf Canada building now stands) loomed over the city skyline. Tuxedo Park, West Hillhurst, Elbow Park and Inglewood were at the edge of the city, with a few scattered houses beyond.

Even when the oil was found, the affluent society came slowly to Calgary. War-time shortages of houses, building materials, cars and even telephones continued into the first years of peace. Into the early Fifties, some Calgary families had to live in "temporary" housing in air force huts left over from the war.

However, a few luckier citizens were advertising for live-in maids for $50 to $60 a month. A teacher might make twice that. T-bone steak was 45 cents a pound back in 1947, but meat was still rationed. Movies still cost less than 50 cents, and you could see movies like The Third Man (1949) or The African Queen (1951) without staying up late or watching a lot of commercials. In 1947, songs called It's Almost Like Being In Love and Papa Won't You Dance With Me sold a lot of 78-rpm records. The LP record wasn't invented until 1948. Speaking of inventions, the transistor was invented in 1947, but hardly anyone noticed at the time.

Lester Pearson, left, receives a Nobel Peace Prize from Gunnar Jahn of the Norwegian Nobel Committee. Pearson proposed the first UN peacekeeping force which supervised a Middle East cease-fire.

By the end of 1960, Calgary had grown to nearly 250,000 people, most of them housed in new suburbs stretching out to Thorncliffe, Haysboro, and Westgate. New buildings, some of them eight or ten storeys high, dotted the city centre. Elveden House at 20 storeys, and the AGT microwave tower, bringing network television to Calgary, now dominated the skyline. The Herald was squeezing more than 75,000 copies a day from a creaky, obsolete plant. The paper still cost only a nickel.

The first suburban shopping centres were open. T-bone steak now cost about 80 cents a pound, but a teacher might average $400 or $500 a month. Anyone who didn't want to stay home and watch television could see Psycho or Saturday Night And Sunday Morning, but the provincial movie censors wouldn't let anyone look at Brigitte Bardot. Elvis Presley was already a star, and his 1956 hits, Blue Suede Shoes, Hound Dog, and Don't Be Cruel were getting to be golden oldies.

After the lean years of the depression and the war, Calgary finally did get some things it had long needed. The Jubilee Auditorium, a gift of the provincial government, made a place for music and drama, which had held forth in highschool gymnasiums and the Stampede Corral. McMahon Stadium gave the Calgary Stampeders a decent place to play, though they did well enough in 1948, winning the Grey Cup after a season of home games in Mewata Stadium. Street-cars were replaced with buses. The 14th Street bridge and the 4th Street underpass were built. It was pleasant, after so long, to have money again. The provincial government even had enough money to pay a $20 a year "dividend" for a couple of years to Alberta citizens. It wasn't exactly the $25 a month William Aberhart had promised in the Thirties, but it was nice to have.

Alberta's Social Credit government ruled serenely through the Fifties, as it had through the Forties and would through the Sixties. Premier Ernest Manning had a mild setback in 1955, when he was reduced to 37 of 65 seats in the Legislature while the Liberals won 15. (The Herald played some part in reducing the Social Credit majority.) However, Manning came back handsomely in 1959, winning 61 seats.

In 1947, the death of R.B. Bennett, the Calgary lawyer who became prime minister of Canada, severed one more link with the city's older days. The following year, Liberal Prime Minister William Lyon Mackenzie King, Canada's most durable politician, retired and was succeeded by Louis St. Laurent. In 1949, Newfoundland became the 10th province in Confederation. Elizabeth II was crowned Queen in 1953, and the first men stood on top of Mount Everest.

In Canadian politics, the pivotal event of the Fifties was the pipeline debate of 1956. The pipeline in question was the TransCanada, which would carry Alberta's new-found reserves of natural gas to Eastern markets; the issue was who would finance it, and who would benefit. The Liberal government used closure to limit debate in the House of Commons, and the storm of protest that followed this move helped to sweep Conservative leader John Diefenbaker into power in 1957. He won a minority, and in 1958 went back to the polls to defeat the new Liberal leader, Lester Pearson, by the largest majority in Canadian history.

In the United States, Harry S. Truman, who had taken

over as president when Franklin D. Roosevelt died, won a term of his own in 1948. Then, in 1952, Dwight D. Eisenhower, the general who had directed the Allied liberation of Europe, was elected president, and re-elected in 1956. His vice-president was Richard M. Nixon, of whom we will hear more.

The Fifties were the time of Cold War. The Second World War, and the coups that followed, had re-drawn the map of Europe, with the eastern half under Communist rule. George Orwell's classic novel 1984, published in 1949, crystallized many people's fears of the future.

Again and again, events provided new grounds for fear of a world-conquering Communist movement. In 1949, Mao Tse-tung's Communists established a government in China, and in the same year the Soviet Union exploded its first atomic bomb. Igor Gouzenko's defection from the Soviet embassy in Ottawa in 1946 had triggered a hunt for Soviet spies, and many were found. Klaus Fuchs, Alan Nunn May, Julius and Ethel Rosenberg were among the spies blamed for speeding the Soviet Union's development of nuclear weapons. In 1950, Communist troops from North Korea invaded South Korea; later Chinese troops would join the war against United Nations forces defending the South. The death of Josef Stalin in 1953 brought only brief encouragement, if any. In 1954, the French lost Vietnam; the one-time French colony was divided into a Communist North and a (temporarily) independent South. In 1956, the Hungarian people rebelled against their Communist government, and the Soviet Union sent in troops to crush the revolt. In 1957, the Soviet Union launched Sputnik, the first artificial earth satellite. The space age had begun, but so had the age of the intercontinental ballistic missile.

In the United States, especially, fear of international Communism spurred a search for Red subversives at home. In the early Fifties the American Senator Joseph McCarthy became the most famous of these Communist-hunters, but he wasn't the first, or the last. The question about all of them was whether they damaged Communism as much as they did democracy. (The Herald, no friend of Communism, had no good words for McCarthy, either.)

Meanwhile, new nations were being born. India and Pakistan emerged from some 200 years of British colonial rule. Later, new African states, among them Ghana and Nigeria, were created from former colonies. Not yet called the Third World, these new nations and others that followed were to become a new force in world politics.

Israel was created in 1948 when the British withdrew from Palestine, which had already been partitioned into Arab and Jewish states by the United Nations. Jordan and Egypt immediately invaded, and seven months of war followed. Fighting broke out again in 1956, over Egypt's seizing the Suez Canal. Britain, France and Israel invaded Egypt. International pressure forced them to withdraw, and Canada was largely responsible for the creation of the first United Nations peacekeeping force, which supervised the cease-fire. Lester B. Pearson, the Canadian architect of the UN peace force, won the Nobel Peace Prize.

Like every decade, the Fifties ended leaving a great deal of unfinished business. If an event can be singled out to mark the end of this era, perhaps the best choice would be the election, in November, 1960, of the first American president born in this century, John F. Kennedy.

Soviet tanks roll into Budapest to suppress the Hungarian uprising of 1956.

Calgary in the Fifties

Locally, the news of the Fifties included the usual ration of fires, floods, crimes, and oddities. There was also a new, continuing, story: the story of a city trying to cope with rapid growth and sudden prosperity. Calgarians marvelled, a little nervously, at the new, hard-driving pace of their town. They watched new buildings spring up, and wondered how the owners would ever find enough tenants. (Many of these buildings have since been torn down to make way for bigger buildings.) Until prosperity really took hold, Calgary—and Alberta—were in some ways astonishingly backward. In 1947 Herald reporter David Stansfield wrote a series of articles on Alberta's child-welfare laws. This series, and a parallel investigation by Charlotte Whitton for the Imperial Order of Daughters of the Empire, led to a royal commission which examined the problem. In the following story, Stansfield described the treatment of Alex Walters (not his real name) who had run away from several foster homes.

Let us see if we cannot convey a more complete picture of life in a juvenile detention home by considering what sort of a life young Alex Walters led during his six weeks' confinement in the South Side Jail in Edmonton this winter.

Alex, 11, lived in a four-by-six cell made of broad strap-iron. It was furnished with two flat sheet metal bunks and nothing else. He shared the use of a dirty old toilet—right out in the open—with whatever other boys happened to be in the place at the same time. He had the use of a basin and a shower—also right out in the open. His meals were served to him on a bare wooden table outside his cage.

Presumably he was well-fed—somebody raised a fuss a few years ago, and now meals are brought into the South Side Jail from a nearby cafe. Presumably he slept well—as well as a child can sleep on a hard sheet-metal shelf with one or two dirty blankets as bedding.

Perhaps he had some fresh air and exercise: the constable on duty when The Herald visited the jail said something vague about exercise and pointed to an open space between the jail and the South Side fire hall; the children in the jail at that time said they were never let out of their cages except for meals and to wash and go to the toilet, and then only into the outer barred room of their prison.

Perhaps he wasn't mistreated; again The Herald doesn't know for sure. An entirely trustworthy informant, who used to be connected with child welfare work in Edmonton a couple of years ago, said that children in the South Side Jail used to be beaten with a large rubber strap for misdemeanors at that time, and that he had personally seen children with their bodies black and blue from beatings.

Whether that practice is still followed we don't know. The children in the jail on May 10 said that Alex Walters had been strapped,

but of course they aren't reliable witnesses.

Physically, Alex may not have been looked after too badly. Educationally, of course, his weeks in prison were a dead loss. No attempt is made to give the children any schoolwork. And that, incidentally, would appear to be an infringement of the province's School Attendance Act—unless being left indefinitely in jail can be considered as an "unavoidable cause" of absence from school under the terms of the act.

For Alex's spiritual welfare, there was a Sunday school teacher in to see him once a week. While one must admire the fortitude of a Sunday school teacher who would venture into such a place, one cannot help wondering what good a children's Sunday school lesson would do a hardened jailbird like Alex.

This is briefly what The Herald has been able to find out about Alex Walters' life in the South Side Jail. It's pretty sketchy. A lot of questions remain unanswered. Isn't it about time the people of Alberta called for a Royal Commission to get the answers to some of these questions?

May 23, 1947

This is one of the more bizarre crimes in Calgary's history, and it remains a puzzle.

City police today are continuing their investigations into the alleged 19-year-old murder of a man of 66 years, missing since March, 1929, whose body was found Saturday evening buried under the floor of a small frame cottage at 1805 20th Ave. N.W.

The body was believed by police to be that of Thomas C. Hall, teamster, who was living alone in the house in March, 1929, and disappeared. There was no police record of his death or of his ever having been reported missing. A newspaper clipping supposed to record his death in an automobile accident in North Dakota in 1930 was being sought.

The body was found about 8 p.m. by Alfred Cecil Pearce who, with his wife and three children, moved into the house that day on return to Calgary from Port Alberni, B.C., where they had been living for the last few months.

While in one of the bedrooms, Mr. Pearce found the floor weak. Returning to the kitchen, he went down into a small dugout cellar and, looking through beneath the bedroom floor, saw two sections of joists had been removed.

He went back to the bedroom, tore up part of the floor and discovered the corpse, lying partly buried in ashes beneath the floor.

The body was of a man of about 66 years of age, wearing a leather jacket, work pants, wool socks and no shoes. His skull was well

preserved and one large jagged hole was visible in his left temple. An envelope was lying beside his arm.

The envelope which was found beside the dead man was addressed to T.C. Hall and the return address was Fred C. Hall, R.R. No. 2, High River, Alta. The postmark was High River, March 6, 1929.

Mr. and Mrs. Pearce were very upset by the incident and refused to stay in the house. Mr. Pearce told The Herald he wanted to get his money back for the place, which he had only purchased two days ago.

Mrs. Pearce said she was afraid of "ghosts" and the children related a tale of a mysterious clammy hand poking one of them prior to the corpse being discovered. They packed up the remainder of the clothing and furniture Sunday and went to stay with friends.

Police investigations indicated that the deceased was likely Thomas C. Hall, who lived in the house from 1924-29 and had not been seen after the month of March, 1929.

Thomas Hall was about 66 years old at the time he disappeared and was separated from his wife—his second—at the time. He worked as a teamster.

July 12, 1948

In the following story the word "gay" is used presumably, in its older sense.

The diary of a "Gay Lothario" in which is listed his romantic conquests over a period of seven years, is in possession of city police after being found on a local street.

Listing the names and addresses of various "lady loves," the diary, neatly and carefully hand-printed, details the pleasures of the company of various women the romantic male has known in Calgary and other centres between 1943 and the present.

The owner may recover his diary by calling at police headquarters and identifying his diary.

October 14, 1950

The man, perhaps predictably, was resourceful.

Calgary's "Gay Lothario" who listed in a diary his romantic experiences over a period of seven years, giving the names and addresses of his "lady loves," is anxious that record be destroyed.

Saturday afternoon two little boys handed police an envelope which, they said, had been given to them by a man who asked them to deliver it at headquarters.

The enclosed note read: "Sirs, Reference diary mentioned in Calgary Herald this afternoon (1st page, 2nd section). Would you kindly destroy these papers as I have no wish to claim them—and naturally suffer very much embarrassment. Sincerely."

The note was not signed but police are certain of its authenticity. It is printed in the same neat manner as the extremely revealing diary.

Police plan to follow the man's request.

October 16, 1950

Winter floods were common in Calgary until the Bearspaw Dam and dredging of the Bow Channel brought the river under control. This flood caused more trouble than most.

Almost 3,000 Calgarians were homeless today and many thousand dollars' damage was caused in the wake of a sudden Bow River flood which swept a wide area in the centre of the city Friday night and early this morning.

Friday at midnight police estimated about 1,200 people had been forced from their homes. This morning city officials, police and firemen estimated the figure at closer to 3,000 flood victims.

Waters of the Bow River, backed up behind an ice jam, Friday night poured through streets and avenues on both sides of the river from Centre St. on the south bank and east of 4th St. N.E. on the north bank.

Despite flood warnings for the past several days and constant patrols by police in the threatened area, the river rose so swiftly that few persons had a chance to flee from their homes before the current started sweeping around buildings at 10:15 p.m.

Twenty below zero weather and slippery footing under the swift and treacherous currents, which swept down streets and avenues, made rescue efforts difficult and boats, tractors and trucks were pressed into service to evacuate persons from threatened homes.

A survey of the area indicated that approximately 435 dwellings, four apartment blocks containing 77 suites, the Cecil hotel and some 40 business premises were in the flooded area.

Many police officers and firemen suffered from frost bitten feet as they ploughed through deep water to rescue householders. A number of firemen whose feet were chilled when icy waters flowed into their waders filled the boots with hot water to keep their feet warm.

So swift was the current at 6th Ave. and 4th St. E., several blocks south of the river, that four policemen pushing a boat loaded with women evacuees almost lost it at about 2:45 a.m. when the flow of water forced the boat down an alley. A tractor pulled the boat and its cargo to safety.

On the north side of the river five men jumped into the current to rescue another boatload of persons when the craft was carried towards the river channel by the swift-moving waters.

East of 4th St. N.E., an area of 16 blocks was under flood waters which in places reached a depth of more than four feet. In this area which reached as far east as 7A St.

The dream car of the Fifties had a long, low look, tail-fins, lots of chrome, push-button automatic transmission, and a big V-8 engine. People laughed at the Volkswagen Beetle, but it outlasted the DeSoto.

N.E., more than 167 households were threatened by the rising waters and the ground floors of five business premises were flooded.

The scene in this area was one of desolation. A few street lights still shone through the eerie grey mist which rose from the city water and here and there house lights flickered. On the streets cars and trucks stood with water and ice floes as high as their fenders.

Adam Stuckert, 737 McDougall Road, testified to the rapidity with which the flood waters had risen. While listening to the 10 p.m. news broadcast he had heard of the rising waters. Going to his front door he looked out and saw a thin trickle of water coming down the street.

By the time he had gone back into the house, put on a pair of shoes, a sweater and a coat it was too late and he had to wait and be rescued by boat.

One fireman carried a small boy to safety and then the child cried at losing his puppy. The fireman went back into the house and saw the dog swimming about the basement.

"When I picked him up he licked my face," the fireman said. "I guess he was never so glad to see anyone before. He was frozen almost solid," the fireman said.

Police who went to one house on 6th Ave. E. found a man sleeping soundly in a second storey bedroom while water lapped at the front door of the home.

When awakened he looked at his watch and drowsily told the officer "Let me sleep. It's still an hour until I have to go to work."

"Okay," the policeman replied, "but I don't know how you're going to get out. The water is already coming in your front door."

"Wait! Wait!" the householder implored.

Officers reported that the sleeper set a new record for getting dressed hurriedly.

December 2, 1950

The good old days.

A "progressive party" is a fine thing, but it's not for the mailman or milk or bread delivery men. At least not while they're on duty.

And a progressive party is just about what some of the delivery men are up against at this time of year. Scotch at one house. Rum at the next, then some wine, and perhaps a small shot of gin at another.

As company officials are quick to point out, no man could be expected to do his best work under such circumstances. So, they urge Mr. and Mrs. Calgary, please don't offer the breadman, milkman or postman a drink.

All agree that hot coffee, tea or cocoa would be gratefully accepted by the men, particularly if the weather is bad.

It is also permissible to present any of the men with a cash gratuity or a small present as thanks for good service if the house owner wants to do this. But no drinks.

Postmaster Robert Stephen said his men had a tough job on their hands and the plea of "just a quick one" could sabotage the whole effort.

December 19, 1951

The Real Oil Boom Begins

"An oil well of the highest order," Leduc No. 1, came in quietly on a February afternoon in 1947. It wasn't greeted with the near-hysteria that followed the Turner Valley discovery in 1914, but the Leduc well marked Alberta's real entry into the petroleum era. In the quarter-century since Leduc No. 1, oil has transformed Alberta's economy, its major cities — and its relations with Ottawa. C.V. Myers, The Herald's oil editor, wrote this report on the well that began Alberta's real oil boom.

Imperial Leduc No. 1, 18 miles southwest of Edmonton is performing with high promise, after kicking off at 4 p.m. Thursday, and is now entitled to be called an oil well, probably an oil well of the highest order.

The well made its debut in somewhat spectacular fashion, snorting and puffing with great bursts of gas and watery oil. They put a flame to the pipe then and the flame rose 30 feet in the air as the well belched only black smoke. With professional perfection it blew a dense black ring in a perfect circle, a ring 30 feet in diameter which rose 50 feet in the air and hung there for several minutes, as the monster puffed and heaved, struggling for breath.

It seemed for a time like the newborn oil well must expire as the flare died to a flicker and for almost an hour the life went weak and the flame went out. Five hundred shivering spectators climbed into their cars and drove away across the frigid plain, blanketed deep in snow.

When all but a few stragglers had left, the new well snorted again. It belched and then roared as the gas burst out and the flare shot skyward almost to a level with the hundred foot derrick. It was an oil well and no one doubted it.

Imperial officials are still reluctant to say too much about their new well, but anyone could see them working hard at efforts of restraint.

The fact is Imperial has found an oil field at last, after 19 years of effort and after an expenditure of $17,000,000. Since 1939 the company has spent in excess of $13,000,000, according to figures released today.

In the last 10 years Imperial has drilled 114 wildcat wells and has done almost half the total of all geological work carried out in Western Canada. It took that to hit the jack-pot — if this is the jack-pot — as indeed it appears to be.

Veteran Turner Valley oil men say this well compares with crude oil wells in that remarkable field.

Walker Taylor, Imperial's western manager, stressed the need for oil in Canada, a country which produces only 11 per cent of its consumption. He especially stressed the need for oil on the prairies, where high freight costs boost the cost of gasoline. He said that new

fields were not being found in the States fast enough to keep up with the rate of depletion. As a result we have had to take the crumbs, whatever type of oil we could get and be thankful for that.

Leduc, February 14, 1947

Sightseers from Edmonton flocked to Leduc No. 1 in February, 1947.

Development at Leduc went full speed, and even a year later the companies had not found the edges of the oil-producing zone. C.V. Myers wrote this anniversary story.

One year ago today Imperial Oil Ltd. struck pay dirt in its Imperial Leduc No. 1. All indications were that a new oil field had been discovered. Today the most optimistic predictions of a year ago stand justified.

An area of 8,100 acres has been proved up as oil land. Today 41 wells are pouring out rich liquid into tanks, stemming the tide of U.S. imports and halting the flow of U.S. dollars southward. Imperial has completed 29 producers and has still to strike its first failure. Independents have completed twelve producers. Imperial, with another 14 wells located, is going full steam ahead.

While more and more wells swell the Leduc field Imperial is rushing work on a 4,000 to 6,000 barrel-a-day refinery in Edmonton, 20 miles away. The plant is being removed from Whitehorse, Yukon.

Meanwhile, Leduc's yield of 5,000 barrels a day is coming south to Calgary.

The development at Leduc in one year has been phenomenal. Already more than half a million barrels of oil have been produced. Turner Valley in its history has produced nearly 90,000,000 barrels, but Imperial estimates of Leduc make it just as large. Calculated recoverable reserves are 100,000,000 barrels.

February 13, 1948

A Herald editorial pointed out that agriculture was still — in 1952 — Alberta's main source of wealth. Even so, the figures for oil income were impressive.

Mention the word "Alberta" and most people, including Albertans, immediately start thinking about oil. Much of the present boom in this province does, of course, derive from oil and the business activity which oil has stimulated. But some figures released this week by the provincial government are a warning to us not to lose our sense of proportion.

In 1951, the total value of petroleum production in Alberta was $116,000,000 and of natural gas about $4,000,000 making $120,000,000 from the two closely-related industries. This is undoubtedly a lot of money, representing about $120 in new wealth for every man, woman and child in the province. And since oil provided the provincial government with around 30 per cent of its total revenues last year, oil has a decided bearing on the problem of keeping provincial taxes down.

Big as oil is, however, it is still dwarfed by Alberta's agriculture enterprises. The value of wheat production alone was nearly double the value of petroleum and natural gas at $225,000,000.

Altogether, agricultural production in Alberta last year (including dairy products, honey, poultry, wool and furs) amounted to $767,323,000. This is not only much bigger than the value of our oil production; it is more than six times as big.

For the time being, at any rate, the foundations of our prosperity are on the land and not underneath it. In many ways, this is comforting; for with wise crop policies and intelligent conservation, the land will go on delivering up its treasure year after year, whereas when you take a barrel of oil or a ton of coal out of the ground it is gone forever.

June 28, 1952

Fred Kennedy described the feat of an Indian girl who deserves at least a footnote in the annals of feminism.

There was no joy in the One Spot family tepee at the Indian camp grounds at Victoria Park Friday night. Eleven-year-old Linder (Linda) One Spot was not only bucked off in the boys wild steer riding event, but she had a headache.

A month ago the 11-year-old daughter of Councillor Eddie One Spot of the Sarcees decided she wanted to compete in the boys steer riding at the Stampede. This event is exclusively for the boys so Linda changed her name to Linder and entered the event.

She practised hard and when the big day came, Linda or Linder was at the chutes all decked up like a real cowboy and with her thick black hair tucked up beneath her big rust-brown cowboy hat.

But right at the outset, Linder, or is it Linda, found the going tough. Try as she might, she couldn't stay aboard the pesky little critters to earn a qualified ride.

But she made progress. On the first steer she survived three jumps and on the second she survived five. Friday was the big day. The whole thing was a secret, until the story appeared in The Herald Friday, and that afternoon every photographer on the grounds was ready and waiting when Linder, or is it Linda, climbed over the chute gate and settled abroad her critter.

"Turn me out, men" yelled Linda as she pulled her hat down over her eyes and spat out her wad of gum.

The chute gates yawned open and out came Linder. For five jumps she rode the critter, but on the sixth she went out the front door and in passing the steer clipped her on the side of the head, knocking off her hat and displaying her profusion of hair topped by two bright blue bows of ribbon.

For several seconds Linder lay on the ground, half dazed and completely mortified. She was so sure that she was going to be able to ride that steer.

With tears streaming down her face she was assisted to the first aid post where it was soon found that she had escaped injury.

Will she try again next year?

Linda doesn't know, but the officials do—the event is exclusively for boys, and girls are banned from competition.

July 12, 1952

This editorial has stood the test of time: it could be printed in today's newspaper and be just as true.

We are becoming confirmed in the belief that citizens of Calgary either lead charmed lives or are sensationally agile. There is no other way to explain why there is not at least one traffic fatality every day, for without a doubt this city harbors more dimwitted dolts who are permitted to drive cars than any other city on the North American continent.

If these mentally retarded individuals

The Duke and Duchess of Windsor at Banff. They occasionally visited the duke's beloved EP Ranch near Calgary, but the duchess never shared his enthusiasm for the place. He had bought the ranch in 1919 when he was Prince of Wales. (He became King Edward VIII, but abdicated to marry in 1938.) He sold the ranch in 1961. He died in 1972 in Paris.

were merely of suicidal bent, and there was no more at stake than the lives which they themselves seem to value so lightly, perhaps it would not matter too much.

If their only wish is, as it seems to be, to smear themselves and their cars over some handy bit of landscape, then most of us would not deny them fulfillment of their maniacal whim.

However, the situation is not that simple. There are people in Calgary, perhaps the majority, who have a keen interest in living out their natural lives, and in seeing their children permitted to grow up alive and unmaimed.

They have a feeling, which frequently amounts to fury, that they should be allowed to do this without the necessity of leaping for their lives out of the paths of monstrous engines of death piloted by feckless jackasses every time they are required to venture forth into the streets.

May 16, 1953

Herald reporter Doug Collins worked for British intelligence services for eight years during and after the Second World War. When Reader's Digest published the story of a Calgarian's supposed exploits as a secret agent, Collins grew suspicious. The resulting story won him a special citation in Canada's National Newspaper Awards, and honorable mention in the Heywood Broun competition in the United States.

The story of George DuPre, as related in the November issue of Reader's Digest, is a fiction.

Millions of people in every country in which the Digest is published will have been taken in by a tale of "The Canadian Who Wouldn't Talk," according to which DuPre worked in France for British Intelligence during the Second Great War and suffered torture at the hands of the Gestapo rather than disclose the secrets of the net of which he was a member.

The truth is that George DuPre was

never in France during the war and never had any connection with Special Operations Executive, the organization which directed all British clandestine activities on the European continent. He was forced to admit this Thursday to a Herald reporter.

The story of DuPre, as told by Quentin Reynolds (a book has been, or is to be published, under the title of "The Man Who Wouldn't Talk") is far removed from the facts of technical operations as conducted by S.O.E.

Briefly, the Digest article implies that DuPre was in France for four years — from 1940 to 1944 — and that during that time he worked in a village (name not disclosed) near the vicinity of St. Lo. Normandy, as a member of the French Resistance, masquerading all the while as an idiot. He was dropped by a Lysander aircraft within 100 paces or so of the farm in which he was to make his first contact with the resistance group, and was briefed to work specifically on the rescue of Allied fliers who had been shot down. He was to work in a service station, and was to assist in sabotage work. He remained in the same village for the whole four years, the article said.

There are so many holes in this that it is hard to imagine DuPre expecting to get away with it.

Here Collins described how DuPre's story contradicted the policy and standard practices of the Special Operations Executive.

DuPre was Thursday interviewed by The Herald "in connection with the publication of the book by Mr. Reynolds." The interview went like this:

REPORTER: "I myself was connected with Intelligence once and may have come across you some time. Which section of S.O.E. were you with? A, B, or C?"

DuPRE: (unhesitantly) "B Section."

REPORTER: "Oh. Then you must have known dear old Col. Kitchingham, who was in charge of that lot at that time."

DuPRE: "Yes, indeed. I knew him well."

REPORTER: "He was a grand old chap, wasn't he? Was an agent himself in the first war, and would never send a chap on a mission he wouldn't have fancied himself."

DuPRE: "That's right."

REPORTER: "And of course you must have known that silly old fool John Cooke, who was liaison between S.O.E. and the R.A.F.?"

DuPRE: "Certainly. What a character he was."

REPORTER: "I suppose you did your paradropping course at the school in Wimborne, Dorset?"

DuPRE: "That's right."

REPORTER: "Those instructors were rotten so-and-so's, weren't they? They never knew what the chaps were in for and always put them through a rough time."

DuPRE: "Yes. I certainly lost a few pounds there myself."

All of this was fine. Except that the reporter had never heard of anyone called Kitchingham, or Cooke, and the parachute training for S.O.E. was not carried out at Wimborne. Neither was there an A, a B or a C section.

In short, DuPre was unable to explain any of the administrative or technical details with which he must necessarily have been acquainted had he in fact ever been an agent in France. He did "confirm" during the interview, that he had been in France four years and this has also been stated in Canadian Press reports.

There is, however, more direct evidence of his duplicity than the largely circumstantial. There are in Alberta three ex-R.C.A.F officers who are prepared to swear affidavits to the effect that they joined up with DuPre. The date? May 15, 1942. Clearly then he could not have been in France at that date.

Further, The Herald was able to obtain from two of these officers photographs of DuPre which were taken in Victoria in June, 1942, one of which was signed by DuPre. Just to make sure that by some mysterious juxtaposition of bodies DuPre was not DuPre but some twin brother; he was asked at the beginning of the interview to provide the reporter with a signed copy of Readers' Digest. The signature is exactly similar to the one on the picture.

DuPre was at first not inclined to admit that his story was fictitious, but eventually did so when it became evident that he knew nothing of Intelligence work and that documentary evidence was at hand to show that he had been in Canada when, according to Reader's Digest, he was in France.

DuPre, asked why he had allowed things to get so far, said he really didn't know, but that things had "grown" since he first started spreading his fiction back in 1946. This original idea, he declared, had been for Mr. Reynolds to write a novel on the basis of his (DuPre's) alleged experiences, but that this had been changed when Mr. Reynolds had heard the full "facts."

DuPre's most oft-repeated sentence when in the hands of the Gestapo was, according to the Digest article, "Je ne sais pas. . . Je ne sais pas."

Asked today by The Herald whether he had any statement to make before the paper went to press, Mr. DuPre said: "Nothing. Except that I have been advised that my story is not a true story."

November 13, 1953

Under the heading "Why we dropped Dick Tracy," publisher Basil Dean explained the disappearance of one of the Herald's more popular comic strips — if "comic" is the word.

Y ou will not find Dick Tracy on our comic page today. This strip has been dropped from the columns of The Calgary Herald.

We have reached this conclusion because in the unanimous opinion of my associates and myself, the creator of Dick Tracy has, on numerous occasions in recent months, overstepped the bounds of good taste by which every reputable newspaper tries to govern itself.

We in this office do not take a namby-pamby view of life or of our responsibilities in the day-to-day conduct of the newspaper. We think a great deal of the talk about crime comics is exaggerated and the agitation for censorship a threat to an important freedom. But at the same time the Dick Tracy strip, on occasion, contains horror sequences which we would rather not have in the paper.

What finally persuaded us was a recent episode in which the current villain, "Rughead", shoved a gun into another man's mouth, and another one in which a man on his deathbed was drilled between the eyes by a revolver bullet. This sort of thing seems like brutality for its own sake.

February 21, 1955

The Dick Tracy comic strip wasn't always this startling. However, during the outcry about crime comics in the Fifties, The Herald felt obliged to cancel the strip.

Before vaccine was developed, polio threatened everyone, especially children, with paralysis or death. There was an annual outbreak of the disease, peaking in summer and tapering off in the fall. Stories like this one were not unusual.

Calgary's third poliomyelitis death in the current outbreak occurred Monday night and three new cases were reported in the city.

Vernon H. Silver, a 31-year-old flying officer from R.C.A.F. Station Claresholm died Monday night in Col. Belcher hospital.

The three new cases admitted to the city Isolation hospital during the night included a 12-year-old boy, nine-year-old boy and a six-year-old girl.

The new cases brought the total number of reported in Calgary and district to date to 61. Of the total 39 were Calgarians and 22 have been from points surrounding the city.

In an effort to check the spread of the disease city health authorities have asked for the closing of all summer camps and the cancellation of all picnics and other unnecessary gatherings of children for the remainder of the polio season.

Children under 16 years old will not be permitted to attend the Clyde Beatty circus scheduled to play here Wednesday and Thursday. Circus officials have agreed to cooperate with the city health department by refusing admission to children under 16 years old.

A charge that provincial government negligence in failing to provide for garbage collection in Montgomery may be responsible for the polio outbreak in that district was made Monday night by a Montgomery school trustee at a political meeting in Bowness.

Dr. L.C. Allan, assistant Calgary medical officer of health, told The Herald this morning that as far as medical authorities knew, there was no direct relation between the sanitary facilities of a community and the polio incidence.

August 5, 1952

In 1954 Salk polio vaccine was tested across North America. To avoid any chance of bias in the tests, half the children were given a neutral injection, and half got real vaccine. In 1955, the good news came; the Salk vaccine was safe and effective.

In Calgary, the Salk anti-poliomyelitis vaccine proved 100 per cent effective, Dr. L.C. Allan assistant city medical health officer said today.

Only one child of more than 2,500 taking part in the 1954 Salk tests contracted polio, and this child received the neutral solution, not the vaccine.

The lone victim is a nine-year-old girl, who is still in the Alberta Red Cross Crippled Children's Hospital.

One other Alberta child taking part in the test also had polio last year, but provincial health authorities have not revealed whether this child received the vaccine or the neutral solution.

Three National Newspaper Award winners from Herald photographers. Jack DeLorme's shot of Calgary firemen rescuing a child (top) won in 1949. Harry Befus won the 1952 prize for a picture of a Stampede wild-horse race. Jerry Ormond's photo of a chuckwagon spill at the Stampede (bottom) was the best news picture of 1957. Befus later become The Herald's photo editor.

Inoculation of more than 5,000 city school children with the Salk poliomyelitis vaccine will start Thursday morning in the city schools barring unforeseen snags.

Dr. L.C. Allan, assistant city health officer, said the code used in the 1954 Salk tests was received by his department Thursday afternoon and is being broken down today.

The breakdown of the code will indicate which children received the vaccine in the 1954 tests and which received the neutral solution.

Children who received the neutral solution last year will be among those receiving the vaccine this year.

At the end of the program scheduled to start next week about 8,000 city school children will have been inoculated with the Salk vaccine.

The groups will include most Grade I's; most in Grade II and the pupils in Grade III and IV this year who were "polio pioneers" last year.

No child will be given the vaccine without consent of parents or guardians.

Dr. Allan said there is virtually no reaction resulting from inoculation with the vaccine. Only in rare instances does a child feel even slightly upset after being inoculated.

April 15, 1955

This story by Denny Layzell of The Herald brought almost immediate results. Two weeks after it appeared, policy was changed so that the mentally ill could be held at the General Hospital.

Scenes which sicken veteran police officers and even hardened criminals are to be found in Calgary almost daily as men and women suffering from mental illness are held in city police cells like common criminals.

For years treatment of the mentally ill against whom warrants have been issued under the Mental Diseases Act has aroused the ire of police officers who regard as "inhuman" the manner in which these persons are handled.

When a warrant under the act is issued it must be served by police and while the officers are sympathetic they have no recourse but to book and lodge the mentally ill in the cell block.

They point out the mentally ill are lodged in separate cells and under constant surveillance but this in no way alters the fact those suspected of insanity are behind bars.

Mentally ill persons are often taken from the psychiatric ward in the General Hospital and lodged in the cells until evidence is produced as to whether or not the patient should be committed to a mental institution.

Many of the men and women held pending a hearing under the provisions of the Mental Diseases Act are aged and have never seen police cells before.

In the women's cell block, they are in a close proximity on numerous occasions, to prostitutes, many of whom are being held as venereal disease suspects, female drunkards and criminals of various types.

In the men's cells, the situation is even more pronounced as there are invariably more male than female prisoners, many of extremely low type including inebriates, perverts and unclean vagrants.

Police say that in many cases the mental patient's condition worsens the moment he or she is placed behind bars.

"If they are not completely mental when they are brought in they usually are before they get out," one officer stated.

Calgary's magistrates and court officials are most sympathetic to the mentally ill and have stated that if arrangements could be made to have the patients held in the psychiatric ward at the General Hospital all officials concerned would be willing to hold court hearings of the cases there.

It is believed that this would do much to ease the mental stress of patients.

Everyone with knowledge of the situation is certain that a change should be made, but as one prominent psychiatrist stated, "the city and the province are equally to blame and it is up to them to change the regulations regarding handling of mental suspects."

February 25, 1957

Bob Shiels wrote a six-part series for The Herald describing Calgary as it saw itself in 1957. Here is an excerpt.

A young lady stopped the conversation the other day. "I love Calgary," she said. "But it gives me indigestion."

The young lady bit her fingernails. The pace here, she explained is too hectic. It could get you down — if you didn't love the place.

Mulling it over later in the day, the boys in the pub (average tenure three hours) agreed that theirs was a frantic existence in the Foothills City.

An old-timer explained it this way:

"Thirty years ago, if I was in a hurry, I would avoid the main streets. I knew too many people and I wasted too much time talking to them. There was that intimacy of association.

"Calgary's structures, ideals and objectives have changed.

"This is no longer a small big town. There is the rush and bustle of big business. It's become a professional operation."

The old-timer believed we in Calgary have lost our intimacy of association. In the hurrying throngs there are fewer whom you see and recognize.

"It brings a great strangeness for those who have lived here some time," he said.

The new Calgary has developed with breathtaking speed. Pedestrians still avoid the main streets, where possible, but only to prevent being pushed off into the gutter.

Calgary, rightly or wrongly, is known as a high-living, free-spending city where telephones jangle, horns honk, money is spent and big decisions are made to a greater extent and on a larger scale than in most other cities, particularly on the prairies. Accurate statistics on sales of the new tranquilizer drugs are not immediately available.

Calgary, on the other hand, is a home-owning community. It is estimated there are 25,000 owner-occupied dwellings in the city, against 16,000 apartments and flats. Forty-five hundred homeowners take in lodgers.

Dissatisfied lodgers are at liberty to compete with tourists and convention-goers at 24 local hotels or approximately 35 Calgary area motels. An ultra-modern hotel-motel, slated to be one of the finest in the West, is under construction at the cloverleaf intersection of the No. 2 and Trans-Canada highways.

Calgarians transact much of their business over 82,623 telephones — the number reported by the AGT as of Jan. 15 of this year.

A recent report indicated that phone-using Calgarians qualify as the most talkative in the world. Colored telephones have been introduced for addicts bored by black ones.

Approximately 60,000 cars and around 16,000 commercial vehicles, most of which can be found at the corner of 8th Ave. and 1st St. W. at 5 p.m. weekdays, are registered in Calgary.

All this indicated that we Calgarians are busy, fairly prosperous (although weekly wage totals fall slightly short of the national average), ambitious, and often harassed.

The primary purpose of this series is to find out just how the modern Calgary came about and what keeps the wheels turning today.

Where, for example, did we get the money and inclination to buy 57,500 Elvis Presley records, which is the number sold here since the Pelvis wiggled into the public view?

Are we too busy to watch our television sets? It's unlikely, because 53,000 have been sold in the Calgary area. There are more than 30,000 it is estimated, in the city itself.

March 25, 1957

The producers of Teacher's Pet, a movie starring Clark Gable and Doris Day, had an inspiration: they needed extras for newsroom scenes, so why not get real newspaper people? Bob Shiels of The Herald was among those chosen. Here is one of his dispatches from Hollywood.

Further footnotes, pertinent and otherwise, on life in cloudland: Thirteen of the 50 out-of town newsmen here for the filming of "Teacher's Pet" had to fly home because their home offices wanted them back.

I stayed on because my home office at this point hasn't said it cares if I never come back at all. . .

Conversation between two newsmen in a cab last night:

"Do you cover movies full time?"

"No, as a matter of fact I cover politics."

"That's odd. How did you come to get this trip?"

Herald reporter Bob Shiels, left, with Clark Gable on the set of the 1957 newspaper movie, Teacher's Pet.

"Politics..."

The filming of "Teacher's Pet" is progressing well ahead of schedule and the need for the visiting news hounds (if there ever was a need for them in the first place) probably will come to an end in about two days.

So far most of us alleged actors are little more than blurs in the background. All my efforts to deliver greetings to the folks in Calgary have been discouraged by the director.

I am possibly the highest-paid blur in the history of movie-making.

I won't go into detail describing the scenes we have on film thus far. There is enough unhappiness in the world as it is.

One thing I can say: The newsroom as created by the Pelberg-Seaton team for Paramount is the most realistic that I've ever seen in a movie.

And I should know. I've worked for quite a few newspapers in my time. Why, I even lasted with one outfit for three years before the management got wise that I wasn't particularly doing anything there.

As for the Shiels Fan Club in Calgary, I would advise that you bring binoculars to whichever theatre is foolhardy enough to offer Teacher's Pet.

I'm not exactly prominent in this show. Some fathead called Gable keeps getting in the way.

Personally, I can't see what this Gable has that I haven't got. The Shiels Fan Club and the Gable Fan Club, which I understand has a small but not-too-alert following, may have to have it out. Gable may have more fans but mine are meaner and tougher.

On seeing the first shots of Teacher's Pet, a visiting lout from Cincinnatti decided "we'll have to rely on Gable to sell this show."

Hollywood, California, May 17, 1957

Bill Gold, who later became a political reporter, an editorial writer and eventually editor of The Herald, got some of his early experience covering the lions. The lions in this case were not a service club.

Nice fellows, those lions. Dropped in to see them after lunch.

Chateau D'or and Tommy were holding court, Chief butler was Edward Kuhn. He's more commonly known to the thousands attending Polack Bros. Circus at the grounds as Captain Eddie, the lion tamer.

Shakily living up to a promise made in the late hours of the night before, this Herald scribe made a tour of the big cage — a quick tour.

As Gold was going in, most of his courage was oozing out.

Seeing I was the guest Mr. Kuhn kindly asked me to step in before the regular occupants arrived. So far it was easy.

Then, escorted by the charming Mrs. Kuhn, Carlene, Tommy loped in. I started to do some loping of my own but someone had quite sensibly closed the cage door.

Anyway Tommy was a little more fussy than that. Disdaining the quivering lump of denim-encased flesh that was The Herald's contribution to the affair he made a bee-line for a pedestal on the other side of the cage and got up on it.

Chateau D'or (Shatow for short, although we didn't get on first name terms) made something of an entrance.

He eyed me. I reciprocated.

Anyone who says all humans can stare down all animals never met me — or this cat. My eyeballs gradually receded into their sockets while visions of being a main course danced through my head.

"Gaarrhhh" quoth pussy.

"My God" breathed I.

Introductions thus over to everyone's satisfaction but mine, Mr. Kuhn invited his charge to take a seat and chat a while.

"Ghaaaar, Grrr," the talkative monster muttered.

"Er, yes," replied the purveyor of public information.

"That's nice," said the captain somewhat untruthfully.

Topics of conversation exhausted, the interview was deemed closed by the captain. Shatow had other ideas.

He jumped off the pedestal, briefly considered using me as one, this scheme being rejected due to the obvious instability of the object, and jumped on to another one.

"Out," said the captain.

"Grr," said the cat.

"Let me out," said Gold.

Shatow reluctantly went, followed by the docile Tommy. Gold went, followed by jet trails. Unnerved but at least uneaten.

July 13, 1957

In his student days, Joe Clark had a summer job as a Herald reporter. He wasn't a flashy writer, but he was always game, as this first-person story shows.

This reporter has tested a new dental service which virtually abolishes pain from tooth fillings.

This new apparatus does not claim to completely eradicate pain. But it does do away with friction between drill and tooth, which ultimately causes much of the pain.

Dr. J.M. Galvin of 707A 14th St. N.W. owns one of these machines. He had it installed last January, and has used it since then.

Commenting on the workings of the new apparatus, the Cavitron, Dr. Galvin says: "Frankly, I don't believe they will ever achieve painless dentistry." However, this machine comes close to that desirable quality. By abolishing actual contact between the tooth and the mechanical apparatus, the Cavitron does away with the friction.

This reporter, long leery of dentists and their instruments, agreed to test the apparatus to see if it really stood up to the claims of those who use it. A lower tooth was filled, and the hole carved without the benefit of freezing.

We would do it again.

The operation is not entirely free from sensation. Occasionally, the mouth experiences a feeling which is on the threshold of pain, but even this feeling seems to slide off. Personally, we sat with dentist and apparatus in mouth and waited to be hit. The stab of pain so often evident even in "prefreeze" jobs did not occur. When the hand-piece was removed, we wondered when the drilling was to begin.

This is not exaggeration. The pain which is so often linked with dentistry and tooth filling actually did not occur. It is missed, though not sorely.

July 22, 1957

Don Mackay's career as mayor of Calgary came to a sad end. The man who made the white hat a symbol of Calgary was defeated at the polls by Harry Hays after a scandal and a judicial inquiry. The inquiry found that Mackay and a number of city administrators had improperly accepted gifts from contractors. However, the best-remembered part of the whole affair was the 35 bags of cement that started it all. Merv Anderson of The Herald covered the Mackay affair.

Mayor D.H. Mackay rode out the roughest political storm in his career Thursday. Council sharply censured him for borrowing city cement, but an all-out attempt to force his resignation failed to carry by two votes.

Aldermen clashed continually during one of the most free-wheeling emotion-tossed meetings in council's lusty history. The Mayor wept.

The dramatic session sprang from Mayor Mackay's admission that 35 bags of cement he borrowed from the city in 1956 were not returned until about 10 days ago.

During the gruelling nine-hour special meeting, council rejected a motion calling for the Mayor's resignation on a 5-7 vote and nullified a motion requesting a judicial inquiry by the attorney-general on a tied 6-6 vote.

The Mayor, who abstained from voting sat with head bowed as aldermen got up to criticize him for "stupidity, foolishness and arrogance."

Tears welling up in his eyes, Mayor Mackay accepted "censorship for this action of mine which has been a pretty poor case of judgment."

But he defiantly refused to resign "because it would be admitting arguments" of some aldermen.

"For whatever years the Lord may grant me," he said in an emotion-choked voice, "I will never admit I have been guilty of anything except lack of judgement."

Ald. James Macdonald took issue with the drama of the Mayor's defence before he began to speak.

"He would make a martyr of himself. He would suggest this is a political move."

Ald. Macdonald also criticized his fellow aldermen, charging them with "a lack of intestinal fortitude.

"Sure he's a nice fellow, but does that condone him using his office for his own benefit?" Ald. Macdonald asked.

Countered Ald. Ernest Munson: "Why should we a council set ourselves up as judges and jury? We didn't elect the Mayor—the general public did."

Council at the end of the long fray approved a motion by Ald. James Macdonald calling for "severest possible censure." It carried 7-5. Another motion by Ald. Milton Harradence provided for setting up of a committee "to investigate and make inquiry into or concerning any matter connected with the good government of the city."

It carried 11-1.

Ald. Mrs. Mary Dover said "There is a certain amount of politics here. For some years there has been an attempt to put the mayor in purely an administrative capacity."

"I can honestly say there's not a bit of

Calgary mayor Don Mackay wore his trademark white hat to a judicial inquiry into his dealings at city hall.

politics in it as far as I'm concerned," Ald. P. N.R. Morrison replied.

Ald. Milton Harradence said "There has been nothing criminal, only stupidity and arrogance."

September 19, 1958

Later that year, Mackay did submit himself to the judgement of the public, and was voted out of office. Before the election, a Herald editorial offered this advice.

This is the most important mayoralty election Calgary has ever faced.

It is also the most inexcusably dull and farcically polite campaign. It has bordered, throughout, on the plain ridiculous.

A painstaking judicial inquiry found Mayor Mackay guilty of taking "improper advantage" of his office. In less formal language that means he misused and abused the high office Calgary's citizens entrusted with him.

The issue, then, is whether Mayor Mackay is a fit person to remain as mayor of

Calgary. The Herald believes he is not.

Why are Mayor Mackay's major opponents avoiding discussion of this very simple but paramount issue?

They are doing it because they are afraid an open attack on Mayor Mackay will drive votes to him rather than against him. Unfortunately, there is some truth in this, particularly in regard to those women voters whose protective instinct is aroused by Mayor Mackay's somewhat juvenile personality. We find this sad, and earnestly hope that before next Wednesday intelligence will triumph over misguided emotion.

Forgiveness is a noble thing, but it should not be debauched into putting a public seal of approval on wrong-doing.

Aside from the shameful findings of the Turcotte report, the plain truth is that Mayor Mackay's administration over many years has been appalling. The carefully-fostered fiction that he has built Calgary practically single-handed is sheer nonsense. Instead of swallowing the patter about how much Mayor Mackay has done for Calgary, it would be more to the point if more people considered what Calgary has done for Mayor Mackay.

His re-election would be an invitation to any city employee so inclined to use his position for personal advantage in the future.

Surely Calgary is not going to do that.

October 8, 1959

Later Judge L.S. Turcotte conducted an inquiry. City council found his report awkward to deal with.

Alderman James Macdonald resigned from City Council Monday night in a dramatic protest against council's "refusal" to take action on the Turcotte report.

In a tense, two-hour debate, a majority of aldermen maintained that the electorate should be the "sole judge and jury" of Mayor D.H. Mackay.

An overflow gallery — spectators were standing four deep at back — applauded and jeered as highlights of Judge L.S. Turcotte's report were reviewed.

In demanding silence, Ald. Isabella Stevens, acting chairman, threatened to "clear the courtroom" if there were any further disturbances.

A motion requesting the Mayor to resign failed on a 5-6 vote. Ald. Milton Harradence described the motion as "futile and puerile" because it carried no legislative weight.

Ald. Macdonald failed to get a seconder for a motion which would have cut off the mayor's salary and a motion for the dismissal of Commissioner E.C. Thomas and Harry Walshaw, streets construction engineer.

Judge Turcotte in his inquiry report, released Friday, declared Mayor Mackay, Commissioner Thomas and Mr. Walshaw had derived "improper advantage" in the form of substantial gifts from firms doing business with the city. The report ruled criminal actions against the officials were not justified.

August 4, 1959

Having a Beer in Alberta

In Alberta, until the late Fifties, beer was the only alcoholic beverage that citizens could drink outside their own home. They could drink it in a beer parlor, and that's about all they could do there: no music, no dancing, no games, no liquor. Just beer. In Calgary and Edmonton, men and women had to go to separate beer parlors. Anyone who wanted a cocktail, or wine with a meal, could present his liquor licence at one of Calgary's two liquor stores, buy a bottle, and take it straight home. As H.D. Surplis of The Herald reported, two armed-services members of the Legislature tried to get the laws amended, just slightly.

A motion by F.C. Colborne (Air Force) and L.D. Ward (Navy), both of Calgary, requesting the government to restore mixed drinking in the cities of Calgary and Edmonton, was defeated 42-10 by the Legislature Tuesday afternoon.

"The question is not one of the merits of alcoholic beverages but simply the question whether the people of Calgary and Edmonton should be denied privileges enjoyed by the rest of the province," said Mr. Colborne in moving the motion. "If we believe in equal rights, now is the time to demonstrate that fact," he challenged the House.

More than 20 years had passed since the people of the province abandoned prohibition as a solution of the liquor problem, Mr. Ward reminded the members, yet little or no change had been made in liquor laws since. "There remains much room for improvement," he declared. Service men had seen how the problem was handled abroad and "they are certainly not contented with some of the conditions prevailing here with respect to the liquor problem." They were determined it was time for a change.

Segregation was "a hangover from early days," he asserted. "Surely the men and women of Calgary and Edmonton are not so dissolute that they may not drink together," he said. "If people are going to drink, let there be facilities for doing it more decently."

Premier E.C. Manning explained that the restriction was introduced primarily because of representations from the police and hotel proprietors. There was nothing to prevent husbands and wives drinking together in their homes. He doubted if those clamoring for mixed drinking were in that category. "As far as I am concerned the province would be far better off if we didn't have this liquor racket at all," he declared.

J. Harper Prowse (Army), Edmonton, declared that the government was perfectly willing to take a $10,000,000 yearly profit from liquor but refused to accept its responsibility. "That responsibility is to see that people drink properly," he said. "It is high time we sat down here, calmly and sanely, and looked the thing over...we have made no attempt whatever to provide people with facilities to drink properly...make them (hotel proprietors) bring the beer parlors up to a standard where a man can bring his wife into one. If in 22 years our pub-keepers haven't learned to handle drunks, then I submit it's high time we got some new pub-keepers," Mr. Prowse declared.

Edmonton, March 26, 1947

An editorial.

It is apparent that the provincial government has made an astounding discovery. Only 27 years after the passing of the Alberta Liquor Control Act, it has received information leading it to believe that Albertans are ignoring the act in "many of its basic details."

How are we ignoring it? Mr. Manning doesn't say. Can it be that some unspeakable villain has taken a flask to a football game? Or consumed liquor in a place other than his own domicile? Or had a drink on a train? Or neglected to enter the full name, address, occupation, telephone number, color of eyes, annual income, Unemployment Insurance number, wife's grandmother's maiden name and height in centimetres of a guest whom he has taken to his club? Perish the thought: such things cannot happen in righteous Social Credit Alberta.

They cannot happen: but we have the government's word for it that they are in fact happening. And as everybody knows the government never speaks anything but the strictest truth. When Mr. Manning says that mixed drinking is bad and sinful in Edmonton and Calgary, but perfectly legitimate and safe in Lethbridge, Medicine Hat, Okotoks and Cochrane, everybody can see the essential justice of his view; it is not necessary for him to explain just why it is right in one place and not in another.

Come, come, fellows: we are letting the side down. Our liquor laws are so tolerant, so sensible, so civilized that we should obey them to the letter. Only the most thick-headed kind of believer in outmoded monetary theories could fail to see the difference between buying his wife a beer in Cochrane and buying his wife a beer in Calgary.

They may tolerate cocktail lounges and other sinks of iniquity down in degenerate Ontario and Quebec; they may allow pubs in decadent, Socialist-ridden Britain; but that is not for us. Out here in the wide-open spaces where the wind is free and the hot air of Social Credit politics warms up our winter days, an all-wise government legislates our morals for us. Furthermore, it makes $11,000,000 a year profit by the simple process of telling us we ought not to drink.

May 26, 1951

The liquor laws weren't always obeyed, but they were enforced, as this letter to the editor describes.

Alberta has a peculiar appeal to my wayward soul. It is my thought that I could live nowhere else as pleasantly and still experience the delightful thrill of close brushes with the law such as occurred recently in one of the better "supper clubs."

The crowd was good, the atmosphere sheer delight, the orchestra excellent, the floor show amusing: ice tinkled pleasantly in glasses of coke or ginger furtively spiked from under the table. The dress and decorum of the guests was equal in every respect to that of the guests at the country club.

O, terrible, terrible is the wrath of a little god! Enter the storm troopers in squads of eight — and the little people about us, those stalwart sinners, all dropped to their knees in what I took to be an attitude of prayer. Not so! Fool that I am, it was merely a scramble for bottles under the table. The music stopped. The sinners sat. And the young couple at the next table lost their "mickey" of rye, back to the gods from whence it came. Shamefully they rose, gathered their friends about them, and with one last longing look behind, left their Eden to return to another year's drudgery.

Ah well, the true God forbade the apple entirely in His Eden. Our little god, more generous, more understanding, sells the apple. And those sinners who fail to live up to the small restrictions imposed on its consumption shall fall by the wayside and suffer accordingly, as will the banished young anniversary couple. Their parting conversation though, is evidence of the confirmed sinner. They were hand in hand hustling out when she said: "They told me the fine is $30. We didn't budget for that, darling." "Don't worry, hon," he assured her. "I'll go without lunches this month." My bottle? Don't be silly! Would you have suspected the six fountain pens in my pocket each contained a shot of rye?

A Voice In The Wilderness, Calgary.

March 19, 1957

In a provincial plebiscite held in 1957, Calgarians voted four-to-one in favor of letting men and women drink beer in the same room. As The Herald reported in February, 1958, "Calgarians obviously had been waiting for mixed drinking with parched throats. Mixed drinking came into effect here Monday, and the response was fantastic. Within a half hour after the doors on the new Ladies and Escorts sections opened, it was literally impossible to get a chair. One manager proposed that the gentlemen remove their hats, in deference to the ladies. Another said that men drinking with ladies seemed to have an anaesthetic effect. Both men and ladies seemed to be less loud." In November the first cocktail lounges opened.

Manning and Diefenbaker

In the fifteen years following the Second World War, Social Credit reached the middle of its long reign in Alberta. Under Premier Ernest Manning, William Aberhart's economic dogma and bitter strife with Ottawa were replaced by quiet, conservative government. Perhaps out of nostalgia for Aberhart's $25-a-month "dividend" (never paid), for a short time every adult Albertan was given $20 a year out of the province's new oil wealth. Some accusations of wrong-doing were lodged against the government, but they came to very little. Social Credit continued to win substantial majorities. Even by the standards of Alberta politics, it was a quiet time. On the federal scene, the Fifties were much more eventful. In 1948, Louis St. Laurent replaced William Lyon Mackenzie King as Liberal leader and prime minister. In 1956, the House of Commons erupted in bitter controversy over the construction of the TransCanada gas pipeline. The new Conservative leader, John Diefenbaker, led an outcry against "Liberal arrogance," and after the 1957 election formed a minority Conservative government. He returned to the polls the following year and won a record majority over the new Liberal leader, Lester B. Pearson. But first, some news of Alberta politics. One of the livelier moments in the provincial legislature was reported by Andrew Snaddon, who later became editor of The Edmonton Journal, and then publisher of The Medicine Hat News.

Alberta Liberal leader J. Harper Prowse.

L ashing out with the charge that Premier E.C. Manning was the "Judas" of the Social Credit movement, J. Harper Prowse, Liberal leader, blasted the calm that had surrounded Friday's budget debate in the legislature.

He immediately ran afoul of the Speaker, Rev. Peter Dawson (S.C.), Little Bow, who charged the Liberal leader with reading a speech he had not himself written.

The fireworks continued throughout Mr. Prowse's speech, one of the fieriest attacks on the government heard in years.

Mr. Prowse opened with the claim that the province had a $59,000,000 cash surplus and would have another $10,000,000 by the end of the fiscal year.

This was reached by the policy of "this government of keeping their own house in order, by turning a deaf ear and blind eye toward the cries for help and the desperate position of our municipal organizations and the mass of provincial taxpayers."

He continued later, "It must indeed be difficult for them (the premier's supporters) to try to follow their leader when they are called upon to try to explain the vacillations of their premier, who is sometimes praying for the poor but these days is more often dining with the rich."

Mr. Prowse then went on to say that there was great sorrow in the province when the late Premier William Aberhart died. "Mr. Speaker, I think it was perhaps a kindness to him that he was taken away at that time, because if he were alive today to see what has happened to the movement he founded, to read in the newspapers praise from the bankers and the heads of great international corporations, and hear at the same time the people for whom he lived and worked groaning under the burden of taxation which they pay: if he could see the youth whom he trained to take his place, showing more concern for the pockets of the bondholders and the investment dealers than for the pockets of the people whose faith voted him into power, then I am sure he would die of a broken heart.

"And if, Mr. Speaker, it would be correct to say that the late Premier William Aberhart was the Messiah of the Social Credit movement, then the present premier is certainly its Judas."

Speaker Dawson here called Mr. Prowse to order. He noted that he had allowed reading of speeches but felt qualified to know when a member was reading something he had not written himself, and this was such a case.

"I take exception to that," said Mr. Prowse in anger.

"It is the ruling of the chair," replied Mr. Dawson.

"You are certainly riding your privilege for all it is worth," the red-faced Mr. Prowse snapped. The Speaker ignored the retort and Mr. Prowse continued.

At the conclusion of the afternoon sitting there occurred a further altercation between the Speaker and Mr. Prowse witnessed by The Herald reporter and another Southam newspaper representative.

All members except Mr. Prowse and his fellow Liberal, Hugh John MacDonald, Calgary, had left the House. The reporters were looking for Speaker Dawson. The Speaker entered the chamber and Mr. Prowse approached him.

"That was an awful thing you did this afternoon, Mr. Speaker," Mr. Prowse remarked. The Speaker asked what he meant. Mr. Prowse said he meant the incident of his speech being called out of order and using a speech not his own. "Harper, I've heard you speak for a good many years and I can tell when it is not your own speech."

"In that case your bad judgment is only exceeded by your conceit," Mr. Prowse replied, turning on his heel and walking from the chamber.

Edmonton, March 11, 1950

This rather technical story by Dick Snell of The Herald was the first pebble in a political avalanche. J. Harper Prowse, Alberta Liberal leader, followed with a series of charges of wrong-doing and bad management by the Social Credit government. Premier Manning called an election, and though Social Credit was returned with 37 seats, the Liberals won 15 and other opposition parties 7. Snell won a National Newspaper Award.

A t least 11 members of the Legislative Assembly of Alberta may have disqualified themselves from that office by virtue of bank dealings with the provincial government treasury branches, The Herald learned today.

Under Section II of the Legislative Assembly Act, any person who contracts with any public office or department of the provincial government is disqualified from sitting and voting in the Legislative Assembly.

The Treasury Branches Act provides that loans and deposits are contracts with a department of the provincial government.

Just prior to adjournment of the current session April 6, an amendment was passed allowing members to do business with the branches but this is not retroactive.

This means that any member who has made a loan or deposit with the provincial treasury branches since the 1952 election and prior to April 6 is disqualified as of the time he entered that contract. Being so disqualified, a writ of election must be issued to fill the seat he vacates.

Investigations by The Herald have shown at least 11 Social Credit members have had deposits with the treasury branches since the election and prior to April 6.

Recently, two other Social Credit MLA's found themselves unseated from the Assembly by reason of having a contract with the provincial government. A Calgary barrister, James D. MacDonald, has brought an action against the pair, R.S. Lee, Taber, and J.C. Landeryou, Lethbridge, seeking the $200 a day penalty they may have to pay for each day they sat illegally in the assembly.

This session the government, possibly discovering the embarrassing position its members had placed themselves in, slipped through an amendment making deals with the treasury branch by members legal.

The amendment, and the way it was put to the legislature, is tantamount to an admission, one lawyer told The Herald.

As the change is now in force, members who had dealings with the branches since just prior to Easter are exempted. However, those who had dealings with the branches prior to that time were then disqualified and are not saved by the new section which is not retroactive.

There is also the possibility that this legislation, and, perhaps other bills, are not properly passed for want of a quorum — at least 20 qualified members.

Because of the number who have disqualified themselves since the election in 1952 by dealing with the branches, lawyers feel the possibility is not remote.

As no division was taken on the question or any record kept of the vote, The Herald was unable to determine whether there were enough qualified members in the legislature at the time to pass the amendment.

May 11, 1955

A royal commission found little to complain of in the Manning government's administration. Bill Drever who was to go on to become managing editor, then associate editor, of The Herald summed up the commission's findings.

With the exception of one major recommendation covering land sales and purchases, Alberta's Social Credit government has been freed on charges of maladministration. The charges were levelled at the government during the 1955 election campaign.

The findings of the Macdonald-Mahaffy Royal Commission, set up last fall to investigate the allegations, were released by Premier E.C. Manning.

Under investigation were the operation of Treasury Branches with respect to loans to members of the Legislature; letting of highway contracts; purchasing and selling of buildings and property; construction of a paved road from the Belmont rehabilitation centre to Edmonton; awarding of public works contracts and specifying of brand-name products; and a minerals rights trade Premier Manning made with the government.

A summary of the findings shows:

1. No preference was shown to MLAs in making loans from the Treasury Branches. (The practice of making loans and taking a sessional indemnity as security was questioned.)

2. The letting of highway contracts is satisfactory providing the government calls for tenders on all projects. (Two specific cases were noted where this had not been done.)

3. A complete re-examination of the government's machinery for buying and selling land and buildings, or purchasing same, should be made.

4. The government played no part in construction of the hard-surface road from the rehabilitation centre to the drive-in partly owned by Lucien Maynard, former attorney-general.

5. The government's system of calling for tenders on public works projects is satisfactory.

6. The government was justified in specifying Pre-cast and Ytong products on buildings investigated.

7. Premier Manning's trade of mineral rights with the government was no different than trades made by about 20 ordinary citizens.

With respect to the major recommendation covering buying and selling of land, Premier Manning said serious consideration will be handled by "one department and should be in the hands of a competent and experienced person."

Premier Manning said the findings "are most gratifying and fully vindicate our position."

Edmonton, June 9, 1956

Social Credit never did achieve its promised $25 a month dividend. The closest it came was $20 a year, given to citizens out of surplus oil royalty revenue. The "dividend" was abandoned the following year. Bob Shiels found that there were plenty of takers on the first day of the program.

The Alberta government's $20 dividend became payable for the first time today and eligible Calgarians wasted no time whatsoever before going after it.

D-Day for dividends found fantastic crowds assembled at nearly all of the main downtown banks.

When the banks' doors opened at 10 a.m., a steady flow of bonus-seekers moved in and kept coming all morning.

To be eligible the applicant must be a Canadian citizen or British subject at least 21 years old prior to Dec. 31, 1957, who has been a resident of Alberta for the immediately preceeding two years and for a total of not less than 10 years.

The banks and treasury branches are taking each applicant's word for it when he signs the necessary declaration.

Bank officials, some of whom were surprised at the early demand, expected that the initial rush will ease off in one or two days.

Altogether, it is estimated approximately 550,000 Albertans are eligible for the dividend.

If everyone applies for the bonus, the payments will use up an $11,000,000 fund, representing one-third of the province's net royalties from oil and gas production.

The fund was established under the Oil and Gas Royalties Dividend Act passed at the last session of the Legislature after stormy debate and strong Opposition protests.

Opponents of the dividend scheme called it "paleface treaty money" designed primarily to win Social Credit votes. They argued that there were innumerably better ways in which the money could be spent.

Most bonus seekers indicated they want not only to collect the $20 right away, but they will also spend most of it without further ado.

"I'll put it right in the bank," said one woman. She was an exception.

One male bonus-seeker said he needed the money to pay the grocery bill. Another had a laundry bill that just about cancelled out any monetary gain.

One honest individual admitted that he was "going out and buying himself four cases of beer."

September 3, 1957

It was a season for landslides, and in 1959 Ernest Manning more than made up for his losses to the Liberals in 1955. Bill Gold summed up the meaning of this Alberta-style majority government.

Alberta Thursday elected 61 Social Crediters to a 65-seat Legislature and wrote another colorful chapter in its political history.

Premier E.C. Manning squashed a threatened Progressive Conservative invasion and all but eliminated his official opposition in the last Legislature, the Liberals.

Mr. Manning did the job even more resoundingly than Social Credit's founder in Alberta, William Aberhart, who obtained only 56 seats in his first election.

The Conservatives had three seats and some predicted they would win a dozen more, but they ended up with only one — Calgarian Ernest Watkins.

The Liberals held 15 seats and some predicted they would lose many of those, but they ended up with only one — Mike Maccagno of Lac La Biche.

The CCF held two seats and they ended up with none.

The election meant that:

1. Mr. Manning is now the strongest provincial premier in all of Canada.

2. Only Prince Edward Island has ever elected a stronger government since confederation, and that was in 1935 when that small province returned 30 Liberals out of 30 seats.

3. Social Credit is in a stronger position than ever before. Premier Manning has established himself as a leader of even greater strength than William Aberhart.

4. Those who contend the last two federal elections would have strong effects provincially have been proved wrong.

5. Social Credit's new five-year mandate will extend its possible tenure in office to 29 years, within one term of the national record.

July 19, 1959

This was the beginning of the famous pipeline debate, and the beginning of the end of 22 years of Liberal government. C.D. Howe's extraordinary use of closure to limit debate before debate had even begun was a major issue in the 1957 election that brought the Conservatives into power. Warren Baldwin of The Herald's Ottawa bureau sent this report.

Trade Minister C.D. Howe applied the gag to Parliament Monday before it had a chance to say "ouch." In a surprise move never before attempted in the House of Commons, he gave notice of closure on the pipelines resolution debate before the debate opened. The motion will be put and carried today by the government's steam-roller majority and one hour past midnight the first stage of the pipelines battle will end. Seven times the gag rule has been used between 1913 and 1932 but never before has a minister given notice before a single opposition member has spoken.

The Conservatives, backed by the CCF, met the move with a challenge to an immediate election.

"The all-Canadian pipeline," Opposition Leader Drew shouted as his party thundered its applause, "is being financed by the Canadian taxpayer only to be handed over to American promoters. Let the government call an immediate election on this issue. Let them go to the people and let the people decide."

The closure motion Monday disposes of the resolution stage. The next would be imposed on Thursday on second reading of the bill to establish the Northern Ontario Pipeline Company and lend the $72,000,000 to Trans-Canada Pipelines Limited for construction of the Winnipeg line. Then there will be committee stage of the bill and third reading, each, if the government wants to cut debate to the minimum, taking two days.

Ottawa, May 15, 1956

In an editorial headed "Sieg Heil! Sieg Heil! Sieg Heil!," The Herald took its stand against closure.

Parliamentary democracy, as free peoples know it, was arrogantly jeered in Ottawa Tuesday when Rt. Hon. C.D. Howe's motion of closure was crushed through Parliament by the obedient and spineless Liberal majority.

Closure was meant to be used to stem filibustering tactics, and repetitious argument on measures which have been thoroughly debated. It was mis-used Tuesday to smash opposition to an expenditure of millions of Canadian dollars for a pipeline project which has now assumed radically different proportions from anything which the Canadian Parliament has discussed before. It was done to choke off opposition protests against a measure which is of vital importance to Canada's future as a nation. It was done before the debate even started.

Closure has been used warily and rarely in past years. Mr. Howe moved his motion before debate even started. Mr. Howe is determined that his chosen instrument for moving Alberta gas, the Trans-Canada Pipe Lines Ltd. company will be given the go ahead, regardless of its past failures to meet its obligations; regardless of the fact that Canadian taxpayers are putting up the majority of the money which will be needed; regardless of Parliament's duty to examine the new measures to the fullest extent, and regardless of the fact that U.S. investors will reap any profits.

Prime Minister St. Laurent, the "leader", said nothing.

Mr. Howe walked out while the Leader of the Opposition spoke. That was not a flip gesture at the personality of the man who faced him. It typified Mr. Howe's cynical disregard for Parliament. It is a supreme example of contempt for Parliament and for the Canadian people.

And the Liberal members cheered. And the Liberal members voted on command. Their allegiance is to Mr. Howe; their feelings for democratic procedure and for the right of the Parliament in which they are supposedly responsible members were as nothing. Their duty as MPs has not bothered them.

It is not the Liberal intention to give Parliament a fair-chance to debate the issue, perhaps then using the closure if necessary after a reasonable time. It is a dangerous precedent.

It is the totalitarian chorus of rubber-stamp followers paying allegiance to a Fuehrer.

May 16, 1956

The use of closure led to prolonged procedural arguments, and to bitter and chaotic scenes in the House of Commons. Reginald Hardy sent this report from The Herald's Ottawa bureau.

Crazy, man! but crazy! those MP dadeeos are cool, real cool. "They're the most!" That was how the bright-eyed youth in the black denim trousers and the motorcycle boots described the exhibition of rock-and-roll which he had just witnessed from a seat in the public gallery of the House of Commons.

As one who is not too hep to the colorful jargon of the juke-box boys I'll not attempt a literal translation.

But I think I know just what the young man meant. Certainly of all the unusual performances which this writer has witnessed in Parliament over the period of the past 15 years Thursday's pipeline follies takes the cracked cookie-jar.

To go along with my jive-happy friend, it was the greatest when the scene was set at 2:30 p.m. Thursday; the galleries were packed with interested taxpayers who had come to see Mr. Howe's guillotine in action. The guillotine was there in the background, all right, suitably draped in black, and the eager spectators leaned forward in their places awaiting the dull thud of the falling knife and the smooth snicker-snack of the blade shearing through Conservative and CCF necks.

But instead of the guillotine they were treated to a new and still more refined method of closure — closure by slow torture. By the rack and the wheel, by the thumb-screw (oh, how they groaned), and by the iron mask.

It was a procedural nightmare. Six divisions and four votes in committee. By the time they locked the booby-hatch up at 10 p.m. all the House had accomplished since 1 a.m. Wednesday, was to postpone discussion on two clauses of Mr. "Executioner Howe's" bill.

When the House finally got into committee, Mr. Howe produced his new formula for closure by thumbscrew. He moved that "further discussion" on clause one of the bill be postponed.

As there hadn't yet been any discussion on the clause this procedure resulted in an immediate uproar. It was an uproar that continued throughout the afternoon and reached its wildest crescendo in the evening when Conservative and CCF members literally dared the chairman and Mr. Speaker to take stringent punitive action.

At one juncture, as deputy speaker W.A. Robinson attempted to report to Mr. Speaker his words were drowned out by the deafening yells of the Opposition, by the slamming of desk tops and by the insistent demands of Opposition members to be allowed to speak.

Speaker Rene Beaudoin, white-faced and grim, eventually found his voice.

"I have never seen this before and I never thought I would see it," he declared.

"Mr Speaker, you leave me no alternative but to defy the chair," shouted Davie Fulton, the Conservative member for Kamloops.

"Now for another half-hour lecture," interjected another member. "What do you do if the chairman is so dumb?" protested Conservative Frank Lennard from Wentworth.

And so it went. At times chairman Robinson and Speaker Beaudoin were clearly at a loss at what to say or do.

When CCF member A.M. Nicholson rose to his feet and chairman Robinson began to wave him down with "I am sorry . . ." CCF leader Coldwell leaped to his feet in protest.

"This whole procedure is an abomination to me," he cried.

"Even Louis XIV would blush," added John Diefenbaker, the Conservative from Prince Albert.

"Is Parliament to be throttled?" asked Mr. Diefenbaker. "Surely because my right hon. friend (Mr. Howe) is an engineer, he cannot ditch, dam and drain Parliament of its privileges in one afternoon."

"Utterly disgraceful proceedings and a crass violation of the rules of this House," said Mr. Knowles.

"The minister is now the lord high executioner of Parliament," added Mr. Diefenbaker.

"It denies the basis of the life of Parliament itself," boomed Conservative leader Drew.

Yes, the people who packed the galleries of the House on Thursday got their money's worth. I'll wager they'll be back in force today, bringing their friends.

Ottawa, May 25, 1956

Six months after the pipeline debate, John Diefenbaker was chosen leader of the Progressive Conservative party. (Quebec's bitterness over the choice was short-lived; in the 1958 election the Conservatives won 50 seats in that province.) Richard L. Sanburn, editor-in-chief of The Herald, reported on the beginning of the Diefenbaker phenomenon.

Amid wild cheers which drowned out part of the announcement itself, John Diefenbaker of Prince Albert was proclaimed the new leader of the Conservative Party at 3:30 p.m. (1:30 p.m. Calgary time) Friday.

He won on the first ballot, as he had freely predicted, over Donald Fleming of Toronto and Davie Fulton of Kamloops, B.C.

It was the third try for the leadership by Mr. Diefenbaker, and it was a man choked with emotion who came to the speakers' podium to pledge himself to the service of his party "and all the people of Canada." At one point, he seemed near tears, visibly fighting for control before he went on with his acceptance speech.

Immediately Mr. Diefenbaker's win was announced, Mr. Fleming moved that his election be made unanimous, and Mr. Fulton seconded the motion.

The only dead spot in the big auditorium was the section seating the 300-odd strong delegation from Quebec. Perhaps a couple of dozen stood up. The rest remained seated and silent.

After it was over Friday afternoon, one Quebec delegate was heard to say, "Well, we say good-bye to our good friends in Ontario; perhaps you will see us again in maybe fifty years."

On every occasion this week when an English-speaking person valiantly attempted a brief sortie into French, the Quebec group rose and sang the inevitable "Il a Gagne ses Epaulets" (he has won his epaulets). But not for Mr. Diefenbaker.

Thursday night, Mr. Diefenbaker spoke in French. There was stony silence in the Quebec section. Friday, in his acceptance speech, Mr. Diefenbaker again spoke French. Again, stony silence. Mrs. Diefenbaker, too, offering her own thanks, spoke briefly in French. Traditional French gallantry was deep in moth balls. Mrs. Diefenbaker got nothing but stony silence from the Quebec section.

It was the sour note of the whole convention.

Ottawa, December 15, 1956

Charles King of The Herald's Ottawa bureau travelled with the Diefenbaker campaign in 1957, and provided this sample of "The Chief's" campaign oratory.

John Diefenbaker carried the Conservative campaign into CCF Saskatchewan today after making a public bet that "third parties" will elect no more than two candidates east of the Manitoba border.

John Diefenbaker in 1957, near the peak of his long, dramatic career. He defeated the Liberals, in power for more than 20 years, and went on to win the largest Parliamentary majority in Canadian history.

The touring national leader of the Tory party displayed growing optimism after an 800-mile trip by air and highway Thursday that wound up his three day visit to Manitoba.

It was the 22nd day of his campaign for the June 10 federal election, and he made his 50th speech to a cheering throng of 1,000 persons who overflowed the biggest hall in the town of Minnedosa, centre of the riding of Liberal Justice Minister Stewart Garson.

Listeners lined the walls and literally hung from the balcony in Minnedosa to hear him lash the Liberal government on foreign policy and agriculture, and deliver his strongest attack yet on what he calls "third parties" — CCF and Social Credit.

"If you take some ideas from the Conservative party and some from the Liberal party, you have a thing called a movement and not a party," he said in a sarcastic reference to Social Credit.

Then, putting it in the language of his farm audience, he poured on the heat:

"Can you mix No. 3 tough and No. 4 smutty and make No. 1 hard by putting them in the same bag?"

His argument was the old one — that if all the voters who oppose the government put their weight behind the Conservative party instead of "diluting their opposition" the Liberals would be thrown out of office June 10.

Flin Flon, a busy mining centre of 12,000 population, delivered an audience of 200 persons in mid-afternoon to hear him speak.

It was Mr. Diefenbaker's signal to talk about labor and the north.

He proposed a program of building "roads to riches" — access highways to hasten the development of northern industry. Many of the country's resources can't be developed because there are no access roads, he said.

At Dauphin, he hit back sarcastically at Liberal claims that the Conservatives couldn't field a cabinet if they ever did win power.

"When I hear such imports as John Whitney Pickersgill (Minister of Citizenship) say 'where would they get a cabinet?' I say we'd get a cabinet without straining ourselves.

"Think of these men — these cabinet ministers. Sometimes I shudder in the face of such greatness."

Kipling, Saskatchewan, May 12, 1957

Diefenbaker won 112 seats in the 1957 election, and formed a minority government. He was the first Conservative prime minister since R.B. Bennett. Alberta elected only three Conservatives; the rest of the province's seats went to one Liberal and 13 Social Crediters. In 1958 Diefenbaker called another election, with spectacular results: his party won 208 out of 265 seats, including 50 in Quebec. All 17 Alberta constituencies went Conservative; federally, Social Credit was temporarily wiped out. (In the election of 1962 Diefenbaker slipped back to where he had been five years earlier: a minority government with 116 seats.)

From the Sports Pages

Barbara Ann Scott, Keith Spaith, Woody Strode, Marilyn Bell, Matt Baldwin — these were some of the big names in Canadian sport in the late Forties and early Fifties. Some of them had a special meaning for Calgary fans. Spaith and Strode belonged to the vintage Stampeder team that won the Grey Cup in 1948. Marilyn Bell, a young Toronto woman, swam Lake Ontario. Matt Baldwin's Alberta rink shone in Macdonald Brier curling. And Barbara Ann Scott became Canada's sweetheart after her Olympic figure-skating championship in 1948. Basil Dean reported her triumph for the Southam newspapers.

Barbara Ann Scott walked, or rather skated, away from her rivals in the free-style contest of the Olympic women's figure-skating championships here this afternoon and was proclaimed Olympic champion for 1948 by the thunderous acclamation of the crowds long before the contest was completed and before the judges had announced their official scores.

She had drawn number 13 in skating order, and performed after the two other leading contenders, England's Jeanette Altwegg and Austria's Eva Pavlik. Since she already led by a clear margin in compulsory figures, she needed only to maintain her lead in order to win the title. But after thousands of spectators had seen her flawless four-minute program, there was no doubt about the result.

Barbara Ann's program was the most deceptively effortless performance I've ever witnessed. Her program in the world's championship in Stockholm last year had the leaping, sparkling grace of a mountain stream. Her program today was more like a quiet river through some lovely bubbling few moments of leaps and spins. It was as perfect as anything she has done.

Her four minutes on the rink were punctuated with sharp bursts of applause for her faultless technique and, incidentally, for her sure-footedness on a very bad ice surface which had been disastrous for several other competitors, including United States' Eileen Seight, who fell three times.

After she left the ice and judges had put up their marks, Barbara Ann was mobbed by at least 200 press and amateur photographers and movie cameramen. She posed for them and then was shepherded back to the ringside, since she was anxious to watch United States' Gretchan Merrill, who skated shortly after Barbara Ann.

Barbara Ann, asked about marriage prospects, said "I haven't even thought about it."

"I practice eight hours a day and as you can see I haven't much time."

Then she turned with a grin to Jimmy Grogan, United States figure skater, and chuckled: "I'm waiting for him." But she hastened to remind reporters:

"You'd better put this in. Jimmy is 16."

Prime Minister W.L. Mackenzie King sent from Ottawa the following message:

"Dear Barbara Ann: The word of your having won the Olympic championship has just been received. From one end of Canada to the other there is great rejoicing at your victory and at the high honor you have brought to yourself and to your country.

"The government joins with the people in extending warm congratulations to you. All are delighted beyond words."

St. Moritz, Switzerland, February 16, 1948

Calgary football fans left their mark on Toronto when they journeyed eastward to see the Stampeders play the Ottawa Rough Riders. Herald sports editor Bob Mamini sent this report.

The Stampeder Special brought a bit of the Old West to staid Toronto today and let the East know that prairie football fans are right back of Calgary's challenge for the historic Grey Cup. Stampeders play Ottawa Rough Riders for the Canadian gridiron championship Saturday afternoon at Varsity stadium.

With cowboy band and 250 travelers off the special joined by 70 who made the trip by air, Union station echoed to the Stampeder victory song — "Put On Your Red and White Sweater" — as cowboys and cowgirls from the great open spaces put on a Western show for Torontonians.

Reels and square dances in the station and in the lobby of the Royal York had pop-eyed easterners looking on in amazement. They thought the Calgary Stampede had moved to the shores of Lake Ontario.

The trip east may not have rivalled the great western trek of the 1870's, but for enthusiasm and spirit those on the Stampede Special agreed there never has been anything to match this trip.

With Jim Macqueen and Neil West carrying the Stampede banner followed by the cowboy orchestra of Oscar Stonewall, Bill Galliardi, Bev Bander and Jac Friedenberg, the cowboys and girls from the prairies, some of them real cowhands, took command of the station and the hotel lobby.

The Ottawa Rough Rider team pulled in at almost the same time and the players merely stood back and watched.

"With that kind of following, Calgary must have a real team," said one of the Ottawans.

Staid Toronto hadn't seen anything like it in years and there was more than one raised eyebrow among homburg-wearing suburbanites on their way to downtown offices.

All the fans, who had come 2,000 miles just to see the Stamps play, were dressed in full cowboy regalia, chaps, clicking spurs and all.

The cowgirls were partial to snow-white 10-gallon headpieces and red silk shirts. All the fans wore kerchiefs with "Stampeders" emblazoned on them and Calgary's red and white colours.

One bow-legged son of the West carried a lasso with which he roped goggle-eyed Toronto girls. One Toronto onlooker said he couldn't figure it out because the Calgary traveling ranch had much the prettier girls.

An accordion ground out music as the Calgarians first sang their city's anthem ("Calgary — Where the Sun Shines All the Day") and then reeled off a square dance.

A reporter asked one westerner timidly: "I suppose it's ridiculous to ask who's going to win Saturday."

There was a cowboy yell and a hand like a side of western steer crashing down on the reporter's back, "It certainly is, son; it certainly is."

Toronto, November 26, 1948.

The Stampeders won their first Grey Cup in 1948 — and their last until 1971. Sports editor Bob Mamini just made The Herald's final edition with the news.

Calgary Stampeders this afternoon won the Grey Cup final. The powerful Red Raiders defeated Ottawa Rough Riders to win the Dominion senior football championship. Rated an 8-5 underdog in the pre-game betting, the triumph was considered a mild upset.

The victory enabled Les Lear's Lambasters to complete the 1948 season with an undefeated record. The win brings to a close the richest season in gridiron history for Calgary. It was way back in 1911 when Calgary won the Western championship and to win again the Western title and go on to lift the Grey Cup was more than many experts expected.

Stampeders took to the air with a brilliant forward offensive to take a 6 to 1 lead in the second quarter.

Keith Spaith pitched the payoff pass to Norm Hill on a sleeper play. Hill fell over the goal line, the ball bouncing out of his hands, and he was sitting on the turf when the ball came right back into his hands. It was a picture play but for a moment it looked as if he had lost possession. Freddie Wilmont kicked the extra point from placement.

The Calgary scoring drive started when Woody Strode snagged Turner's pass on a third down on an end sweep and the Stampeders had possession on their own 45-yard line. Calgary's aerial attack went to work at this point with Hood taking a short toss into the flat. The charging Ottawa line drew a yardage penalty for interference and Spaith came back with a 31-yard forward to Strode.

Play was 11 yards out when the Spaith-to-Hill pass paid off.

Calgary lost possession at the start of the

second half after receiving the kickoff, for illegal interference. Riders then started a sustained march which climaxed when Paffrath crashed over centre from the one-yard line after Riders had gained a first down through a Calgary offside. Chipper booted the extra point to give Riders a 7-6 lead.

Stampeders regained the lead when Woody Strode scooped up a loose Ottawa ball when Paffrath's pass was knocked down. The lanky Stampeder end tossed a lateral to Chikowsky who went to the Rider 10 before being brought down. Thodos scored on the next play and Wilmot converted to give Calgary a 12-7 lead.

A jammed crowd of 20,000 fans was on hand to cheer the Stampeder success. Calgary played terrific football to win against a heavier club which also was given the nod because it had more experienced players.

Several hundred Calgary supporters, many dressed in traditional cowboy fashion, cheered the Red Raiders after traveling 2,500 miles to see the team.

Calgary had plenty of support in the game against Ottawa. One reason possibly was that the Grey Cup this year provided a much different setting than the classic of the past few years. Not only were Toronto Argonauts not on hand to defend their championship but Winnipeg Blue Bombers failed to represent the West for the first time since 1937. Bombers won the Canadian crown three times since 1935.

The triumph came after a long haul by both Coach Lear and his 30 players. The Calgary team started under Lear's direction with spring training. Early in August Stampeders were back at it again and played their initial game August 21. The club got away to a good start and defeated Toronto Beaches-Indians 16-7 in a pre-season game.

From there Calgary racked up 12 consecutive triumphs without a setback, and the only game Stampeders didn't win was when Saskatchewan Roughriders held them to a 4-4 deadlock in the first game of the Western final. Calgary made up for this by defeating Riders 17-6 in the second contest.

Varsity Stadium, November 27, 1948.

Long distance swimmers made sports history in the Fifties. Among them was Canada's Marilyn Bell, who swam Lake Ontario. Not to be outdone, The Herald's John Hopkins swam the Bowness Lagoon. Art Evans sent this report.

PILOT BOAT DISPATCH — Bowness Lagoon has been conquered. The treacherous waters of this world-famous resort near Calgary, which had never been successfully crossed by a long distance swimmer, met their master Monday as John Carmen Hopkins, a spunky, chunky farmboy, stroked his way to fame and fortune.

Hopkins, a powerful swimmer who was first introduced to water when he fell down the well at his father's farm in Bentley, Alberta, refused to give up despite calm

Crowds welcomed the Calgary Stampeders home when the team won the 1948 Grey Cup. They fell a bit short in 1949, but the fans thronged downtown to greet them anyway. The scene above is Centre street and Ninth Avenue, in front of the old CPR station. In those days, even football heroes travelled by train.

water and ideal weather conditions, and in the end victory was his. "I did it for the money," was Hopkins' modest comment as he crawled ashore to be met by three curious children and a stray dog.

It was this reporter's privilege to follow the epic battle of Man against Bowness from the safety of a tipsy canoe and what a spine-tingling fight it was. The issue was always in doubt. At one stage it appeared that all was lost when the gallant swimmer struck his head on the ornamental fountain in the middle of the Lagoon.

However the dogged Hopkins refused to give up. After sinking twice he pushed his way to the surface again and continued in the wrong direction for half an hour before Coach Gorde Hunter got him back on course with the aid of a whaling harpoon. Thereafter a brisk belt with an oar was all that the distance swimmer needed to guide him to his goal.

Alongside Hopkins' amazing feat, the exploits of endurance swimmers like Bert Thomas, Marilyn Bell and Flo Chadwick pale into insignificance. They had learned to swim BEFORE they set out after records. Hopkins has never learned to swim and when a man is afraid to take a bath alone it takes raw courage to test the wild whirlpools of Bowness Lagoon.

That's what Hopkins had plenty of Monday—raw courage. The fact that he had to be thrown bodily into the water by his handlers just to get him started, does not detract in any way from the magnificence of his achievement. In fact his early reluctance to get his feet wet adds lustre to the stature of a major accomplishment. What other swimmer in the world today could extricate himself from a starting position in the mud at the bottom of a shallow lagoon, and fight on to victory?

August 16, 1955.

John Hopkins of The Herald wrote this profile of one of the giants of the curling world. Two days later, Matt Baldwin won the Brier.

The geography books are going to have to be changed. There's a province between Saskatchewan and British Columbia that's named Baldwin. It used to be called Alberta when I was going to school. But that was before Matt Baldwin started blowing up quite a curling storm back in 1954.

Canada can be considered to have two homebrew sports heroes.

One is Maurice Richard who toils splendidly for the Montreal Canadiens.

The other is Baldwin.

His fame is best measured around the Memorial Arena here where the 29th Macdonald Brier, and Baldwin's fourth, is being played.

Ten of the participating rinks are identified by provinces. So in the parlance here, Saskatchewan lost to Manitoba and Northern Ontario defeated British Columbia. But Baldwin defeated New Brunswick.

There are a lot of unfamiliar faces in the Brier, of course. But it's just that the name Baldwin has come to be associated with championship curling.

Early this week he had to move to a secluded hotel in order to foil the well-wishers. And eating has become something of a chore because he hasn't yet mastered the feat of eating with one hand and shaking hands with the other.

The only real privacy he has here is when he's on the ice.

And, to quote an old saw, it couldn't happen to a nicer guy. Fame rests lightly on the shoulders of this 31-year-old magician.

He is, to sum it, a great guy.

Victoria, March 6, 1958.

Battles in the Cold War

The years after the Second World War were shadowed by fears that the Third might be imminent. The weapons ranged on both sides grew more and more deadly. The Soviet Union matched the American atomic bomb; then both sides deployed still more destructive hydrogen bombs. Elaborate plans were made for evacuating whole cities on warning of a bomber attack; these plans were abandoned when the much faster intercontinental ballistic missile was developed. At times international tension was as severe as it had been in the late Thirties. United Nations troops fought Chinese Communists in Korea; Britain and France attacked Egypt in the Suez Canal crisis; Soviet tanks and troops suppressed an uprising in Hungary; an American spy plane was shot down over the Soviet Union. This last episode scuttled the faint hopes for progress at a summit meeting between U.S. President Dwight D. Eisenhower and Soviet Premier Nikita Khrushchev. Early in this troubled time, Peter Inglis of The Herald's Washington bureau filed this report on the growing tension in the United States.

A very high personage, speaking not for attribution, Tuesday succinctly summed up the mood of the American people:

"Not mad at anybody; just very confused and a little hurt."

He might well have added "and exceedingly anxious".

Americans or at least Washingtonians are in a fingernail-chewing mood.

This confused, slightly-hurt anxiety comes largely from the floods of words that have been beating on their ears about wars and rumors of wars; about Communists boring at their government structure; about what would happen if somebody else had the atom bomb; and how somebody else may have it pretty soon. The words flow from all sides: from politicians on Capitol Hill, from soldiers, diplomats, newspaper columnists, and radio's professional viewers-with-alarm.

William C. Bullitt, the bald-domed, one-time ambassador to Russia, brought the word-fest to fever pitch with his statement before the House committee on un-American activities that if the Russians had had the atomic bomb "it would already have been dropped on the United States."

Twenty-four hours later dispatches from Germany quoted a noted physicist newly "escaped" from Russia, as saying the Russians are very near to having the bomb.

General Eisenhower, appearing before a luncheon of the National Press club, tried to pour oil on the troubled waters of American opinion by saying flatly, "no nation at present would deliberately provoke a war — and that includes Russia."

But even he felt compelled to add: "But wars are stupid anyway, and they can always be started stupidly by some immature county that gets itself into a position from which it feels it cannot back down."

Meanwhile, right at home, there was a good start on what might turn into a witch-hunt directed against everybody with ideas to the left of liberal.

Most Americans seemed solidly behind President Truman's plan to "purge" government departments of Communists and fellow travelers. Several Democratic bigwigs, including Secretary of Labor Schwellerbach, had already begun to outshout their chief in their protestations of hatred of Communism — perhaps because the Democratic party itself has on occasion been accused of radicalism by the deeper-dyed Republicans in Congress.

Few Americans seemed to have considered the liberties question involved in such a "purge" — a question which caused the searching of many Canadian hearts during the Dominion's spy inquiry last year.

The committee on un-American affairs rubbed its hands with glee and seemed not at all disposed to heed the warning of American Federation of Labor President William Green — an old Red-hater himself — that persecution might strengthen Communism in the United States or make it pop up under a different name, as it had done in Canada.

Washington, March 26, 1947

There are some familiar names in this report from a China still in the throes of Communist revolution. A correspondent of The Times of London provided this report for Southam newspapers.

The most significant feature of the last few weeks in Peking, which has now become the capital of China again under the Communist regime, has been the sudden openly acknowledged spread of Russian influence.

More than 300 Russian advisers, technicians and educationists have been arriving in Peking and taking part in celebrations. The Soviet ambassador, General Roshin, has arrived there with a large staff.

Refugees from Harbin state that North Manchuria is completely under the Russian thumb, with the Russian consul-general giving orders to the Communist authorities.

The real government of the new "Chinese People's Republic" is the central political council, with Mao Tse-tung as president, six vice-presidents, and 53 members. Under this is the so-called central people's government, with Chou En-lai as prime minister and foreign minister.

The heads of the pro-Russian party now in power are Liu Shao-chi, secretary general of the Communist party; Li Li-san, vice-chairman of the trade unions and former chairman in North Manchuria; and Lo Jung-heng as head of the inspection bureau, presumably corresponding with the Soviet N.K.V.D.

The much-vaunted "land reform" has failed to satisfy a large section of the peasantry, who are also burdened by heavy taxes and over-regimentation and the continued rise in the cost of living, in spite of intensive propaganda and fine promises.

Nevertheless, such discontent is unlikely to have any moderating effect on extremist policies.

Meanwhile Communists stabbed westward today in what may be the death blow to the Nationalists on China's mainland.

Some Allied leaders from the Second World War stayed on to cope with a Cold War world. British prime minister Winston Churchill, back in power after a post-war electoral defeat, conferred in 1952 with U.S. President Harry Truman during a brief visit to Washington.

Chinese newspapers reported that two government armies were routed in a Red thrust at Kweilin in the southwest.

Red General Lin Piao appeared to be trying to split the shattered Nationalist domain in two with a quick knockout of its last big mainland force — the 200,000-man force of General Pai Chung-hsi.

Press accounts said the conqueror of Manchuria, Tientsin and Hankow sent veterans of the Reds' fourth field army straight at Pai's home base, Kweilin. The Kwangsi province city is 250 air miles northwest of Canton.

To the south, another Communist force commanded by General Chen Keng was reported slashing westward from the newly-won Canton area. These troops were said to be less than 50 miles from the Kwangsi border. Their drive was along the West river.

The push on Kwangsi seemed in itself evidence that the Reds are determined to extend their control quickly over the entire mainland.

Tokyo, October 20, 1949

Canadians were part of the United Nations force that fought North Korean and Communist Chinese invaders in South Korea. The Korean war broke out in 1950 and ended in a truce three years later. Bill Boss of the Canadian Press sent back this report on a battle fought by the Princess Patricia's Canadian Light Infantry.

The Chinese had had enough. They withdrew. Throughout Tuesday night and part of Wednesday, the Chinese Communist hordes attacked United Nations positions on a steep hill on this west central sector of the flaming Korean front. They out-flanked and encircled these troops who until now had met with only token resistance as they advanced northward.

But they failed to break a line held by such stalwarts as the sergeant who flung his empty rifle like a spear into the face of the enemy. Or the young company commander who coolly called for mortar and artillery fire upon his own position when his men ran out of ammunition.

These troops held steady as rocks as the enemy in his massed hundreds assaulted their hill from the front, from the flanks and finally from the rear when the flanks gave way under sheer weight of numbers. By 6 a.m. Wednesday the enemy had had enough. He withdrew down the hill and dug in.

But he was only 100 yards away screened by a thick curtain of smoke, behind which he undoubtedly was building up for another attack. But at least for the time being, the enemy had been turned back.

Wave upon wave, following the orders of whistles and bugles to the split second, the enemy hordes surged upon the United Nations' positions late Tuesday night and kept it up almost without cessation until Wednesday morning. It was suicidal, but it evoked this tribute from one sergeant.

"They're good. They were on top of our positions before we knew it.

Canadian soldiers fought in the Korean War of 1950-53, against Communist forces from North Korea and China. It was a nasty little war, involving a lot of close-range fighting with grenades and bayonets.

"They're quiet as mice with those rubber shoes of theirs and then there's a whistle. They get up with a shout about 10 feet from our positions and come in.

"The first wave throws its grenades, fires its weapons and goes to the ground. It is followed by a second which does the same, and a third comes up. They just keep coming."

That was the sergeant who hurled his bayonetted rifle like a spear when his ammunition gave out. Another man hurled his bayonet at the foe.

The sergeant's company held out by dividing the slim remaining supply of ammunition until the enemy pressure eased.

West Control Section, Korea,
April 26, 1951

Peter Inglis of The Herald's Ottawa bureau covered the coronation of Queen Elizabeth II.

Radiant, clothed in majesty and strangely alone in the middle of the bright throng — alone in the awesome, dedicated solitude of monarchy — she sits erect in the chair in which Britain has crowned its kings and queens since the Middle Ages. In absolute silence, the Archbishop of Canterbury takes St. Edward's Crown from the Dean of Westminster, turns and sets it reverently on her head.

The silence shatters. A great shout, three times repeated, rises as one voice from 7,000 throats and reverberates from the ancient vault dimly seen high above the blaze of gold and blue, crimson and scarlet:

God Save the Queen!

The Abbey's bells peal joyously.

Gold and silver flash as princes and princesses, peers and peeresses, don their coronets and caps of state, and the heraldic kings of arms their crowns.

And the trumpets sound, a strident, triumphant fanfare underlining climax.

In this vibrant instant Elizabeth II has been crowned, with God's grace Queen of the United Kingdom of Great Britain and Northern Ireland and of her other Realms and Territories, Head of the Commonwealth.

After the shouting and the trumpets, suddenly there is silence and in it the voice (the archbishop) pronouncing a benediction:

"The Lord give you faithful Parliament and quiet realms; . . . wise counsellors and

A year after her coronation, Queen Elizabeth II and the Duke of Edinburgh made this official appearance, riding around the track at the opening of the 1954 Ascot race meeting.

upright magistrates; leaders of integrity in learning and labor. . .honest, peaceable and dutiful citizens.

"May wisdom and knowledge be the stability of your times, and the fear of the Lord your treasure."

Then anointed, crowned and blessed Queen, she leaves Saint Edward's chair, mounts the golden carpeted steps of the dais and is lifted by the archbishops, the bishops and the lords on to her throne, there to receive their homage.

Then a sudden crash of drums, a fanfare of trumpets and a mighty shout from all the assembly: "God Save Queen Elizabeth! Long Live Queen Elizabeth! May the Queen live forever!"

The archbishop administers Holy Communion, a solemn Te Deum is sung, and the Queen, who has retired to Saint Edward's chapel, returns dressed in her robe of crimson velvet, wearing now the imperial crown, and is escorted in magnificent procession through the Abbey to its West Door.

The ceremony is done.

Westminster Abbey, June 2, 1953

In July, 1956, Egypt's president Nasser seized control of the Suez Canal. After three months of diplomatic protests, Britain and

France invaded Egypt Oct. 31 in an effort to restore international control. Israel had invaded two days earlier as part of a continuing border dispute. Canadian External Affairs Minister Lester B. Pearson won the 1957 Nobel Peace Prize for his part in establishing a UN peace-keeping force. J.R. Walker of Southam News Service sent this report from the UN session that established the force.

A United Nations command or an international police force in the Middle East, to be headed by Canada's Maj. Gen E.L.M. Burns, was approved early this morning by the UN general assembly, voting favorably on a Canadian-inspired resolution.

It was proposed that a battalion or so of Canadian troops, now on NATO duty in Germany, would be used in a non-belligerent fashion, to "secure" the peace in Egypt. The U.S. government, as Ambassador Henry Cabot Lodge said in debate at midnight, "is prepared to help in an important way, as regards airlifts, shipping, transport and supplies."

Canada's External Affairs Minister Lester Pearson rushed home Friday to obtain Cabinet approval, then hurried back here for another special meeting of the assembly Saturday evening.

His resolution, requesting Dag Hammarskjold to submit within 48 hours a plan for setting up a police force for this emergency, was passed 57-0, with 19 abstentions.

Significantly, the Arab bloc, aside from Egypt, voted for it, showing how keen they really are for any big military action in the Middle East.

The British and French who had abstained from both Saturday and Sunday resolutions, were not happy about them, because they gave no opportunity for British and French troops to participate in the actions after a cease fire. They continued, however throughout the weekend to hold off landing operations.

Equally unhappy at the police force plan were the Israelis, who are probably most reluctant to give up any of the territory they have captured in Gaza and the Sinai Peninsula. They are holding out for a new armistice agreement with new boundaries, now.

United Nations, November 5, 1956

Russian tanks and troops crushed the Hungarian uprising in November, 1956. Nearly 200,000 Hungarians fled to other countries, many of them to Canada. Jack Stepler of Southam News Services sent this report from Klingenbach, Austria, on the Hungarian border.

The brief but fierce flame of Hungarian liberty was ground out by the iron heel of the Russian army during the "Black Sunday" of Nov. 4.

I saw that flame die here in the eyes of thousands of Hungarian refugees, just as it died in the Russian bombardment of Budapest.

Ten thousand heartbroken refugees — freedom snatched from their country's grasp — streamed through this Austrian border town Sunday, almost the entire number which succeeded in last-minute flight from the new oppression of a Soviet puppet government, the revived terror of secret police and the wholesale purges of freedom fighters which they are convinced their trapped countrymen now face. And some still ask: "Can the United Nations help Hungary?"

Although they came in pitiful bundles, with half-eaten loaves of bread in string bags with little more than the clothes they wore, they are the fortunate ones.

For they are the only survivors of the Judas kiss of Russian treachery, the "big lie" which the Russians perpetrated on Hungarian patriots from early Friday until Soviet tanks and artillery opened fire on Budapest before dawn Sunday.

I listened to that lie at the resistance headquarters at the university in the Hungarian town of Sopron late Saturday night. Our team of three Commonwealth correspondents travelled five miles into Hungary to Sopron in the dark for what was the final Western contact with insurgent leaders at a local headquarters. We knew the Red army was near, but not how near.

As two professors in the committee hierarchy courteously served us with coffee, they relayed the news which was to become Sunday morning the "Big Lie". Hungarian and Soviet Army chiefs in Budapest were conferring. The Russians had assured them, said Budapest radio, that no more Soviet reinforcements would be brought into Hungary. Soviet troops (already deployed strategically throughout the country) "would be withdrawn from Hungary in three or four days".

Soon afterwards, that Hungarian Army delegation had become Soviet prisoners and the "withdrawing" Russian troops had the country in an iron grip.

We sipped our late night coffee and the grey haired academician who was the spokesman advised us "Soviet tanks are approaching Sopron. The last word we had they were 12 miles away. There has been no resistance so far. The people hope, but cannot know what the Russians intend.

"We have a government which has accepted the demands of the people. Freedom and neutrality for Hungary has been declared. It now depends on what the United Nations does. At the moment we must wait."

With the tall polite student who guided us through the dark from the frontier we left the university to make our way through the ill lighted and muddy streets of the town of 35,000 back to the refuge of this Austrian border town.

We had seen the Russian army slam down the Iron Curtain early Saturday at Hegyeshalorn, the Hungarian frontier post on the main road between Vienna and Budapest. Five hundred yards inside the Hungarian side of the ploughed "no man's land" three Russian tanks in roadside fields had trained their muzzles on the road. All traffic had ceased. Sunday the few Hungarian frontier officials fled to Nickelsdorf on the Austrian side of the border strip, among the few who got out other than through Klingenbach.

As we watched the Russian troops climb above their tanks, an Austrian policeman and an Austrian Red Cross team gave us a foretaste of the Russian brutality which was to erupt in the early hours of Sunday.

The policeman was livid with rage, but explained that he and the Red Cross had hurried to the border to aid a Hungarian woman who had been stabbed by the tankmen in the fields, but that the Russians had refused to allow anyone near her; that she lay bleeding on the ground and the Austrians and Hungarians were powerless to help her.

The pattern of what was to come in a few hours was already forming.

The great tragedy of the collapse of the Hungarian revolt is their faith in the promises of the Russians. The revolt was an inspiring thing to watch grow, just as it was heartbreaking to see suppressed by treachery.

The spark that was ignited by the Budapest rising spread like wild fire all over the country. There was no proper organization. But, inspired by the Budapest bid for freedom, in town after town national committees were formed to fight for Hungarian freedom.

Everywhere the Hungarian army joined the rebels. Eventually they consolidated their organization under the National Council with headquarters in Gyor in

A captured Hungarian secret policeman, hands in the air, waits to be shot in the back by Hungarian rebels in Budapest. Two more, shot earlier, lie where they fell. The Soviet Union was quick and ruthless in suppressing the revolt. Many of the refugees found their way to Canada.

Western Hungary. When the AVO — secret police — slaughtered 80 peaceful demonstrators in nearby Magyarova ten days ago, the freedom fighters routed out, killed or arrested the secret police.

These men hung from lamp-posts in their hundreds. As the rebels gained strength they forced their demands for liberty and Hungarian neutrality on the government of Titoist Imre Nagy, even though they trusted Nagy simply because he was the only man to trust, in the words of the Sopron professor: "His actions in the last few days deserve support."

But the Hungarians were lulled into a sense of false security by their success. They did not expect Russian treachery; forgot that the tommy gun is no match for the tank.

Klingenbach, November 5, 1956

An editorial, taking note of the Russians' launching of the first man-made satellite.

Mankind, through the roaring thrust of a Russian rocket, Friday burst the bonds of gravity and stood on the black, cold threshold of space. The successful launching of the satellite which is even now orbiting through space about the globe is a scientific achievement of the first magnitude and, as such, crosses all frontiers to send a thrill of accomplishment and wonder through men everywhere.

It was, perhaps, inevitable that man would one day shuck off the bonds of his own atmosphere in his restless quest of the unknown which, in this case, began when the first individual lifted up his head and wondered at the immensity above him. Man himself has yet to probe space with his own senses, but this will follow as inevitably as did the first flying machine follow man's envy and interest in the free flight of the birds.

It is inevitable unless, of course, man destroys himself first. And therein lies the fly

which mars the scientific ointment. While the world rejoices at man's unlocking another secret of nature, the free world's jubilation is marred with foreboding and dread.

Moscow to New York in sixteen minutes. That is the rate at which the Russian satellite is moving, and that is the length of time it would take a satellite carrying a nuclear-equipped weapon to travel that distance when — not if — it is possible so to equip and launch such a weapon.

So it is that feeling in the Western world about the Russian feat is tinged with fear; not the honest fear of men standing on the threshold of the unknown, but the sickly fear that this latest advancement of man will be turned upon him as yet another weapon.

The Russians must be saluted for an achievement which is surely one of the great milestones in our recorded history. It gives the rest of the world a new appreciation of the technological advancement in the U.S.S.R.

October 8, 1957

An editorial.

One of the wisest acts the West could perform at this moment is to admit the Communist government of China is the government of that country and officially recognize it as such in UN matters and matters of trade.

The West, and in this case this really means the United States, is going to have to recognize Red China one of these days.

It will be forced to, by sheer weight of logic and of practical conditions. It could be done now without hardship.

This is not to suggest that this would make everything sweetness and light between the democracies and Communist China. That is too much to expect, but it would, at least, avoid some of the friction and remove some of the grounds for distrust.

If the United States cannot be persuaded to see reason as far as China is concerned then Canada and other western countries should do it themselves. It is to the advantage of the West to have trade with China and some basis of understanding.

For it is certain that Red China will be recognized. It is one of the most important facts of international politics.

August 8, 1958

An American U-2 spy plane was shot down over Soviet territory in May, 1960. Its pilot, Francis Gary Powers, survived to stand trial in a Russian court, as J.R. Walker of The Herald's London bureau reported from Moscow. Powers was freed in 1962 in exchange for Rudolph Abel, a Russian spy in the U.S.

To a burst of wild applause the Soviet prosecutor today called upon the court to sentence Francis Gary Powers to 15 years in prison for spying.

Hours later, the American U-2 pilot was sentenced to 10 years.

The state prosecutor, General Roman Rudenko, who argued for the Russians at the Nuremberg trials, told the military court that he would not demand the death penalty because of Powers' "sincere repentance" for his "criminal act."

Powers' defence counsel made a 45-minute plea for leniency because the U-2 pilot was only a tiny cog in the American military machine. Then Powers himself in a 5-minute speech threw himself upon the mercy of the Soviet court.

He admitted that he had committed a "grave crime and I realize I must be punished for it." He asked that all circumstances of his action be considered and that since he never delivered the information to the U.S., he be dealt with leniently. He did not wish to be considered personally as an enemy of the Russian people and was "deeply repentant and profoundly sorry" for what he had done. His plea was listened to in an intense silence, but no one seemed to be particularly moved by his quiet pleading.

It was obvious from the start of Rudenko's summing up speech to the packed hall, that it was President Eisenhower, vice-president Nixon, Secretary of State Herter, and the Pentagon "war mongers" who were really on trial here.

Brandishing the Brinkmanship policy of John Foster Dulles, in one hand and contrasting it with the peaceful co-existence policy of Nikita Khrushchev in the other, Rudenko launched immediately into an attack on what he called "the criminal and aggressive actions of the American criminal circles."

He labelled Powers, who sat quietly doodling with a pencil in the dock, a "nonstop spy pilot in the service of the U.S. military" who "sold himself to American intelligence for $2,500 a month."

Moscow, August 19, 1960

Soviet Premier Nikita Khrushchev waves his fist as he addresses the United Nations General Assembly. Later in the proceedings, he pulled off a shoe and brandished it to emphasize how strongly he disagreed with a ruling of the chairman.

Charles Lynch of Southam News Service was on hand for a disgraceful, but fascinating episode in the United Nations General Assembly.

The president of the General Assembly smashed his gavel and adjourned the session in a huff. Premier Khrushchev of the Soviet Union thumped madly upon his desk, called the Philippine delegate a "jerk", and at one point tore off his shoe and brandished it in the air.

It all happened here Wednesday as the assembly debated whether the issue of colonialism should be discussed before the full assembly or in the political committee.

Veteran observers, their eyes popping, expressed the opinion that had President Frederick Boland of Ireland not wound it up with his gavel-breaking exhibition, there might well have been fisticuffs between the representatives of East and West.

Nothing like it had been seen in these parts since the days when the UN site was a slum known as Hell's Kitchen, inhabited by the Dead End Kids.

Grown men, some of them diplomats, hooted and hollered like teen-agers staging a rumble.

The final blow-up came, ironically, just when Premier Khrushchev was on the threshold of his first voting victory in the General Assembly. It was brought on by one of his henchmen, Eduard Mezincescu, deputy foreign minister of Romania.

Mr. Khrushchev had been getting great mileage all day out of his resolution to have the assembly discuss colonialism. Delegates from all parts of the world, but notably Africa and Asia, flocked to his support—it was like asking a church picnic to come out against sin.

But Mezincescu was provoked by a reference to the lack of full independence in Eastern Europe made by Francis O. Wilcox of the United States.

Mezincescu stomped to the podium and went into a long tirade, aimed first at the United States, but gradually switching to President Boland, whom he accused of being partial to the West.

At this point, Mr. Boland was thumping his gavel so hard it snapped in two, and the head went flying through the air, landing behind the assembly president.

Mr. Boland, fuming, said: "In view of the scene we have just witnessed, the meeting should be adjourned at once and it is hereby adjourned."

Mr. Khrushchev had opened Wednesday's debate with a routine speech introducing his resolution—routine in that it used words no stronger than scum, robbers, slave traders and slave owners to describe the imperialist oppressors and colonialists.

It looked like one of the assembly's calmer days.

The fireworks really started when Lorenzo Sumulong of the Philippines took the floor. He brought in the issue of independence in Eastern Europe, and Mezincescu lit up like a Roman candle.

He demanded that Sumulong be gavelled to order.

But Boland said the Filipino delegate's remarks were a matter of opinion, but not out of order. At this point, Khrushchev, from his seat, took off his shoe and brandished it.

Up to the podium strode the wrathful Mr. Khrushchev, with both shoes on his feet but fire in his eye. He waved the Filipino away from the podium with a rude gesture, which Sumulong met with a mock salute.

Mr. Khrushchev proceeded to call Sumulong a "jerk of American imperialism." (Russian experts said the word could also be rendered as "joker", but the UN interpreter gave it as "jerk.")

Then came Mr. Wilcox of the U.S. and his mention of eastern Europe. He was about to say more about captive governments and about rude and intemperate conduct by the Soviet Union and the "satellite" Romanians.

October 13, 1960

Jokes and Strong Words

Herald columnists flourished in the Fifties. Ken Liddell, railroad fancier and inveterate tourist, covered southern Alberta, turning up fascinating people and places. Art Evans' whimsy and parody brightened many a slow news day. Richard J. Needham, alas, was lured away to Toronto. Best of them all, perhaps, was Richard L. Sanburn. Take It From Here, Sanburn's column on the editorial page, was usually good for a laugh, a cheer, or a purple face, depending on Sanburn's mood and the reader's belief. Here, in his forthright way, he chides a right-wing Social Credit MP.

Last Friday there was an article on this page reprinted from Saturday Night, Toronto, which consisted almost entirely of a tape-recorded telephone interview that publication had with John Blackmore, Social Credit MP for Lethbridge.

In it, Mr. Blackmore beat his soggy old drum again in favor of a full-scale witch hunt after Communists and suspected Communists in Canada.

Rarely have I ever encountered such junk.

And in view of the fact that I have already had various remarks to make in this column about Mr. Blackmore and his hysterical hallucinations, I think I may reasonably have a bash at this particular wild-eyed effusion.

Mr. Blackmore, of course, sees himself as the only bona fide, homogenized, true-blue and one hundred per cent Communist fighter in this country. In this he is amazingly similar to Joe McCarthy in the United States, which isn't really amazing because in many respects Mr. Blackmore is a carbon copy of McCarthy with a few shrill and fanatical trimmings which are of his own devising.

However, let's get on to some of the things Mr. Blackmore said in his interview.

People all over the country, he said, were deeply concerned with this matter (Communism).

Richard L. Sanburn

That's right, Mr. Blackmore, they certainly are. I happen to be one of them. But those people are also concerned with fundamental freedom, human decency and an old-fashioned thing called democracy. And most of us are just as concerned about protecting our way of life from the kind of dictatorship of fear and threatened character assassination being huckstered by the McCarthys and Blackmores as we are about protecting it from Communists. Real Communists, that is, Mr. Blackmore, not the very many thoroughly responsible but liberal-minded people you would probably denounce as Communists largely because they refuse to have any part of your ravings and rantings.

Yes, Mr. Blackmore said, he had "supporters," but wouldn't want their names mentioned. They were "mortally afraid" of being assailed as he has been assailed. "There has evidently been a campaign to intimidate Parliament." (Mr. Blackmore at this point was kind enough to refer to an editorial in The Herald and called it a "standing disgrace" to Canada.)

Really, Mr. Blackmore, you do see the most remarkable things under the bed.

Why not be more specific about the "organization" you suggest "may be behind it"? I'll bet I can guess. Every member of it would have a Semitic name, wouldn't he, or else he would have changed his name so it wouldn't sound Semitic?

I have criticized you, Mr. Blackmore, very forthrightly at times, and will continue to do so whenever the occasion suggests it. There is no "organization" telling me what to write, Mr. Blackmore, although I know you won't believe this. I write what I think, personally, and I think you've got several buttons loose in the brains department.

Just because Parliament tends to laugh you off the stage you bring up this fantastic claptrap about Parliament being "intimidated." Is there no possibility, Mr. Blackmore, that Parliament laughs at you because you're so crazily hepped about witch-hunts that you're funny? Can't anybody hold firm opinions of their own, which are in violent opposition to your opinions, without having been "intimidated"?

And what are all your "supporters" so mortally afraid of? Maybe they're a pretty gutless bunch, like the two who wrote to me once and wouldn't sign their names. I challenged them to crawl out from under their slimy rock, and to this day, I've not heard a peep out of them.

And so you can't see how on earth newspapermen, like myself, can be anything else but pro-Communist because we won't pass the matches while you burn witches at the stake. People you have decided are witches, that is.

I guess it would never occur to you that a lot of people remember that Nazi-Fascist fire is just as brutal, ruthless and fatal as Communist fire.

April 5, 1954

Ken Liddell

Ken Liddell's column, Furrows and Foothills, chronicled his travels through the West, especially southern Alberta, for nearly 25 years. He was a railway buff, and in this column he planted the seed of an idea; four years later, a 5900 locomotive was saved from the scrap-heap and preserved near Mewata Stadium. In 1981, it was moved to Heritage Park.

Because we have let so many things slip away unnoticed is no reason why we should not now start to retain what may soon be only remembered.....so why doesn't Calgary endeavour to obtain a 5900 class locomotive for permanent, public display?

In their day the 5900s were not only the biggest thing of their kind in the British Empire, but they are as closely linked with Calgary's history as were the bull teams because they were built for the sole purpose of chewing the mountains down to size between Calgary and Revelstoke.

They've left their old fields out in the mountains — diesels have taken over — and while some are barking at the miles over the main line prairies to the East, there is a long, lonesome line of them in melancholy retirement at Ogden Shops in Calgary.

Beyond keeping a certain number in repair, what the CPR plans to do with these big, beautiful and powerful creatures, even the CPR does not know for sure.

As scrap (dreadful thought) they would return a pittance and from what I can gather no other roads, such as foreign roads, want to buy them.

There are two reasons for this. One is the impact of dieselization and the other is they are such big brutes few railroads could use them.

In other words, the 5900's were built for Alberta's rugged Rocky Mountains...and Calgary, within whistling distance of their challenge, the Big Hill at Field, is the place where one should be permanently displayed.

You would have no idea how big these things are until you see one standing by itself. You may think you've got a fair sized lot, but the largest of the 5900's (there are three classes and the smallest is only smaller by a foot or so) are those numbered 5900 to 5919 and they are 98 feet long. From rail to top of the smokestack is 15½ feet.

They are on the way to becoming something children born today may never see. Certainly not in action. . . the wonderful sight of them hammering and yammering their way over the mountains under the careful, gloved caress of a single man.

If one was saved people could gaze at it in wonder. If promises of atomic power come about, who knows but what they may even laugh because man — of our age — once built a thing so big to move himself around.

But they'd never hear them panting under exertion or sighing at rest.

And Calgary, for which they were built, may have the opportunity to save one for posterity. . . a great attraction for a city proud of its traditions, but an attraction more tangible than just a spirit.

August 10, 1955

Rock 'n Roll was just getting started in the Fifties, and Richard L. Sanburn was better-equipped than most grown-ups to understand what was happening.

The other evening, purely in the interests of sociological research, I went to a movie.

I went to see "Rock Around the Clock," a percussive melodrama constructed around the musical organization intituled Billy Haley and His Comets.

It deals with what some people are still calling "the phenomenon" of the kind of popular music and dancing known as "rock 'n roll."

And it is the film which has been causing no end of a ruckus in Britain.

In many British cities in which it has been shown, the youthful audiences have been sent into uncontrollable, riotous and destructive spasms by the music in this film. They have practically wrecked theatres, rocked 'n rolled into the streets and stopped traffic, and their unhinged behavior has necessitated calling the cops and the fire department to put out the conflagrations of unbridled young emotions.

I wanted to see what would happen in Calgary.

And I can tell in one word.

Nothing. Sweet nothing at all.

The young fry sat there, enthralled and entranced. I saw some feet tapping ever so quietly on the floor. Nobody squealed, nobody jived. They just sat there quietly, ever-so-well behaved, and soaked it up in pure delight. Good for them.

At this point, I suspect, some of my teenage "fans" are sitting there squint-eyed just waiting for me to express my opinions of rock 'n roll so they can rip up this newspaper and stick another rusty nail in that

miniature effigy of Sanburn they seem to keep handy.

Well, kids, you can simmer down.

I hate to disappoint you, but I had a wonderful time myself. I liked it.

I like it because it filled me with nostalgia. It reminded me almost painfully of part of my own life, when I was young and when I too, played in a dance band. Piano, if you're interested.

You see, chums, we played essentially that same kind of music more than twenty years ago. Not all the time, mind you, but a good healthy dish of it spread through an average evening of dancing. The young people liked it then just as they like it now, because it has rhythm in it you could hang your hat on. There was a good deal more melody to the numbers in my day than there is in 1956 rock 'n roll.

And today, they have the benefit of electronic instruments, which weren't heard of in my time. So that the beat of the guitars and the bull fiddle and so on can build up so that they can be felt as much as they can be heard. As a matter of fact, by the time that film was over I felt as though I'd had a massage with sound-waves.

I did notice, too, that the pianists in both outfits did their stint standing up, with no piano stool, wiggling and jerking as if possessed. Those boys wouldn't have lasted in my league. That stuff's okay for a number or two, but we used to play a solid five hours or more at a go, and at the end of it I was lucky I could get off the stool. On the average, I dropped a good five pounds in weight every dance-night.

But it sure took me way back. And I'll tell you something, kids. . . when you see history coming round for the second time, you don't feel too good.

October 22, 1956

Bruce Phillips has since become famous as a television newsman, but it was The Herald that taught him everything he knows about rats. In an editorial-page column, he described that education.

Another rat has been killed in Alberta, which means there must be at least two or three left.

As usual, the execution was followed by a thorough exposition in the press of all the facts relating to the rodent's demise.

Alberta must be the only place in the world where the death of a rat is front-page news. Usually these stories give the readers all the titillating details, including a note about the instrument used, how many blows were required to polish off the beastie, and whether it had any last words.

The reason for this vital interest in the state of the rat is, as the old-timers know, because Alberta is virtually rat-free. What there is that makes Alberta rat-free, apart from the obvious fact they are so relentlessly hounded by everyone in the province, is not known.

An example of the public preoccupation

Bruce Phillips

with rats occurred on this reporter's very first working day at The Herald, and for that matter in Alberta. I was, of course, uninformed of the rat situation.

A woman called that morning, and in wild excitement bordering on hysteria, shouted into the telephone, "I've killed a rat. A big brown one. I've killed a rat."

Having come from a land where rats are born, live and die natural deaths without incident or public concern, the statement didn't have much impact.

A half an hour or so later I wandered over to the city editor and recounted the strange experience of a woman shouting over the telephone about a rat.

The transformation was immediate and violent. The city editor started calling for a photographer, and hurling questions one after the other without waiting for an answer. Where? When? What color was it?

I could hardly be blamed for beginning to wonder about the woman and the city editor.

When he calmed down enough to explain himself, he was appalled to discover his new boy had failed to obtain any information on the incident. It was a reportorial disgrace that took some time to live down.

A subscriber once telephoned to report having seen a rat; not killed one, mind you. Just sighted one. The story was given top billing on the local page, with a two-column heading, which said "WOMAN SEES RAT".

Satellites may come and go, worlds may tumble, but for pure sustained loyal readership, a good rat story is still an Alberta newspaperman's best bet.

October 26, 1957

Art Evans, a Herald columnist who later moved to The Edmonton Journal, had a love-hate affair with the Burns Avenue bus. One day, after reading a bit too much Ernest Hemingway, he wrote this column.

Hemingway and the Burns Avenue Bus: The cold was a coldness and the coldness was cold. Ralph knew this but he told no-one. There are things a man must lock tightly in his soul as the soul of the sea is locked tightly.

Art Evans

You are Ralph who lives at III Edgerow Road and it is time to go and drive straight and true, the inspector said. He fired a field gun he had brought back from the true war. It was the starting signal and on the other side of town a building collapsed truly in fine dust.

Ralph released the clutch as a true man releases his only true soul. Beneath him, the twisted bowels ground into life-force motion. They were moving. Ralph was driving straight and true. Outside, the cold was a coldness and the coldness was cold.

March 1, 1957

Richard J. Needham

He knew who he was and what he did. He was Ralph and he lived at III Edgerow Road and he drove the Burns Avenue Bus straight and true. Sometimes he said things to himself. I am Ralph and I live at III Edgerow Road and I drive the Burns Avenue bus straight and true. It was good for a man to know these things. He was not angered at the cold for the cold was a coldness and he knew it was.

Ralph patted the true sides of the Burns Avenue bus. It was the true pat of a lover caressing a woman. The bus was a brave bus living as it knew it must live, the only way. Its bowels were twisted and the wholeness had departed, but the bus lived true.

An inspector approached. He had been to the wars, fighting true in the brave mud and now the fighting and the mud were behind him and yet all around him. He was a proud man.

But he could no longer drive straight and true and they had made him an inspector. He suffered the demotion and the hurt in his eyes was a true hurt. But his soul was still driving straight and true, the only way a true soul can drive.

A column by Richard J. Needham.

It may be that there are easy countries in this world, but Canada is not one of them. This is a hard country, and it will only survive so long as it produces hard people. It is easy to forget that in such cities as Toronto and Montreal, even in such cities as Calgary and Edmonton. But once you get out of the cities, once you travel, as we have been doing, through the bush and across the prairie, you are sharply reminded of it.

Life is hard on the prairie, life is hard in the bush, and you can tell it by the faces of the people you see through the train windows. They are hard faces, not in the sense of being mean and cruel, but in the sense of being tough and resourceful. These people do not live by pushing buttons, but by fighting and mastering a hostile environment.

It is from this struggle of man against nature, against climate, against history and geography, that Canada draws her strength. Where life is easy, men and women decay. Adversity is what makes them sturdy and enterprising. Do not expend your sympathy on the children growing up in steam-heated apartments. They are the under-privileged.

There is a strange story being spread around that Canadians have a right to this or that or the other thing. Tell it to the gloomy jackpines; tell it to the deathcold waters of Lake Superior; tell it to the ancient rock. The only right Canadians have is the right to build a nation. We have made a start at that, but only a start: there is harder work before us than behind.

The whistle blows in the sharp air; the smoke drifts over the silent forest; the train beats its way, as a score of others are doing, from ocean to ocean. It's gotta be done, say the wheels: it's gotta be done, it's gotta be done. And so it is done, as everything else is done in Canada, because men have the will and energy to do it.

It is not systems that count: it is men. For a hardy, adaptable people, any system will work: for a slothful, self-pitying one, none at all. What kind of men have we produced in Canada? Look around, you will see their monument. What kind are we producing today?

January 3, 1951

Richard J. Needham said farewell to Calgary in this column, written in 1951.

Writing," says E.B. White, "is hard work and bad for the health." We have been writing these pieces for some eleven years, and while it has not been bad for our health, we will agree that it has been hard work. It is not hard physically, but it is very hard mentally, to choose the right nouns and verbs and put them in the right order.

Some pieces are harder to write than others. This is an especially hard one, because it is the last one of all: a valedictory, if you please, or a swan song. We are leaving Calgary, and Alberta, and the West. Next Saturday evening a train will bear us away to Toronto, where we hope to perform useful services around the office of The Globe and Mail. So ends a 15-year chapter in our life.

It seems much longer, and it seems much shorter. It seems longer because of all the changes we have seen during that time. When we came here, many people still referred to street car routes as the "Red Line" and the "White Line". Social Credit meetings were well attended, and the distribution of dividends looked for at any moment. Coffee cost a nickel at the Bay, and a second cup (said the management, cheerfully) was yours for the asking. For $2,000 cash, you could pick up a nice bungalow on the North Hill. How many centuries ago was that?

It seems shorter because we can remember just about every detail of our arrival in Calgary. It was September, 1936, but it seems like yesterday. Coming from the smoky old East, and seeing Calgary for the first time on one of those blue-and-gold mornings, we were enchanted by the clear, tangy air; by the sense of freedom and adventure; by the feeling that we were spiritually, as well as physically, on top of the world.

The old town was kind of beaten up in those days: nobody had any money. But we think (or we have deceived ourself into thinking) that people had more fun then, that it was a friendlier place, that it had a spaciousness and graciousness which have since contracted. Calgary is half again as big as it was when we came, and the merchants love it, but a lot of Calgarians don't love it, and we can understand why.

Something has been lost. But enough remains to make this, as it has always been, a city with its own distinctive character. It has long seemed to us that this city, not Edmonton, is the true capital of Alberta. It is not a matter of money or politics or population, it is a matter of spirit, and that is what Calgary has. Restless, lucky, casual, hard-living, hard-working, hard-drinking, it is one of the last places in the world where an individualist can feel at home.

We have grown up a little bit in Calgary. We have learned that life flows and changes: nothing remains stable. The mere fact of having anything makes certain that you will lose it. What we have had here — the happiness, the friendships, the adventure — we gracefully and gratefully surrender. We have the memory of them, and perhaps that is better: for memories cannot be lost, and do not ever need to be surrendered.

February 15, 1951

Blockade Test Hours Away As U.S. Fleet Rings Cuba

CABINET MEETS

Tougher Cuba Stand Likely For Canada

RUSSIAN FORCES ON ALERT

Ships May Meet Before Nightfall

WASHINGTON AP — Russia and the United States headed on a collision course today as U.S. ships moved to enforce an arms blockade of Cuba.

HOW LONDON NEWSPAPERS REACTED

Cuban, U.S. Charges Go Before UN Today

TODAY
Inside The Herald

THE CALGARY HERALD
PRICE TEN CENTS
CALGARY, ALBERTA, MONDAY, JUNE 5, 1967
FORTY PAGES
Late City Edition

MID-EAST CRISIS AT A GLANCE

Middle East War Erupts; Land, Air Battles Fought

Israelis, Arabs Clash In Sinai

TEL AVIV — The Middle East was aflame with war today as fighting broke out between Israel and its Arab neighbors for the third time in 30 years.

Blasts Herald War In Cairo

Anti-Aircraft Bursts Seen; Crowds Cheer Radio Bulletins

By DON McGILLIVRAY

CAIRO — The Middle East tinder box burst into flames today and war came to Cairo this morning with the sound of explosions and gunfire.

Women Weep Openly

Airliners Warned Off

HERALD WRITERS COVER BATTLE ZONES

Three As Isr

MOST F FOR SECU

Big Fo Urged

By ROBERT COHEN

THE CALGARY HERALD
PRICE FIVE CENTS
CALGARY, ALBERTA, FRIDAY, NOVEMBER 22, 1963
FORTY-FOUR PAGES
Late City Edition

KENNEDY SLAIN

Assassinated In Dallas

DALLAS, Texas — President Kennedy was slain today.

The 36th president of the United States was shot to death by a hidden assassin armed with a high-powered rifle.

Futile Effort To Save Life

SHOT IN HEAD, KENNEDY SLUMPS IN BACK SEAT OF CAR
Mrs. Kennedy, Security Man Lean

THE CALGARY HERALD
PRICE TEN CENTS
CALGARY, ALBERTA, THURSDAY, AUGUST 22, 1968
FIFTY-SIX PAGES

Soviets Must Pay Colo

By EDWARD CRANKSHAW

LONDON —

'Murderers Go Angry Czechs

Extraordinary Display Of Resistance

They Fought Bare-Handed

By TAD SZULC

FLAG LOWERED Czech border

Quick UN Censure Sought Before Puppet Rule Set Up

By PAUL KIDD

'MISTAKE', SAY ROMANIANS

VIENNA (AP) —

PM Says Russian Move 'Great Leap Backward'

By ROBERT COHEN

OTTAWA —

Hostage Taken At Gunpoint

City Man Held In S

By GORDON STEPTO

THE CALGARY HERALD
CALGARY, ALBERTA, MONDAY, JULY 21, 1969
X PAGE
STOP PRESS EDITION

Man On The Moon

'GIANT LEAP FOR MANKIND'

BULLETIN
HOUSTON — Moon walkers Neil Armstrong and Edwin Aldrin this afternoon brought their tiny lunar module 'Eagle' to a rendezvous and link-up with the command ship piloted by Mike Collins.

Lunar Module Lifts Off Moon
By GEORGE BRIMMELL and BOB COHEN

'It's Unbelievably Perfect', Armstrong's Wife Exclaims

MRS IAN ARMSTRONG CROSSES FINGERS FOR ASTRONAUT

ASTRONA.. ARMSTRONG APPROACHES FIRST STEP ON MOON

Reaction
Canada – Glued To TV Sets

Calgary – Few Left Home

MRS PAT COLLINS   MRS JOAN ALDRIN

Luna Lands On The Moon, But May Have Hit Too Fast

JODRELL BANK, England

MOON STORIES FOR HERALD

Europe – They Jumped To Their Feet And Cheered

The Electrifying Sixties

1961-70

Vietnam, the Beatles, the first men on the moon. Cassius Clay, Pierre Trudeau, and the Rolling Stones. Civil rights, peaceful protest and riots in the cities of America. Heavy drugs, heavy rock, heavy politics. Flower power, black power and student power. The Bay of Pigs, the Cuban missile crisis, the Six-Day War. John F. Kennedy shot, Martin Luther King shot, Robert F. Kennedy shot. The first heart transplant, the first man in orbit, the first supersonic passenger plane. The sexual revolution, the youth revolution, the computer revolution. The Berlin Wall and the invasion of Czechoslovakia. "Smash the state," "Up against the wall," "Black is beautiful," "The light at the end of the tunnel," "Sorry about that." The Sixties. A time of hope and rage — and hopes that fueled more rage.

John F. Kennedy began the decade with his stirring inaugural address in January, 1961. "Let every nation know," he said, "whether it wishes us well or ill, that we shall pay any price, bear any burden, meet any hardship, support any friend, oppose any foe to assure the survival and the success of liberty."

Some of the sharpest skirmishes of the Cold War were fought in the early Sixties. In the spring of 1961, the United States sponsored an invasion of Cuba. Fidel Castro, briefly an American hero after he won power in Cuba, had aligned himself with the Soviet Union. The invasion by American-trained Cuban exiles, supposed to trigger a pro-American uprising in Cuba, was an inglorious failure.

The Communists solved the problem of refugees who were slipping out of East Berlin into the West zone: In August, 1961 they built a wall across the city and killed anyone who tried to leave the East zone without permission.

In the fall of 1962 came the closest approach, so far, to the Third World War. American reconnaissance planes found that Soviet nuclear missiles were being installed in Cuba. Kennedy imposed a naval blockade. Ships bound for Cuba would be stopped and searched. A confrontation between Soviet and American ships could have started a war, and for a tense week the armed forces and civil defence services on both sides stood at the alert. Finally Soviet Premier Nikita Khrushchev backed down and withdrew the missiles from Cuba. U.S. Secretary of State Dean Rusk learned of the Soviet ships turning around and commented: "We're eyeball to eyeball, and I think the other fellow just blinked."

After this triumph, Kennedy had little more than a year to live. In November, 1963, he was shot dead in Dallas, Texas. The alleged assassin, Lee Harvey Oswald, was killed two days later.

The Kennedy years had seen the rise of a non-violent campaign for Negro civil rights in the South. "I have a dream," said Dr. Martin Luther King, leader of the movement, a dream of an America without racial discrimination. White Americans, many of them young, northern and middle-class, joined blacks in a campaign of passive resistance and voter registration to overcome discrimination. Southern authorities responded with fire-hoses, cattle prods and attack dogs to break up the demonstrations. The unofficial response was even more brutal: civil-rights workers, white and black, were slain by guns and bombs. In 1968, King was assassinated by a white man, James Earl Ray. Even before King's death, black extremists were gaining influence. In the middle and late Sixties, rioting, sniping and arson raged through the summer-heated black ghettos of northern U.S. cities.

The Vietnam war, too, divided American society. In the Kennedy years, it seemed an easy war to win. A corps of American military advisers would train the South Vietnamese army to suppress the Communist Vietcong guerrillas. Kennedy's successor, Lyndon Johnson, escalated the war. He sent in the Marines, he sent in the army, he ordered bombing raids on North Vietnam. As the war intensified, so did the violent protests. Johnson, shaken by the bitterness of the reaction against the war, announced that he would not seek a second term in 1968. Robert F. Kennedy, the main hope of the anti-war campaigners, was shot dead before he could run for president. Richard Nixon, the new president, began to withdraw American troops, while still expanding the war. In the protests that followed Nixon's invasion of Cambodia, four students at Kent State University were shot by the U.S. national guard. And the war went on.

There were other struggles and crises in the Sixties: civil wars were fought in Nigeria and the Congo (United Nations Secretary General Dag Hammarskjold died in a plane crash on a mission to the Congo). Rhodesia's white regime broke away from Great Britain rather than grant more power to the black majority and France gave up on a long, nasty struggle and granted Algeria its independence. Canadian troops were part of a UN force that did the sometimes dull, sometimes dangerous job of keeping the peace between Greek and Turkish factions on Cyprus. China was turned upside down by the Red Guards in Chairman Mao Tse-tung's cultural revolution. Britain was shaken by the Profumo scandal, in which a cabinet minister lied about sleeping with Christine Keeler, a prostitute who shared her favors with a Soviet naval attache. Israel triumphed in the Six-Day War with Egypt and Syria in 1967, but this victory planted the seeds of later combat. In Czechoslovakia, a new spirit of liberalism had been growing; the Czechs' hopes of greater freedoms were crushed in 1968 when the Soviet Union sent in tanks and troops to restore its idea of order.

As usual in every era, some giants passed from the scene: Winston Churchill and Dwight D. Eisenhower died; Nikita Khrushchev was removed from power; Pope John XXIII, who had "opened the windows" of the Catholic Church died; so did E.M. Forster and T.S. Eliot and Bertrand Russell.

A heavy decade. Anyone who wanted to get away from the news for a while could go see a movie: *Cleopatra*, with Richard Burton and Elizabeth Taylor; *Dr. Zhivago*; *Dr. Strangelove*; *Lawrence of Arabia*; *The Manchurian Candidate*; *The Sound of Music*; *Tom Jones*; *Guess Who's Coming to Dinner*; *Blow-Up*; *2001: A Space Odyssey*.

Stay-at-homes would find plenty to read. To name only a few books of the Sixties: Joseph Heller's *Catch 22*; Katherine Ann Porter's *Ship of Fools*; Philip Roth's *Portnoy's Complaint*; Ralph Nader's *Unsafe at Any Speed*; Tom Wolfe's *The Electric Kool-Aid Acid Test*; John Updike's *Couples*; Theodore Roszak's *The Making of a Counter-Culture*; Truman Capote's *In Cold Blood*; Marshall McLuhan's *Understanding Media*; Alexander Solzhenitsyn's *One Day in the Life of Ivan Denisovich*.

Like so much else in the Sixties, sex was a focal point of innovation and exaggeration. The pictures in *Playboy* and its imitators became more startling. The mini-skirt and topless bathing suits made their appearance, followed by topless — and bottomless — waitresses and go-go dancers. For some, at least, sex became more free and easy, especially after the development of the birth-control pill. Couples lived together more openly in what used to be called sin. Perhaps by no accident, the women's liberation movement got under way.

Sports fans will remember that wretched poet and brilliant boxer Cassius Clay (later Muhammad Ali). And, in 1968, major-league baseball came to Canada with the Montreal Expos.

The decade produced its share of standard ballads, but the really memorable popular music of the Sixties was something

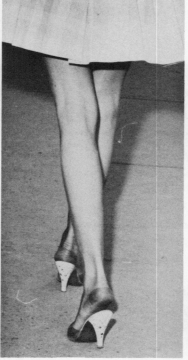

John F. Kennedy, left, in a silk hat for his inauguration; the mini-skirt, which made fashion history; and the Beatles, right, who made musical history.

else entirely. Above all there were the Beatles, the first superstars of the decade. Their early hits, like *I Want to Hold Your Hand*, were some of the most cheerful, innocent things about the whole decade.

As the Sixties rolled on, rock got tougher, and folk music turned to protest. Bob Dylan, Joan Baez, the Rolling Stones, the Jefferson Airplane, Jimi Hendrix, Big Brother and the Holding Company (with Janis Joplin), Country Joe and the Fish — these and many others were the prophets of the Sixties' counter-culture. Dr. Timothy Leary, the high priest of LSD, was another prophet. The counterculture looked on drugs, music and sex almost as sacraments, offering fellowship and revelation — and excluding outsiders.

"The counter-culture" was a catch-all term covering everyone from pacifist, vegetarian hippies to would-be revolutionaries. They may not have known in detail what they wanted, but they knew what they didn't want: safety and comfort purchased at the price of conformity, materialism, war, racism and exploitation. At their worst, they proved that hate and self-righteousness are not exclusively the vices of those over 30; and in the end, they accomplished far less than the purposes they had proclaimed. Still, they were left with a sense that their lives could have been, should have been, different.

Meanwhile, Canada had its own preoccupations, though the larger events of the Sixties did spill across the border. A generation of political leaders passed from the scene. Quebec became the focus of concern about the country's future. The Centennial celebrations of 1967 gave the nation a new, though short- lived, sense of confidence. Pierre Trudeau, then a strange, magnetic figure, became prime minister.

Alberta prospered, though not spectacularly. The province's main problem, which went unsolved in the Sixties, was to find markets for all the oil and gas that it was ready to produce. Oil from Venezuela and the Middle East, at about $3 a barrel, was cheaper than Alberta crude in Eastern Canada. Albertans agitated for an oil pipeline to Montreal, but Alberta oil got no farther than Ontario, where consumers paid a small premium over the import price in order to support the domestic industry. Politically, it was a quiet time. Ernest Manning retired in 1968 after 25 years as premier. A year earlier the Conservatives, under their new leader Peter Lougheed, elected six MLAs.

Calgary grew steadily, from 250,000 in 1961 to 385,000 in 1970, and began to take on its present shape: a small, tight core of tall buildings surrounded by an ever-spreading ring of houses and small apartments. It swallowed the towns of Bowness and Forest Lawn in its outward spread. In 1961, the 20-storey Elveden House dominated the skyline. By 1970, there were office buildings nearly twice as tall, and the Calgary Tower looked down on them all.

John Diefenbaker was still prime minister in the early Sixties, but his government was in trouble. The economy was faltering, and relations with the United States were testy. The election of 1962 destroyed Diefenbaker's majority. He carried on, but in 1963 his government was defeated in the Commons on the issue of providing American-controlled nuclear weapons for Canadian forces.

Lester Pearson and his Liberals, who had become converts to the idea of atomic weapons for Canada, won the 1963 election. Pearson's minority government has some notable, if controversial, achievements on its record: a new Canadian flag, universal medicare, the Canada Pension Plan, the unification of the armed forces.

In 1967, after years of public and private struggle within the Conservative party, Diefenbaker lost the leadership to Robert Stanfield. The following year Lester Pearson retired, and was replaced by Pierre Trudeau, who quickly called an election and won a majority.

Trudeau may have benefited from the euphoria that followed the Centennial celebration, especially the international success of the Montreal world's fair, Expo 67. Canadians were ready for adventure, and Trudeau seemed to offer it. If the usual word for Stanfield was "decent," the word for Trudeau was "brilliant." He was, perhaps, the man for the time. Here was a Quebecer willing to face down the Quebec separatists, and ready to crush the radical FLQ after the kidnappings and murder of October, 1970. Even so, he and Western Canadians soon didn't get along, and in the Seventies this mutual lack of understanding would become a serious problem.

Finally, a word about the achievement of the Sixties that seems most likely to be remembered a few centuries from now, if anything is remembered. In 1961, Yuri Gagarin, a Russian, circled the world for the first time in a man-made satellite. On a summer day in 1969, Neil Armstrong, an American, became the first man to set foot on the moon.

195

The Dangerous Decade

The Bay of Pigs affair, an abortive attempt to overthrow Fidel Castro, was the first notable event of a troubled decade. Worse was to come: the Berlin wall, the Cuban missile crisis, the Vietnam war, the assassinations of John Kennedy, Robert Kennedy, and Martin Luther King, the invasion of Czechoslovakia, a war in the Middle East and numerous riots to protest war and racism. The Bay of Pigs was mild by comparison with what followed. For a short time after he took power in Cuba, Fidel Castro was an American hero. His Communist sympathies soon made Castro intolerable to the United States, which trained and financed a group of Cuban exiles to invade Cuba and overthrow him. The invasion force quickly came to grief on the shore of the Bay of Pigs. In this editorial The Herald asked why, if the job was to be done at all, it wasn't done properly.

A good deal of confusion continues to surround the situation in Cuba, but indications are that the attempted overthrow of the Castro regime by a small invasion force has apparently ended disastrously.

It seems the invaders based their hopes on an anticipated general uprising of anti-Castro citizens throughout the island and this did not materialize.

Such a denouncement leaves a number of serious questions to be answered.

Why, for example, did the United States government, which is reported to have condoned recruitment and perhaps even some training and arming of Cuban counter-revolutionaries on U.S. soil, allow the attempt to go ahead without reasonable certainty that it would succeed? Unless the U.S. can show it was not involved in any way with the pitiful exploit, it is bound to suffer an impairment of prestige throughout the world.

No one can quarrel with President Kennedy's frank confession that U.S. sympathies are with the anti-Castro counter-revolutionary movement.

But U.S. leadership has stated itself in even stronger terms than this. Unless it is prepared to see the counter-revolution in Cuba through to a successful conclusion now, it may find itself in an embarrassing position.

The West did not rally to the side of the Hungarian patriots in their uprising. Other anti-Communist revolts have been stamped out without Western intervention, though it has been said that some of these movements were encouraged to believe they would receive aid.

In future, any groups planning to restore free government in their oppressed countries should be warned unmistakably in advance that they need not expect outside Western aid. And any which do receive encouragement should receive outright help when they need it.

April 24, 1961

Some unfinished business of the Second World War was concluded in the Sixties. Israeli agents found Adolf Eichmann, one of the principal organizers of the Nazis' mass murder of Jews. They kidnapped him from Argentina and brought him to trial in Jerusalem. A wire service report:

A dolf Eichmann intoned the words "not guilty" 15 times today, denying all counts of Israel's indictment naming him as the master destoyer of 6,000,000 Jews.

Attorney-General Gideon Hausner, Eichmann's prosecutor, said the former Nazi officer "still believes he did what was right and proper in destroying millions."

Hausner began with a harsh, emotional outline of the case. He said Eichmann beat a Jewish child to death with his own hands for stealing peaches.

"This is the trial of the destroyer." As he continued tears came to the eyes of some members of the audience.

Eichmann, sitting attentively but showing little emotion, stared at Hausner, unblinking.

The attorney-general continued:

"When I stand before you, judges of Israel, to accuse Adolf Eichmann, I do not stand here alone.

"Here with me stand six million prosecutors. But, alas, they cannot rise and level a finger at the man in the prisoner's dock.

"Their blood cries to heaven but their voices cannot be heard."

Saying that Eichmann truly felt no sense of guilt, Hausner told the court "if swastikas were raised again with shouts of sieg heil, if the hysterical voice of Hitler were to be heard again, if high-tension barbed wire were set up once more, Adolf Eichmann would rise... and go back to his work of oppression and butchery."

The prosecutor outlined the rise of the Nazis to power in Germany in 1933, their use of anti-Semitism as a weapon to advance their objectives in the world and finally the ghastly ordeal visited on the Jews.

Early in his statement, he turned to look at Eichmann in the prisoner's dock and said:

" In this trial, we shall also encounter a new kind of killer, the kind that exercises his bloody craft behind a desk and only occasionally does the deed with his own hands.

"True, we know of only one incident in which Adolf Eichmann actually beat to death a Jewish boy, who had dared to steal fruit from a peach tree in the yard of his Budapest home."

Nothing showed in Eichmann's face.

"We shall find Eichmann describing himself as a fastidious person; a 'white collar worker'," Hausner continued. "To him, the decree of extermination was just another order to be executed."

"Yet he was the one who planned, initiated, and organized, who instructed others to spill this ocean of blood and to use all the means of murder, theft and torture."

On Eichmann's pleas of innocence before the court, Hausner reported that he was as guilty as though Eichmann himself had "knotted the hangman's noose, lashed the victims into the gas chambers, shot in the back and pushed into the open pit every single one of the millions who were slaughtered."

He listed the steps in Eichmann's swift rise to importance in the Gestapo, from a faceless file clerk in an office to the moment when he was placed in charge of what the Nazis called "the final solution of the Jewish problem."

This meant mass extermination.

"He reached out to every corner to carry out the 'final solution', using the methods he found most efficient... and always with one goal in mind — to get hold of the Jews

Adolf Eichmann, behind bullet-proof glass and flanked by guards, faces his accusers in Jerusalem.

and to send them to camps in the east.

"It need not surprise us, therefore, that on Jewish matters he gave orders to men of higher rank than his own."

Eichmann's highest rank in the Gestapo was lieutenant-colonel.

The prosecutor said a "confused and blinded world" had not been alarmed by the fate of the Jews, and did not realize that the persecution of the Jews was only the beginning of the onslaught.

Jerusalem, April 17, 1961

Eichmann was found guilty. His appeal that he was acting under orders from his superiors was rejected, and he was hanged. His body was cremated and the ashes strewn in the Mediterranean. Alvin Rosenfeld of the Herald Tribune News Service wrote this account of Eichmann's last hours.

Adolf Eichmann paid with his life two minutes before midnight Thursday (2:58 p.m. MST) for the lives of 6,000,000 European Jews.

The ex-Gestapo colonel, who played a major role in the Nazi extermination program which sent Jewish men, women and children, to death, met his end by hanging. His victims had been herded into gas chambers, lined up and shot on the edge of mass graves or strung up on the gallows.

The execution took place at Tamle Prison, near Tel Aviv, less than two hours after Israeli President Itzhak Ben-Zvi announced his rejection of the 56-year-old Eichmann's plea for clemency.

Eichmann died bravely, standing erect on the improvised gallows, and refusing the offer of a black hood. "I do not need it," he said.

"After a short while, gentlemen, we shall meet again. So is the fate of all men. I have lived believing in God, and I die believing in God."

Eichmann's spiritual adviser, William L. Hull, a Canadian missionary, visited the death cell for one and a half hours Thursday, and reported that Eichmann was "very hard and bitter at the verdict."

Jerusalem, June 1, 1962

Through the Fifties, East Germany lost many people to the West. Many of these refugees slipped across the boundary between East and West Berlin. In 1961 the East German authorities responded by building a wall across the city, and shooting anyone who tried to cross it without permission. Richard L. Sanburn, editor-in-chief of the Herald, sent this dispatch from the Berlin wall.

Here is The Wall which snakes in all its brutal ugliness for 35 miles through the heart of this city of tension. It has to be felt to be believed. One can look at pictures, and read about it, and not quite believe it still, because The

The Berlin Wall was hastily thrown together, almost overnight. Here East German workers add more height to the original wall, intended to prevent defections to the western zone of the divided city.

Wall is built of more than rough concrete blocks, sloppily applied mortar, barbed wire and broken glass.

It is forbidding physically. It is even more forbidding emotionally. It is built of fear and hatred, callous cruelty and death.

There are visible signs of these invisible ingredients.

The signs are there in the macabre fence-post-and-barbed-wire memorials erected on the sidewalk just a few feet inside the Western sector... memorials to people who died in desperate leaps from their high-up apartment windows as East German Communist police and soldiers battered down the doors behind them.

It was their last chance for freedom. The Communists had come to brick up those windows to prevent just such escapes. It was August 13, 1961, or shortly after. One hears a lot about August 13 in Germany.

Here on the sidewalk, three rough fence posts arranged in a triangle, about six feet high barbed wire draped loosely around them. A black wreath. On the sidewalk, three or four small flower pots with wilting blooms. Higher up, a black cross-bar nailed at an angle, and on it the simple inscription Ida Siekmann, 23/8/02 - 22/8/61.

It was here, on the day before her 59th birthday, that Ida Siekmann died on the sidewalk after jumping from the window of her apartment trying to escape. It was only a few feet across to freedom. But it was too far from three storeys up.

Ida Siekmann's despairing jump to the freedom that was death took place on Bernauer Strasse. Others tried the same thing along Bernauer Strasse, which has many tall

apartment buildings and constitutes the East-West Wall at this point, and there are fence-post-and-barbed-wire memorials to them on the sidewalk, too. They all jumped, but it was too far down to freedom.

Bernauer Strasse is a deathly quiet street now. Here and there, it is possible to see over the top of the Wall, and silent knots of West Berliners frequently stand, just looking. Once in a while, they may see somebody they know... a friend, a brother, a mother.

Incredible in an allegedly civilized world allegedly at peace? More than a million people in the city-prison that is East Berlin, forbidden on pain of death to cross what used to be ordinary streets.

Why did the Communists build The Wall last August 13? They said they did it to defend the German Democratic Republic (Communist Germany) from "open military provocation from West Berlin." They said they did it "to stop the slave-trading, the traffic in human beings in West Berlin and Bonn, to stop the activities of the enticers to flee and the saboteurs." They said they did it to prevent East Berliners from being "degraded" by the glitter of West Berlin.

The "slaves", of course, were the 50,000 or 60,000 East Berliners who used to cross into West Berlin every day to work. The "degradation" means the showy, affluent, busy and gay life of free West Berlin.

The Communists are most solicitous about "protecting their people" from this sort of thing. Now, they shoot them if they try to escape to "slavery and degradation".

West Berlin, July 17, 1962

In the autumn of 1962, the world came dangerously close to war. American U-2 spy planes had found Soviet missile bases being installed in Cuba. The missiles could have delivered nuclear warheads to most of the United States and southern Canada. U.S. President John F. Kennedy responded with a blockade of Cuba, and for a week the world waited tensely. The AP reported:

Russia and the United States headed on a collision course today as U.S. ships moved to clamp an arms blockade on Cuba. A direct confrontation between the two great powers could come by nightfall, in the judgement of Washington officials.

The crisis appeared to be the greatest since the Second World War.

A mighty U.S. fleet fanned across the Atlantic prepared to intercept a large number of Russian cargo ships possibly carrying missiles to Cuba.

The first contact will bring about the first test of President Kennedy's newly-proclaimed arms blockade of Cuba.

The navy was reported keeping a watchful eye out for a big Russian ship, rigged to carry guided missiles. The ship was said to be bound for Cuba and may well be the first vessel intercepted under the blockade order.

Large numbers of Soviet ships were reported moving in the direction of Cuba, but not in convoy. U.S. navy vessels sailed Monday from the Puerto Rico area and east coast ports.

Their orders: hail, stop, search and, if necessary, sink vessels which try to avoid inspection.

In Moscow, the Soviet Union ordered its armed forces placed on alert and cancelled all leaves. In Havana, a broadcast said the Cuban military forces have been mobilized.

The full scope of the crisis broke Monday night when President Kennedy announced Russia's establishment of missile bases in Cuba threatening the United States, Canada and Latin America and disclosed a seven-point program of U.S. action starting with a naval blockade to halt the flow of any offensive arms to Cuba.

While mounting this blockade to keep the offensive weapons such as missiles and bombers out of Cuba, the United States looked to its power elsewhere — just in case the Communists should try some counter-move.

The nuclear jet bombers of the Strategic Air Command and its 144 combat-ready intercontinental ballistic missiles were ready.

U.S. ground, sea and air forces around the globe — including those in Berlin and West Germany — were also ordered to be especially vigilant.

Kennedy was depending on crisis diplomacy to pull the world back from the brink of conflict. Shortly before his address he sent a personal message to Soviet Premier Khrushchev to refrain from any step which would make the situation worse.

The overriding question being asked in government circles here was whether Khrushchev would slow down or turn back Soviet ships on the way, at least to give time for a cooling-off period and avoid an almost immediate show-down.

The Pentagon said Soviet ships now bound for Cuba have no Russian escorts.

The defence spokesman, appearing Monday night at a packed briefing, made it plain that the drastic U.S. blockade was triggered by confirmation that 1,200-mile range mobile ballistic missiles were in place and actually threatening U.S. cities.

The President announced that he had received at 9 o'clock last Tuesday morning "the first preliminary hard information" that a series of "offensive missile sites is now in preparation on that imprisoned island" — Cuba.

Washington, October 23, 1962

Nuclear war was a real possibility during that tense week, and the Alberta government took what few precautions were possible.

Alberta's Emergency Measures Organization has been put on an emergency basis in view of the Cuban situation, Hon. L.C. Halmrast, welfare minister and EMO provincial director, said today.

Mr. Halmrast said the situation is the gravest since the end of the Second World War.

"It's hard to know what instructions we should give now in the event of an alert being sounded," he said. "The best advice we can give right now is that everyone should listen to their radios if sirens are sounded. Radio is our quickest means of communication. Office buildings should be equipped with radios."

Mr. Halmrast said he feels any attack on Alberta would come from manned bombers. He said that in such an event, evacuation of cities would be a possibility.

Edmonton, October 24, 1962

The Soviet Union pulled back from a confrontation. No Soviet ships ventured into the blockade zone, and after a week of intensive

diplomacy Khrushchev agreed to withdraw the missiles from Cuba.

The assassination of an American president stunned the world. This report was compiled from fragmentary bulletins pouring in from wire services.

President Kennedy was slain today. The 36th president of the United States was shot to death by a hidden assassin armed with a high-powered rifle. The president died in Parkland Hospital at 1 p.m. CST (noon Calgary time).

Kennedy, 46, lived about 30 minutes after a sniper cut him down as his limousine left downtown Dallas. Reporters said the shot that hit him was fired about 12:30 p.m. CST.

Soon after Kennedy was assassinated Friday in Dallas, a white man in his mid-twenties was arrested in the Riverside section of Fort Worth in the shooting of a Dallas policeman.

Automatically, the mantle of the presidency fell to Vice-President Lyndon B. Johnson, a native Texan who had been riding two cars behind Kennedy.

Kennedy died at Parkland Hospital, where his bullet-pierced body had been taken in a frantic but futile effort to save his life.

Lying wounded at the same hospital was Governor John Connally of Texas, who was cut down by the same fusillade that ended the life of the youngest man ever elected to the presidency.

Connally and his wife had been riding with the President and Mrs. Kennedy.

Jacqueline Kennedy cradled her dying husband's blood-smeared head in her arms as the presidential limousine raced to the hospital.

"Oh, no," she kept crying.

Connally slumped in his seat beside the president.

Anxious citizens cluster around The Herald's bulletin board for news of the John F. Kennedy assassination.

Lee Harvey Oswald in handcuffs after the Kennedy assassination. Oswald himself was killed two days later, leaving many unanswered questions, although an inquiry concluded Oswald acted alone.

Like President Kennedy's death, it was hard to believe this wasn't just another act in a televised drama. But it was as real and raw as life in Texas apparently is.

I looked at Oswald through a forest of police legs. He was kicking feebly. By now a policeman had him under the arms and a couple of others had his feet.

They hoisted and dragged him back to the door from which he had emerged, moments earlier.

There was no blood — just the brown fedora of the gunman lying on the pavement. In the hatband were the initials J.R.

The man who did the shooting — striptease joint owner Jack Ruby (real name Rubenstein) has been charged with murder.

Almost every policeman in the Dallas force knew Ruby well. But none had noticed him in the garage which had been searched three times within the hour.

I looked at my watch.

Barely five minutes had passed since the time Oswald had first appeared.

Dallas, November 25, 1963

Oswald died within an hour. Jack Ruby was convicted of murder, and died in prison. An inquiry led by United States Chief Justice Earl Warren found that Oswald had acted alone in shooting President Kennedy. This conclusion has been widely disputed; contending theories suggest conspiracies by parties ranging from Fidel Castro and the KGB to the Mafia and the CIA.

One man told the police that the shots had been fired from the window of a warehouse along the parade route. A search of the building revealed a 7.65 German rifle — such as used in the Second World War — on the steps or staircase of the fifth floor. Police also found three spent shells in the chamber of the rifle.

Dallas, November 22, 1963

The day after John F. Kennedy was shot, the alleged assassin was in custody and the events of that terrible day in Dallas were becoming clearer.

Sixteen blocks from the scene of President Kennedy's sudden assassination, a slender, thin-faced former U.S. marine sharp-shooter was under heavy police guard today, formally charged with the murder of the young president whose search for world peace led him to the grave.

While an angry country reacted with a flood of telegrams to Mayor Earl Cabell suggesting among other things that Dallas be burned to the ground, police ended 10 hours of intensive interrogation of 24-year-old Lee Harvey Oswald and then booked the New Orleans native on the murder charge. He likely will be arraigned for grand jury action next week.

Unruffled and seemingly unperturbed, the brown-shirted Oswald, 24, who had defected to Russia in 1959 and had returned in 1962, professed his innocence, saying "I did not shoot anybody."

Police Chief Jesse Curry of Dallas said today Oswald has "readily admitted he is a Communist."

At approximately 12:30 p.m. CST, the slow-moving Kennedy motorcade had rounded a downtown corner to enter a freeway. Three shots rang out.

Detective Ed Hicks said one bullet from a 7.65-millimetre Italian-made rifle, fitted with telescopic sights, hit the back of Kennedy's head and emerged from his throat.

"It made a hole about two inches wide at the back of his head," he said.

Dallas, November 23, 1963

Lee Harvey Oswald was never tried. Two days after the Kennedy assassination, he was shot in the basement garage of Dallas police headquarters while he was being taken to an armored car bound for the county jail. Peter Worthington of the Telegram News Service gave this eye-witness account of the shooting.

Suddenly a stocky man with his hat pulled low over his eyes bounded seven feet across the roadway and, seemingly from nowhere, a gun appeared in his outstretched hand.

I felt the blast of the gun in my lower stomach. Detective Roy Lowr winced and sprang forward. Uniformed policemen and sheriffs in cowboy hats descended on the stocky man, who, it seemed, was fighting desperately to get another shot at Oswald.

"Oh...oh...oh..." Oswald sobbed. Then he crumpled to the pavement, hugging his stomach.

An editorial

What was mortal of Sir Winston Churchill has been taken by death. But that great part of him which was immortal will continue forever to activate the minds and memories of free men.

Sir Winston had passed his ninetieth birthday. The events which shaped him and those he helped shape had receded into history. New scenes and new players had taken over the world stage. And so it was not unexpected to learn at last that death, defied so often in its varied guises by Sir Winston before, had finally managed to subdue the old warrior-statesman in a last confrontation which found implacable time on its side.

But those among us who were also of his time to one degree or another feel pangs of parting just the same. The Grand Old Man is gone. A gap has been left which no other can fill. A seal has been placed on a stirring half century during which it was wonderful to have lived.

It was not only for his deeds on behalf of the free world, as beleaguered Britain's wartime prime minister, that Sir Winston won his remarkable world-wide admiration and affection, though it was these which set his mark on history. There was also about him an aura of human quality which caught the imagination. He was without affectation. He was modest in the exercise of great authority. He was bold in opposition but quick to forgive. It was not in him to be an arrogant victor. He conceived it both decent and practical to help his vanquished opponent to his feet once the battle was over.

Neither as a politician nor as a military strategist was Churchill infallible. He made mistakes, as other men do. Some of them, being within large-scale contexts, were big ones. But he was more often right than most of his contemporaries. He displayed a rare, intuitive grasp of history-making events and an amazing ability to define them in words and put them in the kind of perspective which made it possible for everyone else to understand them too.

His wartime speeches, carried by radio throughout the English-speaking world, were as if inspired and were weighted with tremendous impact and effect. On other occasions, both before and after the war, he spoke with unusual prescience of the future.

Winston Churchill left an enduring mark on history and the stamp of his character as well as his works will long be an inspiration to men who seek after the good and the great.

January 25, 1965.

Charles Lynch of Southam News Service spent several weeks in China in the spring of 1965. He quickly found traces of a Canadian hero, Dr. Norman Bethune, who served as a battlefield surgeon with Mao Tsetung's army during the Chinese revolution.

My tour of the Peking Children's hospital was going along in routine fashion, spiced with the spine-tingling and heart-warming sights and sounds of any institution dedicated to the healing of sick kids, when I mentioned Dr. Norman Bethune.

If I had mentioned Chairman Mao himself, the effect could not have been more electric.

My guide for the hospital tour was a tiny Chinese lady, Dr. Sen Yan-hua, chief medical officer of the hospital, and the mention of Bethune, the Canadian doctor who served with Mao's revolutionary forces and pioneered modern battlefield medicine, sent her off in a torrent of adulation.

Bethune has become a legendary figure in China — though whether he is a medical legend or becoming a political legend is not so clear. The rash of articles on the anniversary of his death last year seems to have shifted the weight of Bethune's Chinese reputation from the medical to the political.

Peking, May 5, 1965

Visiting a Chinese commune, Lynch found its people full of a new pride in their accomplishments.

At the entrance to a little backroad village in the High Bank People's Commune, an archway made of pine boughs had been erected to provide a setting for the village May Day celebrations.

It was a handsome affair, and as we drove beneath it I was struck by the resemblance to the archways you see in old engravings of Ottawa, back in the days when working together was taken as a fact of life in the Canadian capital.

We have become sophisticated since then, and the Chinese are so far behind the times they still believe in helping one another — in fact this is a recent discovery for them and they regard it as something akin to fire or the wheel.

The village archway was of course, a Communist device — erected by Communist villagers in honor of a Communist feast. Thus it takes on a sinister connotation in our eyes — but the only emotion I could detect in the villager about the archway was pride.

And pride was what they seemed to feel, too, about their brick homes, many of them newly-built, and about their light bulbs, clocks, radios and their pigs, both communally and individually owned.

The High Bank People's Commune seems to have brought a sense of well-being to the villagers who comprise it — the same villagers who have always lived on those acres.

The commune, 20 miles east of Shenyang and in sight of the great coal mines of Fushun, occupies a stretch of land between the Hui mountains and the Hang River. It is served by a main highway and a main railroad, and its main job is to feed the hungry mouths of the industrial worker of Shenyang.

This area was "liberated" in 1948, and land reform was carried out swiftly, but individual ownership had its drawbacks.

Columnist Charles Lynch at the New China People's Commune, outside Canton.

Mutual aid teams were started in 1951, and these developed into elementary co-operatives in 1954, and advanced co-operatives in 1956. The commune emerged on September 4, 1958, a red-letter day in these parts. Six years later, the commune is a going concern, as anybody who visits it can plainly see.

The commune is still short of farm machinery, and Mr. Chen says the management side leaves something to be desired. Early in its life the commune, along with most of the rest of China, suffered a series of natural calamities. In this area, they took the form of wind, flood, insects and drought. The crisis was weathered and Mr. Chen thinks the present system of pest controls, dykes, irrigation and windbreaks would enable the commune to meet any future emergency.

There are more than 1,300 new houses on the commune, several of which I visited. They are bright and well-constructed and neat as a pin inside.

Cash income per household averages about $225 a year, and the commune members have their own credit union.

Facts and figures, even when backed by personal observation, don't tell the whole story of the commune — some of the feel of the place may be conveyed in a little poem written by one of the commune members. It goes: "Today, we have light without oil; we plough our land with the iron ox; if there is drought, we can lift water to wet our rice; man's will, not heaven, decides; we listen to radio on our warm bed; today, every member is leading a happy life; our machines process the rice and wheat; collective production brings in the harvest quickly; the old way was like sitting on an oxcart."

"Come back in the golden season," said Mr. Chen, meaning harvest time. "The place is beautiful then." I believed him.

Shenyang, Manchuria, May 10, 1965

War broke out in the Middle East in 1967 soon after the withdrawal of the United Nations peacekeeping force, which had been there since The Suez crisis of 1956. Egypt blocked access to the Israeli port of Elat. Israel, fearing an attack by Egypt, launched what was described as a "preventive" war, and achieved a stunning victory. In six days of fighting Israeli forces shattered the Egyptian army and air force, and inflicted heavy losses on Syria. By the time a cease-fire was arranged by the United Nations, Israel had occupied all of Jerusalem, The Sinai and formerly Jordanian-controlled territory on the West Bank. Bruce Phillips of Southam News sent this report from Tel Aviv halfway through the Six-Day War.

It's the kind of war you can drive to in the morning after breakfast, and if you're lucky, be back in time for dinner over white linen.

Some are not lucky, like Ben Oyserman, a free-lance Israeli photographer whose pictures have been seen on Canadian television in the last few days. I had a drink with him in the plush Hilton Hotel a few days ago,

An Israeli soldier observes a blazing oil refinery at Port Suez, set on fire by an artillery barrage during the Six-Day War. Israel's territorial gains in the 1967 war later became another centre of Mid-East conflict.

but Tuesday his car struck a mine near the city of Gaza and he is dead.

Oyserman's death, the candlelight dinners and desert battles are all part of the incongruous upside down nature of life here today. The war is everywhere and nowhere at the same time. Monday for example, shells were falling in the northeast quarter of Tel Aviv, and we could hear them while we were being briefed by a military press officer. He said they were only 600 yards away, but nobody seemed concerned. The idea seems to be that the war is only important if you are in the middle of it.

The shelling stopped Tuesday, and, as of this writing, there has been a day free of the constant air raid alerts which marked the first day of the conflict. Both of these facts lend weight to Israeli claims to have dealt the Arab air forces a stunning blow and to have captured the Jordanian positions which were firing on the city.

All this points up the fact that in a country as small as this there is no such thing as a single front, or two or three fronts. The whole place is one big front.

For instance I travelled to a pleasant seaside resort called Netanya about 20 miles north of here on the strength of reports it had been bombed. We found a factory and a gas station on the outskirts had been damaged, but the wide shaded streets of the town were untouched. So we left the place, and hours later an Iraqi plane came back and unloaded a couple of bombs on the spot where we had been standing. One woman was killed and several people injured.

Tel Aviv, June 7, 1967

Don McGillivray of Southam News Service reported the Six-Day War from Cairo.

On the third day of the Arab-Israeli war Cairo anxiously awaits news from the battlefield and the United Nations.

The United Arab Republic high command has reported fierce fighting on Arab soil following intervention by Britain and the United States, still claimed here despite denials.

Cairo was calm after a night of blackout and air alert which included heavy attack, ground-to-air rockets, horizon flashes and distant explosions.

There is no bomb damage in central Cairo.

Mahamed Heikal, the editor of an authoritative newspaper and a close friend of President Nasser Tuesday detailed evidence for American-British intervention, including the claim that Israel deployed 400 planes on the Jordanian front during the night, more than the U.A.R. could muster alone after losses.

Heikal said downed Israeli pilots carried copies of British maps and U-2 type photos.

He cited an Israeli pilot confession and claimed American and British volunteer pilots joined the Israelis.

The mood of Cairo shifted Tuesday from the up-beat tempo of Monday's street crowds to a quiet anger at reported intervention of the United States and Britain.

The undercurrent of anger at air support reportedly given Israel flared up only once in a demonstration at the well-guarded United States embassy.

Cairo, June 7, 1967

A second Kennedy might have become president of the United States, but an assassin intervened. When President Lyndon Johnson decided not to run in 1968, Robert F. Kennedy became a strong contender for the Democratic party nomination. He was shot down just after a major triumph, a victory in the California primary.

Senator Robert F. Kennedy was shot in the head today and one of the surgeons who operated on him was quoted as saying "the outcome may be extremely tragic."

The New York senator was officially described as in "extremely critical" condition

and Dr. Henry Cuneo, one of three surgeons who operated on Kennedy said: "he might not make it. There is a slim chance of his recovery."

This morning police identified a Sirhan Sirhan as the gunman who hit Kennedy with three shots shortly after midnight.

The attempted assassination came after Kennedy's biggest triumph in his quest for the Democratic presidential nomination — a victory in the California primary.

Kennedy had proclaimed his win to about 2,000 supporters at an Ambassador Hotel rally and was taking a shortcut through the kitchen to a meeting with reporters when shots rang out.

With stunning rapidity at 12:15 a.m., a man police described as a Caucasian, about 25, five feet five inches tall and 210 pounds, with dark hair and complexion, emptied the chambers of an eight-shot, .22-calibre pistol.

Kennedy fell, hit apparently three times. Five others near him were wounded, none as badly as the presidential candidate.

Kennedy lay for some time on his back in the kitchen, eyes open, the crowd milling around him. Some observers say they heard him say, as he was lifted into the police ambulance: "Oh no. No. Don't."

Roosevelt Grier, beefy tackle for the Los Angeles Rams, grabbed the assailant's arm. Joe LaHive, a local Kennedy campaigner, and Olympic decathlon champion Rafer Johnson lifted the man and spread him on a steel kitchen table.

"Nobody hurt this man!" one of the athletes shouted. "We want to take him alive!"

AP reporter Bob Thomas was in the adjoining press room. He rushed into the kitchen to a scene of horror. Women were screaming "Oh no!" "God, God, not again!"

Los Angeles, June 5, 1968

Senator Robert F. Kennedy, felled like his president brother by an assassin's bullet, died early today.

President Johnson, shocked and dismayed at the shooting, announced in Washington the appointment of a 10-member commission to examine what he called this "tragic phenomenon" of violence and assassination in the U.S.

Los Angeles, June 6, 1968

Sirhan Sirhan, a 25-year-old Jordanian immigrant, was convicted of murdering Kennedy and sentenced to death. The sentence was reduced to life imprisonment, and he will be eligible for parole in 1984.

Robert Kennedy was buried from St. Patrick's Cathedral in New York. A special train took his body to Arlington National Cemetery in Washington, where his brother John had been buried less than five years earlier.

Senator Edward M. Kennedy, the last son of a family that gave three sons to its nation, eulogized his slain brother Robert today, as a

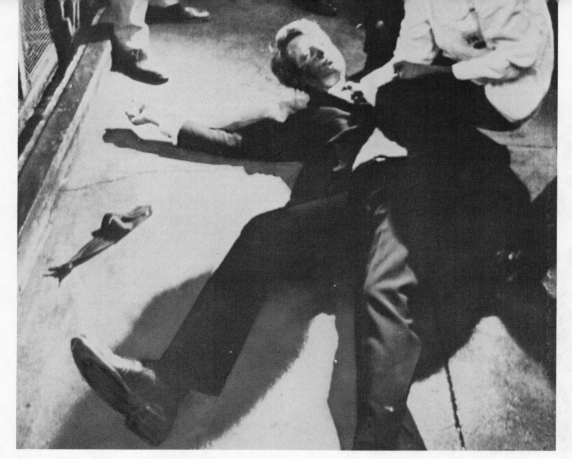

Robert F. Kennedy lies fatally wounded on the floor of a Los Angeles Hotel. He died the following day.

man who "gave us strength in time of trouble," and "will always be by our side."

His voice sometimes near breaking from emotion, Kennedy told mourners in St. Patrick's Cathedral his brother, slain by an assassin Wednesday, "loved life completely and lived it intensely."

Edward Kennedy said the late senator from New York wanted to express "real love" toward his fellow man. He quoted his brother as saying that "real love is something unselfish and involves sacrifice in giving."

Senator Kennedy today asked the world to remember his assassinated brother "simply as a good and decent man who saw wrong and tried to right it."

His voice was broken at the start, but he then declaimed in ringing tones lengthy extracts from the dead senator's 1966 speech to young South Africans, urging youth everywhere to play its full part in shaping a new world without discrimination or oppression.

Then the Massachusetts senator almost broke down.

His voice trembled with emotion and half-stifled sobs, as he said "my brother need not be idealized or enlarged in death beyond what he was in life."

"He should be remembered simply as a good and decent man who saw wrong and tried to right it; who saw war and tried to stop it.

"Those of us who loved him and who take him to his rest today pray that what he wished for us and what he wished for others will some day come to pass for all the world."

New York, June 8, 1968

The student radical movement was nearing its peak in 1968. Poverty, racism, and above all the war in Vietnam, made radicals of many middle-class students. One landmark event in the movement's history was the Chicago Democratic nominating convention. With Robert F. Kennedy dead, Vice-President Hubert Humphrey was nearly certain to be named the Democrats' *presidential candidate. The student left thought he was hopelessly tainted by his part in shaping U.S. policy in Vietnam. Protesters flocked to the Chicago convention. The radical left was not averse to violence in the streets, but in this case it was easily outdone by the Chicago police. J. Anthony Lukas of the New York Times reported on the Chicago riot.*

National guardsmen and police battled young dissidents in downtown Chicago Wednesday night as the week-long demonstrations against the Democratic national convention reached a bloody and violent climax.

Scores of persons were injured and hundreds were arrested as the security forces chased down demonstrators who had broken out of Grant Park on the shores of Lake Michigan in an attempt to reach the International Amphitheatre where the Democrats were meeting.

The police and guardsmen used clubs, rifle butts, tear gas and chemical Mace on virtually anything moving along elegant Michigan Avenue and the narrow streets of The Loop area.

Even elderly bystanders were caught in the furious police onslaught. At one point, police turned on several dozen persons who had been standing quietly behind police barriers in front of the Conrad Hilton Hotel watching the demonstrators across the street.

For no apparent reason, the blue-helmeted policemen charged the barriers, crushing the spectators against the windows of a restaurant in the hotel. Finally the window gave way, sending screaming middle-aged women and children backward through the broken shards of glass.

The police then ran into the restaurant and beat some of the bloodied victims who had fallen through the windows and arrested them.

At the same time, other policemen outside on the broad, tree-lined avenue were clubbing the young demonstrators repeatedly under glaring television lights and in full view of delegates' wives looking out the hotel's windows.

Afterward, newsmen saw shoes, women's purses and torn pieces of clothing lying with shattered bloodied glass on the sidewalk and street outside the hotel and for two blocks in each direction.

Although clearly outnumbered and outclassed by the well-armed security forces, the thousands of anti-war demonstrators, McCarthy supporters and Yippies maintained an air of defiance throughout the evening.

They shouted: "The streets belong to the people," "This land is our land," and "Hell no, we won't go," as they skirmished along the avenue and among the side streets.

When arrested youths raised their hands in the "V for victory" sign, which has become a symbol of the peace movement, other demonstrators would shout "Sieg heil!" or "Pigs!" at the policemen making the arrest.

It was difficult for newsmen to estimate how many demonstrators were in the streets of midtown Chicago during the night.

Estimates of those involved in the evening action ranged between 2,000 and 5,000.

Although some youths threw bottles, rocks and even loaves of bread at the police, most of them simply marched and countermarched, trying to avoid the flying police squads.

Some of them carried flags – the black anarchist flag, the Red flag, the Viet Cong flag and the red and blue flag with the yellow peace symbol emblazoned on it.

Chicago, August 29, 1968

When Czechoslovakia showed signs of a growing independence and liberalization, the Soviet Union sent in tanks and troops to bring its satellite back into line. The Herald commented in an editorial.

Ruthless Communist logic dictated today's take-over of Czechoslovakia by Soviet Russia and its East European satellites. Freedom had begun to flower in Czechoslovakia.

Freedom is the very antithesis of Communist dictatorship. The two cannot survive side by side. So the new Czech liberalization movement had to be rooted out and the new libertarian government in Prague along with it.

Nations where democratic freedoms prevail are shocked today but they need feel little surprise at the invasion of Czechoslovakia by the military forces of its five Communist neighbors.

The only surprising thing is that Moscow leaders have tolerated this long the replacement of a hard-line Communist government in Prague eight months ago by a government committed to such concepts as free speech, a free press and national independence.

Any New Look pretensions Soviet leadership has been trying to assume have been stripped away. It is the same old thing underneath the civilized mask: brutal, totalitarian dictatorship, exercised with the backing of fearsome military might.

Soviet troops in Czechoslovakia, 1968. These seem to be getting a better reception than some of their comrades-in-arms, who were taunted and spat on. Some tanks were attacked with sticks, stones and bare hands. The tanks prevailed, and the brief period of liberalization under Alexander Dubcek ended.

Invidious comparisons with United States efforts to help preserve human liberty abroad undoubtedly will be made. But only those blinded to the truth because they do not choose to see will be subverted by this kind of cynical nonsense.

August 21, 1968

Tad Szulc of the New York Times News reported on the brave, quickly crushed resistance of the Czechs.

Despite pleas of pro-Dubcek radio stations not to resist, the Czechoslovaks fought their invaders Wednesday with Molotov cocktails, stones and sticks and bare hands, as well as with an extraordinary display of passive resistance that seemed to rally much of the nation around Dubcek.

In Prague, a number of Soviet tanks were destroyed.

Soviet infantrymen with submachineguns at the ready stood along downtown streets or patrolled them slowly.

Despite the constant appeals for calm and non-resistance, hundreds of youths built a barricade from two overturned trucks and a red trolley off the old town square. It took three Soviet tanks to ram down the obstacle.

On many occasions, Soviet troops fired submachine-guns and rifle bursts in the air as crowds taunted and insulted them and spat upon them.

Czechoslovaks, many of them weeping, shook their fists at the Soviet troops and tanks. Nazi Swastika signs were painted on several tanks. On Charles Bridge over the Vltava, a huge sign said: Russians Go Home.

The Soviet soldiers seemed bewildered and nervous. One told a group of Czechoslovaks that the Soviet troops had come to protect them. The Czechoslovaks laughed.

Prague newspapers, including the party organ Rude Pravo, distributed free copies with front-page denunciations of the invasion. Later, the newspapers printed leaflets in Russian, German and Polish explaining to the invading troops that they were committing an injustice.

The occupation forces seemed unable to discover and silence radio stations loyal to the Dubcek regime.

The stations switched broadcasting frequencies and moved to clandestine studios after their permanent installations had been captured.

After having gone off the air shortly after noon, a television station, calling itself "the free television station of the Prague district", returned to the air tonight showing lengthy films of Soviet tanks moving through the city, gun emplacements, patrolling soldiers and even anti-Soviet demonstrators running away from the Russians.

Military estimates were that 25,000 Soviet, East German, Polish, Hungarian and Bulgarian troops were occupying the capital, the majority of them Soviet.

According to these estimates, an airborne division, a motorized infantry division, a battalion of T-55 tanks, a battalion of T-62 medium tanks plus artillery and fighter and bomber air support were involved in the occupation of Prague.

Prague, August 22, 1968

Charles Manson and his followers were implicated in at least a dozen murders, notably the grisly slaying of Sharon Tate and four friends at Tate's Los Angeles home. The Manson "family" has been described as the dark side of the hippie phenomenon, but Manson seems to have had more in common with Adolf Hitler than with the Love Generation. George Brimmell of Southam News Service reported a grotesque episode at the trial of Manson and three of his followers.

Monday was another vintage day at the Manson murder trial... the day that Manson tried to attack the judge. Armed with two sharp pencils, Charlie Manson leaped toward the bench and Judge Charles H. Older, only a matter of a few feet away.

But a vigilant deputy-sheriff felled him with a flying tackle, and moments later, Manson was led from the courtroom shouting at his honor "in the name of Christian justice, someone should cut your head off."

Manson's co-defendants, the three female members of his hippie family, were removed from the court, too, after they broke into a chant and wouldn't shut up.

Yesterday's episode was but the latest in a series of courtroom grotesqueries in what will probably go down as one of the strangest murder cases in American history.

At 11:06 a.m., Manson was led in — the "guru"...the head of the "family"...the alleged mastermind of seven gruesome murders.

His appearance is shocking: the long locks, wildly disarrayed; a scraggly beard; rumpled prison denims; extreme pallor.

He is tiny — five feet, four inches...he carries a couple of legal-type note pads, and pencils. There was the brooding face with the hypnotic eyes that had filled the cover of Life magazine.

Then the girls — Leslie van Houten, 20, Patricia Krenwinkel and Susan Atkins, both 22.

Pathetic figures...plain, very plain, no make-up...all have long, lank hair...each has a cross scratched in her forehead... they wear jail issue — blue denim blouses and skirts, blue sweaters, sandals, no stockings.

You have to keep reminding yourself these people and these events are the apotheosis of the American hippie-youth-drugs-violence alienation phenomenon, that has given this case such notoriety and worldwide attention.

The first witness was a detective-sergeant from homicide, but before he could start testifying, Manson began jabbering.

Manson: "The minute you find me guilty, you know what I'm going to do to you?"

Judge: "What are you going to do?"

Manson: "You know..."

Judge: "Be quiet."

Manson: "You order me to be quiet while you kill me in your court."

Judge: "I'm going to have you removed if you don't stop."

Manson: "I'll have you removed if you don't stop — I have my own system..."

And with that he sprang with amazing agility toward the judge, only 12 feet away.

Most of us had been transfixed by this exchange, but Deputy Sheriff Bill Murray leaped through the air, landed on Manson and smashed him to the floor. Other officers piled on.

I expected to see some blood, at least, but Manson got up apparently unhurt, and as he was led out he hurled over his shoulder this final thought for the judge: "In the name of Christian justice, someone should cut your head off..."

Los Angeles, October 6, 1970

Manson and his three disciples were found guilty and sentenced to death. This sentence was reduced to life imprisonment when the U.S. Supreme Court ruled the death penalty unconstitutional.

Idealists and Arsonists

The early sixties saw the rise of a non-violent campaign for civil rights in the southern United States. Black and white Americans marched together, staged sit-ins in segregated stores and restaurants, and conducted voter registration drives among southern blacks. A few whites responded with guns and bombs. One of the victims was Medgar Evers, shot outside his home in Jackson, Mississippi. Bruce Phillips of Southam News Service sent this report.

The blood had barely been washed off the carport pavement at 2332 Guynes St., but Mrs. Medgar Evers could not betray her husband's sacrifice by pointless grief.

She had to tell the world that his life and death in the service of Negro rights must not be in vain, and she did it in one of the simplest and most eloquent declarations of faith this correspondent has ever witnessed.

Short hours before, Mrs. Evers had run out of the bungalow to find her husband mortally wounded, and one of her three children imploring him to "get up, daddy." Mr. Evers was the Mississippi field supervisor of the National Association for the Advancement of Colored People, and a lurking assassin had shot him in the back.

But she showed up Wednesday night at a mass Negro meeting at the Pearl Street African Methodist Episcopal Church, to urge her fellow Negroes to "finish his fight."

And although her husband met his death brutally and violently, the "fight" she urged the Negroes to continue is based on the principle of non-violence, of turning the other cheek, of stirring the conscience of those who would perpetuate the division of human beings on racial lines.

The question that grips Jackson today is whether the Negroes here will be satisfied with her husband's way. His murder has stirred resentments and provoked a unity not known before, and the peaceful demonstrations which had been going on here for a fortnight, with hundreds arrested, might now turn into something worse.

Mrs. Evers had been preceded to the platform in the packed and stifling church by several Negro ministers, most of whom had just come from an afternoon's stint in jail. Fourteen of them had been arrested for "parading" without a permit.

They exhorted the audience to boycott the white merchants on Capitol Street, to wear a black mourning band for a month, and to keep on demonstrating.

But nothing touched the crowd with half the impact of Mrs. Evers' brief appeal. She spoke without a note, with only the suggestion of a tremble in her voice, and this is what she said:

"I come here tonight with a broken heart, but I come because I feel it is my duty to do so. I come to make a plea. No one knows as I know how my husband gave his life for this cause — before he was killed. He lived with this cause 24 hours a day, all day, every day.

"It was his wish that this movement would become the most successful this nation, the world has ever known.

"Sunday evening was his first chance to be home for a few hours. He talked of death. He said he was ready, and if he had to go he would rather go this way than sleep away peacefully.

"He was doing this not only for the Negroes in Jackson, not only for the Negroes in Mississippi, not only for every Negro in the United States, not only for all the colored people in the world, but for every white man, too.

"I am left without his comfort. I am left with three children to rear. I am also left with a strong determination to try to pick up where he left off. I hope by his death all of you are able to draw some of his spirit, some of his strength, some of his courage and some of his determination to finish this fight.

"My main purpose in coming here is to ask of you a favor. Nothing can bring Medgar back, but his cause can live on. I don't want his death to be in vain. That would be as bitter a blow as his death has been. So finish his fight, not only for Jackson, but for your children, for this nation, in memory of my husband."

When she finished, every hand in the church was raised in response to a shouted challenge to "finish his fight."

They also dug into pockets for one and five dollar bills and produced nearly $700 as the beginnings of a fund for the Evers family.

Blame was laid on the local and state politicians. If they had not maintained the "old, rotten ways" Mr. Evers would have been in some other less hazardous occupation.

Jackson, Mississippi, June 13, 1963

In the late Sixties the black ghettos of many American cities exploded into rioting, arson, looting and sniping. It sometimes took days to restore order. Paul Kidd of Southam News Service was in Detroit during the "long, hot summer" of 1967.

The tough, blue-helmeted state trooper crouched beside me and squeezed the trigger of his carbine. Somewhere, out there in the darkness, a sniper was trying to get us in his gunsights.

And the whine of the gunman's bullets indicated their closeness.

The trooper fired another two shots at the spot on the Detroit apartment building roof where he thought the would-be killer was hidden.

Here we were last night, a Michigan policeman and a Canadian correspondent, sharing the side of a car as a gunfire shield at the intersection of Lawton Street and Joy Street in the northwest section of the automobile capital of the world.

The trooper rasped: "As soon as you get the chance, get the hell out of here."

A U.S. Army paratrooper patrols a Detroit street after an outbreak of arson, sniping and looting in 1967.

But that chance was not to come for at least a quarter-of-an-hour.

Meanwhile, the bullets flew over and around the car.

Somehow, the battle seemed almost unreal.

Here, in this city of 1,700,000 population in mid-Twentieth century America, a square-mile area was echoing to the sound of snipers' bullets and the return chatter of army machine guns and the crackle of police carbines.

Tanks and armored personnel carriers rumbled down the blackened, debris-littered streets.

It was almost like a movie set — only the shooting was for real.

How real could be seen in city mortuaries, into which 33 dead men and women have now been carried, and in the wards of Detroit hospitals where more than 200 persons now lie with bullet wounds in their bodies.

I had been chatting with several Negroes sitting on the porches of their homes near riot-blitzed 12th Street when four siren-howling state police cars roared past.

I jumped into my car and sped after the troopers. Suddenly, near the Sacred Heart Seminary at Joy and Lawton Streets, I ran into a police checkpoint.

I had just produced my press credentials when sniper fire, which had been concentrated further inside the area, began to spatter the intersection.

At that moment, the state trooper and I hit the asphalt deck.

Around us the other policemen began shooting out lamps to darken the street — thus blurring the aim of the snipers and, at the same time, making it easier for police spotlights to pick out the rooftop and window-hiding gunmen.

The sniper fire became heavier. A policeman roared through a bullhorn "keep back from the windows or you will be shot."

The answer was more sniper fire.

Suddenly, there was a shifting curtain, a flash of a face in window, and the policeman and national guardsmen sprayed the spot with bullets.

Later, police found 38-year-old Jack Sednor dead beside the window.

Meanwhile, the sniper barrage continued.

There came a lull in the shooting. The trooper next to me muttered: "Now, see if you can make it — but keep your lights off and go like hell."

Keeping low, I inched into the car and turned on the ignition. A split-second later, I floored the accelerator and sped clear.

As I did, gunfire opened up again behind me.

Snipers have a habit of firing at cars without headlights because they think that they are police vehicles.

I entered spacious Grand River Boulevard lined with mile after mile of devastated, burned buildings.

The destruction was almost beyond belief — and, looking at it, one understood how property damage in the United States' costliest riot had been carried to more than $200,000,000.

Detroit, July 26, 1967.

The funeral procession for Dr. Martin Luther King. His coffin was taken to the cemetery in a mule-drawn wagon, symbol of the poor Southern blacks for whom he had campaigned. Thousands of marchers followed.

Martin Luther King, Jr., leader of the moderate civil-rights movement in the United States, was shot to death in Memphis, Tennessee on April 4, 1968. With his death, the moderate wing of the civil-rights movement lost its most eloquent spokesman. George Brimmell of Southam News Service reported from Washington on the reaction to King's death.

The shock and despair that greeted news today of Dr. Martin Luther King's murder were matched here today with the threat of retribution.

Stokely Carmichael, militant Negro leader, called a news conference in which he warned of "retaliation in the streets."

Carmichael called the murder an act of war against the Negro people by "white America" and declared: "We have to retaliate for the execution of Dr. King. Our retaliation won't be in the courtroom but in the streets of America."

Carmichael was among hundreds of demonstrators in Washington where one white man died during several hours of violence.

"When white America killed Dr. King, it declared war on us," Carmichael said. "Black people know that their way is not by intellectual discussions. They know they have to get guns. I think white America made its biggest mistake when she killed Dr. King. She killed all reasonable hope."

In contrast to Carmichael's threats, Congressional reaction suggests that Dr. King's memorial may be a landmark civil rights bill — passage of the long-stalled open housing measure.

Former Alabama Governor George Wallace, possibly King's greatest single adversary, termed the assassination "a senseless, regrettable and tragic act."

Senator Edward Brooke, only Negro in the Senate, said "The crime is unspeakable...the grief is unbearable."

Senator Frank Church: "We are steeped in violence. It is the curse of the land."

Republican presidential candidate Richard Nixon said "The most meaningful and appropriate of all tributes would be a prayerful contemplation of the ghastly consequences of hatred, and a new dedication to the ideals of non-violence for which he stood."

In Kalamazoo, Mich., Negro students at Western Michigan University locked themselves inside the student centre on the campus this morning and refused to admit white students or faculty members. They posted signs, some of which read: "The King is dead, so is peace," and "drop dead, white savages."

Washington, April 5, 1968

An editorial.

Dr. Martin Luther King was a man of courage and of principle. He believed in a cause. He was prepared to die for it. Throughout his years of leadership in the Negro civil rights movement in the United States, he willingly accepted the ever-present prospect of martyrdom.

The world was well aware of Dr. King's own serene composure in the face of possible death. However, this awareness in no way diminishes the horror of his murder in Memphis Thursday night. This is a terrible tragedy, and its implications are frightening.

Dr. King was the apostle of non-violence in the civil rights movement, and yet he died as a result of a wanton act of violence. He was a brave man, of noble purpose. The idea which he represented has not died with him — no gunman's bullet, after all, can kill an idea — but it *is* in jeopardy.

April 5, 1968

The First Men in Space

The Soviet Union's early lead in space technology continued into the Sixties. Yuri Gagarin became the first man to orbit the earth. Through the decade, the American space program gradually pulled ahead, and in 1969 the United States landed the first men on the moon. A wire service report:

A young Russian astronaut has orbited around the world in an hour and a half, radioing back reassurances along the way, and landed safely after the first human conquest of space.

This was disclosed by the Soviet Union today in an open announcement hailing one of history's greatest scientific accomplishments.

Moscow declared the epochal flight of the five-ton space ship took place between 9:07 and 10:55 a.m. (1:07 and 2:55 a.m. MST).

Mankind's first space traveller, Major Yuri Alekseyvich Gagarin, was in orbit one hour and 29 minutes before reverse blasts permitted his ship to settle back to earth by parachute.

This is how Moscow radio described what took place:

The space ship was rocketed into the air at 9:07 a.m. and 15 minutes later the swarthy young pilot radioed: "The flight is proceeding normally. I feel well."

Less than an hour later, as he whistled around the globe at more than 17,000 miles an hour — six times faster than man ever travelled before — he reported he was withstanding his state of weightlessness well.

"I am watching the earth," he said. "The visibility is good. I hear you well."

Scientists throughout the world heaped praise on their Soviet colleagues.

Sir Bernard Lovell, head of Britain's giant Jodrell Bank Observatory had described the launching of the spaceman as "the greatest achievement in the history of man."

Sir George Thomson, president of the British Association for the Advancement of Science said:

"I think this is the date children will have to remember when they come to learn history in 50 or 100 years time."

Gagarin, a 27-year-old father of two young children, one of them born just a month ago, told the official Soviet news agency Tass that everything went as planned both during the flight and on the landing.

Moscow went wild with celebration at the news of Gagarin's successful return to earth. Loudspeakers blared out the announcement throughout the city, students cheered and shouted in Red Square and Moscow Radio broadcast special songs marking the flight.

Moscow, April 12, 1961

Tragedy struck the American space program in 1967. Ironically, the three astronauts died in an earthbound test capsule, not in space.

Sudden fire in a spaceship Friday night killed three astronauts and dealt a severe blow to the United States' plans for getting men to the moon this decade.

Investigators poked today through the charred hulk of the Apollo I moonship, seeking the cause of a searing fire that turned it into a death trap for the three astronauts.

One and one-half miles from Pad 34, site of Friday night's first U.S. spacecraft tragedy, the bodies of astronauts Virgil I. (Gus) Grissom, 40; Edward H. White II, 36; and Roger B. Chaffe, 31, lay in an infirmary.

They were practising for a two-week space mission, the first of the Apollo flights which will culminate in the lunar landing, when the hot blaze snuffed out their lives in an instant.

Space officials said they would push on with the program, but the tragedy which capped a long series of troubles with the Apollo spacecraft will call for a soul-searching look before other lives are risked.

Not a word came from the astronauts when the fire tipped into the explosive pure oxygen atmosphere of the spacecraft. Death, said the space officials, was instantaneous.

Some day, every spaceman knew in his heart, it was bound to happen.

But when it came, they thought, it would be in the far reaches of space, not this way.

Going through a full-scale simulation of the launch that was to carry them aloft Feb. 21 for a two-week ride, Grissom, White and Chaffee were trapped in the spacecraft when it was swept by sudden fire.

The emergency escape system was closed to them, because the entire craft was locked in a protective gantry.

Cape Kennedy, Florida, January 28, 1967

The biggest story since Columbus; the first explorers reach the moon. George Brimmell and Bob Cohen of Southam News Service reported on the Apollo II mission to the moon and it's safe return.

The Eagle has started to fly home to its mother ship after nearly 22 hours on the moon during which man's footprints were left in the lunar dust and in the history of mankind.

The two Apollo II astronauts blasted off from the moon shortly before 11 a.m. MST and within minutes reached the relative safety of lunar orbit — the first time anything had ever rocketed away from the moon.

It was the only aspect of the Apollo II mission that had never been tested — and it had to work, just right, just as it did — or commander Neil Armstrong and pilot Edwin Aldrin would almost certainly have been doomed.

Armstrong and Aldrin immediately began pursuing the command ship circling 69 miles above the surface with astronaut Michael Collins at the controls.

"Beautiful, very smooth," Aldrin commented as Eagle took off from the moon.

"A very quiet ride. There's that one crater down there."

The successful lift-off means that Eagle is manoeuvring for its historic link-up with Collins and Columbia, and a safe ride home, later this afternoon.

Left behind, along with the U.S. flag, the two-ton descent stage of the lunar module, scientific gear, are their overshoes, the portable life support systems that enabled them to walk outside the spaceship, cameras, gloves, and old food containers.

As one scientist-astronaut put it: "The moon will look like a bad picnic."

It was 7:58 p.m. MST on Sunday when Armstrong achieved immortality as he set his left foot gingerly on the surface of the moon.

"That's one small step for man, one giant leap for mankind," were his first words as he stepped on the lunar surface less than seven hours after the Apollo II had made its epic landing.

It had taken roughly 10 minutes for Armstrong to get through the hatch of the lunar module, work his way from its "front porch" down the nine steps to the alien, eerie surface of the moon.

At last there he was — a ghostly figure, his movements like a movie in slow motion — his words crackling back a quarter million miles through the depths of space.

He said: "I'm going to step off the LM now . . ."

And, still holding the ladder with his right hand, moving cautiously in his bulky space suit, Armstrong touched the moon with his foot.

About 20 minutes later Aldrin became the second earthling to plant his footprints on the moon.

And a little after 11 p.m. the two

Yuri Gagarin, first man to orbit the earth.

astronauts were back in Eagle, back with the most precious material ever known to man — samples of the lunar soil.

Their nuggets make the Hope Diamond pale in value. These chunks of the moon, to be transported back to earth for analysis, could hold the key to the solar system's history.

They may well tell the age of the moon...its origin...and explain some of the mysteries of interplanetary relationships.

Armstrong and Aldrin accomplished what men have dreamed of since time immemorial — and all mankind shared in the exhilaration of their discovery.

Earlier — before they had emerged from Eagle — Buzz Aldrin conveyed a moving message to the world. About three hours after the lunar touch-down, Aldrin asked "every person listening in...wherever they may be...to pause and contemplate the events of the last few hours...and to give thanks in his or her own way."

The astronauts raised the stars and stripes — and had a telephone call from the president of the United States.

Richard Nixon, sharing the glory of the hour, told Armstrong and Aldrin their feat on the Sea of Tranquillity "inspires us to redouble our efforts to bring peace and tranquillity to earth."

Armstrong also read aloud the inscription on a plaque which included the words, "We came in peace for all mankind."

Carrying a portable television camera to beam back pictures of uncanny clarity, the astronauts took stock of their exclusive domain. Armstrong, the 38-year-old mission commander, gazed around at the stunning lunar landscape, and radioed back to earth; "It has a beauty of its own. It's very pretty up here."

Armstrong likened the moonscape to the high desert country in his homeland. Later he and Aldrin dragged the television camera around in stages to share the panoramic view with earthbound watchers 250,000 miles away.

The two Americans walked slowly and warily at first, aware that one false move could bring death on the airless, grey desert of the Sea of Tranquillity.

But as their confidence mounted Armstrong and Aldrin jumped, bounced and kangaroo-hopped in front of their landing craft, taking advantage of reduced gravity — one-sixth that on earth.

With television trained constantly on the astronauts, the dream of centuries became almost matter-of-fact routine as Armstrong and Aldrin dug into the moon's surface, scooped up dust and rock samples, and reported their findings back to earth.

The astronauts, standing upright in the tiny moonbug, flew down to the lunar surface controlling Eagle manually. They knocked off computer control when it appeared they would touch down on a boulder-strewn area. They landed on a smoother area some four miles farther than originally selected.

The moon surface easily withstood the shock of the Eagle's landing. The four-legged machine sank only one or two inches into the dust — boding well for future moon landings.

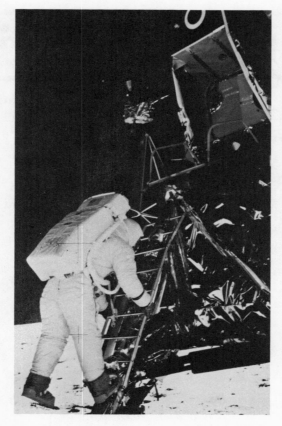

Edwin Aldrin, Jr. leaves the spaceship.

Neil Armstrong, first man to stand on the moon.

With oxygen life packs strapped to their backs, the astronauts went about their work with the calmness of a Sunday afternoon gardener on earth. They set up on the moon instruments that will continue to give scientists on earth information for some time to come.

Through the magic of television, an estimated 500,000,000 people around the world had a ringside seat to man's greatest adventure.

There were memorable utterances during the day of high adventure.

There were Armstrong's words when Eagle separated from the command ship to start the dangerous descent: "The Eagle is flying."

There were Armstrong's — and man's first words from the moon's surface after touchdown: "Houston...Tranquillity Base here. The Eagle has landed."

They unveiled a stainless steel plaque bearing these words:

"Here men from planet earth first set foot upon the moon, July 1969, A.D. We came in peace for all mankind."

They left on the moon a disc on which messages from the leaders of 76 nations including Canadian Prime Minister Trudeau had been recorded. They will return to earth with them the flags of 136 nations, including Russia. And they left behind mementos for three Americans and two Russians who died for the cause of space exploration.

Houston, Texas, July 21, 1969

The Herald's editorial on the moon landing opened with the words of a Canadian pilot, John Gillespie Magee, Jr.

I've topped the wind-swept heights with easy grace,
Where never lark, or even eagle, flew;
And, while with silent, lifting mind I've trod
The high untrespassed sanctity of space,
Put out my hand and touched the face of God.

There's a new meaning today to those soaring words written by a young Canadian air force pilot before he was killed in 1942. Little did he know that the words he wrote describing his own experience were almost prophetic even to the use of the word "eagle".

This is a day on which man might well stand in awe of himself, amid all the exultation, exhilaration, pride and profound admiration for three men as courageous as the world has ever known.

Man has walked on the moon, and the dream-stuff of poets and visionaries down through the ages has become reality.

And by making dream into reality, man has outstripped his very language. What words are left, really, to describe what happened Sunday?

Here is man, with this incredible intellectual ability, surpassing technological skill and vast material resources, able to burst the bounds of earth and set foot on a distant planet, and with all this he is not capable of living in peace with himself.

From the moon's surface, he could look back at his earthly home and know that several wars were raging there, that one of them had been triggered by a silly soccer game.

Truly, God must be shaking His head.

It will be a long time before we learn the full meaning of Sunday's shattering event, but we must know that it cannot be regarded simply as another technological triumph.

It was another major tampering with nature itself. There are deep implications in the fields of philosophy, religion, and politics, not to mention the possible effects on the shifting, grinding masses of power in our native world.

Today, then, at the dawn of a new age, let us all pray that the intelligence which took man to another planet can be used — somehow — to make a better one of his own.

July 21, 1969

Catastrophe in Vietnam

The lessons of the Vietnam war, whatever they may be, have not yet been assimilated. There is still no consensus about how, or whether, the war should have been fought. Perhaps all sides could now agree on this much: it was a disaster for the United States. Right or wrong, the war brought a new, intense bitterness to American politics. The whole affair began quietly: after the French were defeated in Vietnam, the country was divided, north and south, in 1954. In 1960, North Vietnam organized the National Liberation Front, whose Viet Cong guerrillas aimed to overthrow the government of South Vietnam. The United States responded, at first, with a handful of military advisers, then thousands of advisers. As late as 1963, American officials saw it as an easy little war.

U.S. Secretary of State Dean Rusk Friday for the first time gave a strongly-optimistic report on the state of the anti-Communist struggle in Vietnam where 12,000 U.S. advisers are fighting alongside the Vietnamese army.

"We are turning an important corner in South Vietnam in relation to the Viet Cong (Communist) effort," the secretary said.

In documentation of his judgment, Mr. Rusk stated, for example, in recent months the ratio of arms captured has shifted dramatically in favor of the government troops.

He also revealed for the first time that defections from the Viet Cong have grown rapidly.

It has long been the view of experts on Communist warfare that the beginning of the end will come when the Viet Cong itself begins to see that victory is going to go to the other side.

Washington, March 9, 1963

Under Lyndon Johnson, the United States began to take a harder line, as Bruce Phillips of Southam News Service reported. In August, 1964, Johnson won the Gulf of Tonkin resolution from Congress, approving presidential action against further aggression. (North Vietnamese torpedo boats had fired on U.S. destroyers in the Gulf.) The United States never did declare war on North Vietnam; the Gulf of Tonkin resolution was the basis of subsequent U.S. action.

The United States government is prepared to face a full-scale Pacific war if it proves necessary to roll back Communist penetration of Southeast Asia.

It has been learned here that the administration will not entertain any suggestion of a political settlement unless and until there is a complete withdrawal from Laos and South Vietnam of guerrillas from North Vietnam.

In the meantime, the government has resolved to use whatever force is necessary,

and has nearly a quarter of a million troops based at points west of Alaska and Hawaii which are available for duty in Southeast Asia.

The feeling now is that any attempt to achieve a political settlement based on the exciting situation in South Vietnam and Laos, both of which have large areas under rebel control, could only lead ultimately to a complete take-over of the area.

Washington, June 20, 1964

American forces in Vietnam grew quickly. By the time Don McGillivray of Southam News Service filed this report in May, 1965, the U.S. had nearly 75,000 troops there.

The napalm blew out in a searing balloon of white, orange and red flame among the deep greens of the tropical trees. Even from high above it was a fearsome sight. On the ground it must have been like a preview of hell.

I was watching the battle of Ap Truon Trung from a U.S. army helicopter, a UH-1B — generally known as a "Huey" in these parts.

The ground fighting was being done by Army of the Republic of Vietnam (Arvin) troops with U.S. army advisers. I was invited to see it from the command and observation helicopter, swinging high above to maintain a panoramic view of the battle.

The battle of Ap Truon Trung is unlikely to ring through the pages of history. Like a thousand encounters past, and probably a thousand to come in the bewildering Vietnam war, it proved nothing and settled nothing. Perhaps it doesn't deserve to be called a battle.

Ap Truon Trung is one of the countless narrow, jungley villages in the Mekon River delta, a strip of thatched huts bordering one of the canals which cross-hatch the whole rice-growing area. The people of Ap Truon Trung work in the nearby paddy fields, and they live in a Viet Cong controlled area.

Whatever this means in their daily lives, on this particular day it became a life-and-death question because Vietnamese army intelligence had reported three companies of Viet Cong troops in the area. With U.S. advice, the Arvins planned an elaborate operation to trap and destroy them.

The day was bright and almost cloudless. From far away, we could see smoke rising from Ap Truon Trung — evidence that the first air strikes had found some targets. By the end of the dry season, huts made of thatch and wattle are dry and burn like tinder.

We got over Ap Truon Trung in time to see the second air strike.

Silver Skyraiders, flown by Vietnamese pilots, streaked down the length of the village, sowing their deadly seeds.

Then came the napalm. From the point of impact a napalm bomb grows in an instant into an inferno, a storm of fire billowing out to scorch and char anything in its path.

It is jellied gasoline, made in Vietnam from ordinary aviation gasoline with certain additives, and fused to burn on contact.

It's the most fearsome weapon yet put into the Vietnam war. On the few occasions when the tough and disciplined Viet Cong troops have broken and run, making themselves into targets, they've run from napalm.

The Arvin troops, in camouflage uniforms, deployed quickly and efficiently from their helicopters, searching the paddies, the trees and the tall grass for signs of Viet Cong activity. There was no sign.

There had been, in fact, no evidence of Viet Cong except for the few shots fired at the skyraiders and these might have come from the part-time VC warriors who are always everywhere in the delta.

Either the original intelligence report was wrong and there never were three companies of Viet Cong in the area, or they had slipped away in sampans. Or they were still hiding, breathing through bamboo reeds in the murky water. The 3,000 Arvin troops on the ground would continue to search.

"This often happens," explained an American. "We go out and find nothing. But it's like fishing. You don't expect to catch something every time you throw in the bait."

Can Tho, South Vietnam, May 28, 1965

It was a strange war in many ways. For one, there never was a consensus at home that the United States was right, and the enemy wrong. Harrison Salisbury of the New York Times News Service visited North Vietnam and found that intensive American bombing, begun in 1965, was having no decisive effect.

At 3 a.m. last Friday morning, across Long Bien (formerly Paul Doumier) Bridge in Hanoi, moved a procession of women, each with a bamboo pole on a bowed shoulder and burdens balanced on each end.

There was nothing unusual in the sight — nothing for Hanoi and North Vietnam, that is. All through the night, people are carrying heavy burdens on their backs into and out of the city and out along the network of roads and trails that thread through a maze of rice paddies and canals in the Red River delta, moving supplies south and moving food into the city.

To a remarkable extent, North Vietnam has become a night country. It is darkness that provides the greatest protection against U.S. bombers. And it is in the dark hours when movements of supplies and troops are carried out.

A U.S. Marine, wounded in a Viet Cong attack on his tank, is pulled to a helicopter for evacuation. More than 46,000 American servicemen were killed in battle in Vietnam, and another 300,000 were wounded.

It is apparent after even casual inspection that the U.S. air offensive has cost the North Vietnamese heavily. It compels them to commit manpower that otherwise would be available to reinforce the armed services, build up factory production, lift agricultural output or simply convey supplies to the south.

The North Vietnamese undoubtedly will grow leaner and thinner if the war of attrition goes on. But this has been their history for so many years that it is questionable whether it will produce the effect that this policy is designed to produce — a willingness on Hanoi's part to negotiate peace.

Anticipating heavy bombing of Hanoi, the authorities have scattered offices, schools, factories and almost everything moveable into villages and towns nearby. Since the air force has been paying more attention to the environs of Hanoi than to the city itself, substantial casualties have been caused in evacuated schools. The authorities admit this but say they are caught in a dilemma. If the U.S. starts a saturation attack on Hanoi, they do not wish to expose the people to mass casualties. They prefer to risk scattered casualties resulting from the evacuation.

The net conclusion of many foreign residents of Hanoi is that while U.S. bombing has damaged North Vietnam severely, causing heavy material and human losses and compelling the government to invest men and material in neutralizing the attack, it is not likely to provide a decisive factor in maintaining the fight in the south or in compelling Hanoi to capitulate.

Hong Kong, January 13, 1967

Paul Kidd of Southam News Service reported one of the major peaceful protests against the Vietnam war.

In the midnight drizzle, dissident Americans passed a massive judgment on the Vietnam war with a "march against death." One by one, the Vietnam moratorium demonstrators dropped cardboard placards bearing the names of dead Americans and shattered Vietnamese villages into a dozen crude wooden coffins in the shadow of the floodlit United States Capitol.

It began at 6 p.m., this outpouring of national protest against an unpopular war, and it will continue until Saturday.

It was a long, silent procession of mostly young, white Americans carrying candles in paper cups with the placards around their necks, making the pilgrimage from the gates of Arlington National Cemetery to the symbolic coffins on Capitol Hill.

"My son, Timothy Clark," a middle-aged man with tears on his cheeks called out as he strode past the gate of the executive mansion, his slain son's name flapping against his coat.

Washington, November 14, 1969

The My Lai massacre came to be a symbol of everything that was wrong with the war effort in Vietnam: it was brutal, it was pointless, it made a mockery of everything the United States was trying to accomplish. The New York Times News Service sent this report of testimony at the trial of Lieutenant William Calley Jr.

A hushed court Friday heard a former soldier describe in gruesome detail the alleged massacre of South Vietnamese civilians at My Lai and swear that he saw First Lt. William L. Calley Jr. "Blow the head off" a woman who tried to rise from a pile of corpses in a ditch.

Calley, accused of premeditated murder in the slaughter of 102 civilians, glared at the witness, 21-year-old Dennis I. Conti.

Conti spared the court none of the brutal excesses of that tragic day when Charlie Company, First Battalion, 20th Infantry Division, assaulted the hamlet of My Lai 4 on the belief that a Viet Cong battalion was holed up there.

On landing from an assault helicopter he became separated from Calley and lost his bearings, he said, in some tall elephant grass and hedge rows at the western edge of My Lai.

When he found the command post, he testified, Calley ordered him to "round up the people."

Conti said he helped round up about 30, "mostly women and children."

After he had helped take the group of villagers to the command post, Conti testified that "Lt. Calley came out and said 'take care of these people'."

"We said 'okay'," Conti related.

"We stood there and watched them (the prisoners.)

"Calley came back a few minutes later and said 'I thought I told you to take care of them.'

" 'We are,' we told him.

" 'No,' he said, 'I mean, kill them.'

"Lt. Calley said 'Come around this side. We'll get on line and fire into them.'

"I said: 'No. I've got a grenade launcher. I'll watch that tree line.'

"Lt. Calley and Meadlo (Paul D. Meadlo) stood side by side and fired directly into the people.

"The people just screamed and yelled. I guess they tried to get up, too.

"They were pretty well messed up. Lots of heads were shot off and pieces of heads. Pieces of flesh flew off the sides and arms.

"Meadlo fired a little bit and broke down and started crying and said: 'I can't shoot any more people.'

"He stuck his weapon into my hands and said 'here, you do it.'

"I said, 'If they're going to be killed, I'm not going to do it. Let Lt. Calley do it.'

"Meadlo took back his weapon. At that time there was only a few kids standing.

"Lt. Calley killed them one by one."

Fort Benning, Georgia, December 5, 1970

Calley was the only man convicted of the My Lai massacre. He had defenders who argued that he was only a scapegoat. He was imprisoned for 3½ years, three years of that time under house arrest in his bachelor apartment on a military post.

Diefenbaker to Trudeau

In Canada, the political uproar of the Sixties was confined mostly to the House of Commons and the back rooms of Ottawa — until the FLQ crisis in 1970. Both major parties chose new leaders during the Sixties, and a new party was born. The Herald greeted the NDP in this editorial.

Five days of the New Democratic convention in Ottawa are over now, and Canadians will have a chance to assess this new political creature which will soon be soliciting their votes.

From the demonstrations just accorded the nation the NDP emerges as an old hodge-podge of conflicting ideologies, sharp divisions, and plain fuzzy thinking.

The divisions are inherent in any amalgamation of trade unions and Socialist intellectuals. Farmers plump for free trade on one hand and the unions seek protection for their industries on the other. It will be a long time before the grain farmers of Western Canada will be able to erase the bitter feeling generated by last year's strike of grain handlers at Vancouver.

The fuzzy thinking comes out clearly in the words of the party's new leader, Mr. T.C. Douglas, premier of Saskatchewan. He is a man whose surface charm and crowd-pleasing talents are more easy to pin down than his reasoning.

For instance, he announced as though he had thought it up all by himself, that the billions of dollars now spent on tools of war should be spent combating ignorance and poverty. This is the stand, he says, of the NDP. It is also the stand, and Mr. Douglas knows it perfectly well, of any sensible person in the Western hemisphere. The fact is that international Communism is menacing our very existence. We have to arm to save our lives and to protect the way of life we want our children to enjoy.

Mr. Douglas and his friends finally agreed upon a resolution saying they could stay in NATO — if NATO agrees to make itself over in the image preferred by the NDP. Otherwise, the NDP will pack its bags and get out.

That type of thinking simply isn't good enough. And "simply isn't good enough" is a phrase which sums up much of the New Democratic party.

August 5, 1961

By 1963, the Conservative government of John Diefenbaker — which five years before had recorded the biggest landslide in Canadian history — was torn by internal dissension, and close to defeat at the polls. The party's bitterest disputes were over Canadian relations with the United States, especially on the question of nuclear weapons. Diefenbaker and his followers did not want to equip anti-aircraft missiles in

Canada, and Canadian forces in Europe, with nuclear warheads. The strongest proponent of nuclear weapons was Defence Minister Douglas Harkness, MP for Calgary North, who resigned from the government over Diefenbaker's policy. The issue came to a head at a closed session of the Conservative caucus a few days after Harkness's resignation. Charles Lynch of Southam News Service compiled this account of the meeting.

Grown men wept, insults were exchanged, cabinet ministers bared souls and orators preached for their lives at Wednesday's meeting of the Progressive Conservative party here.

The caucus was the climax of two weeks of tension-laden crisis for the party, whose government had been brought down in the House of Commons the night before and whose leader, John Diefenbaker, was now fighting for his political life.

It was one of those miracles that sometimes take place in politics that the members of the caucus, comprising the party's MPs and senators, were able to emerge from the session to announce with great excitement, and at least a measure of truth, that the party was united behind Mr. Diefenbaker's leadership for the election campaign ahead.

Cabinet resignation rumors had been flying like confetti during the preceding week, as various cabinet ministers fought to save the life of the government, if need be by jettisoning Mr. Diefenbaker.

Only one resignation stuck — that of Douglas Harkness, the minister of national defence. His pro-nuclear views were backed by at least half of the members of the cabinet — and like him, they were prepared to accept Mr. Diefenbaker's public statement that Canada had nuclear commitments to NATO and NORAD, and stood ready to fulfill them under certain conditions.

But the stresses and strains on Harkness proved too much for him to tolerate, and

John Diefenbaker, left, and Douglas Harkness, before Harkness broke with Diefenbaker.

when he finally took his resignation action none of his cabinet colleagues followed him.

Harkness's resignation went in Sunday night, after a day described by one of the participants as one of the most incredible in the life of any cabinet, in any country.

When the Harkness resignation was made public on Monday, the pressures mounted. Party emissaries were meeting secretly with Robert Thompson of the Social Credit party, and were even flirting with NDP leader T.C. Douglas, trying to find a way to save the life of the government in Tuesday's confidence vote.

Thompson is quoted as having said the government could expect as much as eight months of grace if Mr. Diefenbaker would step aside and Finance Minister George Nowland were installed as prime minister on an action program.

Conservative informants say Thompson was acting on instruction from Premier Manning of Alberta, who had sent word that the price of continued Social Credit support for the government in the Commons should be the removal of Mr. Diefenbaker.

Manning's weapon over Social Crediters from Quebec, according to these sources, was a threat that contributions to federal Socred funds from Alberta, including the funds of the Quebec wing of the party, would be cut off unless the Quebec members followed Thompson's lead in demanding Diefenbaker's head, and then pressing on to defeat the government when Mr. Diefenbaker hung on.

The terms were not met, and the government went down to defeat.

That left the cabinet with its own internal problems on the eve of an election — a cabinet many of whose members felt they could no longer function under Mr. Diefenbaker's leadership. These men had become convinced that the party could not win the election under Diefenbaker; they dreaded the anti-American note that Mr. Diefenbaker seemed to favor as a campaign technique; and they were dissatisfied with the prime minister's indecision on nuclear weapons.

The gist of the testimony in caucus was that the ministers did not feel they could continue to function under Mr. Diefenbaker if the coming election campaign was going to be waged on a primarily anti-American note. They said they could not be parties to such a campaign.

After these speeches, the pro-Diefenbaker forces began to manifest themselves.

Western MPs and senators came to bat for the Prairie boy who made good — the West, it appeared, stood solid for Diefenbaker and dark threats were made.

But the voices that changed the mood of the caucus came not from the West, but from two Easterners, both senators.

Senator Alfie Brooks of New Brunswick, government leader in the Senate, rose to heights of emotional oratory hitherto unsuspected in support of Diefenbaker's leadership. The caucus gave him a rousing ovation

Herald cartoonist Tom Innes on the Harkness-Diefenbaker dispute: "Gonna be in town long, stranger?" "Nope. Just passin' through."

---

at the end. The gist of his argument, and the most telling point with the ministers who were ready to resign, was that such an action would be fatal to the party.

The party loyalty theme was picked up by the greatest of all Conservative orators, Grattan O'Leary of Ottawa. O'Leary, whose platform prowess is legendary although he has never been an elected politician, was attending his first party caucus.

Those who heard him say they had never witnessed such a performance. Almost single-handed, he rallied the caucus to the side of John Diefenbaker, and by the time he had finished the room was in an uproar. If the party was saved at Wednesday's caucus — and only the election outcome will show whether it was or not — O'Leary gets most of the credit.

Not all the wounds were healed, by any means. But sufficient unity was created for the members of the caucus to present a seemingly united front when they emerged.

Thus ended what one senior Conservative called the most fantastic two weeks in Canadian political history — a fortnight whose full story will not be known until the memoirs are written years hence.

Ottawa, February 7, 1963

Other members of the Conservative cabinet had threatened to resign, and two of them — George Hees and Pierre Sevigny — did quit. That spring, the Liberals, under Lester Pearson, were returned to power as a minority government.

John Diefenbaker's campaign of 1963 was the last whistle-stop tour of Canada. Even then, campaigning from a railway train was an exercise in nostalgia, but it was still possible — barely — to reach many small towns by train. Doug Sagi of The Herald rode the Diefenbaker train through southern Alberta.

John Diefenbaker has turned back the clock and made all Western Canada his "main street" as he takes his special train on his whistle-stopping mission through the Prairies.

The train stops at a hamlet, the rear coach even with the station platform, and the man in the black coat and homburg steps from it.

Shaking hands as he passes through the crowd, he seems unchanged from the solitary Conservative MP who regularly shook hands up and down Second and Central Avenues, the main streets of Saskatoon and Prince Albert, Saskatchewan, 10 and 20 years ago.

The people call him by his first name; he loves it, and occasionally recognizes someone and can call a first name back.

If local officials have a speaking platform set up, he uses it, but only briefly. He is not there, he frequently tells the crowds, to "talk politics."

Saturday, Prime Minister Diefenbaker's "campaign special," a five car Canadian Pacific train, took him electioneering through Southern Alberta.

At Okotoks, the first stop, there were 200 people and he must have shaken hands with half of them. His wife, Olive, managed to get around to the other half while his brother, Elmer, took pictures.

At High River the crowd approached

800 and there was an Indian dance, too.

At Claresholm he mentioned that an uncle of his had once settled there. (There appear to be a great many Diefenbaker ancestors scattered about the country.)

He was given a proclamation of welcome and he promised to treasure it as he does his recently-conferred freedom of the City of London, England.

March 25, 1963

After nearly 80 years of staunch Conservatism, The Herald found it could not stomach John Diefenbaker's policy on nuclear weapons, and the general disarray into which the party had fallen. Much to the disgust of Tory readers, the paper endorsed Lester Pearson's Liberals.

The Calgary Herald believes that, in the national interest, Mr. Lester Pearson and the Liberal party should form the next government of Canada.

Only by electing a strong Liberal government can this country put an end to the instability and uncertainty which have beset it sorely now for at least a year.

The Conservative government is a torn and tattered thing, its record in the past year something that few Canadians can contemplate without a shudder.

Internally, it is sick with disaffection and active animosity.

Externally, it is presenting a facade of bluster and spurious martyrdom which we cannot believe will fool any thinking Canadian who has paid the slightest attention to the spectacle which has unfolded in Ottawa in the past year.

The Herald did not come lightly to this decision to give its full support to the Liberals this time after endorsing the Conservatives so often in the past.

Even a year ago, during the last election, this newspaper had deep reservations about the kind of government the Conservatives had been providing, and expressed these doubts. Nevertheless, we said Mr. Diefenbaker and his government should have another chance. They have had that chance. They have bungled it beyond belief.

March 26, 1963

Less than 20 years ago, the Canadian flag was bitterly dismissed by many loyal citizens as "Pearson's rag." Until the Pearson government introduced the maple-leaf design, Canada's symbol had been the red ensign, which prominently included the British Union Jack. The new flag was condemned by many people as a sell-out to Quebec and a betrayal of the men who had fought under the red ensign. It took some years for the hard feelings to die down and the new design to be generally accepted. Don McGillivray of Southam News Service was in the Commons press gallery on the long, angry night when the new flag was approved.

The red maple leaf flag was forced through the Commons by closure at 2:12 a.m. today in a fantastic, howling climax to six months of struggle.

Before the 163-to-78 vote approved the new flag, Opposition Leader Diefenbaker lost a fight for the final word to Prime Minister Pearson, then spurned a last appeal from the prime minister to rally 'round the new flag.

Spirits were high and tempers up as the House went through 10 hours of impassioned speeches, catcalls and votes. After the end, a Conservative MP socked a Liberal on the jaw near the front door of the Parliament Building while jubilant French-Canadian MPs waved the new flag for TV cameras.

It took four roll-call votes to push the new flag through the house.

When the result was announced, Liberal MPs threw paper in the air and shouted their triumph. French-Canadians jumped up to sing "O Canada" in French as some Tories walked out and others got grudgingly to their feet.

A minute later, the whole house and the public galleries, still jammed despite the late hour, stood together to sing "The Queen" in English.

But the real climax came when Mr. Pearson, having gained the floor by a vote and a speaker's ruling, faced Mr. Diefenbaker and his shouting band of last-ditch Conservatives.

Through a flurry of interruptions, the prime minister paid tribute to the "long, hard and sincere fight" by the Tories but

declared that the "fight is over in this House of Commons."

He asked Mr. Diefenbaker to "forget the passions, the prejudices and the bitterness of the fights of the past few months and rally 'round this Canadian flag and make it an emblem of unity."

"A flag by closure," retorted Mr. Diefenbaker, "imposed by closure."

Then Mr. Pearson asked the Conservatives not to force a recorded vote "so that we will not be in a position in this House of having members vote against what will be our national flag."

"Don't be crazy," said Conservative J. Waldo Monteith. "I want to be recorded."

"All right," Mr. Pearson shouted above the angry noise of many voices. Red-faced and waving a fist for emphasis, he continued:

"We on this side have made the appeal. They have turned it down with jeering and insult. We on this side and a good many on the other side of the House will vote with pride and confidence in the motion you are about to put before the House."

Ottawa, December 15, 1964

The growing tension between French- and English-speaking Canadians was already evident in the early Sixties, years before the Quebec separatists — radical or democratic — became a serious political force. In 1965 the Royal Commission on Bilingualism and Biculturalism issued a warning which is still unfortunately relevant today. J.R. Walker of Southam News Service summarized the commission's preliminary report.

Canada could be destroyed unless the problem of French Canada is resolved. Starkly the Royal Commission on Bilingualism and Biculturalism warned Canadians today of their possible fate in its preliminary but unanimous report, if "the greatest crisis in its history" were not faced.

That crisis, the 10-man commission headed by Davidson Dunton and Andre Laurendeau, stated, lay in Quebec and sprang from French Canadian rejection of the state of affairs established under Confederation in 1867.

"There are hopeful signs; there are great possibilities for Canada. But we are convinced at the present time that the perils must be faced."

The commission said it will recommend concrete "adjustments and accommodations" in its final report.

"But," they added, "a major operation will perhaps be unavoidable. The whole social body appears to be affected. The crisis has reached a point where there is a danger that the will of the people to go on may begin to fail."

Throughout their report, the B&B commissioners revealed the impression, as they said, of listening "not to a dialogue, but to two soliloquies."

Rather than a conflict between a majority and a minority, the commission said, "it is

rather a conflict between two majorities: That which is a majority in all Canada and that which is a majority in the entity of Quebec."

This attitude, the report went on, "goes back to a fundamental expectation for French Canada, that is, to be an equal partner with English-speaking Canada.

"If that idea was not achieved, Separatism was just around the corner.

"An important element in French-speaking Quebec is already tempted to go it alone." And the commissioners noted the Separatists exercise an influence on French Canadian society proportionately higher than their numbers.

The reason for this crisis "now," the commissioners said, "apparently lay in the conflict within generations breaking out in French Quebec." The young and the intellectuals were leading it.

French Canadians' "major grievance, overshadowing all others," was that English-speaking management in Quebec business and commerce prevented a majority of French employees from working in their mother tongue once they reached a certain level. And Quebecers warned the commission this situation could "no longer" be allowed to continue.

The next complaints, according to the B&B report, were against alleged discrimination in the civil service, in transportation, and in the armed forces, especially the air and naval forces.

On the other hand the commissioners found English Canadians "content with Confederation," but lacking knowledge about not only Quebec but other regions of Canada.

The commissioners admitted that the great bulk of English-speaking opinion seemed moderate. "It has no animus against French-speaking Canadians...it tends to be bewildered and often hurt by reports from Quebec."

Ottawa, February 25, 1965

Liberal Justice Minister Lucien Cardin blurted the news of a six-year-old scandal involving Conservative cabinet ministers and a West German woman named Gerda Munsinger, who apparently had contacts in the KGB. The House of Commons, with Lester Pearson's minority government on one side and the disintegrating leadership of John Diefenbaker on the other, was in a surly mood at the best of times; this, as George Brimmell of Southam News Service reported, was not the best of times. The press pounced on Cardin's hint, and found that Mrs. Munsinger, contrary to Cardin's information, was still alive and talking.

Justice Minister Cardin's report of the death of Gerda Munsinger proved to be premature. Gerda is alive, and she came back to haunt the House of Commons Friday.

She's haunting the justice minister, whose resignation was demanded time and again through a fantastic session of the House.

Gerda Munsinger, who may have been a spy, and Pierre Sevigny, who was definitely a cabinet minister.

She's haunting Pierre Sevigny, former associate minister of national defence, whose name was linked with Mrs. Munsinger in the Commons, over the repeated but ineffectual objection of a horde of Conservative MPs.

She's presumably haunting one or more other former Diefenbaker ministers, said to have known her as well, in Canada's very own Profumo-type scandal.

And as the Commons broke for the weekend, the word "adulterer" hung in the air.

It's difficult to convey the atmosphere in the Commons Friday. Not unlike a lynch mob, perhaps, on the opposition side. It was ugly, "sickening" to some members.

They roared, and they shouted — even the prime minister. They raked over past scandals.

In the midst of it all came the bombshell news that Bob Reguly of The Toronto Star, unquestionably Canada's outstanding investigative reporter, had located Gerda Munsinger alive and well in Munich.

The House got the word that though Justice Minister Cardin wasn't prepared to name names — he sat silent through the day's wild scenes — Gerda was. She'd named Pierre Sevigny, for example, and said she was prepared to come back to testify about her friendship with him.

It had been just a week before that Mr. Cardin, then jousting with Opposition Leader Diefenbaker over the Spencer security case, had challenged the former prime minister to justify his actions over what he called "the Monsignor case."

Through the ensuing days, newsmen developed details of the affair, and finally, Thursday, the justice minister called a press conference and made a number of sensational disclosures.

He charged that more than one Tory cabinet minister from the Diefenbaker cabinet was involved with Mrs. Munsinger, a 36-year-old divorcee whom reporter Reguly describes as "tall, blonde and shapely."

He charged that the then prime minister, Diefenbaker, had "mishandled" the affair, and he alleged that Mrs. Munsinger was "a security risk."

He suggested that the Munsinger matter should be looked into by the royal commis-

sion which the government decided last week to set up into security practices in Canada since 1944.

And he declared that the woman had been engaged in espionage before she came to Canada in 1955.

More than that, he said she was now dead. He said that although he had not personally studied the file, he had it from the Mounties she had died of leukemia since her return to Germany in 1961.

The crisis point in Friday's Commons debate came at mid-afternoon.

At that point it was known that The Toronto Star was on the streets with the straight goods about Gerda, and naming Pierre Sevigny.

Ottawa, March 12, 1966

An inquiry by Mr. Justice Wishart Spence of the Supreme Court of Canada found that Diefenbaker, then prime minister, should have removed Sevigny from his job as associate minister of defence in 1960 when he learned about Sevigny's relationship with Munsinger. (The hazard was not pillow-talk about weapons systems, but rather blackmail by enemy agents.) George Hees, another Conservative cabinet minister, had been named in the case, but Spence found his association with Munsinger "not at all improper in character."

Canada's Centennial year, 1967, was the high point of a decade that had been, politically at least, sordid and grouchy. Expo 67, which drew visitors from all over the world and sent most of them home happy, was the centrepiece of the celebration. Canadians everywhere celebrated the accomplishments of a century. The Herald, a mere youth of not quite 84, marked the occasion with this editorial.

The rest of the world will just have to excuse us if we wear our national pride more rakishly than usual tomorrow. On this Dominion Day we have been a nation for 100 years.

Canada has accomplished some mighty achievements in growing from colony to free, independent nationhood and from a group of backwoods settlements to a modern industrial country and important world trader.

The road has more often than not been twisting and rough and its course anything but clear.

Our success in negotiating it gives us plenty of reason for pride as we celebrate the Centennial Dominion Day.

Canadians spent the first 100 years taming a rugged environment and creating the physical sinews of a nation.

What we should be doing now is forging a national character which will knit together the racial and national splits in the Canadian personality.

Our great national resources and technical and industrial development provide grounds for the confident expectation of continued growth and prosperity.

The next 100 years could be even more successful and exciting than the first if we can submerge petty racial and regional differences in the same happy mixture of foresight and optimism our founding fathers used in creating the nation.

June 30, 1967

Charles de Gaulle's sense of destiny was not exactly in tune with that of English-speaking Canada. Tim Creery of Southam News Service reported this jarring note in the Centennial celebrations.

President Charles de Gaulle of France received a thunderous ovation Monday night as he issued an incitement to separatism from a balcony of Montreal City Hall.

"Vive le Quebec libre," he cried. (Long live free Quebec.)

The crowd of about 5,000 dominated by loud, placard-waving members of the separatist Rassemblement Pour l'Independence Nationale, responded rapturously to the president's adoption of their "Free Quebec" slogan. Earlier they had drowned out the singing of O Canada with their booing.

In his fervent address from the pillared balcony high above the throng, Gen. de Gaulle compared the spirit of emancipation he found in Quebec to the spirit in France when it was liberated from Nazi occupation.

"I am going to confide a secret in you," President de Gaulle told the delighted crowd. "This evening here, and all the way along my route, I find myself in an atmosphere of the same kind as that of the liberation."

The response was earsplitting. Later the crowd broke police lines and reached for the hand of the general as he and Premier Daniel Johnson of Quebec rode away from city hall in an open car.

The tumultuous scenes in front of the elegant building in the heart of Old Montreal came at the end of a 10-hour progress along the 160 miles of "The King's Road," from Quebec City to the second largest French speaking city in the world. Mr. Johnson was at the president's side all the way, as the hero of the "free French".

Montreal, July 25, 1967

An editorial.

President Charles de Gaulle of France is living down to all the advance billing in regard to his visit to Canada and Expo.

Within hours of his pompous arrival, he had violated every known ethic of proper behavior by a foreigner visitor to another state.

He stood guilty, almost as soon as he arrived, of the most boorish kind of international behavior.

To say he has been guilty of shocking bad manners is a feeble understatement.

He has openly encouraged subversion by the worst elements in Quebec. He has actively encouraged behavior calculated to damage, if not destroy, the very existence of Canada as a single nation.

Is there any way to un-invite him, and send him back to France?

July 25, 1967

De Gaulle, after a rejoinder by Lester Pearson, cut short his visit to Canada.

The Diefenbaker era came to an end in the autumn of 1967, when a Conservative convention chose Robert Stanfield, premier of Nova Scotia, as its new leader. J.R. Walker of Southam News Service reported on the beginning of this new, never quite successful, period in the party's history.

A new era has dawned in the Conservative party with the election of Premier Robert L. Stanfield to its leadership.

In a wide-open convention, without precedent in the history of the Tory party, the cool and craggy Nova Scotian of the reflective Conservative viewpoint has decisively ended the hectic and disputatious Diefenbaker years.

As the tall, spare, rather scholarly premier leaves today for Halifax to wind up 11 years as head of that successful Conservative government, the wily, old chieftain from the Prairies, one week from his 72nd birthday, will be returning to Prince Albert to brood upon his humiliating but inevitable defeat.

The advent of Premier Stanfield on the national stage is inevitably going to change the look of the Progressive Conservative party, attracting a new breed of men to the top councils of the party and into the House of Commons.

Toronto, September 11, 1967

John Diefenbaker was a fighter to the last, as Southam's Bruce Phillips reported. In the

1967 convention he ran for the leadership he already held, and lost it to Robert Stanfield. Then, though he left the Opposition leader's office and official residence, he stayed on in the House of Commons.

The end for John Diefenbaker was a brutal and shocking thing, but the instinct toward pity was tempered by the knowledge that the manner of his going was knowingly dictated by himself.

He would have had it no other way. Any suggestions that he endured that terrible beating because of a flight from reality are false.

His last hours as leader were so totally in character with the whole of his amazing 50 years in politics that now, with two days in which to ponder those tumultuous events, it is hard to imagine him having chosen any other mode of farewell.

The defeat was as spectacular in its dimensions as all his past triumphs and catastrophes. His final acts were riddled with the ambivalence of a man equally obsessed by power and by ideals which Canadians now recognize so well; and the entire affair was wrapped in the deliberate mysteries he so loves to fashion. The last day, in other words, was consistent with all the others; a distortion of the normal process, a freak occurrence, fascinating and in some respects even admirable, but still just beyond the reach of ordinary understanding.

Like everything else the defeat tests assumptions people make about him which fail to take his character into account. For example, there should have been no surprise that he let his name stand, or any incredulity that he let it remain for a second and even a third ballot while the pathetic scraps of his power melted away.

He is so totally the political animal that any other course would have been unnatural, even a denial of the purpose and meaning of a politician's life as he sees it. To him, a politician's duty is to struggle for power until all life and hope are beaten out of him. No other approach would have sus-

tained him through the many and bitter disappointments of his early life, and it was unthinkable that he could somehow change at the end.

Toronto, September 11, 1967

Expo 67, the world's fair in Montreal, was the centrepiece of Canada's Centennial celebration. Lisa Balfour of Southam News Service wrote this farewell to one of Canada's great successes.

By Sunday night, it will be all over. Expo, that is: the six-month marvel that has materialized as a dazzling example of what the world, and Canada particularly, can achieve when everybody works together.

From start to finish, the 1967 world's fair has been an experimental melting pot for over 60 different national cultures and even more architectural styles.

In fact, it has become a new urban experience and one which in many ways points up the obvious inadequacies of conventional city life.

In any event, the 1,000 acre Montreal exhibition seems to have condensed more into a six-month period than many years of travel and academic study usually do.

Thus, although the fair was originally billed as the icing on our Centennial cake, it has since proved to be much more — in fact, an intellectual and spiritual experience wrapped up in a physically attractive package.

Moreover, it has given Canadians a magnificent excuse to boast about themselves and at the same time, it has given the world in general an opportunity to see this vast country from a new and different point of view.

As a successful trend setter, there seems no doubt that Expo has provided Canada with a new sense of pride in her own worth

After the 1968 election, Herald cartoonist Tom Innes saw Pierre Trudeau as the Pied Piper of Canada.

and – as Montreal Mayor Jean Drapeau says – because it has done this, it has been well worth its cost.

For another thing, Expo has been a fair to beat all fairs, particularly because it has attracted a precedent setting crowd – well over the record chalked up by the Brussels world fair in 1958.

Expo's final attendance of a probable 50,000,000 will make it the attendance leader in world's fairs of comparable size.

Expo has also proved the in-place to go and as such has attracted a record number of crowned heads, presidents, diplomats, and personalities from the world of art and science.

Although Cuba's Castro, Yugoslavia's Tito and Russia's Kosygin failed to show up, Expo did bring Queen Elizabeth II, General Charles de Gaulle and President Lyndon Johnson to Montreal in the course of the summer.

One of the main reasons for the huge public interest – in the Czechoslovakian and telephone pavilions particularly – was the fact that such technically fascinating and spiritually satisfying films were offered.

For that matter, the second most outstanding feature of Expo 67 – apart from the 1,000 acre site itself – was the number of avant garde films that have made so important a contribution to almost every pavilion.

From the fair's very outset, films at Labyrinth, the Ontario pavilion, the Canadian National and Canadian Pacific pavilions and the United Nations pavilion have proved irresistible and in some cases impossible to get into without hours of waiting.

But many of the pavilions which didn't thrive on the reputation of their films did so because they offered the kind of exhibits which caught the public's imagination. For instance the British pavilion – which both stimulated and amused the visitor – proved an obvious example of this kind of attraction.

But here again, Expo broke a record, being the only first-category world's fair to claim a participation of over 60 nations.

Montreal, October 28, 1967

Tim Creery of Southam News reported on the beginning of the Trudeau phenomenon. Lester Pearson had announced his retirement; the Liberals' choice of leader would step into his shoes as prime minister.

The most daring and unconventional bid for the prime ministry in Canada's history was formally launched today by Justice Minister Pierre Trudeau.

Announcing his decision at a packed press conference in the National Press Building, the 46-year-old, left-wing, academic, non-conformist millionaire said he thought his candidacy had been promoted by the press "as a huge practical joke on the Liberal party."

He said he thought the newsmen had been building up a thesis so that they would be able to say, after the Liberal Leadership

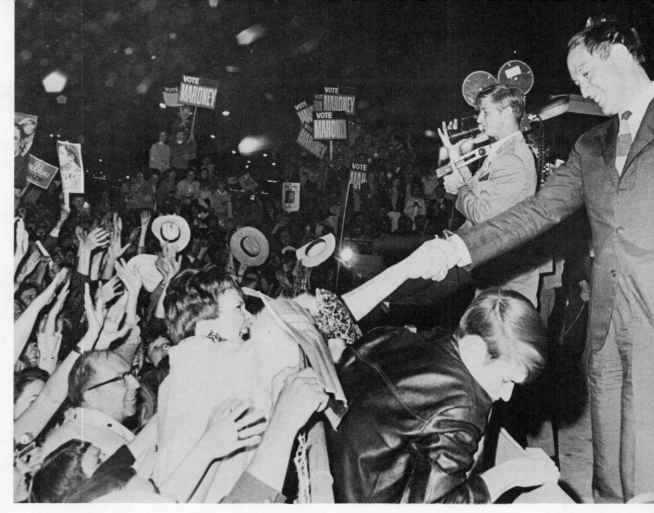

Trudeaumania in Calgary, near the end of the 1968 federal election campaign. The Liberals even won a seat in the city, with Pat Mahoney taking Calgary South.

convention, "they didn't have the guts to choose a good guy because the good guy didn't run."

"The joke blew up in your faces and mine," said Mr. Trudeau, "because people took it seriously."

In his normal witty and relaxed fashion the justice minister told the press conference about his search for "absolute truth," his successful efforts a decade ago to be removed from a U.S. blacklist of people who couldn't enter that country, and his former opposition to Prime Minister Pearson and the Liberals whom he had once called "idiots."

Mr. Trudeau said he would stand by what he had written in the past, mostly in the monthly review, Cite Libre, in which he attacked the Duplessis regime, the nationalism of the quiet revolution, and centralization of government in Ottawa.

But he added "I don't think the analyses I wrote at other times are necessarily applicable today. I was abstracted from the concrete political fight – I was a professor, an essayist.

"You play the game by different rules when you are in the university," said Mr. Trudeau, who taught constitutional law at the University of Montreal. "As a professor you seek absolute truth. In politics you seek to accommodate absolute truth to the facts around you."

Mr. Trudeau said he had heard that he was on the U.S. blacklist before he was due to attend a Commonwealth conference in 1956 or 1957 in Pakistan on behalf of the Canadian Institute of International Affairs. He thought the blacklisting had probably been due to his attendance at a Russian-sponsored economic conference in Moscow in 1952, at the height of Stalinism.

"I went to the American consul in Montreal and he said 'yes, you have been blacklisted.' I said "How do I whiten myself?' He told me."

Asked about the "bleaching" process, Mr. Trudeau said he appealed the decision and then was questioned. It had taken a few

weeks. They probably still felt he was a bit "pink."

Ottawa, February 16, 1968

In the end, of course, Trudeau did win, finally defeating John Turner for the Liberal leadership. He replaced Lester Pearson as prime minister, and in the summer election of 1968 he won the majority that had always eluded Pearson.

The October Crisis of 1970 was the disastrous peak of the activities for the FLQ – the Front for the Liberation of Quebec. Up to this point, the movement's terrorism had been restricted to bombing mail-boxes and armories, sometimes with fatal results. Then, in 1970, it resorted to kidnapping.

Four men, two armed with sub-machine guns and another with a revolver, kidnapped James Richard Cross, British trade commissioner, after entering his house at 8:15 a.m. today.

Police said the British government office here said that the wife of the trade commissioner later received a telephone call from the kidnappers. Contents of the conversation were not divulged by the police.

Chief Detective Inspector Roland Jodoin quoted a witness as hearing one of the four abductors say "We're the FLQ."

The Front de Liberation Quebecois, an underground terrorist organization in Quebec, has been linked to dynamite bombings during the 1960s and to demands for the political independence of the province from Canada.

Montreal, October 5, 1970

The Cross kidnapping was followed by another: Quebec Labor Minister Pierre Laporte was seized by another section of the FLQ. Armed soldiers appeared in Quebec and Ottawa to protect other prospective kidnap victims. Pat O'Callaghan of Southam News Service reported the prime minister's defence of this extraordinary measure.

"It's more important to keep law and order in society than to be worried about weak-kneed people who don't like the looks of an army."

This was Mr. Trudeau's response Tuesday to CBC national affairs reporter Tim Ralfe, who had told the prime minister that he "was worried about living in a town that's full of men with guns running around."

In the course of an interview outside the Parliament Buildings, Mr. Trudeau said "...I think it's more important to get rid of those who are committing violence against the total society and those who are trying to run the government through a parallel power by establishing their authority by kidnapping and blackmail."

When Mr. Ralfe said that his choice was to live in a society that "is free and democratic which means that you don't have people with guns running around in it," Mr. Trudeau replied:

"Well, there's a lot of bleeding hearts around that just don't like to see people with helmets and guns. All I can say is 'go on and bleed'."

Asked just how far he would go, Mr. Trudeau said "Just watch me."

When questioned whether such measures would extend to reducing civil liberties and using wiretapping, Mr. Trudeau said: "Yes, I think that society must take every means at its disposal to defend itself against the emergence of a parallel power which defies the elected power in this country, and I think that goes to any distance.

"So long as there is power here which is challenging the elected representatives of the people, then I think that power must be stopped, and I think it's only, I repeat, weak-kneed bleeding hearts who are afraid to take these measures."

Ottawa, October 14, 1970

The prime minister was indeed willing to take strong measures. He proclaimed the War Measures Act, which in effect suspended all civil rights at the government's discretion. Many Quebecers suspected of FLQ sympathies were arrested and held without being charged and without bail.

Le Front de Liberation du Quebec has been outlawed under the regulations of the War Measures Act proclaimed today by the Trudeau government.

Prime Minister Trudeau tabled the regulations under the emergency legislation — used for the first time in peace time — in the Commons this morning.

Under the regulations, anyone who is a member of the terrorist FLQ organization can be imprisoned for a term not exceeding five years.
Ottawa, October 16, 1970

A soldier stands guard outside Quebec city hall during the FLQ crisis of October, 1970. About 6,000 soldiers were mobilized to protect buildings and prominent politicians in Ottawa and Quebec.

The FLQ responded by murdering Pierre Laporte. He was found dead in the trunk of an abandoned car, strangled with his gold neck chain. The Herald published this editorial.

All decent Canadians today, wherever they may live, are heavy in their hearts with shock, horror and shame.

Savage kidnap and murder. Politics of blood.

Can this be our Canada? Canada, the peaceful country?

Canada, the land of tolerance, democratic procedure, compromise?

Canada, the gentle land, the relaxed land, the envy of so many less fortunate countries?

Must we accept as the signal of the future the barbaric events which have been slashed so cruelly across this nation's face in the past two weeks?

It cannot be and it must not be.

If ever in our history there was a time to unite, for all men of goodwill to say with one voice that these things will not be borne, that time is now.

No thinking person can any longer harbor the slightest doubt that the kidnappers and murderers of recent days are viciously bent on not only splitting this nation, but on destroying it, on bringing down in ghastly chaos everything it has ever been, everything all its citizens ever hoped it would be.

This is no time for any responsible Canadian to rant against "Quebec." That is precisely what the terrorists want.

Instead, our profound sympathy and understanding goes out in fullest measure to those millions of decent Quebecers who, in their agony, most surely feel the shame and the awfulness of these days more, even, than the rest of us.

This is a time for all of us, wherever we are and whatever our ancestry, to be driven together, not ripped apart, as these depraved enemies of civilized society would have it.

October 19, 1970

Nearly two months after he was kidnapped, James Cross was released. Bob Hill of Southam News Service reported on the end of the October Crisis.

James Cross, who described his release from 59 days' captivity as "almost like being out of hell," today rested in hospital where doctors said his condition is excellent in all respects.

The tired-looking but cheerful British diplomat, 22 pounds lighter from his kidnap ordeal, was admitted to the Jewish General Hospital at 12:15 a.m. MST, about an hour after the Canadian Forces plane carrying his abductors and some of their immediate families touched down at Havana airport.

Mr. Cross was driven to hospital under police guard from the Canada Pavilion at the Man and His World site where he was technically in the custody of Cuban officials until the kidnappers reached Cuba, as stipulated in the agreement covering the exchange of Mr. Cross for the abductors' passage to Cuba.

Four men, two women and a child were flown to Havana in a government plane, winding up a dramatic and tense day of negotiations.

In a short film made Thursday during a meeting at the Canadian Pavilion with Justice Minister Jerome Choquette, Mr. Cross expressed delight at seeing the sun again after more than eight weeks in his small, windowless room in the kidnappers' hide-out house in North Montreal.

Aboard the four-engine Yukon to Cuba were two of the prime suspects in the Oct. 5 abduction — Marc Carbonneau, 37, and Jacques Lanctot, 25, both taxi drivers — and Pierre Seguin, a new figure in the case whose name had not been previously mentioned.

Lanctot's wife and daughter were also aboard, along with Jacques Cossette Trudel and his wife (Lanctot's sister.) The group was accompanied by two external affairs department representatives.

Montreal, December 4, 1970

Sports of The Sixties

Cassius Clay, later to become Muhammad Ali, seemed an unlikely contender for the heavyweight boxing championship. Most sports writers dismissed him as a show-off with more mouth than muscle. Then he beat Sonny Liston, who chose to stay in his corner when the seventh round started. Southam News Service sports columnist Jim Coleman summed up the meaning of it all.

The golden virtue of silence has been dealt a death-blow. Cassius Clay, the Louisville loudmouth, has won the world's heavyweight boxing championship by default. Sonny Liston simply surrendered the championship — Clay didn't win it conclusively.

Liston gave up his title sitting puffy-faced on a stool in his corner as the bell rang for the opening of the seventh round.

Sweat, and something suspiciously close to tears of frustration, trickled down Liston's cheeks while Clay erupted in a wild war dance in the centre of the ring.

It was a suitably nutty ending for one of the nuttiest promotions in the history of pugilism. Manager Jack Nilon took the blame (or credit) for stopping the fight, explaining that Liston has been complaining of creeping paralysis up his treelike left arm, which had been injured by a punch in the very first round. Possibly, boxing may be saved by the timely intervention of the United States government. Clay is expecting a military draft call which could remove him from the prize ring for two years. Pugilism may be saved. But the United States Armed Services face disaster. The war department should sound-proof all military installations before Clay is inducted.

All the foregoing can be dismissed as a patently unfair appraisal of Clay who had been holding his own in the first six rounds. He had earned his moment of glorious vindication when he climbed on the first strand of ring ropes and leaned toward the laughing but puzzled reporters, screaming: "Eat your words. Eat your words."

Miami, February 26, 1964

Herald sports editor Gorde Hunter wrote off another Stampeder football season when the hometown team made it to the Western finals, and lost. He datelined this column "Nextyearsville," which is the football fan's name for Calgary.

The sweet dreams of vine-covered cottages surrounded by Grey Cups, carefully nurtured by season-long brilliance, by excitement generated by go-for-broke football, evaporated in the Chinook-warmed air at McMahon Stadium late Saturday afternoon.

The visions of whoop-de-do on Toronto streets, of white hats worn proudly, of chuckwagons and sidewalk cookouts, of hi-jinks, of the re-birth of Grey Cup fun and frolic, all turned to bitter ashes — again.

The dreams vanished not because of any short-comings of myopic officials. Not because of any calls that jobbed the good guys in dying seconds. Not because of any weather vagaries. The weather was beautiful, the officiating as good as I've seen in many a playoff.

They disappeared because the Calgary Stampeders could not live down the tag of not winning the big one. The balloons burst because the Winnpeg Blue Bombers proved beyond any reasonable doubt to be the better team. Because the Bombers possessed the poise of champions.

The Stampeders did not have the poise to overcome costly fumbles at key junctures. They were conned by Kenny Ploen and by a rookie receiver who ran sideline patterns for 30 minutes. Ploen spotted the over-anxiousness of Stampeder defenders and at half-time cooked up a little ambush with young Ken Nielsen.

On the second play of the second half Ploen pulled the string on a 109-yard pass and run play with Nielsen and real championship clubs don't get burned by 109-yard plays. Nielsen had faked the sideline and run an "up." Later, to prove it wasn't a fluke, he did it again for six more points.

Ken Nielsen, drafted by the Stampeders two years ago, but turned back to the inter-collegiate pool because Syd Halter ruled he wasn't eligible for draft that year. Drafted this year by Hamilton because Hamilton has received Edmonton's first choice in a previous deal. An Edmonton boy who wanted to practise his dentistry in Edmonton. Hamilton felt they needed a good split end and traded Nielsen to the Bombers for a guy name of Cloyd Webb. Webb is now back somewhere in the cornfields of Iowa and if ever Bud Grant made a steal, this one deserved a jail term.

I will defend the entertainment the Stampeders gave us from July through November. They were exciting, unpredictable, good and rarely dull. In the final analysis they just weren't as good as the Bombers and this isn't a hanging offence.

There was the usual ostentatious display of champagne in the winner's quarters. A vulgar display of victory to a hard loser entering the laugh-filled room. Yet nobody would have the temerity to deny them their exhilaration. Remember, this club won but one game in 1964 and if this isn't the greatest single-season come-back in the modern era of Canadian football, it will most certainly do until something better comes along.

The pennants, the white hats, the cowboy costumes have been packed away. The hotel and airline reservations cancelled.

Next year, and all that jazz.

November 22, 1965

A young Canadian skier, Nancy Greene, won top honors for Canada at the 1968 Olympics. Later that year, she went on to win her second World Cup Championship. The Canadian Press reported:

Nancy Greene set her mind on the beautiful slopes of this French village last spring. There were two things she wanted — she told an interviewer — the 1967 World Cup and the 1968 gold medal in skiing.

She won the World Cup last year the hard way by spotting her nearest rivals an advantage by returning home to Canada to compete there rather than staying in the European meets where she could pick up points.

Thursday she won the gold medal in the giant slalom in the winter Olympics in a most spectacular fashion.

In turning in an incredible time of 1 minute, 51.97 seconds she gave Canada its first gold medal and became the first Canadian to win two medals in skiing in the Olympics. She had won the silver in the slalom Tuesday.

After her amazing victory she had all these things to say to reporters between gasps:

"I was staggered when I heard the time. I just kept attacking in a bid to get that gold. I was not in the least bit nervous after a fine night's sleep and I felt good before the race. I was determined to win or fall doing it. I was quite confident. I had won nine international giant slaloms in the last two years, and I would have been disappointed if I had not won here. It was not a matter of luck — I don't think there is luck in racing. It was mostly psychology. I was too intense. I learned to relax."

She said the race was probably the greatest of her career.

"I decided just to attack the course. So I worked and I skied and worked so that I didn't have to think of anything else. I really wanted to win it."

Paul Serhenick of the Canadian Amateur Ski Association, once said of Nancy: "This is one tough little gal."

How tough? To keep in shape during the off-season she does deep-knee bends, straightening up to her full 5-feet-4 with her kid brother on her shoulders. Not content with that, she lifts weights.

In the winter of 1966-67 she reached the world-class stature she had been seeking. She went to Europe and was doing well and the World Cup was in sight.

But there was an international event in Canada in its Centennial year. She came home in the middle of the European season, spotting her top rivals six important races that counted toward the cup.

When she was named Canada's top Athlete of the Year in 1967 she said she wanted to repay the honor by winning an Olympic gold medal.

Chamrousse, France, February 16, 1968

Manning, Hippies, Rock

Closer to home, the Sixties were comparatively quiet, though there were local examples of hippies, drugs, war protests, and even a rock festival. In 1961, Herald publisher Basil Dean paid this farewell tribute to the Calgary he had known.

There is something about Calgary which gets into your blood, and I shall not forget the happy years here as long as I live. I have always thought, and I shall continue to think, that this city stands alone in Canada. It has a character, an atmosphere, a way of life all its own; the products, perhaps, partly of the climate, partly of the influence of the ranchers who settled the surrounding countryside, partly the heritage of people like Bob Edwards and other characters who illumined Calgary's history. Whatever the reason the atmosphere is there.

There will be endless memories to recollect in the future. The Stampede, for example, which I tended to shrug off for the first two or three years, and then became progressively more embroiled in — and the more I became embroiled, the more I enjoyed it.

Or the feeling of stepping aboard a DC-8 on a muggy morning in Toronto, and stepping off three-and-a-half hours later in the clear, clean Calgary air. Believe me, there is nothing quite like this feeling.

The Chinook wind constitutes a set of memories all its own. I am quite sure that nobody who hasn't experienced the dramatic changes of temperature which we get here ever believes the stories we tell about them. I didn't believe them myself for the first winter we were here, for the simple reason that there weren't any Chinooks; but I surely believe them now.

Or the sight of the early-morning sun tinting the tops of mountains which you really cannot bring yourself to believe are sixty miles away.

And then the people. Nature endowed this city with one of the most beautiful settings, and certainly the best climate, in the country. But the people either came here on their own free will or were born to it.

It is they who really make Calgary. There is an imaginative quality about the people of this city at their best which is, I think, unmatched.

January 30, 1961

Herald columnist Andrew Snaddon tackled the old, thorny question, "Is Calgary really so friendly?"

What's this, what's this? A Newcomer's Club? Here in Calgary? Calgary, which is famous for its friendliness from coast to coast and further than that, having a club where people can get to know each other because they can't get to know the lovable old residents?

I have always suspected that the old Calgary friendliness was largely a publicity man's dream. Still, being almost a native (nine months of age, got here as quick as I could) I was willing to go along with the old con game. I have rather enjoyed being told by friends in faraway places that they would just love to come to Calgary, where everyone was just everloving, and ready to make with the shake.

I have not believed it and, frankly, have not really cared too much. I like the place and have always feared that if we ever had to live up to the legend it would be intolerable. I hate the thought of going around being wildly enthusiastic about perfect strangers and, even more, I hate being approached by perfect strangers on a bus who want to be cosy-like and talk about the weather.

So it's snowing. So who cares?

Purely and simply the old cowtown is getting bigger. In the earlier days when there were only a few residents in town a newcomer could hardly go unnoticed. There wasn't much to do, or as much to see, and there was undoubtedly a greater sense of the need to band together for community projects.

However, Calgarians were not content to let this legend die. They have been making noises about the unfriendly East for years. Calgarians will tell you, asked or unasked, about how they would rather live here in this nice friendly place than they would in a cold, detached big city such as London.

Well, I have lived in London. People were not always sticking their cotton-picking snouts into other people's business, I'll admit. They had enough good taste to mind their own business. Yet, they were still friendly and they'd come to help a neighbor willingly, if the help was needed and wanted.

What I do say is that it is about time Calgarians of long standing quit peddling this Junior Chamber good cheer about what warm, sociable types they are, as if it is a virtue peculiar to the Stampede City.

April 17, 1961

Peter Lougheed became leader of the Alberta Conservatives when Social Credit was still firmly entrenched. Lynne Cove of The Herald recorded Lougheed's first step to power.

Alberta's new Conservative leader Peter Lougheed Saturday started what will probably be Alberta's longest election campaign.

It began immediately following his election as leader and "it's not going to stop", says the determined 36-year-old grandson of the late Sir James Lougheed, Alberta's first Conservative federal cabinet minister.

Mr. Lougheed, a Calgary lawyer, won the leadership in a two-way battle with another Calgary lawyer, Duncan McKillop, at the leadership convention here Saturday.

Mr. Lougheed has his eye on at least the Opposition leader's spot in the Legislature after the 1967 provincial election, but knows there is a lot of work ahead of him if the Conservatives are to be successful.

"I have no illusions. It's a long tough road."

"Things are beginning to stir, to happen in this province", says Mr. Lougheed. "The voters are getting ready to make a move."

The public wants an alternative to the present Social Credit government and they don't want to vote Conservative just to vote against the present administration, he says.

"The people want to vote for something.

"Let us create a new political force in Alberta politics, a force with tradition but also vitality, a force with enthusiasm but also imagination."

Edmonton, March 22, 1965

Word of the hippies — and the hippies themselves — spread quickly from San Francisco. Herald reporter Krista Maeots found that local hospitality didn't always extend to the love generation.

There are some visitors who do not feel welcome in this city — even at Stampede time. There's Glenn, for example, an 18-year-old traveler from Montreal, who says he has been "threatened by the greasers (local trouble-makers)", stopped by the police nine times, and even hit over the head by an old lady with an umbrella since he arrived four days ago.

The message is simple, he says with a grin.

"They don't want me here. I've got long hair. That means I'm a threat — a dope fiend, a thief or a fairy."

Glenn spurns all these labels, defining himself as "a hippie," and to define "a hippie" he quotes a passage from Winnie-The-Pooh:

"Here is Edward Bear, coming downstairs now, bump, bump, bump, on the back of his head, behind Christopher Robin. It is, as far as he knows, the only way of coming downstairs, but sometimes he feels that there really is another way, if only he could stop bumping for a moment and think of it."

A hippie, the youth says, is "a person who has stopped bumping to think."

Glenn is one of many young people passing through the city this week, on their way East or West.

Several of them had stories to tell at a gathering in a Calgary apartment Thursday, of unpleasant encounters with police officers, local youths and middle-aged citizens.

A small airliner crashed while attempting to land at the Calgary airport. All 15 people aboard survived. Kent Stevenson of The Herald won a 1963 National Newspaper Award for this picture.

"We've been stopped a lot by cops who have asked us what our names are, where we come from, how much money we have, where we're staying and when we're leaving," said 18-year-old Andrew of Ottawa.

"You get the feeling here that if you make the slightest slip, the cops will take advantage of it to give you a rough time," he said.

Paul thought it was the pacifistic attitude of hippies that bothered people.

The youths pointed to an incident that occurred during Monday's Stampede Parade, when a young man with a sign saying "Love, Peace and Freedom" was hauled out of the parade several times, and told that protesters were not allowed.

"When to love peace and freedom means to protest, you can see what bad shape our society is in," one boy said.

The six youths at the gathering all said they were committed to travelling, and gave many reasons for journeying across Canada:

"Because it's there...to get new ideas...because I've always lived in one place, with one kind of life..."

July 15, 1967

When Ernest Manning retired after 25 years as premier of Alberta The Herald paid him this slightly qualified tribute in an editorial.

Alberta has been extraordinarily well-served by Hon. Ernest Manning. It will miss his firm hand on the provincial tiller when he turns over the office of premier to a successor yet to be named in December.

Mr. Manning has been a member of the Social Credit government since it first took office thirty-three years ago. He was chief lieutenant to party founder William Aberhart during the early years and succeeded Mr. Aberhart to the premiership in 1943.

The early years of Social Credit government in Alberta were concerned largely with ineffectual efforts to make an unorthodox brand of economics work on the provincial level. As depression and large-scale unemployment faded out with the onset of the Second World War, Social Credit theories faded out with them. Following Mr. Manning's accession to the leadership, party decisions were ironed out

and the government settled down to the task of orthodox administration of provincial affairs.

Soon after the war, the Leduc oil discovery set off large-scale petroleum exploration and development. It became necessary to create policies and controls which would ensure for Albertans an equitable share of returns from exploitation of the province's natural resources and, further, to make certain that these resources would not be squandered wholesale. With the memory of Turner Valley's rapid resource depletion in mind, policies were evolved to safeguard the interests of future generations of Albertans.

Mr. Manning manoeuvred skilfully between the demands of commercial oil interests and the rights of the people of Alberta which he held in trusteeship. It is fair to say that the interests of both sides have been well looked after. Today, as a result of this kind of management Alberta is considered to be one of Canada's three most affluent provinces.

Naturally, not all of the policies which Mr. Manning's governments have introduced in the past quarter century have won total acclaim. There have been marked differences in viewpoint regarding priorities for expenditure of provincial revenues which have been set from time to time in Edmonton.

The Social Credit government has failed to keep step with the times and give urban populations their fair share of representation in the Legislature, despite the shifts in population which have been occurring. It has maintained old-fashioned complexes in the face of altering social concepts in such spheres as liquor consumption, blue laws and censorship. It has maintained an observable sense of authoritarianism which, at times, has seemed scarcely indistinguishable from the outmoded concept of divine right.

Premier Manning has never seemed to understand the functions, duties and obligations of a free press. He has been notably

Ernest C. Manning retires after 25 years.

219

sensitive to criticism. He has considered opposition parties as being obstructive and a hindrance to governmental administration when, in reality, they are an essential element in government of the people, by the people and for the people.

Small oppositions in Legislature by no means betoken overpowering popular support for the government at election time. Mr. Manning, an extraordinarily capable politician, has never ignored this and it has doubtless served to keep his governments from lapsing into the apathy and decay typical of most one-party regimes.

By and large, no provincial leader has ever earned and won more public respect, confidence and admiration than has been sustained over a remarkably long period by Premier Manning.

Alberta will not seem the same without him.

September 28, 1968

Herald writer Carol Hogg profiled Harold Cardinal, who exemplified the new assertiveness of Canadian native people in the late Sixties.

He speaks softly but he utters bombshells, and he speaks for 10,000 Alberta Indians. He's a young Cree who usually wears a white shirt and tie topped by a beaded jacket, showing that he is both modern and Indian.

He rises at a meeting and calmly moves that 11 whites be asked to leave. It doesn't matter that the whites are there to offer financial assistance.

"The time has come when we as Indians must run our own affairs. Any advisory role white people play, they had better make sure it is just advisory, as anything else is now highly unacceptable to Indians," he says.

Harold Cardinal speaks as president of the Indian Association of Alberta. A lot of changes have been made since he took office four months ago.

At one meeting under Mr. Cardinal's chairmanship, the IAA abolished a long-standing committee of white advisers to the organization.

"We don't need them anymore," Mr. Cardinal stated simply.

The militant young Cree, who has been working to exclude whites from Indian meetings and organizations, is now declaring war against the department of Indian affairs.

"The present policy of Indian affairs toward assimilating Indians or making them nice little brown white men is doomed to failure.

"Unless they are willing to accept our culture and our identity, they, the bureaucrats, the faceless, anonymous decision-makers for the federal government, will continue to multiply the social problems they have created, instead of solving them," Mr. Cardinal charges.

He is impatient to have Indians take control of their own affairs.

"What we need now, not ten years from now, is the assumption of certain roles and responsibilities by the Indian organizations existing around the country.

"We cannot hope to solve all our problems today, next month, next year or even possibly in my lifetime, but for God's sake let us start now."

He is in increasing demand as a speaker. He has spoken at political conventions, national forums and on national television.

People are listening to him. At a recent conference in Toronto, he received a five-minute ovation from an audience of 500 whites.

But more importantly, Indians are listening to him and supporting him. The Indian membership in IAA has risen from 150 to 10,000 during the four months Mr. Cardinal has been president.

Mr. Cardinal says he is not a radical.

"The statements I make are really very moderate in view of what has happened to Indians in the past 100 years. My views seem radical because Canadians haven't had many radical statements from Indians in the past," he explains.

Far from being a radical, Mr. Cardinal says he is working to prevent an upsurge of violence in Alberta.

"What do we do if we don't get what we want? When people are backed into a corner, what can they do? Sometimes it's difficult for whites to realize the urgency of the situation. I'm rather afraid of what might happen — especially when you see what the Negroes are doing in the United States.

"That's why people like me are involved at this time — to prevent a Watts in Canada. We must work to avoid violence."

November 2, 1968

All through the Sixties, Herald associate editor Parker Kent kept the faith with conservatism. In this column, he pronounced his maledictions on what he had found a thoroughly unsatisfactory decade.

The world is going to the dogs because of the spread of romantic idealism, in my opinion. Idealistic nonsense is being spouted on every hand. Real values are held in low esteem. Nonsense is paid respect. The world looks to ignorant youth for wisdom. The other side is right, our side is wrong. Affluence is corrupt, poverty is pure and wholesome. Disarm and your enemy will follow suit.

Socialist philosophy is gaining ground. Everyone will be taken care of. It matters not what you do for the state, it is what the state will do for you which counts. Shorter hours, higher pay for everyone, and no private bosses or owners to resist demands for more, more and more.

No more spending on costly armament. Let virtue stand straight and strong and no one will dare attack. No more party politics. Let there be one party, an honest party which will do all things for all people all the time. Peace, it's wonderful.

This sort of clap-trap is being preached today by all manner of adult men and women. No wonder our young people are so confused. Better housed, better surrounded by material aids and comforts than any generation of youth before, they are given the impression there is no challenge left, nothing for them to do but turn back the clock. They gain the idea that their parents made a mess of the world and many of their teachers and many of the politicians eagerly agree. The world isn't perfect and, to the new generation, this can only mean that it's completely all wrong. Take things as they are and try to improve them? Oh no, that would take too much time. Why not turn everything upside down and see if that works better?

It took millions of years for man, crawling painfully and slowly upward, to get us to the point where we now are in the Western countries. Compared to where man has been, this is a pretty good point to be at. But it isn't perfection. There has to be more change yet. The decision this present generation faces is whether that change will be further advancement or retrogression. The trend at the moment is toward retrogression.

October 2, 1969

Rod Sykes, who combined a sharp mind with a sharp tongue, was one of Calgary's more memorable mayors. He seemed to enjoy a brisk fight, and found many people who were willing to oblige him on that score. Herald columnist John Hopkins found the man's quieter side, and wrote this piece about "the other mayor Sykes."

He's a voracious reader, always has been. Learned to read very early in life, reads quickly ("I get through a couple of whodunnits on the plane between here and Montreal") and retains most of what he reads. "Books are my personal nightmare," he says. "I think maybe I ran for mayor of Calgary so that I wouldn't have to move. I've got so many books it's unreal. They're all over. I've read them all, but I've never got around to providing bookshelves for them."

His favorite authors? Probably Charles Dickens and Anthony Trollope. ("Dickens caricatured, Trollope portrayed.") He feels that Trollope was overshadowed by Dickens, and unfairly so. He has read something like 25 of Trollope's 70 or so books; would like to read more but they aren't that available.

He's a mystery fan, places Ellery Queen high on his personal list. Agatha Christie he enjoys; also John Dickson Carr. He finds the whodunnits a tremendous release. For periodicals he likes Punch (although his subscription has lapsed), The New Yorker and The Saturday Review ("the finest of them all"). He also enjoys Mad ("if my sons didn't buy it, I would") and The Financial Post. Time magazine doesn't interest him ("I find it almost as inaccurate as The Herald") but the comics do. Peanuts he enjoys but thinks Pogo is "trying too hard." He collects, avidly, old issues of Boys' Own Annual and Chums.

Rod Sykes hears that he's Calgary's 31st mayor.

He doesn't enjoy television, he insists, and has absolutely nothing in the way of favorite programs. Radio he enjoys, he says, although he talks in terms of The Shadow, The Green Hornet, Jake and the Kid and the Prairie Gardener.

He is quite skilled as a carpenter ("I wouldn't say that I'm of cabinetmaker calibre but I am very good with wood") and is in the process, which will be a lengthy one, of renovating his home. He's also an enthusiastic gardener "but I'm not happy with just cosmetic gardening. When I garden I want to change the landscape. It's a great feeling of power."

He buys cars for transportation and, in fact, has never owned a new one. His present vehicle is a 1965 Dodge Wagon "and it should last another ten years, maybe even more if I wash it."

His biggest fault?

"My impatience with idiots."

May 26, 1970

Festival Express, a trainload of musicians that included Janis Joplin, Gordon Lightfoot and The Band, made a two-day stop in Calgary. Jacques Hamilton of The Herald was in the crowd at McMahon Stadium for the show.

Calgary has just spent two days as the rock music capital of Canada. It appears that the city, with a little cleaning up and some help from its uniformed friends, might just recover.

Thousands of young people are on the roads out of town today in an exodus as peaceful as the weekend rock festival that brought them here.

Despite scuffles between gate-chargers and police, Festival Express was every bit as "cool" an event as optimists had hoped during the tense weeks that preceded the show.

Most of the credit has to go to Calgary police who spent their time inside McMahon Stadium bouncing babies instead of teens and looking the other way at some open use of alcohol and drugs.

The only times the police had problems were when they had to keep the Festival Express from turning into a "free" show for gate-crashers. Saturday, and Sunday, hundreds of determined young people made spontaneous attempts to fight their way in through the stadium gates and wall panels.

Verbal abuse from the angry young people who couldn't — or wouldn't — pay the $14 price of admission was heavy, but there was little physical contact.

The promoters have declined to say just how big the peaceful crowd inside the gates was for each of the 12-hour shows Saturday and Sunday. Public relations representatives

made claims that Sunday's crowd was "over 20,000," but more conservative sources suggested a figure of 9,000 for each show.

Inside, the policeman was a "cool guy" who strictly followed a pattern of not interfering with the crowd in any way. So good was the police image that, on one occasion, when two youths began yelling "pig" at an officer they had the crowd turn on them.

The 90 to 100 uniformed officers inside the stadium largely ignored wine and beer drinking and the odor of burning marijuana. Some sources estimated that as many as one of every three people in the crowd were using some kind of drug. Drug Information Centre personnel on duty reported that everything from LSD to cocaine and morphine was circulating in the packed playing field.

So open was the use of drugs that, when announcer Terry David Mulligan made a half-joking appeal for "some grass for the stage," he was answered with a shower of marijuana cigarettes.

The openness apparently lulled some young people into a false sense of confidence. Before Saturday night had ended, the Royal Canadian Mounted Police — whose undercover agents were circulating in the crowd — had arrested four persons on charges of trafficking. One was reported to have had more than $2,000 on him when he was arrested. There were no charges, however, of possession.

For the promoters, it was a successful finish to an otherwise dismal tour. The show, in both Toronto and Winnipeg, drew only a fraction of the predicted attendance.

July 6, 1970

Near the end of a decade filled with violent change, it did not seem utterly absurd to think of a revolution sweeping across the Western democracies. To many people revolution was a live issue. Nicholas von Hoffman of the Washington Post News Service summed up this state of mind when it was at its peak.

It is impossible to date a mood, a psychological era. But if the beginnings are lost it is retrospectively obvious that some time in the middle years of the last decade Americans began to feel differently about themselves. They began to relish and cultivate a sense of doom and revenge: they spoke of the "fire next time" and they liked the feelings the thought of fear induced; they spoke of Armageddon and Apocalypse like people who wanted what the rest of mankind dreads.

They ascended the helix of violence, crime, confrontation, counter-confrontation, riot, arson, and assassination as though they were going through a sexual experience. They enjoyed it. They proclaimed themselves the sick society with a necrophiliac delight in the pathology of pathology. After each act of blood-letting they were not content with seeing it on the tv screen; they had commissions to

dredge it up again, show the killing in new lights and use the analysis of the latest acts of savagery as grounds to predict yet more.

One phenomenon is the talk of revolution. Six or seven years ago only paranoid reactionaries gabbled about revolution. For everybody else the subject was laughable. Now the word is used everywhere and all the time, and not merely as metaphor or hyperbole as in the sexual revolution.

People say the word again and again, meaning they expect in some vague, indefinite, but not too far future time, a violent, political upheaval will come to pass. The word is tossed around thoughtlessly but with the connotation that it will solve our problems, take care of everything, make us well. If you try to pin people down as to how this last and most awful political act is going to make anything better, you don't get answers; you get emotional expectations. Their words in reply suggest that a great welling up and solidifying of masses of people will provide a purging, a burning and a purification of the great, collective, social soul. They talk like people drained of energy who see the revolution as a dynamo of massive, undifferentiated human force which recharges and revives them.

The prevalence of revolutionary talk has sprung up in two or three years. Maybe it's simply a fashion and, like bell-bottom trousers, people will tire of it, but that's not certain. We don't know much about revolutions, but what we do know makes it impossible to shrug off the conversations as of no consequence.

But people with the revolutionary rage in them take freedom and civil liberties for granted in their justifiable anguish over such questions as racism, war and poverty. What they forget is that there is no reason to think pulling down the formal, governmental structure of the country can solve these problems while there is every reason to believe the revolution will add new ones.

The great problem a revolution would bring with it would be the establishing of any other kind of government that the American people could accept as legitimate. It doesn't matter how much good can be said for it; the fact is that every revolutionary government goes through the tortures of the damned trying to achieve the legitimation and acceptance which bring stability and the possibility of going forward with any social or economic program.

Washington, January 30, 1970

'NOW' FOR LOUGHEED

36-year Socred reign is over
By Kevin Peterson and Don Sellar

Liberal party leader lost

Lougheed's first tasks
Bill of Rights given priority

MANNING REJECTS DEMISE OF PARTY

THE CALGARY HERALD

DAILY—10c   SATURDAY—15c   CALGARY, ALBERTA, TUESDAY, AUGUST 31, 1971   SIXTY PAGES   LATE CITY EDITION

SEAT RUNDOWN		
	1971	1967
PC	49	6
SC	25	55
NDP	1	0
Lib	0	3
Ind	0	1
Total	75	65

HOW CALGARY RIDINGS WENT

Calgary-Bow — Roy Wilson (SC).
Calgary-Buffalo — Roy Glitter (PC).
Calgary-Currie — Fred Peacock (PC).
Calgary-Egmont — Mary Leitch (SC).
Calgary-Elbow — x Dave Russell (PC).
Calgary-Foothills — x Len Werry (PC).
Calgary-Glenmore — x Bill Dickie (PC).

Calgary-McCall—George Ho Lem (SC).
Calgary-McKnight — Cal Lee (PC).
Calgary-Millican — x Art Dixon (SC).
Calgary-Mountain View — x Albert Ludwig (SC).
Calgary-North Hill — Roy Farran (PC).
Calgary-West — x Peter Lougheed (PC).
x—denotes incumbent

POPULAR VOTE	
PC	296,946 (46.5 per cent)
SC	262,900 (41.2 per cent)
NDP	71,073 (11.1 per cent)
Lib	7,460 (1.2 per cent)

Stunning Alberta upset puts PCs in power

THE CALGARY HERALD

LATE CITY EDITION
CALGARY, ALBERTA, THURSDAY, AUGUST 8, 1974
PRICE — 15c

July climb only .8%
Inflation gallop slows slightly
By Don Sellar

Nixon ready to step down; plans tv address tonight

House GOP head reveals decision
WASHINGTON (CP)

RICHARD NIXON on way out

GERALD FORD AND WIFE BETTY at home

Canadians in midst of Cyprus battle
NICOSIA (CP)

PARTIES BY SEATS				PARTY PERCENTAGES OF POPULAR VOTE			

Calgary	Alberta

THE CALGARY HERALD

WEDNESDAY, MAY 23, 1979

...ends 16-year drought for Tories
By Christopher Young
OTTAWA — Charles Joseph Clark

Charles Joseph Clark

Reporter, 1957   PC leader, 1976   PM-elect, 1979

Joe has done well as admitted non-entity
By Don Sellar
SPRUCE GROVE, Alta

Transition decisions in Rockies
JASPER

Sensitive period

Little action expected on Petro-Canada

Business welcomes new team
By Ron Nowell

THE CALGARY HERALD

WEDNESDAY, SEPTEMBER 2, 1981
25 CENTS

Canada 'winner' in oil pact
By David Hatter
OTTAWA

RCMP miners missed China
OTTAWA (CP)

Materials reused

Peter Lougheed and Pierre Trudeau took time for small talk before signing

The highlights
OTTAWA (CP) — Highlights of the oil agreement

Home heating costs will soar

Deal removes recovery roadblock
By Don McGillivray
News Analysis

A Time of Change

1971-82

Quiet as the last dozen years may seem when compared with the Sixties, they were eventful enough to satisfy most people's taste for news. Richard Nixon resigned, one jump ahead of impeachment for the Watergate cover-up; the Vietnam war ended with a Communist victory; fighting broke out again in the Middle East; Northern Ireland was torn by sectarian strife; Lebanon suffered a civil war; Chile elected a Marxist government and lost it in a military coup; the Shah was chased out of Iran; the Soviet Union invaded Afghanistan, and martial law stifled Solidarity's hope for a more democratic Poland.

In Canada our troubles were smaller, but we made the most of them. Alberta and Ottawa argued for eight years over the price of oil and the sharing of resource revenues.

Peter Lougheed won wide support in Alberta for his tough attitude on resources. Separatists from Quebec and the West proposed to dismantle the country. There was some bitterness over bilingualism; Ottawa tried to make a larger place for French across Canada, while Quebec tried – more effectively – to make a smaller place for English within its borders. The Canadian economy, never dramatically sick in the Seventies, was never in glowing health: inflation and unemployment held on at disturbingly high levels; interest rates doubled in a decade; the Canadian dollar sank below 85 U.S. cents. All in all, it wasn't the best of times for Canada – though it was hardly the worst.

Terrorist groups and lone assassins made news in the Seventies. Ronald Reagan was shot; Pope John Paul II was shot; both survived. Egypt's president, Anwar Sadat, was shot and killed; so was John Lennon, of Beatles fame. Terrorists bombed, hijacked and kidnapped – for causes ranging from a unified Ireland to a Palestinian homeland to an independent Croatia.

It's probably too soon to draw any large conclusions about the meaning of the years since 1970. However, at least two trends, feminism and concern for the environment, seem likely to influence the way we think for a long time to come. The women's liberation movement, as its name might suggest, was a product of the Sixties, but it proved more durable than most of the ideas that came out of that decade. As the Seventies wore on, the movement was dominated by moderates who wanted equal respect, equal pay and equal opportunity for women; safer birth control; better day-care; and a fairer share for women in divorce settlements. Abortion was the most hotly-debated feminist issue – one of the few policy issues in recent decades to be argued as a question of morality, not economics.

"Spaceship Earth" became a catch-phrase of the environmentalists, the general idea being that the world is a closed, balanced system whose inhabitants will perish if they foul or waste the earth's limited resources of air, earth, energy and water. The Limits to Growth, a report commissioned by the Club of Rome, predicted a short, nasty future for humankind; a growing population with rising expectations fatally polluting the environment as it exploits dwindling resources to feed and shelter itself. The report's computer-based predictions have been criticized, chiefly for underestimating the capacity of technology to conserve resources, discover new supplies, and control pollution. Even so, the report may have captured some of the spirit of the past decade: mistrust of technology, a suspicion that we have taken the wrong turn in pursuing economic growth, and a preference for limits rather than possibilities.

Meanwhile, the inside pages of the newspapers recorded the usual run of fads, hits and nine-day wonders, some funny, some grim. A little-known American writer, Clifford Irving, attempted the boldest fraud of the decade. He told his trusting publishers that he had ghost-written the autobiography of the secretive billionaire Howard Hughes. The publishers bought the manuscript, and gave Irving an advance payment intended for Hughes. Irving's wife, posing as "Helga R. Hughes," cashed the cheque, made out to H.R. Hughes, in a Swiss bank. Alas for Irving, Hughes and the Swiss bank broke their

usual habit: they talked. Hughes, in a telephone press conference, denounced the fake autobiography. The bank said H.R. Hughes was a woman. And the Irvings went to jail.

Newspaper heiress Patricia Hearst was kidnapped in San Francisco by something called the Symbionese Liberation Army, a leftover from Sixties radicalism. From captivity she denounced her parents as "pigs," and joined her kidnappers in a bank robbery. The SLA, more a platoon than an army, was smashed in a bloody shoot-out, but Hearst stayed at large. In 1975, she was arrested; despite her plea that she had been brainwashed, she was convicted of the robbery.

At the movies, not so long ago, we could see Love Story, The Sting, Jaws, One Flew Over The Cuckoo's Nest, Star Wars, Annie Hall and Saturday Night Fever. Disco was to be the next big thing in popular music – or maybe Punk, or New Wave, or perhaps Country and Western was to be the next big thing. There were quite a few next big things in Seventies music.

For Alberta, certainly, the Seventies and the beginning of the Eighties have been a time of change. In 1971 came one of the political upheavals that Alberta voters produce once every few decades. The Conservatives, under Peter Lougheed, won the provincial election. After 36 years in power, always with safe majorities, Social Credit had finally been defeated.

At that time, the province was comfortably prosperous, but not spectacularly so. Oil was selling at about $4 a barrel, a figure that didn't produce huge royalties for the provincial government. Then the world price of oil began to rise, under pressure from OPEC, the cartel of major producing countries. In Canada, the question was how high the domestic price should be, and who should get the revenue. After eight years of bitter wrangling between Alberta and Ottawa, a long-term agreement was finally reached in 1981. During that time, the price of Alberta oil increased about five-fold, but it still lagged far behind the world figure set by OPEC. Albertans complained that they were once again being exploited for the benefit of central Canada.

Whether the price was fair or not, it brought a huge amount of money to Alberta. Provincial government spending rose sharply. Even so there was enough money left to start the Alberta Heritage Trust Fund, which now holds more than $10 billion. This fund is one aspect of Lougheed's strategy: get as much money as possible to help build a more diversified economy. The Eighties will be the testing time for this program.

The long fight with Ottawa probably strengthened Lougheed's support in Alberta. To put it in the terms of Eastern editorial writers and cartoonists, the blue-eyed sheiks rallied around Prince Peter, the ruler of Saudi Alberta. In 1979, he won a third term with 74 out of 79 seats in the Legislature.

A lot of Alberta's new prosperity found its way to Calgary. People and money flooded into the city. From 1971 to 1981, the population grew by 50 per cent, to about 600,000. By 1981, the growth rate was more than 30,000 a year. The city spread outward and upward. Midnapore, which started as a one-grain-elevator town south of Calgary, was swallowed by the city. In 1981, the city issued more than $2 billion worth of building permits – as much as Metro Toronto or Houston, Texas. A local joke says that Calgary's official bird is the crane

– the kind that perches on top of unfinished high-rises.

This growth has been a mixed blessing. The city offers more variety, more excitement, more opportunity, but it's not as easy to live in as it used to be. Housing costs more, commuting takes longer, crowds are bigger, crime is a problem. And yet the local boosters of 80 and 100 years ago, who predicted such a brilliant future for their little town, would be proud and astonished to see how right they were.

Pierre Trudeau, in his many variations, dominated Canadian political life in the Seventies. He was:

–The bored dilettante who nearly lost the 1972 election to Robert Stanfield;

–The political mechanic who kept his minority government going with the NDP's support until 1974, when he won another majority;

–The economist who pooh-poohed wage and price controls in 1974, and enforced them in 1975;

–The campaigner for Canadian unity who may not have understood the West, but did his mighty best against Rene Levesque and the Parti Quebecois campaign for sovereignty-association;

–The tired, jaded politician who lost to Joe Clark;

–The game fighter who quickly brought down Clark's minority government and went on to win yet another election;

–The statesman who won the provinces' agreement on bringing the constitution to Canada from Britain, after so many before him had failed.

It was all very interesting to watch, but there was a pervasive feeling, at least in the West, that Canada wasn't working very well. The economy was sluggish. Federal-provincial relations were testy. Ottawa spent more, without seeming to accomplish more. Even a basic service like the post office was run badly. Nevertheless, to a sufficient number of Canadian voters, Trudeau and his government looked like the best choice from the available talent. Joe Clark, the young man from High River, Alberta, just couldn't gain and hold the voters' confidence. He may have been a good compromise choice as tory leader, he may have been adept in the backrooms of politics, but a charismatic leader he was not.

Probably the most significant international event of the Seventies was the end of the Vietnam war. Richard Nixon called it "peace with honor" when a settlement with North Vietnam was reached in 1973 after some 1.5 million people had died. Henry Kissinger, Nixon's foreign affairs specialist, won the 1973 Nobel Peace Prize. Le Duc Tho, the North Vietnamese negotiator, turned down his share of the prize, on the grounds that peace had not yet been achieved. He was right: the fighting continued for two years after the U.S. withdrew its troops, and ended with the North Vietnamese conquest of the South in 1975.

Nixon might have been remembered today as the statesman who extricated the United States from a futile, costly war, the man who could outgrow his beliefs of the Fifties and see the need for detente with the Soviet Union and diplomatic relations with Communist China. Instead, he's remembered chiefly for the Watergate scandal. Senior men on his staff had plotted a burglary to bug the offices of Nixon's Democratic opponents. When the burglars were caught, Nixon ordered an

Pierre Trudeau and his bride, the former Margaret Sinclair. Both made headlines in the Seventies, although in rather different ways.

all-out effort to hide their links with the White House. Then he struggled for two years to conceal this cover-up; in the end he failed, undone by the bugs he had installed in his own office.

The Middle East continued to be a trouble spot through the Seventies. In 1973, Egypt and Syria launched a surprise attack on Israel. In spectacular tank battles larger than any fought in the Second World War, the invaders regained some of their former territory, but these gains were mostly undone by a ceasefire agreement. Despite intense diplomatic efforts since then, there has been no solution to the question of Israel's right to the land it occupied in the Six-Day War of 1967.

Early in 1979 the Shah was driven out of Iran by Islamic fundamentalists who opposed his secular form of oppression. Later that year militant students seized the American embassy in Tehran and took staff members hostage. An American rescue raid failed disastrously, and most of the hostages were held for more than 400 days before their release was negotiated. The Canadian ambassador to Iran, Ken Taylor, became a hero when he and his staff hid some American diplomats and smuggled them out of the country.

These are some of the events that have brought us to the present day. Limited space precludes a full account of all the notable characters and happenings of recent years. Historians will do them justice eventually, dismissing some as ultimately unimportant, rescuing others from undeserved obscurity. Meanwhile, for the loose ends, for the unfinished business – for the news – there are still the newspapers.

The Politics of Petroleum

In 1973 OPEC, the Organization of Petroleum Exporting Countries, finally organized an effective cartel, and began forcing the price of crude oil upward. In Canada, eight years of bitter dispute followed. The issues were what the price of Canadian oil and natural gas should be, and who should get the huge revenue resulting from higher prices. The producing provinces (for practical purposes, Alberta) cited provincial ownership of natural resources, and the need to provide for the province's future when cheaply-producible oil runs out. The federal government argued that confederation means sharing, and that the domestic price should be kept below the world price – which meant a subsidy for Eastern consumers of imported oil. The oil companies said that they should be rewarded for their exploratory risk-taking, and that they needed more money to find new oil. Ottawa responded to the OPEC increases with a tax on the then-large exports of Alberta crude to the United States. Don Sellar of Southam News sent this report.

With dramatic suddenness, the Trudeau government announced plans Thursday to levy a new export tax on Canadian crude oil shipments to the United States starting Oct. 1.

The measure, announced by Energy Minister Donald Macdonald, effectively creates a two-price system for Canadian oil under which U.S. customers will pay higher prices.

For the month of October alone, American buyers will pay an extra 40 cents a barrel above the Canadian domestic price, contributing a healthy $15 million to the Trudeau government's coffers.

Mr. Macdonald conceded the oil industry was "not wildly enthusiastic" about the principle of a two-price system under which government would collect the price differential.

The Canadian Petroleum Association indicated it wants not just a slice of the pie but all of it. "We are seriously concerned that the oil industry which takes all the risks is now being denied the opportunity to obtain full market values for its production," CPA president John Poyen said in a statement.

Ottawa, September 14, 1973

Alberta Premier Peter Lougheed vowed to fight against the new measure, which he called "the most discriminatory . . . in the entire history of Confederation." The Herald commented in an editorial.

The federal government has finally come to the logical conclusion of its recent behavior. It has told the oil industry and the province of Alberta to go to hell. The interests of the hinterland are to serve the interests of the Ontario-Quebec consumers.

The forty-cent-a-barrel export tax will create a two-price system. Canadians will receive the existing price. Americans will pay extra. Ottawa pockets the difference.

No extra revenue flows to the producers of crude oil. Where do they get the millions of dollars – the hundreds of millions of dollars – necessary to explore for and find the new oil reserves the country so desperately needs in the long term?

Ottawa chose to act unilaterally. Its methods are crude and rude. Its policy is bad. It is bad because it frustrates development of the industry. It is bad because it denies the true owners of the asset – Albertans – potential revenue opportunities. It is bad because it will lead to a new and meddlesome federal presence in the industry. It is bad because it represented an opportunity for genuine consultation and that opportunity is now lost.

Finally, the policy is bad because it seeks to insulate the central regions of Canada from the realities of the market, without properly understanding the equally powerful realities of the producing region.

September 15, 1973

The sentiment of some Albertans was expressed by a bumper sticker, which was notorious though never, in fact, widely distributed.

Calgary mayor Rod Sykes says he was ashamed of the widely-publicized bumper sticker "Let the Eastern Bastards Freeze in the Dark," distributed in Alberta.

In a speech here Wednesday, he said the sticker did not represent the true feelings of Calgarians – that they are Canadians first.

Instead, he unveiled a new bumper sticker that read:

"That Eastern Bastard is My Brother."

Toronto, December 6, 1973

Prime Minister Trudeau held on to NDP support in the Commons with a dramatic new policy.

In a bold bid to make Canada self-sufficient in oil and gas before 1980, Prime Minister Trudeau has announced sweeping policy changes which will prolong the life of his minority government.

The Liberal leader defused a threatened withdrawal of New Democratic party support by promising to continue the freeze on domestic oil prices until spring, build the Montreal pipeline and create a National Petroleum Corporation capable of entering the oil production field.

The price freeze, implemented for five months last September, would be extended because the government concluded there is "neither need nor justification" to change the price of domestic oil this winter.

Ottawa, December 7, 1973

As Sid Tafler of The Herald reported, Trudeau was not made welcome when he visited the heart of the Canadian oil industry. Though he won no Alberta seats in the 1974 election, he won a majority in the Commons. Earlier in 1974 Ottawa and Alberta had compromised on a price of $6.50 a barrel for oil, well below the OPEC price.

Prime Minister Pierre Trudeau stepped out of his brown limousine and right into a red-hot demonstration organized by angry oil industry employees as he campaigned in Calgary Wednesday.

A well-disciplined crowd of about 1,000 persons confronted the prime minister on the steps of the Palliser Hotel, shouting "We want your head," and waving blatantly anti-Liberal signs.

The protest appeared to be a carefully-orchestrated effort by oil company workers to voice demands for more lenient tax treatment for their employers during Mr. Trudeau's only campaign swing through southern Alberta.

Mr. Trudeau came up smiling as he was jostled by the crowd which completely blocked traffic on 9th Ave. for about 20 minutes.

He was taunted and jeered at as police quickly escorted him from his car to the front steps of the hotel.

At the top of the stairs, Mr. Trudeau paused to turn and wave and was almost struck by a grapefruit-sized ball of paper thrown from the street.

The preponderance of oil employees in the crowd of protesters was humorously noted by a police officer, who shouted through his loud-hailer as the demonstration dispersed:

"Time to go and drill some oil."

June 6, 1974

In 1974, Finance Minister John Turner's budget dealt the oil companies another blow. They would have to pay corporate income tax on the royalties they paid to the Alberta government. Lougheed called this tax on a tax "the biggest ripoff of any province in Canadian history." On the federal side, Donald Macdonald contributed some heavy artillery to the war of words.

Energy Minister Donald Macdonald Thursday described Premier Peter Lougheed's reaction to federal thinking on resource control as "vicious," and a speech Tuesday by Intergovernmental Affairs Minister Don Getty as "dripping with venom."

Facing hostile Progressive Conservatives in the Commons, the energy minister also indicated he couldn't understand how an otherwise moderate and rational man such as Edmonton-Strathcona MP Doug Roche could align himself with the attitude that Alberta is being victimized to the benefit of Central Canada.

Mr. Getty had accused Ottawa of sacrificing development in Alberta because it was too oriented to protecting heavily industrialized Central Canada and couldn't stand not having the oil and natural gas necessary to fuel that industry under federal control.

The federal minister used the term "antipathy" several times in reference to Mr. Getty. His comments about Mr. Lougheed being "vicious" apparently stemmed from the premier's various statements on protecting Alberta priorities.

He scorned the suggestion that Alberta should get a world price for its oil. Alberta had never received a world price. For some 15 years Eastern Canadian consumers had subsidized the development of the Alberta oil industry by paying between $1.25 and $1.50 a barrel more than the world price.

"There are only skyscrapers in Calgary and Edmonton today because of federal policies," he said.

Ottawa, December 6, 1974

In December, 1974, the Alberta government announced that it would refund to the oil companies the province's share of the income tax on royalties. In February, 1975, Ottawa, Alberta and Ontario agreed to take shares of the financially troubled Syncrude oil sands project. In March, Lougheed won 69 of 75 Legislature seats, after campaigning for an "energy mandate."

The energy dispute boiled on, with federal-provincial talks breaking down, then resuming to reach short-term agreements on further price increases. By July 1, 1977, the price was $10.75 a barrel, but the Canadian price was still below the world level. And, as Gordon Jaremko of The Herald's Edmonton bureau reported, Lougheed continued to warn that there was little time left to restructure Alberta's oil-based economy.

With a pledge never to quit seeking a new deal for Alberta, Premier Peter Lougheed has set 1985 as the deadline to make the province independent of oil in its economic base.

Albertans' prosperity is precarious and "it's no time for complacency or to coast," the premier told his Conservative party's annual convention during the weekend.

He promised work on five fronts: moving economic power west, overcoming federal obstruction, getting international prices for resources, winning favorable freight rates and finding export markets.

The deadline could be tighter, Lougheed told a news conference Sunday. It's a moving target and could be 1983 or 1987, depending on rates of depletion of oil and gas and new discoveries.

The reasons for the mid-1980s deadline surfaced in Provincial Treasurer Merv Leitch's budget address earlier this month.

Crude oil production has declined 27 per cent since 1973 and is expected to be half the rate of four years ago by 1985. Gas

production is expected to peak in 1981, then slip slowly.

In the mid-1980s, the government will know if it has been successful by checking its own ledgers and the sources of new jobs created through economic expansion, Lougheed said.

Nearly half the treasury's income now comes from royalties and fees from sales of depleting natural resources.

Edmonton, March 28, 1977

Herald columnist Pat McMahon toured Eastern Canada to find out what the rest of the country thought of Alberta. Though he found a good deal of sympathy for the province's position, he didn't find much of it in Sarnia, the heart of the Canadian petrochemical industry.

It is widely believed that Ontario Premier William Davis plans to fight his next provincial election using Alberta as a surrogate Satan.

If he does, Sarnia and Toronto will probably turn out to be his most fertile fields.

After visiting six Ontario cities, I'm convinced that most people in this province haven't been swayed by the steady stream of vitriol that has been directed at Alberta recently by Davis, NDP leader Ed Broadbent and the Toronto media.

But I definitely found some hostility in this smoky southwestern Ontario industrial city and a lot of it in Toronto.

People here were incensed when Lougheed, in effect, warned that Alberta might even cut off the oil supply, stating that Petrosar would be "ill-advised" to count on Alberta supplying the fuel it would need.

"If Lougheed had his way, all the plants here would dry up and the whole industry would move to Alberta," growled an aging boilermaker.

"Frankly, I feel damned hostile toward Alberta for raising the price of my gasoline and heating oil," a young IBM computer salesman told me. "Oil is part of a country's wealth, not a province's."

It was a theme I heard over and over.

"Don't even talk to me about Alberta," snarled a big man in work clothes who turned away and stomped off as his wife looked back at me with an apologetic shrug.

A businessman complained, "I wasn't aware my Canadian passport was only good up to the border of Alberta." I thought he'd coined a pretty good line until I saw it in a letter-to-the-editor in that day's Toronto Star. It was one of three anti-Alberta letters in that edition.

"Selfish" is the word I heard used most often. And nobody, absolutely nobody I met in Toronto, wanted to hear how Ontario has enjoyed freight-rate, tariff and other advantages over western provinces ever since confederation. People there argue, with some justification, that what happened yesterday is not relevant to a discussion about today's energy prices.

Sarnia, Ontario, December 24, 1979

Joe Clark's short-lived Conservative government claimed to be near an oil-pricing agreement with Alberta, but the agreement would have cost consumers another 18 cents a gallon at the gas pumps. As Ben Tierney of the Southam News bureau in Ottawa reported, Pierre Trudeau made the most of the issue in Eastern Canada, promising a smaller price increase and a larger share of the revenue for the federal government.

If the first few days of Pierre Elliot Trudeau's campaign are any indication, the Liberal party believes the quickest way to the Canadian voter's heart is through his gas and/or fuel-oil tank.

Trudeau's opening speeches – all of them prepared in advance, and all of them carefully read – have had one theme more dominant than any other – the higher cost of energy under the Clark government and the impact that higher cost will have on ordinary Canadians, particularly those who live and vote in the East.

Alberta joined the Clark government and the multinational oil companies as one of Trudeau's villains in his tell-'em-how-much-it's-gonna-hurt strategy. His recall of the good old days – Liberal days before John Crosbie's budget – is about as subtle as a two-by-four between the eyes.

The Crosbie budget would raise an extra $90 billion in oil and gas revenues between 1980 and 1983, he said in a recent speech in Montreal. But only a very small amount of that – $17 billion – would ever find its way into the federal treasury. The rest would be divided up between the province of Alberta and the multinational oil companies.

"Ninety billion dollars is a great deal of money to use in reaching self-sufficiency in oil," said Trudeau. "But if you immediately hand over $73 billion to Peter Lougheed and the oil magnates, and let them spend it as they wish, there isn't much left over to put a Canadian energy policy in place."

Ottawa, January 7, 1980

Trudeau came back with a majority in February, 1980. As Gordon Jaremko of Southam news reported, Energy Minister Marc Lalonde soon repeated the constant theme of the Liberals' energy-pricing policy: "sharing."

Energy minister Marc Lalonde, saying "The nation is in a bind," appealed Tuesday to Alberta Premier Peter Lougheed to show some generosity in oil price and revenue negotiations.

"Sharing is what this country is all about," said Lalonde, countering Lougheed's refusal, which was widely noted here, to let "patriotic euphoria" over Quebec's vote to stay in Canada affect Alberta's demands for higher returns on its resources.

Speaking at the annual meeting of the Canadian Manufacturers Association, Lalonde said "We just came out of a referendum in which we fought hard for a united Canada. We defeated those (in Quebec) who wanted political sovereignty with economic association.

"We did not carry out this difficult bat-

When in Rome . . . federal Energy Minister Marc Lalonde dressed Western for a Stampede-week visit to the Calgary Petroleum Club in 1981.

tle to get economic sovereignty with political association."

Lalonde served notice that the federal government refuses to honor Lougheed's claims that Alberta has the right to demand world prices and the bulk of the proceeds for its resources because the constitution says the province owns its fuel resources.

"We're simply emphasizing that the nation is in a bind and that province-building shouldn't be at the expense of nation-building."

The federal minister further rejected Alberta claims that the province has already paid its dues since 1973 as a result of agreements which have kept oil and gas prices well below international rates.

Lalonde said, "Confederation isn't a totting up of who owes what. It's a balancing of strengths and weaknesses as they rise and fall over time."

Ottawa, May 28, 1980

Talks between Lalonde and Alberta Energy Minister Merv Leitch had already broken down, largely over a proposed federal tax on natural gas exports. Late in July, with oil and gas pricing agreements due to expire in a week, last-minute negotiations between Trudeau and Lougheed failed over oil pric-

ing and the gas export tax. On August 1, Alberta unilaterally increased its crude oil price by $2 a barrel to $16.75. In the October budget, Ottawa responded unilaterally, imposing a natural gas tax and a schedule of oil price increases. Bob Bragg of The Herald's Edmonton bureau reported the Alberta reaction.*

The federal budget's energy program is "nothing more or less than a takeover" of Alberta's oil and gas, says Provincial Treasurer Lou Hyndman.

Both Hyndman and Energy Minister Merv Leitch reacted strongly against the budget in a Tuesday night news conference.

Although they refused to go into many details both ministers attacked the budget's imposition of a tax on natural gas and the unilateral setting of oil price increases. Leitch said the tax on natural gas, while not simply an export tax, represents a wellhead tax which the province has consistently resisted as an intrusion on provincial rights.

And Hyndman said that the oil price schedule, along with the tax on gas, moves decision making on natural resources, which Albertans own, from Alberta to Ottawa permanently.

Leitch attacked the proposed oil price increases because they are below the rate of inflation for the first two years and are "saying to Albertans that they will have to sell the oil at less than half its value for a number of years."

Edmonton, October 29, 1980

Lougheed responded swiftly and dramatically to the federal budget. Geoff White of The Herald's Edmonton bureau summarized the premier's television address.

Premier Peter Lougheed inflicted heavy losses on both the Alberta and federal treasuries Thursday night as he announced cuts in oil production in a province-wide television address.

In retaliation against this week's federal budget, the premier said he will obtain from the legislature the authority to cut Alberta's oil production by 15 per cent in three 90-day stages.

The move, which will reduce Alberta's oil sales to the rest of Canada by 180,000 barrels a day, or 15 per cent, within nine months, will result in a loss in provincial royalty revenues of about $260 million in the next year.

"What is ownership all about?" Lougheed asked his audience. "The Ottawa government has without negotiation, without agreement, walked into our home and occupied the living room, and I guess I feel pretty strongly about that."

Describing the federal budget as "an outright attempt to take over the resources of the province owned by . . . all two million of us," Lougheed said the government's plans represent "a practical, sound and measured response."

Lougheed assured his audience that Canadians would not suffer if the federal government is unable to obtain extra oil supplies on the international market to

cover the shortfall which Alberta's move will create. In the face of a shortage, he said, the province will lift its production cuts.

October 31, 1980

Finally, a long-term energy agreement was hammered out. David Hatter of The Herald was in Ottawa for the end of the long fight.

The federal-provincial energy war is over with a peace treaty which will bring a progression of higher prices for consumers over the next five years.

Premier Peter Lougheed and Prime Minister Pierre Trudeau signed a pact on oil pricing and revenue sharing here Tuesday afternoon, plotting the five-year course for staggering price increases in gasoline and home heating oil and smaller ones for natural gas.

Under the agreement – which provides substantially higher well-head prices for oil – the price of gasoline at the pump will at least double by the end of 1986 to about $2.70 a gallon (approximately 60 cents per litre) from the current $1.40 per gallon (about 29 cents per litre).

Total energy revenues until the end of 1986 are estimated at $212.8 billion – about $32 billion more than under the National Energy Program (NEP).

Of this Alberta gets $64.3 billion (30 per cent) through its royalties; Ottawa gets $54.3 billion (25 per cent); and industry $94.2 billion (45 per cent), although out of its share it must pay its exploration and operating costs.

Federal Energy Minister Marc Lalonde said that of the $32 billion in extra revenues, Ottawa takes $15 billion, industry gets $10 billion, and Alberta $8 billion.

However, in return for the higher prices and removal of the gas export tax, Alberta had to concede on a number of key points:

– Provincial royalties will be frozen. This means that as new oil – which has a lower royalty rate – accounts for an ever bigger portion of the province's production, the average over-all royalty rate will decline from 42 per cent to 36 per cent.

– Alberta will contribute $4.3 billion during the next five years to pay for the Petroleum Incentive Program within the province. This is the program whereby exploration grants are provided to companies on the basis of their Canadian ownership.

– Alberta has accepted an increased federal Petroleum and Gas Revenue Tax, the new incremental oil revenue tax (effectively a windfall profits tax) as well as the natural gas tax on domestic sales.

– Alberta has accepted Canadianization of the oil industry. Not only will it administer the PIP program but it will also create a $600-million fund to encourage Canadianization of oil sands projects.

Lougheed, however, pointed to three key benefits for Alberta in this new package – higher prices, higher provincial revenues, and a new atmosphere of certainty for the oil industry.

Ottawa, September 2, 1981

New Faces Rise to Power

The Seventies and early Eighties were an eventful period in Canadian politics. Pierre Trudeau's fortunes rose and fell and rose again. Quebec flirted with separatism. Joe Clark led the Conservatives back into power in Ottawa – briefly. One of the rare turning-points in Alberta politics came in 1971. Kevin Peterson (who later became managing editor of The Herald) and Don Sellar (who joined Southam News) covered the victory of the Progressive Conservatives.

Peter Lougheed led a band of 49 Tories into the new Alberta Legislature Monday, unceremoniously tossing Premier Harry Strom and Social Credit's 36-year-old administration out of power.

The Conservatives left the Socreds with only 25 seats as their upset paved the way for Alberta's first Tory government.

New Democratic party leader Grant Notley gained personal election in Spirit River-Fairview to add a third political voice to the Legislature debate.

Edmonton and Calgary voters swept Mr. Lougheed to victory. In the capital, the Tories captured all 16 seats, while in Calgary they took 9 of 13.

In their wake, they left eight defeated cabinet ministers as they gained 24 seats from Social Credit and 8 of the 10 new seats created by redistribution.

Accompanying the Tory upset was a solid majority for Daylight Saving Time in Alberta with 62.75 per cent of the electorate in favor.

A buoyant Mr. Lougheed, flanked by his wife Jeanne and their four children, saluted his opponents for 36 years of public service and promised to accept his new responsibilities in "the greatest darned province in the world and let's just make it a better one."

While the Tories were most impressive in the two big cities, they grabbed a majority in Alberta's smaller cities and defeated the Socreds in central and northern Alberta.

The only area which stayed Socred was southern Alberta below Calgary where the new government failed to win a seat.

The Conservatives leaned on three catchy themes to pull off the upset: "Time for a Change," "People before party," and simply "Now!"

Mr. Lougheed's victory immediately roused speculation that the premier-elect may have to resist a draft from the national Conservative party when it chooses a successor to Robert Stanfield.

Asked about the leadership of the federal party, the giant-killer repeated his oft-stated denial of personal interest in federal politics.

Despite a heavy emphasis on the leader's face and personality in province-wide advertising, Mr. Lougheed contended it was the "door-to-door and farmyard-to-farmyard" work of his candidates that made the difference in the election.

However, just as radio carried William

Peter Lougheed and his wife Jeanne, election night, 1971. After trying for 66 years, the Progressive Conservatives finally formed a government in Alberta. They've won huge majorities in the two elections since.

Aberhart to the first Social Credit victory in 1935, television was probably the biggest factor in Mr. Lougheed's ending the Socred skein of victories at nine.

August 31, 1971.

Prime Minister Trudeau surprised the nation by marrying a young Vancouver woman, Margaret Sinclair. After three children and some painfully public crises, the marriage broke up, but at the time, Margaret Trudeau was "the most envied woman in Canada." Patrick O'Callaghan of Southam News (later publisher of The Edmonton Journal) sent this report in happier days.

Margaret (Sinclair) Trudeau next week moves into the Ottawa scene as the most envied woman in Canada. She steps from comparative obscurity into the full glare of publicity as not only the newest, but the youngest Parliamentary bride.

She takes on the role of giving wifely support to a man who has jealously guarded his private life in those rare off-moments away from the political spotlight.

The vibrant, auburn-haired 22-year-old beauty – daughter of former Liberal cabinet minister James Sinclair and a political science graduate of Simon Fraser University – has been a companion of Trudeau on a number of occasions since they first met three years ago on a Tahiti holiday.

The most noted picture of the two was taken at a skating party at the governor-general's residence about a year ago.

Since then, however, Canada's swinging prime minister has had several dates with Barbara Streisand, estranged wife of Elliot Gould.

Miss Streisand and Trudeau have been seen together at a number of gala functions, and the screen star has also been a guest at 24 Sussex Drive – the prime ministerial residence in Ottawa.

But all that is over now and a young West Vancouver woman has become Canada's most envied woman.

Ottawa, March 5, 1971

In 1972, Pierre Trudeau was looking slightly tarnished. During the election campaign of that year, Conservative supporters waited impatiently for their leader, Robert Stanfield, to put some fire in his dry, quiet style. Charles Lynch of Southam News was on hand when it happened.

Can't somebody slip Mr. Stanfield a pep pill?" a lady asked. I said I doubted it would have much effect, but then somebody did slip him one, and when the reaction set in it was like a jolt of speed.

The old turtle was off and running, breathing steam out his nostrils and his ears, acting and sounding for all the world like a man who really feels he is going to win this election.

He would have had to be a man of stone not to be stimulated by this week's figures on mounting unemployment and climbing inflation, two of the heaviest blows fate could deal a government on the eve of an election, and two of the finest gifts the gods could bestow on an opposition.

Stanfield's moving now, as I've never seen him move before.

He has a snap in his voice and a gleam in his eye as he says the country is drifting rudderless, and accuses the Trudeau government of a long list of sins of omission and commission, including the intriguing one of "arrogant silence."

He says stubborn stupidity had driven unemployment and inflation to their present high levels; Trudeau's plan to raise personal income taxes in January was "unjust, unnecessary and totally inappropriate."

"We have no intention of letting the government get away with this," he says, in the tone of a man who has his opponent on the hook.

"I've had enough," Stanfield grates into the microphone. "I'm fed up with seeing enterprise and hard work down-graded. I've had enough of seeing effort and achievement down-graded. I've had enough of unemployment and burdens on old age pensioners. We need changes in Ottawa."

Coupled with his sharpened attacks on the Trudeau government, Stanfield is at last beginning to develop the theme of the kind of government he would provide if elected.

It has the makings of an appealing program, including cuts in personal income taxes, assorted anti-inflation measures including a wage and price freeze if inflation continues to gallop; increased payments to old age pensioners; cuts in the size and cost of the federal bureaucracy, and an end to make-work programs, which would be replaced by solidly-based programs planned jointly with provincial and municipal governments, in line with provincial and municipal priorities.

Peterborough, Ontario, October 13, 1972

Stanfield almost made it. He won 107 seats to Trudeau's 109. The Liberals ruled with a minority government, under heavy pressure from their NDP supporters, until they won a majority in the 1974 election.

Joe Clark and his wife Maureen in a moment of triumph at the Conservative leadership convention in 1976. Clark, 36, defeated Claude Wagner on the third and final ballot for the leadership of the party.

Having lost three elections to Pierre Trudeau – 1968, 1972, 1974 – Robert Stanfield stepped down as Conservative leader. His successor, as Nicholas Hills of Southam News reported, was a surprise to almost everyone.

In an astonishing political upset 36-year-old Charles Joseph Clark won the national leadership of the Progressive Conservative party Sunday by a slim 65 votes on the fourth ballot over Quebec's Claude Wagner, who had led all the way until his defeat.

Joe Clark, as he is more commonly known, took votes from almost every candidate and from every region of the country to become the party's youngest leader in its history, and the 14th since Confederation.

The final count, one of the closest ever in national politics, was 1,187 for Mr. Clark to 1,122 for Mr. Wagner, a one-time Quebec Liberal justice minister who switched parties in 1972.

A rank outsider at the outset of the convention, the MP from Rocky Mountain House riding, put together a coalition of the progressive forces in the party as the voting went along, and with his victory sustained the middle-of-the-road policies of retired leader Robert Stanfield.

It was a stunning victory for the grassroots of the party. His campaign had been largely run by young Tories who had quit their jobs or their university education for what seemed to be a hopeless cause. His organization was sustained by personal loans and only a month ago it appeared to be on the rocks. He won in the end because he had fewer enemies than any other candidate and genuinely wider appeal.

The youngest of the 12 candidates, he somehow overcame the problem of his age by a strong sustained performance during the convention and through a network of political friends built up during nearly 20 years of service and work for the party on both the provincial and national levels.

Mr. Clark, the first Conservative leader with a fluent command of both French and English, broke into a broad grin and leaped to his feet in triumph after the final result was declared.

A career politician who has worked briefly as a university lecturer and a journalist, Mr. Clark said he campaigned for unity within the party and country.

"That is now the message of my leadership."

Ottawa, February 23, 1976

Mary Gilchrist of The Herald went to High River, Joe Clark's home town south of Calgary, to find out what the young Conservative leader had been like as a boy.

A serious, studious and stubborn boy – who never did learn to tie a reef knot – made High River a proud town Sunday.

Townsfolk, glued to their television sets all weekend to follow the fortunes of native son Joe Clark in the Tory leadership race, were jubilant when he emerged winner.

"It's incredible! I can hardly believe it," said boyhood friend Jim Howie, "I went to school with the next prime minister of Canada!"

At his house, as in other High River homes Sunday evening, celebration combined with reminiscences to draw a picture of the boy born and educated here.

He's remembered as "a very intelligent boy, very clever," by a school principal.

His cubmaster remembered him as the boy who would not give up.

A political associate described him as an able political organizer and campaigner.

His cousin John Soby said Joe had always known his political goal – and he isn't there yet.

"When the rest of us sat around talking about what we wanted to be when we grew up, he always wanted to be prime minister of Canada."

Don King, editor of The High River Times, once the Clark newspaper, remembers the eight-year-old Joe Clark. Mr. King was his scout master.

For weeks, Mr. King tried to teach him his knots.

"Poor Joe. He just couldn't get them. He never gave up. He never got discouraged . . . And he never did get the knots."

Another boyhood friend, Don Tannas, remembers Joe as "a little more serious than most boys."

The Clark family has been long established in High River. His father, Charles, was editor and publisher of The High River Times, a newspaper founded by his grandfather in 1905. Always interested in politics and Canadian history, friends pinpoint a trip to Ottawa as a teenager as a single most important influence.

The High River Rotary Club sponsored the trip where Clark and other young Canadians toured the capital and met members of the Senate and Parliament.

February 23, 1976

Promising that it would work for something called "sovereignty-association," the Parti Quebecois, led by Rene Levesque, won a surprising victory in the 1976 Quebec election. Bill Fox and James Ferrabee of Southam News reported on an election night that – for a while – seemed to threaten Canada's future as a single country.

Rene Levesque's separatist Parti Quebecois turned the political situation in Quebec – and Canada – upside down Monday with a stunning majority win in the Quebec election.

In a campaign which began as a two-party race between the ruling Liberals and the Parti Quebecois, a rejuvenated Union Nationale party played the spoiler in at least 25 of 30 ridings – siphoning off enough Liberal votes to allow PQ candidates to capture 66 of 110 seats in Quebec's National Assembly.

Tom Innes won a National Newspaper Award for this November, 1981 editorial cartoon illustrating Prime Minister Trudeau's difficulties in trying to hammer out a new constitution while the "fall-out" from his efforts bounced off the native people and women, and gave Quebec Premier Levesque a large headache.

The Robert Bourassa-led Liberals, who held 96 seats when the election was called, were decimated – holding 27 seats.

An emotional Mr. Levesque told jubilant PQ supporters who jammed an east-end arena to the rafters his new government would "work as hard as we can to make Quebec a country for all Quebecers who live in it and love it."

Clearly the euphoric thousands who jammed streets in east-end Montreal to celebrate the PQ win consider the vote the dawning of a new era; independence a foregone conclusion in their minds.

But while he told the cheering throng the "clear PQ majority" would enable his government to hold a referendum on separation within a year or two, premier-elect Levesque also tried to reassure "all those voters who might have feared a PQ victory."

As the victory became clear, cavalcades of deliriously excited Parti Quebecois supporters travelled around Montreal into today's early hours.

Many rode on the roofs and hoods of cars and trucks, unfurling blue-and-white fleur-de-lis flags and waving pictures of PQ candidates.

Horns blaring, they made for the traditional gathering place of young Quebecois, Place Jacques Cartier, the cobbled square on a hill in Old Montreal.

There, they gave vent to their plainly-expressed feelings that francophone Quebec's national hour had come.

However, most federal politicians and business spokesmen who commented on the election said they interpreted the election of the Parti Quebecois as criticism of the Liberal administration of Mr. Bourassa, not as a vote in favor of independence.

"I am confident that Quebecers will continue to spurn separatism because they believe in an indivisible Canada," Prime Minister Trudeau said.

Montreal, November 16, 1976

The Berger hearings about the proposed Mackenzie Valley natural gas pipeline were a dramatic sign of a new attitude toward economic growth. Ten or twenty years earlier, a pipeline down the Mackenzie River valley to deliver natural gas from Alaska might have seemed unquestionably good. But Justice Thomas Berger listened to objections from native people in the area, and from those concerned about the environmental effects of the line. His recommendations did much to tip the scales in favor of the less controversial Alaska Highway pipeline route. John Howse, Herald business editor, filed this report.

For 19 months Mr. Justice Thomas Berger listened to the views of northern natives on the pipeline. He visited 35 communities, travelled 17,000 miles, heard evidence in seven languages from 1,000 witnesses, filling 32,353 pages of inquiry transcript.

In Tuktoyaktuk, whaler Vince Steen summarized the history of the Inuit:

"A lot of people seem to wonder why the Eskimo don't take the white man's word at face value any more . . . well, from my point of view it goes way back, right back to when the Eskimos first saw the white man . . . the Eskimo is asking for a land settlement because he doesn't trust the white man any more to handle the land that he owns, and he figures he's owned for years and years."

Robert Andrew, at Arctic Red River, said "We are saying we have the right to determine our own lives . . .

"We are saying we are a distinct people, a nation of people and we must have a special right within Canada.

"We have our own system, our own way of life, our own cultures and traditions. We have our own language, our own laws and a system of justice . . . Land claims mean our survival as a distinct people."

Peter Thrasher, of Aklavik, expressed an Inuit viewpoint: "In many ways I inherit what my grandfather and my father have

Justice Thomas Berger with his report.

given me; a place to live in, a place to own, something I have a right to. I would like to give something for the future generations of my children so they will have something to live on, and they also should have the right to inherit this country." .

Natives often voiced fear about the prospect of a pipeline coming to the Territories.

Fred Rabiska said at Fort Good Hope: "If the pipeline is built we will be very unhappy people. We will drift farther from each other as well as from our land."

At Fort McPherson, Elizabeth Colin, who had worked with the Peel River Alcoholics Anonymous Centre told the inquiry: "Right now we are trying to get back on our feet, as natives trying to help ourselves. But what will happen if the pipeline comes through and there is going to be a lot of money and a lot of Indians are going to be affected by alcohol?"

At Fort Good Hope, Cassien Edgi echoed these sentiments: "What is going to happen if the pipeline goes through Fort Good Hope? Drugs, booze, family break-up and trouble. In the past we have a handful of white men. Now, how many girls have kids without fathers and live on welfare? If the pipeline goes through there will be thousands and thousands of white people."

It's evident from his report that Berger did exactly what he promised the natives, he listened to them.

Ottawa, May 10, 1977

In the middle of the federal-provincial disputes of the seventies, editor William Gold explained in a column that The Herald could love Canada without feeling much affection for the current federal government.

The Herald has consistently supported the concept of a united Canada and has never at any time condoned or contemplated the prospect of Quebec separating, or, even worse and even sillier, the prospect of Alberta separating.

Yet, we find ourselves accused from time to time with being "anti-East" and going out of our way to heap ridicule and scorn on all matters of federal concern.

Certainly, we haven't agreed with everything Ottawa has done. It has finally taken the Supreme Court of Canada to clear up and put a stop to Ottawa's incredibly gratuitous meddling in Alberta's acquisition of Pacific West Airlines. Sure, we criticized Ottawa on that one. But people tend to forget that we also criticized Alberta's Peter Lougheed for buying the airline in the first place and still think he ought to sell it.

Certainly, we criticized Ottawa in the matter of the oil export tax. Without so much as a by-your-leave, hundreds of millions of dollars were simply taken from this province, in order to subsidize fuel costs elsewhere. We weren't consulted. There was no co-operative federalism. We were simply the subject of executive fiat and everyone with a grain of political sense knows perfectly well that if Alberta had elected a dozen Liberal members to the House of Commons it simply wouldn't have happened that way.

We have frequently called down abuse on the general competence with which Canada is run by the present Liberal government. There are people selling vegetables off push carts with greater administrative talent than is frequently exhibited by members of the Trudeau cabinet, or some of its specially created upper echelon civil servants.

Finally, we have objected violently to quite blatant attempts by the Liberals to confine the argument about the future evolution and preservation of federalism to terms that permit only the Liberal party to participate. In point of fact, Joe Clark and the Conservative party are more broadly representative of all Canadians apart from those in Quebec and are probably, in the last analysis, every bit as competent to discuss with Quebec the questions of the new arrangements and accommodations that will have to be made to preserve a form of federation that will leave this country in fact a country.

But that last point is the fundamental one. It has to be a country. Canada from sea unto sea is one of the most glorious concepts of the last couple of hundred years. The fact that slightly more than 20 million people of a whole mixture of cultures can operate and develop this enormous land mass, bordered by three vast oceans and bisected by one of the greatest lake and river systems in the world, not only poses a unique challenge for those of us active today but endows us with the capacity to bequeath our children and to their children after them a legacy of civilization and personal prosperity beyond the comprehension of the vast majority of the world's billions of people.

There will be squabbling in Canada, raucous, clamorous, and even joyous as long as it exists.

Let there be no doubt about one thing, though, The Calgary Herald is a federalist newspaper committed totally to the Canadian whole.

February 24, 1977.

Once more, for the first time since John Diefenbaker, the people of Canada chose a Conservative and a Westerner for their prime minister. Don Sellar of Southam News reported on the beginning of Joe Clark's short-lived triumph.

Joe Clark stood on the platform at the Arena, his long bony fingers flashing the double V for victory salute – a new trademark.

Beside him was his wife Maureen McTeer, doing her very best to hold back the tears of pride – and only narrowly succeeding.

"Let's get Canada working again," the Tory band played. "Joe is Number One," a hand-lettered placard proclaimed. "For he's a jolly good fellow," the jubilant crowd of 2,000 roared.

It was a moment in history – the toasting of a man who is not yet 40 but who will be, within the next few days, the sixteenth prime minister of Canada.

Make no mistake about it. Clark, a man who once described himself as a "nonentity," who was elected Tory leader as if by mistake, had earned his place on that stage Tuesday night.

Regardless of what he achieves as prime minister, Clark has managed, by sheer determination and hard work to do a pretty good job of knocking off Pierre Elliott Trudeau.

It was a rough, two-month campaign in which he flew about 65,000 kilometres "from coast to coast to northern coast" as he put it in his speeches.

Goodness knows how much more Clark travelled by bus, hammering away at the 11-year Trudeau government record and the failings of the charismatic man himself.

His strategists – and the man himself – knew Clark could not be sold to voters as a prophet or a magician. He had to be the consensus leader, the team man, running against the "one-man band."

In the end, he will have to prove himself as a consensus leader who can make Parliament work even though he is a handful of seats short of a parliamentary majority.

It was not easy for Clark – son of a High River weekly newspaper publisher – to prove to the Tories that his real ability lay as an organization man.

But when Trudeau finally called his plebiscite on his 11-year-old leadership and mocked Clark's "high school" rhetoric, Charles Joseph Clark proved to hold all the best cards in Canadian politics.

Spruce Grove, Alberta, May 23, 1979

The Clark government vanished in less than a year. Too many blunders, too long a delay in calling Parliament, too much bad news in the budget – many reasons have been suggested. It was the budget, especially the extra 18 cents a gallon on gasoline, that finally brought the government down in Parliament. In the election in February, 1980, Pierre Trudeau won a majority again, and the results were disturbing for everyone: Trudeau won only two seats in the West, Clark only one in Quebec.

In 1980 the Parti Quebecois government held its long-promised referendum on "sovereignty-association" for Quebec, and lost. Apparently a small majority of French-speaking voters rejected the proposal; with English and other minority-language voters in Quebec, they added up to a 59 per cent vote against the government's plan to negotiate independence for Quebec and an economic union with the rest of Canada. Crosbie Cotton of The Herald went back to his home town in Quebec and filed this story on reactions to the vote.

Louise Landry, battling hard to fight back tears, was bitter and angry as she flung quart bottles of beer down on the arborite tables. The people the barmaid served at the only hotel in nearby St. Francois Xavier had planned a raucous evening of celebration, but this night they were crying in their beer.

"How can people be so stupid?" lashed out the ardent supporter of the 'oui' vote in the Quebec referendum. "People didn't understand."

"I can't understand them, the people who voted 'no'," said the 25-year-old, who has four older brothers now living in Calgary.

"Quebecers had a chance, but now there is no hope left. The people who voted 'no' will have to explain, but they can't because they don't know why they did it. They are too stupid to have a reason."

Louise had worked all day at the polls for the 'oui' forces, and then headed optimistically to her part-time job at the hotel, where more than 300 people were expected for a victory party.

Few showed up.

While Louise, the youngest of eight children, was openly disappointed, her mother Jacqueline Langlois was ecstatic.

"I thought the vote was going to be closer, but this is really good," said Langlois, a nurse who voted against giving Premier Rene Levesque a mandate to negotiate sovereignty-association.

Nervously perched in front of the television at her home in this Eastern Townships city, about 20 kilometres from where her married daughter lives, Langlois said:

"It proves that French Canadians want to be something more than just Quebecers, they want to be part of the beautiful country of Canada."

She realized her daughter would be downhearted in defeat, but said time would heal wounds suffered Tuesday night.

"There have to be losers. I'm glad I was on the winning side," said Langlois, whose three other children still living in Quebec also supported the 'non' side.

Her four children in Calgary had also said they would vote in favor of Canada if they had remained residents of Quebec.

In this region, where many of the young men and women have fled to other parts of Canada in search of employment, the victors talked of re-establishing the harmony between francophones and anglophones that once existed.

There was no dancing in the streets. People were more anxious to stay at home and dream about the tranquility they have longed for.

But Louise Landry was not among them. Her dreams of a new life, one in which Quebecois would control their own destiny, were defeated at the ballot box.

"There is no future, nothing else to do. People were just too stupid to understand," she said, uncapping another beer amid party-goers who had nothing to celebrate.

Sherbrooke, Quebec, May 21, 1980

Prime Minister Trudeau's role in the history texts remains to be seen. Perhaps he will be remembered, finally, for the compromise that – over Quebec's objections – will make the Canadian constitution a Canadian law. Aileen McCabe of Southam News reported on the final hour of the constitution debate.

Canada's constitution is coming home after 114 years. Members of Parliament from every party joined together Wednesday to vote 246 to 24 to patriate the British North America Act with an amending formula and an entrenched charter of rights.

It was probably among the most historic and emotional moments ever to take place in the House of Commons.

It was preceded by 18 months of rancorous federal-provincial debate which cut to the very heart of the country and left Quebec and its francophone majority once more isolated in Confederation.

Premier Rene Levesque ordered flags in the province to be flown at half-mast Wednesday.

For Prime Minister Trudeau it was a personal victory.

The Liberal caucus cheered as he stood to cast the first vote for the resolution he fought for so tenaciously.

But his victory was tinged, first by the compromises forced on him by nine provinces, and then Wednesday, by the Liberals who opposed him.

Five Liberals stood against him to protest against the shortcomings that will be cast in stone by the British Parliament at Westminster.

Conservative leader Joe Clark, whose opposition over the last year resulted in significant changes in the resolution, also led a divided caucus when he stood to vote.

Seventeen of his MPs broke ranks, a difficult blow made worse by the fact they also diametrically opposed each other.

Roch LaSalle, the lone Tory from Quebec, voted against the resolution because it isolated his province, but some of his colleagues said afterwards that they opposed it because it gave too much to Quebec.

New Democratic chief Ed Broadbent saw three of his 32 MPs bolt the party line.

But for the uneasiness, there was a certain festive atmosphere as the Commons bells rang for nearly an hour to call MPs to vote.

The Commons moved on to "other business" immediately following the vote.

Ottawa, December 3, 1981

A resolution that would bring the Canadian constitution home was sent to London just before Christmas, 1981. Perhaps it was rather late in the century to celebrate Canada's prospective escape from the last trace of British rule; in any case, Lawrie Joslin, Herald editorial page editor, found the final ceremony less than inspiring.

Commentators described the scene as emotional when the governor general received the constitutional documents at Rideau Hall Tuesday night and sent them on their way to the Queen in London with his private secretary.

But the emotionalism seemed to be missing from the views flashed on home television screens. The turning-over ceremony came across to me as somehow anticlimactic.

Possibly no one even thought about a ceremony until the last minute. After 50-odd years of trying unsuccessfully to patriate the constitution, who would sit down and write this unusual episode of the Canadian story until they were certain there was going to be a purpose?

So it turned out to be a prosaic affair. The nearest we got to inspirational language – the kind of thing we might recount to those who missed the historic moment – came when an alert microphone picked up Prime Minister Trudeau's barely audible, apparently off-the-cuff, "That's great."

The whole business of constitutional rebirth has been work-a-day from the beginning. Perhaps if one of the leading players had been able to inspire the first ministers they might have got the job done a lot sooner. If anyone can be said to have come anywhere close it would be Justice Minister Chretien, but he kept tripping over the politics of the matter in his role as Great Persuader.

The phrasing of the new constitution has been described as plodding, even bureaucratic, coming nowhere near the lyrical quality of the United States constitution.

That depends to a considerable degree on the way one reads the two documents. The criticism moved me to attempt a comparison. I found a classic economy in the passages of the U.S. constitution that seems missing from the new Canadian counterpart.

In any case, constitutions are legal documents which must be couched in legalese not noted for launching the mind into flights of emotional fancy.

It is also possible that reason lies in our history for our inability to display emotion about constitutions. The Americans do give their constitution a more exalted place in their hearts than we have given ours. But their constitution was shaped by emotions born of perceived oppression and subsequent revolution. Most of us probably consider it fortunate our forbears didn't have to undergo such severe testing even if it means our emotions are not to be easily moved in these matters.

At least the document went first-class, although no champagne could be found on the defence department aircraft for toasts.

December 11, 1981

The Struggle to the Top

It wasn't the classiest football game ever played, but when the Calgary Stampeders came off a soggy field in Vancouver, they were the 1971 Grey Cup champions. They owed the 14-11 score to a pair of blunders in the last minutes of the game. Toronto's Leon McQuay fumbled on the Stampeder eight-yard line, and Reggie Holmes pounced on it. Herald sports editor Hal Walker wrote the fumble-by-fumble account of the Stamps' second Grey Cup victory.

They looked like winners; then they looked like sure losers; they looked like winners again and it seemed that Dick Thornton had turned it all around for Argos with only 2:26 left on the clock when he returned an interception 54 yards to the Stampeders' 11-yard line.

But a gutsy Calgary defence dug in and rescued the entire province from the precipice it seemed it might topple over. They did it many times, but their enjoyment of it heightened with every shot they got at Joe Theismann, the Argonaut quarterback. Theismann was sacked twice by Craig Koinzan, twice by John Helton, once by Fred James and once by Dick Suderman, the best front in Canadian football. They grounded the high-priced Toronto rookie for a total loss of 82 yards. And they broke Joe's nose, too.

Theismann was collared by Wayne Harris and Joe Forzani on a play pass action in the third quarter and his nose bent under the impact. His eyes kept watering from the fractured proboscis and he took himself out of the game. His replacement, Greg Barton, the ex-Detroit Lion, couldn't get anything moving, either, in this whacky contest which was replete with something else than excellent football. Defence had it all over offence and Jim Duncan acknowledged, with thanks, the great heart of the Stampeder defence.

Leo Cahill made no bones about trying to buy a Grey Cup and did an excellent job recruiting people like Theismann, Barton and the most sought-after of all, Leon McQuay. The irony is that it was McQuay's fumble at the Calgary eight-yard line with one minute and three seconds left and Empire Stadium in a tumultuous, emotional uproar. But a lot of people were measured for goat's horns in this wild finale to the season and they weren't all outfitted in Argonaut white jerseys. Jim Illye challenged a punt by Zenon Andryushan in the third quarter and fumbled the ball to Joe Vijuk who lateralled to Charlie Scales for a 39-yard touchdown gallop. It brought Argos to a 10-14 closure and then Ivan MacMillan, Argos' field goal expert, missed a 31-yard try and Argos came away with only one point.

This was such an incredibly bizarre wind-up that you couldn't believe it, but antlers were ready for Harry Abofs, the Argonaut punt returner who came up with what was perhaps the biggest goof of the game. On a pressure punt by Jim Furlong which bounced around at the Argonaut 49

yard line, Abofs, who is German-born but went to Tennessee Tech on a football scholarship, kicked the ball out of bounds.

He was unaware, he said afterwards, that by doing this it meant Argonauts had to give up possession of the ball.

"I did the same thing earlier this year in the East," he told reporters, "and no call was made against me." This deprived Argos of their last gasp chance to try and mount an offence.

Vancouver, November 29, 1971

The 1972 Canada-Russia hockey series was supposed to answer the question: Can Canada's professionals beat Russia's state-supported amateurs? The answer was "yes," though later series provided other answers. Jim Coleman of Southam News reported on a game that was an athletic — though not diplomatic — triumph for Canada.

I don't know what the heck you were worrying about. I kept telling you that Canada would make a clean sweep of this series on Moscow ice. I can hardly wait to get home to have a few words with those wisenheimers who have been sending me all that charming mail.

Mind you, there were a few occasions last night when the confidence of even the most loyal Canadian wavered. At the end of the second period, when the Soviets were leading 5-3, things looked so bleak that a couple of us went up to the press bar on the fourth floor of the Moscow Sports Palace and ordered some of those salami sandwiches that they import from Minsk. They only import the bread from Minsk — the salami runs wild around here.

We were washing down the salami with a stout drencher of chloride of lime when a courier dashed in with the news that Phil Esposito had reduced the margin to 5-4 on a pass from Pete Mahovlich.

"Order me a double vodka," said my

Canadian companion, "this is the only place to get a really dispassionate view of the game."

He was just downing his double vodka when the courier rushed back with the further intelligence that Rodrique (Mad Dog) Gilbert, the comely rightwinger, had scored a clean-cut fistic decision over Eugeni Mishakov at 3:41. The courier panted the news that both players were serving major penalties.

"Crimey," bawled my Canadian companion, as he coughed the raw vodka through the gaps in his front teeth.

Well, we got back to our seats soon enough to see Alan Eagleson logging more ice time than Don Awrey and Marcel Dionne have logged in this series.

The Eagle flew down from his perch, screaming wildly, when the goal judge failed to turn on the red light as Yvan Cournoyer tied the score at 12:56. (This was the same goal judge who flashed the red light only for a split second when Paul Henderson scored the winner in the sixth game on Tuesday night.)

Anyhow, a full platoon of Soviet militia grabbed Eagleson as he left his seat. They were giving him the heave-ho right out of the ruddy building when the Canadian hockey players, brandishing their hickory staves, converged on the spot where the Eagle was going down for the third time.

Peter Mahovlich vaulted the boards and plunged into the crowd of militia. The other Canadian players were ready to follow Pete when — suddenly and inexplicably — at least 10 militiamen retreated, leaving Eagleson resembling a pile of garbage. The players picked up Eagleson as, pale-faced and badly shaken, he was almost entirely a passenger while they propelled him clear across mid-ice to the other side of the rink and the security of the Canadian team's bench.

Eagleson's feet hadn't even dried out, after his first trip across the ice when he had bounded over the boards again. This time, Alan and almost every member of the Canadian hockey contingent were slithering

Soviet player takes to the air during the momentous final game of the 1972 Canada-Russia hockey series.

and sliding madly to converge on the doorstep of the Russian net, where Paul Henderson had just finished scoring the winning goal of the entire damn series at 19:26.

Once again, the same goal judge didn't flash the red light as Henderson picked up his own rebound and shoved the puck under the shell-shocked Vladislav Tretiak.

The two referees didn't need the glow of the red light to tell them that the puck was in the net. At least 30 Canadian lunatics were pointing at the puck. They were yelling deliriously and clouting Henderson until his skull was ringing like a Chinese gong.

After the game, Phil Esposito, among others, complained about the referees. Coleman agreed.

Mr. Joseph Kompalla, a West German alleged hockey referee, must be the last word in cloth-headed guffins. Kompalla almost penalized the Canadians out of the rink in the first period and the lid blew off when he gave Jean-Paul Parise a very, very questionable interference penalty at 4:10.

Parise lost his head when Kompalla added a misconduct penalty. Kompalla almost lost his head, too, because Parise rushed at him with his stick raised high over his left shoulder and he acted as if he would decapitate the referee. Kompalla ordered Parise to the dressing room with a match penalty.

Around the Canadian bench, the occupants almost went insane. In fact, a few did take leave of their senses. A Canadian trainer threw a chair onto the ice, where it disintegrated.

Fortunately for the prestige of Canadian hockey, the game was continued to its successful conclusion. (The Soviets were leading 1-0 at the time of Parise's expulsion.) But it must be acknowledged that the display around the Canadian bench did little to enhance our reputation in world diplomatic circles.

Moscow, September 29, 1972

Herald sports columnist Larry Wood pondered on fame and money and Howard Cosell in the world of pro sport.

I've never been a disciple of Howard Cosell but it's likely I've simply been following the flow. Howard thrives on being disliked and that makes it easy. His cultured approach to sport can be nauseating, and I suspect there's something of a bloated ego there that demands constant feeding.

I don't know. Maybe I've been shortchanged in the culture department. Or maybe it's just that I can't afford the brand of Havanas that Howard smokes.

Nevertheless, there's a facet of Cosell's makeup that commands the respect of people in my business. Those, at least, who abide by the principles of journalism. Howard tells it like he thinks it is, however embellished, and I've never heard the guy accused of being a shill.

Skier Scott Finlay takes a near-fatal tumble in the 1978 Canadian downhill championships at Lake Louise. Herald photographer John Colville won a National Newspaper Award for this picture.

I've never argued, either, with his perspective of the entire sports sphere. He calls it "the toy department of life," and I doubt if you'll improve on the metaphor. Think about it.

A guy who finds anything of earth-shattering significance in these pages, any day, is existing in a somewhat deluded state. Nothing that happens in the realm of sport will ever change the course of world history.

Sport, plain and simple, is an outlet for some, and an escape for others, and entertainment for vast numbers. But you're kidding yourself if you view it on a higher plane.

Based on my views of the passing sports scene, I've been labelled a cynic, a skeptic, and as late as last week, a clown. You can take your pick. It doesn't bother me much because, in my business, it's the only way to go. A too-positive approach, all of the time, inevitably leads to fooling yourself, and that leads to attempts to fool the public.

When pro athletes are paid more for their services than are world leaders, it's difficult to consider sports in any category other than fantasy. But reconciling the attitudes of athletes as to their importance is one thing. How do you digest the inanity of owners who grant these values?

Sure, and you can argue that guys like me contribute to the absurdity of it all by publicizing the modest accomplishments of pro athletes. The sports pages have been known to manufacture false heroes, not unlike movie magazines. But I don't necessarily think Liz Taylor is worth $2 million, or whatever, for one film role, either.

I guess it's all part of the international penchant to be entertained. But that doesn't mean that we have to take it seriously. Not 99 44/100 per cent.

And Howard Cosell doesn't. I respect him for that.

April 13, 1978

NHL hockey finally came to Calgary in 1980. Crosbie Cotton of The Herald joined the crowd in the undersized Stampede Corral for the Calgary Flames' first home game.

Fans came in tuxedoes, and they came in jeans. The sold-out crowd jammed the old Corral to the rafters for The Big Event.

Hockey magic had lured them, caught them and conquered them on the night the National Hockey League came to Calgary to stay.

"Pinch me, I can't believe this is happening," said television play-by-play announcer Ed Whalen, moments before Flames goaltender Dan Bouchard burst onto the ice through a large poster of the club's emblem.

But, it was happening.

By the time the first puck was dropped Thursday night, the voices of many ardent fans were hoarse.

They cheered Nelson Skalbania, the man who had made a dream come true when he brought the team from Atlanta. They applauded former NHL president Red Dutton when he signed the ceremonial first face-off, current NHL president John Zeigler at his side.

"I've seen them play three exhibition games and I think they'll do well this year," said former hockey great Bert Olmstead, now a Black Diamond farmer.

The game turned out to be a ho-hum affair, with the Flames blowing a 4-1 lead to finally settle for a 5-5 tie with the Quebec Nordiques.

Few fans were disappointed. Peter and Henry Eichler hadn't even expected to be on hand inside the league's smallest arena. The two had tried unsuccessfully to scalp their $21 ducats for $100 before the game.

"This game is really great," they remarked between the second and third periods. "We're really glad we came."

October 10, 1980

The Watergate Scandal

The Watergate affair began with what a White House spokesman disdainfully called a "third-rate burglary." It ended with President Richard Nixon forced to resign, and with many of his senior aides facing jail terms.

Disclosure that a salaried Nixon-campaign security expert was one of five men arrested during a break-in at the Democratic national headquarters has prompted Democratic accusations of "political espionage" and Republican denials of involvement.

Police said the men apparently were planning to install electronic bugging devices and photograph papers in the files at Democratic headquarters in the Watergate office complex.

Former attorney-general John Mitchell, chairman of the committee for re-election of the president, said in a statement that the five men were "not operating either on our behalf or with our consent."

Washington, June 19, 1972

The 1972 election campaign ended in a landslide victory for Richard Nixon. Meanwhile, a handful of reporters, notably Bob Woodward and Carl Bernstein of The Washington Post, followed up the thin leads provided by the burglary. They found evidence of illegal contributions to the Republican election campaign, and of spying and harassment against the stronger contenders for the Democratic nomination. There were signs, too, that senior Nixon officials had a hand in planning the burglary. Nixon, under increasing pressure, accepted responsibility but not blame for the Watergate affair, and accepted the resignations of his two top aides, H.R. Haldeman and John Ehrlichman. He also fired his counsel, John Dean. Dean came back to haunt him at hearings of a special Senate investigating committee.

John Dean had his say Monday. Now it's up to seven senators and their lawyers to test his accusations that President Nixon and the White House hierarchy were involved in the Watergate affair.

In a 245-page statement read before the Senate Watergate committee Monday, Dean, fired by Nixon as White House counsel, droned through his long-awaited account of how a break-in at Democratic national headquarters grew into a widespread conspiracy to head off a potentially disastrous scandal.

Dean described the pre-campaign atmosphere of a White House staff that worried constantly about anti-Nixon demonstrators, paid spies to tail political opponents and contemplated plans to break the law in search of information.

As his story unfolded, he implicated in the cover-up the president; John Mitchell, former attorney-general; Richard Moore,

Senator Sam Ervin of the Watergate Committee.

special presidential counsel; Charles Colson, former special presidential counsel; Patrick Gray, former acting head of the FBI; and a host of aides and assistants.

Dean's account is in direct conflict with earlier statements by the president on a number of crucial points.

After the election, consideration was given to putting out the facts "to get rid of the Watergate," Dean said.

But, when he told senior presidential aide H.R. Haldeman that could result in indictments against Mitchell, Haldeman, White House staffers John Ehrlichman, Dean and Gordon Strachan, and campaign deputy Jeb Stuart Magruder, Haldeman decided to continue the cover-up, Dean recounted.

Washington, June 26, 1973

The Senate committee soon stumbled on evidence that could conclusively prove what part – if any – Nixon had played in covering up White House involvement in the Watergate burglary.

President Nixon had listening devices in the White House that would have automatically recorded his conversations with John W. Dean and other key figures in the Watergate case, a former White House official disclosed Monday.

The microphones and telephone taps were installed with Nixon's knowledge and concurrence and operated all the time, Alexander Butterfield, a former presidential assistant, told the Senate Watergate committee.

The recordings became the immediate focus of the central investigation by the Senate panel into the role Nixon may have played in the Watergate cover-up.

The tape recordings, which Butterfield said were stored in the Executive Office Building by the Secret Service, theoretically could prove or disprove the explosive – but undocumented – charge by Dean, former counsel to the president, that Nixon was deeply involved in the Watergate cover-up.

Washington, July 17, 1973

As Duart Farquharson of the Southam News bureau in Washington reported, Senator Sam Ervin, chairman of the Senate investigating committee, began to look like one of the few bright spots in a sordid affair.

For all the White House horrors, the Watergate scandal may be producing what this country likes most of all – a genuine folk hero.

The new Uncle Sam is fat and jowly, old and wise, with a fatherly twinkle in his eye.

Senator Sam Ervin, the country lawyer from North Carolina, is a far cry from the lean, steely-eyed Uncle Sam of the old days, pointing a finger from a poster and ordering "Uncle Sam wants you."

But Senator Sam's 76-year-old face is beginning to peer out from posters too, to say nothing of buttons, T-shirts and television screens.

Chairman Sam, with his silent harrumphs and fluttering eyebrows,when he's angry, and his salty, self-effacing humor when he wants to draw a gentle point, is the antithesis of the young button-down, Nixon White House characters appearing before his committee.

Nicholas von Hoffman, a usually scathing radical columnist in The Washington Post, says that despite the chairman's Southern conservative background, "we love Sam and need him just now.

"He reeks of the decency and kind justice we incorrigibly associate with our rural past. And those of us who are so snidely contemptuous of Nixon's public pieties, his recourse to cheap patriotism, adore those same traits in our Senator Sam."

Washington, July 21, 1973

A criminal investigation was running in parallel with the Senate hearings. Nixon moved dramatically to head off its aggressive quest for his tapes, but the so-called "Saturday night massacre" cost him heavily in public support. More and more Americans wondered what was on the tapes that he was so desperate to hide.

Members of Congress, shocked and confused over President Nixon's sudden firing of his tough special Watergate prosecutor, were returning today to a Washington suddenly alive with talk of impeachment.

These were the events which touched off the crisis:

Fired – Watergate special prosecutor Archibald Cox, Harvard law professor who has served under four presidents in special assignments and who vowed to pursue the Watergate case "wherever the trail might lead" – even into the White House.

Fired – William Ruckelshaus, deputy attorney-general, former head of the Environmental Protection Agency and one-time acting head of the FBI – the man who refused to fire Cox under presidential order.

Resigned – Attorney-General Elliott Richardson, former defence secretary and head of the department of health, education and welfare, who also refused to fire Cox.

The train of events was set in motion Saturday, after Nixon came into direct confrontation with Cox.

Ordered by the Appeal Court to produce secret tape recordings made in the White House and said to concern Watergate, the president replied he would make available a summary of the information contained in the tapes. He ordered Cox not to pursue the matter in the Supreme Court.

Richardson resigned rather than fire Cox. Ruckelshaus followed, sending in his resignation even as his dismissal notice was on its way.

Across the U.S., calls for impeachment mingled with cries of amazement in an emotional outpouring of reaction from Americans.

And, outside the White House, the normal weekend quiet was shattered by motorists spontaneously demonstrating their support of sidewalk pickets who flashed placards reading "Honk for Impeachment."

Washington, October 22, 1973

Little by little, under pressure from the courts, the crucial tapes came out. As Farquharson reported, the most damning tapes were the missing or partly-erased ones.

For President Nixon the pattern is painfully clear. Every time he launches another Watergate counter-attack, the White House tape recordings rise up again to crush his credibility.

There are the tapes that are missing and the tapes that hum mysteriously, the tapes that play back profanities, honking horns and whistles, and the tapes that present the president's voice, sometimes garbled.

As evidence of innocence or guilt they are probably already virtually worthless.

But, in the way Mr. Nixon and his men have handled them, the tapes imperil a presidency. Coincidence builds on coincidence to confound the public mind.

The fact that President Nixon taped every meeting and phone call without the knowledge of the participants emerged almost by accident during the Senate Committee hearings last July.

Many Americans were upset by this secret presidential invasion of other people's privacy, but the real shockers were still ahead.

Citing the sanctity of executive privilege, President Nixon refused to hand Watergate-related tapes over to the Special Prosecutor, Archibald Cox, or even to Judge John Sirica as ordered by the appeal court.

He changed his mind only after what one of his top aides called the "firestorm" of public opinion which greeted the firing of Mr. Cox and the forced resignations of the attorney-general and his deputy.

The first damaging revelation came Oct. 31 when presidential counsel Fred Buzhardt said in court that two of the nine promised tapes never existed.

The next day White House counsel Buzhardt nervously informed Judge Sirica that 18 minutes of conversation on one of those available seven tapes was impossible to hear because of a mysterious "audible tone."

The talkless segment of the tape occurs in the middle of a June 20, 1972, conversation between the president and former top aide H.R. Haldeman.

Notes taken by Mr. Haldeman, now in the possession of the court, indicate that the topic discussed in the tape portion which now plays back a hum was the need to counter-attack after the discovery of the Watergate break-in three days before.

Washington, November 30, 1973

By the summer of 1974, yet another investigation was closing in on Nixon. The House of Representatives judiciary committee was weighing the grounds for impeaching him. The process would have led to a trial in the Senate, and to Nixon's removal from office if he were found guilty. As Farquharson reported, even some Republicans were abandoning the president.

Joined by one more influential Republican, the House judiciary committee has voted a second time to recommend the impeachment and removal from office of President Nixon.

Voting with the 28-to-10 majority Monday night was Robert McClory of Illinois, second-ranking Republican on the committee.

Saying "the president has failed us," Rep. McClory supported the second article of impeachment charging that Mr. Nixon had repeatedly misused his presidential powers to violate the constitutional rights of U.S. citizens.

The Republican congressman had opposed the first article passed 27-to-11 Saturday, which accused the president of obstruction of justice in connection with the Watergate cover-up.

Monday's vote, following on the criminal indictment of his former treasury secretary, John Connally, was another blow for the embattled president.

Informed of the result, a White House spokesman said "our position remains the same . . . we're confident the House will assess the facts and not vote for impeachment."

Washington, July 30, 1974

The House committee soon passed a third article of impeachment, accusing Nixon of refusal to supply materials it had subpoenaed, but impeachment soon became an academic issue. The Supreme Court finally forced Nixon to release the crucial tape of June 23, 1972, which recorded his approval of the Watergate cover-up less than a week after the burglary. Here was the "smoking pistol" – proof that he had obstructed justice. Nixon resigned immediately. In this news analysis, Farquharson commented on the fall of a president.

He rose so high yet fell with so little a thud. Richard Nixon fought incredible odds to reach a presidency which had already become imperial. Campaigning as a globe-trotting emperor he returned for a second term with popular support unprecedented in the history of the republic.

Now he is gone, with 897 days still to run, and many Americans seem hardly to care.

The tapes did him in. The tape recordings of his own spontaneous words stripped him of his trappings.

"Let's make the next four years the best in American history," the president proclaimed to the affectionate multitude in his hour of victory.

"I think we are going to fix the son-of-a-bitch," the ruler told his courtiers about the same time in the privacy of the Oval Office, speaking of a Democratic opponent. "Believe me. We are going to."

In his second inaugural the public president promised "We shall answer to God, to history and to our conscience for the way in which we use these years."

The private president muttered different thoughts to his accomplices. "We are all in it together. This is war."

Contrary to his Watergate disclaimers the president was obsessed with every detail of politics throughout the re-election campaign.

Debt-ceiling legislation was dismissed contemptuously because "there ain't a vote in it."

He didn't "give a (expletive deleted) about the Italian lira."

As for culture, ". . . the arts, you know – they're Jews, they're left-wing – in other words stay away."

Once the transcripts started coming out last spring the fall of Richard Nixon seemed inevitable.

But it took the Supreme Court to remind the nation that no citizen is above the law when it ordered him to deliver the most fateful tape.

So far had his perspective of himself slipped that he waited an unbelievable eight hours to announce that he would comply with the highest tribunal in the land.

The president made public the June 23 tape of his own duplicity last Monday, on the demand of his own lawyer who had recently learned of its existence.

His supporters in Congress immediately knew the game was up. So did top aides.

Thursday, to the relief of the nation, he removed himself and saved his pension.

Washington, August 9, 1974

237

Terrorism and Strife

If it hadn't been for the Watergate scandal, U.S. President Richard Nixon might be remembered best for opening American relations with Communist China. It was an historic move, and a surprising one, perhaps, for such a veteran of the Cold War as Nixon.

President Nixon opened his dialogue for peace with China's leaders today, holding his first meetings with Mao Tse-tung and Chou En-lai. He appealed to them to join him in "a long march" toward universal peace.

"Not in lock step," the president said in reply to Chou at a banquet in the Great Hall of the People, "but on different roads leading to a common goal – a world structure of peace and justice in which all men stand together."

Nixon said if he and Chinese leaders can find common ground to work together, "the chance for world peace is immeasurably increased."

"Let us recognize at the outset we have had great differences today . . . neither of us will compromise our principles. But while we cannot do this, we can try to bridge them so that we may be able to talk together."

Premier Chou preceded Nixon to the rostrum at the banquet and said the visit provides an opportunity for normalization of relations and exchange of views on questions of concern.

"The American people are a great people. The Chinese people are a great people. The people of our two countries have always been friendly to each other, but owing to reasons known to all, the contacts between the two people were suspended for over 20 years."

Now, "the gates to friendly contact have finally opened."

The unexpected meeting between President Nixon and Chairman Mao, almost immediately after the president had landed at the start of his eight-day visit, caused a 90-minute delay before Nixon's session with Premier Chou.

White House Press Secretary Ronald Ziegler said the two leaders, meeting for the first time had a serious and frank discussion lasting 60 minutes, but refused to give any details.

This description of the talks was used also by the official New China news agency.

In Communist phraseology, "serious and frank discussions" indicate disagreement. The term for agreement usually is "cordial and friendly."

Peking, February 21, 1972

Palestinian terrorists carried their campaign against Israel far outside the Middle East. One of the grimmest episodes of terrorism occurred at the 1972 Olympic Games.

The Olympic Games resumed today under the shadow of Arab terrorism and police action which together left 17 men dead.

An Arab raid on the Israeli athletes' quarters and a later shootout at the Munich military airport had killed 11 of the Israelis' Olympic team, five terrorists and a West German policeman.

German officials started an inquiry into all circumstances of the airport shooting, but said there was no alternative to the police action there.

Premier Golda Meir of Israel thanked the West German government for trying to free nine Israeli hostages who died at the airport. She endorsed the German decision to use force.

Interior Minister Hans-Dietrich Genscher told reporters that German authorities became convinced "a flight out of this country would have meant certain death for the athletes."

The shootout flared after German authorities, unwilling to give in to terrorist demands and convinced the terrorists would kill the hostages set up an ambush at an air base outside Munich.

The terrorists and hostages had been flown there from Olympic Village in two German army helicopters apparently believing they would be flown to Cairo.

Details of the fight in the sealed-off air base were still not complete but eyewitnesses said shooting started when two terrorists stepped from a helicopter to inspect a Boeing 727 jetliner they expected to use.

German sharpshooters hit one of the terrorists. Other terrorists started shooting the hostages, officials said.

One Arab blew himself up with a hand grenade, starting a fire in one of the helicopters where hostages were trapped blindfolded with their hands tied.

Firetrucks attempting to approach to rescue them were driven back by terrorist fire.

Bullets whipped across the field and people jumped from the helicopters and fled in all directions.

Suddenly one helicopter was ripped apart by an explosion and before police were able to douse the flames it was burned to a blackened hulk.

Munich, West Germany, September 6, 1972

President Salvador Allende of Chile, the first Marxist to achieve power peacefully (he won 36 per cent of the vote in a three-way contest) was overthrown by a coup in 1973 and replaced by an exceptionally cruel military dictatorship. Charles Lynch of Southam News recalled his meeting with Allende.

When I interviewed President Salvador Allende of Chile last January, the way to his office led through an anteroom containing a big poster of Che Guevara, with the slogan: "Che Lives!"

But Che, who agreed with Chairman Mao Tse-tung that power comes from the barrel of a gun, was dead.

And now Allende, the Marxist who believed power came from the ballot boxes, is dead, too – a suicide in the very crimson-walled office in which he received me, in the ornate Monada Palace, the heart of the great grey city of Santiago.

His revolution is in ruins, though historians will never agree on what ruined it. The signs of failure were everywhere in Chile at the start of 1973, and Chilenos –

East meets West, as U.S. president Richard Nixon and Chinese Premier Chou En-lai toast each other at the end of a banquet in Peking. Nixon's visit marked a turning-point in Sino-American relations.

more of whom opposed Allende than ever supported him – were arguing fiercely about what was wrong.

Certainly, the United States of America has much to answer for, or to boast about – the machinations of the Central Intelligence Agency and the International Telegraph and Telephone Company had much to do with bringing Allende down.

But moderates and extremists alike will blame Allende himself: moderates will say that he and his incompetent aides wrecked the economy, while extremists will say he was foolish to think he could conduct a revolution by democratic means, even in a country with Chile's long democratic traditions.

Certainly, in revolutionary terms, Allende's fate supports the thesis that revolutions are best carried forward by getting rid of one's opponents, quickly and violently. Allende had no taste for such solutions – in any case they were denied him, because of the sheer numbers of his opponents in Chile, and the political neutrality of the armed forces.

The 65-year-old Allende and his young, idealist ministers put politics before practicality in seeking to nationalize Chile's economy and her industries – the result was chaos, shortages, and hardships for the very people the revolution was designed to help. Among those turning on the president were large numbers of the workers themselves. Most Chilean women opposed him bitterly.

Now this diminutive, good-humored medical doctor joins Che Guevara in the ranks of martyrs to the cause of social betterment for the masses. It is a sad fact that, despite a lifetime of selfless toil, Allende left Chile's masses in worse shape than they were when he came to power.

Ottawa, September 13, 1973

By the middle of 1971, most American ground forces had been withdrawn from the Vietnam war, though the U.S. continued to bomb North Vietnam. Secret negotiations by American Secretary of State Henry Kissinger led to a settlement signed in January, 1973. "Peace with honor," President Nixon called it, but the fighting went on, with each side accusing the other of violating the treaty. North Vietnamese forces pressed south, and by the spring of 1975 they were near Saigon. The last Americans in the country were evacuated on the last day of South Vietnam's independence.

U.S. helicopters landed on Saigon rooftops and at Tan Son Nhut air base today and began evacuating all but a few of the remaining 800 to 900 Americans who fought off South Vietnamese trying to flee before Communist-led forces take over.

United States Marines and armed civilians used pistols and rifle butts to smash the fingers of Vietnamese trying to claw their way over the 10-foot wall at the U.S. embassy as helicopters lifted off the roof. At the airport, angry Vietnamese guards fired at busloads of evacuees and shouted: "We want to go, too."

Some tried to jump over the wall at the embassy and landed on the barbed wire. A man and woman lay on the wire, bleeding. People held up their children, asking Americans to take them over the fence.

The evacuation was ordered after a heavy Viet Cong shelling of the air base before dawn and a radio speech by President Duong Van Minh ordering all Americans assigned to the U.S. defence attache's office out of the country within 24 hours.

The U.S. defence and state departments announced in Washington that President Ford ordered the evacuation because the military situation around Saigon, and particularly at the airport, had deteriorated.

Civilian officials of the South Vietnamese government also were reported fleeing as rumors spread that the Viet Cong and North Vietnamese would soon march into the city.

Defence secretary James Schlesinger said in Washington about 4,000 Americans and South Vietnamese were evacuated within the first three hours after the U.S. airlift began.

U.S. fighter-bombers flew air cover high over the city for the evacuation. Officials said the U.S. embassy will close soon, ending 30 years of official American involvement in the Indochina war.

While most Americans were pulling out, a few remained behind. Among them were a handful of reporters and missionaries.

Saigon, April 29, 1975

The next day the Viet Cong flag was reported flying over Saigon.

Charles Manson's hold on his followers didn't necessarily end when he went to prison. A member of his cult reappeared in the news years after the Manson slayings.

Intelligence agencies knew Lynette Fromme, a disciple of mass murderer Charles Manson, was in town. But she still got within two feet of President Gerald Ford Friday with a loaded .45-calibre pistol. Miss Fromme, 26, who kept in close touch with Manson even after he was sent to San Quentin Prison, was charged with attempted murder of the president.

The thin, red-haired woman was wrestled to the ground after she aimed the pistol at Ford and screamed "It didn't go off."

The firing chamber of the army Colt was empty, but there were four live rounds of ammunition in the clip.

As agents backed Miss Fromme up against a tree and Ford was hustled away by his bodyguards, a witness heard her repeat over and over: "He is not a public servant. He is not a public servant."

A reporter's tape recorder also showed that she yelled "This country is a mess! The man is not your president."

Ford was shaking hands with spectators as he walked through a park near the

Lynette "Squeaky" Fromme under arrest.

California legislature for a meeting with Gov. Edmund Brown Jr.

"I saw a hand coming up behind several others in the front row. And obviously there was a gun in the hand," the president said.

"I then saw almost instantly, very quick and very effective action by the Secret Service in taking care of the matter."

A Secret Service agent stationed in Sacramento said Miss Fromme had not been under surveillance because she had never expressed any interest in the president. He also said it was impossible to keep an eye on everyone who is "a little out of the ordinary."

Sacramento, California, September 6, 1975

Fromme was sentenced to life imprisonment.

Terror and counter-terror continued through the Seventies. One of Israel's major victories in this undeclared war came at Kampala, Uganda.

Israel gloried today in the commando rescue of more than 100 hijacking victims from the Ugandan airport where pro-Palestinian terrorists held them captive for nearly a week.

The 2,400-mile three-plane raid into the heart of East Africa Saturday night was Israel's most prideful military accomplishment since the Six-Day War in 1967. There was nationwide rejoicing.

Israeli officials said 102 hostages were brought back to Israel, but at least 11 of them were taken to hospital. They said three hostages, one of the commandos and seven hijackers were killed, and one hostage was left behind because she had been taken to hospital in Kampala before the rescue.

At sunset Saturday night two Israeli air force 707 jets and a C-130 transport took off for Entebbe. Aboard was an elite commando unit trained in anti-guerrilla warfare. Various sources gave this account of the operation.

The hostages had been imprisoned all week in the lounge of an unused old terminal building several hundred feet from the airport control tower. At least seven terrorists were guarding them Saturday night, and about 70 Ugandan troops were on the second floor of the building or on guard duty outside.

The commandos split into two groups, one to storm into the building and rescue the hostages, the other to take care of any opposition outside.

A diversionary explosion, possibly the bombing of an oil tank, was set off to distract the Ugandans' attention. The Israelis also opened fire on Ugandan air force MIG fighters parked in the open and set six to 10 of them on fire.

"There wasn't too much shooting – the terrorists didn't have a chance to get off a shot," said one of the raiders when he returned to Tel Aviv.

General Mordechai Gur, the Israeli chief of staff, said resistance lasted for only a few minutes.

Tel Aviv, July 5, 1976

Religious cults of all kinds flourished in the seventies. Sometimes their other-worldliness had a sinister aspect – never more so than in the mass suicide of Rev. Jim Jones and his followers at their settlement in Guyana. Feeling threatened by an inquiring American Congressman and the reporters with him, Jones' followers killed five investigators and then lined up to get doses of cyanide-loaded fruit drink. More than 900 people, including Jones, died at Jonestown. Charles Krause of the Times-Post News Service visited Jonestown.

When the Rev. Jim Jones learned Saturday that Rep. Leo J. Ryan had been killed but some members of the congressman's party had survived, Jones called his followers together and told them that the time had come to commit the mass suicide they had rehearsed several times before.

"They started with the babies," administering a portion of Kool-aid mixed with cyanide, Odell Rhodes recalled Monday when I visited Jonestown to view the horrifying sight of 409 bodies – men, women and children, most of them grouped around the altar where Jones himself lay dead.

Rhodes is the only known survivor of Jonestown who witnessed a part of the suicide rite before managing to escape. He was helping Guyanese authorities identify the dead.

Most of those who drank the deadly potion served to them by a Jonestown doctor, Lawrence Schact, and by nurses, did so willingly, Rhodes said. Mothers often would give the cyanide to their own children before taking it themselves, he said.

But others who tried to escape were

Mass suicide at Jonestown. Followers of the Reverend Jim Jones lined up for a fruit drink laced with cyanide, served from the tub in the foreground.

turned back by armed guards who ringed the central pavilion where the rite was carried out, Rhodes said. They were then forced to drink the poisoned Kool-aid and shortly after the mass killings began, Rhodes said, "It just got all out of order. Babies were screaming, children were screaming and there was mass confusion."

It took about five minutes for the liquid to take its final effect. Young and old, black and white, grouped themselves, usually near other family members, often with their arms around each other, waiting for the cyanide to kill them.

They would go into convulsions, their

eyes would roll upward, they would gasp for breath and then fall dead, Rhodes said.

All the while, Jones was talking to them, urging them on, explaining that they would "meet in another place." Near the end, Rhodes said, Jones began chanting, "mother, mother, mother" – an apparent reference to his wife who lay dead not far from the altar.

Of the 409 who died, Jones and two others were shot rather than poisoned, according to C.A. Robert, the chief Guyanese police official at Jonestown Monday.

Port Kaituma, Guyana, November 21, 1978

Strife between Catholics and Protestants in Northern Ireland claimed nearly 2,000 lives in the Seventies, and the decade brought little or no hope of peace. Nicholas Hills of Southam News reported on the young people of Northern Ireland who may provide the next generation of snipers and bombers.

The children of Ulster are the children of violence. Ten years of "the troubles" have produced a new breed of teen-ager whose real vandalism is not breaking school windows or even throwing stones at British soldiers – but, now, delivering bombs for the godfathers of the IRA.

Of all that has shattered Northern Ireland over the past decade this is the most shattering.

Behind the pale, gaunt but still innocent-looking faces of these boys – and girls – is another child altogether, born to hate, taught to hate, and still hating.

"We have taught them this," says a noted Ulster psychiatrist sadly, "and therefore we are going to have another generation of bigots."

The most terrible thing is that when some kind of political settlement finally comes, these children will not be able to switch off.

"They are as indoctrinated as they were

Belfast youths pelt a British armoured car which has broken through their road-block.

five years ago," says Dr. Alex Lyons, "and the powers-that-be have taken little recognizance of this problem."

It is a harsh but almost certainly valid judgment on a harsh situation. For, at a time when violence generally has been diminishing and some form of normality has come back to the community, the children still seem largely to be living in the nether world of sectarian divisiveness and violence.

The comparative ease with which the stricken IRA leadership turns to the young to provide the new messengers of injury and death is a terrible testament to what the old Irish establishment of church and family have really inflicted upon the future of Ulster.

At this time, as some corners are being turned in the seemingly unending struggle, the architects of compromise see that it is the children that must be helped – but that realization has come awfully late.

New efforts are being made to convince the young of Belfast, in particular, that there is another world around the bend.

The Labor government at Westminster has been funnelling a lot of money into health and recreation programs in a serious attempt to bring the youth of Ulster back to some kind of normality. On top of this, the Royal Ulster Constabulary has returned to neighborhood policing in an attempt to convince the kids that they are not "fascist pigs."

Yet as one neighborhood policeman says: "I am not sure whether we are doing anything for today, let alone tomorrow."

These children have become the enigma.

They are not in majority, even in their own peer group. There are many more who have somehow survived their violated environment to grow up to become relatively stable and sensible citizens.

But then terrorists are never in the majority – and the IRA, as it is driven further and further into a corner, shows that a small minority can in such circumstances do all that is necessary to keep Ulster in an unnatural state.

And so, a small minority of children can do the same . . . however much effort is finally expended to rehabilitate a stricken generation.

Belfast, April 26, 1979

President Anwar Sadat of Egypt was gunned down by men of the Egyptian army, but no coup followed. A Canadian diplomat gave this eyewitness account a day later.

I t was quite frantic. I didn't know if the president had been shot, but I could see people being shot down. It was horror . . ."

The words are those of Robert Elliot, Canada's ambassador to Egypt. He was sitting on the reviewing stand in Cairo on Tuesday when a joyful holiday turned into a horrible nightmare with the assassination of Egyptian President Anwar Sadat.

The Regina-born diplomat described the incident in a telephone interview.

"I guess I was about 50 feet from the president – to his right, facing the same direction seated a little above him.

"The parade had been going for about two hours . . . it was a splendid day, hot, bright, a light breeze, a perfect autumn day. It was quite impressive, with gaily decorated tents set up along the route, flags everywhere, a flypast of aircraft, tanks and troops and trucks, and wonderful Egyptian bands.

"The first thing I saw was the lorry, the truck . . . it was part of the artillery section of the parade. It was a regular army truck, a closed one, and it was carrying a piece of field artillery behind it.

"It stopped in front of the VIP section. Then a soldier leapt from the cab of the truck – I only remember two of them in the truck at first, the driver and a passenger.

"He ran toward the rostrum, pulled a grenade from his pocket, and threw it. It fell short of the president, a long way short . . . But it was a signal of some sort for everything else.

"Suddenly there was shooting, grenades going off, immediate great explosions, the presidential guards and the attackers exchanging fire. By this time there were more than two attackers, but I don't remember seeing them come out of the truck.

"I could see people being shot at, shot down, people getting hit by stray bullets – it was quite frantic. I didn't know if the president had been shot, but I could see people being shot down. It was horror . . .

"And there was no place for anyone to go – the square was crowded, the parade route was lined with thousands of people, we were packed pretty close in the stands, on moveable chairs. You couldn't really go anywhere.

"I think it lasted – the shooting, I mean – about four or five minutes. That's my best estimate, but it seemed forever."

Cairo, October 7, 1981

A few weeks before martial law was imposed in Poland, Christopher Young of Southam News sent this report on the Solidarity movement, which was still hopeful and, it seemed, potentially triumphant.

More a movement than a union in the normal sense, Solidarity is open to anyone with a full-time job, which includes philosophers as well as factory hands.

Only 14 months old, Solidarity this week demonstrated its power by successfully calling out most of the country's work force in a one-hour general strike to protest food shortages and harassment of union activists.

The government was angry but apparently powerless in the face of Solidarity's popular support. It is struggling with an economic crisis and shortages unparalleled since the terrible '40s, when six million Poles died at the hands of Germans and Russians.

"There is no other country in the world in which living conditions of the population have deteriorated so rapidly over one year as they have in Poland," said a statement from the cabinet Thursday.

"Such an avalanche of strikes has no parallel elsewhere. The strike terror is inflicted on a society harassed by economic crisis, which the strikes aggravate. The strike blackmail escalates tension, shattering the sense of security of the Poles. This begs the question of where is Solidarity really heading."

But the bulk of the working population, to judge by the strikes themselves, blames the government for the crisis, has no respect for the Polish United Workers Party (the governing Communists), and supports the strikes as a weapon to force the government to change its methods.

An opinion poll among Solidarity members in one of Poland's regions, published this week, asked the question "Whom do we trust?" and reported the following answers:

Solidarity, 100 per cent; Roman Catholic church, 90.5; army, 71.6; parliament, 47.4; police, 24.2; departmental trade unions (the traditional pre-Solidarity kind) 21; government, 17.3; Polish United Workers Party, 4.2.

But although it is clear that Solidarity represents the opinions and holds the trust of Polish citizens, Poles are still unable to answer the question raised by the cabinet: Where is Solidarity heading?

The government has gone as far as it thinks it can, and certainly much farther than it wanted to go a year ago, towards meeting Solidarity's demands – on paper. But Solidarity members do not trust the government and see no evidence that it is really working for economic reform.

The problem, as one foreign diplomat sees it, is that no one seems to have thought through such questions as how materials would be allocated, how products would be distributed, who would coordinate the needs and output of the various segments of the economy, how the country would manage its foreign trade.

The greatest irony is that things have changed so much in Poland in the last year – especially in a vastly widened freedom of expression – that Westerners who live here think it's a lot, and that maybe it's time to stop and digest what has been gained. But Solidarity is on a crusade, and crusaders don't stop half-way.

Warsaw, October 30, 1981

Good news for newspapers. Clark Kent, alias Superman, returned to the public prints in 1979 after a short spell as a television news reporter.

Several comparatively young men who had captured the public's imagination in very different ways died in the Seventies and early Eighties. Dave Billington of The Herald wrote this memoir of Elvis Presley and his meaning to the young of the early Fifties.

There were half a dozen of us who hung around the same street corner every night aimlessly idling away those late adolescent years until, to paraphrase the words of a song of the era, wedding bells broke up that old gang of ours.

We were all high school dropouts, indolently condescending of those who were still in school, and more than a little in awe of those who had been working long enough to own a car that was less than a decade old.

Nowadays we see a caricature (and a very poor one at that) of ourselves in the person of Happy Days' Fonzie camping across the TV screens. But in those days we had no idols and no models after which to pattern ourselves.

The age of the formalized "teenager" had not yet dawned. Ours was a true subculture inasmuch as it did not exist except in the cloudy reaches of our adolescent minds. One thing we did know for sure – our separation from the society in which we lived was as complete as if we lived on another planet.

Rebels without causes or symbols or heroes – until one memorable Monday night.

Hanging around as usual telling lies about our weekends one guy asked if anybody had seen the Dorsey show that Saturday. (The Dorsey Brothers – Tommy and Jimmy – had a weekly big band show on a U.S. network.)

None of us had. And our informant began describing Elvis Presley in terms which would have rivalled Paul's description of the vision he'd had on the road to Damascus.

Our curiosity aroused by our friend's description of Presley we gathered in his front room the following Saturday to view this phenomenon and perhaps sneer yet again at another false prophet.

We did not sneer. We cheered. (Silently of course because in those days overt displays of emotion were not cool.)

We cheered primarily because one of ours had made it and made it big. There we were, greasy hair, curled lip and barely concealed aggression sticking it to them.

Now, the tidy world of The McGuire Sisters, Perry Como, Rosemary Clooney and Patti Page, had been invaded by a real live, genuine, don't give-a-damn hood whose actions spoke a lot louder than the words we didn't have.

With the benefit of 20-20 hindsight, Presley's musical innovations and impacts were, at best slight. Most of his songs were light, almost warm, when compared to the screams of ghetto-cat rage that came from the throat of Little Richard and others like him.

But this is not to underestimate the importance of Presley either as a musical or social phenomenon – for he was both in a way in which no other single postwar entertainer has been.

True his career went on through countless bubblegum movies which often made the Monkees look like high art. But Elvis Presley was the quintessential 1950s hood. Part fantasy, part reality.

All deaths are untimely since we all believe we and those close to us are immortal. Presley's death was no more untimely than that of an anonymous drunk who probably died the same day in some alley.

But Presley's death, for many of us, was a pointed reminder not only of the way we were, but the way we are. . .and why.

August 20, 1977

John Lennon's death, at 40, was a milestone, of sorts, for a generation that had rallied around the Beatles' music.

Former Beatle John Lennon, who catapulted to stardom with the long-haired British rock music group in the 1960s, was shot dead late Monday as he and wife Yoko Ono entered their luxury Manhattan apartment building.

Police have charged Mark Chapman, 25, a free-lance photographer from Hawaii with murder. He was described by one official as "a wacko."

There was no chance to save Lennon. Doctors said he had seven severe wounds in his chest, back and left arm.

Chief of Detectives James Sullivan said Lennon and his wife were walking through the Dakota's big, arched entryway about 10:50 p.m. when a man approached them and fired five shots from a .38-calibre pistol.

Police say that as Lennon left his car, a man called out "Mr. Lennon?" and pulled a gun. Crouching down into a combat stance, he fired at the singer-songwriter.

Lennon groaned "I'm shot", staggered up a few steps into the building and collapsed.

Sullivan said the assailant dropped the gun and was waiting quietly when police arrived.

Police spokesman Anthony Palma said officers found Lennon lying face down in the office of the nine-storey apartment building and carried him to a patrol car.

Ono was taken to the hospital in another car, he said.

Police say she was hysterical on the way to the hospital. "Tell me it isn't true," she cried. "Tell me he's all right."

After word of the shooting spread, hundreds of people gathered outside the entrance to the apartment, many of them weeping.

Lennon earned fame in the early 1960s when he and fellow Britons Paul McCartney, George Harrison and Ringo Starr introduced a new sound that changed the course of rock 'n' roll.

Lennon, who turned 40 Oct. 9, was responsible for writing many of the group's songs.

Lennon and McCartney together wrote more hit songs than any composer in modern history.

Lennon was considered the most politically aware of the Beatles and was described as the group's intellect.

New York, December 9, 1980

A footnote to the death of a superstar.

Mark David Chapman, who is serving a 20 year sentence for gunning down ex-Beatle John Lennon, has asked his lawyer to proceed to court and retrieve possession of Lennon's record album Chapman held when he fired the fatal shots.

Earlier on the night of the shooting, Lennon had autographed the album's jacket for Chapman. The signature was Lennon's last and reports say the jacket is worth $100,000.

September 29, 1981

An editorial marking the death of Terry Fox, a young athlete who made his own losing fight against cancer into something much bigger.

Terry Fox is dead but his personal record of courage and the inspiration he gave to millions will stay with us. Terry's personal fight against cancer and his unique national crusade against the disease was a high point in human experience, a testimonial to what can be achieved by one individual with pluck and determination and a high objective to shoot for.

The young amputee runner's dogged day by day marathon run across Canada, cut short by the recurrence of cancer, became a symbol of hope and a source of pride and inspiration for millions of people around the world. The $23 million which his effort raised for cancer research will be of huge benefit in seeking a cure for one of man's most dreaded scourges. But the personal example which a gallant and determined young Canadian offered to all of us is an even greater legacy.

His memory will be cherished because he refused to be defeated and even death cannot take away the bright victory of the human spirit which he gave to the world.

June 25, 1981

Disturbers of the Peace

As a fast-growing, affluent city, Calgary suffered its share of major crime. Murder and armed robbery became more frequent, and occasionally the peace was broken by more spectacular crimes. When an Air Canada flight out of Calgary was hijacked, Don Sellar and Jack Gorman compiled this report from the findings of a platoon of Herald reporters.

An Air Canada pilot's fire-axe blow to the skull of a bomb-carrying hijacker ended an eight-hour sky drama aboard a DC-8 jetliner late Friday over fog-shrouded southern Alberta.

The hijacker, who claimed to belong to the Irish Republican Army, was thwarted in a desperate bid to exchange the lives of 118 passengers on Flight 812 for $1.5 million in ransom money and safe passage to Ireland.

Veteran Captain Vernon Ehman belted the hijacker on the back of the head as the aircraft approached Calgary from Great Falls, Montana, where the passengers had been traded for $50,000 in cash.

When the jet landed at Calgary International Airport minutes before midnight, police, fire units, a bomb expert and a rescue squad swarmed over the runway apron to unload the crew and its captive.

Police have identified Paul Joseph Cini, 27, of Calgary as the man being held in connection with Friday's hijacking.

RCMP Inspector J.R. Bentham said the man was struck in the head with the broad side of an emergency fire axe.

The Calgary landing ended an unprecedented Canadian hijacking saga during which the plane zig-zagged through skies over Montana, Saskatchewan and Alberta.

Inspector Bentham, RCMP officer in charge of the tense airport operations, told The Herald a sawed-off shotgun, a makeshift bomb and $50,000 were recovered from the craft.

Eyewitnesses from the hijacked airliner confirmed that one shot was fired into a partition near the first-class compartment about an hour after the Vancouver-Toronto flight left Calgary at 3:30 p.m., but it injured no one.

After firing the blast, the gunman outlined his ransom demands and told Capt. Ehman he was prepared to die for his cause.

The hijacker, believed to have boarded the plane at Calgary with 101 other passengers, pointed his weapon at stewardess Anna-Mae Smith and demanded that the plane fly to Great Falls and then to Ireland.

During the one-hour diversion and two hours of circling the Montana city of 70,000, the hijacker held the gun to Mrs. Smith's head while Great Falls bankers gathered the ransom money.

In the next phase of the bizarre hijacking, the gunman allowed the plane to land in Great Falls after he was assured a courier would deliver $1.5 million.

A policewoman placed a briefcase con-

Stewardess Mary Dohey kept hijacker calm.

taining $50,000 on the aircraft, which refuelled and immediately took off for Regina where the hijacker had agreed to release the passengers.

Apparently changing his mind after the crew convinced him there was no flight crew at Regina qualified to make the Ireland trip, the hijacker ordered the DC-8 back to Great Falls.

When the plane landed there the second time, he allowed the 113 passengers to deplane. He then ordered the crew to fly to Calgary, where enough fuel could be taken on to take the craft non-stop to Ireland.

As the aircraft approached Calgary at 3,000 feet, the hijacker was overpowered and subdued by a clout from the fire axe, believed stored behind Captain Ehman's seat.

November 13, 1971.

In fact, Cini had no connection with the IRA. He was found sane, and sentenced on seven counts, four of them carrying terms of life imprisonment. Mary Dohey, a stewardess on the flight, was awarded Canada's highest decoration for bravery, the Cross of Valor. Purser John Joseph Arpin was awarded a Star of Courage and Captain Vernon Ehman a Medal of Bravery.

A routine piece of police work erupted into violence and tragedy, as Ted Kelly reported.

The slaying of a veteran city policeman and wounding of seven others Friday was the final dreadful chapter in a lengthy history of an ex-convict with a record of rape, glue sniffing and weapons use.

"Just say he was mental," a close relative said of the gunman who died in a hail of bullets from police guns.

When he died, while sprinting for a new sanctuary after a Canadian Forces armored personnel carrier had demolished his garage fortress, Philippe Gagnon left behind a legacy of senseless violence.

Detective Hugh Boyd Davidson, 43, the father of five children, was killed when a bullet smashed through two walls of an adjacent garage and found him, seconds after he had shotgunned out the windows in Gagnon's garage.

The windows had to be blasted out in order to lob in tear gas bombs.

The tragic drama unfolded when Constables Thomas R. Dick and Harvey K. Gregorash investigated a routine complaint in the Grandview area of 9th Street S.E. The woman proprietor of a small grocery store reported she had been threatened when she refused to sell a man some glue.

Ann Choma of 1040 9th Street S.E. was hanging clothes in her yard about 1:15 p.m. when a police cruiser pulled into the lane behind her house and entered a garage living quarter two houses north at 1034.

She heard shots and saw the policemen run out. Gagnon had pulled a .22 rifle on them without warning and started firing. A ricocheting bullet caught Constable Gregorash in the scalp but Constable Dick was saved when a bullet lodged in a rear-pocket wallet, bruising him.

Fellow officers swarmed to the scene following this. Det. Davidson, who worked full time on the city's arson squad, was among the first to arrive. He was a veteran of close to 25 years on the Calgary force.

Gagnon fired random shots from two rifles, the other thought to be a .30-.30 calibre gun. Retreating to a cement pit six feet deep in the centre of the garage, he was virtually invincible as police bullets and tear gas failed to dislodge him.

Perhaps at that point, it was decided to call in the military. The result was a tank-like armored personnel carrier.

At 3:40 p.m. the carrier headed up the gravel lane to the garage, climbing a small hill. Fifteen minutes later it was all over in a fantastic barrage of gunfire.

The armored vehicle rammed the garage five times and after the final run Gagnon sprinted toward the house on the property. He never made it.

December 21, 1974.

Ted Drabick's long fight with his bank culminated in a hostage-taking incident that lasted nearly five days. Herald reporters kept a vigil on the story.

I have the hostage and I'm heading downtown." The voice crackled over the police radio and the hostage drama which had kept the city on edge for five days was over.

It was exactly 2:31 a.m. Sunday morning, 112½ hours after sheriff's bailiffs Bob Redfern and Mark Pollard had arrived at the yellow-colored, split-level house at 211 Margate Close in the Marlborough neighborhood to deliver an eviction notice.

Three days earlier on Wednesday night, Redfern had been released.

And now, after eight hours of almost steady negotiations between a lawyer and the gunman who held Calgary in the palm of his hand for almost a week, a weary-looking Pollard was walking out the front door of the hostage house, down the steps to a waiting police cruiser.

Then the attention turned back to Ted Drabick.

At 2:39 a.m. the police radio said "He walked out of his house with his hands over his head."

At 2:40 a.m. the radio said: "Mr. Drabick is in the police car."

The trial of nerves was over.

It began quietly on Tuesday.

Bailiffs Bob Redfern, 42, and Mark Pollard, 32, arrived at 211 Margate Close to serve an eviction notice on the family of Ted and Anne Drabick.

Ted Drabick, a television repairman who had once owned an RCA dealership and repair shop in the nearby Eastport Shopping Centre, had been feuding with the Toronto-Dominion Bank for four years over his mortgage and the dispute had culminated last fall, with the bank's foreclosure.

It's unclear exactly how the two bailiffs were taken hostage, but when two furniture movers showed up at 10:30 a.m. to seize the family's personal possessions, the drama had begun.

Drabick told police he was heavily armed, had a large cache of food and had wired his house with explosives – a claim which turned out to be untrue.

Wednesday should have been one of celebration for Ted Drabick. It was the day he turned 50.

He marked the occasion with a threat, breaking the stillness of the early morning hours by broadcasting a message over a loudspeaker attached to his house.

"Anyone trying to approach the house is running a very high risk. I have laced it with explosives," he warned.

But, less than 24 hours later, Bob Redfern, 42, a 20-year veteran of the RCMP, walked out the front door of the Drabick house and down one block to a waiting police car at 10:40 p.m., capping a day highlighted by an unprecedented television appearance by his captor.

In his televised statement – most of which detailed his dispute with the bank over a mortgage – Drabick said he didn't plan to "instigate any shots...they will have to come from their (the police's) direction."

Thursday was the agonizing day, the day nothing happened.

Communications with Drabick following the release of Redfern the night before had slowed, to the point where he cut off his telephone link with the three-man police negotiating team.

On Friday the uneasy silence that had fallen over Margate Close led police to take a gamble that paid off.

Ted Drabick tells his story on television.

Anxious to get Drabick talking again, police arranged to have the apologies by banker Denis Linton and bank lawyer Murray McGown, taped and played to the gunman two days earlier, aired on television.

That public apology, in which the two urged him not to hurt innocent people and admitted their fault in his mortgage tangle, put Drabick on a "super-high" and prompted him to allow hostage Pollard to telephone his wife.

Better yet, Drabick was talking to police negotiators again.

Late Saturday Drabick's brother Ed, acting on advice from police, contacted Webster Macdonald Jr., one of the city's top criminal lawyers.

Macdonald joined the negotiating team at 6 p.m. and worked out the final details of Drabick's surrender in an eight-hour session.

For Drabick, there was to be immunity for his wife, a new mortgage – at 10 per cent over 10 years – and a way out from behind his financial eight-ball.

For hostage Pollard, there was to be freedom.

For police, the end of the longest siege in the city's history.

January 19, 1981

Ted Drabick was sentenced to six years in prison for unlawful confinement and extortion. He told the court that he still thought he had done the right thing. Two private citizens lent Drabick a total of $35,000 to pay off his debt to the Bank of Commerce and the Toronto-Dominion Bank. The apologies to Drabick were withdrawn.

On the day Calgary lawyer Peter Petrasuk was sentenced to ten years in prison for taking more than $2.3 million from his clients, The Herald published a long account of the case – the man, the money, the victims. Herald writers Howard Solomon and Joanne Ramondt began by summing up a life in ruins.

Peter Petrasuk tried three times to be mayor of Calgary and failed three times. There were those who said he couldn't win because he couldn't be trusted. But, until now, no one could prove that Peter Petrasuk was a crook.

For some, the cost of putting their trust in him was their life savings.

He craved power, adulation, public acceptance. Now he's bankrupt, divorced, suspended as a lawyer, an object of pity or disgust.

His money – and the money of his friends and clients – was wasted in a disastrous housing plan in the prairie town of Carseland, and his dreams were crushed.

A solid but unimaginative alderman, he could never be mayor but fought desperately three times for the chance to preside over the city he loved.

A hardworking Liberal, he tried three times for election in provincial or federal campaigns but couldn't win.

He had the educational credentials – degrees in engineering and law.

He had the energy – 12-hour days, six or seven days a week, toiling in his law office, then countless community functions. He learned hard work from his parents, and learned to thrive on it.

He commanded a certain respect – seldom admiration – for his business moxy, and was able to wheel and deal, for a time, with the cream of Calgary's business crop.

But, in the end, the man who raced from business deal to legal wrangle to political gathering had outrun even his own ambition.

He swindled grandmothers out of their life savings – grandmothers who share his mother's Slavic heritage, grandmothers who cry now when they realize their hard-earned money – in many cases, the money left them by hard-working husbands – is gone.

November 25, 1981

The Petrasuk affair took an especially bitter turn a few weeks after the trial, as Joanne Ramondt reported.

Peter Petrasuk's elderly widowed mother claims her son owes her $100,000 and has left her with monthly mortgage payments of $1,500 on a house she thought she owned outright.

The Herald has learned that Doris Petrashuyk has submitted a claim with the Law Society of Alberta, stating that her son's handling of her affairs has left her with $99,948 owing on her northwest Calgary home.

In her claim, she says she gave her son $12,440 on March 28, 1979, directing him to pay out the existing mortgage on the house at 8 Cromwell Ave. N.W.

She said she directed him to do so in his capacity as her lawyer.

The Ukrainian native said her son asked her on May 22 this year to sign a number of documents relating to her home.

Although she believed she was signing documents to complete the discharge of the mortgage, she said she now understands that she signed a document transferring the home to Petrasuk.

Title of the house has since been transferred back to her, but she claims that in the meantime, a $100,000 mortgage has been taken out on the property.

December 19, 1981

Calgary's Varied Moods

Locally, The Herald kept its eye on every-thing from stray cats to singles bars. No newspaper would be complete without a stray-cat story now and then. Gillian Lind-gren filled the need with the saga of Norton, named for the Art Carney character in the Honeymooners television series of long ago. Needless to stay, Norton found a new home the next day.

Norton's story could probably be told by hundreds of other Calgary cats. The cats who have been left to fend for themselves in garbage dumps, vacant lots and back alleys.

But Norton, a 15-year-old grey and white part-Persian, so named because he was found in a sewer, is a bit luckier than most because someone finally cared enough to take him to a veterinarian for treatment and food.

Wendy Miller of Wheatland Ave. S.W. couldn't stand watching Norton crawl out of a sewer every morning — sometimes when temperatures were as low as 20 below zero.

"When it started to get cold he would crawl down into the sewer at night and in the morning he was so stiff he could hardly crawl out," she said.

During the day Mrs. Miller would leave dry dog food out for Norton — and he was so hungry he ate it.

When she finally took pity on him and delivered him to the Wildwood Veterinary Clinic, the ends of his ears had fallen off because they had been frozen, as had part of his tail.

But Norton isn't completely out of danger. He may yet have to end his days at the hands of the gas man at the SPCA.

Mrs. Miller already has two dogs and a horse, besides an allergy to cats, in the family. So if no one wants Norton he'll have to take that one-way trip to the SPCA.

November 20, 1973

The Calgary skyline, 1981. It was a record year for building permits: more than $2 billion worth of construction was approved. Downtown, only a few buildings survive from Calgary's sandstone era.

The Saturday kids' movie matinee has almost vanished, a victim of television and economics. Herald writer Carol Hogg caught the phenomenon at one of its last high points. The original, full-length version of her article won a National Newspaper Award for feature writing.

It's a block-long line-up in front of the cinema. It's eating two boxes of popcorn, a bag of Smarties and an orange pop. It's screaming during the monster fight.

It's hooting during the love scene.

It's getting away from your parents.

It's a phenomenon known as the kids' matinees.

And it's dying.

Like church, like the fox-trot and other institutions dear to the hearts of North Americans, the kids' matinee is struggling to stay alive.

The thing is, it no longer pays. And that's a fatal ailment.

Only six of Calgary's 24 theatres still show regular children's matinees. And it's not a paying proposition, even in these few theatres.

Pressed for a reason why they continue something that, at best, breaks even financially, cinema executives don't come up with any very convincing answers.

Jim Moore, city supervisor for Odeon Theatres, says, "We do it because we've always done it. It's a traditional part of running a theatre.

"I don't know how long it will be before somebody farther up in the corporation says 'Hey, this isn't paying — why are we doing this?' "

During a recent school holiday for a teachers' convention, local theatres brought in special attractions that drew capacity audiences reminiscent of the hey-day of the matinee.

A visit to the matinee at such a time is like a trip back to childhood.

A line-up of waist-high patrons starts to coagulate at the theatre door at 12:05. The first feature is scheduled to begin at 1:30, when Godzilla, the monster with the heart of gold, will settle things once and for all with the (gulp) Smog Monster.

There is a protocol involved in attending a matinee. You do not simply take your seat and wait for the feature to begin.

You race to your seat, deposit your coat, jump on and off your seat three times in rapid succession to make sure the spring-up device functions satisfactorily. Then, trailing your muffler, you make a dash for the snack bar, struggling up the aisle against other incoming bodies, letting out the odd shriek. At the snack bar you buy a popcorn and a pop. Balancing one of these in each hand, you go the bathroom...

All of this is well under way before the average adult can accomplish his blinking adjustment to the theatre gloom after the afternoon sunshine.

The roar cannot be described as dull. It has a distinctly piercing quality. When the theatre lights go out and the screen lights up, this roar does not subside, it intensifies — to a peak beyond measurement in mere decibels.

At such a time, the matinee phenomenon looks as healthy as ever. But a number of special circumstances were at work. The teachers' convention made it a four-day weekend. That made it worthwhile for theatre management to bring in special attractions such as Godzilla Versus the Smog Monster and the Wizard of Oz, which are so good that they draw full houses even at 75 cents a head.

The situation on an average Saturday is quite different. The price of admission drops to 50 cents a head, and even then, theatres are less than half-full.

"Quite frankly, when it comes to the financial side of kids' matinees, I don't like to look too closely," Mr. Moore says.

"As recently as two or three years ago, the matinee was still a paying proposition. Then audiences began to dwindle, and this year it's just no good at all."

Part of the problem is that movies suitable for matinee use are no longer being produced in any numbers. Most of the films made today are violent and/or sexy and have a Restricted or Adult rating.

Although special features can withstand a 75-cent admission price, parents object to having to give their children more than 50 cents admission on an average Saturday. After all, the kids can stay home and watch TV for free.

But although television is an ever-present competition to movie matinees, theatre operators do not single it out as a major factor in the decline of matinees. Movie-houses continued to fill up with kids long after TV came on the scene.

After all, kids don't really go to matinees because of what's on the screen. Rather, they go because it is an exclusive club which welcomes only those under the age of 13 in possession of two quarters. In short, it is a place where a kid can be a kid.

Adults are not made welcome – either by the kids or by theatre management.

"We always warn an adult at the box-office that he likely won't enjoy the experience. If he insists on going in, we usually ask him to sit in the back row – to isolate him for his own sake, and also for the sake of the kids who like to get away from adults for a while," says Mr. Moore.

It is this "kids'-club" mystique which enabled the Saturday afternoon matinees to withstand the advent of TV.

What has really written The End to the phenomenon of kids' matinees is the shift of residential neighborhoods. Many theatres are located in areas which no longer have many children living there.

Mr. Moore has a special warm spot in his heart for the kids' matinee as an institution. He was a manager of a city theatre in the heyday of the Saturday afternoon children's matinee.

"I guess when you ask why we continue to have kids' matinees, if I were honest, I would say just for the love of it. Like a lot of other people, I'm terribly sentimental about it. Sentimentality is the only reason left for carrying on.

"The way it's going, I suppose the kids' matinee is going to disappear. It looks like it's coming to an end, and I don't want it to come to an end. It should be a protected species. We've tried a lot of different things but nothing seems to work.

"There's no use asking where it's going – it's gone."

March 1, 1974

Before reviewing a Calgary Philharmonic concert Herald critic Jamie Portman once reviewed the audience. (The program consisted of works by Ralph Vaughan Williams, Gustav Holst, Manuel De Falla and Aaron Copland.)

The Calgary Philharmonic patron was in a complaining mood as she left the Jubilee Auditorium. Those of us within her vicinity couldn't help overhearing her as she registered her objections to what she had just heard.

The trouble with contemporary music, she declared, was that it all sounded the same and that it went on and on and on. Why, she asked plaintively, couldn't the orchestra have played some Strauss waltzes?

Well, the Calgary Philharmonic Orchestra will be playing Strauss Saturday night at the first of its series of 1975 pop concerts. Unfortunately, it's obvious that some CPO audience members would like a steady diet of Strauss even for its main-series concerts.

And that point of view is terribly, terribly depressing, especially when it's voiced in the aftermath of a concert as good as the one presented Sunday afternoon. Furthermore, one has the depressing hunch that more than a few so-called local music lovers subscribe to such a philosophy.

At the risk of being labelled an elitist snob, I would venture to suggest that if the average CPO audience member found Sunday's concert to be dull and inaccessible, then maybe we shouldn't bother with having an orchestra at all.

For my money, Sunday's concert appealed, not merely because of the playing of the orchestra under Maurice Handford, but because of the wonderful variety and appeal of the programming.

Indeed, it was the type of program which would automatically sell out in many cities. Here, it attracted perhaps 1,200 persons, less than half the auditorium's capacity.

January 13, 1975

Look, up in the sky. It's a country singer, it's a bag of manure, it's 100 country records. Barry Nelson of The Herald reported on Cal Cavendish's one-man air show.

The Calgary Tower and the control tower at Calgary International Airport were both evacuated Friday evening as a 34-year-old country singer staged what he later called "an aerial ballet" over the city.

Cal Cavendish explained buzzing the tower, circling the 625-foot restaurant, flying between downtown buildings and dumping 100 pounds of manure on the city, along with 100 copies of his recording "Government Inspected", as a calculated protest at losing his pilot's licence rather than a suicidal mission or thoughtless stunt.

He surrendered to RCMP at Brooks after landing his single-engine Luscombe 8A in the dark on a dirt road near Duchess.

About 6:40 p.m. he approached the Calgary International Airport, flying "just above the grass," buzzed the control tower, circled it twice and flew towards the city centre.

He circled the Calgary Tower twice, passing close enough to the restaurant to "see the faces and hands of the people inside."

He also flew between the block-apart towers of Place Concorde at an altitude which would have allowed an eighth-floor resident to look down on his plane.

Police ordered the Calgary Tower restaurant and lounge evacuated about 6:45 p.m. Patrons waited in the ground level lobby until they were allowed to return about 7:25 p.m.

Feeling it was possible Cavendish might repeat the buzzing and unsure of his location, the police evacuated the tower again about 9 p.m.

The radio in Cavendish's plane was not working and the flyer never communicated with police or air traffic controllers.

Cavendish opened the door of the plane and dropped manure and records on the downtown area.

Cavendish, who said he used 100 pounds of manure and 100 records to "celebrate Calgary's centennial," claimed that "it is more dangerous to drive down Macleod Trail in a car than to do what I did."

April 12, 1975.

The courts were not amused. Cavendish was fined $3,000.

Cal Cavendish, singer, song-writer, guitarist, stunt flyer, and amateur bombardier.

Pollution and wasted resources became important issues in the Seventies, but warnings had been sounded decades before. Locally some of these warnings came from Grant MacEwan, historian, conservationist, mayor of Calgary, lieutenant-governor of Alberta – and the author of a weekly Herald column, Our Natural Heritage. In 1975, he noted a milestone.

This marks the one thousandth consecutive weekly column to appear with my name in the Calgary Herald. The first one, under the date of December 8, 1956, noted:

"Within the last few days Canadians have read or heard about an alarming decline in northland caribou, tragic forest losses by burning, a threat to west coast salmon fishing and an extension of dustbowl conditions which have gripped the Southern States for five years. These warnings should make every Canadian realize that virgin newness is no longer a characteristic of our continent – that it is time to think and talk and act sensible conservation."

"A course of lectures on conservation or a newspaper series by itself will not achieve a great deal. What is needed is a country-wide movement with educational institutions, churches, service clubs and all organizations interested in public welfare taking a part to promote a conservation philosophy, recognizing a responsibility to the years ahead."

"We have heard those economists who scoff at aspects of conservation, contending that when we cut down the forest and use up all the oil, something better will take their places. But the history of other lands tells a different story, a convincing and sad story of nation after nation rising to greatness with the development of resources, then declining and disappearing when those natural riches were ravished and neglected. Scores of once-prominent nations have gone down to oblivion when they neglected what might be regarded as good housekeeping in handling their resources."

It does not seem like a thousand weeks, at least not until the change in public attitude is noted. Canadians are beginning to embrace conservation principles, recognizing the crucial importance of a dedicated stewardship in the handling of their great natural inheritance.

December 1, 1975

The custom of giving the city's distinguished visitors a white hat occasionally gets out of hand. One such visitor fought back, as Patrick Tivy reported.

Prince Philip made sure he couldn't be given another white hat when he visited the Commonwealth Games shooting range in Calgary Thursday.

The Prince, who has been put through three "white hat" ceremonies on previous visits to the Stampede city, brought a white hat of his own.

Prince Philip arrives, complete with white hat.

The hat was atop the Prince's head for only a few seconds after he arrived at Calgary International Airport, but it made him virtually unrecognizable as he emerged from his private plane.

He removed the hat as he reached the bottom of the stairs, and carried it the 10 paces to the black limousine waiting for him.

Once inside the vehicle he tossed it onto the back window ledge, where it remained for the duration of his visit.

The subtle flash of Royal wit came as the latest in a running battle with hat-crazy Calgarians.

White hats have been presented to important visitors to the city for almost three decades, although the custom has lately shown some signs of dying out.

The Prince suffered silently through two hat ceremonies, but rebelled at the third.

"Not another one!" he exclaimed to then-Mayor Rod Sykes when the hat was brought out. He did accept the gift, but refused a photographer's request to pose with it. "I'm no clown," he retorted.

August 11, 1978.

Herald columnist Suzanne Zwarun paid this tribute to one of the last of the old-time newsmen.

My sister spoke to Doug MacRae only once, on the telephone, and he so utterly enchanted her, she never forgot him and still, years later, inquires after him.

He was one of the last of the old time newspapermen, who worked for the helluv it, instead of the money, and who delighted in being an eccentric in an age of university-trained reporters. He drank some. He infuriated the people he worked for and the people who worked for him. But he was a fine newspaperman.

Doug came to Calgary from a stint with the Ottawa Citizen, where he became something of a minor legend as a newspaperman. A friend who worked against him on the police beat delights in reciting the sagas of a reporter who embarrassed him constantly by being just too good for him.

Once, during a shoot-out on a quiet Ottawa street, cowering policemen were astonished to see MacRae, meandering along with his rubbery gait, shoulders hunched, hands in pockets, whistling happily to himself, sauntering across the lawn in front of the house from where the bad guys were shooting at anything that moved.

MacRae wandered around to the back of the house and rapped on the basement window. When one of the three gunmen, somewhat taken aback opened the window, MacRae allegedly said: "Hi, I'm Doug MacRae of the Citizen. Got a minute?" And the stunned gunman let him in. When the police finally stormed the place, MacRae was found on a couch in the basement, taking notes.

When Liz Taylor and Richard Burton were having their fiery affair – ending in marriage – in the 60s, it was MacRae who found them and got the first interview after their wedding.

He bribed a room service clerk, borrowed his uniform and serving tray, knocked on the door, and when Burton opened it, he swept into the room, set down the tray and said: "Hi, I'm Doug MacRae of United Press . . . got a minute?" He got his interview.

But the changes and modernizations in the newspaper business did not sit well with MacRae. Computers in the newsroom were more than he could cope with, ties on city editors made him grind his teeth.

MacRae didn't write much after coming to The Herald for the first time 11 years ago. When his old police beat crony from the Ottawa Journal pressed him on that one night several years ago, he said, rather sadly, "You and I are just too damned old to be chasing fire engines." He'd conceded to progress. The business had passed him by and he realized it.

Last week, he drowned in a New Brunswick river. He was 42.

To those of us who knew and worked with him, his death puts a final "30" to the era of The Front Page.

June 26, 1979

Some of the "boat people" – refugees from the Communist regime in Vietnam – found a new home in Calgary. Kathryn Warden of The Herald described the ordeal of a typical refugee family.

For five Vietnamese refugee children who arrived in Calgary two weeks ago, the International Year of the Child has been a year of misery.

The children – 10-year-old twin boys and their three cousins aged 10 to 13 – still have nightmares about their 10-day ordeal on the South China Sea and their three-month stay in Malaysian refugee camps.

The three cousins – Lan, Trinh and Thuan – watched helplessly as their mother and two sisters drowned when their boat began to sink off the Malaysian coast.

The two brothers, Doug and Hoa, lost

their nine-year-old brother when their father, Dan Pham, lost his grasp on the boy in the churning waters.

Pham, who asked that his real name not be used, and the children are among 124 survivors of a boatload of 240 persons who left Vietnam in mid-March in what they considered a flight to freedom.

The escape had been planned for almost a year, but it took that long for Pham to raise the roughly 283 grams (10 ounces) of gold that he had to pay the boat owner, whom Pham believes was in the pocket of the government.

Pham had to assume a Chinese name because only ethnic Chinese were allowed to buy their way to freedom, he said. He was one of only 16 passengers who weren't ethnic Chinese.

During the first four days of the voyage, the boat was robbed six times by pirate fishermen from Thailand. Pham said he lost nothing because he had virtually nothing with him, but others lost all they owned.

When they approached the Malaysian coast they were towed back out to sea by the Malaysian navy. When the boat's motor broke down, they were left to drift for three days with no water or supplies. Eight children and one old man died because there was no water. "We had to throw them into the sea," Pham said.

With a makeshift paddle created out of the boat's bamboo roof, they managed to paddle back to within sight of land. However, they were again towed out to sea.

This time the boat sank and about half the passengers drowned before the Malaysian navy boat, which was standing by, decided to make a rescue.

July 25, 1979

Feminism was the major social revolution. Catherine Butlin of The Herald reviewed some of the changes that a decade had brought.

The seventies, for better or for worse, belonged to women. The decade now drawing to a close saw the women's movement survive and flourish, where other movements that had their roots in the radical sixties, withered away.

But even though women took greater strides in the seventies than in preceding centuries, Calgary feminists say they still walk several paces behind men in arenas of economic, political and social power.

"I believe a revolution in thought is occurring," said Maria Eriksen, a Calgary psychologist and women's activist.

"And that is the only real kind of revolution there is."

Eriksen shares with many Calgary women's advocates a sense of optimism while looking back at the seventies.

"The most important thing is the number of women who have entered various professions and trades," she said.

"There is a profound change in the way women are treated today. There is a real discomfort with treating women as sex objects."

But the statistics are less encouraging.

A recent study by University of Calgary management professor Al Cahoon showed that women hold only three per cent of the top jobs, nine per cent of middle managerial and 12 per cent of lower supervisory jobs in Calgary – even though women make up 34 per cent of the work force here.

Women have failed to make significant inroads on the Canadian political scene as well.

Only six of Alberta's 79 MLAs are women at the end of 1979.

Only 10 of 282 seats in Parliament are filled by women, none of whom are from Alberta.

And, in the 50 years they have been eligible, only 18 women have been appointed to the Senate.

On a more positive note, Calgary feminists point to this year's celebration of the persons case as a benchmark of the seventies that has set a tone and pace for the women's movement in the eighties.

The persons case, decided 50 years ago by the British Privy Council, made women eligible for senate appointments in Canada.

Because of these invasions of former male ground, women's advocates say the greatest impact of feminism in the seventies has been on behavior rather than economics.

"It is inevitable that the lives of men will be affected," said Carolyn Larsen, co-founder of Calgary's Contemporary Woman program.

"The women's movement has given rise to men's liberation so that now, as we go into the eighties, we are looking at equality for all people and fighting for not just women's but human rights," Larsen said.

December 31, 1979

A Calgary boy who grew up to be a diplomat became an American hero, at a time when Americans very much wanted a hero. Ken Taylor, the Canadian ambassador to Iran, and three of his staffers, hid six American diplomats and slipped them out of the country on Canadian passports. Meanwhile, scores of Americans were being held hostage by Iranian militants who seized the U.S. embassy after the Ayatollah Khomeini's regime overthrew the Shah. Some Americans were released early, but most had to endure 444 days of captivity until their release was negotiated. Dave Margoshes of The Herald reported on Taylor's homecoming.

Ken Taylor is an unlikely, unassuming uncomfortable hero. For one thing, the 45-year-old career diplomat is too short, too slight, too well-dressed, too good-looking to be a real hero except on the silver screen or the pages of a comic book.

What he really is, Taylor has been telling people who gush over what Ald. Craig Reid artfully described Monday as his "act of bravery, I guess you would call it," is a good neighbor, not a swashbuckler.

But events have a way of catching up

Diplomat, hero, Ken Taylor.

with people. And Ken Taylor, a bright Calgary kid who went into the diplomatic corps because of the appeal of "the diversity, the constant change of scenery," is having to learn to live with "a very heightened sensation" of being, if not a genuine hero, at least a celebrity.

"What I did was no different than what any of my colleagues would have done," Taylor says modestly, "but most people don't get the chance."

Still, reluctant or not, Taylor has become a hero, at least in some people's eyes.

"He's done more for Canada than all the politicians put together," observed a Mountie on hand at the airport as Taylor and his wife arrived early Monday morning.

And an American woman who had dropped by to greet the ambassador put her finger squarely on it this way: "He got involved and this day and age, that's something to be proud of."

Back in Ottawa, the letters are piling up. Most are from Americans, who have taken Taylor to their breast in a way that Canadians are usually embarrassed to do. Many of them are from school children.

"You're my number one Valentine," one of the letters said, Taylor recalled over a beer Monday afternoon.

"I think I'd be brave, too, but I'm not sure," said another child's letter.

Playing a hero's role hasn't had a chance to really sink in yet, though it's been over two weeks now since Taylor, Canada's ambassador to Iran, and three of his staff spirited six Americans they'd been harboring in their embassy out of the country.

In the past few years, he pointed out, there's been a string of American envoys assassinated, embassies burned, hostages taken.

"The diplomatic life," he said diplomatically, "has become a more suspect one. It's become a focal point for dispute."

Does that mean one has to be braver to be an ambassador these days? "More foolhardy, perhaps," Taylor said, laughing.

February 12, 1980

Some of the thousands of people who flocked to Calgary looking for work found only bitter disappointment, as Joanne Ramondt reported.

East is meeting West in Calgary in a way the two parts of the country have never come together before. It's in the courthouses, flophouses and jail cells that the two are shaking hands and introducing themselves as wary, unwilling strangers.

No one is surprised that as 1,500 newcomers arrive in the city each month, some will be involved in crime. But certain recent incidents and trends are disturbing. Police blame a 60 per cent increase in armed robberies on recent arrivals. However, not all of the recent arrivals who find themselves involved in crime are coming to the city intentionally to rip it off.

Although provincial court Judge Hubert Oliver says most of the recent arrivals he sees passing through his court have criminal records, there are some new arrivals who police, crown prosecutors and judges agree are stealing to survive.

Recently, provincial court Judge Douglas McDonald halted legal proceedings in his court to gather more information about why he is seeing so many young people from other provinces charged with stealing small amounts of food from supermarkets.

Many of these young people hadn't committed criminal offences in the past, and that they do now disturbs him, as it should disturb others when Calgary is such a magnet for the young.

A report gathered for the judge showed many newcomers are looking for the cliche: streets paved with gold.

When they find, instead, high rents and few jobs for unskilled, untrained people, and run out of money, they may arrive on the doorstep of the Calgary Welcome Centre during the day, or the Single Men's Hostel, both in downtown Calgary and designed to help those in need.

"The image of a lot of people in the rest of the country is that all you have to do is walk inside the city limits and you'll find a job," says Rev. Alan Billington, who, as director of the Welcome Centre, sees the new arrivals when they need companionship, a cup of coffee or sandwich.

"It's as hard in Calgary, or perhaps even harder because of the influx of skilled people, to find a job as it is anywhere in the country."

March 15, 1980

Herald writer Catherine Butlin met Cary Grant, but she was born 30 years too late to appreciate the occasion fully.

Eat your heart out, Mom. I had coffee Wednesday morning with Cary Grant. And while at age 76, he didn't quite fill the billing you gave him as "a great lover-boy, so good-looking he didn't have to act," he is certainly looking tanned, fit and healthy on the occasion of his second visit to the Calgary Stampede.

Cary Grant talks with Calgary reporters during a visit to the Stampede.

Grant, the ultimate smoothie, smooched and sparred his way through some of heyday Hollywood's greatest hits, with some of its sexiest actresses.

But the tall, white-haired actor turned a cold, Garbo-like shoulder to the movies after making his last, Walk Don't Run, a box office flop.

He came to Calgary with his daughter Jennifer, a stunning beauty at 14, and the equally attractive Barbara Harris, Grant's companion.

Grant, who first visited the Stampede in 1967, would just as soon you controlled those autograph-seeking impulses if you see the debonair stranger, with cowboy hat pulled low to hide those famous features, strolling through the grounds.

But he doesn't really expect to be hounded by adoring fans at Stampede '80.

"I don't get mobbed anymore," said the still-suave Grant. "They treat this venerable old gentleman with respect."

Even though Grant has led what to many would read as a fairytale existence, thanks to the movies, he doesn't think people "should waste their time watching them."

"What do you really care who ends up getting the girl or who did the murder?" he asked in an interview at a downtown hotel room.

"Life is the good stuff. I don't waste my time reading fiction or watching films. I don't have the time."

There are queries about his favorite movie and his favorite leading lady, to which he replies "I can't remember," in his famous mid-Atlantic drawl (which he describes as old Cockney), "It's been so long since I did them."

There's no doubt, though, about who was the sexiest leading lady he ever loved on the silver screen.

"I guess I'd have to say Sophia," said Grant in a thoughtful tone.

July 10, 1980

In a city full of young strangers, in a time of greater sexual openness, singles bars flourished. Mark Hallman of The Herald looked at the phenomenon. (He changed the names of the people interviewed.)

Darting eyes comb the room, furtively, sometimes boldly, assessing who's worth the time. Not bad over there. Hmm . . . Could be better, could be worse . . .

It's a calculating, if not cynical, method of weighing the merits of an evening's "entertainment," but almost every man or woman who steps into a singles bar sizes up the odds in just such a way.

"Let's be realistic – everybody checks everybody out," says Jan, a 23-year-old Calgary secretary, as she coolly scans the bar, puffing intently on her cigarette.

But Jan, garbed in a revealing top and tight-fitting jeans, insists she's come to the bar with two female friends only "to meet people, to have a good time – that's all."

She and her friends have displayed a clear determination to have fun. She's waited more than half an hour to get in the bar, an elaborately furnished room panelled with wood and spotted with leafy ferns, antiques and assorted bric a brac.

After work, the three-piece suit and the work-a-day dress are not uncommon in such establishments, but as the evening wears on, the clothing becomes not only more casual, but relentlessly more trendy.

The men tend to undo a few more shirt buttons – some still display gold medallions draped around their necks – while the women squeeze into tighter clothing, revealing substantially more cleavage and thigh.

In the singles bar scene, however, where brave facades, calculated indifference and light-hearted conversation prevail, it's next to impossible to find anyone willing to talk about anxieties or disappointments with the opposite sex.

But in a rare, candid moment, one man did just that.

Jake, a 29-year-old teacher, said he's had an unnerving experience with a woman he'd met in a singles bar.

Everything clicked and Jake found himself really taken by the woman. She invited him to her apartment, making it plain she wanted to make love to him.

But as they climbed into bed, she made it clear this was a "one night stand" – she didn't want to see him after they parted the next morning.

Jake eventually found out that she wanted the satisfaction of fooling around on her boyfriend, who constantly did the same thing to her.

Jake said the experience revealed an important personal truth – it showed him he needs sex within the context of a relationship or with a woman who can reciprocate his affection.

Few women in singles bars are blatant about hustling the opposite sex, but there are those who overcome convention and stake their claim.

"It depends on whether the guy interests me enough to go over and talk to him," said Jane, 24, a comely brunette, who works as a secretary in a downtown office.

"If I got to know him and liked him enough, I'd go home with him. But there'd have to be something more to it than a one-nighter."

October 18, 1980

With your help I would like to contact the gentleman who was sitting front row right reading the newspaper by the lights that illuminated the stage at a matinee performance of John Murrell's play, Memoir, on Sunday, Feb. 15.

Since I was unable to read the newspapers that day I would like him to send me the articles that he was reading with such absorption.

In return, I will send him a copy of the pieces of the play that he missed. I was the lady who was on stage at the time, playing Sarah Bernhardt.

Joy Coghill,

Vancouver, B.C. March 4, 1981

The streetcar rides again. Just before the C-Train put Calgary commuters back on the rails, Sheila Pratt of The Herald wrote this piece, looking forward – and back, to the streetcars of 1908.

Calgarians will be railroaded into a transit revolution Monday when the sleek, smooth C-Train glides down the big steel rails into downtown.

Switching commuters back to a track that began with clangy, wooden streetcars decades ago, Light Rail Transit will shunt

Cartoonist Tom Innes found extra sunshine in the Winter Olympics victory.

buses from the mainline to make room for transit's modern miracle.

For transportation planners, completion of the 12.5-kilometre south line from Anderson Road to 7th Avenue S. is the realization of a 15-year-old dream scoffed at years ago when a move from "rubber back to rail" seemed like a U-turn from progress.

Skeptics and critics, many of them provincial MLAs, say the city isn't big enough to support a "hopped-up streetcar" system that so far has cost $175.3 million. They predict it will be an unwanted burden to taxpayers who will still cry for more roads.

But transit enthusiasts, like Mayor Ralph Klein, say the C-Train is "definitely the right track for the future" and this is just the beginning of a five-leg network that will span the city.

While it takes one bus driver to carry 75 people, the C-Train with one operator, can carry 450 and make the journey in less time.

Whether the LRT gamble pays off remains to be seen. But Bill Kuyt, assistant commissioner of transportation, is optimistic.

"They worried about exactly the same thing at the council meeting in 1908 trying to decide whether to plunge into the streetcar system," says Kuyt.

"And that $544,000 gamble for a 12-car system paid off."

May 23, 1981

After a lot of work and several disappointments, Calgary won the right to play host to the Winter Olympics. Herald reporter Crosbie Cotton reported the reaction in Baden-Baden, where the decision was made.

The International Olympic Committee ushered Calgary into a new era today when it awarded the 1988 Winter Games to the city.

Jubilant Calgary delegates tossed white hats in the air amid the glittering European elegance of the opulent casino where IOC president Juan Antonio Samaranch announced the decision at 9 a.m. Calgary time.

At first mention of their city's name in the announcement, Mayor Ralph Klein was hugged by a grinning Frank King, president of the Calgary Olympic Development Committee (CODA).

Some of the 100 or so CODA members cried with joy when they learned Calgary had won over Cortina d'Ampezzo, a small resort in northern Italy and Falun-Are, two Swedish towns that had entered a joint bid. Most of them had come at their own expense to witness the historic announcement.

When it came, they shouted with joy, hugged and kissed each other. It was the end of a tiring journey that began almost three years ago when an unknown man named Frank King announced he would lead the bid.

Calgary won on the second ballot in the secret session behind closed doors. It first captured 35 votes from the International Olympic Committee delegates, compared with 25 for Falun and 18 for Cortina.

With the Italian opponents surprisingly out of the second round, Calgary overcame the Swedish bid 48 votes to 31.

"Hallelujah," shouted an ecstatic Frank King.

"I was nervous to the last second," said Premier Peter Lougheed, who was involved in Calgary's last Olympic bid.

"I'm proud of the support of the people of Calgary. It will help in terms of Canadian unity."

"There will be a new civic purpose, a new civic focus," said King.

"I'm convinced that Calgary will put on the greatest Games the world has ever seen."

CODA president Bob Niven, the head of a small oil company, who dedicated thousands of hours in pursuit of the city's Olympic dream, was overjoyed.

"The bringing of the Winter Olympics is going to do much for the development of sport, not only in Calgary but in Canada and western North America."

Today's winning bid was the seventh time Calgary has headed to the Olympic well seeking the Winter Games, and tonight CODA volunteers will drink champagne.

Baden-Baden, West Germany, September 30, 1981.

Prosperity and fast growth have been a mixed blessing for Calgary, as Herald editorial writer Catherine Ford found on her return from a stay in Toronto.

To newcomers who bought the local myth; to each stranger without friends and family in Calgary – my sympathy. It's tough living in a cold city.

Today's Calgary is not the city of my childhood, or even the city I left two years ago.

It's a city long on money, and short on heart.

In a few years, we've managed to destroy – almost – its environmentally fragile beauty, and the famous Western friendliness is disappearing.

There are a lot of questions I'd like to ask for the strangers who arrive here to find the reality harsh indeed.

(Before that, for all the merchants and businessmen, for all the companies and landlords who have absorbed bum cheques and midnight sneaks and vandalism and destruction – I realize it isn't easy dealing with a transient population.)

But somewhere there must be a civilized middle of the road.

Without it, we'll end up with all the problems of Toronto and Montreal – and none of the ambience. We're well on the way. (The Calgary of the early 1980s is almost a carbon copy of Toronto in the late 1950s.)

This is progress? This is the land of opportunity?

A city which planned to advertise for easterners to stay away, until someone suggested that might be a tad unfriendly?

This city where the council seems hellbent on destroying whatever beauty is left downtown, turning it into a steel and glass wasteland?

Cynical? You bet I'm cynical.

Not just about the city itself, but also about businessmen who make a living hawking their wares. If there is justice, one day the customer will cry "enough," and demand more for his money than ill temper, discourtesy and unconcern.

Reality is to a stranger moving here an attitude of such conspicuous consumption that the customer is no longer right, just tolerated.

What does the merchant care? Somebody else will be clamoring to buy.

The stranger trying to furnish a home, buy groceries or get any kind of service in this city is in for a rude shock.

Why does living in Calgary these days resemble something akin to open warfare? Tell me how somebody who doesn't know anyone in this city manages? How do you cash a cheque when your driver's licence doesn't have a picture on it (a blatant invasion of privacy), and you can't produce a photo identification card?

How do you rent an apartment when you're young and just starting out? (If you can find an apartment to rent.)

How do you come to love a city which has winter in its heart?

December 7, 1981.

Mayor Ralph Klein made it clear that some newcomers are more welcome than others in Calgary.

Bums" and "unskilled people" aren't welcome in Calgary, Mayor Ralph Klein told a dinner meeting of the Calgary Newcomer's Club Wednesday night.

Many of the approximately 150 women sat in surprised silence as the mayor lashed out against transients and unskilled labor from Eastern Canada, blaming some recent arrivals for rising crime in his city.

Klein promised tough action at the club meeting – a social group of recent arrivals in the city.

The mayor, speaking from a prepared text and later answering questions, said the majority of Calgarians have to be protected from "a lot of creeps" even if it takes some "cowboy techniques" to control anti-social behavior.

"Even if we have to put them all in jail, on top of one another, we have to do it," Klein said.

Admitting he was "a bit of a redneck" on the issue, the mayor noted that for the first time statistics show there are more Quebecers than native Indians now in Calgary jails.

No exact figures were used during the speech.

Klein told the meeting that while "it might sound elitist, we want highly skilled people, educated people, people with technological skills."

He said these people often come to the city with guaranteed jobs and guaranteed accommodation, so they are welcome.

"But what we don't want," he said, "are unskilled workers who often come without jobs, without accommodation and without money to take care of themselves."

January 7, 1982

Finally, a farewell to some of Calgary's minor landmarks. Herald columnist Allan Connery said goodbye to half a city block that had stood through boom and bust and war and finally succumbed to the boom of the Seventies.

If downtown Calgary is haunted, surely it's the ghosts of buildings, not people, whose uneasy presence lingers. A ghost from early Calgary, if it tried to return to the bedroom where it died, might find itself haunting the lobby of an office building. Better to imagine the building haunted by the house whose place it took.

No archaeologist will ever dig up Calgary layer by layer, as ancient Troy was brought to light. Here we scrape the site flat and start over. The layers remain, though, in the pages of the Calgary city directory, recording year by year who lived, who did business, in buildings we'll see no more.

Dig down 10 years, and walk along the south side of 7th Avenue, eastward from Eaton's, which is still a landmark. (Today that side of the street is occupied by Oxford Square, already renamed the Toronto-Dominion Centre.)

At the corner, where Eddie Bauer, 10 years later, will outfit the well-dressed outdoorsman, stands the Caribbean Bakery. Why Caribbean? Too late to ask, 10 years later.

Next, the Towne Cinema, which will later find a new home on the site of another demolished building.

Stop now and look at the $200 suits in Don Forster's window. Two hundred dollars for a suit. How many ambitious young men must have vowed they someday would wear $200 suits. Inflation alone will give them their wish in 10 years.

Beside the suits in the window is the entrance to the Frontier Apartments, 30-odd of them on two floors above a row of stores. The people there don't shop at Forster's even though it's handy.

Then the Havana Tea and Coffee Room. No beatniks inside – you'd have to dig down another 10 years for them. Ten years later, the Toronto-Dominion Bank will have inherited the site. Music goes well with nostalgia, haven't you

found? Past the espresso machine, then, through the wicker basket chairs, to the juke-box. Richard Harris: "MacArthur Park is melting in the dark..."

But onward. Past the wig shop, the florist's (house plants on the sidewalk in fine weather), the sporting-goods store (those are hiking boots in the window; you'll be seeing more of them), the Venice Salon, the House of Japan (incense, chess sets and paper lanterns), the carpet store, the leather clothing boutique (no, the kind you'd wear on the street, even in Calgary), another men's clothing store (Coachman) and a sewing-machine store.

Pause, finally, at the entrance of the Wales Hotel beverage room. (In 10 years, perhaps the cocktail lounge of the Corkscrew Restaurant will be haunted by the ghost of a 20-cent draft beer, alone and aghast.)

And so to the corner of 7th Avenue and 2nd Street S.W. Watch for the traffic, but don't look back: you can't walk down that street again.

August 12, 1978

Allan Connery may not have been around when the first Calgary Herald was cranked out on a tiny press that last day of August in 1883. But he does have a native son's perspective of the events from that day onward. Connery was born in Calgary on March 7, 1943 and has spent most of his working life in this city.

He started his reporting career at the Herald in 1964, but after a brief beginning, left to work on The Toronto Globe and Mail in its Ottawa bureau ("I was a glorified copy runner and file clerk," he recalls) and later with the Beacon-Herald in Stratford, Ont. before deciding the West was the place to be after all. In March of 1968, Connery returned to The Herald to stay.

He has been a reporter, copy editor, night city editor and editorial writer. In 1977 his well-known wit was put to good use as he became a full-time columnist on the editorial page, specializing in the lighter side of the news.

Connery worked 18 months on this book. "I travelled through many a mile of microfilm," he says of his massive research undertaking. The result is "a sort of scrapbook, a condensed version of all kinds of memorable events, also some of the nuttier things that gave some flavor to the times."

He's now back writing the column with the same perceptive eye for the nuttier things that give flavor to the times today.